Revenue Statistics in Africa

1990-2016

Statistiques des recettes publiques en Afrique

1990-2016

This work is published under the responsibility of the Secretary-General of the OECD, the Executive Secretary of ATAF and the Chairperson of the AUC. The opinions expressed and arguments employed herein do not necessarily reflect the official views of the member countries of the OECD or its Development Centre, or of the member countries of the African Union or of ATAF.

Cet ouvrage est publié sous la responsabilité du Secrétaire général de l'OCDE, du Secrétaire Exécutif de l'ATAF et du Président de la CUA. Les opinions et les arguments exprimés ici ne reflètent pas nécessairement les vues officielles des pays membres de l'OCDE ou de son Centre de développement, ou des pays membres de l'Union africaine ou de l'ATAF.

This document, as well as data and any map included herein, are without prejudice to the status of or sovereignty over any territory, to the delimitation of international frontiers and boundaries and to the name of any territory, city or area.

Ce document ainsi que les données et cartes qu'il peut comprendre sont sans préjudice du statut de tout territoire, de la souveraineté s'exerçant sur ce dernier, du tracé des frontières et limites internationales, et du nom de tout territoire, ville ou région.

Please cite this publication as:
OECD/ATAF/AUC (2018), *Revenue Statistics in Africa 2018*, OECD Publishing, Paris.
http://dx.doi.org/10.1787/9789264305885-en-fr

Merci de citer cet ouvrage comme suit :
OCDE/ATAF/CUA (2018), *Statistiques des recettes publiques en Afrique 2018*, Éditions OCDE, Paris.
http://dx.doi.org/10.1787/9789264305885-en-fr

ISBN 978-92-64-30587-8 (print/*imprimé*)
ISBN 978-92-64-30588-5 (PDF)

Photo credits: Cover © some of the graphic elements in the main cover illustration were adapted from Freepik.com.

Corrigenda to OECD publications may be found on line at: *www.oecd.org/about/publishing/corrigenda.htm*.
Les corrigenda des publications de l'OCDE sont disponibles sur : *www.oecd.org/about/publishing/corrigenda.htm*.

Foreword

Revenue Statistics in Africa *is a joint publication by the OECD Centre for Tax Policy and Administration, the OECD Development Centre, the African Tax Administration Forum and the African Union Commission, with the technical support of the African Development Bank, the World Customs Organisation and the Cercle de réflexion et d'échange des dirigeants des administrations fiscales and the financial support of the European Commission.*

The report presents detailed, internationally comparable data on both tax and non-tax revenues for 21 African countries. Its approach is based on the well-established methodology of the OECD Revenue Statistics *database, which has become an essential reference source for OECD member countries and many more. Comparisons are also made with the average for OECD economies and for the economies featured in* Revenue Statistics in Latin America and the Caribbean.

The term "taxes" in this publication is confined to "compulsory, unrequited payments to general government". As outlined in the Interpretative Guide to the Revenue Statistics, taxes are "unrequited" in the sense that benefits provided by government to taxpayers are not normally in proportion to their payments. The OECD methodology classifies a tax according to its base: income, profits and capital gains (classified under heading 1000), payroll (heading 3000), property (heading 4000), goods and services (heading 5000) and other taxes (heading 6000). Compulsory social security contributions paid to general government are treated as taxes, and classified under heading 2000. Much greater detail on the tax concept and the classification of taxes is set out in the OECD Interpretative Guide in Annex A.

The term "non-tax revenue" includes all general government revenue that does not meet the OECD definition of taxation. Revenues that do not constitute taxation include grants (e.g. foreign aid), returns on government market investments, rents on the extraction of resources from public lands, sales of government-produced goods and services, and the collection of fines and forfeits. More details on these types of revenues, as well as an explanation of the use of cash or accrual basis of reporting in the publication, are available in Annex B.

Chapter 1 and Chapter 2 of this report provide an overview of the main tax-revenue and non-tax revenue trends respectively in the 21 participating countries from 2000 to 2016. A special feature on the Strategy for the Harmonisation of Statistics in Africa (SHaSA) is contained in Chapter 3, while Chapter 4 explores the level of tax revenues by main tax categories and how the respective tax structures of the 21 countries have evolved since 1990. Chapters 5 and 6 contain detailed information on tax and non-tax revenues respectively on a country-by-country basis as well as a comparison of the non-tax revenues mix over time in the 21 countries.

Avant-propos

Les Statistiques des recettes publiques en Afrique *est une publication conjointe du Centre de politique et d'administration fiscales de l'OCDE, du Centre de développement de l'OCDE, du Forum sur l'administration fiscale africaine (ATAF), et de la Commission de l'Union Africaine, avec l'assistance technique de la Banque africaine de développement, de l'Organisation mondiale des douanes et du Cercle de réflexion et d'échange des dirigeants des administrations fiscales et le soutien financier de la Commission européenne.*

Le rapport fournit des données détaillées et comparables à l'échelle internationale, sur les recettes fiscales et non fiscales de 21 pays africains. Son approche repose sur la méthodologie bien établie des Statistiques des recettes publiques de l'OCDE, *devenue une source de référence essentielle pour les pays membres de l'Organisation et au-delà. Des comparaisons sont également effectuées avec la moyenne des économies de l'OCDE et avec celle des économies couvertes par les* Statistiques des recettes publiques en Amérique latine et dans les Caraïbes.

Dans cette publication, le terme « impôts » fait référence uniquement aux « versements obligatoires sans contrepartie aux administrations publiques ». Comme indiqué dans le Guide d'interprétation pour les Statistiques des recettes publiques, les impôts sont « sans contrepartie » en ce sens que les prestations fournies par les administrations aux contribuables ne sont pas normalement proportionnelles à leurs paiements. La méthodologie de l'OCDE consiste à classer les impôts en fonction de l'assiette : le revenu, les bénéfices et les gains en capital (rubrique 1000), les salaires et la main-d'œuvre (rubrique 3000), le patrimoine (rubrique 4000), les biens et les services (rubrique 5000) et autres impôts (rubrique 6000). Les cotisations obligatoires de sécurité sociale versées aux administrations publiques sont aussi traitées comme des impôts et classées dans la rubrique 2000. Des informations plus détaillées sur la notion d'impôt et sur la classification des impôts sont présentées dans le Guide d'interprétation de l'OCDE figurant à l'annexe A.

Le terme « recettes non fiscales » recouvre toutes les recettes des administrations publiques qui ne sont pas considérées comme des « impôts » selon la définition de l'OCDE. Les recettes non fiscales incluent les dons (comme l'aide extérieure), les rendements d'investissements publics, les rentes tirées de l'extraction de ressources du domaine public, la vente de biens et de services produits par le secteur public, et les amendes et confiscations. On trouvera, à l'annexe B, des informations plus détaillées sur ces catégories de recettes ainsi qu'une explication de l'utilisation de l'enregistrement sur la base des décaissements ou des droits constatés.

Le chapitre 1 et le chapitre 2 du rapport offrent une vue d'ensemble des grandes tendances de 2000 à 2016 dans les 21 pays participants des recettes fiscales et non fiscales respectivement. Une étude spéciale sur la Stratégie pour l'harmonisation des statistiques en Afrique (SHaSA) est incluse dans le chapitre 3. Le chapitre 4 examine le niveau des recettes fiscales par principaux types d'impôts et l'évolution des structures fiscales des 21 pays depuis 1990. Les chapitres 5 et 6 fournissent respectivement des données détaillées sur les recettes fiscales et non fiscales par pays ainsi qu'une comparaison des structures des recettes non fiscales dans le temps dans les 21 pays.

Acknowledgements

Revenue Statistics in Africa has been jointly produced by the Organisation for Economic Co-operation and Development (OECD) Centre for Tax Policy and Administration (CTP), the OECD Development Centre (DEV), the African Tax Administration Forum (ATAF) and the African Union Commission (AUC), with the technical support of the African Development Bank (AfDB), the World Customs Organisation (WCO), the Cercle de réflexion et d'échange des dirigeants des administrations fiscales (CREDAF) and the European Commission. The staff from these organisations with responsibility for producing the publication were: Emmanuelle Modica, Leonie Beisemann, Talita Yamashiro Fordelone, Michael Sharratt and Michelle Harding of CTP under the supervision of the Director Pascal Saint-Amans, the Deputy Director Grace Perez-Navarro and the Head of the Tax Policy and Tax Statistics Division David Bradbury; Sébastien Markley, Bakary Traoré, Arthur Minsat and Alexander Pick of DEV under the supervision of the Director of the Development Centre and Special Advisor to the OECD Secretary-General on Development Mario Pezzini, and of the Senior Communications Manager Henri-Bernard Solignac-Lecomte; Director of Research at ATAF Nara Monkam; Dossina Yeo, Senior Statistician and Jose Awong Alene, Statistician at the AUC under the Director of Economic Affairs Dr. René N'guettia Kouassi; Chaouch Anouar Statistician at AfDB under the Director of Statistics Department Charles Leyeka Lufumpa and Koua Louis Kouakou at AfDB heading the Division of Economic and Social Statistics; Technical Officer Thomas Cantens at WCO under the direction of Head of Research and Strategies Unit Robert Ireland; Secretary General Didier Cornillet of CREDAF; Policy Officer Vincent Bigot, Head of Domestic Revenue Mobilisation Sector Stefan Agne and Head of Budget Support, Public Finance Management, Domestic Revenue Mobilisation Unit Erica Gerretsen at the European Commission. Dossina Yeo and Jose Awong Alene (AUC) authored the Special Feature (Chapter 3). Elizabeth Nash, Delphine Grandrieux, Antonela Leiva, Justina La and Julia Peppino at DEV and Alexandra Le Cam and Marie-Aurélie Elkurd at CTP assisted with the production and publication of this report and Stephanie Coic produced the cover.

The authors would like to thank their colleagues working in national entities with whom they have consulted regularly. These institutions include finance ministries, national tax agencies and national statistical institutes of Botswana, Burkina Faso, Cabo Verde, Cameroon, the Republic of the Congo, the Democratic Republic of the Congo, Côte d'Ivoire, Egypt, Eswatini, Ghana, Kenya, Mali, Mauritius, Morocco, Niger, Rwanda, Senegal, South Africa, Togo, Tunisia and Uganda. They also wish to give their appreciation to DEV and CTP colleagues for commenting on drafts and providing technical assistance.

Finally, the partners would like to thank the European Commission, ATAF and the AUC that hosted, organised and funded the technical workshop in Addis Ababa, Ethiopia (October 2017).

This document was produced with the financial assistance of the European Commission. The views expressed herein can in no way be taken to reflect the official opinion of the European Union or of its member countries.

Remerciements

La publication des *Statistiques des recettes publiques en Afrique* a été produite conjointement par le Centre de politique et d'administration fiscales (CPAF) de l'Organisation de coopération et de développement économiques (OCDE), le Centre de développement de l'OCDE (DEV), le Forum sur l'administration fiscale africaine (ATAF), et la Commission de l'Union Africaine (CUA), avec l'assistance technique de la Banque africaine de développement (BAfD), de l'Organisation mondiale des douanes (OMD), du Cercle de réflexion et d'échange des dirigeants des administrations fiscales (CREDAF), et de la Commission européenne. Les agents de ces organisations auxquels la responsabilité de la publication a été confiée sont : Emmanuelle Modica, Leonie Beisemann, Talita Yamashiro Fordelone, Michael Sharratt et Michelle Harding du CPAF sous la supervision du Directeur du Centre Pascal Saint-Amans, de Grace Perez-Navarro, Directrice adjointe du CPAF et de David Bradbury, Chef de la Division des politiques fiscales et statistiques ; Sébastien Markley, Bakary Traoré, Arthur Minsat et Alexander Pick de DEV sous la supervision du Directeur du Centre de développement et Conseiller spécial auprès du Secrétaire général de l'OCDE sur le développement Mario Pezzini, et de Henri-Bernard Solignac-Lecomte, Chef de la communication ; Nara Monkam, Directrice de recherche à l'ATAF ; Dossina Yeo, principal statisticien, et Jose Awong Alene statisticien de la CUA, sous la supervision de René N'guettia Kouassi, Directeur des affaires économiques ; Chaouch Anouar, statisticien à la BAfD, sous la supervision de Charles Leyeka Lufumpa, Directeur du département des statistiques et Koua Louis Kouakou, de la BAfD, à la tête de la Division des statistiques économiques et sociales ; Thomas Cantens, Administrateur technique à l'OMD, sous la direction de Robert Ireland, Chef de l'Unité Recherche et stratégies ; Didier Cornillet, Secrétaire général du CREDAF ; Vincent Bigot, chargé de mission ; Stefan Agne, Chef du secteur de la mobilisation des ressources intérieures et Erica Gerretsen, Chef de l'unité de l'appui budgétaire, gestion des finances publiques, et mobilisation des ressources intérieures à la Commission européenne. Dossina Yeo et Jose Awong Alene (CUA) ont écrit l'Étude Spéciale (Chapitre 3). Elizabeth Nash, Delphine Grandrieux, Antonela Leiva, Justina La et Julia Peppino de DEV et Alexandra Le Cam et Marie-Aurélie Elkurd du CPAF ont aidé à la production de la publication sous forme imprimée et électronique et Stephanie Coic a produit la couverture.

Les auteurs tiennent à remercier leurs collègues des institutions nationales avec lesquels des consultations ont eu lieu régulièrement. Ces institutions sont notamment les ministères des Finances, les administrations fiscales nationales et les instituts statistiques nationaux de l'Afrique du Sud, du Botswana, du Burkina Faso, du Cabo Verde, du Cameroun, de la République du Congo, de la République démocratique du Congo, de la Côte d'Ivoire, de l'Égypte, de l'Eswatini, du Ghana, du Kenya, du Mali, du Maroc, de Maurice, du Niger, de l'Ouganda, du Rwanda, du Sénégal, du Togo et de la Tunisie. Ils souhaitent également exprimer leur reconnaissance aux agents de DEV et du CPAF pour leurs commentaires sur les projets de texte et leur assistance technique.

Enfin, les partenaires ont à cœur de remercier la Commission européenne, l'ATAF et la CUA d'avoir accueilli, organisé et financé les ateliers techniques à Addis-Abeba, Éthiopie (octobre 2017).

Ce document a été produit avec le soutien financier de la Commission européenne. Les opinions exprimées dans ce présent rapport ne peuvent en aucun cas refléter l'opinion officielle de l'Union européenne ou de ses pays membres.

Table of contents

Table des matières

LIST OF TABLES/LISTE DE TABLEAUX

Chapter 2/Chapitre 2
Non-tax revenue trends, 1990-2016/Tendances des recettes non fiscales, 1990-2016

Chapter 3/Chapitre 3
Special feature/Étude spéciale

Chapter 4/Chapitre 4
Tax levels and tax structures, 1990-2016/Niveaux et structures des impôts, 1990-2016

LIST OF FIGURES/LISTE DE GRAPHIQUES

Chapter 1/Chapitre 1
Tax revenue trends, 2000-2016/Tendances des recettes fiscales, 2000-2016

Chapter 2/Chapitre 2

Non-tax revenue trends, 1990-2016/Tendances des recettes non fiscales, 1990-2016

Revenue Statistics in Africa 1990-2016/Statistiques des recettes publiques en Afrique 1990-2016
© OECD/ATAF/AUC 2018/© OCDE/ATAF/CUA 2018

Executive summary

Achieving the United Nations' Sustainable Development Goals (SDGs) and implementing the Addis Ababa Action Agenda requires mobilising additional finance, in particular domestic resources, to fund public goods and services. This report presents internationally comparable indicators on tax and non-tax revenues that can be used to track progress on domestic resource mobilisation and to inform tax policy and reforms.

Revenue Statistics in Africa provides data on 21 African countries: Botswana, Burkina Faso, Cabo Verde, Cameroon, the Republic of the Congo, the Democratic Republic of the Congo, Côte d'Ivoire, Egypt, Eswatini, Ghana, Kenya, Mali, Mauritius, Morocco, Niger, Rwanda, Senegal, South Africa, Togo, Tunisia and Uganda. It includes a special chapter on the African Union's "Strategy for the Harmonisation of Statistics in Africa (SHaSA)" and the role of *Revenue Statistics in Africa* in this Strategy.

Tax revenues

In 2016, the average tax-to-GDP ratio for the 21 countries in this publication (the "Africa (21) average") was 18.2%. The tax-to-GDP ratio refers to total tax revenue, including social security contributions, as a percentage of gross domestic product (GDP). The Africa (21) average is below the Latin American and the Caribbean (LAC) average of 22.7% and the OECD average of 34.3%. Across countries, tax-to-GDP ratios ranged from 7.6% in the Democratic Republic of the Congo to 29.4% in Tunisia in 2016, with two-thirds of the countries falling between 13.0% and 20.0%. In six countries, the tax-to-GDP ratio exceeded 20% (Mauritius, Morocco, Senegal, South Africa, Togo and Tunisia).

Tax revenues have increased significantly since 2000 in almost all countries in the publication, driven by strong increases in revenues from taxes on income and profits (2.6 percentage points on average) and from VAT (2.0 percentage points on average). Consequently, the Africa (21) average tax-to-GDP ratio has increased by 5.0 percentage points since 2000, a similar increase to the LAC average (4.7 percentage points) and higher than the OECD average (0.4 percentage points over this period). Between 2015 and 2016, while African economic growth slowed and commodity prices continued to decline, the Africa (21) average tax-to-GDP ratio remained unchanged.

The greatest source of tax revenues among countries featured in this publication are taxes on goods and services, which accounted for 54.6% of total tax revenues on average in 2016, with VAT alone contributing 29.3% of tax revenues. Taxes on income and profits accounted for a further third (34.3%) of average tax revenues. This is a similar tax structure to that of the average LAC country, except in relation to social security contributions. Social security contributions in LAC as a percentage of GDP are more than twice as high as in Africa, accounting for much of the difference in the regions' respective average tax-to-GDP ratios.

Taxes on goods and services were the principal source of tax revenues for 17 countries in 2016 (ranging from 35.8% of tax revenues in Tunisia to 74.6% in Togo). For the four remaining countries (Botswana, Egypt, Eswatini and South Africa), taxes on income and profits accounted for the principal share of total tax revenue. The share of social security contributions in total tax revenue was highest in Tunisia (31.6% of total revenues), Morocco (17.1%) and Egypt (12.6%).

Non-tax revenues

In 2016, total non-tax revenues were lower than tax revenues in all countries except Botswana and were below 5% of GDP for 12 countries. The highest shares were seen in Botswana (18.2% of GDP) and Eswatini (11.2%) – both of which are net recipients of funds from the Southern African Customs Union (SACU) – followed by the Republic of the Congo, which reported grants and oil revenues amounting to 9.4% of GDP.

Non-tax revenues tend to vary more between years than tax revenues due to changing commodity prices and the variability of grants. However, non-tax revenues have been on a downward trend in recent years: in 2016, all but four countries had lower non-tax revenue to GDP ratios than in the previous year, and this indicator was lower than ten years previously in all but six countries.

The sources of non-tax revenues vary across the 21 countries in the report. For six countries (Côte d'Ivoire, the Democratic Republic of the Congo, Niger, Rwanda, Togo and Uganda), grants provided the majority of non-tax revenues. For Cameroon and the Republic of the Congo, rents and royalties contributed the majority of non-tax revenues while for Ghana most non-tax revenues were generated by sales of goods and services. For Eswatini, SACU revenues amounted to 82% of non-tax revenues.

Special feature

In recent years, African countries have committed to reducing poverty and improving living conditions, notably through the adoption of the African Union's Agenda 2063 and the SDGs. Monitoring progress against these goals requires good quality, timely, and harmonised statistical data that allow for cross-country comparisons. However, the production of quality statistics in the continent faces several challenges, including lack of resources, low institutional capacity and poor co-ordination across statistical bodies.

The African Union's "Strategy for the Harmonisation of Statistics in Africa" (SHaSA) aims to overcome these challenges. Its vision is to establish an efficient statistical system that covers the political, economic, social, environmental and cultural development and integration of Africa. It has four strategic themes: to produce quality statistics; to co-ordinate the production of quality statistics; to develop the sustainable institutional capacity of the African Statistical System; and to promote a culture of quality policy and decision-making.

Revenue Statistics in Africa is an important contributor to SHaSA. It improves the quality and comparability of revenue statistics in the continent through a product tailored to the needs of tax policymakers, maintaining consistency with international standards. It also allows countries and international organisations to track progress and shape strategies to increase public revenues in Africa in a sustainable, equitable and efficient way. Moreover, it builds statistical capacity among participating countries and provides valuable lessons for harmonisation of statistics in the continent.

Résumé

La réalisation des Objectifs de développement durable (ODD) des Nations Unies et la mise en œuvre du Programme d'action d'Addis-Abeba exigent la mobilisation de fonds supplémentaires, notamment des ressources intérieures, pour financer les biens et services publics. Ce rapport présente un ensemble d'indicateurs comparables à l'échelle internationale sur les recettes fiscales et non fiscales, qui peuvent servir à mesurer les progrès accomplis par les pays pour mobiliser leurs ressources intérieures et élaborer leurs politiques et réformes fiscales.

La publication *Statistiques des recettes publiques en Afrique* fournit des données sur 21 pays d'Afrique : Afrique du Sud, Botswana, Burkina Faso, Cabo Verde, Cameroun, République du Congo, République démocratique du Congo, Côte d'Ivoire, Égypte, Eswatini, Ghana, Kenya, Mali, Maroc, Maurice, Niger, Ouganda, Rwanda, Sénégal, Togo et Tunisie. Elle comprend également un chapitre spécial consacré à la « Stratégie pour l'harmonisation des statistiques en Afrique » (SHaSA) de l'Union africaine et à la place occupée par les *Statistiques des recettes publiques en Afrique* dans cette stratégie.

Recettes fiscales

Le ratio moyen impôts/PIB dans les 21 pays d'Afrique couverts par la publication (« moyenne d'Afrique (21) ») s'est établi à 18.2 % en 2016. Le ratio impôts/PIB correspond aux recettes fiscales totales (y compris les cotisations de sécurité sociale) exprimées en pourcentage du produit intérieur brut (PIB). La moyenne pour l'Afrique (21) a été inférieure à celle des pays d'Amérique latine et des Caraïbes (22.7 %) et des pays de l'OCDE (34.3 %). Dans les différents pays, les ratios impôts/PIB observés vont de 7.6 % en République démocratique du Congo à 29.4 % en Tunisie, deux tiers des pays ayant enregistré un ratio compris entre 13.0 % et 20.0 %. Six pays ont affiché un ratio supérieur à 20 % (Afrique du Sud, Maroc, Maurice, Sénégal, Togo et Tunisie).

Les recettes fiscales ont sensiblement augmenté depuis 2000 dans presque la totalité des pays considérés. Cet accroissement s'explique par les fortes hausses des recettes tirées des impôts sur le revenu et les bénéfices (2.6 points de pourcentage en moyenne) et des recettes de TVA (2.0 points de pourcentage en moyenne). Le ratio moyen impôts/PIB des pays d'Afrique (21) a ainsi progressé de 5.0 points de pourcentage depuis 2000. Cette progression est comparable à celle enregistrée en moyenne dans la région d'Amérique latine et des Caraïbes (ALC) (4.7 points de pourcentage) et plus élevée que dans les pays de l'OCDE (0.4 points de pourcentage sur la période). Ce ratio est resté stable entre 2015 et 2016, alors que la croissance économique en Afrique a reculé et que les prix des matières premières ont continué à baisser.

Les pays couverts par la publication tirent l'essentiel de leurs recettes fiscales des impôts sur les biens et services, qui ont représenté en moyenne 54.6 % du total des recettes fiscales en 2016. Les recettes de la TVA à elles seules représentent 29.3 % du total. Les impôts sur le revenu et les bénéfices quant à eux constituent un tiers (34.3 %) des recettes fiscales moyennes. Cette structure fiscale est comparable à celle de la moyenne des pays de la région ALC, sauf pour ce qui concerne les cotisations de sécurité sociale. Ces dernières y sont en effet plus de deux fois plus élevées qu'en Afrique, et expliquent pour l'essentiel l'écart entre les ratios moyens impôts/PIB respectifs de ces deux groupes.

Les impôts sur les biens et services ont constitué en 2016 la principale source de recettes fiscales pour 17 pays (de 35.8 % des recettes en Tunisie à 74.6 % au Togo). Dans les quatre pays restants (Afrique du Sud, Botswana, Égypte et Eswatini) la plus grande partie des recettes fiscales provient des impôts sur le revenu et les bénéfices. La part des cotisations de sécurité sociale dans le total des recettes fiscales est la plus élevée en Tunisie (31.6 %), au Maroc (17.1 %) et en Égypte (12.6 %).

Recettes non fiscales

En 2016, les recettes non fiscales totales ont été inférieures aux recettes fiscales dans tous les pays à l'exception du Botswana, et ont représenté moins de 5 % du PIB dans 12 pays. C'est au Botswana et en Eswatini, qui sont tous deux bénéficiaires nets des recettes de l'Union douanière d'Afrique australe (SACU), que la part des recettes non fiscales a été la plus élevée, s'élevant respectivement à 18.2 % et à 11.2 % du PIB. La République du Congo, dont la part des recettes provenant des dons et du pétrole s'élève à 9.4 % du PIB, se classe en troisième position.

Les recettes non fiscales perçues varient généralement plus, selon les années, que les recettes fiscales du fait des fluctuations des prix des matières premières et de la variabilité des dons. Ces recettes ont toutefois suivi ces dernières années une trajectoire descendante. Les ratios recettes non fiscales/PIB ont ainsi été inférieurs en 2016 à ceux de 2015 dans tous les pays sauf quatre, et en-deçà des niveaux observés dix ans auparavant dans l'ensemble d'entre eux à l'exception de six pays.

L'origine des recettes non fiscales diffère d'un pays à l'autre. Les dons ont fourni la majorité des recettes non fiscales dans six des 21 pays couverts par ce rapport (Côte d'Ivoire, République démocratique du Congo, Niger, Rwanda, Togo et Ouganda). Le Cameroun et la République du Congo tirent pour leur part la majorité des recettes non fiscales de loyers et de redevances, tandis qu'au Ghana, elles proviennent essentiellement de la vente de biens et services. Dans le cas de l'Eswatini, les recettes de la SACU représentent 82 % des recettes non fiscales.

Étude spéciale

Ces dernières années, les pays africains se sont engagés à faire reculer la pauvreté et à améliorer leurs conditions de vie, notamment au travers de l'adoption de l'Agenda 2063 de l'Union africaine et des ODD. Le suivi des progrès réalisés au regard de ces objectifs exige des données statistiques de bonne qualité, actualisées et harmonisées permettant des comparaisons entre pays. Néanmoins, la production de statistiques de qualité sur le continent africain se heurte à différents obstacles, comme l'insuffisance de ressources et de capacités institutionnelles et le manque de coordination entre les organes statistiques.

La « Stratégie pour l'harmonisation des statistiques en Afrique » (SHaSA) vise à lever certains de ces obstacles. Elle porte la vision d'un système statistique efficace couvrant toutes les dimensions – politique, économique, sociale, environnementale et culturelle – du développement et de l'intégration du continent africain. Elle s'articule autour de quatre thèmes stratégiques : i) produire des statistiques de qualité pour l'Afrique ; ii) coordonner la production de telles statistiques ; iii) renforcer durablement les capacités institutionnelles du système statistique africain ; et iv) promouvoir une culture de la qualité en matière de politiques publiques et de prise de décision.

La publication *Statistiques des recettes publiques en Afrique* constitue un élément essentiel de la stratégie SHaSA. Il s'agit d'un produit adapté aux besoins des responsables de la politique fiscale, qui permet d'améliorer la qualité et la comparabilité des statistiques des recettes publiques du continent africain, tout en garantissant la cohérence avec les normes internationales. Elle aide également les pays et organisations internationales à suivre les progrès accomplis et à définir des stratégies visant à accroître les recettes publiques d'une manière durable, équitable et efficiente. Enfin, elle vient renforcer les capacités statistiques des pays participants et constitue une source d'enseignements précieux à l'appui de l'harmonisation des statistiques en Afrique.

Chapter 1

Tax revenue trends, 2000-2016

Chapitre 1

Tendances des recettes fiscales, 2000-2016

Chapter 1

Tax revenue trends, 2000-2016

Achieving the United Nations' Sustainable Development Goals (SDGs) and implementing the Addis Ababa Action Agenda calls for mobilising additional finance, in particular domestic resources, to fund public goods and services. Taxation provides a predictable and sustainable source of government revenue, in contrast with the volatility of official development assistance and mineral royalties. This report presents an internationally-comparable set of indicators on tax and non-tax revenues which can be used to track progress on domestic resource mobilisation (as envisaged in the SDGs, the Addis Ababa Action Agenda as well as related initiatives such as the Addis Tax Initiative) and to inform tax policy and reforms.

This chapter discusses the trends of the tax-to-GDP ratio, the tax structure and the share of tax revenue by level of government in 21 African countries: Botswana, Burkina Faso, Cabo Verde, Cameroon, the Republic of the Congo, the Democratic Republic of the Congo, Côte d'Ivoire, Egypt, Eswatini[1], Ghana, Kenya, Mali, Mauritius, Morocco, Niger, Rwanda, Senegal, South Africa, Togo, Tunisia and Uganda. The discussion supplements the detailed country information on tax revenue in Chapter 5.

This chapter provides cross-country comparisons of tax revenue data for the countries included in this publication. It also compares the averages of the 21 African countries with that of 25 Latin American and Caribbean (LAC) countries (OECD/ECLAC/CIAT/IDB, 2018[1]) and that of 35 OECD countries (OECD, 2017[2])[2].

Tax-to-GDP ratios

Tax-to-GDP ratios in 2016

The average tax-to-GDP ratio in the 21 African countries in this publication (referred to as the "Africa (21) average") was 18.2% in 2016 (Figure 1.1). The tax-to-GDP ratio is measured as tax revenues (including social security contributions paid to general government) as a proportion of gross domestic product (GDP). The Africa (21) average needs to be interpreted with caution due to the incompleteness or unavailability of data for social security contributions in some African countries in this publication.[3] In comparison, the LAC and the OECD average tax-to-GDP ratios were 22.7% and 34.3% respectively in 2016.

In 2016, tax-to-GDP ratios varied widely across the countries included in this publication. They ranged from 7.6% in the Democratic Republic of the Congo to 29.4% in Tunisia. Two-thirds of the countries had a ratio between 13.0% and 20.0% in 2016 (Botswana, Burkina Faso, Cabo Verde, Cameroon, the Republic of the Congo, Côte d'Ivoire, Egypt, Eswatini, Ghana, Kenya, Mali, Mauritius, Niger, Rwanda and Uganda). Six countries (Mauritius, Morocco, Senegal, South Africa, Togo and Tunisia) had tax ratios greater than 20% in 2016.

If social security contributions (SSCs) are excluded, the tax-to-GDP ratios show a different distribution. For example, the five countries with the highest tax-to-GDP ratios including SSCs (Morocco, Senegal, South Africa, Togo[4] and Tunisia) still have tax-to-GDP ratios above 20% when SSCs are excluded but the relative positions of the countries change.

South Africa has the highest ratio without SSCs, at 28.2% of GDP, due to comparatively low tax revenues from SSCs as a percentage of GDP. In contrast, Tunisia, where SSCs equate to 9.3% of GDP, has the fifth-highest tax-to-GDP ratio of African countries if SSCs are excluded.

Figure 1.1. **Tax-to-GDP ratios and total tax revenue (excluding social security contributions) as percentage of GDP, 2016**

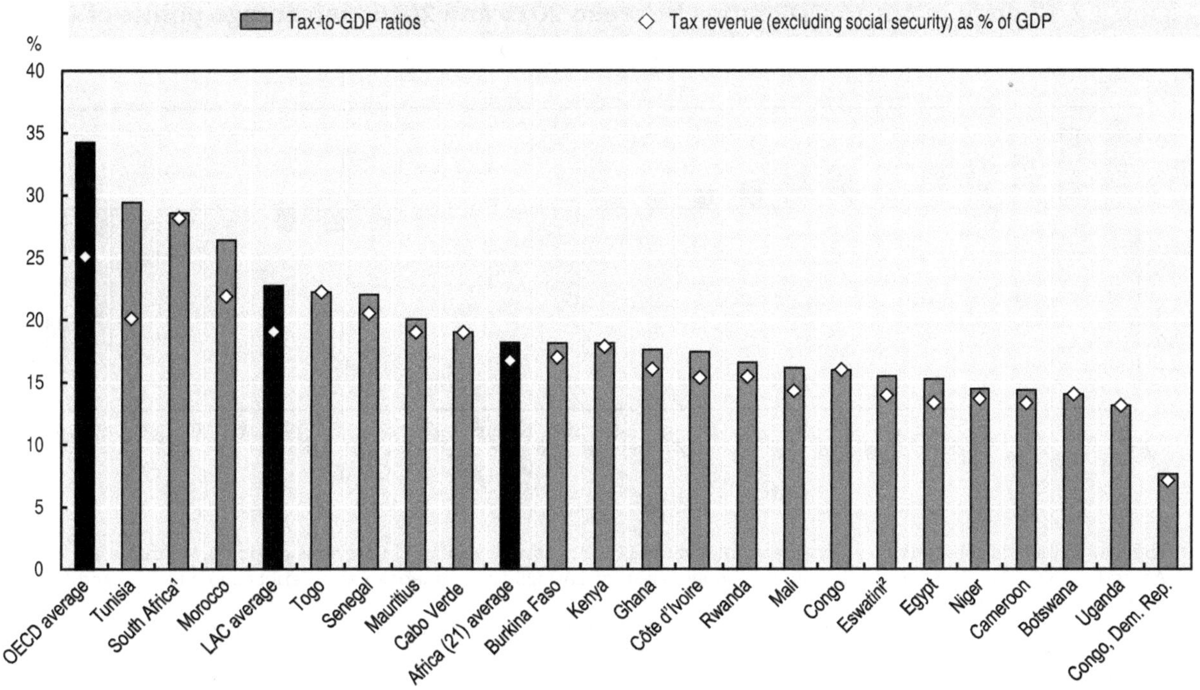

Notes: The figures include sub-national government tax revenues for Eswatini (Swaziland in previous editions), Mauritius, Morocco and South Africa for 2002-2016. The Africa (21) average, the averages for LAC (25 Latin American and Caribbean countries) and the OECD (35 countries) are unweighted.

The Africa (21) average should be interpreted with caution as data on social security contributions are not available for the Republic of the Congo, the Democratic Republic of the Congo (prior to 2012), Togo and Uganda and are only partially available in Cameroon and Senegal. Social security contributions for Botswana are deemed to be null as they do not meet the criteria to be classified as social security contributions set out in the OECD classification of taxes in the Interpretative Guide. See the country tables in Chapter 5 for further information.

1. The tax-to-GDP ratio should be interpreted with caution as it includes payments made by South Africa to the Southern African Customs Union (SACU) pool.
2. Previously Swaziland.

Source: Tables 4.1 and 4.2 in Chapter 4 and (OECD/ATAF/AUC, 2018[3]), "Revenue Statistics in Africa: Comparative tables", *OECD Tax Statistics* (database), *http://dx.doi.org/10.1787/be755711-en*, for the LAC average.

StatLink *https://doi.org/10.1787/888933818777*

Changes in tax-to-GDP ratios between 2015 and 2016

The tax-to-GDP ratio for the Africa (21) average remained stable between 2015 and 2016 (Figure 1.2), in the context of a slowdown in economic activity in Africa. Amid a sustained decline in commodity prices and weak global economic conditions, GDP growth across Africa as a whole fell from 3.6% in 2015 to 2.2% in real terms in 2016 (AfDB/OECD/UNDP, 2017[4]). In comparison, the LAC tax-to-GDP ratio average decreased by 0.3 percentage points and the OECD average increased by 0.3 percentage points over the same period.

The relative stability of the Africa (21) average is a result of two distinct situations within the group of countries: 11 countries recorded an increase in their tax-to-GDP ratio in 2016 whereas 10 countries recorded a decrease (Figure 1.2). Changes of over 1.0 percentage points occurred in countries with low tax-to-GDP ratios (below 17.0%): Botswana registered the highest increase (1.3 percentage points) followed by Mali (1.2 percentage points). The largest decreases (of over 2.0 percentage points) occurred in the Democratic Republic of the Congo and Niger. These countries aside, there were no other changes of more than one percentage point in either direction.

Figure 1.2. **Change in tax-to-GDP ratios between 2015 and 2016 (percentage points of GDP)**

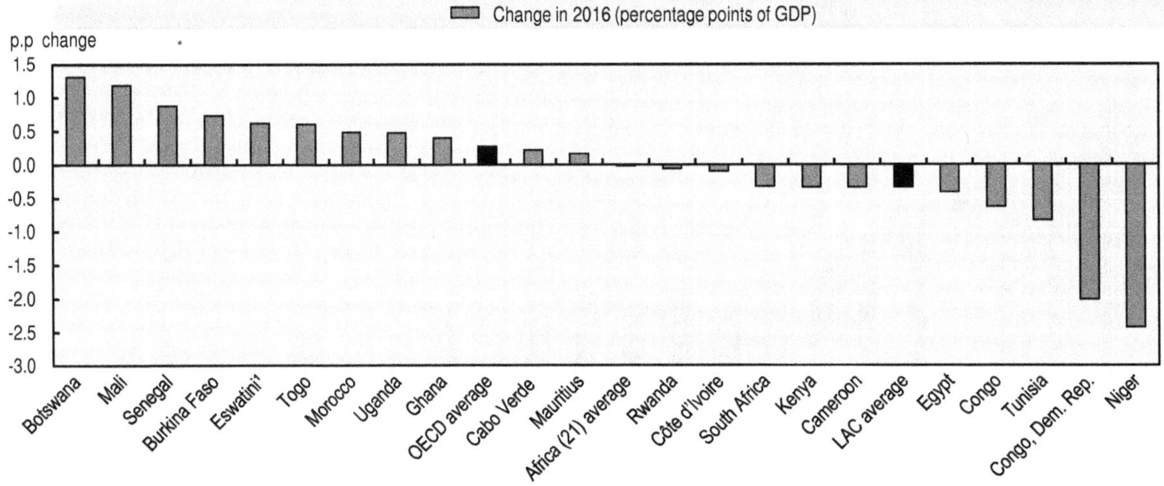

Notes: The figures include sub-national government tax revenues for Eswatini (Swaziland in previous editions), Mauritius, Morocco and South Africa for 2002-2016. The Africa (21) average, the averages for LAC (25 Latin American and Caribbean countries) and the OECD (35 countries) are unweighted.

The change in the Africa (21) average should be interpreted with caution as data for social security contributions are not available or are partial in a few countries. See the country tables in Chapter 5 for further information.

1. Previously Swaziland.

Source: Authors' calculations based on data in Table 4.1 in Chapter 4 and (OECD/ATAF/AUC, 2018[3]), "Revenue Statistics in Africa: Comparative tables", *OECD Tax Statistics* (database), *http://dx.doi.org/10.1787/be755711-en*, for the LAC average.

StatLink *https://doi.org/10.1787/888933818796*

The main tax revenue categories (as a percentage of GDP) also remained stable between 2015 and 2016 but there was great heterogeneity among countries. In the two countries that recorded the biggest increases between 2015 and 2016 – Botswana and Mali – the tax revenue categories that drove the increases differed. An increase in income tax revenue equivalent to 1.1% of GDP was the main driver of the increase of Botswana's tax-to-GDP ratio. In Mali, the increase in the tax-to-GDP ratio was explained principally by a 0.5 percentage point increase in revenues from value added tax (VAT) and a 0.3 percentage point increase in social security contributions.

In Botswana, the increase in income tax revenue as a percentage of GDP (of 1.1 percentage points) was entirely driven by the "mineral tax", an income tax on companies in the mineral sector (predominantly diamonds). Sales of diamonds increased significantly in 2016, resulting in a large increase in Botswana's mineral exports and fiscal revenues (IMF, 2017[5]).

In Mali, the overall increase in the tax-to-GDP ratio was 1.2 percentage points between 2015 and 2016, well above the target set by the government of 0.75% of GDP. Mali has implemented various reforms to expand the tax base, reduce exemptions and improve revenue-collecting agencies' civic-mindedness (IMF, 2016[6]). For example, in recent years the Direction General of Taxes of Mali has operated targeted audits in companies not usually entitled to claim VAT refunds. These audits have resulted in an increase in the number of businesses effectively paying VAT and helped to increase VAT revenue by 0.5% of GDP in 2016, an increase that accounted for 43% of the total increase in the tax-to-GDP ratio.

Figure 1.3. **Change in tax-to-GDP ratios by main tax heading between 2015 and 2016 and by country (percentage points of GDP)**

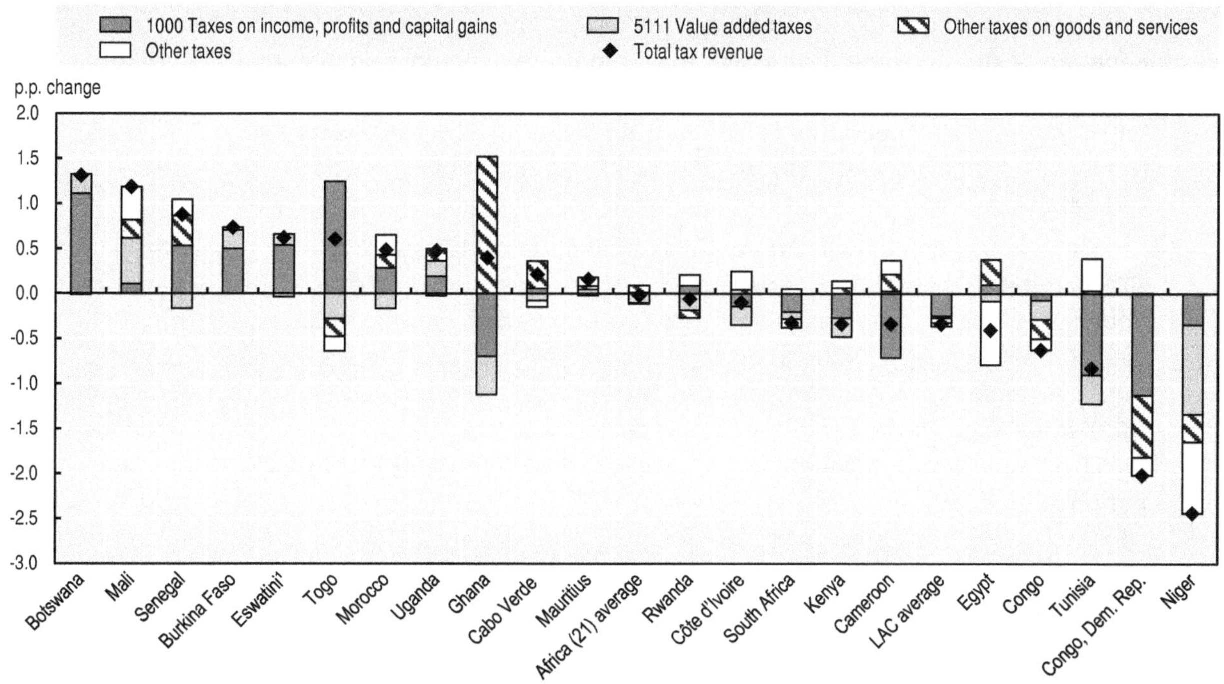

Notes: The figures include sub-national government tax revenues for Mauritius, Morocco, South Africa and Eswatini (previously Swaziland). The Africa (21) average, the averages for LAC (25 Latin American and Caribbean countries) and the OECD (35 countries) are unweighted. The Africa (21) average should be interpreted with caution as data for social security contributions are not available or are partial in a few countries. See the country tables in Chapter 5 for further information.

1. Previously Swaziland.

Source: Authors' calculations based on data in (OECD/ATAF/AUC, 2018[3]), "Revenue Statistics in Africa: Comparative tables", *OECD Tax Statistics* (database), *http://dx.doi.org/10.1787/be755711-en*, for the LAC average.

StatLink https://doi.org/10.1787/888933818815

The Democratic Republic of the Congo and Niger registered the largest decreases among the 21 countries included in this publication in their tax-to-GDP ratio, of 2.0 and 2.4 percentage points respectively. In Niger, the decreases in tax revenue as a percentage of GDP occurred across all the main categories, particularly VAT (1.0 percentage points) and other taxes such as registration fees (0.8 percentage points). In the Democratic Republic of the Congo, decreases in income tax revenues (equivalent to 1.1% of GDP) and in other taxes on goods and services[5] (0.7% of GDP) explained the overall decrease in the tax-to-GDP ratio.

Some countries showed significant increases in certain tax types between 2015 and 2016. Ghana's revenues from other taxes on goods and services increased by 1.5% of GDP following the introduction of new excise measures included within the Energy Sector Levies Act passed in December 2015. New levies on petroleum products, the energy debt recovery levy and the price stabilisation and recovery levy, were introduced and the road fund and the energy fund — levied on diesel and petrol — were revised upwards. The increase in excises compensated for drops in revenues from the other tax categories (by 0.7% of GDP for income taxes and 0.4% for VAT). A decrease in crude oil production contributed to a decline in corporate income tax (CIT) (hellenicshippingnews, 2017[7]).

The decrease in Niger's tax-to-GDP ratio in 2016 was largely attributable to lower activity among large companies, particularly in the mining, oil and telecommunications sectors. In addition, the depreciation of the Naira in Nigeria – following Nigeria's economic slowdown caused by the drop in international oil prices in 2014 – resulted in a drop in Niger's exports of petroleum products to Nigeria (IMF, 2017a[8]).

Declines in oil prices reduced revenues from the mining sector in the Democratic Republic of the Congo and affected all the main tax categories (such as CIT, VAT and import duties). In addition, the government implemented a reform exempting import VAT for companies operating in the mining sector, leading to a decrease of revenues from VAT on imports equivalent to 1.1% of GDP (though this was offset by a decrease in VAT refunds).

Changes in revenues from personal income tax (PIT) and CIT as a percentage of GDP between 2015 and 2016 varied significantly across the 21 countries included in this publication (Figure 1.4). Changes in CIT revenue varied more than revenues from PIT. In 2016, Cameroon, the Democratic Republic of the Congo and Tunisia recorded decreases in CIT revenues of at least 0.5% of GDP. Tunisia registered the largest decrease (1.6% of GDP) while Togo showed the largest increase (1.1% of GDP). In contrast, most changes in PIT revenue were equivalent to between -0.1% of GDP and 0.4% of GDP over the same period.

Figure 1.4. **Annual changes in revenue from taxes on income and profits, by sub-category and by country between 2015 and 2016 (percentage points of GDP)**

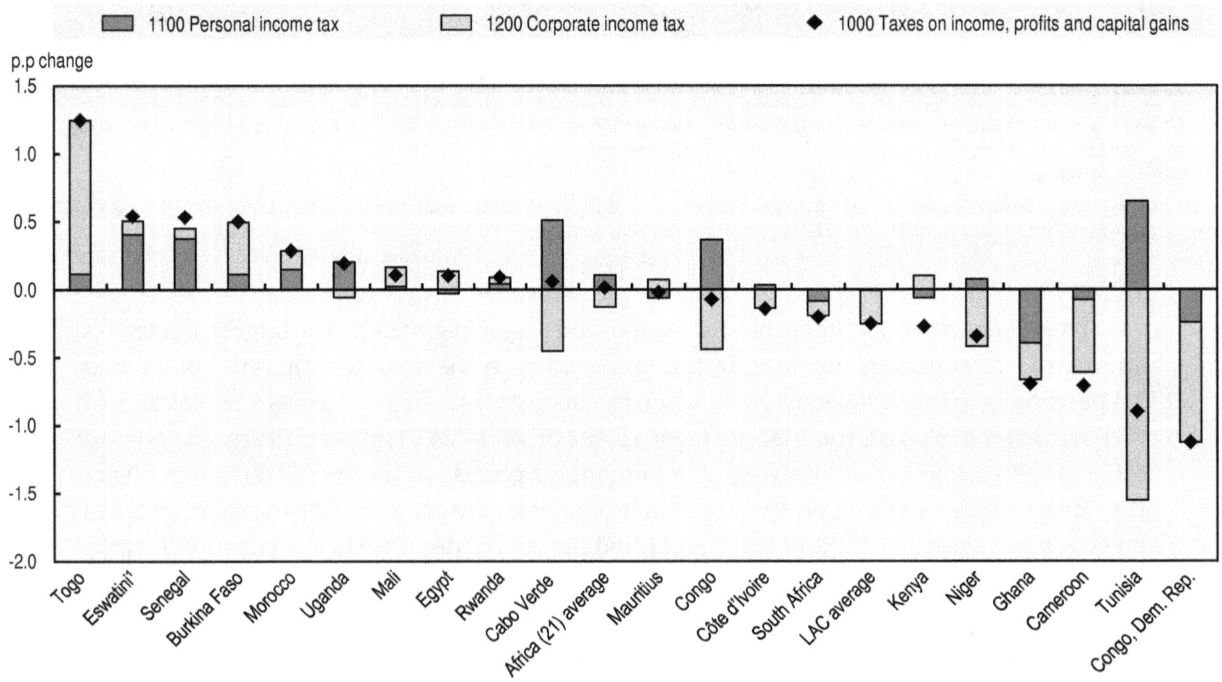

Notes: The Africa (21) average, the averages for LAC (25 Latin American and Caribbean countries) and the OECD (35 countries) are unweighted. Botswana is not included as the breakdown of income tax by 1100 personal income tax and 1200 corporate income tax is not available.

1. Previously Swaziland.

Source: Authors' calculations based on data in (OECD/ATAF/AUC, 2018[3]), "Revenue Statistics in Africa: Comparative tables", *OECD Tax Statistics* (database), *http://dx.doi.org/10.1787/be755711-en.*

StatLink https://doi.org/10.1787/888933818834

Evolution of tax-to-GDP ratios since 2000

With the exception of the period between 2008 and 2010, the average tax-to-GDP ratio for the Africa (21) rose more or less steadily between 2000 and 2015, before stalling in 2016 (Figure 1.5). It increased by 5.0 percentage points across the period as a whole, from 13.1% in 2000 to 18.2% in 2016. This growth reflects favourable macroeconomic conditions, changes in tax policy and strengthening of tax administrations. This trend is similar to that of LAC countries, where the average tax-to-GDP ratio increased by 4.7 percentage points over the same period. The performance of the 21 countries included in this publication and LAC contrasts with OECD countries, where the average tax-to-GDP ratio was 34.3% in 2016, 0.4 percentage points above its level in 2000.

The global financial crisis resulted in a decrease of the average tax-to-GDP ratio across the Africa (21) of 0.3 percentage points between 2008 and 2010. A slowdown in economic activity and lower commodity prices contributed to this decrease. Over the same period, a number of the 21 countries implemented measures to stimulate the economy. For example, Morocco reduced the CIT rate by 5 percentage points in 2008 to improve companies' competitiveness and enhance their resilience during the financial crisis (see Box 1.1).

The LAC average also decreased between 2008 and 2010, by 0.4 percentage points. In contrast, the OECD average was affected by the crisis mainly between 2007 and 2009, registering a decrease in the tax-to-GDP ratio of 1.4 percentage points over that period. OECD countries also recovered more slowly; the average tax-to-GDP ratio returned to its pre-crisis level of 33.7% in 2014, whereas the Africa (21) average exceeded its pre-crisis level (16.6% in 2008) in 2011.

Figure 1.5. **Average tax-to-GDP ratios for Africa (21), LAC and OECD, 2000-16**

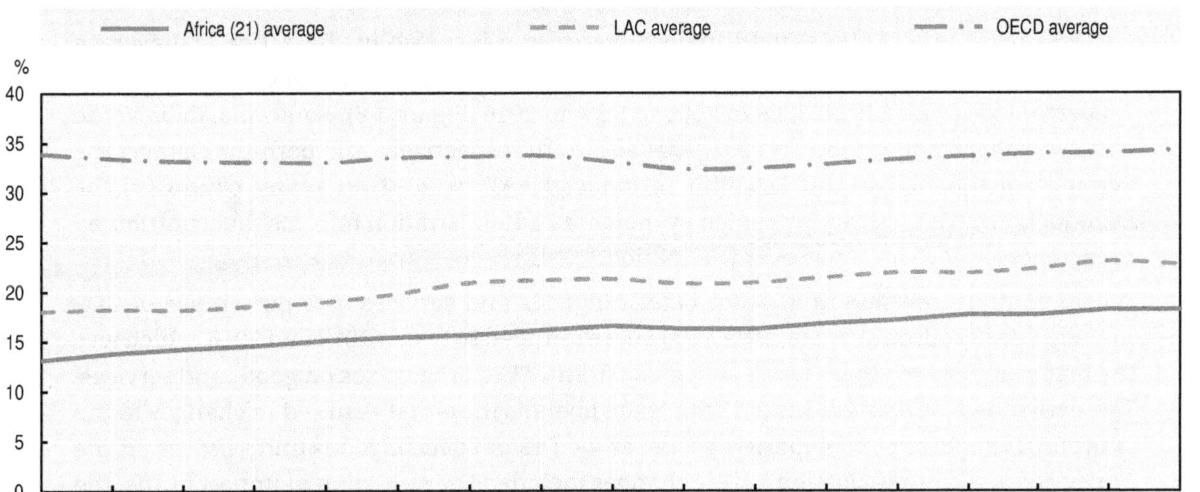

Notes: The figures include sub-national government tax revenues for Eswatini (Swaziland in previous editions), Mauritius, Morocco and South Africa for 2002-2016.

The Africa (21) average, the average for LAC (25 Latin American and Caribbean countries) and the OECD average (35 countries) are unweighted.

The Africa (21) average should be interpreted with caution as data for social security contributions are not available or are partial in a few countries. See the country tables in Chapter 5 for further information.

Source: Table 4.1 in Chapter 4 for the OECD and Africa (21) averages and (OECD/ATAF/AUC, 2018[3]), "Revenue Statistics in Africa: Comparative tables", *OECD Tax Statistics* (database), *http://dx.doi.org/10.1787/be755711-en*, for the LAC average.

StatLink *https://doi.org/10.1787/888933818853*

Since 2000, a large number of African countries have implemented major structural reforms of their tax administrations and have undertaken significant changes to their tax systems. For many countries, reforms were aimed at strengthening and modernising tax administrations. Among the reform initiatives introduced were taxpayer offices specialising in large and/or medium-sized companies; self-assessment systems; taxpayer segmentation and modern risk management (Kloeden, 2011[9]); (Fossat; Bua, 2013[10]). Some countries undertook reforms to expand their tax base, eliminating certain exemptions and simplifying tax legislation. These changes were often accompanied by programmes to educate taxpayers about tax systems and to improve taxpayer services, for example through the introduction of electronic tax service facilities.

Extensive reforms carried out by Rwanda since 2000, for example, have increased tax revenues significantly (AfDB, 2010[11]). The objective of these measures was to expand the tax base by registering informal businesses and simplifying compliance processes. Other reforms contributing to the increase in tax revenues included the introduction of a VAT in 2001, new income tax laws and new tax rates in 2005 and 2006 as well as the strengthening of the compliance enforcement system and internal collection processes. The compliance rate of large taxpayers — who contribute around 75% of total domestic tax revenues — has risen to 97% following these reforms. Morocco has also implemented an extensive tax reform agenda since 2004 (see Box 1.1).

Revenue from income taxes contributed the most to the increase of the average tax-to-GDP ratio of the Africa (21) between 2000 and 2016. Income tax revenues increased by 2.6% of GDP over this period to reach 6.2% of GDP in 2016, driven mainly by CIT revenue, which increased by 1.4 percentage points from 1.4% to 2.8% of GDP. PIT revenue as a percentage of GDP has increased steadily since 2000 and reached its highest-ever level of 3.0% in 2016 versus 2.1% in 2000.

VAT revenue was the second main driver of the increase in the Africa (21) average tax-to-GDP ratio between 2000 and 2016. VAT revenue as a percentage of GDP increased by 2.0 percentage points, from 3.3% in 2000 to 5.3% in 2016 (Figure 1.6). Botswana, Cabo Verde and Rwanda introduced VAT in 2002, 2004 and 2001, respectively, and both the Democratic Republic of the Congo and Eswatini introduced VAT in 2012. In many countries, the introduction of VAT was accompanied by major tax administration reforms that contributed to increases in VAT revenues over that period.

In contrast, revenue from other taxes on goods and services as a percentage of GDP initially decreased, on average, after 2000 but rebounded between 2013 and 2016, which was the first year in which there was a shift away from VAT to other taxes on goods and services. The earlier decline was associated with trade liberalisation that resulted in changes to the taxation of imported and exported goods, as well as of specific goods and services, in the 21 countries of this publication. These changes included the reduction of import tariffs, the narrowing of the base of products and services subject to excises and the elimination of taxes on exports.

Trends observed for these different tax types in the 21 African countries are on average similar to those recorded in the LAC region. The Africa (21) average revenue from taxes on income and profits recorded a higher increase than the LAC average between 2000 and 2016 (2.6 percentage points compared to 1.8 percentage points in LAC). In contrast, the Africa (21) average for VAT revenue as a percentage of GDP grew by less than the LAC average (2.0 percentage points compared to 2.1 percentage points). As happened for the

Africa (21) average, the LAC average for revenues from taxes on other goods and services declined up to 2013 since when it has slightly increased. In contrast, revenues from taxes on income and profits and from taxes on other goods and services as percentage of GDP were relatively flat over this period for OECD countries; VAT revenues increased slightly, by 0.3 percentage points.[6]

Box 1.1. **Tax reforms in Morocco between 2004 and 2013**

Between 2004 and 2013, Morocco undertook a number of key tax policy reforms, which were accompanied by a reorganisation and strengthening of its tax administration. These reforms contributed to an increase in total tax revenues from 23.1% of GDP in 2004 to 28.1% in 2013.

The most substantial reforms concerned VAT; changes to the VAT system occurred nearly every year and included measures to expand the tax base, simplify taxation rules for certain products and reduce the number of products subject to exonerations and reduced rates. The number of VAT rates was also reduced. Between 2004 and 2013, VAT revenue as a percentage of GDP increased by 2.8 percentage points, accounting for 56% of the total increase in tax revenue over this period.

Reforms were made to the CIT (impôt sur les sociétés) in 2008, 2011 and 2013, with a view to improving competitiveness and assisting companies during the financial crisis. The main measures included:

- reducing the CIT rate from 35% to 30% and the tax on profits on the financial sector from 39.6% to 37% in 2008;
- the reduction of the CIT rate for small companies whose turnover did not exceed 3 million Dirhams in 2011; and
- further exonerations and reduced CIT rates for targeted small companies in 2013.

As a result of these reforms and the financial crisis, CIT revenues decreased by 2% of GDP between 2008 and 2013. However, between 2004 and 2013, CIT revenues increased by 1.5% of GDP, due to exceptional revenue growth resulting from enforcement measures and strong economic growth prior to the financial crisis.

The PIT system (impôt sur le revenu) was reformed in 2007, 2009 and 2010 with the goal of improving the purchasing power of households. Over this period, marginal PIT rates were reduced, tax scales were restructured and the threshold for exempt income increased significantly. The Direction Générale des Impôts (DGI) estimated that these measures led to a total reduction in revenue of 11 billion Dirhams over the period. As a percentage of GDP, PIT revenues declined by 1.0 percentage points between 2007 and 2010.

Significant improvements were made to tax administrations between 2004 and 2013. Targeted taxpayer services were created in 2005 (for large taxpayers and small companies, for example) to meet the needs of these groups and provide them with more tailored services. These efforts led to an increase in the number of taxpayers registered for VAT, CIT and PIT of 8%-13% in 2007. In addition, responsibility for CIT and VAT collection was passed to the DGI, resulting in an estimated growth in CIT revenue of 19% between 2004 and 2005. Finally, tax audits and inspections were reinforced, leading to an increase in compliance by companies.

Source: Lakhal, H., Moroccan Ministry of Finance (DGI), based on an analysis undertaken while on secondment at the OECD.

Figure 1.6. **Revenue from taxes on income and profits, VAT and other tax headings as a percentage of GDP, 2000-16**

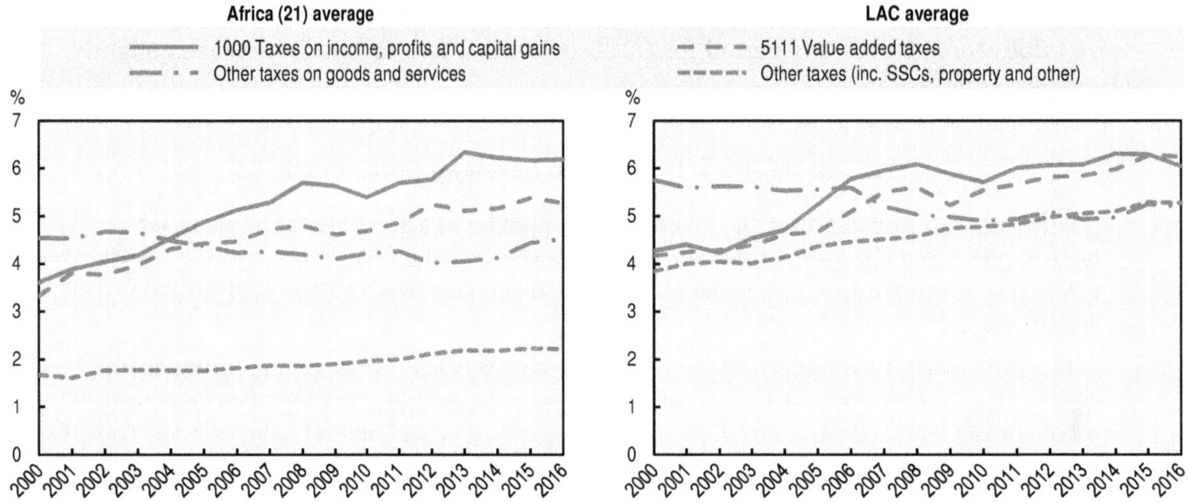

Notes: The figures include sub-national government tax revenues for Eswatini (Swaziland in previous editions), Mauritius, Morocco and South Africa for 2002-2016.

The Africa (21) average, the averages for LAC (25 Latin American and Caribbean countries) and the OECD (35 countries) are unweighted. Due to lack of data availability, the Africa (21) average does not include Botswana prior to 2004, Egypt prior to 2002 and Kenya prior to 2001. The Africa (21) average for other taxes should be interpreted with caution as data for social security contributions are not available or are partial in a few countries. See the country tables in Chapter 5 for further information.

Source: Table 4.1 in Chapter 4 for the OECD and Africa (21) averages and (OECD/ATAF/AUC, 2018[3]), "Revenue Statistics in Africa: Comparative tables", *OECD Tax Statistics* (database), *http://dx.doi.org/10.1787/be755711-en*, for the LAC average.

StatLink *https://doi.org/10.1787/888933818872*

While the trends in income taxes, VAT and other goods and service taxes were very similar between the Africa (21) and the LAC averages, revenue from social security contributions, property taxes and other taxes evolved differently between 2000 and 2016, explaining the difference in the tax-to-GDP ratio between the two groups. In 2016, revenue from social security contributions, property taxes and other taxes amounted to 2.2% of GDP on average among the 21 countries included in this publication compared to 5.3% of GDP in the LAC region.

In 2016, social security contributions as a percentage of GDP in the LAC region stood at 3.7% compared to the Africa (21) average of 1.7%.[7] Social security contributions in the LAC region as a percentage of GDP increased by 1.1 percentage points between 2000 and 2016 whereas the Africa (21) average increased by 0.4 percentage points[8]. From the 1980s onwards, many LAC countries have made substantial reforms to their social security systems that contributed to the increase of revenues from social security contributions.

The evolution of tax-to-GDP ratios was different for each country among the 21 countries included in this publication between 2000 and 2016 (Figure 1.8). The Republic of the Congo and Togo recorded the highest increases of more than 10 percentage points. Over this period, and in particular since 2006, Togo has made significant efforts to improve the processes of its three revenue administrations and to establish stronger revenue authorities. Measures implemented by Togo between 2010 and 2012 included initiatives to increase the number of tax offices; tackle fraud and tax evasion; establish the monitoring of revenue systems; increase the number of registered taxpayers; modernise information systems; and reinforce staff capacity. Another reform was the establishment of the OTR (Office togolais des recettes) in 2014, which unified customs and tax services into a single administration. These reforms contributed to Togo increasing its tax revenues as a percentage of GDP by 7.2 percentage points between 2010 and 2016, which represents 57% of the total increase since 2000.

Figure 1.7. **Change in tax-to-GDP ratios (incl. and excl. SSCs) between 2000 and 2016 (percentage points of GDP)**

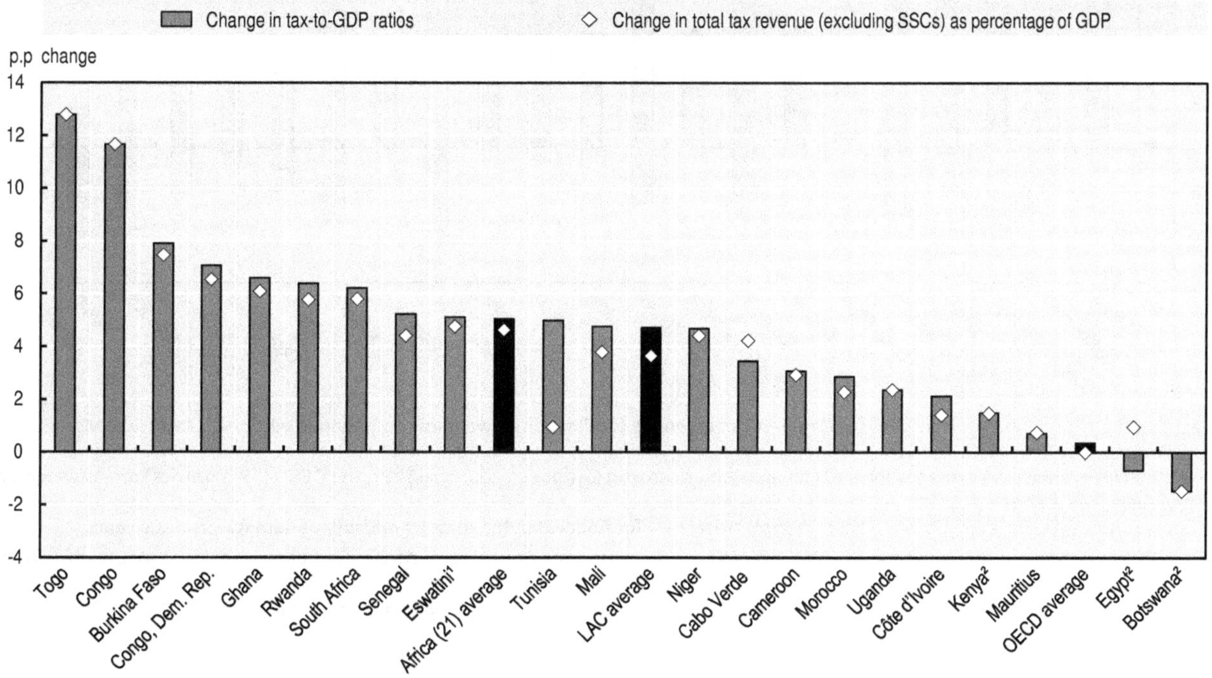

Notes: The figures include sub-national government tax revenues for Eswatini (Swaziland in previous editions), Mauritius, Morocco and South Africa for 2002-2016.

The Africa (21) average, the averages for LAC (25 Latin American and Caribbean countries) and the OECD (35 countries) are unweighted.

1. Previously Swaziland.
2. Change since 2001 for Kenya, since 2002 for Egypt, since 2004 for Botswana due to unavailability of data for previous years

Source: Tables 4.1 and 4.2 in Chapter 4 for the OECD and Africa (21) averages and (OECD/ATAF/AUC, 2018[3]), "Revenue Statistics in Africa: Comparative tables", *OECD Tax Statistics* (database), *http://dx.doi.org/10.1787/be755711-en*, for the LAC average.

StatLink *https://doi.org/10.1787/888933818891*

The principal contributors to the change in tax-to-GDP ratios between 2000 and 2016 varied across countries. VAT was the main contributor for 10 countries (Figure 1.8). The biggest increases in VAT revenue (over 3 percentage points of GDP) occurred in three countries that introduced VAT in the 2000s (Cabo Verde, Rwanda and Eswatini) and in Burkina Faso, the Republic of the Congo and Togo (respectively 3.2, 3.2 and 5.7 percentage points). For the other countries, the main contributors varied between PIT (3 countries), CIT (2 countries), social security contributions (2 countries), other taxes on goods and services (3 countries) and other taxes (1 country).

Figure 1.8. **Change in tax-to-GDP ratios by main tax headings between 2000 and 2016 and by country (percentage points of GDP)**

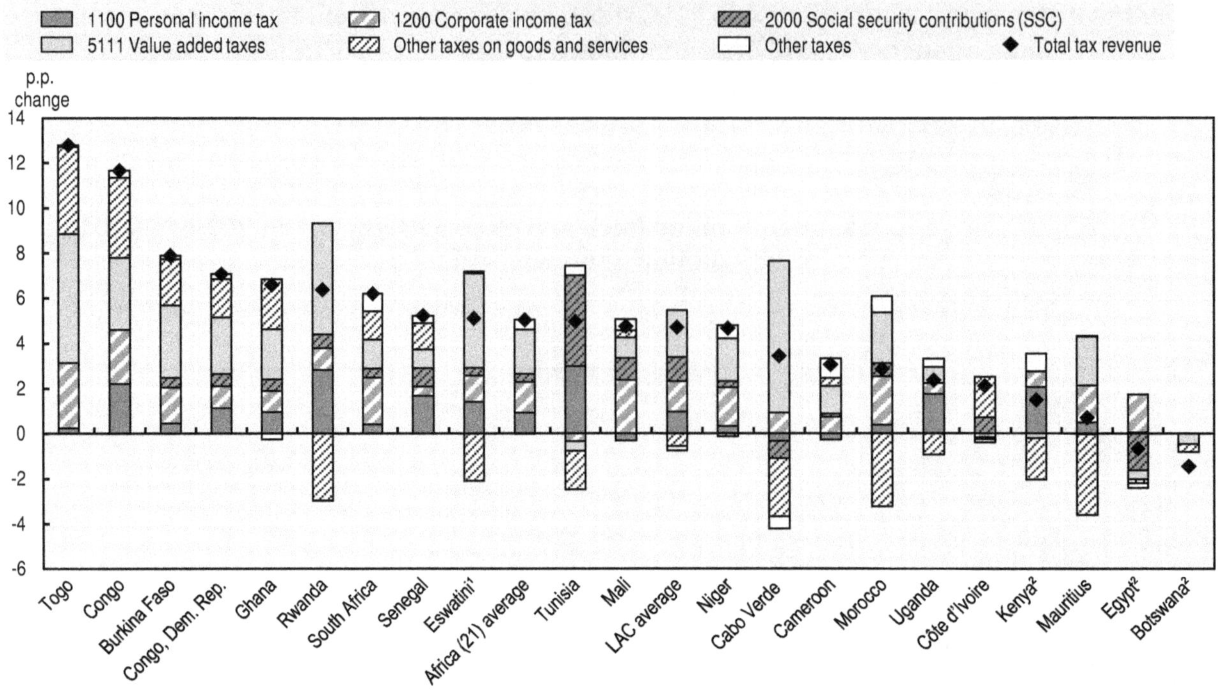

Notes: The figures include sub-national government tax revenues for Eswatini (Swaziland in previous editions), Mauritius, Morocco and South Africa for 2002-2016.

The Africa (21) average, the averages for LAC (25 Latin American and Caribbean countries) and the OECD (35 countries) are unweighted.

1. Previously Swaziland.

2. Change since 2001 for Kenya, since 2002 for Egypt, since 2004 for Botswana due to unavailability of data for previous years

Source: Authors' calculations based on (OECD/ATAF/AUC, 2018[3]) "Revenue Statistics in Africa: Comparative tables", *OECD Tax Statistics* (database), *http://dx.doi.org/10.1787/be755711-en.*

StatLink *https://doi.org/10.1787/888933818910*

Box 1.2. **Changes in tax-to-GDP ratios in African regions**

Most of the 21 countries included in this publication belong to regional organisations whose members adopt common tax and external tariff rules and form a customs union. Kenya, Rwanda and Uganda belong to the East Africa Community (EAC), which also includes Burundi, South Sudan and Tanzania. Burkina Faso, Côte d'Ivoire, Mali, Niger, Senegal and Togo belong to the West African Economic and Monetary Union (WAEMU, also known by its French acronym, UEMOA). This union also includes Benin and Guinea-Bissau.

The evolution of different tax types between 2000 and 2016 in these two regions has differed. Since 2000, revenues from taxes on other goods and services in EAC countries have declined significantly whereas the reverse is observed in the WAEMU countries over this period. The decreases in the EAC countries ranged from 0.9% of GDP in Uganda to 3.0% of GDP in Rwanda. In contrast, these revenues decreased only slightly in Niger (by 0.1% of GDP) and increased in all other WAEMU countries. Togo registered the highest increase since 2000 (equivalent to 3.8% of GDP).

WAEMU introduced common external tariffs (CET) in 2000 whereas CET were implemented in EAC countries in 2005, and so occurred during the period considered in this analysis. This explains the significant reduction of revenues from other goods and services in EAC countries compared to WAEMU countries over this period.

Box 1.2. **Changes in tax-to-GDP ratios in African regions** *(cont.)*

PIT has increased significantly as a percentage of GDP in EAC countries since 2000, by 1.8 percentage points or more in all countries. In contrast, increases in PIT were modest in most WAEMU countries, with the exception of Senegal, which recorded an increase equivalent to 1.7% of GDP, and Mali, where PIT revenues decreased as a percentage of GDP.

CIT as percentage of GDP increased more in the WAEMU countries in this publication than in EAC countries between 2000 and 2016. Increases exceeded 1.5% of GDP in Burkina Faso, Mali, Niger and Togo whereas they did not exceed 1.0% of GDP in any of the EAC countries. Burkina Faso, Mali, Niger and Togo derive some of their tax revenues from mineral resources[a]; the boom in commodity prices in the previous decades contributed to the large increases of CIT revenue over this period.

Figure 1.9. **Change in tax-to-GDP ratios by main type of tax categories for EAC and WAEMU countries in this publication between 2000 and 2016 (percentage points of GDP)**

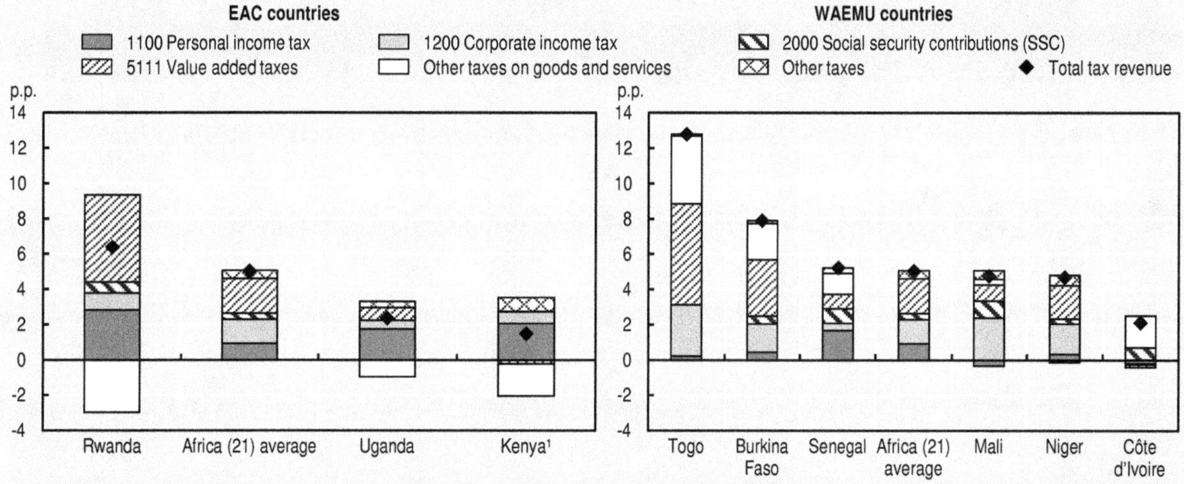

Notes: The figures include sub-national government tax revenues for Eswatini (Swaziland in previous editions), Mauritius, Morocco and South Africa for 2002-2016.

The Africa (21) average, the averages for LAC (25 Latin American and Caribbean countries) and the OECD (35 countries) are unweighted.

1. Change since 2001 for Kenya due to unavailability of data.

Source: Authors' calculations based on (OECD/ATAF/AUC, 2018[3]), "Revenue Statistics in Africa: Comparative tables", *OECD Tax Statistics* (database), *http://dx.doi.org/10.1787/be755711-en*.

StatLink *https://doi.org/10.1787/888933818929*

a. WAEMU member States benefit from natural minerals resources. Gold is the most important export in Burkina Faso and Mali. Niger and Togo are ones of the biggest producers and exporters of uranium and phosphates respectively. (WTO, 2018[25])

Factors influencing tax-to-GDP ratios

Tax-to-GDP ratios are influenced by a variety of domestic and international factors. Domestically, macroeconomic characteristics such as the importance of agriculture in the economy, resource endowments, openness to trade and the size of the informal economy can influence tax-to-GDP ratios. The power of tax administrations, the levels of corruption and tax morale (or willingness of people to pay taxes) are also strongly linked to the level of tax revenues (OECD, 2014[12]). Geographic location is relevant: landlocked countries are less able to impose taxes on goods and services entering the country than island countries. In addition, international factors, including the tax policies of other countries, can impact tax-to-GDP ratios.

Tax-to-GDP ratios tend to be higher in high-income countries: in general, OECD countries collect a higher amount of tax revenues than non-OECD countries, measured as a percentage of GDP. Several of the 21 countries included in this publication have lower income and development levels and lower tax-to-GDP ratios than LAC countries (Figure 1.10). African countries show a wider range of GDP per capita compared with LAC and OECD countries.

Figure 1.10. **Tax-to-GDP ratios and GDP per capita (in PPP) in African countries, LAC, OECD and selected Asian countries, 2016**

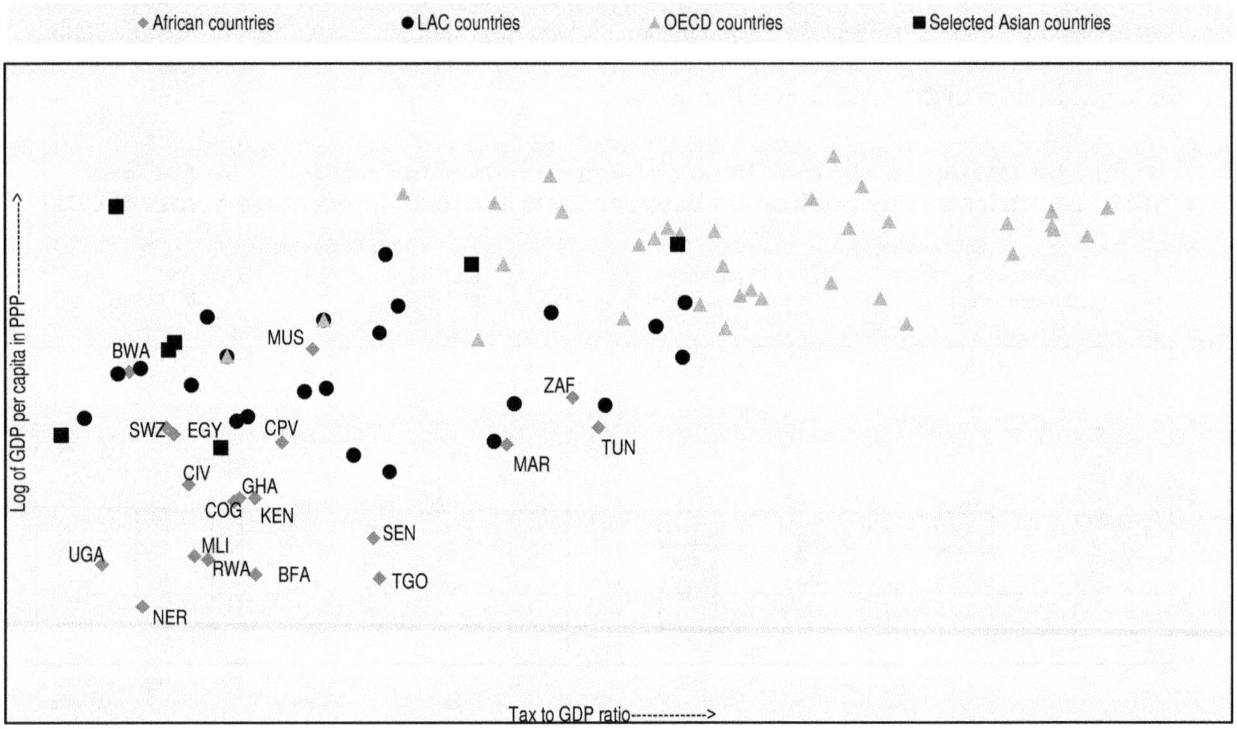

Notes: The y-axis is on a logarithmic scale. The purchasing-power-parity (PPP) between two countries is the rate at which the currency of one country needs to be converted into that of a second country to ensure that a given amount of the first country's currency will purchase the same volume of goods and services in the second country as it does in the first. The implied PPP conversion rate is expressed as national currency per current international dollar. An international dollar has the same purchasing power as the US dollar has in the United States. An international dollar is a hypothetical currency that is used as a means of translating and comparing costs from one country to the other using a common reference point, the US dollar (definitions derived from IMF, 2018 and (WHO, 2015[13]).

Source: (IMF, 2018[14]) for figures of GDP per capita. Tax-to-GDP ratios are sourced from the regional *Revenue Statistics* publications.

StatLink https://doi.org/10.1787/888933818948

Higher shares of agriculture in GDP are associated with lower tax-to-GDP ratios in many studies (Addison and Levin, 2012[15]) (Profeta and Scabrosetti, 2010[16])). This reflects the fact that agriculture is a challenging sector to tax in many countries:

- In developing economies, most people working in this sector receive low incomes and many are not registered for tax purposes (PEAKS, 2013[17]).
- There is less taxation of the agricultural sector in Africa due to a high level of informality and a low level of monetisation (AfDB/OECD/ECA, 2010[18]).
- The agriculture sector often benefits from numerous tax exemptions.

Countries that receive substantial revenues from oil exports for example often exhibit low tax ratios. Countries with more revenues from natural resources tend to resort less to politically-demanding forms of taxation such as income taxes (AfDB/OECD/ECA, 2010[18]) and have relatively narrow tax bases. The three countries (Botswana, Cameroon, and the

Republic of the Congo) that collected oil and mineral royalties and dividends amounting to more than 10% of non-tax revenues in 2016 all had tax ratios below the Africa (21) average. These kinds of revenues, which are not classified as taxes, are discussed in detail in Chapter 2.

Tax structures

A country's tax structure identifies the composition of tax revenues by different tax types. This is an important indicator since different taxes have different economic and social effects. The composition of taxes varies widely across 21 countries included in this publication, reflecting countries' different policy choices, economic structures and conditions, tax administration capabilities and historical factors.

Evolution of tax structures

The Africa (21)'s average tax structure shifted towards VAT and taxes on income and profits between 2000 and 2016. VAT revenue accounted for the highest share of tax revenues in 2016 at 29.3% (5.3% of GDP), an increase of 4.9 percentage points from 2000 (Figure 1.11). The revenue share of other taxes on goods and services was the second highest at 25.3% of total tax revenue in 2016 (4.5% of GDP), although it has declined by 11.5 percentage points since 2000. The share of total tax revenues generated by CIT and PIT grew by 3.3 and 0.8 percentage points respectively, to 15.3% (2.8% of GDP) and 15.8% (3.0% of GDP) over the same period.[9]

Figure 1.11. **Tax structure, Africa (21) average as percentage of total tax revenue and percentage of GDP, 2000 and 2016**

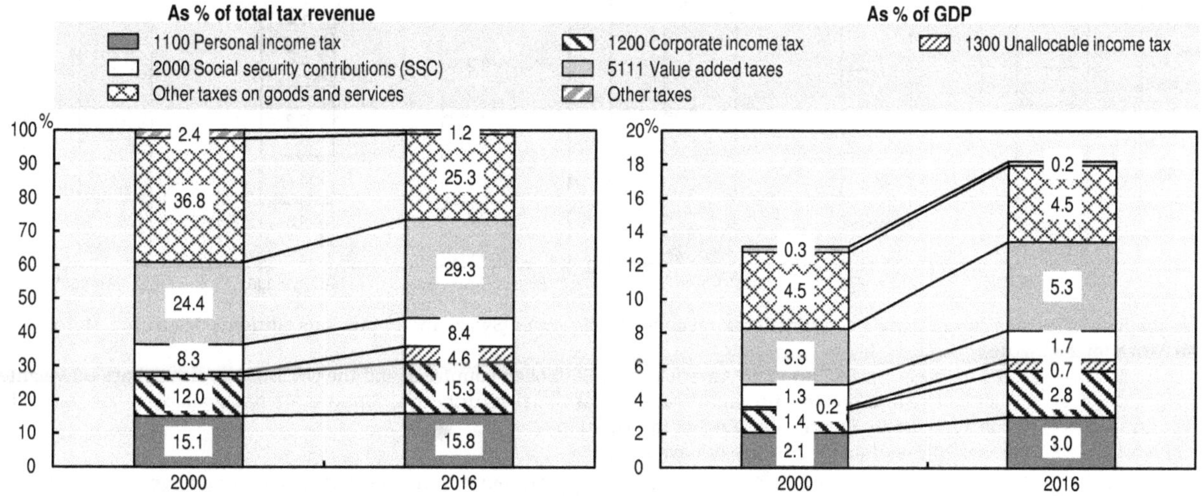

Notes: The figures include sub-national government tax revenues for Eswatini (Swaziland in previous editions), Mauritius, Morocco and South Africa for 2002-2016.

The Africa (21) average, the averages for LAC (25 Latin American and Caribbean countries) and the OECD (35 countries) are unweighted. They should be interpreted with caution as data for social security contributions are not available or are partial in a few countries. See the country tables in Chapter 5 for further information.

Due to lack of data availability, the Africa (21) average does not include Botswana prior to 2004, Egypt prior to 2002 and Kenya prior to 2001.

Source: Authors' calculations based on data on (OECD/ATAF/AUC, 2018[3]), "Revenue Statistics in Africa: Comparative tables", *OECD Tax Statistics* (database), *http://dx.doi.org/10.1787/be755711-en*.

StatLink https://doi.org/10.1787/888933818967

Tax structures in 2016

VAT's contribution to total tax revenues across 21 countries included in this publication on average was the same as its average contribution in LAC and about 10 percentage points higher than the OECD average (20.0%). However, as a percentage of GDP, VAT revenues for the Africa (21) average are lower than the LAC average (6.2%) and OECD average (6.7%) (Figure 1.12).

The Africa (21) average share of CIT revenues in total tax revenue amounted to 15.3% in 2016 (similar to the LAC average at 15.4%) and was higher than the OECD average of 8.9% (2015 figure). Reported as a percentage of GDP, the Africa (21) average and the OECD average have the same share of CIT revenues at 2.8% of GDP; these were lower than the LAC average at 3.4% of GDP (Figure 1.12).

In contrast, the Africa (21) average share of PIT revenues to total tax revenue at 15.8% was lower than the OECD average of 24.4% (2015 figure) but higher than the LAC average (9.7%). As a percentage of GDP, the share of PIT revenues of the OECD average (8.4%) was more than double the Africa (21) average (3.0%).

Figure 1.12. **Tax structure for the Africa (21), LAC and OECD averages as a percentage of total tax revenues and as a percentage of GDP, 2016**

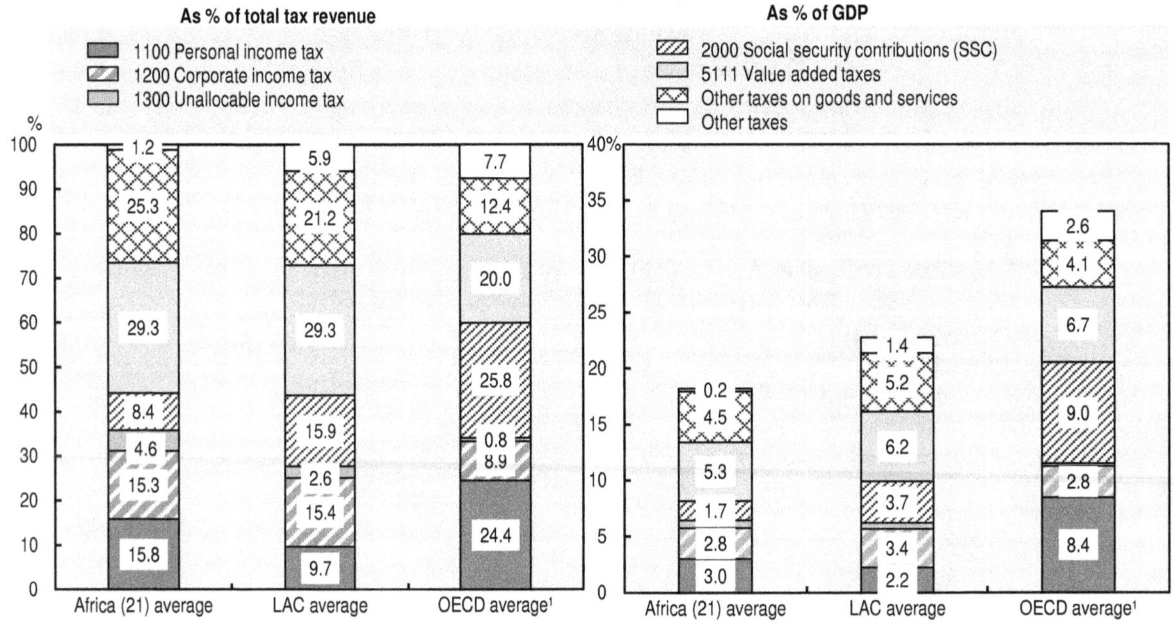

Notes: The figures include sub-national government tax revenues for Eswatini (Swaziland in previous editions), Mauritius, Morocco and South Africa for 2002-2016.
The Africa (21) average, the averages for LAC (25 Latin American and Caribbean countries) and the OECD (35 countries) are unweighted.
The Africa (21) average y should be interpreted with caution as data for social security contributions are not available or are partial in a few countries. See the country tables in Chapter 5 for further information.
The data for the OECD are for 2015 as data for 2016 are not available.

Source: Authors' calculations based on data on (OECD/ATAF/AUC, 2018[3]), "Revenue Statistics in Africa: Comparative tables", *OECD Tax Statistics* (database), *http://dx.doi.org/10.1787/be755711-en*.

StatLink *https://doi.org/10.1787/888933818986*

Tax structures vary considerably among the countries covered in this publication. Figure 1.13 shows the decomposition of tax revenues between income taxes (both personal and corporate), social security contributions, and taxes on goods and services (including VAT and other goods and services taxes).

Taxes on goods and services were the principal source of tax revenues for 17 of the countries, where they ranged from 35.8% of tax revenues in Tunisia to 74.6% of tax revenues in Togo. For these countries, VAT was the main component of revenue from taxes on goods and services except in Côte d'Ivoire, Ghana, Kenya and Uganda, which rely more on other taxes on goods and services.

Figure 1.13. **Tax structures, 2016**

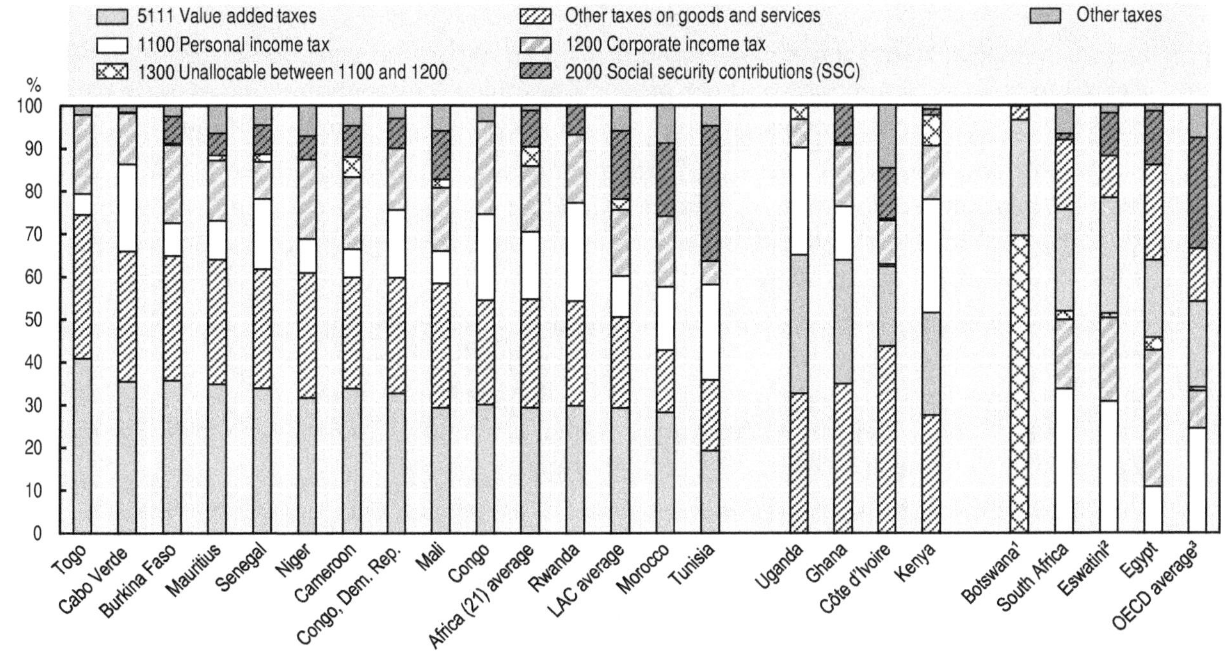

Notes: Figures include sub-national government tax revenues for Eswatini (Swaziland in previous editions), Mauritius, Morocco and South Africa for 2002-2016. The Africa (21) average, the averages for LAC (25 Latin American and Caribbean countries) and the OECD (35 countries) are unweighted.

The Africa (21) average should be interpreted with caution as data for social security contributions are not available or are partial in a few countries. See the country tables in Chapter 5 for further information.

1. The breakdown of revenue from income tax by 1100 personal income tax and 1200 corporate income tax is not available.
2. Previously Swaziland
3. The data for the OECD are for 2015 as data for 2016 are not available.

Source: Authors' calculations based on data on (OECD/ATAF/AUC, 2018[3]), "Revenue Statistics in Africa: Comparative tables", *OECD Tax Statistics* (database), *http://dx.doi.org/10.1787/be755711-en*.

StatLink *https://doi.org/10.1787/888933819005*

Among the four remaining countries (Botswana, Egypt, Eswatini and South Africa), taxes on income and profits accounted for the principal share of total tax revenue and in all four countries represented a greater share of tax revenues than for the OECD and LAC averages. Among these countries, income tax revenues ranged from 45.7% of total tax revenue in Egypt to 69.5% in Botswana. Within the income tax category, South Africa was the only country with a ratio of PIT revenue to GDP that exceeded the average for the OECD.

The importance of social security contributions[10] varies greatly across the 21 countries participating in this publication. The share of social security contributions in total tax revenue is highest in Morocco and Tunisia but they account for a smaller proportion of total tax revenue in the remaining countries, ranging from less than 1.5% in Botswana, Cabo Verde, Kenya and South Africa to above 10% in Côte d'Ivoire, Egypt and Mali. This variation reflects the diversity of the social security programmes and contribution rates in African countries.

For example, social security contributions in South Africa consist only of contributions to the Unemployment Insurance Fund. Other social risks, such as old age and disability, are covered by tax-financed social assistance programmes. In contrast, social security schemes in Morocco and Tunisia are modelled on the French system and cover a wide range of risks including old-age, disability, sickness and maternity, work injury (Tunisia), unemployment (Morocco) and family benefits (SSA, 2015[19]).

Excise taxes

As in most OECD countries, excise taxes are both an important source of tax revenues and are used to influence consumer behaviour. Many countries levy taxes on tobacco and/or alcohol to reduce consumption of these products or impose environmental taxes (such as taxes on transport fuels) to reduce pollution and other negative environmental externalities.

Where possible, the 21 countries participating in this publication have provided a detailed breakdown of their excises by type of products. Excises were classified into seven types: fuel and other petroleum products, mining, tobacco, beverages (both alcohol and soft drinks), vehicles, communication and other.

Excises as a proportion of total tax revenue and of GDP vary greatly across the nine countries (Botswana, Burkina Faso, the Democratic Republic of the Congo, Egypt, Eswatini, Mali, Mauritius, Senegal and Tunisia) for which a detailed breakdown of excise revenue is available. In 2016, they ranged from 1.8% of total tax revenue in Botswana to 18.7% in Mauritius (equivalent to 0.3% and 3.7% of GDP, respectively).

Although the composition of excises is different for each country, the breakdown presented in Figure 1.14 should be treated with caution as it may not cover all products. All nine countries tax fuel and other petroleum products; this category contributed about 25% of total revenues from excises in five countries and two-thirds or more in four countries in 2016 (Figure 1.14). The two other categories that represent a significant share of excises are tobacco and beverages. Revenues from excises on tobacco exceeded 25% of total excise revenues in Egypt, Tunisia and Mauritius and revenues from excises on beverages exceeded 25% of total excise revenues in Botswana, Burkina Faso, the Democratic Republic of the Congo and Mauritius.

Figure 1.14. **Composition of excise taxes in selected African countries, 2016**

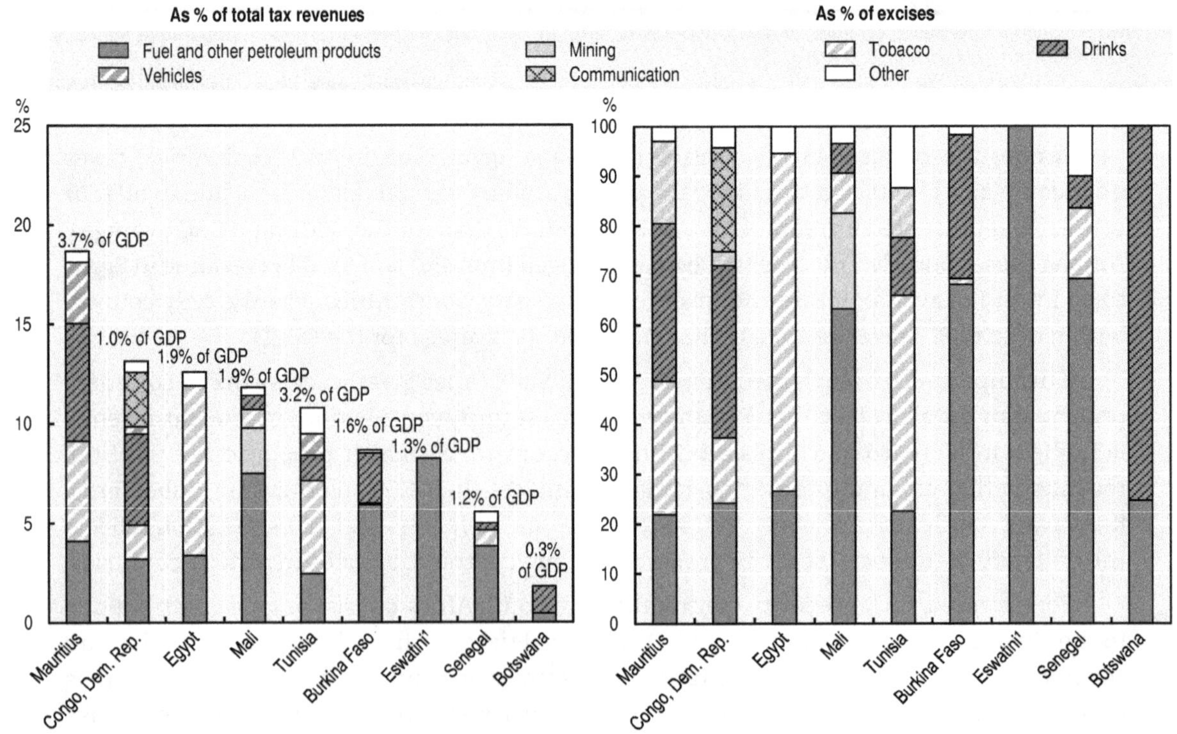

1. Previously Swaziland.

Source: Authors' calculations based on data on (OECD/ATAF/AUC, 2018[3]) from the individual country tables.

StatLink https://doi.org/10.1787/888933819024

Taxes by level of government

Analysis of taxation by level of government for the 21 countries participating in this publication is limited by the fact that data on sub-national tax revenues were only available in four countries: Eswatini, Mauritius,[11] Morocco and South Africa. Revenues collected at sub-national levels are considered to be low in the 21 African countries. AfDB/OECD/UNDP (2015[20]) states that "in Africa, on average, the weight of local government revenue is 7% of the total revenue of local, regional and national governments combined". In 2016, sub-national government revenues as a percentage of total tax revenues were low in the four countries for which data exist: less than 1% in Eswatini and Mauritius, 3.5% in Morocco and 5.0% in South Africa.

Revenues from property taxes are the most important source of tax revenue for sub-central governments in Eswatini, Mauritius, Morocco and South Africa. They represented more than 80% of total tax revenues collected locally in the four countries. Most of the remainder derives from taxes on goods and services. There are wide differences in local taxation among African countries and many of them do not levy any local taxes on buildings and landholdings, or on economic activities (AfDB/OECD/UNDP, 2015[20]).

Sub-central governments generally have limited tax collection responsibilities and most tax revenue is collected at the central government level. AfDB/OECD/UNDP (2015[20]) observed that "Many local governments receive a significant share of their total revenues from central government transfers".

Local governments across Africa have limited resources and their tax administrations are not appropriately equipped to collect taxes efficiently or to properly account for them. This results in high collection costs and an extensive number of low-yield taxes. Moreover, the processing of data on revenue collections and the exchange of information with other public institutions is poor and there is usually little co-operation with the central government. This leads to the duplication of taxes or taxes that are contrary to national objectives (such as local taxes on export crops). Apart from South Africa, appropriate property registers are lacking, which is a major challenge for the collection of property taxes (Fjeldstad; Chambas; Brun, 2014[21]). In Mauritius, for instance, property tax provides a low yield partly due to outdated cadastres and valuations of property (IMF, May 2014[22]).

Although many African countries have undertaken major reforms of their central tax legislation and administrations over the last decades, less has been done at the local government level. Central government taxation has been a greater priority because of the need to reduce national fiscal deficits. It is also easier and less costly to reform central tax legislation and systems than those for local taxes and the potential revenue gains from tax reform at a national level are greater.

Morocco has been reforming local government tax systems and administrations since 2007 to strengthen local tax revenue (Boisard; de Freitas; Hidouci, 2014[23]). South Africa has successfully decentralised urban property tax collection and has developed a modern system to collect property tax revenue. Municipal governments there benefit from appropriate expertise and resources (Monkam and Moore, 2015[24])

Notes

1. Previously Swaziland.
2. Lithuania became an OECD member country on 5 July 2018. Data for Lithuania will be included for the first time in the *OECD Revenue Statistics* publication that will be released in November 2018.

3. Data on social security contributions are not available for the Republic of the Congo, the Democratic Republic of the Congo (prior to 2012), Togo and Uganda; and are only partially available in Cameroon and Senegal. Social security contributions for Botswana are deemed to be null as they do not meet the criteria to be classified as social security contributions set out in the OECD classification of taxes in the Interpretative Guide. See the country tables in Chapter 5 for further information).
4. This ranking should be interpreted with caution as social security contributions data are missing for Togo.
5. These represent mainly excises, customs and import duties
6. Change between 2000 and 2015 as data for 2016 are not available.
7. The Africa (21) average for social security contributions as a percentage of GDP should be interpreted with caution due to the unavailability and incompleteness of social security contributions data in some African countries in this publication.
8. The Africa (21) average should be interpreted with caution as data for social security contributions are not available or are partial in a few countries. Specifically, social security contributions are not available for the Republic of the Congo, the Democratic Republic of the Congo (prior to 2012), Togo and Uganda and are only partially available in Cameroon and Senegal.
9. The Africa (21) average for the corporate income and personal income tax revenue as a percentage of GDP and as a percentage of the total tax revenue should be interpreted with caution as a proportion of income tax revenue could not be allocated within corporate income tax and personal income tax revenue (0.7% of GDP and 4.9% of total tax revenue in 2016).
10. The data for social security contributions are unavailable for the Democratic Republic of the Congo (prior to 2012), Togo and Uganda and are incomplete for Cameroon and Senegal [figures include social security contributions from the Institution de Prévoyance Retraites du Sénégal (IPRES) and data from the Caisse de Sécurité Sociale (CSS). The latter are only available from 2012].
11. Data from Mauritius were derived from financial statements produced by Statistics Mauritius.

References

Addison, T. and J. Levin (2012), *The Determinants of Tax Revenue in Sub-Saharan Africa*, Swedish Business School at Örebro University, Örebro, Sweden, *http://oru.diva-portal.org/smash/record.jsf?pid=diva2%3A570456&dswid=4207.* [15]

AfDB (2010), *Domestic Resource Mobilization for Poverty Reduction in East Africa: Rwanda case study*, African Development Bank, Abidjan, *http://www.afdb.org/fileadmin/uploads/afdb/Documents/Project-and-Operations/Rwanda%20case%20study%20paper%20final.pdf.* [11]

AfDB/OECD/ECA (2010), *African Economic Outlook 2010: Domestic Resource Mobilisation and Aid*, OECD Publishing, Paris, *http://dx.doi.org/10.1787/aeo-2010-en.* [18]

AfDB/OECD/UNDP (2017), *African Economic Outlook 2017: Entrepreneurship and Industrialisation*, OECD Publishing, Paris, *http://dx.doi.org/10.1787/aeo-2017-en.* [4]

AfDB/OECD/UNDP (2015), *African Economic Outlook 2015: Regional Development and Spatial Inclusion*, OECD Publishing, Paris, *http://dx.doi.org/10.1787/aeo-2015-en.* [20]

Boisard; de Freitas; Hidouci (2014), *Renforcer les recettes fiscales locales pour financer le développement urbain en Afrique*, Fonds Mondial pour le Développement des Villes (FMDV), Paris, *http://delog.org/web/wp-content/uploads/2016/03/Etude-FMDV-Fiscalite%CC%81-locale-Villes-Afrique-8-Cas.pdf.* [23]

Fjeldstad; Chambas; Brun (2014), *Local government taxation in Sub-Saharan Africa: a review and an agenda for research*, 2, Chr. Michelsen Institute, Bergen, *http://www.cmi.no/publications/file/5098-local-government-taxation-in-sub-saharan-africa.pdf.* [21]

Fossat; Bua (2013), *Tax administration reform in the francophone countries of sub-Saharan Africa*, International Monetary Fund, Washington, DC, *http://www.imf.org/external/pubs/ft/wp/2013/wp13173.pdf.* [10]

hellenicshippingnews (2017), "Ghana: Crude Oil production declined in 2016", *hellenicshippingnews*, *https://www.hellenicshippingnews.com/ghana-crude-oil-production-declined-in-2016/.* [7]

IMF (2018), *World Economic Outlook*, IMF. [14]

IMF (2017), *World Economic Outlook*, International Monetary Fund, Washington, DC, *http://www.imf.org/en/Publications/WEO/Issues/2017/04/04/world-economic-outlook-april-2017.* [5]

IMF (2016), *Sixth review under the extended credit facility arrangement and request for modification of a performance riterion—debt sustainability analysis*, *https://www.imf.org/external/pubs/ft/dsa/pdf/2016/dsacr16375.pdf*. [6]

IMF (May 2014), *Mauritius: 2014 article IV consultation-staff report (2014b)*, International Monetary Fund, Washington, DC,, *http://www.imf.org/external/pubs/ft/scr/2014/cr14107.pdf*. [22]

IMF (2017a), *Niger : 2016 Article IV Consultation and Request for a Three-Year Arrangement Under the Extended Credit Facility-Press Release; Staff Report; and Statement by the Executive Director for Niger*, *https://www.imf.org/en/Publications/CR/Issues/2017/02/24/Niger-2016-Article-IV-Consultation-and-Request-for-a-Three-Year-Arrangement-Under-the-44704*. [8]

Kloeden, D. (2011), *Revenue administration reforms in anglophone Africa since the early 1990s*, IMF Working Paper, WP/11/162,, *http://www.imf.org/external/pubs/ft/wp/2011/wp11162.pdf*. [9]

Monkam, N. and M. Moore (2015), *How Property Tax Would Benefit Africa*, Africa Research Institute, *http://www.africaresearchinstitute.org/publications/property-tax-benefit-africa*. [24]

OECD (2017), *Revenue Statistics: 1965-2016*, OECD Publishing, Paris, *https://doi.org/10.1787/9789264283183-en*. [2]

OECD (2014), *Development Co-operation Report 2014: Mobilising Resources for Sustainable Development*, OECD Publishing, Paris, *http://OECD* Publishing, Paris,. [12]

OECD/ATAF/AUC (2018), *Revenue Statistics in Africa: Comparative tables*, OECD Publishing, Paris,, *http://dx.doi.org/10.1787/be755711-en*. [3]

OECD/ECLAC/CIAT/IDB (2018), *Revenue Statistics in Latin America and the Caribbean*, OECD Publishing, Paris, *http://dx.doi.org/10.1787/rev_lat_car-2017-en-fr*. [1]

PEAKS, E. (2013), *Taxation and Developing Countries*, Overseas Development Institute training notes, London, *http://www.odi.org/sites/odi.org.uk/files/odi-assets/events-documents/5045.pdf*. [17]

Profeta, S. and S. Scabrosetti (2010), *The Political Economy of Taxation: Lessons from Developing Countries*, Edward Elgar Publishing, *https://books.google.fr/books?isbn=1849805490*. [16]

SSA (2015), *Social Security Through the World: Africa*, SSA Publication Social Security Administration, Washington, DC, *http://www.ssa.gov/policy/docs/progdesc/ssptw/2014-2015/africa/ssptw15africa.pdf*. [19]

WHO (2015), *Purchasing Power Parity 2005*, World Health Organization, *http://www.who.int/choice/costs/ppp/en/*. [13]

WTO (2018), *WT/TPR/S/362 • WAEMU member countries*, *https://www.wto.org/english/tratop_e/tpr_e/s362-00_sum_e.pdf*. [25]

Chapitre 1

Tendances des recettes fiscales, 2000-2016

Pour atteindre les Objectifs de développement durable (ODD) des Nations Unies et mettre en œuvre le Programme d'action d'Addis-Abeba, il est nécessaire de mobiliser des fonds supplémentaires, et notamment des ressources intérieures, afin de financer l'offre de biens et de services publics. L'impôt représente une source de recettes publiques prévisible et stable, contrairement à l'aide publique au développement et aux redevances minières, marquées par une forte volatilité. Le présent rapport contient un ensemble d'indicateurs internationalement comparables sur les recettes fiscales et non fiscales qui peuvent servir à mesurer les progrès en matière de mobilisation des ressources intérieures (comme le prévoient les ODD, le Programme d'action d'Addis-Abeba ainsi que des initiatives connexes telles que l'initiative fiscale d'Addis-Abeba) et à éclairer les politiques et les réformes fiscales.

Ce chapitre examine l'évolution du ratio impôts/PIB, de la structure fiscale et de la part des recettes fiscales par niveau d'administration dans 21 pays d'Afrique : Afrique du Sud, Botswana, Burkina Faso, Cabo Verde, Cameroun, République du Congo, République démocratique du Congo, Côte d'Ivoire, Égypte, Eswatini[1], Ghana, Kenya, Mali, Maroc, Maurice, Niger, Ouganda, Rwanda, Sénégal, Togo et Tunisie. L'analyse proposée vient compléter les informations détaillées par pays consacrées aux recettes fiscales figurant au chapitre 5.

Ce chapitre livre des comparaisons internationales sur les recettes fiscales des pays couverts par cette publication. Il compare également les moyennes des 21 pays d'Afrique avec celles des 25 pays d'Amérique latine et Caraïbes (ALC) (OCDE/CEPAL/CIAT/BID, 2018[1]) et des 35 pays de l'OCDE (OCDE, 2017[2])[2].

Ratios impôts/PIB

Ratios impôts/PIB en 2016

Le ratio moyen impôts/PIB dans les 21 pays d'Afrique couverts par la publication [désigné ci-après « moyenne des pays d'Afrique (21) »] s'est établi à 18.2 % en 2016 (graphique 1.1). Le ratio impôts/PIB correspond aux recettes fiscales (y compris les cotisations de sécurité sociale versées à l'administration générale) exprimées en pourcentage du produit intérieur brut (PIB). Il convient d'interpréter la moyenne des pays d'Afrique (21) avec prudence en raison du fait que les données relatives aux cotisations de sécurité sociale sont incomplètes ou indisponibles pour certains pays africains considérés[3]. À titre de comparaison, les ratios impôts/PIB moyens pour la région ALC et pour la zone OCDE étaient respectivement de 22.7 % et 34.3 % en 2016.

En 2016, les ratios impôts/PIB ont affiché de grandes variations entre les pays couverts par la publication, allant de 7.6 % en République démocratique du Congo à 29.4 % en Tunisie. Deux tiers des pays ont enregistré un ratio compris entre 13.0 % et 20.0 % en 2016 (Botswana, Burkina Faso, Cabo Verde, Cameroun, République du Congo, Côte d'Ivoire, Égypte, Eswatini, Ghana, Kenya, Mali, Niger, Ouganda et Rwanda). Six pays (Afrique du Sud, Maroc, Maurice, Sénégal, Togo et Tunisie) ont obtenu des ratios supérieurs à 20 %.

Si l'on exclut les cotisations de sécurité sociale (CSS), les ratios impôts/PIB présentent une répartition différente. Par exemple, les cinq pays obtenant les ratios impôts/PIB les plus élevés en tenant compte des CSS (Afrique du Sud, Maroc, Sénégal, Togo[4] et Tunisie) affichent toujours des ratios supérieurs à 20 % lorsqu'on exclut les CSS, mais la position relative de ces pays change. Ainsi, l'Afrique du Sud obtient le ratio le plus élevé hors CSS, soit 28.2 % du PIB, en raison du niveau relativement faible des recettes fiscales provenant des CSS en pourcentage du PIB. À l'inverse, la Tunisie, où les CSS représentent 9.3 % du PIB, se place au cinquième rang des pays d'Afrique quand on exclut les CSS.

Graphique 1.1. **Ratios impôts/PIB et total des recettes fiscales (hors cotisations de sécurité sociale) en pourcentage du PIB, 2016**

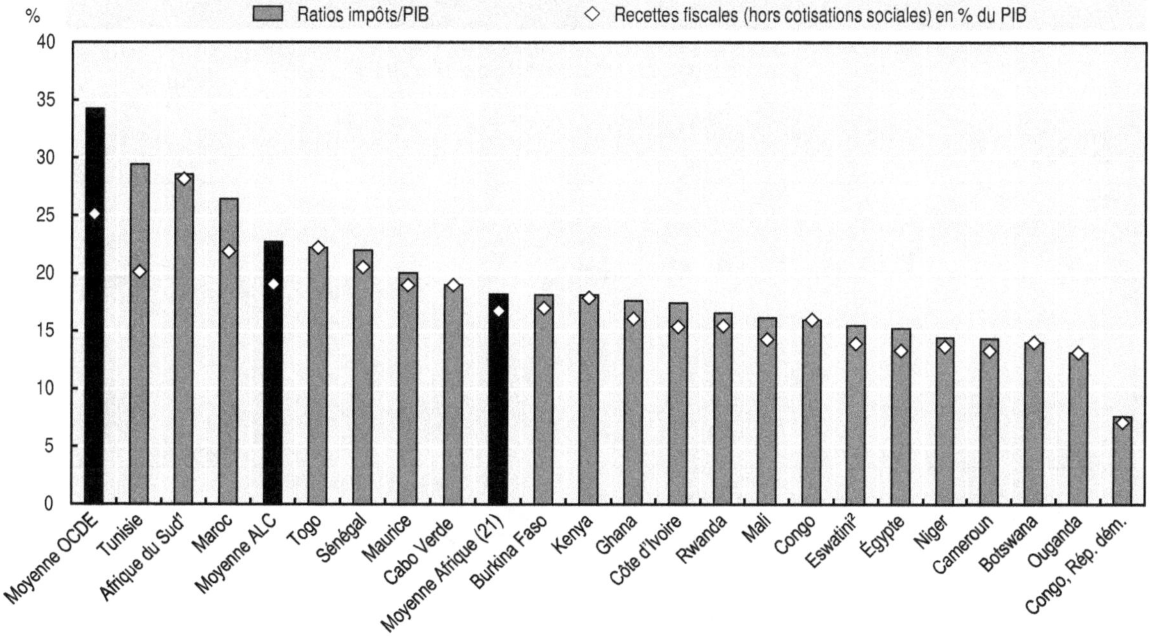

Note : Les chiffres prennent en compte les recettes fiscales des administrations infranationales pour l'Afrique du Sud (pour la période 2002-2016), l'Eswatini (Swaziland dans les éditions précédentes), le Maroc et Maurice. La moyenne Afrique (21) et les moyennes ALC (25 pays d'Amérique latine et Caraïbes) et OCDE (35 pays) sont des moyennes non pondérées.

Il convient d'interpréter la moyenne Afrique (21) avec précaution car des données relatives aux cotisations de sécurité sociale sont indisponibles pour la République du Congo, la République démocratique du Congo (avant 2012), le Togo et l'Ouganda et sont incomplètes pour le Cameroun et le Sénégal. Les cotisations de sécurité sociale pour le Botswana sont égales à zéro dans la mesure où elles ne remplissent pas les critères retenus pour être considérées comme des cotisations de sécurité sociale, selon la classification des impôts de l'OCDE figurant dans le Guide d'interprétation. Pour plus de précisions, se reporter aux tableaux par pays présentés dans le chapitre 5.

1. Il convient d'interpréter le ratio impôts/PIB avec prudence car il prend en compte les sommes recouvrées par l'Afrique du Sud au profit de l'Union douanière de l'Afrique australe (SACU).
2. Anciennement Swaziland.

Source : Tableaux 4.1 et 4.2 figurant au chapitre 4 et (OCDE/ATAF/CUA, 2018[3]), « Recettes fiscales en Afrique : Tableaux comparatifs », *Statistiques fiscales de l'OCDE* (base de données), *https://doi.org/10.1787/7f54581d-fr*, pour la moyenne des pays ALC.

StatLink https://doi.org/10.1787/888933819043

Variation des ratios impôts/PIB entre 2015 et 2016

Le ratio moyen impôts/PIB pour les pays d'Afrique (21) est resté stable entre 2015 et 2016 (graphique 1.2), dans un contexte de ralentissement de l'activité économique en Afrique. Face au déclin constant des prix des matières premières et à la faiblesse de la conjoncture mondiale, la croissance du PIB du continent africain a fléchi de 3.6 % en 2015 à 2.2 % en volume réel en 2016 (BAfD/OCDE/PNUD, 2017[4]). Par comparaison, la moyenne des pays ALC a baissé de 0.3 point de pourcentage et la moyenne de l'OCDE a augmenté de 0.3 point au cours de la même période.

La stabilité relative de la moyenne des pays d'Afrique (21) est la conséquence de deux configurations distinctes dans ce groupe de pays : 11 pays ont enregistré une hausse de leur ratio impôts/PIB en 2016, tandis que dix pays ont connu une baisse (graphique 1.2). Des variations supérieures à 1.0 point de pourcentage se sont produites dans des pays affichant des ratios impôts/PIB faibles (moins de 17.0 %) : c'est au Botswana que le ratio a le plus fortement augmenté (1.3 point de pourcentage), suivi du Mali (1.2 point). Les baisses les plus marquées (plus de 2.0 points) ont été constatées en République démocratique du Congo et au Niger. Ces pays mis à part, il n'y a pas eu d'autre variation supérieure à un point de pourcentage dans un sens ou dans un autre.

Graphique 1.2. **Variation des ratios impôts/PIB entre 2015 et 2016 (en points de pourcentage du PIB)**

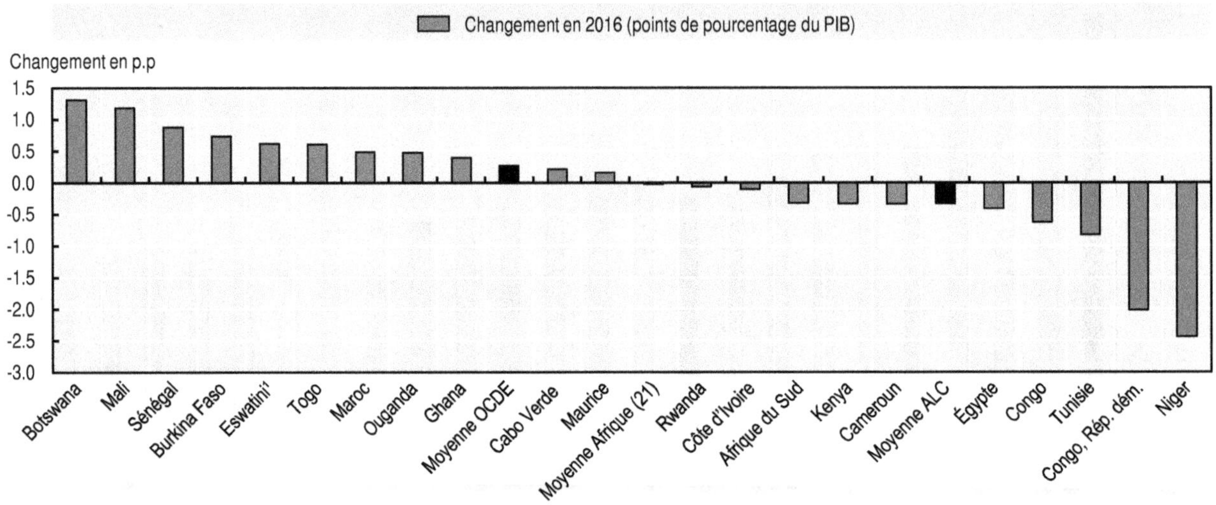

Notes : Les chiffres prennent en compte les recettes fiscales des administrations infranationales pour l'Afrique du Sud (pour la période 2002-2016), l'Eswatini (Swaziland dans les éditions précédentes), le Maroc et Maurice. La moyenne Afrique (21) et les moyennes ALC (25 pays d'Amérique latine et Caraïbes) et OCDE (35 pays) sont des moyennes non pondérées.

Il convient d'interpréter l'évolution de la moyenne des pays d'Afrique (21) avec précaution car des données relatives aux cotisations de sécurité sociale sont indisponibles ou incomplètes pour quelques pays. Pour plus de précisions, se reporter aux tableaux par pays présentés dans le chapitre 5.

1. Anciennement Swaziland.

Source : Calculs des auteurs basés sur les données figurant dans le tableau 4.1 au chapitre 4 et (OCDE/ATAF/CUA, 2018[3]), « Recettes fiscales en Afrique : Tableaux comparatifs », *Statistiques fiscales de l'OCDE* (base de données), *https://doi.org/10.1787/7f54581d-fr*, pour la moyenne des pays ALC.

StatLink https://doi.org/10.1787/888933819062

Les principales catégories de recettes fiscales (en pourcentage du PIB) sont également restées stables entre 2015 et 2016 s'agissant de la moyenne des 21 pays d'Afrique de cette publication. On observe néanmoins une forte hétérogénéité entre pays. Dans les deux pays qui ont enregistré les hausses les plus marquées entre 2015 et 2016 – le Botswana et le Mali –, les catégories de recettes fiscales à l'origine de la progression du ratio impôts/PIB ne sont pas les mêmes. Une augmentation des recettes provenant de l'impôt sur le revenu et les bénéfices équivalente à 1.1 % du PIB a été le principal moteur de la hausse du ratio impôts/PIB au Botswana. Au Mali, l'augmentation du ratio impôts/PIB s'explique principalement par la hausse de 0.5 point de pourcentage des recettes tirées de la taxe sur la valeur ajoutée (TVA) et par l'accroissement de 0.3 point de pourcentage des cotisations de sécurité sociale.

Au Botswana, l'augmentation des recettes générées par l'impôt sur le revenu et les bénéfices en pourcentage du PIB (1.1 point de pourcentage) provient entièrement de l'impôt sur les ressources minérales, l'impôt sur les bénéfices des entreprises du secteur minier (qui pour l'essentiel produisent des diamants). Les ventes de diamants ont sensiblement augmenté en 2016, ce qui s'est traduit par une forte hausse des exportations minières et des recettes fiscales du Botswana (FMI, 2017[5]).

Au Mali, la hausse globale du ratio impôts/PIB a atteint 1.2 point de pourcentage entre 2015 et 2016, soit bien plus que l'objectif de 0.75 % du PIB fixé par le gouvernement. Le Mali a mis en œuvre diverses réformes visant à élargir sa base d'imposition, supprimer des exemptions et améliorer le civisme des organismes chargés du recouvrement de l'impôt (FMI, 2016[6]). Par exemple, la Direction générale des impôts du Mali a procédé ces dernières années à des vérifications ciblées d'entreprises qui n'étaient en principe pas éligibles à réclamer un remboursement de TVA. Ces vérifications ont abouti à une hausse du nombre d'entreprises qui ont effectivement acquitté la TVA et ont contribué à accroître les recettes de TVA de 0.5 % du PIB en 2016, une hausse qui représentait 43 % de la progression totale du ratio impôts/PIB.

Graphique 1.3. **Variations des ratios impôts/PIB observées entre 2015 et 2016 par principales rubriques d'impôts et par pays (en points de pourcentage du PIB)**

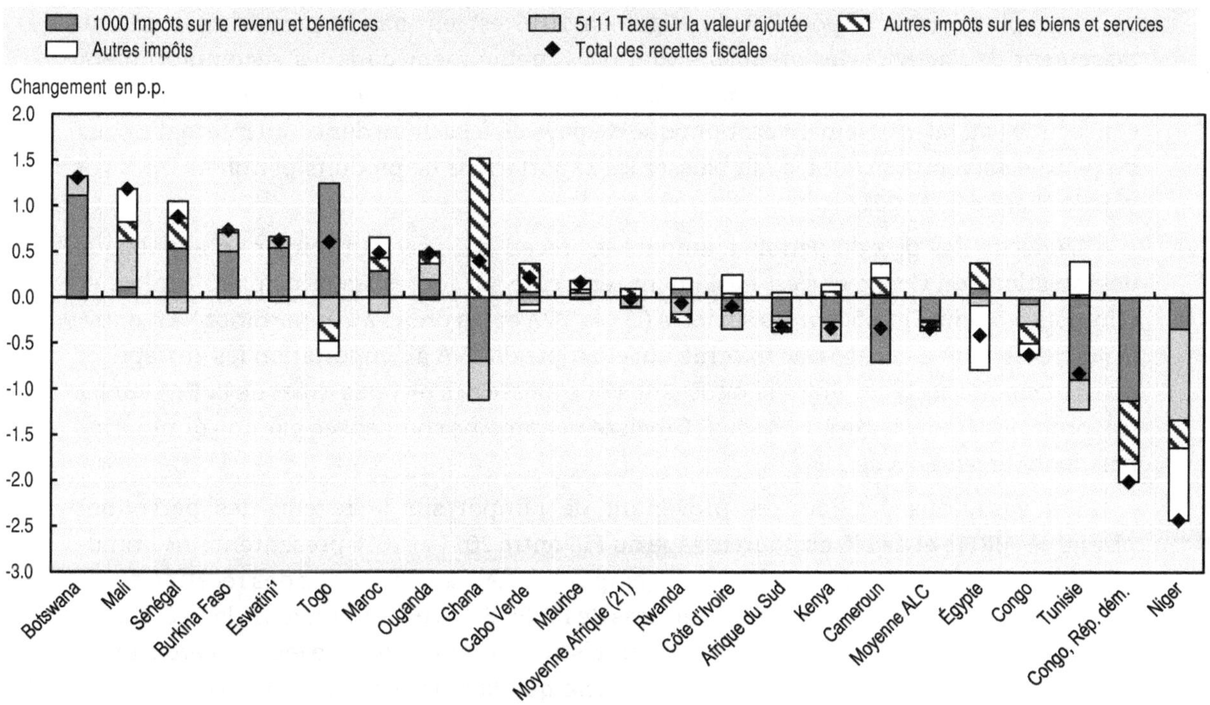

Notes : Les chiffres prennent en compte les recettes fiscales des administrations infranationales pour l'Afrique du Sud, l'Eswatini (anciennement Swaziland), le Maroc et Maurice.
La moyenne Afrique (21) et les moyennes ALC (25 pays d'Amérique latine et Caraïbes) et OCDE (35 pays) sont des moyennes non pondérées. Il convient d'interpréter la moyenne des pays d'Afrique (21) avec précaution car des données relatives aux cotisations de sécurité sociale sont indisponibles ou incomplètes pour quelques pays. Pour plus de précisions, se reporter aux tableaux par pays présentés dans le chapitre 5.
1. Anciennement Swaziland.

Source : Calculs des auteurs basés sur les données figurant dans (OCDE/ATAF/CUA, 2018[3]), « Recettes fiscales en Afrique : Tableaux comparatifs », *Statistiques fiscales de l'OCDE* (base de données), *https://doi.org/10.1787/7f54581d-fr*, pour la moyenne des pays ALC.

StatLink *https://doi.org/10.1787/888933819081*

La République démocratique du Congo et le Niger sont, des 21 pays d'Afrique, ceux qui ont accusé les plus fortes baisses de leur ratio impôts/PIB, de respectivement 2.0 et 2.4 points de pourcentage. Au Niger, le recul des recettes fiscales en pourcentage du PIB a concerné toutes les principales catégories d'impôts, et en particulier la TVA (1.0 point de pourcentage) et d'autres prélèvements tels que les droits d'enregistrement (0.8 point de pourcentage). En République démocratique du Congo, la diminution des recettes de l'impôt sur les bénéfices (équivalente à 1.1 % du PIB) et d'autres impôts sur les biens et services[5] (0.7 % du PIB) explique la contraction globale du ratio impôts/PIB.

Dans plusieurs pays, les recettes générées par certains types d'impôt ont beaucoup progressé entre 2015 et 2016. Ainsi, au Ghana, les recettes provenant d'autres impôts sur les biens et services se sont accrues de 1.5 % du PIB après la mise en place de nouveaux droits d'accise dans le cadre de la Loi sur les prélèvements dans le secteur de l'énergie votée en décembre 2015. De nouveaux prélèvements sur les produits pétroliers, la taxe de remboursement de la dette du secteur énergétique et la taxe de stabilisation des prix ont été instaurés, tandis que les impôts alimentant les fonds routiers et le fonds des énergies — levés sur l'essence et le gazole — ont été revus à la hausse. L'augmentation des droits d'accise est venue compenser la chute des recettes provenant d'autres catégories d'impôts (de 0.7 % du PIB pour les impôts sur le revenu et les bénéfices et de 0.4 % pour la TVA). Le recul de la production de pétrole brut a contribué à l'érosion des recettes de l'impôt sur les bénéfices des sociétés (Hellenic Shipping News Worldwide, 2017[7]).

Le repli du ratio impôts/PIB du Niger en 2016 est en grande partie imputable au tassement de l'activité des grandes entreprises, notamment dans les secteurs miniers, pétrolier et des télécommunications. En outre, la dépréciation du naira au Nigéria, consécutive au ralentissement économique du pays dû à la chute des cours internationaux du pétrole survenue en 2014, a fait baisser les exportations de produits pétroliers du Niger vers le Nigéria (FMI, 2017a[8]).

Le déclin des prix du pétrole a amputé les recettes du secteur minier en République démocratique du Congo et s'est également répercuté sur toutes les principales catégories d'impôts (comme l'impôt sur les sociétés (IS), la TVA et les droits à l'importation). En outre, le gouvernement a engagé une réforme qui exempte de TVA à l'importation les entreprises opérant dans le secteur minier, aboutissant à une baisse des recettes tirées de la TVA sur les importations équivalente à 1.1 % du PIB (baisse néanmoins compensée par une diminution des remboursements de TVA).

Les variations des recettes provenant de l'impôt sur le revenu des personnes physiques (IRPP) et de l'IS en pourcentage du PIB entre 2015 et 2016 présentent une grande hétérogénéité dans les 21 pays d'Afrique (graphique 1.4). Les variations des recettes de l'IS ont été plus marquées que celles des recettes de l'IRPP. En 2016, le Cameroun, la République démocratique du Congo et la Tunisie ont enregistré une diminution de leurs recettes tirées de l'IS de plus de 0.5 % du PIB. C'est en Tunisie que la baisse est la plus forte (1.6 % du PIB) et au Togo que la hausse est la plus prononcée (1.1 % du PIB). En revanche, au cours de la même période, l'évolution des recettes de l'IRPP était généralement comprise entre -0.1 % et 0.4 % du PIB.

Évolution des ratios impôts/PIB depuis 2000

À l'exception de la période 2008-2010, le ratio moyen impôts/PIB dans les 21 pays d'Afrique a progressé de façon plus ou moins soutenue entre 2000 et 2015, avant de s'interrompre en 2016 (graphique 1.5). Il a gagné cinq points de pourcentage sur l'ensemble de la période, passant de 13.1 % en 2000 à 18.2 % en 2016, grâce à des conditions macroéconomiques favorables, à des évolutions dans l'orientation de la politique fiscale et la conception de la fiscalité, et au renforcement des administrations fiscales. Cette tendance fait écho à celle mise en évidence dans les pays ALC, où le ratio moyen impôts/PIB a augmenté de 4.7 points de pourcentage pendant la même période. La situation des 21 pays d'Afrique de cette publication et de la région ALC tranche avec celle des pays de l'OCDE, où le ratio moyen impôts/PIB s'élevait à 34.3 % en 2016, soit 0.4 point de pourcentage de plus que son niveau en 2000.

Graphique 1.4. **Variations annuelles, entre 2015 et 2016, des recettes tirées des impôts sur le revenu et les bénéfices, par sous-rubrique et par pays (points de pourcentage du PIB)**

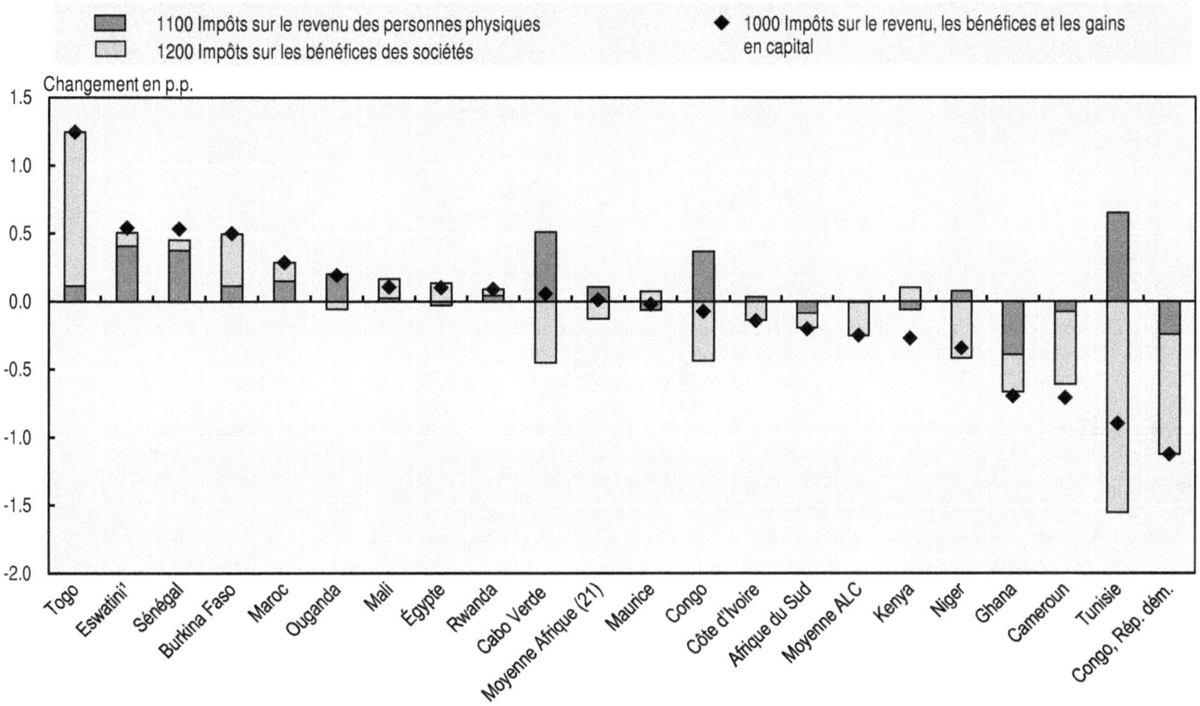

Notes : La moyenne Afrique (21) et les moyennes ALC (25 pays d'Amérique latine et Caraïbes) et OCDE (35 pays) sont des moyennes non pondérées. Le Botswana n'est pas inclus car la ventilation de l'impôt sur le revenu entre la rubrique 1100 Impôt sur le revenu des personnes physiques et la rubrique 1200 Impôt sur les bénéfices des sociétés n'est pas disponible.

1. Anciennement Swaziland.

Source : Calculs des auteurs basés sur les données figurant dans (OCDE/ATAF/CUA, 2018[3]), « Recettes fiscales en Afrique : Tableaux comparatifs », *Statistiques fiscales de l'OCDE* (base de données), *https://doi.org/10.1787/7f54581d-fr*.

StatLink *https://doi.org/10.1787/888933819100*

La crise financière mondiale a fait baisser le ratio moyen impôts/PIB dans les pays d'Afrique (21) de 0.3 point de pourcentage entre 2008 et 2010, le déclin de l'activité économique et des prix des matières premières expliquant en partie cette évolution. Pendant cette période, certains des 21 pays considérés ont mis en œuvre des mesures visant à stimuler l'activité économique. Le Maroc par exemple a réduit le taux de l'impôt sur les bénéfices des sociétés de 5 points de pourcentage en 2008 en vue d'améliorer la compétitivité de ses entreprises et de les aider à devenir plus résistantes pendant la crise financière (voir l'encadré 1.1).

La moyenne des pays d'Amérique latine et des Caraïbes a reculé de 0.4 point de pourcentage entre 2008 et 2010. La moyenne de l'OCDE en revanche a surtout subi le contrecoup de la crise entre 2007 et 2009. C'est pendant cette phase que le ratio impôts/PIB a été le plus nettement altéré, avec une contraction se chiffrant à 1.4 point de pourcentage. La zone de l'OCDE s'est aussi remise plus lentement puisqu'elle n'a dépassé qu'en 2014 le niveau d'avant la crise, soit 33.7 %, alors que la moyenne Afrique (21) est parvenu dès 2011 à dépasser le ratio de 16.6 % en 2008.

Graphique 1.5. **Ratios moyens impôts/PIB pour l'Afrique (21), l'ALC et l'OCDE, 2000-16**

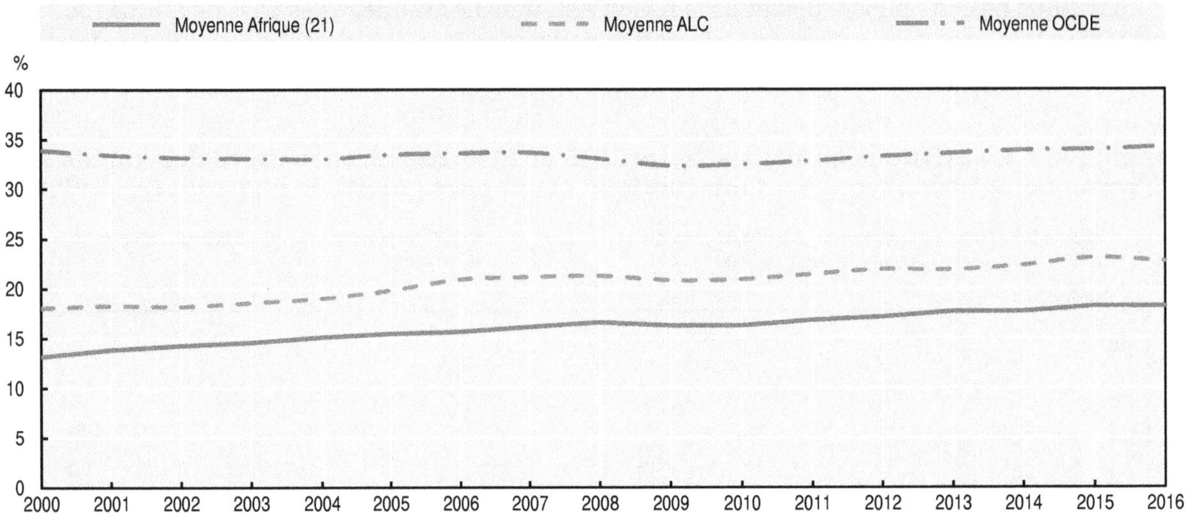

Notes : Les chiffres prennent en compte les recettes fiscales des administrations infranationales pour l'Afrique du Sud (pour la période 2002-2016), l'Eswatini (anciennement Swaziland), le Maroc et Maurice.

La moyenne Afrique (21) et les moyennes ALC (25 pays d'Amérique latine et Caraïbes) et OCDE (35 pays) sont des moyennes non pondérées.

Il convient d'interpréter la moyenne des pays d'Afrique (21) avec précaution car des données relatives aux cotisations de sécurité sociale sont indisponibles ou incomplètes pour quelques pays. Pour plus de précisions, se reporter aux tableaux par pays présentés dans le chapitre 5.

Source : Tableau 4.1 au chapitre 4 pour les moyennes de l'OCDE et de l'Afrique (21) et (OCDE/ATAF/CUA, 2018[3]), « Recettes fiscales en Afrique : Tableaux comparatifs », *Statistiques fiscales de l'OCDE* (base de données), *https://doi.org/10.1787/7f54581d-fr*, pour la moyenne des pays ALC.

StatLink *https://doi.org/10.1787/888933819119*

Depuis 2000, de nombreux pays africains ont procédé à des réformes structurelles majeures au sein de leurs administrations fiscales et entrepris de modifier radicalement leurs systèmes fiscaux. Pour nombre de pays, les réformes ont eu pour but de renforcer et de moderniser les administrations fiscales. Parmi les réformes adoptées, on compte l'introduction de bureaux des gros contribuables et/ou des moyens contribuables, des systèmes tels que l'impôt déclaratif, le ciblage des contribuables et une gestion moderne des risques (Kloeden, 2011[9]) ; (Fossat; Bua, 2013[10]). Certains pays ont engagé des réformes fiscales en vue d'élargir la base imposable, d'éliminer certaines exonérations et de simplifier la législation fiscale. Ces changements se sont souvent accompagnés de programmes destinés à éduquer les contribuables et à améliorer les services aux contribuables, notamment grâce à l'informatisation des services fiscaux.

Par exemple, les réformes de grande ampleur menées par le Rwanda depuis 2000 ont permis d'accroître sensiblement les recettes fiscales (BAfD, 2010[11]). L'objectif de ces mesures était d'élargir la base d'imposition en obtenant l'immatriculation des entreprises du secteur informel et en simplifiant les procédures imposées aux contribuables pour l'exécution de leurs obligations fiscales. D'autres réformes ont contribué à l'accroissement des recettes fiscales, notamment l'adoption de la TVA en 2001, l'application d'une nouvelle législation sur l'imposition des revenus et de nouveaux taux d'imposition en 2005 et 2006, ainsi que le renforcement du système en place pour faire respecter la législation fiscale et des procédures internes de recouvrement. Le taux de respect de leurs obligations fiscales par les gros contribuables – qui procurent environ 75 % du montant total des recettes fiscales du pays – a atteint 97 % à l'issue de ces réformes. Le Maroc déploie lui aussi un important programme de réformes fiscales depuis 2004 (voir l'encadré 1.1).

Encadré 1.1. **Réformes fiscales conduites au Maroc entre 2004 et 2013**

Entre 2004 et 2013, le Maroc a entrepris un certain nombre de réformes fiscales essentielles qui ont été menées parallèlement à une réorganisation et un renforcement de l'administration fiscale. Ces mesures ont contribué à accroître le montant total des recettes fiscales qui ont été portées de 23.1 % du PIB en 2004 à 28.1 % en 2013.

La majeure partie des réformes de fond ont concerné la TVA qui a fait l'objet de modifications pratiquement chaque année, ayant notamment pour but d'élargir la base d'imposition, de simplifier les règles applicables à certains produits et de réduire le nombre d'exonérations et de produits soumis à des taux réduits. Le nombre de taux de TVA applicables a également été réduit. De 2004 à 2013, les recettes de TVA, exprimées en pourcentage du PIB, ont augmenté de 2.8 points de pourcentage, pour représenter 56 % de l'accroissement total des recettes observé pendant cette période.

L'impôt sur les sociétés a également fait l'objet de réformes en 2008, 2011 et 2013, réformes destinées à doper la compétitivité des entreprises et à les aider lors de la crise financière. Les principales mesures prises ont notamment consisté :

- en 2008, à ramener le taux de l'IS de 35 % à 30 % et de l'impôt sur les bénéfices dans le secteur financier de 39.6 % à 37 % ;
- en 2011, à abaisser le taux de l'IS applicable aux petites entreprises dont le chiffre d'affaires est inférieur à 3 millions MAD ; et
- en 2013, à accorder de nouvelles exonérations et à appliquer des taux réduits d'IS à certaines petites entreprises ciblées.

À la suite de ces réformes et de la crise financière, les recettes tirées de l'impôt sur les bénéfices des sociétés, exprimées en pourcentage du PIB, ont reculé de 2 points entre 2008 et 2013. Sur la période 2004 à 2013, elles ont cependant progressé de 1.5 point de PIB grâce aux recettes exceptionnelles recouvrées pendant les années ayant suivi l'application de mesures répressives et une phase de bons résultats économiques avant la crise financière.

Le système d'imposition des personnes physiques a été réformé en 2007, 2009 et 2010 afin d'améliorer le pouvoir d'achat des ménages. Pendant cette période, les taux d'imposition marginaux des revenus des personnes physiques ont été abaissés, les barèmes d'imposition réaménagés et le seuil d'exonération des revenus relevé sensiblement. La Direction Générale des Impôts (DGI) estime que ces réformes sont à l'origine d'une diminution des recettes de 11 milliards MAD au total pendant la période considérée. En pourcentage du PIB, les recettes issues de l'impôt sur le revenu des personnes physiques ont diminué de 1.0 point de pourcentage entre 2007 et 2010.

Les administrations fiscales ont été sensiblement améliorées entre 2004 et 2013. Des services ciblés au contribuable ont été créés en 2005 (à l'intention notamment des gros contribuables et des petites entreprises) afin que l'administration fiscale puisse mieux gérer les affaires de ces contribuables et leur offre des services plus adaptés à leurs besoins. Ces efforts ont permis un accroissement de la proportion de contribuables immatriculés à la TVA et de contribuables payant l'IS et l'IRPP entre 8 % et 13 % en 2007. En outre, c'est la DGI qui a été chargée du recouvrement de l'impôt sur les bénéfices des sociétés et de la TVA : il en est résulté une hausse estimée à 19 % des recettes provenant de l'impôt sur les sociétés entre 2004 et 2005. Enfin, les vérifications et contrôles fiscaux ont été renforcés, ce qui a amélioré la discipline fiscale des entreprises.

Source : Lakhal, H, Direction Générale des Impôts (DGI), à partir d'une analyse entreprise pendant un détachement auprès de l'OCDE.

Les recettes générées par les impôts sur le revenu et sur les bénéfices ont le plus contribué à l'accroissement du ratio moyen impôts/PIB des pays d'Afrique (21) entre 2000 et 2016. Pendant cette période, ces recettes ont augmenté de 2.6 % du PIB pour atteindre 6.2 % du PIB en 2016, principalement grâce à la hausse des recettes de l'IS, qui ont gagné 1.4 point de pourcentage, passant de 1.4 % à 2.8 % du PIB. Les recettes de l'IRPP en pourcentage du PIB ont régulièrement progressé depuis 2000 et ont atteint leur niveau le pus élevé de 3.0 % en 2016, contre 2.1 % en 2000.

Les recettes de TVA étaient le deuxième principal moteur de l'augmentation du ratio moyen impôts/PIB de la moyenne Afrique (21) entre 2000 et 2016. Les recettes de TVA en pourcentage du PIB ont progressé de 2.0 points de pourcentage, passant de 3.3 % en 2000 à 5.3 % en 2016 (graphique 1.6). Le Botswana, le Cabo Verde et le Rwanda ont institué une TVA respectivement en 2002, 2004 et 2001, et la République démocratique du Congo et l'Eswatini ont fait de même en 2012. Dans de nombreux pays, la mise en place de la TVA s'est accompagnée de réformes de grande ampleur des administrations fiscales qui ont contribué à l'accroissement des recettes de TVA pendant la période considérée.

Graphique 1.6. **Recettes tirées des impôts sur le revenu et les bénéfices, de la TVA et d'autres rubriques d'impôt, en pourcentage du PIB, 2000-16**

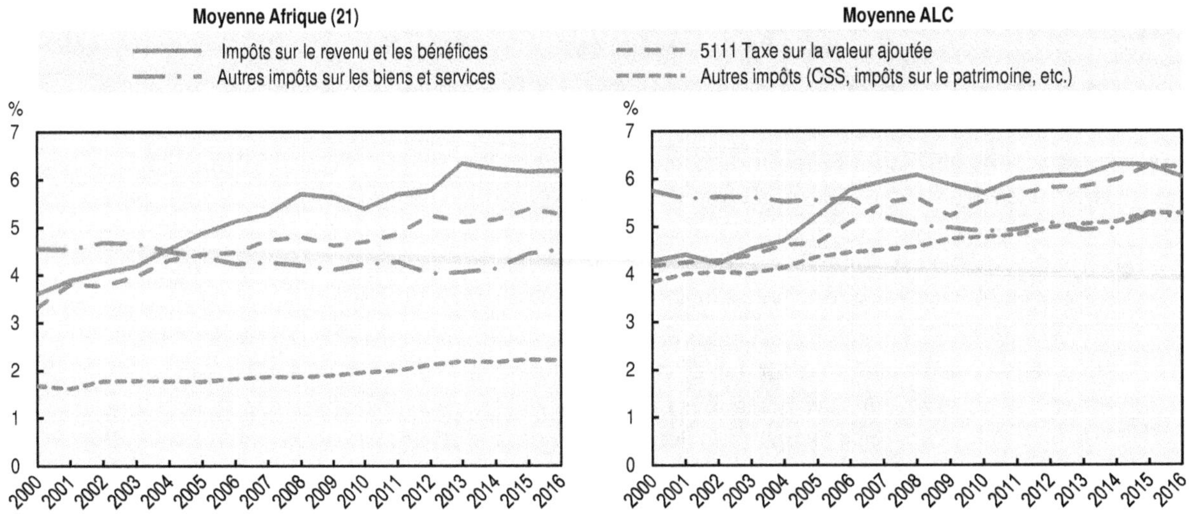

Notes : Les chiffres prennent en compte les recettes fiscales des administrations infranationales pour l'Afrique du Sud (pour la période 2002-2016), l'Eswatini (anciennement Swaziland), le Maroc et Maurice.

La moyenne Afrique (21) et les moyennes ALC (25 pays d'Amérique latine et Caraïbes) et OCDE (35 pays) sont des moyennes non pondérées. Faute de données disponibles, la moyenne des pays d'Afrique (21) exclut le Botswana avant 2004, l'Égypte avant 2002 et le Kenya avant 2001.

Il convient d'interpréter avec précaution la moyenne des pays d'Afrique (21) concernant d'autres impôts car des données relatives aux cotisations de sécurité sociale sont indisponibles ou incomplètes pour quelques pays. Pour plus de précisions, se reporter aux tableaux par pays présentés dans le chapitre 5.

Source : Tableau 4.1 au chapitre 4 pour les moyennes de l'OCDE et de l'Afrique (21) et (OCDE/ATAF/CUA, 2018[3]) « Recettes fiscales en Afrique : Tableaux comparatifs », *Statistiques fiscales de l'OCDE* (base de données), *https://doi.org/10.1787/7f54581d-fr*, pour la moyenne des pays ALC.

StatLink *https://doi.org/10.1787/888933819138*

En revanche, les recettes provenant d'autres impôts sur les biens et services en pourcentage du PIB ont dans un premier temps fléchi en moyenne après 2000, avant de rebondir entre 2013 et 2016, première année durant laquelle s'est opéré un transfert de la TVA vers d'autres impôts sur les biens et services. Le fléchissement initial est allé de pair avec la libéralisation des échanges qui a entraîné des modifications de l'imposition des biens importés et exportés et de l'imposition de biens et services spécifiques dans les pays d'Afrique (21), à savoir notamment un abaissement des droits à l'importation, une réduction de l'assiette pour les produits et services soumis à des droits d'accise et l'élimination des taxes sur les exportations.

Les tendances observées pour ces différents types d'impôt dans les 21 pays d'Afrique couverts sont en moyenne similaires à celles qui se sont dessinées dans les pays d'Amérique latine et des Caraïbes. Entre 2000 et 2016, les recettes moyennes tirées des impôts sur le revenu et les bénéfices dans les pays d'Afrique (21) ont crû plus vite que celles des pays ALC (2.6 points de pourcentage contre 1.8 point dans les pays ALC). À l'inverse, la moyenne des recettes de TVA en pourcentage du PIB a moins augmenté pour les pays d'Afrique (21) comparé à celle des pays ALC (2.0 points de pourcentage contre 2.1 points de pourcentage). Comme pour la moyenne Afrique (21), dans les pays d'Amérique latine et des Caraïbes les recettes moyennes provenant d'autres impôts sur les biens et services se sont repliées jusqu'en 2013, avant de se redresser légèrement. En revanche, les recettes tirées des impôts sur le revenu et les bénéfices et d'autres impôts sur les biens et services sont restées relativement stables sur la période en pourcentage du PIB dans la zone OCDE ; les recettes de TVA ont légèrement augmenté, de 0.3 point de pourcentage[6].

Si les tendances observées concernant les impôts sur le revenu, la taxe sur la valeur ajoutée et d'autres impôts sur les biens et services ont été très similaires, au vu des moyennes, dans les pays d'Afrique (21) et de la région ALC, les évolutions entre 2000 et 2016 ont en revanche été différentes en ce qui concerne les recettes provenant des cotisations de sécurité sociale, des impôts sur le patrimoine et autres impôts, ce qui explique l'écart entre les ratios impôts/PIB pour les deux groupes de pays. En 2016, ces recettes représentaient 2.2 % du PIB en moyenne dans les 21 pays d'Afrique contre 5.3 % dans la région d'Amérique latine et des Caraïbes.

La part des recettes provenant des cotisations de sécurité sociale, en pourcentage du PIB, s'est maintenue en 2016 à 3.7 % dans les pays ALC, contre 1.7 % en moyenne dans les pays d'Afrique (21)[7]. Les recettes tirées des cotisations de sécurité sociale, en pourcentage du PIB, ont augmenté de 1.1 point de pourcentage dans la région ALC entre 2000 et 2016 alors qu'en moyenne en Afrique (21), elles n'ont progressé que de 0.4 point de pourcentage[8]. À partir des années 80, un grand nombre de pays de la région ALC ont conduit de vastes réformes de leurs systèmes de sécurité sociale qui ont contribué à l'essor des recettes provenant des cotisations de sécurité sociale.

Les ratios impôts/PIB ont évolué différemment dans chacun des 21 pays d'Afrique entre 2000 et 2016 (graphique 1.8). La République du Congo et le Togo ont enregistré les plus fortes hausses, supérieures à 10 points de pourcentage. Au cours de la période étudiée, et plus particulièrement depuis 2006, le Togo a déployé d'importants efforts pour améliorer les procédures de ses trois administrations des finances publiques et se doter d'autorités fiscales plus fortes. Les mesures déployées par le Togo entre 2010 et 2012 comprenaient des initiatives visant à densifier le réseau des centres des impôts ; lutter contre la fraude fiscale ; mettre en place un mécanisme de suivi des recettes ; augmenter le nombre de contribuables recensés ; moderniser les systèmes d'information ; et renforcer les capacités des agents. En 2014, le pays a par ailleurs regroupé ses services douaniers et fiscaux au sein d'une même administration, avec la création de l'Office Togolais des Recettes (OTR). Ces réformes ont permis au Togo d'accroître ses recettes fiscales en pourcentage du PIB de 7.2 points de pourcentage entre 2010 et 2016, soit 57 % de la progression cumulée depuis 2000.

Graphique 1.7. **Évolution des ratios impôts/PIB (avec et sans CSS) entre 2000 et 2016 (en points de pourcentage du PIB)**

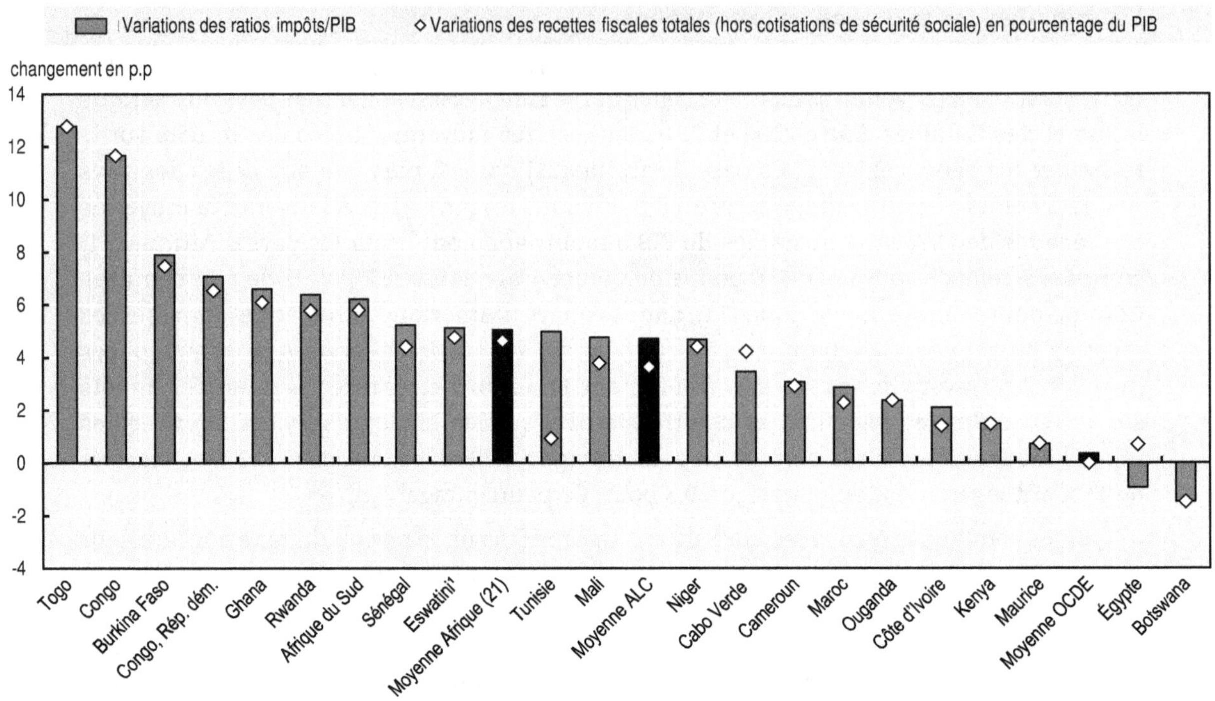

Notes : Les chiffres prennent en compte les recettes fiscales des administrations infranationales pour l'Afrique du Sud (pour la période 2002-16), l'Eswatini (Swaziland dans les éditions précédentes), le Maroc et Maurice.

La moyenne Afrique (21) et les moyennes ALC (25 pays d'Amérique latine et Caraïbes) et OCDE (35 pays) sont des moyennes non pondérées.

1. Anciennement Swaziland.
2. Évolution intervenue depuis 2001 pour le Kenya, depuis 2002 pour l'Égypte et depuis 2004 pour le Botswana faute de données disponibles pour les années antérieures.

Source : Tableaux 4.1 et 4.2 au chapitre 4 pour les moyennes de l'OCDE et de l'Afrique (21) et (OCDE/ATAF/CUA, 2018[3]), « Recettes fiscales en Afrique : Tableaux comparatifs », *Statistiques fiscales de l'OCDE* (base de données), *https://doi.org/10.1787/7f54581d-fr*, pour la moyenne des pays ALC.

StatLink https://doi.org/10.1787/888933819157

Les catégories d'impôts qui ont le plus contribué aux changements des ratios impôts/PIB entre 2000 et 2016 varient d'un pays à l'autre. La TVA arrivait en tête dans 10 pays (graphique 1.8). Les hausses les plus marquées des recettes tirées de la TVA (plus de 3 points de pourcentage de PIB) se sont produites dans trois pays qui ont mis en place un système de TVA dans les années 2000 (Cabo Verde, Eswatini et Rwanda) ainsi qu'en Burkina Faso, République du Congo et au Togo (respectivement 3.2, 3.2 et 5.7 points de pourcentage). Dans les autres pays, les plus fortes progressions du ratio impôts/PIB provenaient de l'IRPP (3 pays), de l'IS (2 pays), des cotisations de sécurité sociale (1 pays), et d'autres impôts sur les biens et services (3 pays) et d'autres impôts (1 pays).

Facteurs ayant un effet sur les ratios impôts/PIB

Les ratios impôts/PIB sont influencés par divers facteurs de portée nationale et internationale. Sur le plan national, des caractéristiques macroéconomiques telles que l'importance de l'agriculture dans l'économie, les dotations en ressources, l'ouverture aux échanges et la taille de l'économie informelle peuvent agir sur les ratios impôts/PIB. Le pouvoir de l'administration fiscale, le niveau de corruption et le civisme fiscal (le consentement à l'impôt) sont aussi étroitement liés au niveau des recettes fiscales (OCDE, 2015[12]). L'emplacement géographique peut exercer une influence sur les niveaux d'imposition : par exemple, les pays enclavés peuvent plus difficilement taxer les biens et services au port d'entrée que les pays ayant un accès à la mer. Enfin, des facteurs internationaux, y compris les politiques fiscales d'autres pays, peuvent se répercuter sur les ratios impôts/PIB.

Graphique 1.8. **Variation des ratios impôts/PIB par principales rubriques d'impôt entre 2000 et 2016 et par pays (points de pourcentage du PIB)**

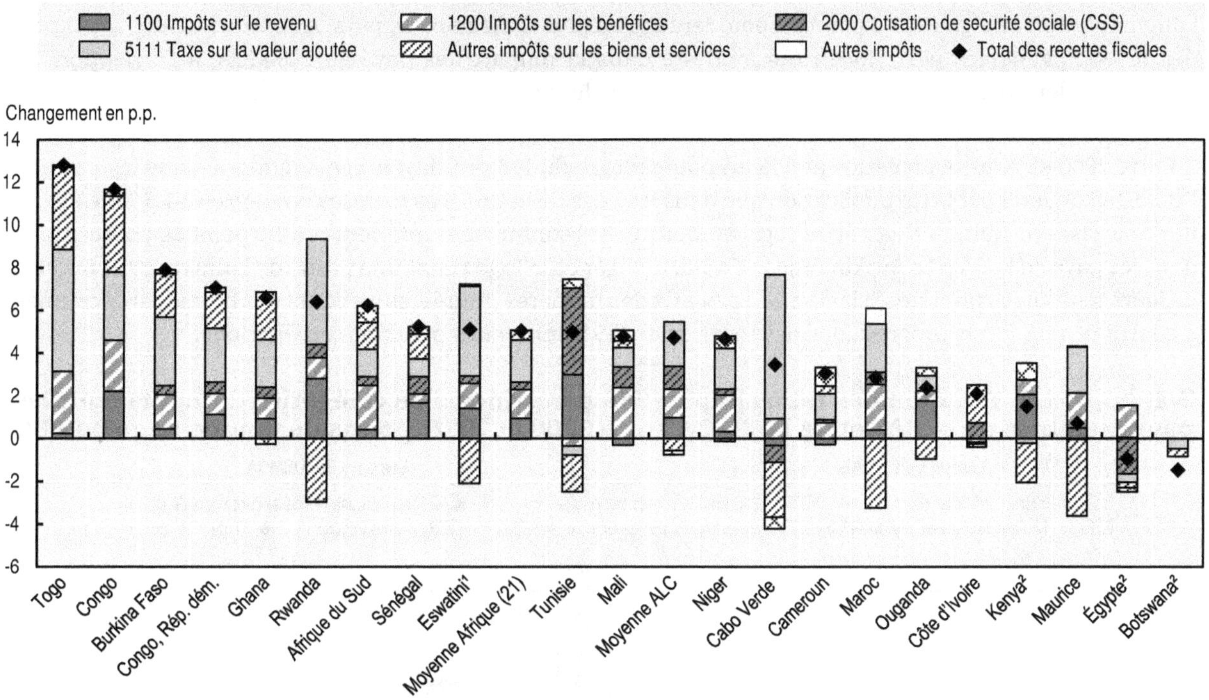

Notes : Les chiffres prennent en compte les recettes fiscales des administrations infranationales pour l'Afrique du Sud (pour la période 2002-16), l'Eswatini (Swaziland dans les éditions précédentes), le Maroc et Maurice.

La moyenne Afrique (21) et les moyennes ALC (25 pays d'Amérique latine et Caraïbes) et OCDE (35 pays) sont des moyennes non pondérées.

1. Anciennement Swaziland.

2. Évolution intervenue depuis 2001 pour le Kenya, depuis 2002 pour l'Égypte et depuis 2004 pour le Botswana faute de données disponibles pour les années antérieures.

Source : Calculs des auteurs basés sur les données figurant dans (OCDE/ATAF/CUA, 2018[3]), « Recettes fiscales en Afrique : Tableaux comparatifs », *Statistiques fiscales de l'OCDE* (base de données), *https://doi.org/10.1787/7f54581d-fr*.

StatLink *https://doi.org/10.1787/888933819176*

Encadré 1.2. **Variations des ratios impôts/PIB dans les régions africaines**

La plupart des 21 pays d'Afrique de cette publication appartiennent à des organisations régionales dont les membres adoptent des règles communes en matière fiscale et douanière et forment une union douanière. Le Kenya, l'Ouganda et le Rwanda sont membres de la Communauté d'Afrique de l'Est (CAE), à laquelle adhèrent également le Burundi, le Soudan du Sud et la Tanzanie. Le Burkina Faso, la Côte d'Ivoire, le Mali, le Niger, le Sénégal et le Togo adhèrent à l'Union économique et monétaire ouest-africaine (UEMOA). Cette union englobe également le Bénin et la Guinée-Bissau.

Les recettes générées par les différents types d'impôts ont suivi une évolution différente entre 2000 et 2016. Depuis 2000, les recettes provenant d'autres impôts sur les biens et services dans les pays de la CAE ont sensiblement baissé, tandis que la situation inverse s'est produite dans les pays de l'UEMOA au cours de la même période. Dans les pays de la CAE, le recul s'échelonnait entre 0.9 % du PIB en Ouganda et 3.0 % du PIB au Rwanda. En revanche, ces recettes n'ont que légèrement décliné au Niger (0.1 % du PIB) et ont crû dans tous les autres pays de l'UEMOA. Le Togo a affiché la plus forte hausse depuis 2000 (équivalente à 3.8 % du PIB).

Encadré 1.2. **Variations des ratios impôts/PIB dans les régions africaines** *(suite)*

L'UEMOA a instauré des tarifs extérieurs communs (CET) en 2000 et les pays de la CAE ont fait de même en 2005, soit pendant la période analysée. Cela explique la forte baisse des recettes tirées d'autres impôts sur les biens et services dans les pays de la CAE par rapport aux pays de l'UEMOA au cours de cette période.

Les recettes de l'IRPP ont sensiblement progressé en pourcentage du PIB dans les pays de la CAE depuis 2000, l'augmentation atteignant 1.8 point de pourcentage ou plus dans tous les pays. A contrario, l'augmentation des recettes générées par l'IRPP a été modeste dans la plupart des pays de l'UEMOA, à l'exception du Sénégal, où leur progression a été équivalente à 1.7 % du PIB, et du Mali, où les recettes de l'IRPP ont fléchi en pourcentage du PIB.

Entre 2000 et 2016, les recettes de l'IS en pourcentage du PIB ont davantage augmenté dans les pays de l'UEMOA couverts par cette publication que dans les pays de la CAE. Les hausses ont dépassé 1.5 % de PIB au Burkina Faso, au Mali, au Niger et au Togo, tandis qu'elles sont restées inférieures à 1.0 point de pourcentage dans les pays de la CAE. Le Burkina Faso, le Mali, le Niger et le Togo tirent une partie de leurs recettes fiscales de leurs ressources minières[a] ; la flambée des prix des matières premières au cours des dernières décennies a contribué aux fortes progressions des recettes de l'IS intervenues pendant cette période.

Graphique 1.9. **Variation des ratios impôts/PIB par principales catégories d'impôts pour les pays membres de la CAE et de l'UEMOA entre 2000 et 2016 (points de pourcentage du PIB)**

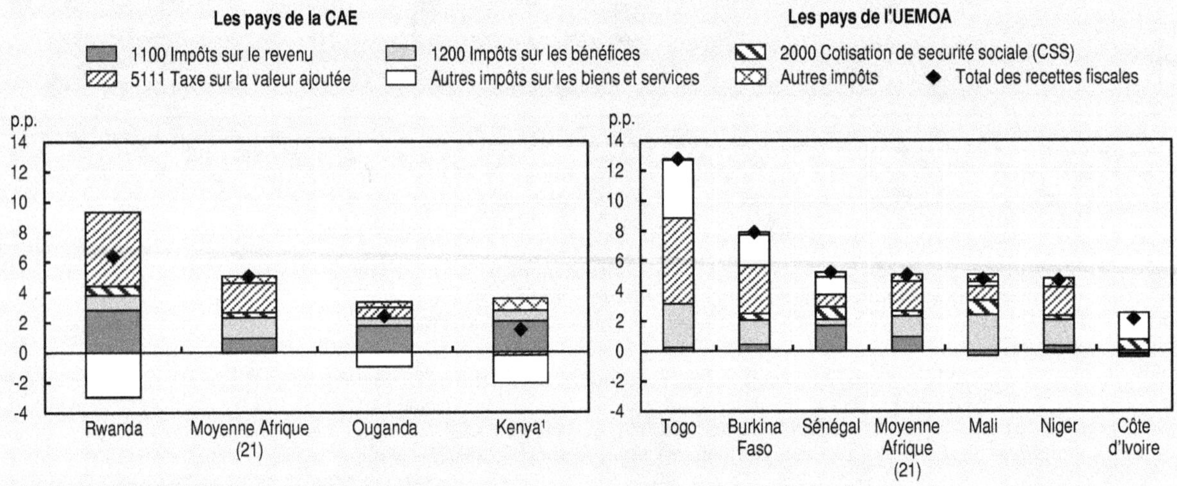

Notes : Les chiffres prennent en compte les recettes fiscales des administrations infranationales pour l'Afrique du Sud (pour la période 2002-2016), l'Eswatini (Swaziland dans les éditions précédentes), le Maroc et Maurice.

La moyenne Afrique (21) et les moyennes ALC (25 pays d'Amérique latine et Caraïbes) et OCDE (35 pays) sont des moyennes non pondérées.

1. Évolution depuis 2001 pour le Kenya faute de données disponibles.

Source : Calculs des auteurs basés sur les données figurant dans (OCDE/ATAF/CUA, 2018$_{[3]}$), « Recettes fiscales en Afrique : Tableaux comparatifs », *Statistiques fiscales de l'OCDE* (base de données), *https://doi.org/10.1787/7f54581d-fr*.

StatLink https://doi.org/10.1787/888933819195

a. Les États membres de l'UEMOA bénéficient de ressources minérales naturelles. L'or est le principal produit d'exportation au Burkina Faso et au Mali. Le Niger et le Togo comptent respectivement parmi les principaux producteurs et exportateurs d'uranium et de phosphates (OMC, 2018$_{[25]}$).

Les niveaux d'imposition sont généralement supérieurs dans les pays à haut revenu : en général, les pays de l'OCDE collectent des recettes fiscales plus importantes que les pays hors OCDE, en pourcentage du PIB. Plusieurs pays africains parmi les 21 étudiés affichent des niveaux de revenu et de développement plus faibles et des ratios impôts/PIB plus bas que les pays d'Amérique latine et des Caraïbes (graphique 1.10). Les pays africains présentent une fourchette de PIB par habitant plus large que les pays d'Amérique latine et des Caraïbes et ceux de l'OCDE.

Graphique 1.10. **Ratios impôts/PIB et PIB par habitant (en PPA) dans les pays d'Afrique, d'Amérique latine et des Caraïbes, dans les pays de l'OCDE et dans certains pays d'Asie, 2016**

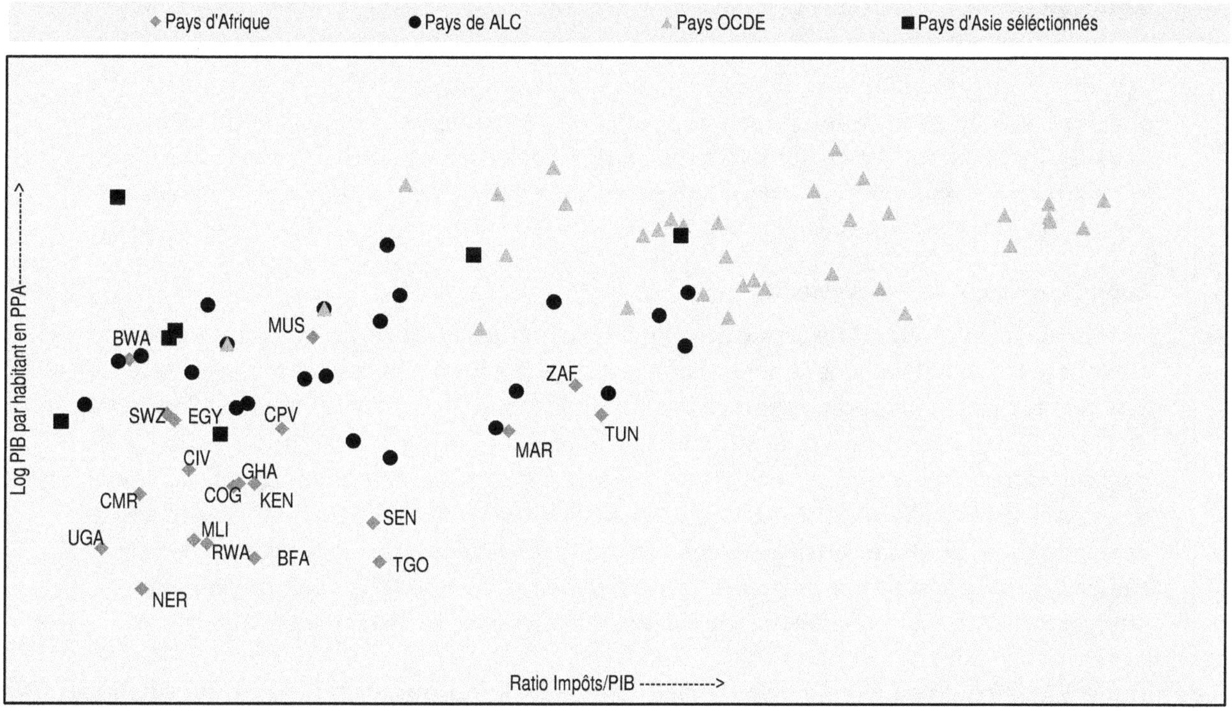

Notes : L'axe y est sur une échelle logarithmique. La parité de pouvoir d'achat (PPA) entre deux pays est le taux auquel la monnaie d'un pays doit être convertie dans celle d'un second pays pour qu'un volume donné de monnaie du premier pays permette d'acheter la même quantité de biens et de services dans chaque pays. Le taux de conversion PPA est le taux utilisé pour convertir une monnaie nationale en dollar international courant. Un dollar international a le même pouvoir d'achat que le dollar US aux États-Unis. Un dollar international est une monnaie hypothétique utilisée comme moyen pour convertir et comparer les coûts d'un pays à l'autre grâce à un point de référence commun, le dollar US (définitions issues de FMI, 2018 et (OMS, 2015[13]).

Source : (FMI, 2018[14]) pour les chiffres du PIB par habitant. Les ratios impôts/PIB proviennent des éditions régionales des Statistiques des recettes publiques.

StatLink https://doi.org/10.1787/888933819214

Dans de nombreuses études, un pourcentage plus élevé du PIB généré par l'agriculture est associé à un ratio impôts/PIB plus faible (Addison et Levin, 2012[15]) (Profeta et Scabrosetti, 2010[16]). Cela traduit le fait que, dans de nombreux pays, l'agriculture est un secteur difficile à traiter :

- La plupart des personnes qui travaillent dans le secteur agricole dans les économies en développement perçoivent de faibles revenus et ne sont pas déclarées (PEAKS, 2013[17]).
- En outre, le secteur agricole en Afrique est moins taxé en raison de l'ampleur de l'activité informelle et du faible degré de monétisation (BAfD/OCDE/UNCEA, 2010[18]).
- Le secteur agricole bénéficie souvent de nombreuses exemptions d'impôt.

Les pays qui tirent des recettes substantielles des exportations de pétrole ont souvent un faible ratio impôts/PIB. Les pays qui tirent d'importantes recettes de leurs ressources naturelles ont généralement moins recours à des formes d'imposition plus contraignantes politiquement, comme l'impôt sur le revenu (BAfD/OCDE/UNCEA, 2010[18]), et leurs bases d'imposition sont relativement étroites. Les trois pays, le Botswana, le Cameroun et la

République du Congo, qui ont collecté des redevances et dividendes tirés du pétrole et autres minéraux pour plus 10 % des recettes non fiscales ont tous des ratios impôts/PIB inférieurs à la moyenne des pays d'Afrique (21). Ces recettes qui ne sont pas considérées comme des recettes fiscales sont examinées plus en détail au chapitre 2.

Structures fiscales

La structure fiscale d'un pays mesure la composition des recettes fiscales en fonction des différents types d'impôts. Il s'agit là d'un indicateur important, car différents impôts ont différents effets économiques et sociaux. La composition des impôts varie beaucoup dans les 21 pays étudiés, ce qui reflète des différences concernant leurs choix politiques, leurs structures et situations économiques, les capacités de leur administration fiscale et d'autres facteurs historiques.

Évolution des structures fiscales

En moyenne, la structure fiscale des 21 pays d'Afrique étudiés révèle une progression des recettes tirées de la TVA et des impôts sur le revenu et sur les bénéfices entre 2000 et 2016. La TVA représentait la plus grande part en 2016, avec 29.3 % du total des recettes fiscales (5.3 % du PIB), soit une augmentation de 4.9 points de pourcentage depuis 2000 (graphique 1.11). La part des autres impôts sur les biens et services arrivait en deuxième position, soit 25.3 % des recettes fiscales totales en 2016 (4.5 % of GDP), malgré un recul de 11.5 points de pourcentage depuis 2000. La part des recettes tirées des impôts sur les bénéfices des sociétés et sur le revenu des personnes physiques a progressé respectivement de 3.3 et 0.8 points de pourcentage, atteignant 15.3 % (2.8 % du PIB) et 15.8 % (3.0 % du PIB) au cours de la même période[9].

Graphique 1.11. **Structure fiscale, moyenne Afrique (21) en pourcentage du total des recettes fiscales et en pourcentage du PIB, 2000 et 2016**

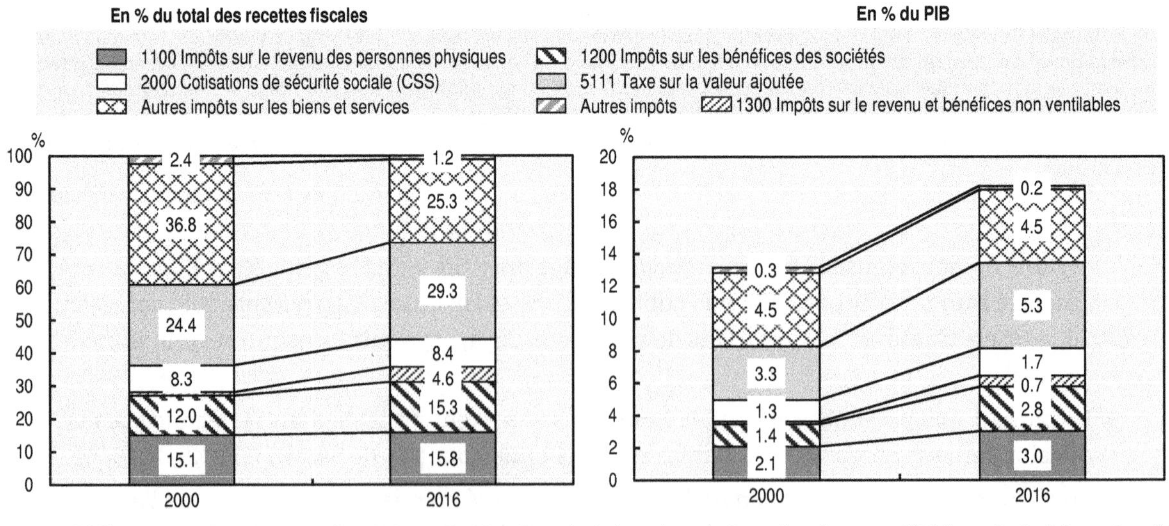

Notes : Les chiffres prennent en compte les recettes fiscales des administrations infranationales pour l'Afrique du Sud (pour la période 2002-2016), l'Eswatini (Swaziland dans les éditions précédentes), le Maroc et Maurice.
La moyenne Afrique (21) et les moyennes ALC (25 pays d'Amérique latine et Caraïbes) et OCDE (35 pays) sont des moyennes non pondérées. Elles doivent être interprétées avec précaution car des données relatives aux cotisations de sécurité sociale sont indisponibles ou incomplètes pour quelques pays. Pour plus de précisions, se reporter aux tableaux par pays présentés dans le chapitre 5.
Faute de données disponibles, la moyenne Afrique (21) exclut le Botswana avant 2004, l'Égypte avant 2002 et le Kenya avant 2001.
Source : Calculs des auteurs basés sur les données figurant (OCDE/ATAF/CUA, 2018[3]), « Recettes fiscales en Afrique : Tableaux comparatifs », *Statistiques fiscales de l'OCDE* (base de données), *https://doi.org/10.1787/7f54581d-fr*.

StatLink https://doi.org/10.1787/888933819233

Structures fiscales en 2016

En moyenne, la contribution de la TVA au total des recettes fiscales dans les 21 pays d'Afrique de cette publication était la même que dans les pays d'Amérique latine et des Caraïbes et environ 10 points de pourcentage supérieure à la moyenne de l'OCDE (20.0 %). Toutefois, en pourcentage du PIB, les recettes de TVA des pays d'Afrique (21) sont inférieures à la moyenne ALC (6.2 %) et OCDE (6.7 %) (graphique 1.12).

En 2016, la part moyenne des recettes de l'impôt sur les bénéfices des sociétés dans le total des recettes fiscales dans les pays d'Afrique (21) s'élevait à 15.3 % (soit un niveau comparable à la moyenne ALC de 15.4 %) et dépassait la moyenne de l'OCDE de 8.9 % (chiffre de 2015). Exprimées en pourcentage du PIB, la part des recettes issues de l'impôt sur les bénéfices des sociétés était 2.8 % pour la moyenne de l'Afrique (21) et la moyenne OCDE ; ces pourcentages sont néanmoins inférieurs à la moyenne ALC de 3.4 % du PIB (graphique 1.12).

Graphique 1.12. **Structure fiscale pour la moyenne des pays d'Afrique (21), ALC et OCDE en pourcentage du total des recettes fiscales et du PIB, 2016**

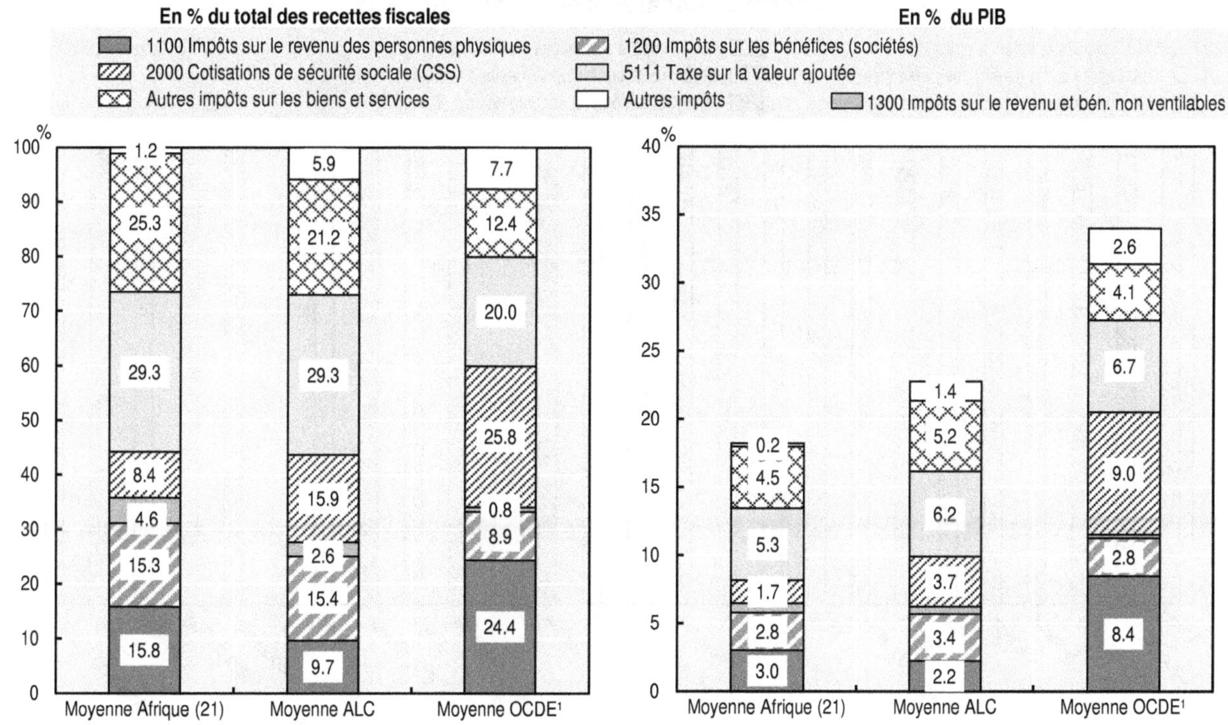

Notes : Les chiffres prennent en compte les recettes fiscales des administrations infranationales pour l'Afrique du Sud (pour la période 2002-2016), l'Eswatini (Swaziland dans les éditions précédentes), le Maroc et Maurice.

La moyenne Afrique (21) et les moyennes ALC (25 pays d'Amérique latine et Caraïbes) et OCDE (35 pays) sont des moyennes non pondérées. Elles doivent être interprétées avec précaution car des données relatives aux cotisations de sécurité sociale sont indisponibles ou incomplètes pour quelques pays. Pour plus de précisions, se reporter aux tableaux par pays présentés dans le chapitre 5.

Les données concernant l'OCDE portent sur l'année 2015 car les données de 2016 ne sont pas disponibles.

Source : Calculs des auteurs basés sur les données figurant dans (OCDE/ATAF/CUA, 2018[3]), « Recettes fiscales en Afrique : Tableaux comparatifs », *Statistiques fiscales de l'OCDE* (base de données), *https://doi.org/10.1787/7f54581d-fr*.

StatLink https://doi.org/10.1787/888933819252

En revanche, la part moyenne, dans les 21 pays d'Afrique, des recettes de l'impôt sur le revenu des personnes physiques dans le total des recettes fiscales, soit 15.8 %, était inférieure à la moyenne de l'OCDE de 24.4 % (chiffre de 2015) mais supérieure à la moyenne ALC (9.7 %). En pourcentage du PIB, la part des recettes de l'impôt sur le revenu des personnes physiques de la moyenne des pays de l'OCDE atteignait 8.4 %, soit plus du double de la moyenne Afrique (21) de 3.0 %.

Les structures fiscales sont très variables d'un pays africain à l'autre de cette publication. Le graphique 1.13 illustre la ventilation des recettes fiscales entre impôts sur le revenu (personnes physiques et sociétés), cotisations de sécurité sociale et impôts sur les biens et services (y compris la TVA ainsi que les autres impôts sur les biens et services).

Les impôts sur les biens et services constituaient la principale source de recettes fiscales pour 17 des pays, allant de 35.8 % des recettes en Tunisie à 74.6 % au Togo. Dans ces pays, la TVA représentait le principal poste de recettes tirées des impôts sur les biens et services, sauf en Côte d'Ivoire, au Ghana, au Kenya et en Ouganda, qui ont davantage recours à d'autres impôts sur les biens et services.

Graphique 1.13. **Structures fiscales des pays d'Afrique (21), 2016**

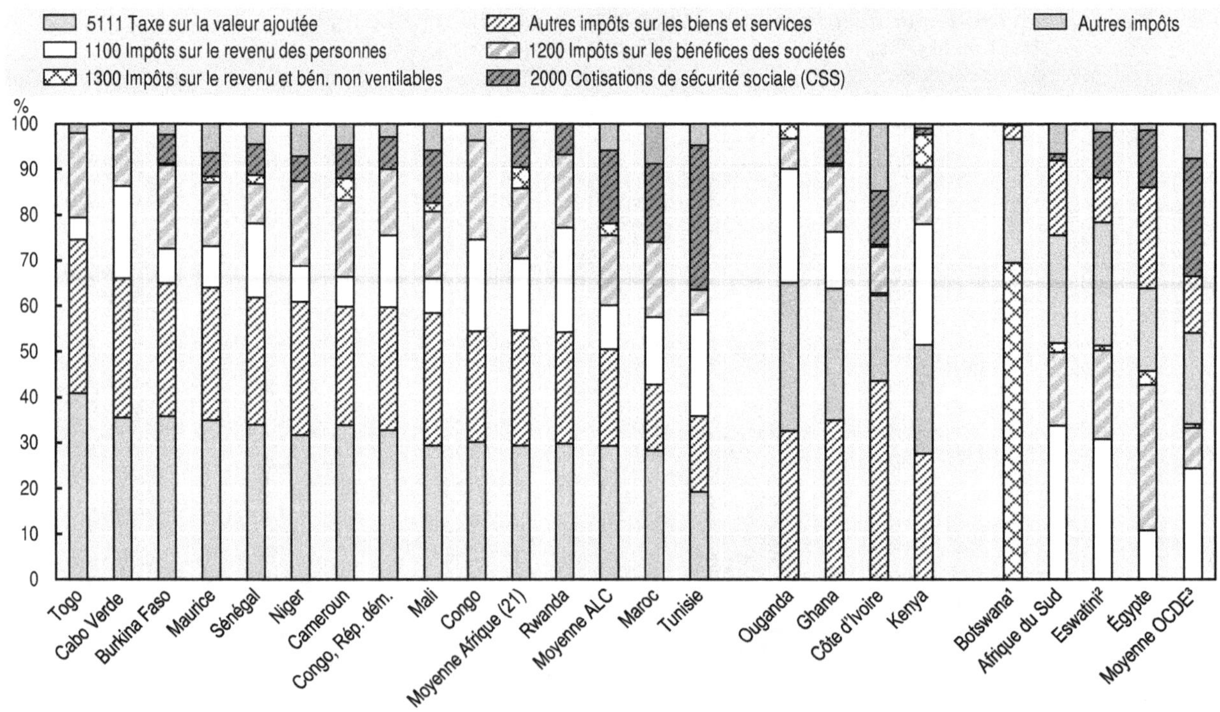

Notes : Les chiffres prennent en compte les recettes fiscales des administrations infranationales pour l'Afrique du Sud (pour la période 2002-2016), l'Eswatini (Swaziland dans les éditions précédentes), le Maroc et Maurice. La moyenne Afrique (21) et les moyennes ALC (25 pays d'Amérique latine et Caraïbes) et OCDE (35 pays) sont des moyennes non pondérées.

Il convient d'interpréter avec précaution la moyenne des pays d'Afrique (21) car des données relatives aux cotisations de sécurité sociale sont indisponibles ou incomplètes pour quelques pays. Pour plus de précisions, se reporter aux tableaux par pays présentés dans le chapitre 5.

1. La ventilation des recettes tirées des impôts sur le revenu et sur les bénéfices entre la rubrique 1200 Impôt sur les bénéfices des sociétés et la rubrique 1100 Impôt sur le revenu des personnes physiques n'est pas disponible.
2. Anciennement Swaziland.
3. Les données concernant l'OCDE portent sur l'année 2015 car les données de 2016 ne sont pas disponibles.

Source : Calculs des auteurs basés sur les données figurant dans (OCDE/ATAF/CUA, 2018$_{[3]}$), « Recettes fiscales en Afrique : Tableaux comparatifs », *Statistiques fiscales de l'OCDE* (base de données), *https://doi.org/10.1787/7f54581d-fr*.

StatLink *https://doi.org/10.1787/888933819271*

Les quatre pays restants (Afrique du Sud, Botswana, Égypte et Eswatini) ont mobilisé la plus grande partie de leurs recettes fiscales grâce aux impôts sur le revenu et les bénéfices, soit une fraction plus élevée que la moyenne des pays de l'OCDE et ALC. Parmi ces pays, les recettes générées par l'impôt sur le revenu étaient comprises entre 45.7 % du total des recettes fiscales en Égypte et 69.5 % au Botswana. Dans la catégorie de l'impôt sur le revenu, l'Afrique du Sud est le seul pays où les recettes de l'IRPP en pourcentage du PIB était supérieure à la moyenne de l'OCDE.

L'importance des cotisations de sécurité sociale[10] est très variable entre les 21 pays couverts par ce rapport. La part des cotisations de sécurité sociale dans le total des recettes fiscales est la plus élevée au Maroc et en Tunisie mais elles occupent une place plus modeste dans le total des recettes fiscales dans les autres pays, allant de moins de 1.5 % en Afrique du Sud, au Botswana, au Cabo Verde et au Kenya à plus de 10 % en Côte d'Ivoire, en Égypte et au Mali. Cette hétérogénéité reflète la diversité des régimes de sécurité sociale et des taux de cotisation dans les pays d'Afrique.

Par exemple, les charges de sécurité sociale en Afrique du Sud se composent uniquement des cotisations au Fonds d'assurance chômage. Les autres risques sociaux, tels que la vieillesse et l'invalidité, sont couverts par des programmes d'aide sociale financés par l'impôt. À l'inverse, les régimes de sécurité sociale marocain et tunisien sont calqués sur le système français et couvrent un large éventail de risques, y compris la vieillesse, l'incapacité, la maladie, la maternité, les accidents du travail (Tunisie), le chômage (Maroc) et les allocations familiales (SSA, 2015[19]).

Taxes d'accise

Comme dans la plupart des pays de l'OCDE, les taxes d'accise constituent à la fois une source importante de recettes fiscales et servent à influencer le comportement des consommateurs. La plupart des pays prélèvent des taxes sur le tabac et/ou l'alcool en vue de réduire la consommation de ces produits, ou imposent des taxes environnementales (sur les carburants par exemple) pour lutter contre la pollution et d'autres externalités environnementales négatives.

Dans la mesure du possible, les 21 pays d'Afrique de cette publication ont fourni une ventilation détaillée de leurs taxes d'accise par type de produits. Les accises relèvent de sept catégories : carburants et autres produits pétroliers, produits miniers, tabac, boissons (alcoolisées et non alcoolisées), véhicules, communication et autre.

En proportion du total des recettes fiscales et du PIB, les accises varient fortement entre les neuf pays (Botswana, Burkina Faso, République démocratique du Congo, Égypte, Eswatini, Mali, Maurice, Sénégal et Tunisie) pour lesquels on dispose d'une ventilation détaillée des recettes qu'elles génèrent. En 2016, elles étaient comprises entre 1.8 % du total des recettes fiscales au Botswana et 18.7 % à Maurice (soit l'équivalent de 0.3 % et 3.7 % du PIB).

Bien que la composition des accises diffère d'un pays à l'autre, la ventilation présentée au graphique 1.14 doit être interprétée avec précaution car elle ne couvre pas nécessairement tous les produits. Les neuf pays imposent les carburants et autres produits pétroliers ; cette catégorie a généré environ 25 % du total des recettes tirées des accises dans cinq pays et les deux tiers ou plus dans quatre pays en 2016 (graphique 1.14). Les deux autres catégories qui génèrent une fraction importante de droits d'accise sont le tabac et les boissons. Les recettes tirées des accises sur le tabac dépassaient 25 % du total des recettes d'accises en Égypte, à Maurice et en Tunisie, et les recettes tirées des accises sur les boissons dépassaient 25 % du total des recettes d'accises au Botswana, au Burkina Faso, en République démocratique du Congo et à Maurice.

Graphique 1.14. **Composition des taxes d'accise dans une sélection de pays africains, 2016**

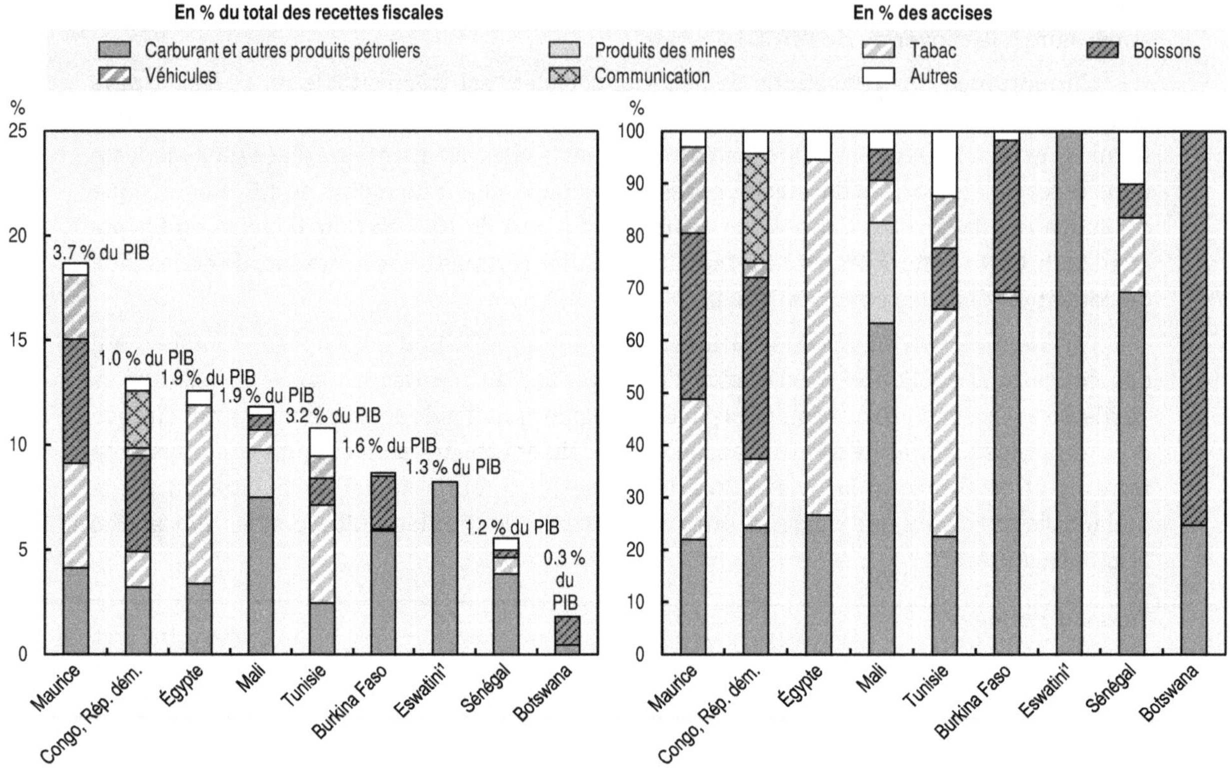

1. Anciennement Swaziland.

Source : Calculs des auteurs basés sur les données figurant dans (OCDE/ATAF/CUA, 2018[3]), et extraites des tableaux par pays.

StatLink https://doi.org/10.1787/888933819290

Impôts par niveaux d'administration

L'analyse de la répartition des impôts par niveaux d'administration dans les 21 pays d'Afrique de cette publication est limitée par le fait que les données sur les recettes fiscales perçues par les administrations infranationales étaient disponibles dans quatre pays seulement : Afrique du Sud, Eswatini, Maroc et Maurice[11]. Les recettes fiscales des collectivités locales sont considérées comme faibles dans les 21 pays africains. Selon la (BAfD/OCDE/PNUD, 2015[20]), « en Afrique, en moyenne, le poids des recettes des administrations locales équivaut à 7 % des recettes totales perçues par les collectivités locales et régionales et l'administration centrale combinées ». En 2016, les recettes des administrations infranationales en pourcentage du total des recettes fiscales étaient faibles dans les quatre pays pour lesquels des données existent : moins de 1 % en Eswatini et à Maurice, 3.5 % au Maroc et 5.0 % en Afrique du Sud.

Les impôts sur le patrimoine constituent la plus importante source de revenu pour les administrations infranationales en Afrique du Sud, en Eswatini, au Maroc et à Maurice. Ils représentent plus de 80 % du total des recettes fiscales dans les quatre pays. Le solde se compose principalement des impôts sur les biens et services. On observe de grandes disparités en la matière, et de nombreux pays africains ne lèvent aucune taxe locale sur le foncier bâti et non bâti, ni même sur les activités économiques (BAfD/OCDE/PNUD, 2015[20]).

Les compétences fiscales dévolues aux administrations infranationales sont généralement limitées, et la responsabilité du recouvrement de l'impôt incombe avant tout à l'administration centrale. (BAfD/OCDE/PNUD, 2015[20]) observent que « de nombreuses administrations locales perçoivent une fraction importante de leurs recettes totales grâce aux transferts opérés par l'administration centrale ».

Les collectivités locales dans la plupart des pays d'Afrique se heurtent à des contraintes de ressources et les outils dont disposent leurs administrations fiscales sont inadaptés pour procéder à un recouvrement efficient des impôts et les imputer correctement en comptabilité. Cette situation entraîne des coûts de recouvrement élevés et un grand nombre d'impôts peu productifs. En outre, le traitement des données relatives aux recettes collectées et l'échange de renseignements avec d'autres institutions publiques sont peu développés, et les administrations locales coopèrent généralement peu avec l'administration centrale. Cela se traduit par des impôts en double ou qui vont à l'encontre des objectifs nationaux (comme des taxes locales sur les cultures d'exportation). À l'exception de l'Afrique du Sud, les registres fonciers en bonne et due forme font défaut, ce qui entrave la collecte des impôts fonciers (Fjeldstad, Chambas, Brun, 2014[21]). À Maurice, par exemple, la taxe foncière est peu productive en partie à cause de cadastres périmés et de valeurs de biens qui ne sont plus à jour (FMI, mai 2014[22]).

Bien que de nombreux pays africains aient entrepris de vastes réformes de leur administration fiscale centrale et de la législation correspondante au cours des dernières décennies, il n'y a guère eu d'initiatives de ce genre au niveau des administrations locales. On a donné la priorité aux recettes perçues par l'administration centrale parce que c'est à cet échelon que la nécessité de réduire les déficits budgétaires s'est fait sentir le plus. Par ailleurs, il est plus simple et moins coûteux de réformer la législation et les systèmes fiscaux au niveau national qu'au niveau local, et les avantages potentiels de la réforme fiscale à un niveau national en termes d'accroissement des recettes sont plus importants.

En 2007, le Maroc a lancé une réforme du système fiscal et des administrations fiscales locales en vue d'augmenter les recettes générées par les impôts locaux (Boisard, de Freitas, Hidouci, 2014[23]). L'Afrique du Sud a décentralisé avec succès le processus de recouvrement de la taxe foncière urbaine. Elle a mis en place un système moderne de collecte des recettes de la taxe foncière et les autorités municipales reçoivent un appui approprié en termes d'expertise et de moyens (Monkam et Moore, 2015[24]).

Notes

1. Anciennement Swaziland.
2. La Lituanie est devenue membre de l'OCDE le 5 juillet 2018. Les données concernant la Lituanie seront incluses pour la première fois dans la publication *Statistiques des recettes publiques de l'OCDE* qui paraîtra en novembre 2018.
3. Les données sur les cotisations de sécurité sociale sont indisponibles pour la République du Congo, la République démocratique du Congo (avant 2012), le Togo et l'Ouganda, et sont incomplètes au Cameroun et au Sénégal. Les cotisations de sécurité sociale pour le Botswana sont égales à zéro dans la mesure où elles ne remplissent pas les critères retenus pour être considérées comme des cotisations de sécurité sociale, selon la classification des impôts de l'OCDE figurant dans le Guide d'interprétation. Pour plus de précisions, se reporter aux tableaux par pays présentés dans le chapitre 5.

4. Ce classement doit être interprété avec précaution car les données relatives aux cotisations de sécurité sociale sont manquantes pour le Togo.
5. Il s'agit principalement de droits d'accise, de droits de douane et de droits à l'importation.
6. La variation est calculée sur la période 2000-15 car les données de 2016 ne sont pas disponibles.
7. La moyenne des pays d'Afrique (21), pour les cotisations de sécurité sociale rapportées au PIB, doit être interprétée avec précaution compte tenu du fait que les données relatives aux cotisations de sécurité sociale sont incomplètes ou inexistantes pour certains pays africains couverts par cette publication.
8. Il convient d'interpréter la moyenne des pays d'Afrique (21) avec précaution car des données relatives aux cotisations de sécurité sociale sont indisponibles ou incomplètes pour quelques pays. Aussi, en République du Congo, en République démocratique du Congo (avant 2012), en Ouganda et au Togo, les données sur les cotisations de sécurité sociale sont indisponibles, et elles sont incomplètes au Cameroun et au Sénégal.
9. La moyenne des pays d'Afrique (21), pour les recettes de l'impôt sur les bénéfices des sociétés et de l'impôt sur le revenu des personnes physiques rapportées au PIB et en pourcentage du total des recettes fiscales, doit être interprétée avec précaution compte tenu du fait qu'une fraction des recettes de l'impôt sur le revenu n'a pas pu être imputée à la catégorie des recettes de l'impôt sur les bénéfices des sociétés et de l'impôt sur le revenu des personnes physiques (0.7 % du PIB et 4.9 % du total des recettes fiscales en 2016).
10. Les données relatives aux cotisations de sécurité sociale sont indisponibles pour la République démocratique du Congo (avant 2012), l'Ouganda et le Togo et sont incomplètes pour le Cameroun et le Sénégal. Pour ce dernier les chiffres tiennent compte des données relatives aux cotisations de sécurité sociale communiquées par l'Institution de Prévoyance Retraites du Sénégal (IPRES) et des données émanant de la Caisse de Sécurité Sociale (CSS). Ces dernières ne sont disponibles qu'à partir de 2012.
11. Les données concernant Maurice proviennent des états financiers établis par le Bureau des statistiques de Maurice.

Références

Addison, T. et J. Levin (2012), *The Determinants of Tax Revenue in Sub-Saharan Africa*, Örebro University School of Business, Örebro, Suède, *http://oru.diva-portal.org/smash/record.jsf?pid=diva2%3A570456&dswid=4207*. [15]

BAfD (2010), *Domestic Resource Mobilization for Poverty Reduction in East Africa: Rwanda case study*, Banque africaine de développement, Abidjan, *http://www.afdb.org/fileadmin/uploads/afdb/Documents/Project-and-Operations/Rwanda%20case%20study%20paper%20final.pdf*. [11]

BAfD/OCDE/PNUD (2017), *Perspectives économiques en Afrique 2017 : Entrepreneuriat et industrialisation*, Éditions OCDE, Paris, *http://dx.doi.org/10.1787/aeo-2017-fr*. [4]

BAfD/OCDE/PNUD (2015), *Perspectives économiques en Afrique 2015 : Développement territorial et inclusion spatiale*, Éditions OCDE, Paris, *https://doi.org/10.1787/aeo-2015-fr*. [20]

BAfD/OCDE/CEA (2010), *Perspectives économiques en Afrique 2010*, Éditions OCDE, Paris, *https://doi.org/10.1787/aeo-2010-fr*. [18]

Boisard, de Freitas, Hidouci (2014), *Renforcer les recettes fiscales locales pour financer le développement urbain en*, Fonds Mondial pour le Développement des Villes (FMDV), Paris, *http://delog.org/web/wp-content/uploads/2016/03/Etude-FMDV-Fiscalite%CC%81-locale-Villes-Afrique-8-Cas.pdf*. [23]

Fjeldstad, Chambas, Brun (2014), *Local government taxation in Sub-Saharan Africa: a review and an agenda for*, 2, Chr. Michelsen Institute, Bergen, *http://www.cmi.no/publications/file/5098-local-government-taxation-in-sub-saharan-africa.pdf*. [21]

FMI (2018), *Perspectives de l'économie mondiale*, FMI. [14]

FMI (2017), *Perspectives de l'économie mondiale*, Fonds monétaire international, Washington, DC, *http://www.imf.org/fr/Publications/WEO/Issues/2017/04/04/world-economic-outlook-april-2017*. [5]

FMI (2016), *Mali : Sixième revue de l'accord au titre de la facilité élargie de crédit et demande de modification d'un critère de réalisation—analyse de viabilité de la dette*, *https://www.imf.org/en/Publications/CR/Issues/2016/12/31/Mali-Sixth-Review-Under-the-Extended-Credit-Facility-Arrangement-and-Request-for-44445*. [6]

FMI (mai 2014), *Mauritius: 2014 article IV consultation-staff report*, Fonds monétaire international, Washington, DC, *http://www.imf.org/external/pubs/ft/scr/2014/cr14107.pdf.* [22]

FMI (2017a), *Niger : Consultations de 2016 au titre de l'article iv et demande d'accord triennal au titre de la facilité élargie de crédit — communiqué de presse, rapport des services du FMI et Déclaration de l'administrateur pour le Niger*, *https://www.imf.org/en/Publications/CR/Issues/2017/02/24/Niger-2016-Article-IV-Consultation-and-Request-for-a-Three-Year-Arrangement-Under-the-44704.* [8]

Fossat; Bua (2013), *Tax administration reform in the francophone countries of sub-Saharan*, Fonds monétaire international, Washington, DC, *http://www.imf.org/external/pubs/ft/wp/2013/wp13173.pdf.* [10]

Hellenic Shipping News Worldwide (2017), « Ghana: Crude Oil production declined in 2016 », *Hellenic Shipping News Worldwide*, *https://www.hellenicshippingnews.com/ghana-crude-oil-production-declined-in-2016/.* [7]

Kloeden, D. (2011), *Revenue administration reforms in anglophone Africa since the early 1990s*, IMF Working Paper, WP/11/162, *http://www.imf.org/external/pubs/ft/wp/2011/wp11162.pdf.* [9]

Monkam, N. et M. Moore (2015), *How Property Tax Would Benefit Africa*, Africa Research Institute, *http://www.africaresearchinstitute.org/publications/property-tax-benefit-africa.* [24]

OCDE (2017), *Statistiques des recettes publiques : 1965-2016*, Éditions OCDE, Paris, *http://dx.doi.org/10.1787/9789264283206-fr.* [2]

OCDE (2015), *Coopération pour le développement 2014 : Mobiliser les ressources au service du développement durable*, Éditions OCDE, Paris, *https://doi.org/10.1787/dcr-2014-fr.* [12]

OCDE/ATAF/CUA (2018), *Recettes fiscales en Afrique : Tableaux comparatifs*, Statistiques fiscales de l'OCDE (base de données), *https://doi.org/10.1787/7f54581d-fr.* [3]

OCDE/CEPAL/CIAT/BID (2018), *Revenue Statistics in Latin America and the Caribbean*, Éditions OCDE, Paris, *http://dx.doi.org/10.1787/rev_lat_car-2017-en-fr.* [1]

OMC (2018), WT/TPR/S/362 • *Pays membres de l'UEMOA*, *https://www.wto.org/french/tratop_f/tpr_f/s362-00_sum_f.pdf.* [25]

OMS (2015), *Purchasing Power Parity 2005*, Organisation mondiale de la santé, *http://www.who.int/choice/costs/ppp/en/.* [13]

PEAKS, E. (2013), *Taxation and Developing Countries*, Overseas Development Institute training notes, Londres, *http://www.odi.org/sites/odi.org.uk/files/odi-assets/events-documents/5045.pdf.* [17]

Profeta, S. et S. Scabrosetti (2010), *The Political Economy of Taxation: Lessons from Developing Countries*, Edward Elgar Publishing, *https://books.google.fr/books?isbn=1849805490.* [16]

SSA (2015), *Social Security Through the World: Africa*, SSA Publication Social Security Administration, Washington, DC, *http://www.ssa.gov/policy/docs/progdesc/ssptw/2014-2015/africa/ssptw15africa.pdf.* [19]

Chapter 2

Non-tax revenue trends, 1990-2016

Chapitre 2

Tendances des recettes non fiscales, 1990-2016

Revenue Statistics in Africa 1990-2016/Statistiques des recettes publiques en Afrique 1990-2016

Chapter 2

Non-tax revenue trends, 1990-2016

Introduction

Governments generate revenues through mechanisms that do not meet the definition of taxes used in this report. These are known as non-tax revenues and can be a very important source of financing; two countries may generate similar levels of taxes but their public spending might differ significantly due to the different levels of non-tax revenues they collect. This is particularly the case among African countries, many of which obtain a substantial portion of their public finances from resource rents or grants.

A clear picture of government finances must therefore reflect both tax and non-tax revenues, despite the challenges associated with collecting data on the latter (Box 2.1). This chapter provides cross-country comparisons of non-tax revenue data for the countries included in this publication.[1]

The main categories of non-tax revenues[2] included here are:

- Grants from foreign governments or international organisations (budget aid, food aid, capital transfers, current transfers, project grants, programme grants, international debt relief, etc.);
- Property income (such as mining royalties and returns on government investment);
- Sales of goods and services (which include some administrative fees);
- Fines and penalties;
- Miscellaneous and unidentified revenues (non-tax revenues that cannot be classified according to the other categories).

Non-tax revenues as percentage of GDP

In 2016, non-tax revenues as a percentage of GDP varied significantly among the 21 countries included in this publication. They ranged from 18.2% of GDP for Botswana to 0.5% of GDP for South Africa. In every country except Botswana, non-tax revenues were lower than tax revenues (Figure 2.1).

Figure 2.1. **Total tax and non-tax revenue by country as a percentage of GDP, 2016**

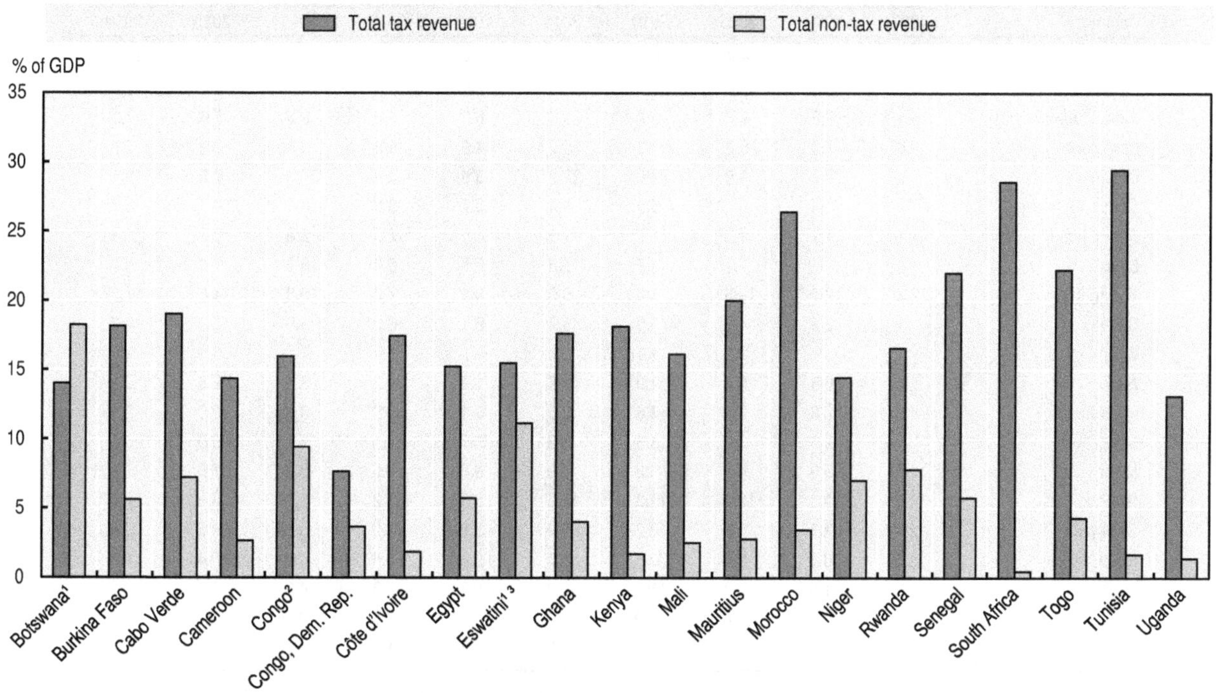

Note: Non-tax revenue figures include sub-national non-tax government revenues for Eswatini, Kenya, Mauritius and Morocco, the only countries for which such revenues are reported. In 2016, these represented, respectively, 4%, 30%, 6% and 45% of all non-tax revenue collected for each country. South Africa reported some local and regional taxes, but no local and regional non-tax revenues.

1. Non-tax revenues for Botswana and Eswatini include funds from excises and customs duties collected by South Africa and then transferred to Botswana and Eswatini through the Southern African Customs Union (SACU) revenue-sharing agreement.
2. Figures presented here are grant revenues and oil revenues reported by the IMF in its April 2018 *World Economic Outlook*. Other types of non-tax revenue were not obtained for the Republic of the Congo.
3. Previously Swaziland.

The tax-to-GDP ratios and non-tax-to-GDP ratios need to be interpreted with caution for some countries, due to incomplete data. Data on social security contributions are not available for Botswana (but are deemed to be null as they do not meet the criteria to be classified as social security contributions set out in the OECD classification of taxes in the Interpretative Guide), the Republic of the Congo, the Democratic Republic of the Congo (prior to 2012), Togo or Uganda. Data on social security contributions are only partially available for Cameroon and Senegal. Data on property taxes are not available for Ghana and Uganda. See the country tables in Chapters 5 and 6 for further information.

Source: Table 4.1 in Chapter 4 and Table 6.1 in Chapter 6.

StatLink https://doi.org/10.1787/888933819309

While the Africa (21) average tax-to-GDP ratio has increased by 5 percentage points since 2000, non-tax revenues have declined in most of these countries in recent years (Table 2.1). Of the 21 countries, all but four had lower non-tax revenues as a proportion of GDP in 2016 than in 2015 and all but six had lower non-tax revenues as a proportion of GDP than 10 years earlier.

Table 2.1. **Total non-tax revenue by country as a percentage of GDP, 1997-2016**

Country	1997	2000	2005	2010	2011	2012	2013	2014	2015	2016
Botswana[1]	..	..	26.6	19.1	20.0	22.4	22.3	22.8	18.4	18.2
Burkina Faso	..	8.6	5.6	5.7	6.9	7.0	8.0	6.3	6.2	5.6
Cabo Verde	16.1	7.6	9.2	9.7	5.6	6.0	6.2	5.3	7.6	7.2
Cameroon	5.0	7.3	6.3	4.3	5.7	4.6	4.5	3.9	3.9	2.7
Congo	..	20.7	31.9	29.0	33.2	33.0	33.5	27.3	7.9	9.4
Congo, Dem. Rep.[2]	..	..	..	6.5	4.4	5.7	3.6	6.4	4.7	3.7
Côte d'Ivoire	1.4	1.1	2.3	1.7	1.5	1.9	2.5	2.6	3.3	1.9
Egypt	..	..	7.1	8.7	5.8	6.5	6.0	10.2	7.3	5.7
Eswatini[1, 3]	12.3	12.1	15.5	8.0	6.6	19.1	17.0	16.8	14.6	11.2
Ghana	..	2.2	4.2	5.0	5.3	6.1	6.2	5.6	6.2	4.0
Kenya	..	..	3.2	1.1	..	..	1.4	1.5	2.0	1.7
Mali	..	6.8	5.4	4.9	5.6	1.4	4.2	3.3	2.8	2.5
Mauritius	4.0	2.8	2.5	3.8	3.5	3.1	3.2	3.0	2.9	2.8
Morocco	..	2.2	3.0	3.6	3.9	3.7	4.1	3.8	3.9	3.5
Niger	..	5.5	8.2	6.3	4.9	8.0	9.5	8.0	7.6	7.0
Rwanda	7.5	11.8	12.7	12.3	12.3	8.8	11.2	9.4	8.9	7.8
Senegal	2.4	2.7	2.3	3.2	2.9	3.8	4.2	5.2	4.5	5.8
South Africa	0.5	0.4	0.5	0.6	0.6	0.6	0.6	0.5	0.4	0.5
Togo	..	1.8	2.7	11.2	9.3	6.3	5.3	4.3	4.1	4.3
Tunisia	..	2.5	2.6	2.9	4.0	3.5	3.6	2.4	2.1	1.7
Uganda	..	..	5.7	2.3	2.5	1.7	1.3	1.5	1.7	1.4

Notes: ".." indicates that the data are incomplete for the country in the particular year.
Non-tax revenue figures include sub-national government revenues for Eswatini, Kenya, Mauritius and Morocco, the only countries for which data on such revenues are reported.
1. Non-tax revenues for Botswana and Eswatini include funds from excises and customs duties collected by South Africa and then transferred to Botswana and Eswatini through the Southern African Customs Union (SACU) revenue-sharing agreement.
2. Figures presented here are grant revenues and oil revenues reported by the IMF's April 2018 *World Economic Outlook*. Other types of non-tax revenue were not obtained for the Republic of the Congo.
3. Previously Swaziland.
Source: Table 6.1 in Chapter 6.

StatLink https://doi.org/10.1787/888933819632

Non-tax revenue collections tend to vary more between years than tax revenues, as demonstrated by the coefficient of variation[3] of tax and non-tax revenues over the most recent ten years of data (Figure 2.2). However, in some countries (Botswana, Burkina Faso, the Republic of the Congo, Rwanda and Niger) tax revenues were almost as variable as non-tax revenues.

Over the past decade, 11 of the 21 countries in this publication showed at least one year-on-year increase in non-tax revenue equivalent to 2% of GDP or more while 14 countries registered a decrease of similar magnitude.

- The largest spike occurred in Niger, where non-tax revenues as a percentage of GDP rose from 8.2% in 2005 to 47.0% in 2006 and then declined to 6.7% the subsequent year.
- In the Republic of the Congo, combined revenues from grants and oil jumped from 36.5% of GDP in 2007 to 47.2% of GDP in 2008, before declining by 25.7 percentage points the following year; between 2014 and 2015, these revenues dropped from 27.3% of GDP to 7.9%, almost 20 percentage points.
- Eswatini also had single-year changes in non-tax revenues equivalent to at least 10% of GDP.

Such fluctuations are often driven by resource rents, due to swings in commodity prices, or by grant revenues, due to the shorter duration and lower predictability of grant flows in comparison to tax revenues. However, other sources of non-tax revenue, for example Southern African Customs Union (SACU) revenues in Eswatini, have also proven to be highly variable.

Figure 2.2. **Coefficients of variation (CV) for tax and non-tax revenues, 2007-16**

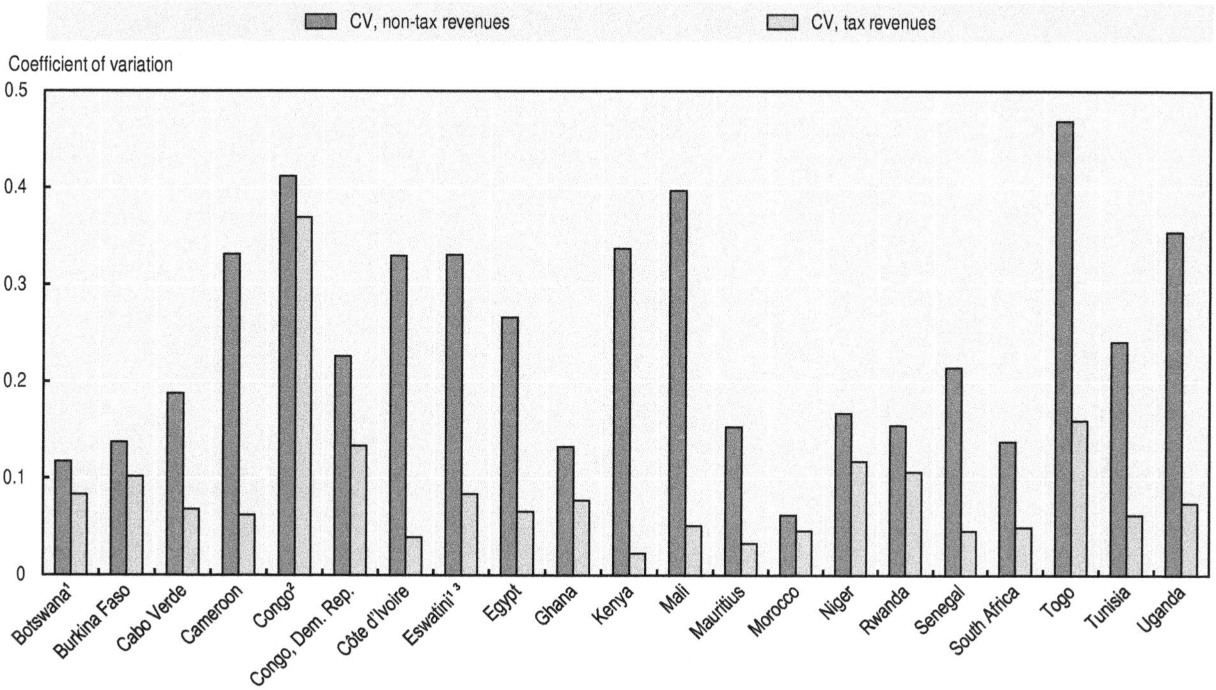

Note: Non-tax revenue figures include sub-national government revenues for Eswatini, Kenya, Mauritius and Morocco, the only countries for which data on such revenues are reported.

1. Non-tax revenues for Botswana and Eswatini include funds from excises and customs duties collected by South Africa and then transferred to Botswana and Eswatini through the Southern African Customs Union (SACU) revenue-sharing agreement.
2. Figures presented here are grant revenues and oil revenues reported by the IMF's April 2018 *World Economic Outlook*. Other types of non-tax revenue were not obtained for the Republic of the Congo.
3. Previously Swaziland.

Source: Table 4.1 in Chapter 4 and Table 6.1 in Chapter 6.

StatLink https://doi.org/10.1787/888933819328

Box 2.1. **Non-tax revenues and data reliability**

Data on non-tax revenues is often not as detailed as tax revenue data. For example, some countries have aggregate figures for total non-tax revenues but do not break this information down beyond grants and other non-tax revenues categories. This may be due to the fact that data on non-tax revenues often come from several different sources. *Revenue Statistics in Africa* indicates cases where total non-tax revenues are reported but may be incomplete.

It is also possible that non-tax revenue data are not subject to the same level of scrutiny as tax revenues. Many types of non-tax revenue are not part of the main budget process and not subject to the same oversight mechanisms as tax revenues. Moreover, they are not always under the responsibility of the custodians of tax statistics.

Grants, legal settlements and mining and oil contracts often involve large payments by external entities such as multinational corporations and foreign governments that are not always transparent to the government or to the population. Some aspects of these deals may be kept secret, for example when large contracts with resource extraction companies contain confidentiality clauses (AfDB/OECD/ECA, 2010[1]). In addition, some countries negotiate large payments that cover many categories of both tax and non-tax revenue, making detailed breakdowns less feasible.

Structure of non-tax revenues

Table 2.2 shows the contribution of each sub-category of non-tax revenue to total non-tax revenue as a percentage of GDP in 2016 for each country included in this publication.

Table 2.2. **Non-tax revenues by sub-category as a percentage of GDP, 2016**

Category	Botswana	Burkina Faso	Cabo Verde	Cameroon	Congo[2]	Congo, Dem. Rep.	Côte d'Ivoire	Egypt	Eswatini[3]	Ghana	Kenya
Total non-tax revenue	**18.2**	**5.6**	**7.2**	**2.7**	**9.4**	**3.7**	**1.9**	**5.7**	**11.2**	**4.0**	**1.7**
-Grants	0.0	2.7	2.8	0.3	0.9	2.5	1.2	0.1	0.2	0.7	0.5
-Property income	10.7	1.1	0.7	2.1	8.6	0.6	0.3	2.8	1.3	1.1	0.3
-Rents and royalties	1.9	0.7	..	2.0	8.6	0.6	0.3	0.3	0.0	0.5	0.0
-Interest and dividends	8.8	0.4	..	0.1	..	0.1	0.0	2.5	0.8	0.6	0.3
-Other property income	0.0	0.0	..	0.0	..	0.0	0.0	0.0	0.4	..	0.0
-Sales of good and services	0.7	0.7	3.1	0.2	..	0.4	0.2	1.1	0.4	2.3	0.7
-Fines, penalties and forfeits	0.0	0.9	0.4	0.1	..	0.2	0.0	0.1	0.1	0.0	0.0
-Miscellaneous and unidentified revenue[1]	6.8	0.3	0.3	0.1	..	0.0	0.2	1.5	9.2	0.0	0.2
Total tax revenue	*14.0*	*18.1*	*19.0*	*14.4*	*16.0*	*7.6*	*17.4*	*15.2*	*15.5*	*17.6*	*18.1*
Total sum of tax and non-tax revenue	*32.2*	*19.9*	*26.2*	*17.0*	*25.4*	*11.3*	*19.3*	*19.1*	*26.7*	*21.7*	*19.9*

Category	Mali	Mauritius	Morocco	Niger	Rwanda[4]	Senegal	South Africa	Togo	Tunisia	Uganda
Total non-tax revenue	**2.5**	**2.8**	**3.5**	**7.0**	**7.8**	**5.8**	**0.5**	**4.3**	**1.7**	**1.4**
-Grants	1.2	0.1	0.0	6.1	5.1	2.8	0.0	2.9	0.1	1.1
-Property income	0.4	1.2	0.9	0.7	..	1.0	0.3	0.8	1.0	0.0
-Rents and royalties	0.0	0.2	0.4	0.4	..	0.4	0.1	0.1	0.4	0.0
-Interest and dividends	0.4	0.2	0.5	0.3	..	0.6	0.1	0.7	0.6	0.0
-Other property income	0.0	0.8	0.0	0.0	..	0.0	0.0	0.0	0.0	0.0
-Sales of good and services	0.7	0.9	1.5	0.1	..	0.0	0.1	0.3	0.0	0.3
-Fines, penalties and forfeits	0.2	0.1	0.3	0.1	..	0.0	0.1	0.0	0.3	0.0
-Miscellaneous and unidentified revenue[1]	0.1	0.5	0.8	0.1	2.7	2.0	0.0	0.3	0.2	0.0
Total tax revenue	*16.1*	*20.0*	*26.4*	*14.4*	*16.6*	*22.0*	*28.6*	*22.2*	*29.4*	*13.1*
Total sum of tax and non-tax revenue	*18.5*	*22.8*	*29.9*	*21.5*	*24.4*	*27.8*	*29.0*	*26.5*	*31.1*	*14.6*

Notes: ".." indicates that the data are incomplete for the country in the particular year.

The figures include sub-national government non-tax revenues for Eswatini, Kenya, Mauritius and Morocco.

1. Including capital transfers not elsewhere classified and voluntary transfers other than grants.
2. Complete non-tax revenue figures were not available for the Republic of the Congo. Revenues only include grant revenue and oil revenue obtained from the IMF's April 2018 *World Economic Outlook*.
3. Previously Swaziland.
4. Non-tax revenues aside from grants were not disaggregated in the data and are therefore classified as miscellaneous and unidentified revenues.

Source: Table 6.2 in Chapter 6.

StatLink https://doi.org/10.1787/888933819651

Figure 2.3 shows the contribution of each sub-category to total non-tax revenues. It combines revenues from interest and dividends with other property income to yield a value for all property income not explicitly identified as rents and royalties. Five distinct groups of countries are apparent when the non-tax revenue mixes for the 21 countries covered in this publication are shown side-by-side:

- The Democratic Republic of the Congo, Côte d'Ivoire, Niger, Rwanda, Togo and Uganda receive a majority of their non-tax revenue in the form of grants;
- Both Cameroon and the Republic of the Congo receive a majority of reported non-tax revenue from rents and royalties (mostly oil revenues), although there is no data on non-tax revenues for the Republic of the Congo beyond oil revenues and grants;

- Ghana is the only country that receives a majority of its reported non-tax revenues from sales of goods and services (government production of market goods and services, as well as administrative fees);
- Eswatini receives 82% of its non-tax revenue from the miscellaneous and unclassified category, which almost entirely comprises SACU revenues. The only other country in the publication that receives SACU revenues is Botswana, where these account for 37.5% of non-tax revenues. Although South Africa is a member of the SACU revenue-sharing agreement, it is a net-contributor to the funding pool and therefore does not report SACU revenues.
- Eleven countries have no single category accounting for a majority of non-tax revenue. Among these countries, Burkina Faso, Mali and Senegal receive a plurality of their non-tax revenue from grants; Botswana, Egypt, Mauritius, South Africa and Tunisia receive a plurality from rents and royalties (mostly oil and mining royalties); and Cabo Verde, Kenya and Morocco receive a plurality of their revenues from sales of goods and services.

Figure 2.3. **Non-tax revenue mix, 2016**

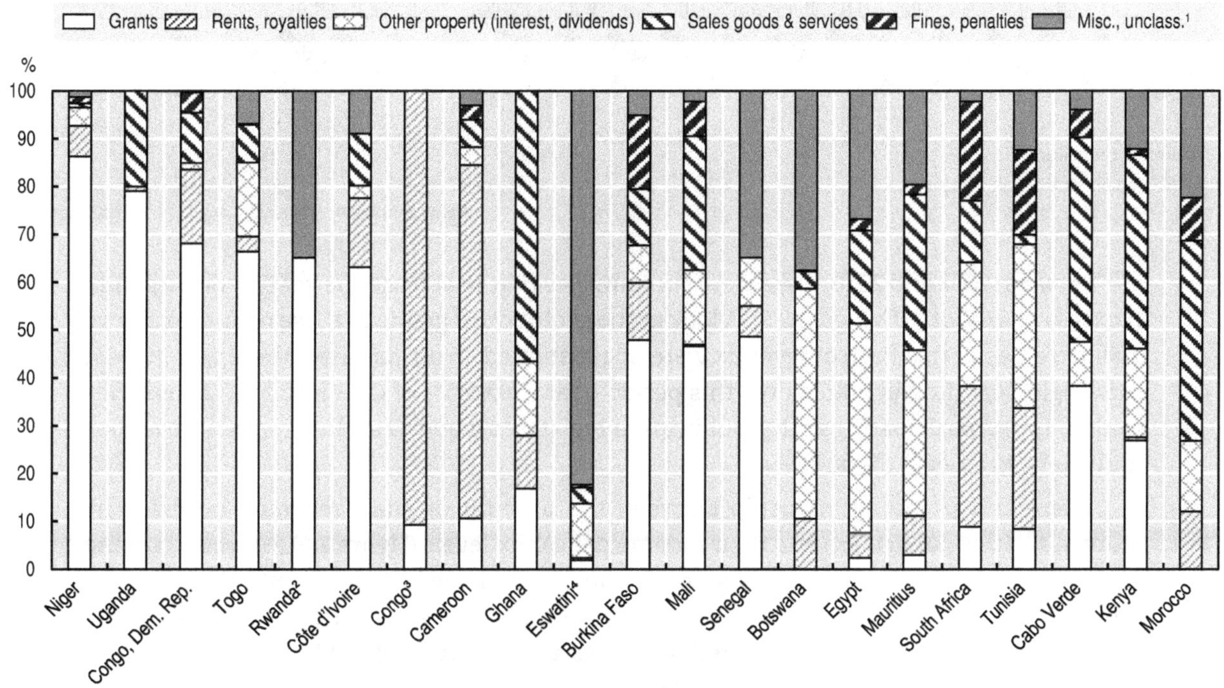

Note: The figures include sub-national government non-tax revenues for Eswatini, Kenya, Mauritius and Morocco.

1. Includes capital transfers not elsewhere classified and voluntary transfers other than grants.
2. Non-tax revenues aside from grants were not disaggregated in the data and are therefore classified as miscellaneous and unidentified revenues.
3. Complete non-tax revenue figures were not available for the Republic of the Congo. Figures reported here represent only grant revenue and oil revenue obtained from the IMF's April 2018 *World Economic Outlook*.
4. Previously Swaziland.

Source: Table 6.2 in Chapter 6.

StatLink https://doi.org/10.1787/888933819347

Grants

The amount of grants received in 2016 by countries included in this publication varied from negligible or none reported (Botswana, Morocco and South Africa) to over 5% of GDP (Niger and Rwanda) (Figure 2.4).

Figure 2.4. **Grants as a percentage of GDP, 2016**

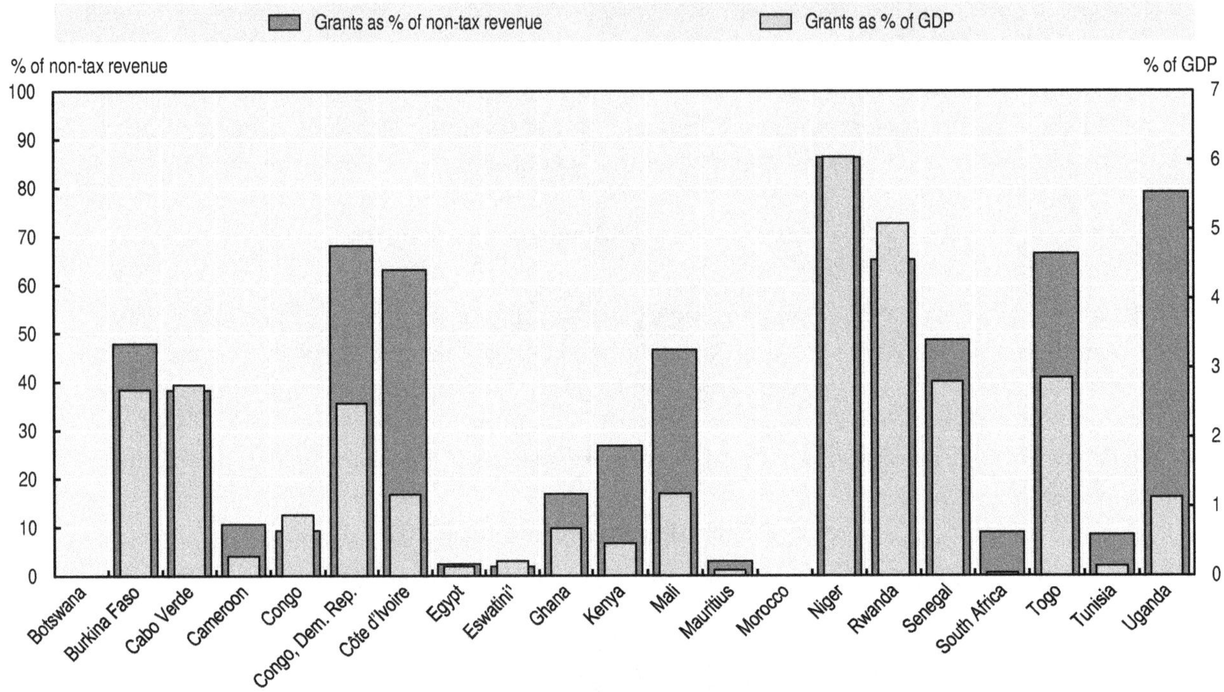

1. Previously Swaziland.

Source: Tables 6.2 and 6.3 in Chapter 6.

StatLink https://doi.org/10.1787/888933819366

Between 2007 and 2016, there were six countries that in at least one year received grants in excess of 6.0% of GDP (Figure 2.5). A look at the evolution of grants in these countries shows that increases in this form of revenue were not sustained. In all six cases, there was at least one single-year drop in grants over this period of at least 2.5% of GDP. In total, 12 countries among the 21 participating in this publication registered a one-year drop in grant revenues equivalent to at least 1% of GDP.

There is a partial relationship between the amount of grant revenues received by countries in this publication and their income per capita levels (Figure 2.6). However, among these countries grant revenues vary among countries with low GDP per capita. For example, Mali, Rwanda and Uganda have similar levels of GDP per capita (in purchasing power parity terms [PPP]) but in 2016 they reported grants as a percentage of GDP ranging from 1.1% (Uganda) and 1.2% (Mali) to 5.1% (Rwanda).

One important source of variation in grant revenues to African governments is debt relief programmes such as the Heavily-Indebted Poor Countries (HIPC) programme. This was launched in 1996 by the IMF and the World Bank as a successor to the Multilateral Debt Relief Initiative (MDRI) with the objective of alleviating the debt burden of lower-income countries facing significant debt distress.

Of the 39 countries deemed eligible for this programme, 33 were in sub-Saharan Africa. Twelve countries in this publication (Burkina Faso, Cameroon, the Republic of the Congo, the Democratic Republic of the Congo, Côte d'Ivoire, Ghana, Mali, Niger, Rwanda, Senegal, Togo and Uganda) received debt relief under HIPC and MDRI (IMF, 2016[2]). This led to spikes in grant revenues in some cases. In the case of Niger, grant revenues rose to 46.3% of GDP in 2006 following a significant debt write-off.

Figure 2.5. **Grants as a percentage of GDP for selected countries, 2007-16**

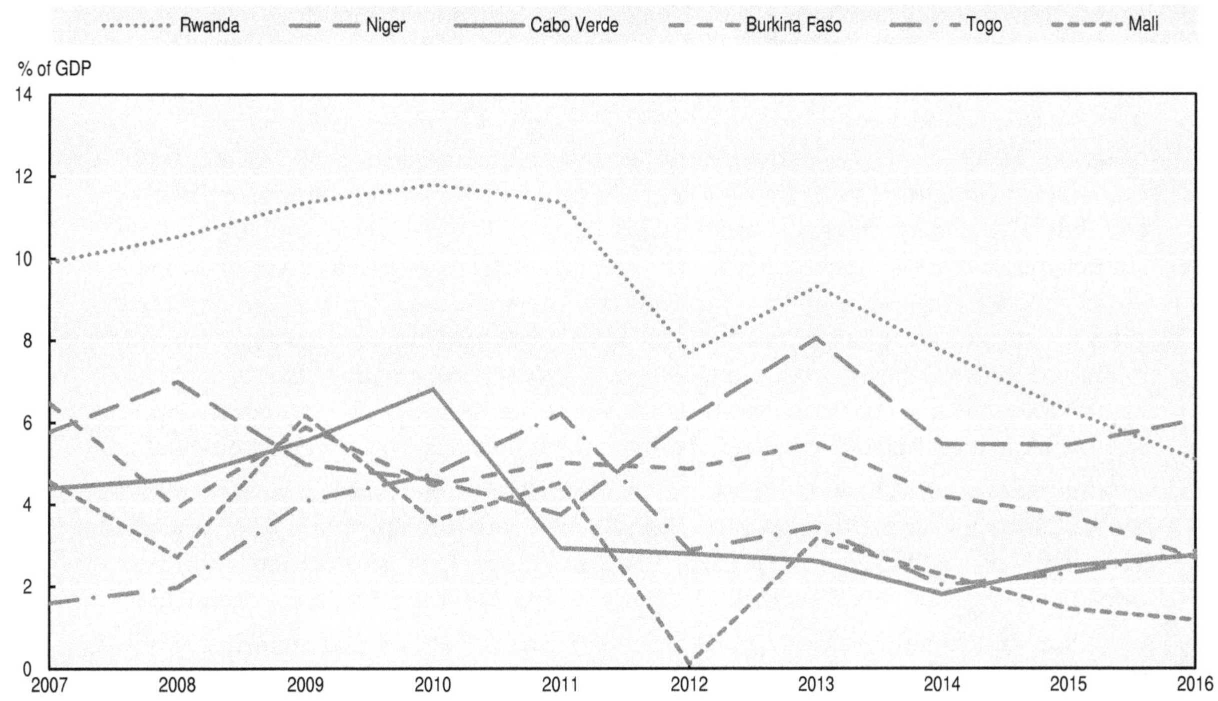

Source: Revenue Statistics in Africa comparative data available at *http://dx.doi.org/10.1787/be755711-en.*

StatLink https://doi.org/10.1787/888933819385

Figure 2.6. **Grants as a percentage of GDP vs GDP per capita in PPP dollars, 2016**

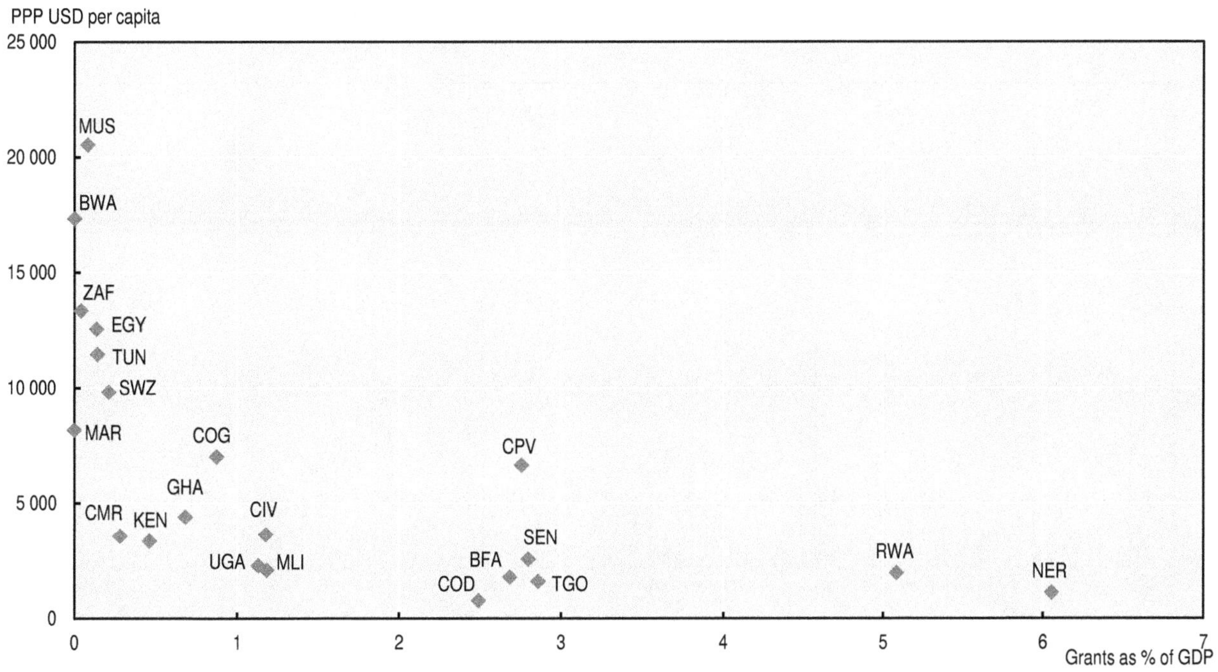

Source: Table 6.2 in Chapter 6 and IMF, *World Economic Outlook*, April 2018 for PPP GDP per capita figures.

StatLink https://doi.org/10.1787/888933819404

Grant revenues to African governments have some overlap with Official Development Assistance (ODA) as defined by the OECD Development Assistance Committee (DAC).[4] However, grants and ODA are not exactly the same. Grants covered by this publication focus on *revenues received* by countries from foreign governments and international organisations whereas ODA is essentially a *measure of donor countries' efforts to support development in low and middle-income countries*. ODA covers flows captured under "grants" in this publication (budget aid, food aid, capital transfers, current transfers, project grants, programme grants, international debt relief, etc.), but ODA also encompasses concessional loans, in-kind technical assistance, in-donor administrative costs, in-donor refugee costs and scholarships as well as other activities that do not generate a (net) revenue flow to the country. Therefore, the volume of ODA received by a given country will be different from – and usually higher than – the volume of grants reported in *Revenue Statistics*. However, research has shown (OECD, Forthcoming$_{[3]}$) that countries with higher GDP per capita tended to receive less ODA as a percentage of GDP than other countries and therefore must find other sources of development financing when their income rises.

Statistics on ODA flows to African countries include public flows from all members of the DAC and some countries outside the DAC,[5] as well as major international organisations such as the World Bank, the IMF and the UN. Statistics on ODA development co-operation from some large non-OECD economies, such as China, India and Brazil, are not included.

Comparing grant revenues to ODA inflows (Figure 2.7) shows that countries receiving the most ODA tend to receive more grant revenues. However, the relationship is not linear; Niger received the highest share of grant revenue as a percentage of GDP in 2016 but Rwanda received the most ODA as a percentage of GDP.

Figure 2.7. **Grants vs net ODA received in 2016, as a percentage of GDP**

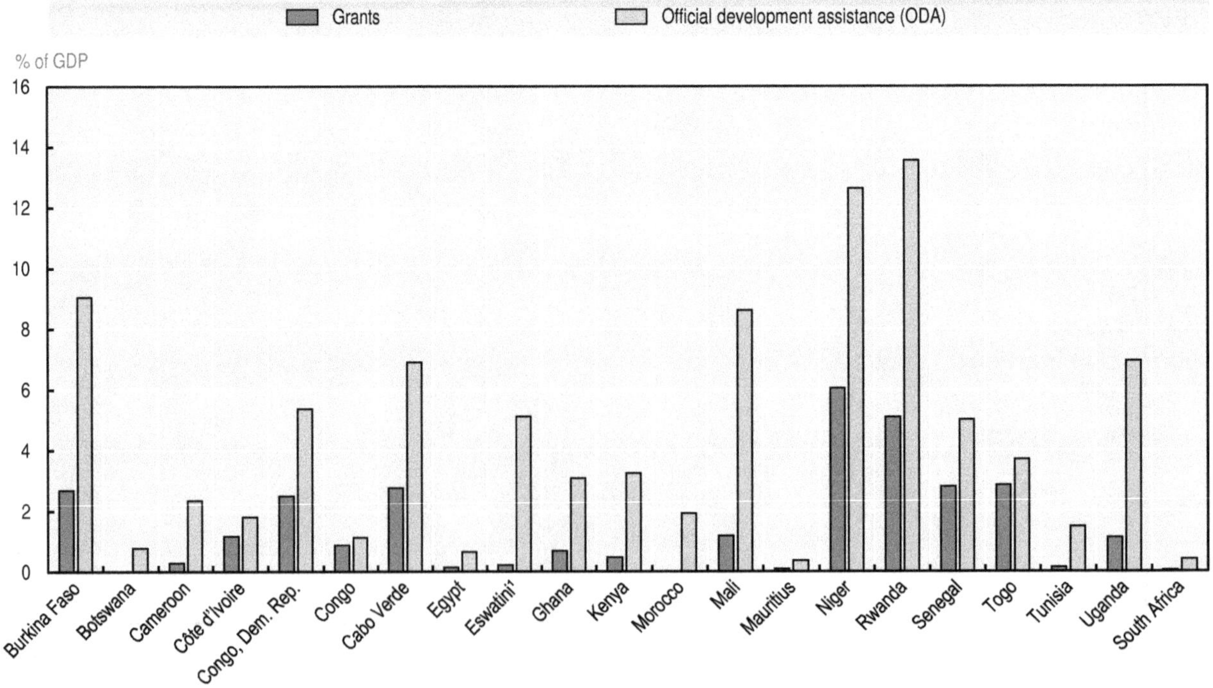

1. Previously Swaziland.

Source: OECD Development Assistance Committee (DAC) 2018 for the ODA data.

StatLink https://doi.org/10.1787/888933819423

Property income revenue

Property income is divided into three categories:

- Rents and royalties;
- Interest and dividends;
- Other and unallocable property income.

Rents and royalties are revenues generated from the land the government owns, usually by prospecting and extracting non-renewable resources from public lands or from harvesting government-owned farms and forests, while interest and dividends are returns on government-owned investments in corporations. In 2016, total property income exceeded 1% of GDP for ten countries out of the 21 in this publication (Figure 2.8). Botswana and the Republic of the Congo reported the highest levels of property income at 10.7% and 8.6% of GDP, respectively. Interest and dividends accounted for over 80% of property income in Botswana, whereas the only data on property income for the Republic of the Congo available concerned rents and royalties (oil revenues, in this case). Seven countries in this publication (Burkina Faso, Cameroon, the Republic of the Congo, the Democratic Republic of the Congo, Côte d'Ivoire, Niger and South Africa) reported a majority of their property income coming from rents and royalties in 2016.

Figure 2.8. **Property income as a percentage of GDP, 2016**

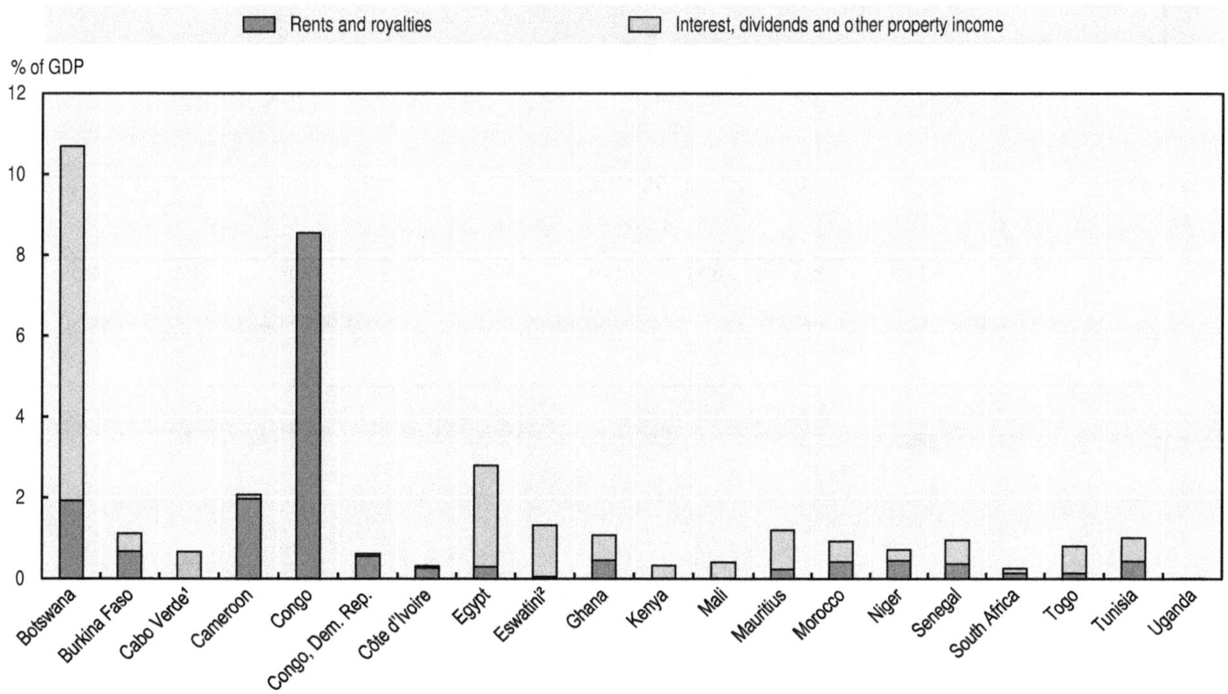

Note: Rwanda is excluded as the data are not available.

1. Cabo Verde property income is not disaggregated.
2. Previously Swaziland.

Source: Authors' calculations based on Tables 6.5-6.25 and Table 4.17.

StatLink https://doi.org/10.1787/888933819442

Revenues from natural resources

Rents and royalties among the 21 countries participating in this publication consist mostly of mineral and oil revenues. In 2016, over half the rents and royalties they collected were oil revenues (royalties and revenues from revenue-sharing agreements with oil companies), which accounted for a majority of rents and royalties for Cameroon, the Republic of the Congo, Egypt and Tunisia. Meanwhile, non-oil minerals were the source of most rents and royalties for Botswana, Burkina Faso, Ghana, Kenya and South Africa. About 3% of total rents and royalties for the 21 countries were not resource-related; these included revenues from the construction and operation of airports in Kenya and Togo, for example.

Natural resource revenues tend to be a highly volatile source of financing. Five countries among the 21 generated rents and royalties from natural resources equivalent to more than 1% of GDP over the past ten years and they all registered substantial year-on-year declines in these revenues at some point over this period (Figure 2.9). In the Democratic Republic of the Congo and Côte d'Ivoire, rents and royalties dropped to less than a quarter of their peak. Cameroon's rents and royalties dropped to 32.8% of their peak value, a difference amounting to over 4% of GDP.

Figure 2.9. **Rents and royalties as a percentage of GDP for selected countries, 2006-16**

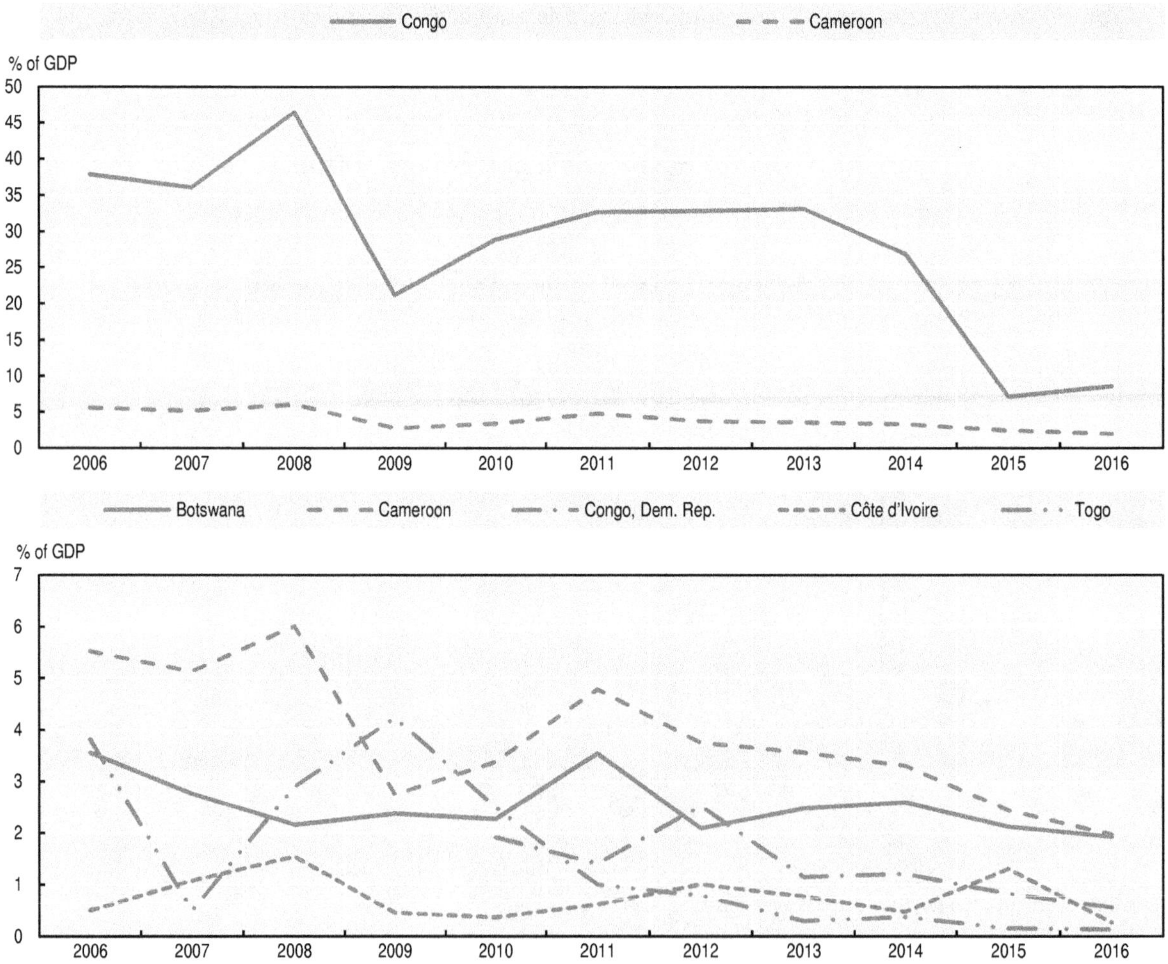

Note: Data for the Democratic Republic of the Congo are only available for the 2010-16 period. Figures for the Republic of the Congo cannot be presented using the same scale as the one used for the other selected countries. Cameroon is featured in both charts in order to serve as a reference.

Source: Authors' calculations based on Tables 6.5-6.25 and Table 4.17.

StatLink https://doi.org/10.1787/888933819461

Rents and royalties for the Republic of the Congo are on a different scale than for other African countries and the impact of the volatility of resource rents is far larger. In the 10 years before 2010, rents and royalties were between five and ten times higher as a percentage of GDP in the Republic of the Congo than in any other country included here. As a result of the size of these revenues as a percentage of GDP, drops in oil prices in 2008-09 and 2014-15 coincided with drops in oil revenues and therefore drops in total non-tax revenues equivalent to 20% of the country's GDP.

The substantial impact of resource rents on government finances among some of the reporting countries reflects a dependence on natural resources that has implications for both the country's finances and their economic development. A recent report (AUC/OECD, 2018$_{[4]}$) characterised four countries (the Republic of the Congo, the Democratic Republic of the Congo, Egypt and Togo) as being "resource-rich" based on their significant underground natural resource production as a percentage of their GDP over the past decade. Resource-rich countries have shown occasionally high rates of economic growth but this growth has not been sustained during periods of lower commodity prices (AUC/OECD, 2018, p. 8$_{[4]}$). In a context where natural resources can have both positive and negative impacts on a country's economy, there are multiple mechanisms by which governments can capture some of this wealth in order to finance investments as part of a more sustainable economic development strategy (see Box 2.2).

Box 2.2. **Natural resources and public finances**[a]

There are various mechanisms by which natural resources can generate revenues or savings for government:

Rents and royalties are the most direct form of revenue relating to natural resource wealth. The government charges fees to companies and individuals in exchange for the right to access government lands. It does this in its capacity as landowner and these fees are generally decided through negotiation. These are recorded under property income.

Payment for services provided by the government is another source of non-tax revenue collected from businesses in the primary sector. This can include, for example, payments for environmental inspections by government officials or payments for the construction of infrastructure. These are recorded under sales of goods and services.

Public ownership (full or partial) of a corporation that exploits natural resources on the government's behalf results in government revenues in the form of profits and dividends. These are recorded under property income.

Taxes or levies can be designed to target companies or individuals who access natural resources. It may sometimes be difficult to make a distinction between a tax on companies operating on public lands and a royalty charged to such companies.

Taxes targeting the activity of natural resource exploitation could be introduced, such as an excise tax on the sale of materials extracted from public lands or a tax on mining that targets the activity, rather than the individual or company exploiting natural resources. These, too, will be recorded as taxes.

Companies and individuals exploiting natural resources are generally subject to the same taxes (such as income taxes and value-added taxes) as the rest of the population. Revenues from these general taxes will be included in government financial statements but not necessarily attributed to sectors exploiting natural resources.

Companies and individuals may use some of the wealth they obtain from natural resource extraction to build infrastructure or provide services. Where this satisfies demand for public investment or services, it could result in savings on government expenditure but it would not be recorded as revenue. In some cases, as a condition for access to publicly-owned natural resources, governments may demand that companies and individuals provide certain services, for example paying for at least part of the cost of constructing and maintaining roads to mines.

a. Mansour and Rota-Graziosi (2013) note that taxes on oil extraction can include corporate income tax, excise taxes on energy products, un-refunded sales taxes such as VATs and non-tax revenue can include royalties, profit sharing, dividends received from state enterprises, and other investment income received from government direct participation in extractive enterprises.

There is a great deal of variation both in terms of the size and the nature of the natural resource endowments of African countries. The contribution of this natural wealth to countries' GDP also varies, as does its impact on government budgets. For example, according to World Bank estimates of the amount of wealth generated by natural resource extraction per country,[6] the Republic of the Congo (mostly oil), Ghana (mostly forest) and South Africa (mostly minerals) were the three countries that generated the highest natural resource wealth per person in 2016. However, due to South Africa's larger and more diversified economy, natural resources in that country accounted for less than 5% of GDP (Figure 2.10) and resource rents were among the smallest of the 21 countries in this publication as a proportion of total revenue.

Figure 2.10. **Estimated natural resource extraction as a percentage of GDP, 2016**

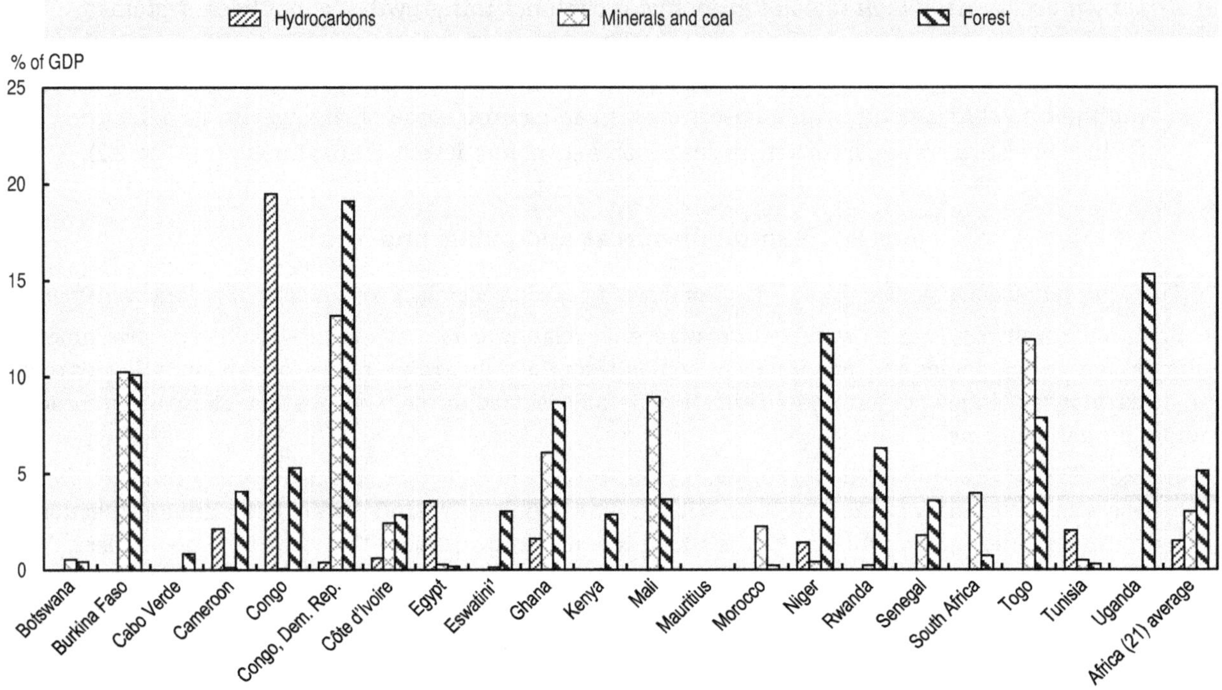

1. Previously Swaziland.

Source: World Bank (2018), *World Development Indicators* for estimates of the total value of natural resource production in each country.

StatLink https://doi.org/10.1787/888933819480

The impact of countries' natural resource endowment on their public finances also varies greatly. Countries such as Botswana, Cameroon and the Republic of the Congo have generated significant public revenues from their substantial natural wealth, while countries such as Togo and Uganda had natural resource wealth production over 15% of GDP but reported government revenues from natural resource rents equivalent to no more than 0.1% of GDP.

In four countries (Burkina Faso, the Democratic Republic of the Congo, Niger and Uganda) wealth generated by forests exceeded 10% of GDP but, as noted above, these did not contribute much to their governments' natural resource revenues. Although some countries, such as Cameroon and Niger, did collect some royalties on logging, forest revenues were a small part of the non-tax revenues for the countries in question.

A number of the 21 African countries are heavily impacted by swings in the prices of individual commodities (Figures 2.11 and 2.12 and Table 2.3). For example, since 2000, the price of gold has risen by as much as 28.1% over the previous year and has fallen by as much as 15.5%. The price of oil was 36.4% higher in 2008 than it was a year earlier, while in 2015, it was 47.3% lower than the previous year.

Figure 2.11. **Top commodity exports from African countries, as a percentage of GDP**

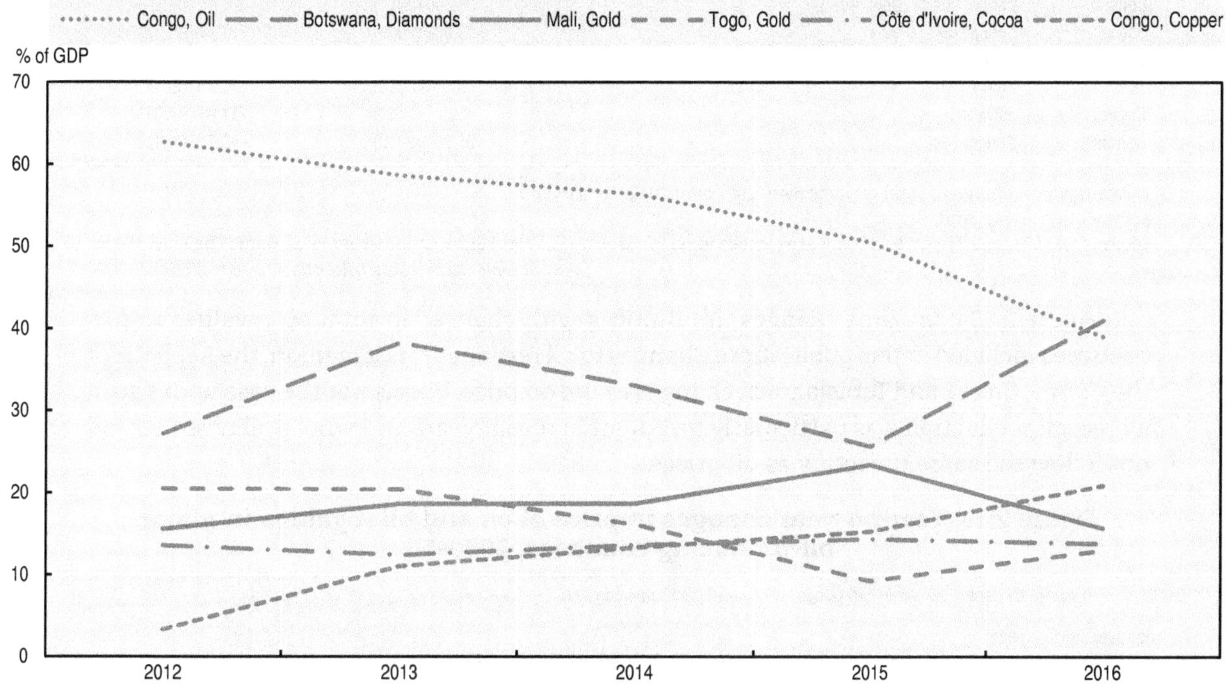

Source: Author's calculations based on COMTRADE WITS Online Database.

StatLink https://doi.org/10.1787/888933819499

Figure 2.12. **Prices of main commodities, 2000-16**

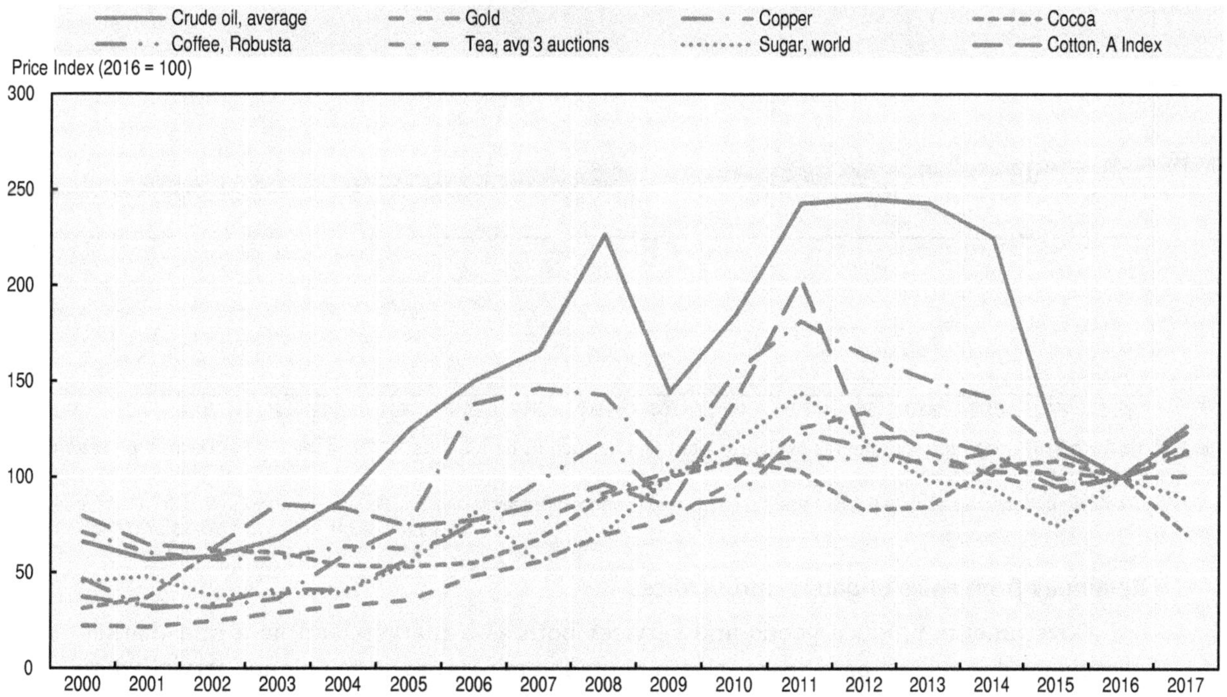

Source: World Bank Commodity Price Data (The Pink Sheet).

StatLink https://doi.org/10.1787/888933819518

Table 2.3. **Notable changes in commodity prices, 2000-16**

Commodity	Producing countries[1]	Maximum YoY increase	Maximum YoY decrease
Crude oil	Cameroon, Congo, Egypt, Ghana	36.4% (2008)	-47.3% (2015)
Gold	Burkina Faso, Ghana, Mali, Niger, Senegal, South Africa, Togo	28.1% (2011)	-15.5% (2013)
Copper	Congo, Congo (Dem. Rep.)	46.3% (2010)	-26.0% (2009)
Cocoa	Côte d'Ivoire, Ghana	32.0% (2008)	-19.7% (2012)
Coffee	Rwanda, Uganda	38.7% (2011)	-29.2% (2009)
Tea	Kenya	18.9% (2008)	-4.9% (2014)
Sugar	Eswatini[2]	41.8% (2009)	-31.8% (2007)
Cotton	Burkina Faso	65.2% (2010)	-40.9% (2012)

1. Average percentage of total exports over the years 2012-16 is over 15%.
2. Previously Swaziland.
Source: COMTRADE WITS Online Database (accessed on 21 June 2018), World Bank Commodity Price Data (The Pink Sheet).
StatLink *https://doi.org/10.1787/888933819670*

Figure 2.13 compares changes in oil prices with changes in total oil royalties in five countries included in this publication. Changes to oil revenues for Cameroon, the Republic of the Congo, Ghana and Tunisia track changes in the oil price. This is not the case with Egypt, whose oil production was particularly turbulent in recent years and whose oil revenues did not follow the same trajectory as oil prices.

Figure 2.13. **Year-on-year changes in price of oil and oil royalties in major oil-producing countries, 2000-16**

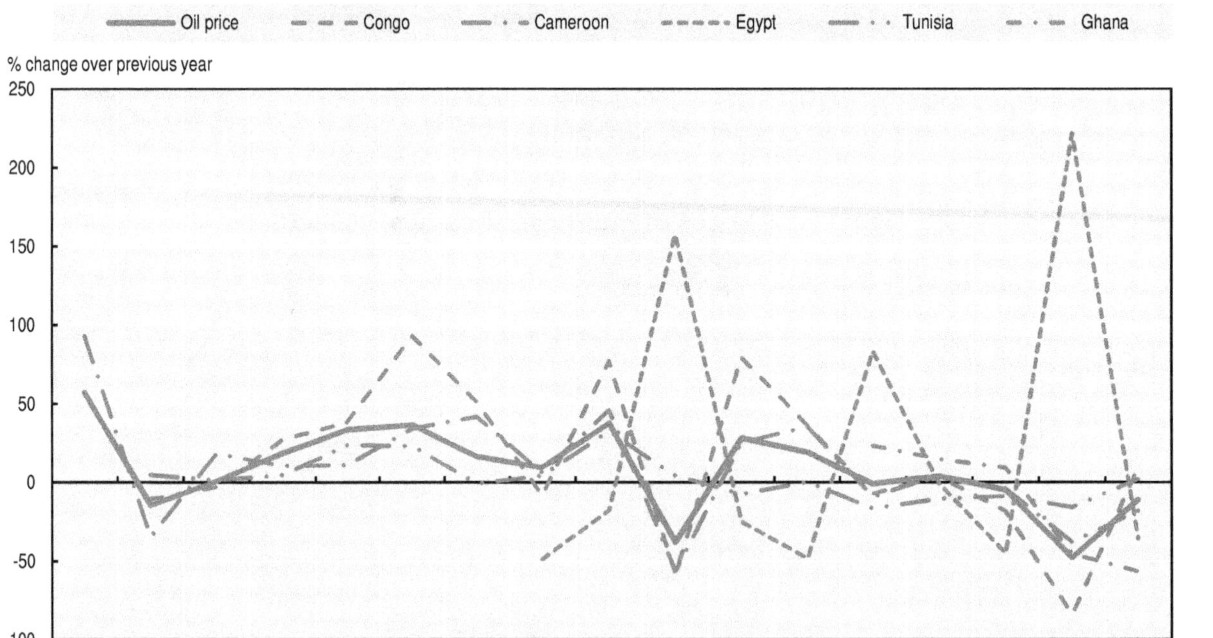

Note: Figures for oil royalties represent figures explicitly identified as such in national data. This does not necessarily represent all oil revenues for the countries in question.
Source: Authors' calculations based Tables 6.5-6.25 and Table 4.17 and Economic Research Division, Federal Reserve Bank of St. Louis for oil prices.
StatLink *https://doi.org/10.1787/888933819537*

Revenues from sales of goods and services

Governments produce goods and services both as a market- and as a non-market participant. As a market participant, governments sometimes provide goods and services that can be obtained from private companies (such as selling food or providing transportation). At the same time, they also provide services in the course of administering programmes and executing laws that are unique to the function of government. Fees charged for these non-market services are generally classified as administrative fees.

Administrative fees are often difficult to classify since they occupy a grey area between payments for services (which are non-tax revenues) and compulsory unrequited payments collected during government operations (which are taxes).[7] Court fees and fees for driver's licences, passports, patent registrations and marriage certificates tend to be classified as non-tax revenues. When administrative fees are classified as taxes, they are typically assigned to one of the following categories:

- 4400 Taxes on financial and capital transactions (for example, taxes on sales of land);
- 5200 Taxes on use of goods and performing activities (for example hunting licences, vehicle registrations);
- 6000 Other taxes (for example, sales of fiscal stamps, where stamps are used to pay for taxes and administrative fees).

Four countries generated revenues from sales of goods and services and administrative fees equivalent to at least 1% of GDP in 2016 (Figure 2.14): Cabo Verde (3.1% of GDP), Egypt (1.1% of GDP), Ghana (2.3% of GDP) and Morocco (1.5% of GDP)

Figure 2.14. **Sales of goods and services and administrative fees as a percentage of total non-tax revenues and as a percentage of GDP, 2016**

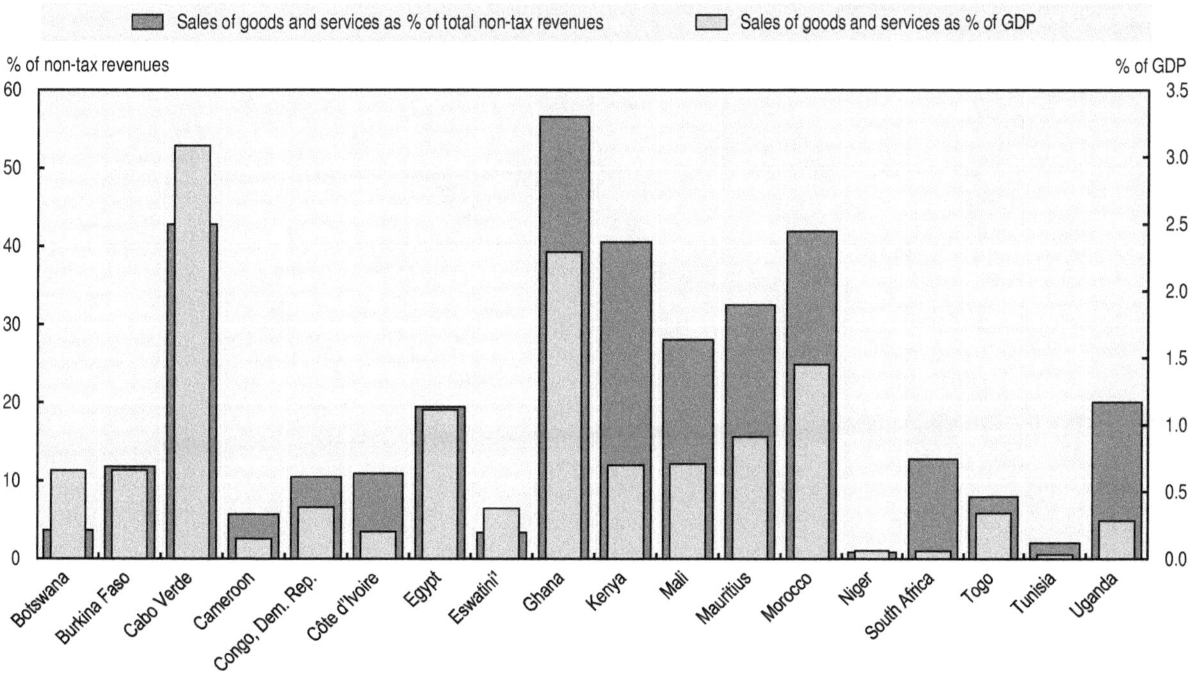

Note: Figures include sub-national government non-tax revenues for Eswatini, Kenya, Mauritius and Morocco.
1. Previously Swaziland.
The Republic of the Congo and Rwanda are excluded as data are not available. Senegal reported no revenue from sales of goods and services.
Source: Tables 6.2 and 6.3 in Chapter 6.

StatLink https://doi.org/10.1787/888933819556

Six countries collect over a quarter of their non-tax revenues from sales of goods and services and administrative fees: Cabo Verde, Ghana, Kenya, Mali, Mauritius and Morocco. In Morocco, 66% of revenue from government sales of goods and services are collected at the local level. Fees made up 94% of revenues listed under sales of goods and services for Cabo Verde. In Ghana, most revenues listed as sales of goods and services were fees and charges collected by MDAs (Municipalities, Departments and Agencies) or MMDAs (Metropolitan, Municipal and District Assemblies).

In Mauritius, 19% of sales of goods and services were collected at the local level and 4% by social security funds. It included a large number of different fees for various government services including route air navigation, police services, as well as receipts from the sale of a range of different products including ground water, animal feed and forest produce. Kenya did not generate high amounts of revenue through sales of goods and services, but this constituted over two fifths of total non-tax revenue in 2016.

Fines and forfeits

Fines and forfeits can be an important, if volatile, source of revenue. Some small fines are obtained on a regular and a predictable basis. In some countries, a proportion of these revenues is used to finance local governments and are not necessarily reported in federal budget statistics. In general, most of the 21 countries included in this publication generate negligible revenues from fines, forfeits and penalties, although revenues from this category in Burkina Faso, Senegal and Tunisia have risen above 0.5% of GDP in recent years (Figure 2.15).

Figure 2.15. **Fines, penalties and forfeits as a percentage of GDP, 2012-16**

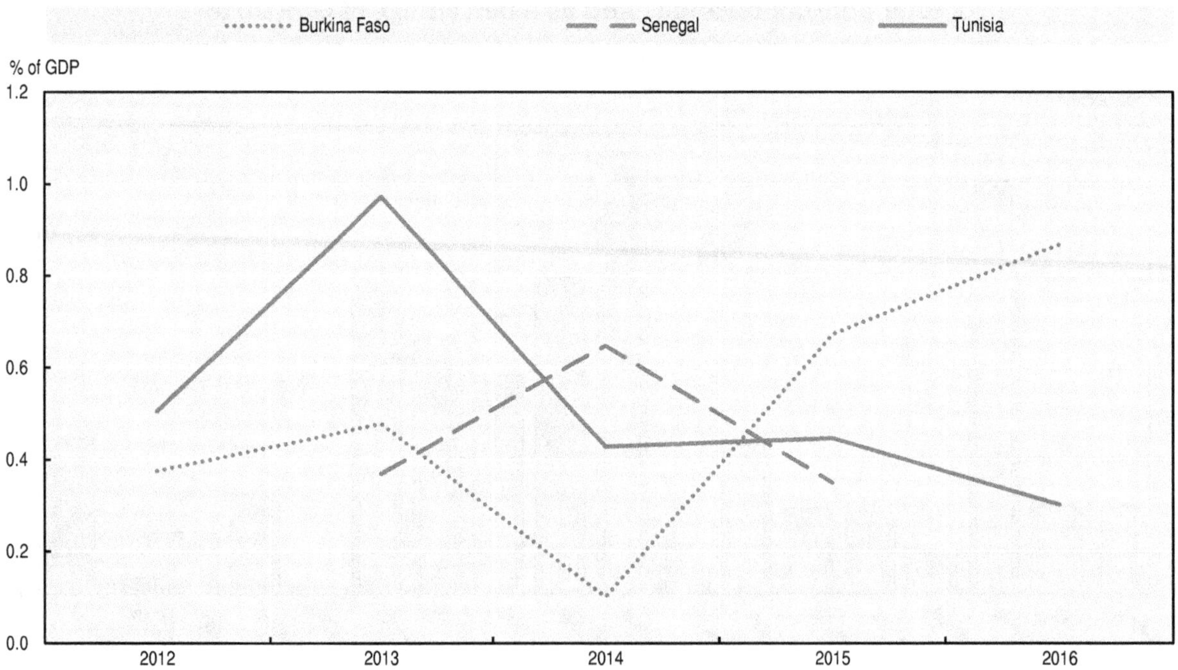

Source: Revenue Statistics in Africa comparative data available at *http://dx.doi.org/10.1787/be755711-en.*

StatLink https://doi.org/10.1787/888933819575

Miscellaneous or unidentified revenue

Some notable categories of non-tax revenue do not fit within any of the categories listed above. These include:

1. Capital transfers not included elsewhere;
2. Voluntary donations to government agencies from individuals or private corporations (not including donations from international organisations, which are classified as grants);
3. Insurance claims paid to government agencies;

4. Payments covering different categories in the classification list where a breakdown is not available;
5. Payments whose proper classification is unknown due to a lack of data. Rwanda did not disaggregate non-tax revenue outside of grants, so these were included in this category;
6. SACU revenues to Botswana and Eswatini.

Miscellaneous and unidentified revenues can be a significant component of non-tax revenues in certain countries (Figure 2.16). These include exceptional voluntary contributions to government in Tunisia, capital transfers from special statutory funds in Mauritius and in Morocco, payments made to government in exchange for the right to compete with state institutions in the provision of services. SACU revenues account for over 90% of all Eswatini's non tax revenues in most years.

Figure 2.16. **Miscellaneous and unidentified revenue as a percentage of total non-tax revenue, 2000-16**

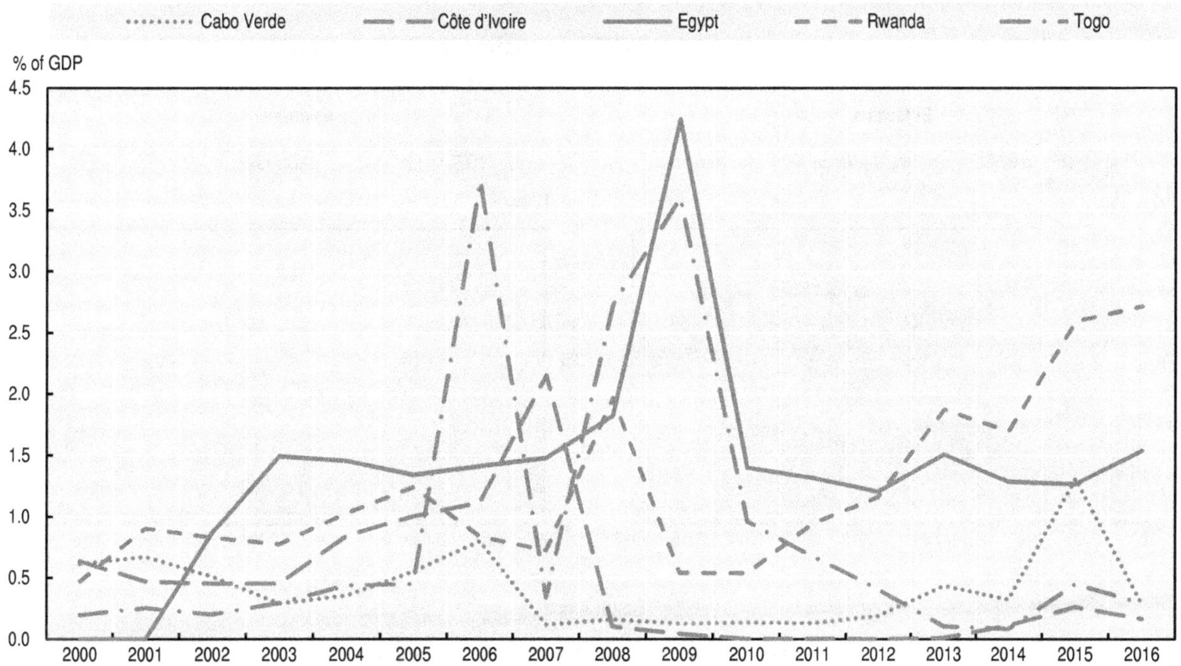

Note: For Rwanda, data for property income, sales of goods and services and fines, penalties and forfeits are included in miscellaneous and unidentified revenue. These data could not be disaggregated to allocate revenue to the relevant non-tax revenue categories.

Source: Authors' calculations based on Tables 6.5-6.25 and Table 4.17.

StatLink https://doi.org/10.1787/888933819594

The volatility of miscellaneous and unidentified revenues shown in Figure 2.16 may be due to large capital transfers, revenue streams that are short-lived or funds that are reclassified as unidentified due to lack of information. The higher values for this category could reflect uncertainty as to the true amount of revenue within the other non-tax revenue classifications. Available data are insufficient to analyse this variation.

There were four countries outside SACU that received unidentified or miscellaneous non-tax revenues that were equivalent to more than 2% of GDP at least once since 2000. In the cases of Cabo Verde, Côte d'Ivoire and Togo, these were brief spikes: there were no more than three years in which these revenues were equivalent to more than 1% of GDP. For Rwanda, unidentified and miscellaneous revenues included all recorded non-tax revenues outside of grants and have been on a steadily increasing trend over the past five years, reaching 2.7% of GDP in 2016. Unidentified or miscellaneous non-tax revenues for Egypt have remained above 1% of GDP in every year since 2003 and in 2009 these reached 4.2% of GDP, higher than any other country in this report.

Southern African Customs Union revenues

The Southern African Customs Union has five member countries, including Lesotho, Namibia and three countries included in *Revenue Statistics in Africa*: Botswana, Eswatini and South Africa (see Box 2.3). The SACU agreement entails the joint collection and sharing of all customs and excise revenues; these revenues have a different impact on each member countries included in this publication.

Eswatini's SACU revenues exceeded its tax revenues in all but eight of the past 20 years and reached 23% of GDP in 2006 (Figure 2.17). South Africa's SACU revenues have never exceeded 4.5% of GDP or 18% of tax revenues. Botswana also receives significant SACU revenues but these were exceeded by other non-tax revenues in 11 of the last 13 years.

Figure 2.17. **Tax, non-tax revenues and SACU revenues in Botswana, Eswatini[2] and South Africa as a percentage of GDP**

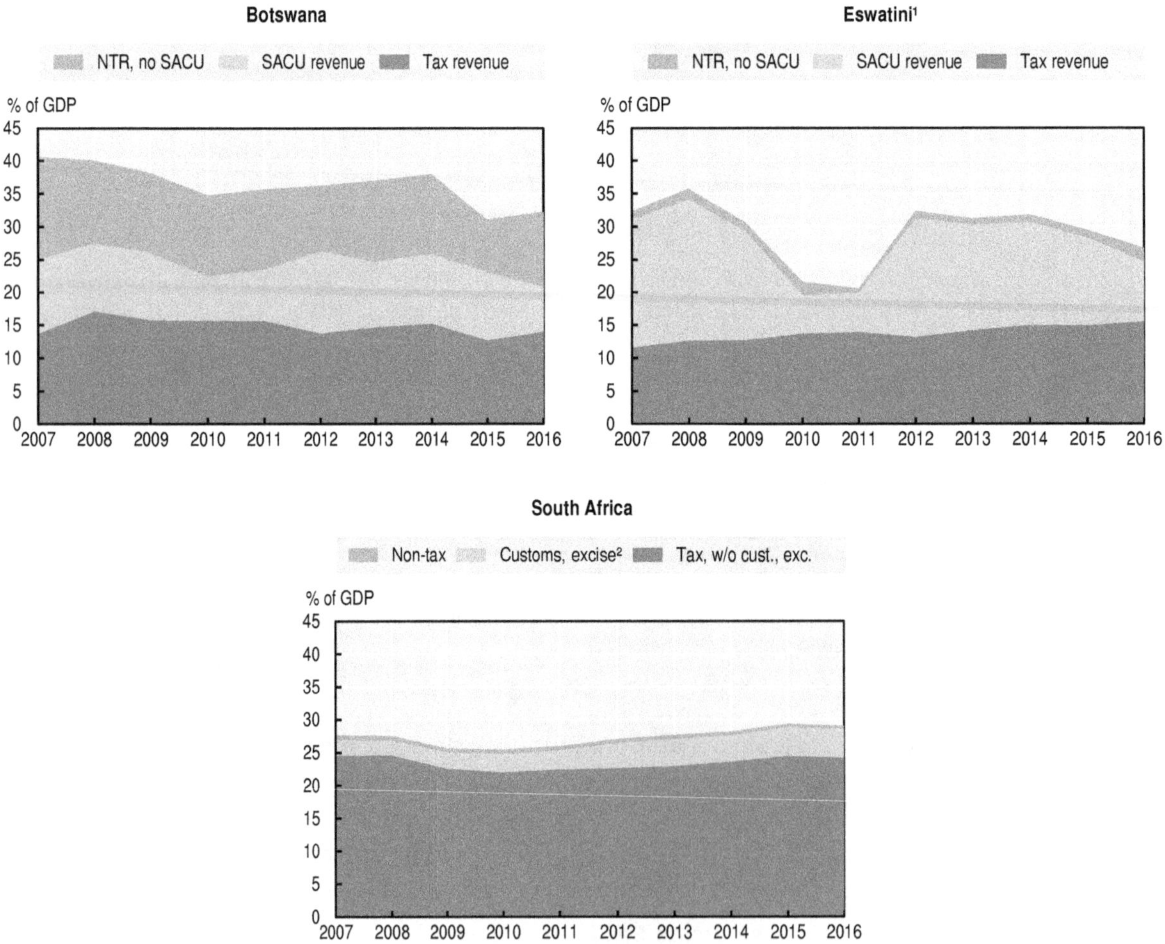

1. Previously Swaziland.

2. Customs and excises as a percentage of GDP include SACU payments made by South Africa to other SACU partner countries, which are not considered revenue under OECD definitions. Payments made to the SACU pool represent around 1% South Africa's GDP.

Source: Revenue Statistics in Africa comparative data available at *http://dx.doi.org/10.1787/be755711-en*.

StatLink https://doi.org/10.1787/888933819613

When comparing Botswana, Eswatini and South Africa, the treatment of SACU revenues must be considered with care. All three countries contribute to the SACU pool and receive a revenue share determined by the same funding formula. However, Botswana and Eswatini are net recipients of the SACU pool whereas South Africa's payments into the SACU pool exceed its level of receipts.

Box 2.3. **SACU revenue**

The Southern African Customs Union (SACU) incorporates Botswana, Eswatini, Lesotho, Namibia and South Africa. It is headquartered in Windhoek, Namibia. Its vision is "an economic community with equitable and sustainable development, dedicated to the welfare of its people for a common future".

SACU is the oldest customs union in the world, having been founded in 1899 between the British colony of Cape of Good Hope and the Orange Free State Boer Republic. Subsequent agreements in 1910 and 1969 included Botswana, Eswatini and Lesotho. Following Namibia's independence in 1990 and the end of apartheid in South Africa in 1994, new negotiations led to the current SACU agreement, which was signed in 2002.

The SACU agreement provides for free movement of SACU manufactured products within the union, without application of tariffs or duties. It also provides for common external tariffs and for the payment of customs and excise duties into a common pool to be shared between the SACU countries under the revenue sharing formula set out in the Annex to the agreement.

The revenue-sharing agreement includes three components:

- A customs component, which divides the gross amount of customs duties according to the value of goods each country imports from other SACU countries in a given year (as a percentage of intra-SACU imports);
- An excise component, which divides the gross amount of excise duties according to each country's GDP as a percentage of SACU's combined GDP; and
- A development component, which is funded from 15% of the excise component and is weighted toward less developed SACU countries using a formula based on GDP per capita.

In this publication, revenue from excises, tariffs and customs duties are included as tax revenues in the country that collected the revenue. They are included under headings 5121 (Excises) and 5123 (Customs and import duties) in the tax revenue tables. Revenues received from the SACU pool are included as miscellaneous revenue in the non-tax revenue tables, as seen in Table 6.13 for Eswatini. In the case of South Africa, where payments exceed the revenue share received from the SACU pool, the payments net of the share received are recorded as a memorandum item in the non-tax revenue table (Table 6.22).

Sources: (SACU, 2017[5]), (SACU, 2014[6]).

Notes

1. There are no comparison with the averages of 25 Latin American and Caribbean (LAC) countries (see (OECD/ECLAC/CIAT/IDB, 2018[8])) and that of 35 OECD countries (see (OECD, 2017[7])) (OECD, Forthcoming[3])) as these publications do not cover non-tax revenues.
2. Please see the Interpretative Guide to non-tax revenue in Annex B of this report for the definitions of these revenue categories.
3. The coefficient of variation is a standard measure of dispersion representing the ratio of the standard deviation over the mean.
4. The official definition of ODA is: "flows to countries and territories on the Development Assistance Committee List of ODA Recipients and to multilateral institutions which are provided by official agencies, including state and local governments, or by their executive agencies. In addition, each transaction must be administered with the promotion of the economic development and welfare of developing countries as its main objective; and be concessional in character and conveys a grant element of at least 25% (calculated at a rate of discount of 10%)". Further information is available at: *www.oecd.org/dac/financing-sustainable-development/index-terms.htm#ODA*

5. A full list of countries and organisations reporting statistics to the DAC is available at : *www.oecd.org/dac/financing-sustainable-development/development-finance-standards/dacdatasubmitters.htm*
6. The World Bank refers to this "natural resource rents". This is calculated as the difference between the value of natural resource production in the countries according to commodity prices and the estimated cost of resource extraction. It is not to be confused with the definition of resource rent used by the OECD, for which it is defined as a form of government revenue. Please see the Interpretative Guide for more details.
7. See paragraphs 9-13 of the OECD Interpretative Guide in Annex A for an explanation of how administrative fees are classified in this publication.

References

AfDB/OECD/ECA (2010), *African Economic Outlook 2010: Domestic Resource Mobilisation and Aid*, OECD Publishing, Paris, *http://dx.doi.org/10.1787/aeo-2010-en.* [1]

AUC/OECD (2018), *Africa's Development Dynamics 2018: Growth, Jobs and Inequalities*, African Union Commission/OECD Publishing, Addis Ababa/Paris, *https://doi.org/10.1787/9789264302501-en.* [4]

IMF (2016), *Heavily indebted poor countries (HIPC) initiative and multilateral debt relief initiative (MDRI): Statistical update*, International Monetary Fund, *http://www.imf.org/en/Publications/Policy-Papers/Issues/2016/12/31/Heavily-Indebted-Poor-Countries-Initiative-and-Multilateral-Debt-Relief-Initiative-PP5024.* [2]

OECD (2017), *Revenue Statistics: 1965-2016*, OECD Publishing, Paris, *https://doi.org/10.1787/9789264283183-en, http://dx.doi.org/10.1787/9789264283183-en.* [7]

OECD (forthcoming), *Global Outlook on Financing for Development*, OECD Publishing, Paris. [3]

OECD/ECLAC/CIAT/IDB (2018), *Revenue Statistics in Latin America and the Caribbean*, OECD Publishing, Paris, *http://dx.doi.org/10.1787/rev_lat_car-2018-en-fr.* [8]

SACU (2017), *Southern African Customs Union Agreement 2002 (As amended on 12 April 2013)*, *http://www.sacu.int/list.php?type=Agreements.* [5]

SACU (2014), *Implementing a Common Agenda Towards Regional Integration: 2014 Annual Report*, *http://www.sacu.int/docs/reports_annual/2014/annual_report.pdf.* [6]

Revenue Statistics in Africa 1990-2016/Statistiques des recettes publiques en Afrique 1990-2016

Chapitre 2

Tendances des recettes non fiscales, 1990-2016

Introduction

Les États perçoivent des recettes au moyen de mécanismes qui ne correspondent pas à la définition des impôts utilisée dans le présent rapport. Il s'agit de recettes dites non fiscales qui peuvent représenter une source de financement très importante ; deux pays peuvent présenter des ratios impôts/PIB similaires et réussir à financer des dépenses publiques de montants sensiblement différents grâce aux différents niveaux de recettes non fiscales qu'ils perçoivent par ailleurs. C'est particulièrement vrai pour les pays africains dont beaucoup tirent une proportion non négligeable de leurs recettes publiques de rentes de ressources ou de dons.

Pour brosser un tableau fidèle des finances publiques d'un pays, il faut donc prendre en considération les recettes fiscales et non fiscales et ce, malgré les difficultés particulières que pose le recueil de données relatives aux recettes non fiscales (encadré 2.1). Ce chapitre propose des comparaisons entre les données relatives aux recettes non fiscales des différents pays couverts par la présente publication[1].

Les principales catégories de recettes non fiscales[2] examinées ici sont les suivantes :

- dons émanant de pays étrangers ou d'organisations internationales (aide budgétaire, transferts de capitaux, transferts courants, subventions de projets, dons au titre de programmes, allégement de la dette internationale, etc.) ;
- revenus de la propriété (redevances minières, produits d'investissements publics par exemple) ;
- ventes de biens et de services (ce qui inclut certains frais administratifs) ;
- amendes et pénalités ;
- recettes diverses non identifiées (recettes non fiscales qui ne peuvent être classées dans les autres catégories).

Recettes non fiscales exprimées en pourcentage du PIB

Dans les 21 pays couverts par la présente publication, les recettes non fiscales, exprimées en pourcentage du PIB, ont largement varié, en 2016, allant de 0.5 % du PIB en Afrique du Sud à 18.2 % du PIB au Botswana. Dans tous les pays à l'exception du Botswana, les recettes non fiscales sont inférieures aux recettes fiscales (graphique 2.1).

Graphique 2.1. **Recettes fiscales et non fiscales totales par pays en pourcentage du PIB, 2016**

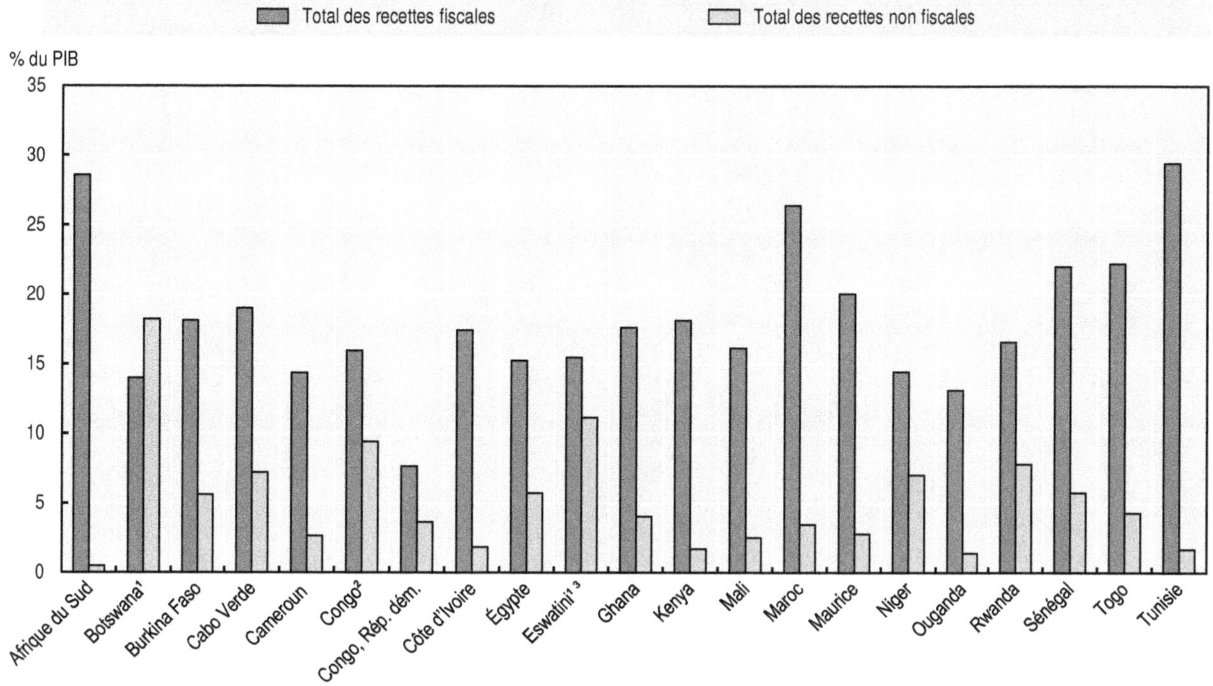

Note : Les données relatives aux recettes non fiscales prennent en compte les recettes non fiscales perçues par les administrations infranationales pour l'Eswatini, le Kenya, le Maroc et Maurice, les seuls pays pour lesquels les données correspondantes sont disponibles. En 2016, les recettes non fiscales perçues par les administrations infranationales représentaient, pour chacun de ces pays, respectivement 4 %, 30 %, 45 % et 6 % des recettes non fiscales totales. L'Afrique du Sud a déclaré percevoir quelques taxes locales et régionales, mais n'a pas fait état de recettes non fiscales locales ou régionales.

1. Pour le Botswana et l'Eswatini, les recettes non fiscales prennent en compte les montants au titre des droits de douane et d'accise recouvrés par l'Afrique du Sud, puis reversés au Botswana et à l'Eswatini en vertu de la formule de partage des recettes de l'Union douanière d'Afrique australe (SACU).
2. Les chiffres présentés ici correspondent à des dons et à des recettes pétrolières figurant dans les *Perspectives de l'économie mondiale* du FMI d'avril 2018. Il n'a pas été possible d'obtenir des chiffres relatifs aux autres catégories de recettes non fiscales pour la République du Congo.
3. Swaziland dans les éditions précédentes.

Les recettes fiscales rapportées au PIB et les recettes non fiscales rapportées au PIB sont des données dont l'interprétation exige de la prudence pour certains pays car elles sont incomplètes. On ne dispose pas de données relatives aux cotisations de sécurité sociale pour le Botswana (où elles sont supposées nulles car elles ne correspondent pas aux critères permettant de les classer dans la catégorie des cotisations de sécurité sociale selon la classification des impôts de l'OCDE figurant dans le Guide d'interprétation), la République du Congo, la République démocratique du Congo (avant 2012), l'Ouganda et le Togo. Les données relatives aux cotisations de sécurité sociale concernant le Cameroun et le Sénégal ne sont que partiellement disponibles. On ne dispose pas de données relatives aux impôts sur le patrimoine pour le Ghana et l'Ouganda. Pour plus de précisions, se reporter aux tableaux par pays présentés dans les chapitres 5 et 6.

Source : Tableau 4.1, chapitre 4, et tableau 6.1, chapitre 6.

StatLink https://doi.org/10.1787/888933819689

Si le ratio moyen impôts/PIB a progressé en Afrique (21) de 5 points de pourcentage depuis 2000, les recettes non fiscales ont en revanche reculé ces dernières années dans la plupart des pays du continent (tableau 2.1). Sur 21 pays, tous sauf quatre ont enregistré des recettes non fiscales, exprimées en pourcentage du PIB, plus faibles en 2016 qu'en 2015, et tous, sauf six, des recettes non fiscales, toujours en pourcentage du PIB, plus faibles que dix ans auparavant.

Les recettes non fiscales perçues varient généralement plus, selon les années, que les recettes fiscales, comme le montre le coefficient de variation[3] des recettes fiscales et non fiscales pour les dix dernières années pour lesquelles on dispose de données (graphique 2.2). Dans certains pays cependant (Botswana, Burkina Faso, République du Congo, Niger et Rwanda), les recettes fiscales ont presque autant fluctué que les recettes non fiscales.

Tableau 2.1. **Recettes non fiscales totales par pays en pourcentage du PIB, 1997-2016**

Pays	1997	2000	2005	2010	2011	2012	2013	2014	2015	2016
Afrique du Sud	0.5	0.4	0.5	0.6	0.6	0.6	0.6	0.5	0.4	0.5
Botswana[1]	..	..	26,6	19,1	20,0	22,4	22,3	22,8	18,4	18,2
Burkina Faso	..	8.6	5.6	5.7	6.9	7.0	8.0	6.3	6.2	5.6
Cabo Verde	16.1	7.6	9.2	9.7	5.6	6.0	6.2	5.3	7.6	7.2
Cameroun	5.0	7.3	6.3	4.3	5.7	4.6	4.5	3.9	3.9	2.7
Congo	..	20.7	31.9	29.0	33.2	33.0	33.5	27.3	7.9	9.4
Congo, Rép. dém.[2]	..	..	..	6.5	4.4	5.7	3.6	6.4	4.7	3.7
Côte d'Ivoire	1.4	1.1	2.3	1.7	1.5	1.9	2.5	2.6	3.3	1.9
Égypte	..	..	7.1	8.7	5.8	6.5	6.0	10.2	7.3	5.7
Eswatini[1, 3]	12.3	12.1	15.5	8.0	6.6	19.1	17.0	16.8	14.6	11.2
Ghana	..	2.2	4.2	5.0	5.3	6.1	6.2	5.6	6.2	4.0
Kenya	..	..	3.2	1.1	..	..	1.4	1.5	2.0	1.7
Mali	..	6.8	5.4	4.9	5.6	1.4	4.2	3.3	2.8	2.5
Maroc	..	2.2	3.0	3.6	3.9	3.7	4.1	3.8	3.9	3.5
Maurice	4.0	2.8	2.5	3.8	3.5	3.1	3.2	3.0	2.9	2.8
Niger	..	5.5	8.2	6.3	4.9	8.0	9.5	8.0	7.6	7.0
Ouganda	..	..	5.7	2.3	2.5	1.7	1.3	1.5	1.7	1.4
Rwanda	7.5	11.8	12.7	12.3	12.3	8.8	11.2	9.4	8.9	7.8
Sénégal	2.4	2.7	2.3	3.2	2.9	3.8	4.2	5.2	4.5	5.8
Togo	..	1.8	2.7	11.2	9.3	6.3	5.4	4.3	4.1	4.3
Tunisie	..	2.5	2.6	2.9	4.0	3.5	3.6	2.4	2.1	1.7

Notes : Le symbole « .. » signale des données incomplètes concernant le pays pour une année donnée.

Les données relatives aux recettes non fiscales prennent en compte les recettes non fiscales perçues par les administrations infranationales pour l'Eswatini, le Kenya, le Maroc et Maurice, les seuls pays pour lesquels les données correspondantes sont disponibles.

1. Pour le Botswana et l'Eswatini, les recettes non fiscales prennent en compte les montants au titre des droits de douane et d'accise recouvrés par l'Afrique du Sud, puis reversés au Botswana et à l'Eswatini en vertu de la formule de partage des recettes de l'Union douanière d'Afrique australe (SACU).
2. Les chiffres présentés ici correspondent à des dons et à des recettes pétrolières figurant dans les *Perspectives de l'économie mondiale* du FMI d'avril 2018. Il n'a pas été possible d'obtenir des chiffres relatifs aux autres catégories de recettes non fiscales pour la République du Congo.
3. Swaziland dans les éditions précédentes.

Source : Tableau 6.1, chapitre 6.

StatLink https://doi.org/10.1787/888933820012

Ces dix dernières années, 11 des 21 pays couverts par la présente publication ont enregistré une hausse des recettes non fiscales, en glissement annuel, équivalant à au moins 2 % du PIB, et 14 pays, ont essuyé une baisse d'une ampleur similaire.

- L'augmentation la plus forte s'est produite au Niger, dont les recettes non fiscales sont passées de 8.2 % du PIB en 2005 à 47.0 % en 2006, avant de retomber à 6.7 % l'année suivante.
- En République du Congo, les recettes cumulées provenant des dons et du pétrole ont grimpé pour atteindre 47.2 % du PIB en 2008, contre 36.5 % du PIB en 2007, avant de reculer de 25.7 points de pourcentage l'année suivante ; entre 2014 et 2015, elles ont chuté, ramenées de 27.3 % à 7.9 % du PIB, soit un repli de près de 20 points de pourcentage.
- L'Eswatini a aussi connu des variations des recettes non fiscales équivalant à au moins 10 % du PIB sur une année.

Ces fluctuations sont souvent imputables aux rentes de ressources, qui subissent les effets des variations des prix des matières premières, ou aux recettes provenant de dons, lesquels donnent lieu à des apports moins prévisibles et s'inscrivant dans des durées plus courtes que les recettes fiscales. Néanmoins, d'autres sources de recettes non fiscales, notamment les recettes versées à l'Eswatini par l'Union douanière d'Afrique australe, se sont aussi révélées très sujettes à des variations.

Graphique 2.2. **Coefficients de variation (CV) des recettes fiscales et non fiscales, 2007-16**

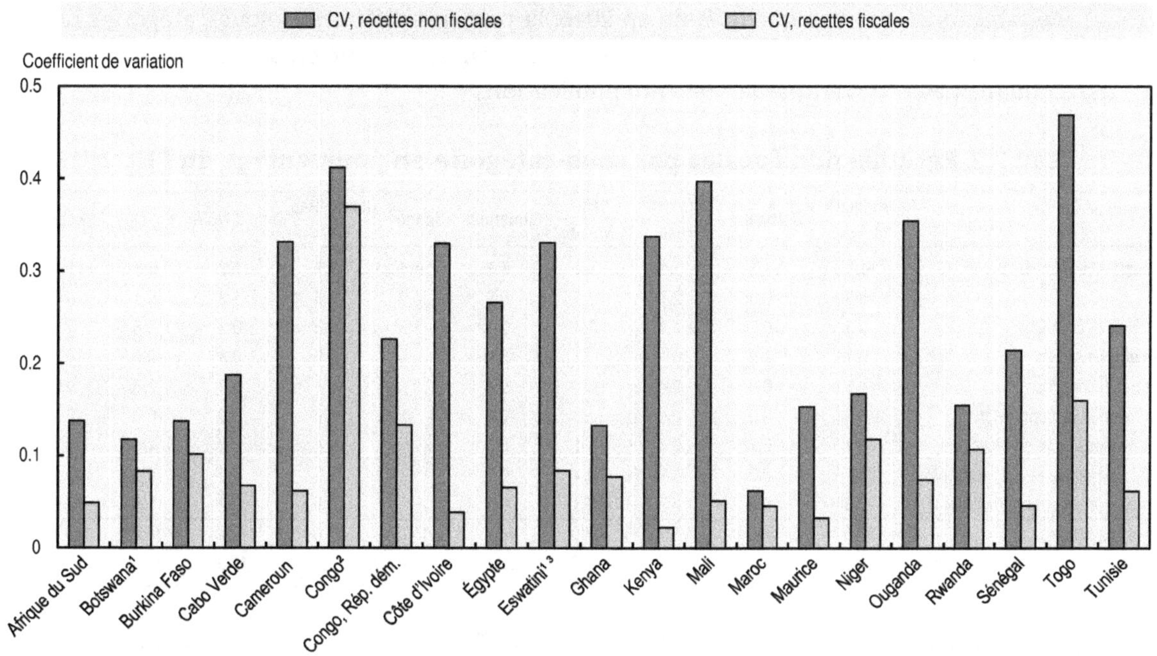

Note : Les données relatives aux recettes non fiscales prennent en compte les recettes non fiscales perçues par les administrations infranationales pour l'Eswatini, le Kenya, le Maroc et Maurice, les seuls pays pour lesquels les données correspondantes sont disponibles.

1. Pour le Botswana et l'Eswatini, les recettes non fiscales prennent en compte les montants au titre des droits de douane et d'accise recouvrés par l'Afrique du Sud, puis reversés au Botswana et à l'Eswatini en vertu de la formule de partage des recettes de l'Union douanière d'Afrique australe (SACU).
2. Les chiffres présentés ici correspondent à des dons et à des recettes pétrolières figurant dans les *Perspectives de l'économie mondiale* du FMI d'avril 2018. Il n'a pas été possible d'obtenir des chiffres relatifs aux autres catégories de recettes non fiscales pour la République du Congo.
3. Swaziland dans les éditions précédentes.

Source : Tableau 4.1, chapitre 4, et tableau 6.1, chapitre 6.

StatLink https://doi.org/10.1787/888933819708

Encadré 2.1. **Recettes non fiscales et la fiabilité des données**

Les données relatives aux recettes non fiscales sont rarement aussi détaillées que celles relatives aux recettes fiscales. Certains pays, par exemple, fournissent pour certaines années un total agrégé de leurs recettes non fiscales, sans autre détail à part la répartition entre les aides sous formes de dons et les autres catégories de recettes non fiscales. L'explication peut être que les données relatives aux recettes non fiscales proviennent souvent de plusieurs sources différentes. Les *Statistiques des recettes publiques en Afrique* indique les cas où le montant total des recettes non fiscales est communiqué, mais où les données sont parfois incomplètes.

Il est par ailleurs possible que les données sur les recettes non fiscales ne fassent pas l'objet de vérifications aussi strictes que celles relatives aux recettes fiscales. Nombre de ces recettes ne sont pas prises en compte aux fins du processus budgétaire principal et les données correspondantes ne sont pas soumises aux mêmes mécanismes de contrôle que dans le cas de recettes fiscales. En outre, elles ne relèvent pas toujours de la responsabilité des services chargés d'établir les statistiques fiscales.

Les dons, les règlements de différends juridiques, les contrats d'exploitation minière ou pétrolière donnent souvent lieu à des versements importants de la part d'entités extérieures telles que des entreprises multinationales ou des administrations qui ne sont pas toujours transparents pour l'administration ou le grand public. Ces accords peuvent inclure des dispositions tenues secrètes, par exemple lorsqu'un contrat important signé avec une entreprise exploitant des ressources naturelles est assorti de clauses de confidentialité très strictes (BAfD/OCDE/CEA, 2010[1]). De plus, il est plus difficile d'établir des découpages détaillés dès lors qu'un pays négocie un versement élevé qui recouvre plusieurs catégories de recettes, fiscales et non fiscales.

Structure des recettes non fiscales

Le tableau 2.2 montre quelle était, en 2016, la part des différentes sous-catégories de recettes non fiscales dans le total des recettes non fiscales, exprimé en pourcentage du PIB, dans chaque pays couvert par la présente publication.

Tableau 2.2. **Recettes non fiscales par sous-catégorie en pourcentage du PIB, 2016**

Catégorie	Afrique du Sud	Botswana	Burkina Faso	Cabo Verde	Cameroun	Congo[2]	Congo, Rép. dém.	Côte d'Ivoire	Égypte	Eswatini[3]	Ghana
Total recettes non fiscales	**0.5**	**18.2**	**5.6**	**7.2**	**2.7**	**9.4**	**3.7**	**1.9**	**5.7**	**11.2**	**4.0**
-Dons	0.0	0.0	2.7	2.8	0.3	0.9	2.5	1.2	0.1	0.2	0.7
-Revenus de la propriété	0.3	10.7	1.1	0.7	2.1	8.6	0.6	0.3	2.8	1.3	1.1
-Loyers et redevances	0.1	1.9	0.7	..	2.0	8.6	0.6	0.3	0.3	0.0	0.5
-Intérêts et dividendes	0.1	8.8	0.4	..	0.1	..	0.1	0.0	2.5	0.8	0.6
-Autres revenus de la propriété	0.0	0.0	0.0	..	0.0	..	0.0	0.0	0.0	0.4	..
-Ventes de biens et de services	0.1	0.7	0.7	3.1	0.2	..	0.4	0.2	1.1	0.4	2.3
-Amendes, pénalités et confiscations	0.1	0.0	0.9	0.4	0.1	..	0.2	0.0	0.1	0.1	0.0
-Recettes diverses et non identifiées[1]	0.0	6.8	0.3	0.3	0.1	..	0.0	0.2	1.5	9.2	0.0
Total recettes fiscales	*28.6*	*14.0*	*18.1*	*19.0*	*14.4*	*16.0*	*7.6*	*17.4*	*15.2*	*15.5*	*17.6*
Total recettes fiscales et non fiscales	*29.0*	*32.2*	*19.9*	*26.2*	*17.0*	*25.4*	*11.3*	*19.3*	*19.1*	*26.7*	*21.7*

Catégorie	Kenya	Ouganda	Mali	Maroc	Maurice	Niger	Rwanda[4]	Sénégal	Togo	Tunisie
Total recettes non fiscales	**1.7**	**1.4**	**2.5**	**3.5**	**2.8**	**7.0**	**7.8**	**5.8**	**4.3**	**1.7**
-Dons	0.5	1.1	1.2	0.0	0.1	6.1	5.1	2.8	2.9	0.1
-Revenus de la propriété	0.3	0.0	0.4	0.9	1.2	0.7	..	1.0	0.8	1.0
-Loyers et redevances	0.0	0.0	0.0	0.4	0.2	0.4	..	0.4	0.1	0.4
-Intérêts et dividendes	0.3	0.0	0.4	0.5	0.2	0.3	..	0.6	0.7	0.6
-Autres revenus de la propriété	0.0	0.0	0.0	0.0	0.8	0.0	..	0.0	0.0	0.0
-Ventes de biens et de services	0.7	0.3	0.7	1.5	0.9	0.1	..	0.0	0.3	0.0
-Amendes, pénalités et confiscations	0.0	0.0	0.2	0.3	0.1	0.1	..	0.0	0.0	0.3
-Recettes diverses et non identifiées[1]	0.2	0.0	0.1	0.8	0.5	0.1	2.7	2.0	0.3	0.2
Total recettes fiscales	*18.1*	*13.1*	*16.0*	*26.4*	*20.0*	*14.4*	*16.6*	*22.0*	*22.2*	*29.4*
Total recettes fiscales et non fiscales	*19.9*	*14.6*	*18.5*	*29.9*	*22.8*	*21.5*	*24.4*	*27.8*	*26.5*	*31.1*

Notes : Le symbole « .. » signale des données incomplètes concernant le pays pour une année donnée.
Les chiffres prennent en compte les recettes non fiscales perçues par les administrations infranationales pour l'Eswatini, le Kenya, le Maroc et Maurice.
1. Y compris les transferts de capitaux non classés ailleurs et les transferts volontaires autres que des dons.
2. On ne dispose pas de chiffres complets concernant les recettes non fiscales pour la République du Congo. Les chiffres présentés ici correspondent à des dons et à des recettes pétrolières figurant dans les *Perspectives de l'économie mondiale* du FMI d'avril 2018.
3. Swaziland dans les éditions précédentes.
4. Les recettes non fiscales autres que les dons ne sont pas ventilées par sous-catégories et sont donc classées dans les recettes diverses et non identifiées.
Source : Tableau 6.2, chapitre 6.

StatLink https://doi.org/10.1787/888933820031

Le graphique 2.3 montre la part de chaque sous-catégorie dans le total des recettes non fiscales. Les recettes correspondant à des intérêts et dividendes et les autres revenus de la propriété sont cumulés de sorte que la valeur obtenue correspond à l'ensemble des revenus de la propriété qui ne sont pas explicitement identifiés comme des loyers et des redevances. Lorsqu'on met en regard les recettes non fiscales perçues par les 21 pays que couvre la présente publication, on distingue cinq groupes de pays :

- La République démocratique du Congo, la Côte d'Ivoire, le Niger, l'Ouganda, le Rwanda et le Togo perçoivent la majeure partie de leurs recettes non fiscales sous forme de dons.

- Le Cameroun et la République du Congo tirent la majeure partie des recettes non fiscales déclarées de loyers et de redevances (il s'agit principalement de recettes pétrolières) même si pour la République du Congo, on ne dispose pas de données relatives aux recettes non fiscales hors recettes pétrolières et dons.
- Le Ghana est le seul pays qui tire la majeure partie des recettes non fiscales qu'il déclare de la vente de biens et de services (production par l'État de biens et de services marchands et redevances administratives).
- Dans le cas de l'Eswatini, 82 % des recettes non fiscales proviennent de la sous-catégorie des recettes diverses et non identifiées, qui sont quasi exclusivement constituées de recettes reçues de l'Union douanière d'Afrique australe (SACU). Le seul autre pays figurant dans la présente publication qui perçoit des recettes de la SACU est le Botswana, pour lequel elles représentent 37.5 % des recettes non fiscales. Bien que l'Afrique du Sud fasse partie de l'accord de partage des recettes de la SACU, elle est un contributeur net et ne déclare donc pas de recettes reçues de la SACU.
- Onze pays n'enregistrent pas comptablement dans une catégorie unique la majeure partie des recettes non fiscales. Parmi ces pays, le Burkina Faso, le Mali et le Sénégal perçoivent une multitude de recettes non fiscales sous forme de dons ; l'Afrique du Sud, le Botswana, l'Égypte, Maurice et la Tunisie perçoivent une multitude de loyers et de redevances (principalement des redevances pétrolières et gazières) ; et Cabo Verde, le Kenya et le Maroc tirent une multitude de recettes de la vente de biens et de services.

Graphique 2.3. **Structure des recettes non fiscales, 2016**

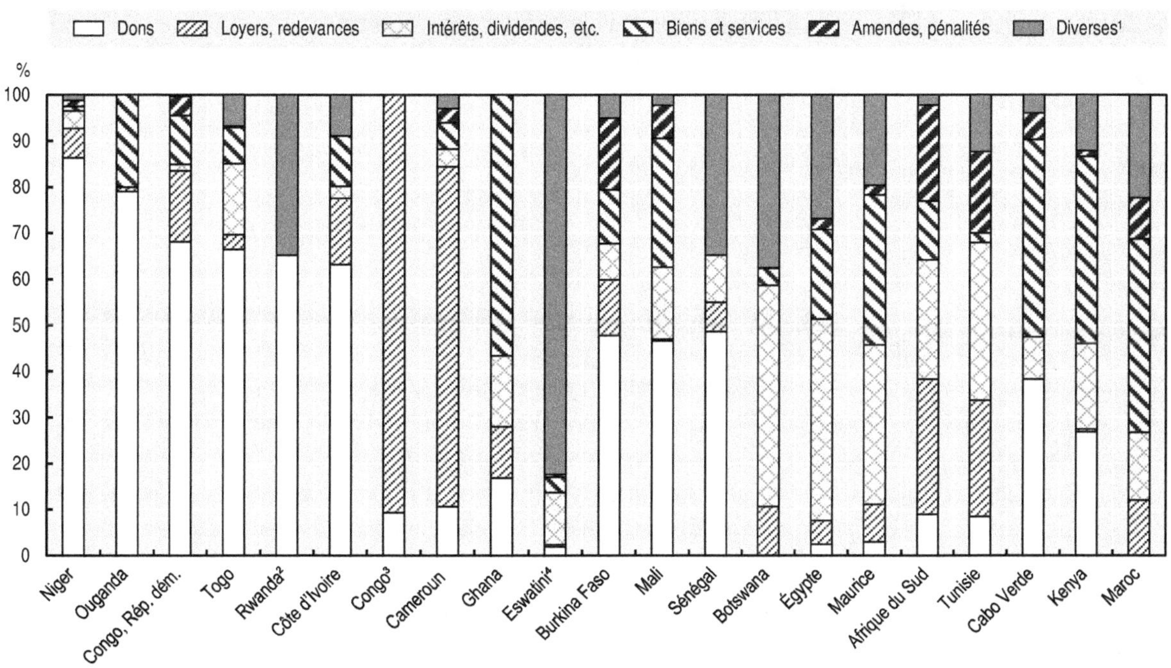

Note : Les chiffres prennent en compte les recettes non fiscales perçues par les administrations infranationales pour l'Eswatini, le Kenya, le Maroc et Maurice.

1. Y compris les transferts de capitaux non classés ailleurs et les transferts volontaires autres que les dons.
2. Les recettes non fiscales autres que les dons ne sont pas ventilées par sous-catégories et sont donc classées comme des recettes diverses et non identifiées.
3. On ne dispose pas de chiffres complets concernant les recettes non fiscales pour la République du Congo. Les chiffres présentés ici correspondent à des dons et à des recettes pétrolières figurant dans les *Perspectives de l'économie mondiale* du FMI d'avril 2018.
4. Swaziland dans les éditions précédentes.

Source : Tableau 6.2, chapitre 6.

StatLink https://doi.org/10.1787/888933819727

Dons

Les dons reçus en 2016 par les pays que couvre la présente publication varient entre des montants négligeables, voire nuls (Afrique du Sud, Botswana, Maroc) et des montants représentant plus de 5 % du PIB (Niger et Rwanda) (graphique 2.4).

Graphique 2.4. **Dons en pourcentage du PIB, 2016**

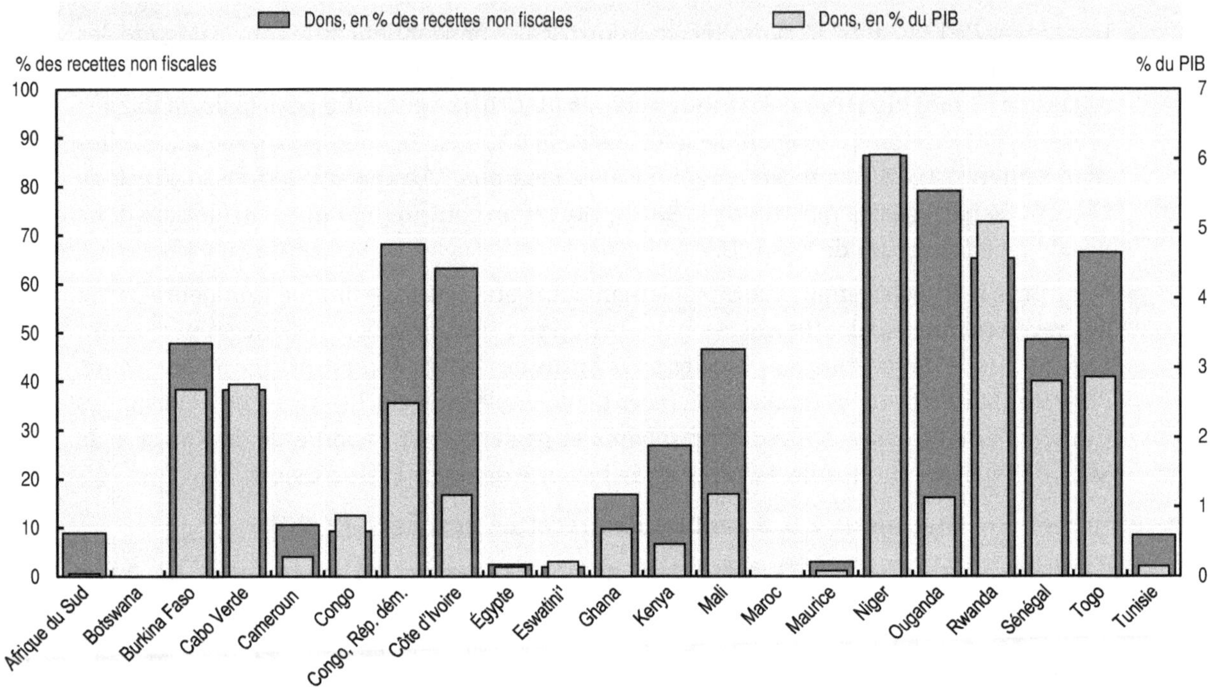

1. Swaziland dans les éditions précédentes.

Source : Tableaux 6.2 et 6.3, chapitre 6.

StatLink https://doi.org/10.1787/888933819746

Entre 2007 et 2016, six pays ont enregistré au moins une fois des recettes annuelles sous forme de dons représentant plus de 6.0 % du PIB (graphique 2.5). Il ressort d'un examen de l'évolution des dons dans ces pays que les hausses de ce type de recettes ne se sont jamais inscrites dans la durée. Dans les six cas mentionnés précédemment, on a observé sur la période considérée au moins une baisse des recettes tirées de dons de 2.5 % du PIB ou plus sur une année. Au total, 12 pays parmi les 21 couverts par la présente publication ont enregistré un repli des recettes annuelles sous forme de dons équivalant à au moins 1 % du PIB.

Il existe une corrélation partielle entre le montant des recettes sous forme de dons perçues par les pays couverts par la présente publication et le niveau de revenu par habitant (graphique 2.6). Cependant, parmi ceux d'entre eux qui affichent un faible PIB par habitant, les recettes tirées de dons sont variables. Le Mali, l'Ouganda et le Rwanda par exemple affichent des PIB par habitant (en parité de pouvoir d'achat [PPP]) de niveaux similaires, mais en 2016, les dons qu'ils ont déclarés ont représenté, en pourcentage du PIB, de 1.1 % (Ouganda) et 1.2 % (Mali) á 5.1 % (Rwanda).

Graphique 2.5. **Dons en pourcentage du PIB, dans quelques pays, 2007-16**

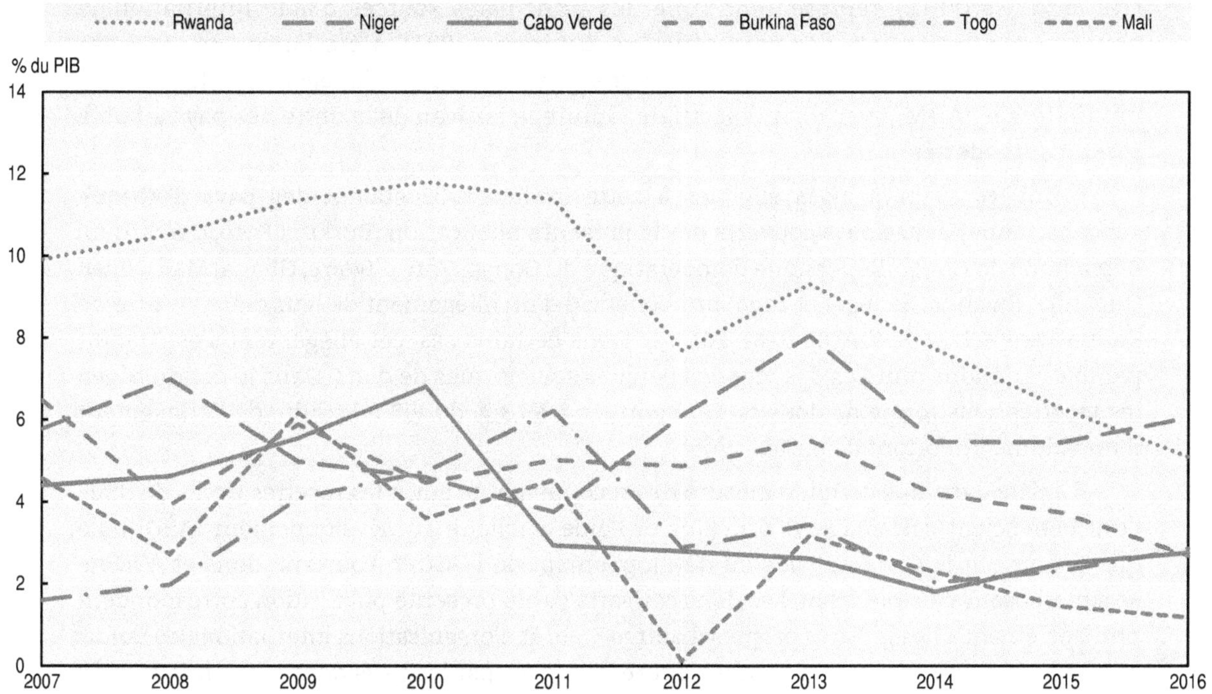

Source : Données comparatives des *Statistiques des recettes publiques en Afrique* disponibles à *https://doi.org/10.1787/7f54581d-fr*.

StatLink *https://doi.org/10.1787/888933819765*

Graphique 2.6. **Dons en pourcentage du PIB au regard du PIB par habitant en dollars US, 2016**

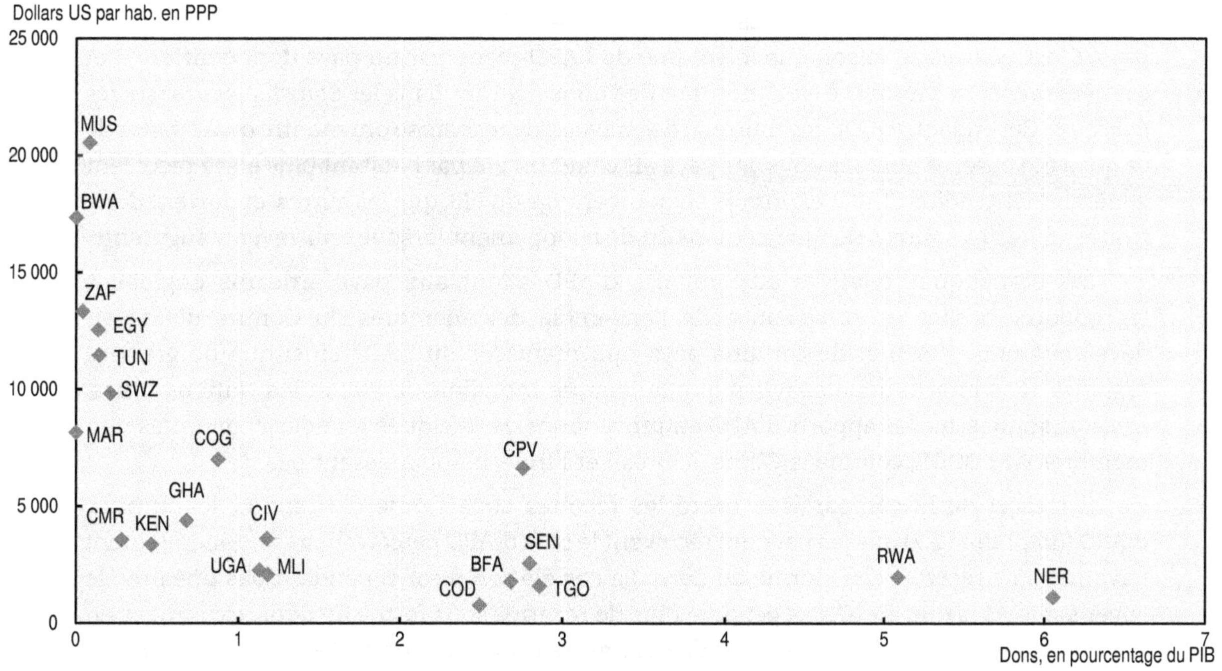

Source : Tableau 6.2, chapitre 6, et FMI, *Perspectives de l'économie mondiale*, avril 2018, pour les valeurs du PIB par habitant en PPP.

StatLink *https://doi.org/10.1787/888933819784*

Les programmes d'allégement de la dette, comme l'Initiative en faveur des pays pauvres très endettés (PPTE), représentent l'une des principales sources d'aide internationale pour les gouvernements des pays africains. L'initiative PPTE a été lancée en 1996 par le FMI et la Banque mondiale dans la lignée de l'Initiative d'allégement de la dette multilatérale (IADM), avec pour objectif de réduire le fardeau de la dette des pays à faible revenu surendettés.

Parmi les 39 pays jugés éligibles à cette initiative, 33 étaient des pays d'Afrique subsaharienne. Douze pays couverts par la présente publication (Burkina Faso, Cameroun, République du Congo, République démocratique du Congo, Côte d'Ivoire, Ghana, Mali, Niger, Ouganda, Rwanda, Sénégal et Togo) ont bénéficié d'un allégement de leur dette au titre de l'initiative PPTE et de l'IADM (FMI, 2016[2]). Dans certains cas, cet allégement s'est traduit par des variations brutales des recettes perçues sous formes de dons. Dans le cas du Niger, les recettes sous forme de dons ont été portées à 46.3 % du PIB à la suite de l'effacement d'un volume important de dettes.

Il existe dans une certaine mesure des recoupements entre les recettes tirées de dons dont bénéficient certains pays africains et l'aide publique au développement (APD) telle que définie par le Comité d'aide au développement de l'OCDE[4]. Pourtant, dons et APD ne se superposent pas tout à fait. Les dons couverts par la présente publication correspondent principalement à des recettes perçues d'autres États et d'organisations internationales tandis que l'APD mesure essentiellement les efforts déployés par les pays donneurs en faveur du développement dans les pays à faible revenu et à revenu intermédiaire. L'APD recouvre les apports considérés comme des « dons » dans la présente publication (aide budgétaire, transferts de capitaux, transferts courants, subventions de projets, dons au titre de programmes, allégement de la dette internationale), mais elle englobe également les prêts assortis de conditions libérales, l'assistance technique en nature, les dépenses administratives supportées par les donneurs, le coût des réfugiés dans les pays donneurs et les bourses d'étude ainsi que d'autres activités ne générant pas d'entrées de recettes (nettes) dans le pays. C'est pour cette raison que le volume de l'APD reçue par un pays donné diffère – et est généralement plus élevé – du montant des dons figurant dans les *Statistiques des recettes publiques*. Cependant, (OCDE, à paraître[3]) des travaux de recherche ont montré qu'à l'instar de ce qui a été observé pour les dons, les pays affichant un PIB par habitant plus élevé reçoivent généralement moins d'APD, exprimée en pourcentage du PIB, que les autres, et doivent donc trouver d'autres sources de financement du développement lorsque leur revenu augmente.

Les statistiques relatives aux apports d'APD allant aux pays africains englobent les apports publics en provenance de l'ensemble des membres du Comité d'aide au développement (CAD) et de certains pays non membres du CAD[5] ainsi que de grandes organisations internationales telles que la Banque mondiale, le FMI et les Nations unies. Les statistiques sur les apports d'APD en provenance de quelques grandes économies non membres de l'OCDE, comme la Chine, le Brésil et l'Inde, n'apparaissent pas.

Il ressort de la comparaison entre les recettes sous forme de dons et les entrées d'APD (graphique 2.7) que les pays qui reçoivent le plus d'APD perçoivent aussi généralement davantage de recettes sous forme de dons. La corrélation n'est cependant pas linéaire ; le Niger est le pays qui, en 2016, a perçu le plus de recettes sous forme de dons, exprimées en pourcentage du PIB, mais c'est le Rwanda qui a attiré le plus d'apports d'APD, en pourcentage du PIB.

Graphique 2.7. **Dons et APD nette perçus en 2016 en pourcentage du PIB**

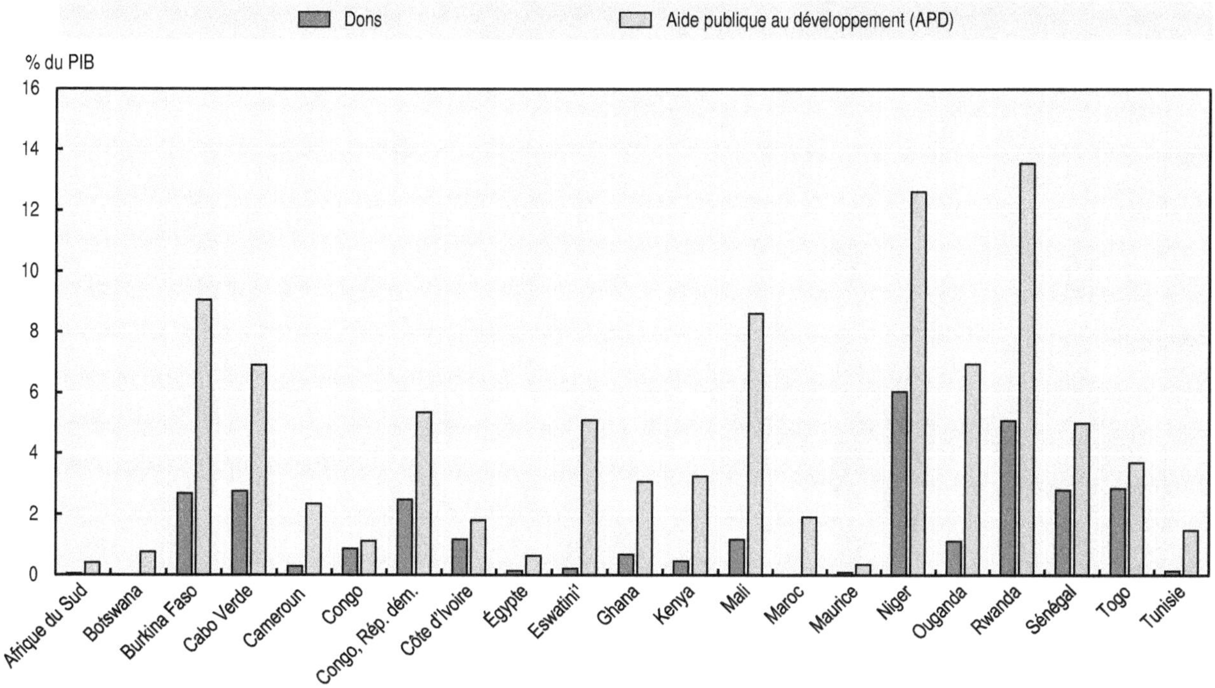

1. Swaziland dans les éditions précédentes.

Source : Comité d'aide au développement (CAD) de l'OCDE, 2018 pour les données relatives à l'APD.

StatLink https://doi.org/10.1787/888933819803

Revenus de la propriété

On distingue ici trois grandes sous-catégories de recettes :

- les loyers et redevances ;
- les intérêts et dividendes ;
- les autres revenus de la propriété non affectés.

Les loyers et redevances sont des recettes générées en contrepartie d'activités de prospection et d'exploitation de ressources naturelles non renouvelables sur des terres appartenant au domaine public, ou de l'exploitation de fermes et de forêts détenues par l'État tandis que les intérêts et dividendes sont une rémunération d'investissements réalisés par l'État dans des sociétés. En 2016, le montant total des recettes perçues au titre de revenus de la propriété a dépassé 1 % du PIB dans dix des 21 pays considérés dans la présente publication (graphique 2.8). Le Botswana et la République du Congo sont ceux qui ont enregistré les niveaux les plus élevés de revenus de la propriété, soit 10.7 % et 8.6 % du PIB respectivement. Les intérêts et dividendes ont représenté plus de 80 % des revenus de la propriété au Botswana. Les seules données dont on dispose sur les revenus de la propriété en République du Congo concernent les loyers et redevances (recettes pétrolières en l'espèce). Sept pays figurant dans la présente publication (Afrique du Sud, Burkina Faso, Cameroun, République du Congo, République démocratique du Congo, Côte d'Ivoire et Niger) ont indiqué que la majeure partie de leurs revenus de la propriété était issue de loyers et redevances en 2016.

Graphique 2.8. **Revenus de la propriété en pourcentage du PIB, 2016**

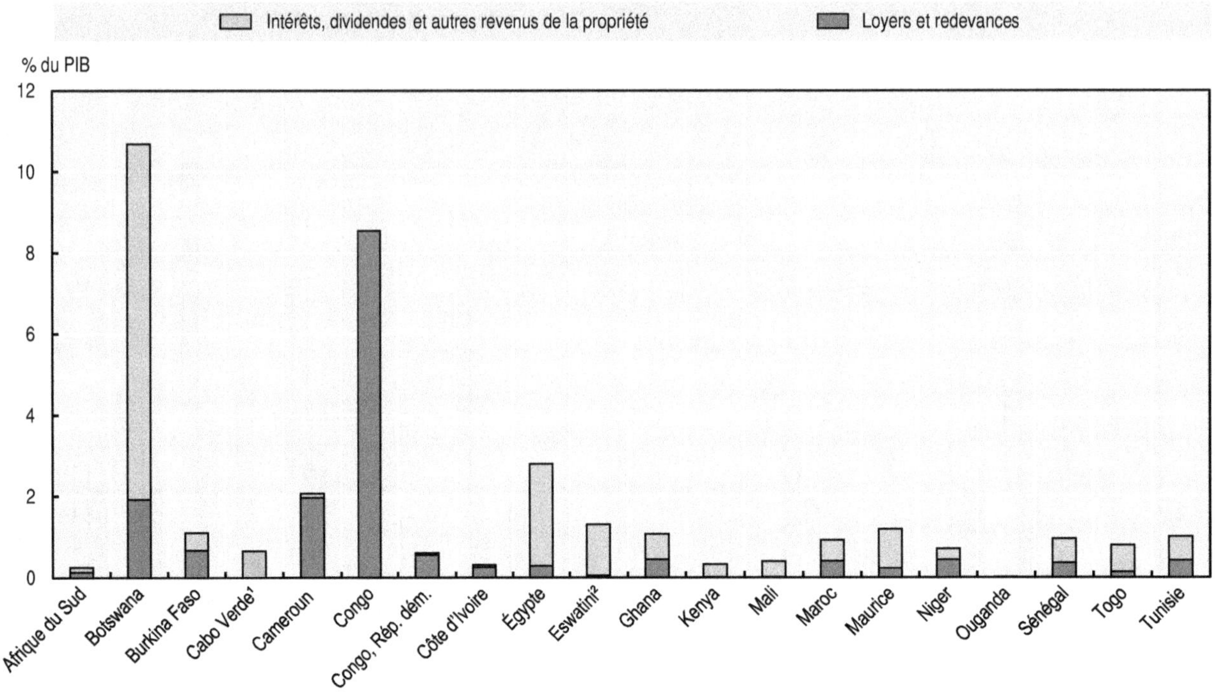

Notes : Le Rwanda n'apparaît pas dans ce graphique faute de données disponibles.
1. Les données relatives aux revenus de la propriété pour le Cabo Verde n'ont pas été ventilées.
2. Swaziland dans les éditions précédentes.

Source : Calculs des auteurs à partir de données présentées dans les tableaux 6.5-6.25 et tableau 4.17.

StatLink https://doi.org/10.1787/888933819822

Recettes des ressources naturelles

Dans les 21 pays considérés dans la présente publication, les loyers et redevances correspondent principalement à des recettes minières et pétrolières. En 2016, plus de la moitié des loyers et redevances perçus par ces pays provenait de recettes pétrolières (redevances et recettes perçues au titre d'accords de partage des recettes conclus avec des compagnies pétrolières), celles-ci représentant la majeure partie des loyers et redevances engrangés par le Cameroun, la République du Congo, l'Égypte et la Tunisie. Parallèlement, les ressources minières hors pétrole constituaient la source de la majeure partie des loyers et redevances perçus par l'Afrique du Sud, le Botswana, le Burkina Faso, le Ghana et le Kenya. Environ 3 % du montant total des loyers et redevances perçus par les 21 pays considérés ne sont pas affectés à une source en particulier ; il s'agit notamment de recettes tirées de la construction et de l'exploitation d'aéroports, au Kenya et au Togo par exemple.

Les recettes issues de ressources naturelles constituent une source de financement qui se caractérise souvent par une forte volatilité. Ces dix dernières années, cinq des 21 pays considérés ont perçu des recettes au titre de loyers et redevances liés à des ressources naturelles équivalant à plus de 1 % du PIB, et dans tous, ces recettes ont subi des contractions sensibles, en glissement annuel, à un moment ou à un autre de la période considérée (graphique 2.9). En République démocratique du Congo et en Côte d'Ivoire, ces recettes ont baissé pour se situer à moins d'un quart de leurs valeurs maximales respectives. Au Cameroun, ces recettes s'établissent à 32.8 % de leur valeur maximale, soit une baisse équivalant à plus de 4 % du PIB. Or ces fluctuations ont un impact massif sur les finances publiques.

En République du Congo, les loyers et redevances se situent sur une échelle différente des autres pays africains, et les effets de la volatilité des loyers tirés des ressources du pays ont une ampleur bien supérieure. Pendant la décennie qui s'est achevée en 2010, les loyers et redevances étaient, en pourcentage du PIB, cinq à dix fois supérieurs en République du Congo à ce qu'ils étaient dans tous les autres pays considérés. En raison du volume considérable de ces recettes, en pourcentage du PIB, les baisses des prix du pétrole enregistrées en 2008-09 et 2014-15 ont occasionné des baisses des recettes pétrolières et, de ce fait, des contractions du montant total des recettes non fiscales équivalant à 20 % du PIB du pays.

Graphique 2.9. **Loyers et redevances en pourcentage du PIB dans quelques pays, 2006-16**

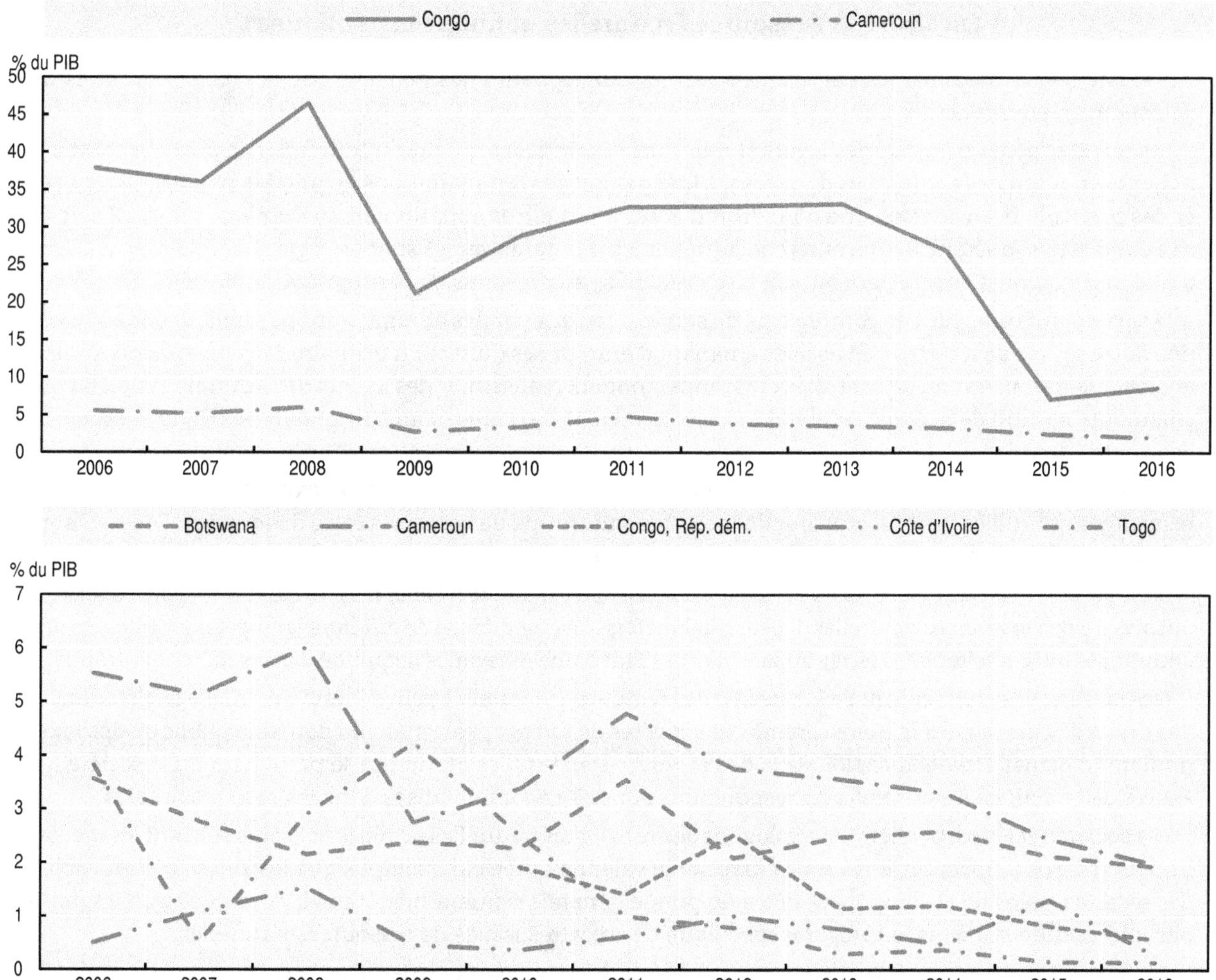

Note : Pour la République démocratique du Congo, les données disponibles couvrent uniquement la période 2010-16. Les chiffres concernant la République du Congo ne peuvent être représentés sur la même échelle que celle utilisée pour les autres pays. Le Cameroun figure sur les deux schémas à titre de référence.

Source : Calculs des auteurs à partir de données présentées dans les tableaux 6.5-6.25 et tableau 4.17.

StatLink https://doi.org/10.1787/888933819841

L'impact non négligeable sur les finances publiques des loyers tirés de leurs ressources par certains des pays ayant fourni des données est le signe d'une dépendance à l'égard des ressources naturelles qui a des conséquences tant pour les finances des pays concernés que pour leur développement économique. Dans une étude récente (CUA/OCDE, 2018[4]), quatre pays (la République du Congo, la République démocratique du Congo, l'Égypte et le Togo) présentent des caractéristiques amenant à les considérer comme « richement dotées en ressources » au regard de la production importante, en pourcentage du PIB, de ressources naturelles issues de leur sous-sol pendant les dix dernières années. On a pu voir des pays richement dotés en ressources afficher des taux de croissance économique élevés, mais cette croissance ne s'est pas poursuivie pendant les périodes de repli des prix des matières premières (CUA/OCDE, 2018, p. 8[4]). Dans un contexte où les ressources naturelles peuvent avoir des effets positifs comme négatifs sur l'économie d'un pays, les pouvoirs publics peuvent recourir à de multiples mécanismes pour consacrer une partie des richesses produites au financement d'investissements dans le cadre d'une stratégie de développement économique plus durable (voir encadré 2.2).

Encadré 2.2. **Ressources naturelles et finances publiques**[a]

Il existe divers mécanismes par lesquels les ressources naturelles peuvent être sources de recettes ou d'économies pour les États :

Les recettes perçues au titre des loyers et redevances sont celles qui présentent le lien le plus direct avec la richesse en ressources naturelles d'un pays. L'État perçoit des rémunérations acquittées par des entreprises et des particuliers en contrepartie d'un droit d'accès à des terres appartenant au domaine public. Il agit en sa qualité de propriétaire des terrains concernés et les montants versés sont en règle générale fixés à l'issue d'une négociation. Ces recettes sont ensuite rattachées aux revenus de la propriété.

Les paiements effectués en contrepartie de services fournis par des administrations publiques constituent une autre source de recettes non fiscales émanant d'entreprises du secteur primaire. Ils peuvent notamment englober la rémunération de contrôles environnementaux réalisés par des agents de l'administration ou des paiements au titre de la construction d'infrastructures. Ces recettes sont comptabilisées dans la catégorie des ventes des biens et services.

Le fait, pour l'État, de détenir une partie ou la totalité du capital d'une société exploitant en son nom des ressources naturelles peut lui procurer des recettes sous forme de bénéfices et de dividendes. Celles-ci sont ensuite comptabilisées dans les revenus de la propriété.

Il est possible d'instituer des taxes ou des droits conçus de manière à cibler les sociétés ou les particuliers qui ont accès à des ressources naturelles. Il peut quelquefois s'avérer difficile de différencier une taxe appliquée aux entreprises qui exploitent des terres appartenant à l'État d'une redevance acquittée par ces mêmes entreprises.

Des taxes et des droits ciblant l'exploitation des ressources naturelles peuvent être mis en place, notamment des droits d'accise sur les matières premières extraites de terres appartenant au domaine public ou des taxes minières ciblant l'activité d'exploitation des ressources naturelles plutôt que le particulier ou la société qui exerce cette activité. Les revenus correspondants sont alors comptabilisés dans les recettes fiscales.

Les sociétés et les particuliers qui exploitent des ressources naturelles acquittent le plus souvent les mêmes impôts et taxes (impôts sur le revenu et taxe sur la valeur ajoutée par exemple) que les autres contribuables. Les recettes tirées de ces impôts et taxes de portée générale figurent bien dans les comptes publics, mais pas nécessairement dans la catégorie spécifique des recettes issues de ressources naturelles.

Par ailleurs, il arrive que des sociétés et des particuliers consacrent une partie de la richesse qu'ils retirent de l'extraction de ressources naturelles à la construction d'infrastructures ou à la fourniture de services. Dès lors que ces infrastructures ou services répondent à une demande d'investissements ou de services publics, il peut en résulter une économie sur les dépenses publiques, qui toutefois ne sera pas comptabilisée comme une recette pour l'État. Dans certains cas, l'État impose, comme condition à l'accès aux ressources naturelles dont il est propriétaire, que les entreprises et particuliers concernés fournissent certains services, par exemple en prenant à leur charge une partie au moins du coût de la construction et de l'entretien des routes desservant les mines.

a. Mansour et Rota-Graziosi (2013) indiquent que les recettes fiscales liées à l'extraction pétrolière peuvent englober l'impôt sur les bénéfices des sociétés, les droits indirects sur des produits énergétiques ainsi que des montants non remboursés de taxes sur les ventes comme la TVA, tandis que les recettes non fiscales peuvent correspondre à des redevances, des participations aux bénéfices, des dividendes des entreprises publiques, et d'autres revenus d'investissements perçus au titre de participations directes de l'administration au capital des entreprises qui réalisent des activités d'extraction.

On observe des différences marquées entre les pays africains tant en ce qui concerne le volume que la nature des ressources naturelles dont ils sont dotés. La contribution des richesses naturelles au PIB est également variable selon les pays, de même que leur impact sur les budgets publics. Selon par exemple des estimations de la Banque mondiale portant sur les richesses générées par l'exploitation des ressources naturelles[6], l'Afrique du Sud (minerais principalement), la République du Congo (ressources pétrolières principalement) et le Ghana (ressources forestières principalement) étaient les trois pays produisant le plus de richesse issue de ressources naturelles par habitant en 2016. Cependant, parce que l'économie de l'Afrique du Sud est de plus grande taille et plus diversifiée, les ressources naturelles représentaient dans ce pays moins de 5 % du PIB (graphique 2.10) et le chiffre des loyers tirés de ces ressources, en pourcentage des recettes totales, était le plus faible des 21 pays couverts par la présente publication.

Graphique 2.10. **Recettes publiques tirées de ressources naturelles en pourcentage du PIB, 2016**

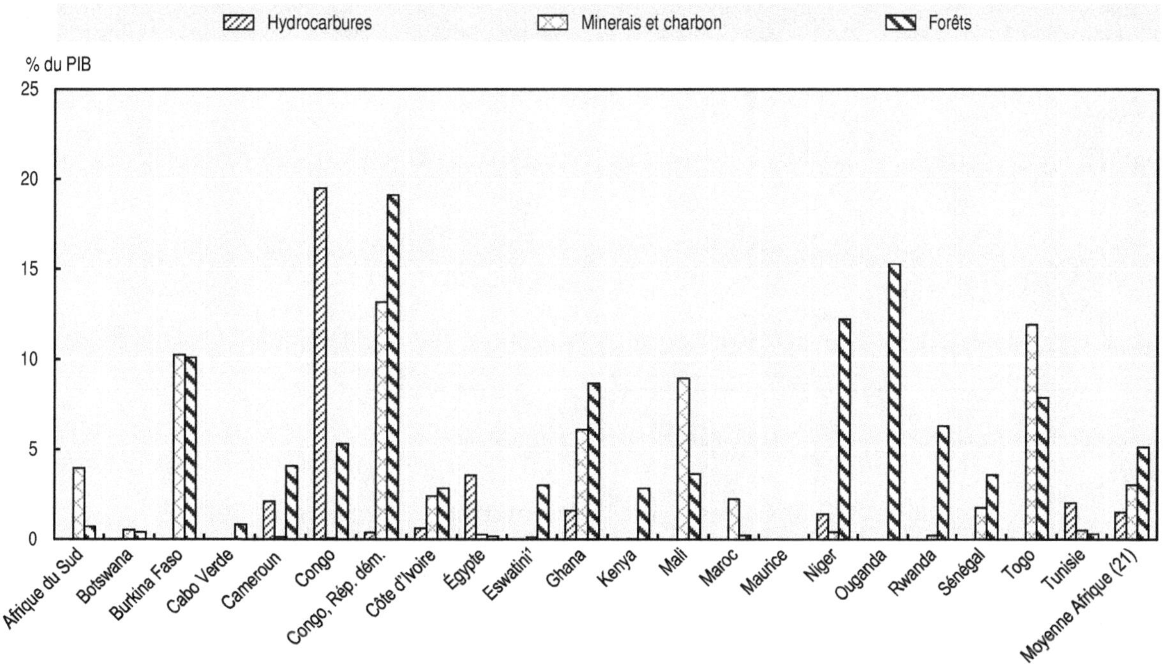

1. Swaziland dans les éditions précédentes.

Source : Banque mondiale (2018), *Indicateurs du développement dans le monde* pour les estimations de la valeur totale de la production de ressources naturelles de chaque pays.

StatLink https://doi.org/10.1787/888933819860

Les effets des ressources naturelles sur les finances publiques de chaque pays varient aussi considérablement. Des pays tels que le Botswana, le Cameroun et la République du Congo ont tiré des recettes publiques importantes des richesses naturelles considérables qu'ils possèdent tandis que d'autres, comme l'Ouganda et le Togo, dont la richesse en ressources naturelles représente plus de 15 % du PIB, n'ont déclaré des recettes publiques correspondant à des loyers tirés de ressources naturelles que pour un montant équivalant à 0.1 % du PIB.

Dans quatre pays (Burkina Faso, République du Congo, Niger et Ouganda), les richesses produites par les forêts ont représenté plus de 10 % du PIB, mais, comme indiqué précédemment, leur part des recettes tirées de ressources naturelles a été modeste. Bien que quelques pays, comme le Cameroun et le Niger, aient perçu de redevances au titre de l'exploitation de leurs forêts, les recettes forestières ont tout de même représenté une petite part des recettes non fiscales des pays en question.

Un certain nombre des 21 pays africains considérés ont durement subi les effets des fluctuations des prix de certaines matières premières (graphiques 2.11 et 2.12 et tableau 2.3). Depuis 2000 par exemple, le cours de l'or a connu des hausses qui ont pu atteindre 28.1 % d'une année sur l'autre et des baisses qui ont pu atteindre 15.5 %. Le prix du pétrole a progressé de 36.4 % en 2008, par rapport à l'année précédente, et en 2015, il a baissé de 47.3 %.

Graphique 2.11. **Principales exportations de matières premières des pays africains en pourcentage du PIB**

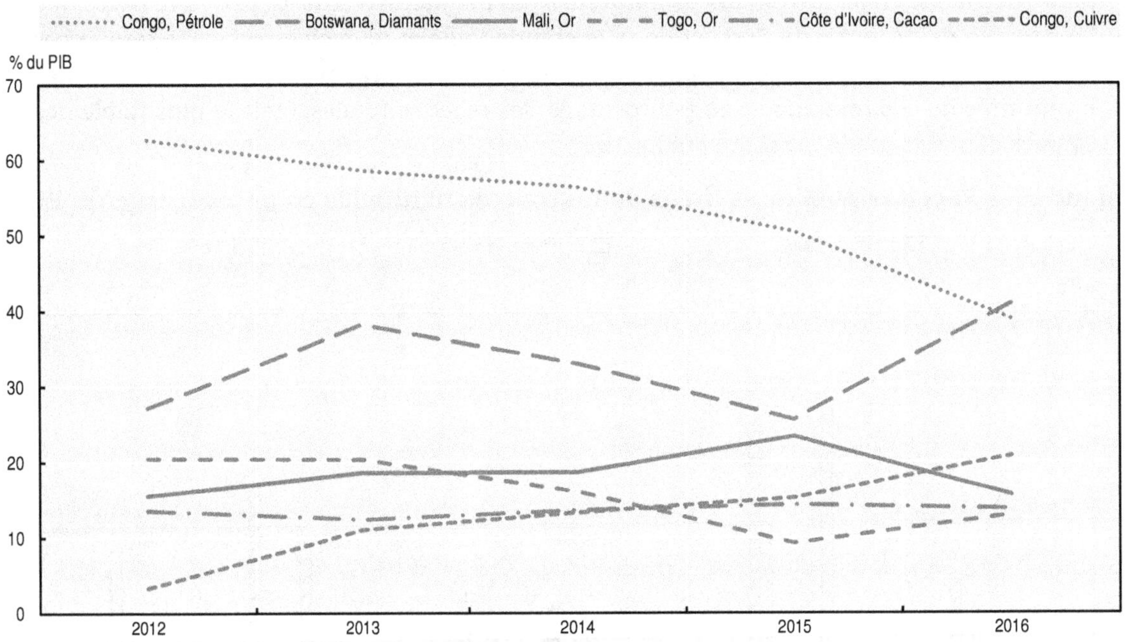

Source : Calculs des auteurs à partir de la base de données en ligne COMTRADE du site WITS.

StatLink https://doi.org/10.1787/888933819879

Graphique 2.12. **Prix des principales matières premières, 2000-16**

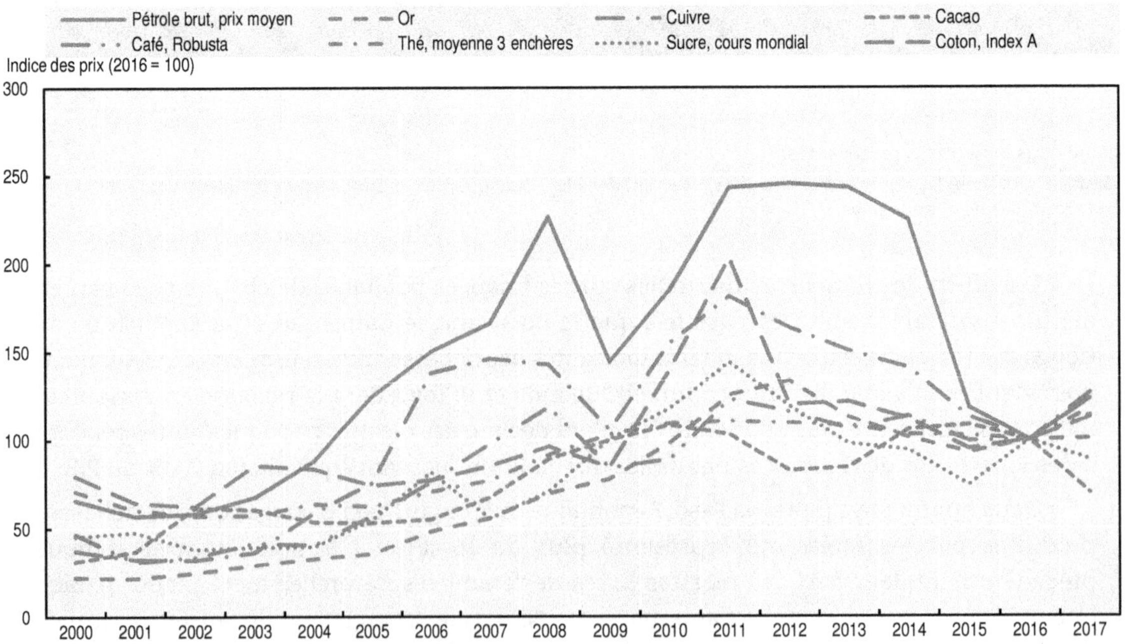

Source : Banque Mondiale, données sur les prix des matières premières (« *The Pink Sheet* »).

StatLink https://doi.org/10.1787/888933819898

Tableau 2.3. **Variations notables des prix des matières premières, 2000-16**

Matière première	Pays producteurs[1]	Hausse maximum en glissement annuel	Baisse maximum en glissement annuel
Pétrole brut	Cameroun, Congo, Égypte, Ghana	36.4 % (2008)	-47.3 % (2015)
Or	Afrique du Sud, Burkina Faso, Ghana, Mali, Niger, Sénégal, Togo	28.1 % (2011)	-15.5 % (2013)
Cuivre	Congo, Congo (Rép. dém)	46.3 % (2010)	-26.0 % (2009)
Cacao	Côte d'Ivoire, Ghana	32.0 % (2008)	-19.7 % (2012)
Café	Rwanda, Ouganda	38.7 % (2011)	-29.2 % (2009)
Thé	Kenya	18.9 % (2008)	-4.9 % (2014)
Sucre	Eswatini[2]	41.8 % (2009)	-31.8 % (2007)
Coton	Burkina Faso	65.2 % (2010)	-40.9 % (2012)

1. Le pourcentage moyen des exportations totales sur la période 2012-16 est supérieur à 15 %.
2. Swaziland dans les éditions précédentes.

Source : Base de données en ligne COMTRADE du site WITS (consulté le 21 juin 2018), *World Bank Commodity Price Data (The Pink Sheet).*

StatLink https://doi.org/10.1787/888933820050

Le graphique 2.13 a pour objet de rapprocher les variations du prix du pétrole de celles du montant total des redevances pétrolières dans cinq pays couverts par la présente publication. Les variations des recettes pétrolières du Cameroun, de la République du Congo, du Ghana et de la Tunisie suivent la courbe des prix du pétrole. Ce n'est pas le cas pour l'Égypte dont la production de pétrole a été particulièrement erratique ces dernières années et dont les recettes pétrolières n'ont pas suivi la même trajectoire que les prix du pétrole.

Graphique 2.13. **Variations, en glissement annuel, des prix du pétrole et des redevances pétrolières des principaux pays producteurs de pétrole, 2000-16**

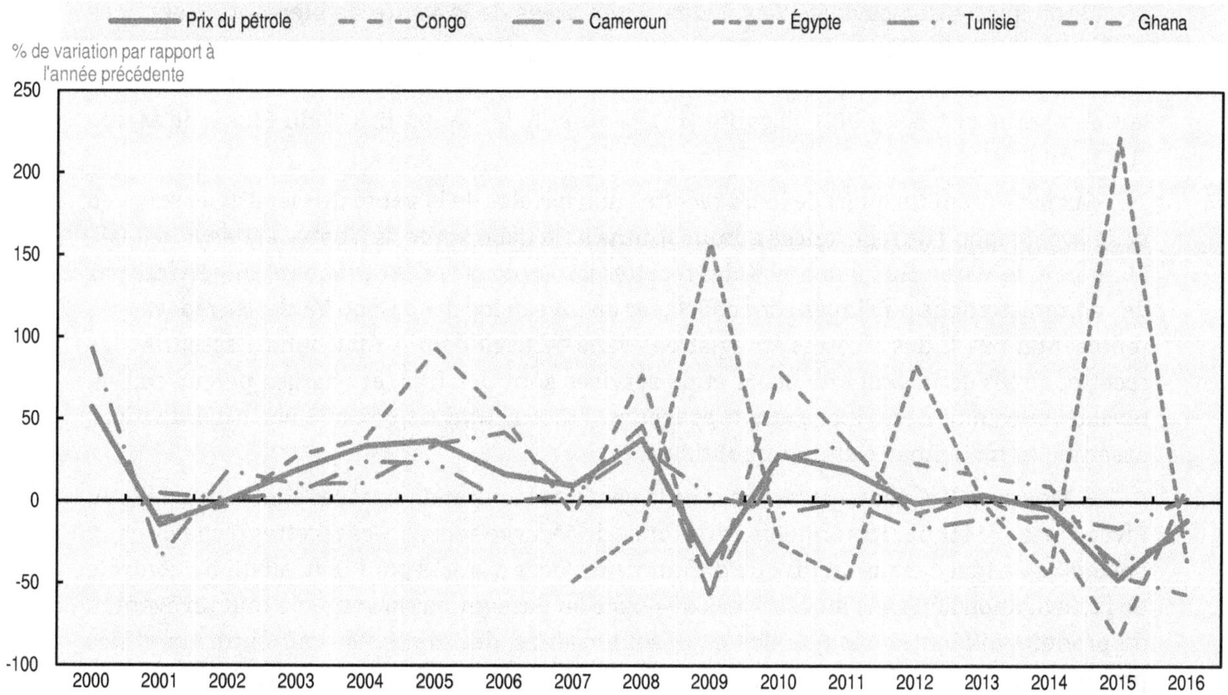

Note : Les chiffres pour les redevances pétrolières sont ceux expressément identifiés comme tels dans les données nationales. Ils ne représentent pas nécessairement l'ensemble des recettes pétrolières des pays concernés.

Source : Calculs des auteurs à partir de données présentées dans les tableaux 6.5-6.25 et tableau 4.17 et *Economic Research Division, Federal Reserve Bank of St. Louis* pour les prix du pétrole.

StatLink https://doi.org/10.1787/888933819917

Recettes tirées de la vente de biens et de services

Les administrations peuvent produire des biens et des services relevant aussi bien du secteur marchand que non marchand. Lorsqu'elles interviennent dans le secteur marchand, elles fournissent parfois des biens et des services que peuvent également procurer des entreprises privées (c'est le cas notamment lorsqu'elles vendent des denrées alimentaires ou assurent des services de transport). Parallèlement, elles assurent, lorsqu'elles gèrent des programmes ou garantissent le respect de la loi, différents services qui sont du seul ressort de l'État. Les frais facturés pour ces services non marchands sont le plus souvent considérés comme des redevances administratives.

Les redevances administratives sont souvent difficiles à classer, car elles se situent dans une zone grise, à mi-chemin entre les rémunérations de services (qui sont des recettes non fiscales) et les prélèvements obligatoires effectués sans contrepartie au profit d'administrations publiques (qui sont des recettes fiscales)[7]. Les frais de justice, ainsi que les frais de dossiers pour les permis de conduire, passeports, enregistrements de brevets et certificats de mariage sont très souvent classés dans les recettes non fiscales. Lorsqu'ils sont considérés comme des recettes fiscales, ils sont en principe rattachés à l'une des catégories suivantes :

- 4400 – Impôts sur les transactions mobilières et immobilières (taxes sur les transactions foncières, par exemple) ;
- 5200 – Impôts sur l'utilisation des biens et l'autorisation d'exercer des activités (permis de chasse, enregistrement des véhicules, par exemple) ;
- 6000 – Autres impôts (vente de timbres fiscaux, dans les cas où ces timbres sont utilisés pour le paiement de taxes et frais administratifs, par exemple).

Dans quatre des pays étudiés, les recettes tirées de la vente de biens et de services et de la perception de redevances administratives représentaient au moins l'équivalent de 1 % du PIB en 2015 (graphique 2.14). Les pays ayant totalisé le plus de recettes étaient : le Cabo Verde (3.1 % du PIB), l'Égypte (1. 1 % du PIB), le Ghana (2.3 % du PIB) et le Maroc (1.5 % du PIB).

Six pays tirent un quart de leurs recettes non fiscales de la vente de biens et de services et de la perception de redevances administratives : le Cabo Verde, le Ghana, le Kenya, le Mali, Maurice et le Maroc. Au Maroc, 66 % des recettes issues de la vente de biens et de services par des administrations publiques sont collectées au niveau local. Au Cabo Verde, les redevances représentent 94 % des recettes enregistrées dans cette catégorie. Au Ghana, l'essentiel des recettes tirées de la vente de biens et de services sont des frais et charges perçus soit au niveau des communes, départements et agences administratives, soit au niveau des districts, assemblées municipales et métropolitaines.

À Maurice, 19 % des recettes tirées de la vente de biens et de services sont recouvrées au niveau local, et 4 % par l'intermédiaire de fonds de sécurité sociale. Ces recettes recouvrent un ensemble de frais perçus au titre de différents services assurés par l'État, allant du contrôle de la navigation aérienne aux services de police en passant par la vente de tout un éventail de produits différents tels que des eaux souterraines, des aliments pour animaux et des produits forestiers. Le Kenya n'a pas tiré de recettes importantes de la vente de biens et de services, mais celles-ci ont tout de même représenté plus des deux cinquièmes du montant total de ses recettes non fiscales en 2016.

Graphique 2.14. **Ventes de biens et de services et redevances administratives, en pourcentage du PIB et en pourcentage du total des recettes non fiscales, 2016**

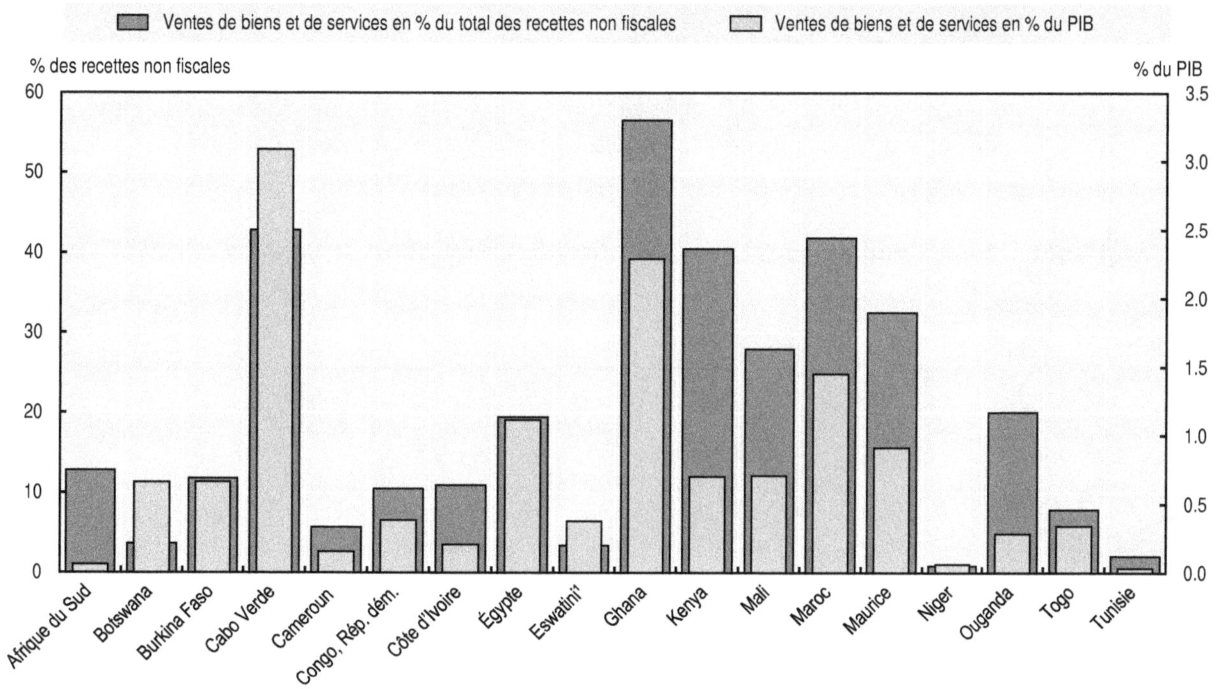

Note : Les chiffres prennent en compte les recettes non fiscales perçues par les administrations infranationales pour l'Eswatini, le Kenya, le Maroc et Maurice.

1. Swaziland dans les éditions précédentes.

La République du Congo et le Rwanda ne figurent pas faute de données disponibles. Le Sénégal n'a déclaré aucune recette provenant de la vente de biens et de services.

Source : Tableaux 6.2 et 6.3, chapitre 6.

StatLink https://doi.org/10.1787/888933819936

Amendes et confiscations

Les amendes et confiscations peuvent représenter une source importante de revenus, toutefois très volatile. Certaines amendes de faibles montants procurent des flux de recettes réguliers et prévisibles. Dans certains pays, une part de ces recettes est utilisée pour financer les administrations locales et elles n'apparaissent donc pas nécessairement dans les statistiques relatives au budget fédéral. De façon générale, les 21 pays couverts par la présente publication ne tirent pour la plupart que des sommes négligeables des amendes, confiscations et sanctions pécuniaires infligées même si ces recettes ont augmenté ces dernières années pour devenir supérieures à 0.5 % du PIB au Burkina Faso, au Sénégal et en Tunisie (graphique 2.15).

Recettes diverses ou non identifiées

Certaines recettes non fiscales représentent des montants significatifs, mais ne relèvent d'aucune des catégories citées ci-dessus. Il s'agit notamment :

1. des transferts de capitaux non pris en compte par ailleurs ;
2. des dons volontaires à des organismes publics de la part de particuliers ou de sociétés (à l'exception des dons émanant d'organisations internationales comme le FMI, qui relèvent de la catégorie des dons) ;

3. des indemnités d'assurance versées aux administrations publiques ;
4. des versements couvrant différentes catégories de la classification et pour lesquels aucune ventilation n'est disponible ;
5. des paiements qu'il n'est pas possible de classer de façon appropriée faute de données pertinentes. Le Rwanda n'a pas fourni de ventilation de ses recettes non fiscales, en dehors des dons, de sorte que ces paiements ont été comptabilisés dans cette catégorie ;
6. des recettes versées par la SACU au Botswana et à l'Eswatini.

Graphique 2.15. **Amendes, pénalités et confiscations en pourcentage du PIB, 2012-16**

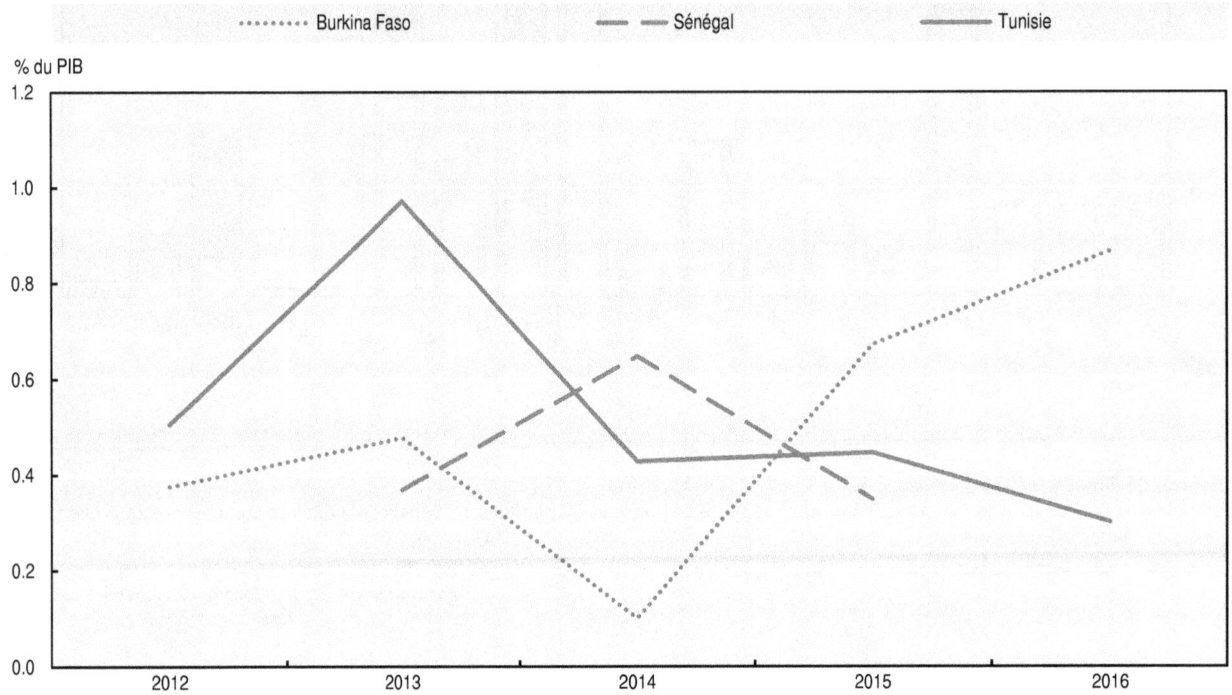

Source : Données comparatives des *Statistiques des recettes publiques en Afrique* disponibles à *https://doi.org/10.1787/7f54581d-fr.*

StatLink *https://doi.org/10.1787/888933819955*

Les recettes diverses et non identifiées peuvent représenter une composante non négligeable des recettes non fiscales de certains pays (graphique 2.16). Elles recouvrent notamment les contributions volontaires exceptionnelles versées à l'administration en Tunisie, les versements effectués au bénéfice de l'administration en contrepartie du droit à entrer en concurrence avec des institutions publiques pour la fourniture de services au Maroc, et les transferts de capitaux depuis des fonds statutaires spéciaux à Maurice. Les recettes reversées par la SACU représentent plus de 90 % du total des recettes de l'Eswatini au titre de la plupart des années considérées.

La variabilité des recettes diverses et non identifiées qui ressort du graphique 2.16 peut être imputable à des transferts de capitaux importants, à des entrées de recettes éphémères ou à des reclassifications de fonds dans la catégorie des recettes non identifiées en raison de l'absence de données. La présence de montants élevés dans cette rubrique pourrait conduire à s'interroger sur la précision des montants inscrits dans les autres catégories de recettes non fiscales. Les données disponibles sont insuffisantes pour mener une analyse concluante des écarts constatés.

Graphique 2.16. **Recettes diverses et non identifiées en pourcentage du total des recettes non fiscales, 2000-16**

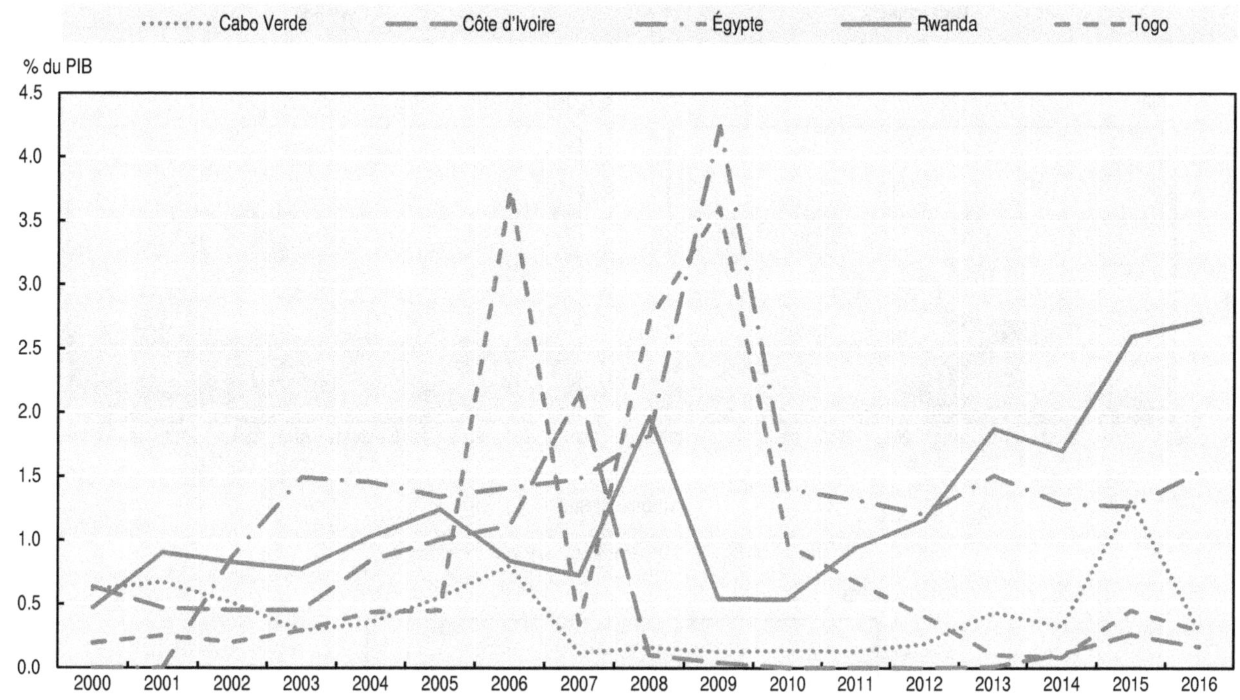

Note : Pour Rwanda, les chiffres relatifs aux revenus de la propriété, aux ventes de biens et de services et aux amendes, pénalités et confiscations sont pris en compte dans les recettes diverses et non identifiées. Ces données n'ont pu être désagrégées aux fins d'affecter les recettes aux catégories de recettes non fiscales concernées.

Source : Calculs des auteurs à partir de données présentées dans les tableaux 6.5-6.25 et tableau 4.17.

StatLink *https://doi.org/10.1787/888933819974*

Quatre pays non membres de la SACU ont perçu des recettes non fiscales diverses et non identifiées équivalant à plus de 2 % du PIB au moins une fois depuis 2000. Dans le cas du Cabo Verde, de la Côte d'Ivoire et du Togo, on a observé des hausses de courte durée : ces recettes n'ont pas représenté l'équivalent de plus de 1 % du PIB pendant plus de trois ans. Pour le Rwanda, les recettes non identifiées et diverses incluaient toutes les recettes non fiscales enregistrées en dehors des dons et ont connu une tendance à la hausse ces cinq dernières années, atteignant 2.7 % du PIB en 2016. Les recettes non fiscales diverses ou non identifiées pour l'Égypte sont restées supérieures à 1% du PIB chaque année depuis 2003 et, en 2009, elles ont atteint 4.2 % du PIB, soit plus que tout autre pays dans ce rapport.

Recettes liées à l'Union douanière d'Afrique australe

L'Union douanière d'Afrique australe compte cinq pays membres, à savoir le Lesotho, la Namibie et trois pays couverts par les *Statistiques des recettes publiques en Afrique*, l'Afrique du Sud, le Botswana et l'Eswatini (voir encadré 2.3). Elle prévoit la perception conjointe et le partage de l'ensemble des droits de douane et d'accise ; les recettes correspondantes n'ont pas les mêmes effets sur les différents pays membres de l'Union douanière couverts par la présente publication.

Les recettes reversées à l'Eswatini par la SACU ont été inférieures aux recettes fiscales recouvrées par le pays sur seulement 8 des 20 dernières années et elles ont représenté jusqu'à 23 % du PIB en 2006 (graphique 2.17). Les recettes reversées par la SACU à l'Afrique du Sud n'ont jamais excédé 4.5 % du PIB, ni 18 % de ses recettes fiscales. Le Botswana a perçu des recettes non négligeables de la part de la SACU, mais celles-ci ont été inférieures à d'autres recettes non fiscales sur 11 des 13 dernières années.

Graphique 2.17. **Recettes fiscales, recettes non fiscales et recettes provenant du fonds SACU pour l'Afrique du Sud, le Botswana et l'Eswatini[2] en pourcentage du PIB**

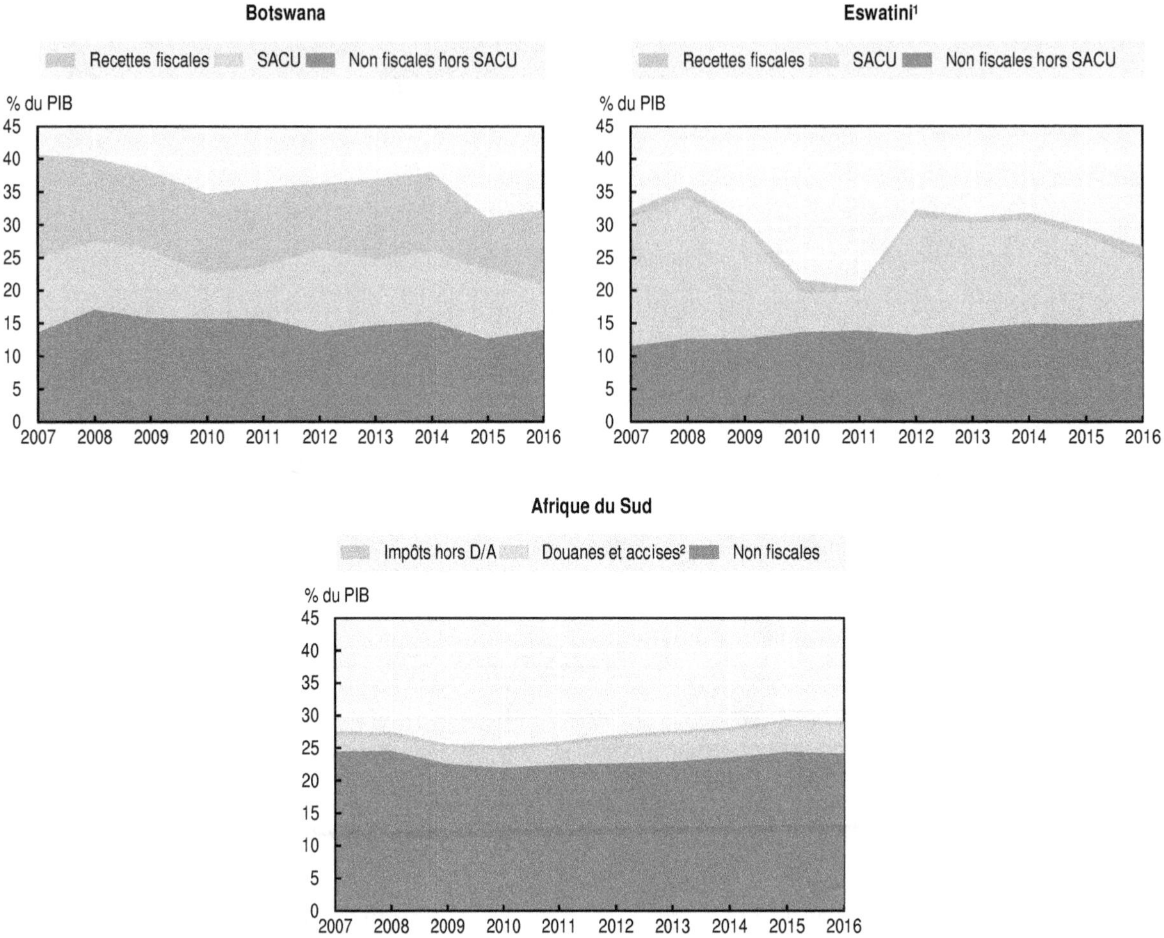

1. Swaziland dans les éditions précédentes.
2. Les droits de douane et d'accise, exprimés en pourcentage du PIB, prennent en compte les paiements effectués par l'Afrique du Sud en faveur des autres pays membres de la SACU qui ne sont pas considérés comme des recettes selon la définition de l'OCDE. Les paiements effectués au bénéfice de la SACU représentent environ 1 % du PIB de l'Afrique du Sud.

Source : Données comparatives des *Statistiques des recettes publiques en Afrique* disponibles à *https://doi.org/10.1787/7f54581d-fr*.

StatLink *https://doi.org/10.1787/888933819993*

Lorsque l'on compare l'Afrique du Sud, le Botswana et l'Eswatini, le traitement des recettes reversées par la SACU doit être considéré avec prudence. Les trois pays participent au système de regroupement et de redistribution des recettes de la SACU, et la fraction de ces recettes qu'ils perçoivent est calculée en appliquant la même formule. Cependant, le Botswana et l'Eswatini sont des bénéficiaires nets des recettes centralisées par la SACU alors que l'Afrique du Sud reverse davantage de recettes à la SACU qu'elle n'en reçoit d'elle.

Encadré 2.3. **Recettes issues de l'Union douanière d'Afrique australe**

L'Union douanière d'Afrique australe (South African Customs Union, SACU) regroupe l'Afrique du Sud, le Botswana, l'Eswatini, le Lesotho et la Namibie, et son siège est établi à Windhoek, en Namibie. Cette union douanière vise à établir « une communauté économique qui favorise un développement équitable et durable, au service du bien-être des peuples, pour construire un avenir commun ».

La SACU, qui est la plus ancienne union douanière au monde, a été créée en 1899 entre la colonie britannique du Cap de Bonne-Espérance et la République boer de l'État libre d'Orange. Des accords conclus par la suite, en 1910 puis en 1969, ont marqué l'adhésion du Botswana, de l'Eswatini et du Lesotho. À la suite de l'accession à l'indépendance de la Namibie, en 1990, et à la fin de l'apartheid en Afrique du Sud, en 1994, de nouvelles négociations ont été ouvertes pour aboutir à la conclusion, en 2002, de l'accord en vigueur à ce jour.

Cet accord prévoit la libre circulation entre les pays membres de la SACU de tous les produits manufacturés fabriqués dans ces pays, en franchise de droits. Il définit également des droits de douanes extérieurs communs et la mise en commun des droits de douane et d'accise, en vue de leur partage entre les pays membres de la SACU suivant la formule de répartition des recettes qui figure en annexe à l'Accord.

Les règles de partage des recettes comprennent trois composantes :

- une composante douanière, qui divise le montant brut des droits de douane en fonction de la valeur des marchandises importées par chaque pays depuis les autres pays membres de la SACU au cours de l'année considérée (en pourcentage des importations totales intra-SACU) ;
- une composante portant sur les droits d'accise, qui divise le montant brut de ces droits selon le ratio correspondant au PIB de chaque pays rapporté au PIB total de la SACU ; et
- une composante de développement, financée par 15 % de la composante liée aux droits d'accise, et pondérée en faveur des pays moins développés de la SACU selon une formule fondée sur le PIB par habitant.

Dans la présente publication, les recettes tirées des droits de douane et d'accise sont comptabilisées dans les recettes fiscales du pays qui les a collectées. Elles sont rapportées dans les rubriques 5121 (accises) et 5123 (droits de douane et droits à l'importation) des tableaux des recettes fiscales. Les montants redistribués par la SACU sont classés dans les tableaux des recettes non fiscales, dans la catégorie des recettes diverses et non identifiées, comme le montre le tableau 6.13 dans le cas de l'Eswatini. Pour l'Afrique du Sud, qui est un contributeur net au mécanisme de la SACU, les contributions, nettes des reversements perçus, sont mentionnées pour mémoire dans le tableau des recettes non fiscales (tableau 6.22).

Sources : (SACU, 2017[5]), (SACU, 2014[6]).

Notes

1. Il n'y a pas de comparaison possible avec les moyennes des 25 pays d'Amérique latine et des Caraïbes (ALC) (voir (OCDE/ECLAC/CIAT/IDB, 2017[8])) et de 35 pays de l'OCDE (voir (OCDE, 2017[7])) car les publications correspondantes ne couvrent pas les recettes non fiscales.
2. Se reporter au Guide d'interprétation sur les recettes non fiscales figurant à l'annexe B du présent rapport pour la définition de ces catégories de recettes.
3. Le coefficient de variation est un indicateur de dispersion obtenu en divisant l'écart-type par la moyenne arithmétique.

4. La définition officielle de l'APD est la suivante : tous les apports de ressources qui sont fournis aux pays et territoires figurant sur la Liste des bénéficiaires d'APD établie par le Comité d'aide au développement ou à des institutions multilatérales et qui émanent d'organismes publics, y compris des États et des collectivités locales, ou d'organismes agissant pour le compte d'organismes publics, sachant que chaque opération doit en outre avoir pour but essentiel de favoriser le développement économique et l'amélioration du niveau de vie des pays en développement, et être assortie de conditions favorables et comporter un élément de libéralité au moins égal à 25 % (sur la base d'un taux d'actualisation de 10 %). On peut trouver d'autres informations utiles à l'adresse suivante : *www.oecd.org/dac/financing-sustainable-development/index-terms.htm#ODA*
5. Une liste complète des pays et organisations qui notifient des statistiques au CAD peut être trouvée à l'adresse suivante : *www.oecd.org/dac/financing-sustainable-development/development-finance-standards/dacdatasubmitters.htm*
6. La Banque mondiale fait référence aux « bénéfices tirés des ressources naturelles ». Ceux-ci correspondent à la différence entre la valeur des ressources naturelles produites dans les pays qui est fonction des prix des matières premières et le coût estimé de l'extraction des ressources. Il convient de ne pas confondre avec la définition de « rente de ressource » utilisée par l'OCDE pour laquelle il s'agit d'une recette publique. Pour plus de détails, veuillez-vous reporter au Guide d'interprétation.
7. Pour plus de précisions sur la classification des redevances administratives, consulter, à l'annexe A, les paragraphes 9 à 13 du Guide d'interprétation de l'OCDE.

Références

BAfD/OCDE/CEA (2010), *Perspectives économiques en Afrique 2010*, Éditions OCDE, Paris, *http://dx.doi.org/10.1787/aeo-2010-fr*. [1]

CUA/OCDE (2018), *Dynamiques du développement en Afrique 2018 : Croissance, emploi et inégalités*, Commission de l'Union Africaine/Éditions OCDE, Addis Abeba/Paris, *https://doi.org/10.1787/9789264302525-fr*. [4]

FMI (2016), *Heavily indebted poor countries (HIPC) initiative and multilateral debt relief initiative (MDRI): Statistical update*, Fonds monétaire international, *http://www.imf.org/en/Publications/Policy-Papers/Issues/2016/12/31/Heavily-Indebted-Poor-Countries-Initiative-and-Multilateral-Debt-Relief-Initiative-PP5024*. [2]

OCDE (2017), *Statistiques des recettes publiques : 1965-2016*, Éditions OCDE, Paris, *http://dx.doi.org/10.1787/9789264283206-fr*. [7]

OCDE (à paraître), *Global Outlook on Financing for Development*, Éditions OCDE, Paris. [3]

OCDE/ECLAC/CIAT/IDB (2017), *Revenue Statistics in Latin America and the Caribbean*, Édition OCDE, *http://dx.doi.org/10.1787/rev_lat_car-2017-en-fr*. [8]

SACU (2017), *Southern African Customs Union Agreement 2002 (As amended on 12 April 2013)*, *http://www.sacu.int/list.php?type=Agreements*. [5]

SACU (2014), *Implementing a Common Agenda Towards Regional Integration: 2014 Annual Report*, *http://www.sacu.int/docs/reports_annual/2014/annual_report.pdf*. [6]

Chapter 3

SPECIAL FEATURE

Strategy for the Harmonisation of Statistics in Africa (SHaSA): 2017-2026

Chapitre 3

ÉTUDE SPÉCIALE

Stratégie pour l'harmonisation des statistiques en Afrique (SHaSA) : 2017-2026

Revenue Statistics in Africa 1990-2016/Statistiques des recettes publiques en Afrique 1990-2016

Chapter 3

SPECIAL FEATURE

Strategy for the Harmonisation of Statistics in Africa (SHaSA): 2017-2026

The Strategy for the Harmonisation of Statistics in Africa (SHaSA) was adopted with its action plan, financing plan and resource mobilisation strategy by the 30th Summit of Heads of State and Government of the African Union, 28-29 January 2018, Addis Ababa, Ethiopia, as the single continental programme for statistical development in Africa for the next 10 years. It is the result of the efforts of the African Statistics System[1] under the auspices of Pan-African organisations (African Union Commission, African Development Bank, United Nations Economic Commission for Africa and African Capacity Building Foundation). *Revenue Statistics in Africa* is a tool for the development of tax policy and an important area of SHaSA.

Background and rationale of SHaSA

Many African countries have made tremendous efforts to lift their people out of poverty and improve their living conditions. Great strides have been made in various domains. The African continent has achieved the second-highest economic growth rate in the world, behind only Southeast Asia; at the same time, the poverty rate has reduced and socioeconomic indicators have improved in recent years. Despite these improvements, over 40% of African populations continue to live in conditions of extreme poverty and many countries are struggling to reap the benefits of growth. This is due to the fact that African growth is largely driven by the export of raw materials and is not experienced equally across African societies. Most youth are unemployed or working in the informal sector.

Mindful of this disturbing situation, during the celebration of the Fiftieth Anniversary of the African Union in May 2013, Africa recommitted itself through Agenda 2063 to focus on its people in order to define the Africa of tomorrow. Agenda 2063 was then adopted in 2015, as a long-term strategic framework which aims essentially at building a prosperous, integrated and peaceful Africa. The same year, the international community adopted the 2030 Agenda for Sustainable Development which aims at eradicating poverty in all its forms and dimensions and ensuring sustainable development. Alongside these international agendas, many countries and Regional Economic Communities (RECs) are pursuing the implementation of Agenda 2063 and 2030 Agenda through their own development vision and plans.

However, the scarcity of financing has always been a major constraint to development in many African countries where traditional sources of financing have not proven to have an effective impact on development because of unreliability, inadequacy and lack of sustainability. Many development plans and programmes have failed because of the lack of adequate financial resources for their implementation. Domestic resources mobilised through tax collection remain insufficient. In 2016, the average tax-to-GDP ratio for the 21 African countries participating in *Revenue Statistics in Africa* was 18.2%, which is largely below the ratios in developed economies. Only three African countries have tax-to-GDP levels above the average of Latin American countries, at 22.7%. Although aid for development from external partners has been beneficial in supporting development programmes in the region, it is, however, below expectation and its future prospect is uncertain because of the economic slowdown in many of external partners. As a result, there are enormous unmet financing needs to achieve sustainable development in developing countries.

To implement these ambitious agendas in the continent, it is essential to reform the tax system and promote tax culture among the population in order to improve tax-to-GDP ratios in all African countries to provide resources to achieve sustainable development.

Furthermore, the monitoring and evaluation of the implementation of these agendas with a view to attaining the objectives and measuring the results, not only requires African countries to produce quality disaggregated statistical data, accessible in a timely manner to ensure that nobody is left behind, but also to produce harmonised data across the continent to allow for cross-country comparisons.

In recent years, many development initiatives on statistics in Africa have been undertaken. This has led to breakthroughs notably in the domain of the production of quality statistics to enlighten political decisions and to support the implementation of national programmes, and continental and international development agendas.

Despite the progress made, there are still a number of difficulties faced by the African Statistics System in terms of measuring topical issues such as governance, peace and security, environment, climate change, public revenue, etc. Statistics are produced based on methodologies that do not always reflect African realities and are not always comparable from one country to another. This situation is linked to a certain number of obstacles including in particular: insufficient resources allocated to statistical activities, lack of institutional capacity, the low production and quality of statistics on the continent, insufficient statistical coverage in the different sectors, inadequate coordination of statistical activities and insufficient consideration given to African specificities during the definition of international norms. The statistics harmonisation programmes of Regional Economic Communities (REC) vary from one region to the other and scarcely meet the needs for harmonised statistics. It is therefore expected that the African Statistics System will make increased efforts towards the continental integration of statistics in order to meet the needs of the continent in the domain of harmonised and quality statistical information.

The review and updating of SHaSA aims at addressing all of these attendant challenges and at supporting the African integration programme alongside national, regional, continental and international development agendas. *Revenue Statistics in Africa* is key in the implementation of SHaSA, as it improves the quality and comparability of revenue statistics in the region through a product tailored to the needs of tax policy makers in African countries, while maintaining consistency with international standards.

Strategy for the Harmonisation of Statistics in Africa: Vision, themes and strategic objectives

The vision of the African Statistical System has been defined as an efficient statistical system that generates reliable, harmonised and timely statistical information covering all dimensions of political, economic, social, environmental and cultural development and integration of Africa.

The vision is based on four strategic themes, which are to: (i) produce quality statistics for Africa; (ii) co-ordinate the production of quality statistics for Africa; (iii) develop sustainable institutional capacity of the African Statistical System; and (iv) promote a culture of quality policy and decision making.

Themes and strategic objectives

SHaSA aims at achieving the vision outlined above by pursuing the strategic themes and objectives that are set out in the table below.

Table 3.1. **Strategic themes and objectives of SHaSA**

Code	Strategic theme	Objectives
1	Strategic theme 1	Produce quality statistics for Africa
1.1	*Strategic objective 1.1*	*Expand the statistical information base*
1.2	*Strategic objective 1.2*	*Transform the existing statistics for comparability*
1.3	*Strategic objective 1.3*	*Harmonise the standards and methods of statistical production*
2.	Strategic theme 2	Co-ordinate the production of quality statistics for Africa
2.1	*Strategic objective 2.1*	*Establish effective co-ordination and collaboration mechanisms*
2.2	*Strategic objective 2.2*	*Define the statistical priorities for the implementation of the integration and development agendas*
3.	Strategic theme 3	Develop sustainable institutional capacity in the African Statistical System
3.1	*Strategic objective 3.1*	*Reform and enhance national statistical systems*
3.2	*Strategic objective 3.2*	*Reform and enhance regional and continental statistical systems*
3.3	*Strategic objective 3.3*	*Develop sustainable statistical capacities*
3.4	*Strategic objective 3.4*	*Establish an effective technological environment*
4.	Strategic theme 4	Promote a culture of quality policy and decision-making
4.1	*Strategic objective 4.1*	*Drive evidence-based decisions through the increased use of statistics*
4.2	*Strategic objective 4.2*	*Improve the communication of statistical information*

(i) Strategic theme 1: Produce quality statistics for Africa

The first strategic theme is a clear approach to ensure the availability of information in all domains of development and integration.

Strategic objective 1.1: Expand the statistical information base: to cover all the domains of development and integration, as well as to adapt the production of statistics to align to the economic structures and activities of Member States of the African Union. This will entail a number of varied approaches, namely: the regular conduct of surveys on population and households, agricultural censuses, economic surveys, the strengthening and exploitation of administrative sources, including civil status registration, the development of trade registers, geographic frames, big data, and local administrative sources.

Strategic objective 1.2: Transform the existing statistics for comparability: This requires the adoption of methodologies for reprocessing and adjustment, and the production and validation of comparable data, enabling quality decision-making in support of development programs and integration.

Strategic objective 1.3: Harmonise the norms and methods of the production of statistics: This objective seeks to adapt international norms and methods to African realities to increase availability of harmonised statistical data, in support of the integration and development programmes.

(ii) Strategic theme 2: Co-ordinate the production of quality statistics for Africa

Uncoordinated interventions of different actors not only lead to the duplication of activities, but also to the ineffective use of the scarce resources.

Strategic objective 2.1: Put in place effective co-ordination and collaboration mechanisms. This implies (i) the implementation of a protocol defining the roles and responsibilities of each actor of the African Statistical System, (ii) the strengthening of the African Statistical Coordination Committee and (iii) the co-operation between the different actors.

Strategic objective 2.2: Define the statistical priorities for the implementation of the integration and development agendas. The identification of priority statistics and the selection and definition of statistical indicators will lead to a harmonised work programme for the African Statistical System.

(iii) Strategic theme 3: Develop the sustainable institutional capacity of the African Statistical System

Building the capacity of the African Statistical System lies at the heart of this strategy because in its absence, the members of the African Statistical System will not be able to produce and disseminate quality and harmonised statistics that are necessary for development and the integration process.

Strategic objective 3.1: Reform and strengthen national statistical systems. Activities at the national level include: the adoption of statistics laws and regulatory frameworks conforming to the African Charter on Statistics; the development of a professional Code of Ethics for African statisticians; the integration of statistics into national development processes; the development and implementation of National Strategies for the Development of Statistics (NSDSs), leading to better planning, sustainable development, and improved co-ordination of statistical activities.

Strategic objective 3.2: Reform and strengthen regional and continental statistical systems, including: the creation of units in charge of statistics in the Secretariats of RECs that do not yet have them (CEN-SAD, IGAD); the strengthening of the statistical functions of RECs; and the operationalisation of the Institute of Statistics of the African Union (STATAFRIC). The key expected outcomes are harmonised programmes and better co-ordination of statistical development across the continent.

Strategic objective 3.3: Develop sustainable statistical capacity through the development of a harmonised training programme; the establishment and strengthening of in-service training centres within National Statistical Offices (NSOs); the strengthening of statistics and demographic training schools and centres; the operationalisation of the Pan-African Training Center for Statistics; etc.

Strategic objective 3.4: Establish an effective technological environment; for example, Management Information Systems (MIS) to ensure (i) the monitoring of the integration programme; (ii) the creation of a statistical database; and (iii) the standardisation of dissemination tools and platforms.

(iv) Strategic theme 4: Promote a culture of quality policy and decision-making

A lack of appreciation of the importance of statistics can lead to underfunding by governments of crucial statistical initiatives, leading to the low level of up-to-date and reliable statistics across the continent.

Strategic objective 4.1: Take decisions based on facts through the increased use of statistics. This objective will be realised by approaching decision-makers and policy makers to advocate for the use of statistics in their speeches and policy making.

Strategic objective 4.2: Improve the communication of statistical information. This implies the development of a strategy for the dissemination of data and a communications plan, which will culminate in the increased use of statistics and an improvement in the quality of policies and decisions.

SHaSA, *Revenue Statistics in Africa* and domestic resource mobilisation

In the same spirit as SHaSA, *Revenue Statistics in Africa* originated from the need to have high-quality statistics to inform public policy and reforms. It connects two broad objectives for African countries: improving tax statistics and mobilising domestic resources, both of which are highlighted in the African Union's *Agenda 2063* as well as in the Sustainable Development Goals. Improving statistics on government revenues will allow countries and international organisations to track progress and shape strategies to increase public revenues in a sustainable, equitable and efficient way. The harmonisation of revenue data also enables countries to compare their tax structures and revenue flows over time and with other countries, creating appetite and opportunities for peer learning.

The availability of free, easy-to-access data also increases transparency and creates an opportunity for greater public accountability both at the national and international levels, which in turn can incentivise better governance and policies in participating countries. Finally, participating in an international initiative can enhance the credibility and strengthen the ability of African countries to raise additional development resources with international investors and external partners.

Revenue Statistics in Africa promotes the vision of the African Statistical System and the four strategic themes of SHaSA. In particular, it contributes to:

- produce quality statistics for Africa through the transformation of national statistics into a set of comparable statistics on tax- and non-tax revenues for African countries. These statistics are produced according to the classification principles of the OECD Interpretative Guide, which is harmonised with all major national accounting standards. Once harmonised, the statistics allow for direct comparisons among African countries and with countries from other regions participating in *Revenue Statistics*. The data also feeds into a single database publicly available for free.
- co-ordinate the production of quality statistics for Africa through the collaborative approach between African countries and regional partner organisations whereby they collectively build and validate the data for each country, with processes, deliverables, roles and responsibilities clearly defined for each party. The success of the approach lies in continuous and iterative dialogue that is completed with the final validation by countries on their statistics.
- develop sustainable institutional capacity of the African Statistical System through an annual training provided during technical workshops for African statistical and tax officials. Regular technical exchanges with each country on the classification of their revenue categories builds capacity of African tax administrations on the harmonisation of data.
- promote a culture of quality policy and decision-making through the easily accessible presentation of comparable revenue statistics across countries and the monitoring of the impacts of key policy reforms on revenue mobilisation. By examining the quantitative impacts of these reforms from a granular to an aggregated level of revenue category and over time, tax policy makers are better equipped to plan tax policy and administration reforms. They are also better able to compare themselves with countries in their region and beyond.

In sum, the *Revenue Statistics' Interpretative Guide* presents a framework for Pan-African harmonisation of revenue statistics. This provides a concrete framework that can inform and support SHaSA, which is a major step forward in providing a common and exhaustive framework for the harmonisation of statistics in all areas of public policy across Africa.

SHaSA governance and implementation

Governance

A framework of governance structures has been developed for the implementation, monitoring and evaluation of SHaSA, as well as regular reporting on its implementation progress. This mechanism defines the roles of governance organisations, taking into account their existing capacities and their particular areas of expertise and strengths, in accordance with the principle of subsidiarity.

Implementation mechanism

Specialised Technical Groups (STGs): They will be revitalised in order to continue their activities in each identified statistical area under the co-ordination of countries and the responsibility of the AU Statistical Institute. The STGs will prepare and implement sectoral action plans for statistical harmonisation in the area concerned; they will develop and/or adopt international standards and methodological guidelines for statistical harmonisation in their respective fields. The AU Institute for Statistics will assist African countries in the implementation of these standards and methodologies. The STG on Public finance, Private Sector and Investment statistics which include revenue statistics should start its work in order to come up with a roadmap including concrete activities to define and adopt norms, methods, and classifications to produce quality and harmonised revenue statistics across all African countries.

Lead countries or champions: The lead countries or champions will be designated to lead on the STGs. Pan-African institutions will provide the secretariat for the various groups. STATAFRIC will establish the programmes of activities of the STGs (see unabridged SHaSA-2 document for list of countries).

The African Union Institute for Statistics (STATAFRIC): It will be the Secretariat for SHaSA implementation. It will co-ordinate the work of the STGs, carry out technical audits of RECs. Harmonisation, production, and validation of official statistical data across Africa will be the exclusive responsibility of STATAFRIC.

The Pan-African Statistical Training Centre: It will be a complementary structure to existing schools and training centres and will fill the missing links in training programmes.

Enhanced partnerships for the implementation of SHaSA

This new statistical landscape calls for other types of partnerships, notably with the private sector, which can contribute to the financing of statistics, foundations, civil society, development partners, researchers, academics, media and journalists, and users, among others, both inside and outside the African continent. *Revenue Statistics in Africa* is an example of a new type of partnership, where a new community of practice and new relationships can be built from a focus on a concrete goal and tangible results. This serves not only to fulfil current data needs but also to set up more efficient processes for future projects.

Political will, leadership and behaviour change

To ensure that the African Statistical System works as effectively and efficiently as possible over the coming years and is able to meet the increased demand for data, political leaders will be required to prioritise quality, timely, reliable, and harmonised statistical production across the continent.

Fostering political will and commitment

To signal political will and commitment, the African Union Commission will continue to advocate for all countries that have not yet ratified the African Charter on Statistics to do so as soon as possible; and to invite Member States to adapt their national statistical laws to the requirements of the Charter.

It is widely accepted that large-scale statistical activities such as censuses and surveys require considerable resources. Over the past 30 years, 7 countries have not conducted any population and housing census, and 19 countries have failed to take a census regularly every 10 years (AfDB/OECD/UNDP, $2015_{[1]}$). However, there are countless less costly activities that are necessary to ensure the effective functioning of statistical systems, such as the promotion of the utilisation of administrative data sources.

The decision of the Heads of State and Government to allocate 0.15% of the national budget each year to statistical activities is therefore welcome. However, to make commitments such as this will not be sufficient to create sustainable statistical systems unless it is put into action and made concrete in budget decisions, as recalled at the 4th Conference of African Ministers responsible for Civil Registration and Vital Statistics in Nouakchott, December 2017. South Africa has met this target by allocating 0.19% of its 2018 budget to statistics.

Political commitment to increased resource allocation would help to revolutionise the production of statistics. However, political leaders must also commit to improved advocacy for statistics and their effective use. Political actors have an important role to play in elevating the importance of statistics by promoting their use in key policy- and decision-making processes.

Leadership

At the national level, it is firstly incumbent on NSOs Directors-General to play the role of co-ordinators and ensure the harmonisation of statistics across the entire national statistical systems (NSS). This activity is one of the major priorities – if not the most important priority – of SHaSA. At present, the low level of political commitment to statistics has resulted in the continent facing a chronic deficit in statistical financing, with only about 20% of the needs provided for by national resources. This high dependence on external resources does not allow for efficient strategic planning of statistical activities and makes it very difficult to implement NSDSs. Moreover, outsourcing production of national statistics may undermine countries' capacity to build their own statistical infrastructure over time.

In the chain of continental harmonisation and co-ordination, RECs have an important role to play through the implementation of their integration policies, which are often accompanied by regional convergence mechanisms. It must be recognised however that at present, some RECs have little statistical capacity of their own.

At the continental level, mindful of the fact that SHaSA constitutes the roadmap for STATAFRIC and the Pan-African Centre for Statistics Training, Pan-African institutions should continue to work in a complementary manner. In this regard, the AUC, which has been mandated to assume political leadership of the African Statistical System and which has elevated the role of statistics to the highest level of Heads of State and Government of the continent, will continue to play this role for the implementation of SHaSA.

Behaviour change

Implementation of SHaSA calls for profound behaviour change across the African Statistical System, most notably among statisticians themselves, particularly at the national level. Approaching their work as unbiased scientists with a commitment to a clear explanation of working methods and utilising methodologies in a transparent way, statisticians must begin to see their role as integral to the functioning of country economies and societies. In addition, they must ensure that statistical products are delivered to users in a timely manner and according to pre-agreed and communicated timetables in order to increase the relevance and credibility of these products.

While the new demands being placed on statisticians are considerable, statisticians should also view the elevated importance placed on statistics as an opportunity to improve statistical production. They should, therefore, be open to embracing innovations. As NSS become more inclusive, it will be necessary for statisticians and managers of statistical systems to build and sustain partnerships with diverse actors drawn from academia, the media, development partners, civil society, and the private sector. The NSS leadership must capitalise on political will and ensure that statistics are prioritised at the highest levels and remain an issue of national sovereignty.

At the regional level, members of the statistical divisions at the RECs must prioritise the drafting and implementation of Regional Strategies for Statistics Development in line with their regional integration programmes, and interact more effectively with Member States of the African Union throughout these processes.

At the continental level, all actors involved in supporting institutions must continue to regard statistical development and harmonisation as matters of the highest priority, with resulting actions such as the resourcing of the continental institutions.

Conclusion

While responding to the demand of policy makers and users to have harmonised quality statistics necessary for the implementation of the integration and development programmes of the continent, SHaSA also responds to the need for the African Statistical System to have a tool for the harmonisation of statistical activities in Africa. The successful implementation of SHaSA depends on: (i) the need for the political will at the highest level of the continent; (ii) the commitment of the members of the African Statistics System including the heads of national, regional and continental statistical systems, (iii) the operationalisation of the AU Institute for Statistics and the Pan-African Statistical Training Centre, (iv) the change of behaviour of statistical actors on the continent, (v) the implementation of the roadmap for the data revolution; and (vi) the mobilisation of adequate resources to finance the implementation of the action plan. Continuous and active advocacy at all levels, dissemination and monitoring and evaluation of SHaSA with regular reports of the governance bodies are also critical for its effective implementation.

In the area of public revenues, *Revenue Statistics in Africa* is already helping to advance the implementation of SHaSA and can provide useful lessons for harmonisation of statistics in other areas of public policy. It provides comprehensive and high-quality statistics on public revenues for African countries, it is based on a framework for harmonisation of revenue statistics that could be expanded to the entire continent, it builds statistical capacity through annual training on classifying public revenues and it informs evidence-based policy and decision-making in participating countries.

Note

1. According to article 1 of the African Charter on Statistics (entry into force: February 2015), the African Statistical System is: "the partnership composed of national statistical systems (data providers, producers and users, statistics research and training institutes and statistics coordination bodies, etc.), statistics units in the Regional Economic Communities (RECs), regional statistics organisations, regional training centres, statistics units of continental organisations and co-ordination bodies at continental level." (*https://au.int/sites/default/files/treaties/7794-treaty-0037_-_african_charter_on_statistics_e.pdf*)

Reference

AfDB/OECD/UNDP (2015), *African Economic Outlook 2015: Regional Development and Spatial Inclusion*, OECD Publishing, Paris, *https://doi.org/10.1787/aeo-2015-en*. [1]

Revenue Statistics in Africa 1990-2016/Statistiques des recettes publiques en Afrique 1990-2016

Chapitre 3

ÉTUDE SPÉCIALE

Stratégie pour l'harmonisation des statistiques en Afrique (SHaSA) : 2017-2026

La Stratégie pour l'harmonisation des statistiques en Afrique (SHaSA), ainsi que son plan d'action, son plan de financement et sa stratégie de mobilisation des ressources, ont été adoptés par l'Assemblée des chefs d'État et de gouvernement de l'Union Africaine lors de sa 30e Session ordinaire, à Addis-Abeba, en Éthiopie, à titre de programme unique de développement de la statistique à l'échelle du continent africain pour les dix prochaines années. C'est le résultat des efforts déployés par le Système statistique africain[1], sous l'égide des organisations panafricaines (Commission de l'Union Africaine, Banque africaine de développement, Commission économique de l'ONU pour l'Afrique et Fondation pour le renforcement des capacités en Afrique). Les *Statistiques des recettes publiques en Afrique* sont un outil pour élaborer la politique fiscale, et couvrent un important domaine de la SHaSA.

SHaSA : Contexte et justification

De nombreux pays africains ont déployé des efforts considérables pour sortir leur population de la pauvreté et améliorer leurs conditions de vie. Des progrès significatifs ont été accomplis dans divers domaines. Ainsi, la croissance économique du continent africain se classe au deuxième rang mondial, n'étant précédée que par celle de l'Asie du Sud-Est. Dans le même temps, le taux de pauvreté a reculé, et les indicateurs socioéconomiques se sont améliorés ces dernières années. En dépit de ces améliorations, plus de 40 % de la population africaine continue de vivre dans l'extrême pauvreté, et nombre de pays ne profitent guère des fruits de la croissance. La raison en est que la croissance africaine est en grande partie tirée par les exportations de matières premières et n'est pas également répartie dans les sociétés africaines. Qui plus est, la plupart des jeunes n'ont pas d'emploi ou travaillent dans le secteur informel.

Face à cette situation préoccupante, à l'occasion de la célébration du cinquantième anniversaire de l'Union Africaine, en mai 2013, l'Afrique s'est réengagée, au travers de son Agenda 2063, à se concentrer sur sa population pour définir l'Afrique de demain. Adopté en 2015, l'Agenda 2063 est un cadre stratégique à long terme qui vise, pour l'essentiel, à construire une Afrique prospère, intégrée et en paix. La même année, la communauté internationale a adopté le Programme de développement durable à l'horizon 2030, dont le but est d'éradiquer la pauvreté sous toutes ses formes et dimensions et d'assurer un développement durable. Parallèlement à ces plans d'action internationaux, de nombreux pays et Communautés économiques régionales (CER) poursuivent la mise en œuvre de l'Agenda 2063 et du Programme 2030 au travers de leurs propres visions et plans de développement.

Cependant, le manque de financement a toujours été un frein majeur au développement pour de nombreux pays d'Afrique, où les sources classiques de financement n'ont pas produit d'effet réel sur le développement parce qu'elles se sont avérées peu fiables, insuffisantes et non durables. Nombre de plans et programmes de développement ont échoué à cause du manque de ressources financières pour les mettre en œuvre. Les ressources fiscales mobilisées par les pays demeurent insuffisantes. En 2016, le ratio moyen impôt/PIB, pour les 21 pays africains participant aux *Statistiques des recettes publiques en Afrique*, se montait à 18.2 %, c'est-à-dire un ratio largement inférieur à ce qu'il est dans les pays industrialisés. Seuls trois pays africains ont un ratio impôt/PIB comparable au ratio moyen des pays d'Amérique latine, soit 22.7 %. Bien que l'aide au développement fournie par les partenaires extérieurs ait été utile pour soutenir les programmes de développement sur le continent, elle est néanmoins inférieure aux attentes, et les perspectives en la matière sont incertaines, en raison du ralentissement économique enregistré par nombre de partenaires extérieurs. Par conséquent, il existe d'immenses besoins de financement non satisfaits, freinant la réalisation d'un développement durable dans les pays d'Afrique.

Pour que ces ambitieux programmes puissent se concrétiser, il est essentiel de réformer le système fiscal sur le continent et de promouvoir la culture de l'impôt dans la population, ce qui permettrait d'élever le ratio impôt/PIB dans tous les pays d'Afrique afin de dégager des ressources au profit du développement durable.

De plus, le suivi et l'évaluation de la mise en œuvre de ces programmes, qui permettront d'atteindre les objectifs et de mesurer les résultats, exigent non seulement que les pays africains produisent des données statistiques ventilées de bonne qualité, accessibles dans des délais raisonnables pour que personne ne soit laissé pour compte, mais aussi que des données harmonisées soient produites à l'échelle du continent à des fins de comparaisons internationales.

Ces dernières années, de nombreuses initiatives ont été lancées en matière de statistiques en Afrique. Elles ont abouti à des avancées notables, en particulier dans la production de statistiques de qualité, permettant d'éclairer les décisions politiques et de soutenir la mise en œuvre de programmes nationaux ainsi que de grands programmes de développement à l'échelle du continent et du monde entier.

En dépit des progrès accomplis, le Système statistique africain reste confronté à un certain nombre de difficultés pour mesurer des aspects qui se rapportent à des thématiques actuelles, comme la gouvernance, la paix et la sécurité, l'environnement, le changement climatique, les recettes publiques, etc. Les statistiques sont produites à l'aide de méthodes qui ne reflètent pas toujours les réalités africaines et qui ne sont pas toujours comparables d'un pays à l'autre. Cette situation est liée à un certain nombre d'obstacles, dont en particulier : l'insuffisance des ressources allouées aux activités statistiques, la pénurie de capacités institutionnelles, la faible production et qualité des statistiques sur le continent, le manque de couverture statistique dans les différents secteurs, le manque de coordination des activités statistiques et le fait que les spécificités de l'Afrique ne sont pas assez prises en considération au stade de la définition des normes internationales. Les programmes d'harmonisation des statistiques mis en œuvre par les CER varient d'une région à l'autre et ne répondent guère aux besoins de statistiques harmonisées. Il est donc attendu du Système statistique africain qu'il redouble d'efforts pour réaliser l'intégration des statistiques à l'échelle du continent, afin de répondre aux besoins d'informations statistiques harmonisées et de bonne qualité.

L'examen et la mise à jour de la stratégie SHaSA sont destinés à relever tous ces défis et à soutenir le programme d'intégration africaine parallèlement aux programmes de développement nationaux, régionaux, continentaux et mondiaux. Les *Statistiques des recettes publiques en Afrique* constituent un instrument clé dans la mise en œuvre de la SHaSA, car il s'agit d'un produit adapté aux besoins spécifiques des administrations fiscales des pays africains qui va améliorer la qualité et la comparabilité des statistiques des recettes publiques en Afrique tout en préservant la cohérence avec les normes internationales.

Stratégie pour l'harmonisation des statistiques en Afrique : Vision, thèmes et objectifs stratégiques

La vision stratégique pour le Système statistique africain est celle d'un système statistique efficient, qui génère des données fiables, harmonisées et disponibles en temps utile, couvrant toutes les dimensions – politiques, économiques, sociales, environnementales et culturelles – du développement et de l'intégration du continent africain.

Cette vision s'articule autour de quatre thèmes stratégiques, consistant à : i) produire des statistiques de qualité pour l'Afrique ; ii) coordonner la production de statistiques de qualité pour l'Afrique ; iii) renforcer durablement les capacités du Système statistique africain ; et iv) promouvoir une culture de la qualité en matière de politiques publiques et de prise de décision.

Thèmes et objectifs stratégiques

La SHaSA a pour but de réaliser la vision décrite ci-dessus en poursuivant les thèmes et objectifs stratégiques figurant dans le tableau ci-dessous.

Tableau 3.1. **Thèmes et objectifs stratégiques de la SHaSA**

Code	Thème stratégique	Objectif
1	Thème stratégique 1	Produire des statistiques de qualité pour l'Afrique
1.1	Objectif stratégique 1.1	Élargir la base de l'information statistique
1.2	Objectif stratégique 1.2	Transformer les statistiques existantes pour en assurer la comparabilité
1.3	Objectif stratégique 1.3	Harmoniser les normes et les méthodes de production statistique
2.	Thème stratégique 2	Coordonner la production de statistiques de qualité pour l'Afrique
2.1	Objectif stratégique 2.1	Mettre en place des mécanismes efficaces de coordination et de collaboration
2.2	Objectif stratégique 2.2	Définir les priorités statistiques en vue de la mise en œuvre des programmes d'intégration et de développement
3.	Thème stratégique 3	Renforcer durablement les capacités institutionnelles du Système statistique africain
3.1	Objectif stratégique 3.1	Réformer et renforcer les systèmes statistiques nationaux
3.2	Objectif stratégique 3.2	Réformer et renforcer les systèmes statistiques régionaux et continentaux
3.3	Objectif stratégique 3.3	Renforcer durablement les capacités statistiques
3.4	Objectif stratégique 3.4	Mettre en place un environnement technologique efficace
4.	Thème stratégique 4	Promouvoir une culture de la qualité en matière de politiques publiques et de prise de décision
4.1	Objectif stratégique 4.1	Encourager la prise de décisions fondées sur des données factuelles grâce au recours accru à la statistique
4.2	Objectif stratégique 4.2	Améliorer la communication des données statistiques

i) Thème stratégique 1 : produire des statistiques de qualité pour l'Afrique

Le premier thème stratégique constitue une approche claire visant à assurer la disponibilité de données statistiques dans tous les domaines du développement et de l'intégration.

Objectif stratégique 1.1 : Élargir la base de l'information statistique pour couvrir tous les domaines du développement et de l'intégration, mais aussi pour adapter la production des statistiques en fonction des structures et activités économiques des États membres de l'Union Africaine. Diverses approches seront suivies à cet effet : conduite régulière d'opérations de recensement de la population et d'enquêtes auprès des ménages, recensement agricole, enquêtes économiques, renforcement et exploitation des sources administratives dont l'état civil, développement de l'enregistrement des sociétés, cadres géographiques, données massives, et sources administratives locales.

Objectif stratégique 1.2 : Transformer les statistiques existantes pour en assurer la comparabilité. Cet objectif exige l'adoption de méthodologies de retraitement et d'ajustement, ainsi que la production et la validation de données comparables, ce qui contribuera à une prise de décision éclairée à l'appui des programmes de développement et de l'intégration.

Objectif stratégique 1.3 : Harmoniser les normes et les méthodes de production statistique. Cet objectif vise l'adaptation des normes et méthodes internationales aux réalités africaines pour accroître la disponibilité de données statistiques harmonisées à l'appui des programmes de développement et de l'intégration.

ii) Thème stratégique 2 : Coordonner la production de statistiques de qualité pour l'Afrique

Les interventions non coordonnées des différents acteurs conduisent non seulement à la duplication des activités, mais également à l'utilisation inefficace des ressources.

Objectif stratégique 2.1 : Mettre en place des mécanismes efficaces de coordination et de collaboration. Il s'agit i) de mettre en œuvre un protocole définissant les rôles et les responsabilités de chaque acteur du Système statistique africain ; ii) de renforcer le Comité de coordination de la statistique en Afrique (CCSA) ; et iii) d'établir une coopération entre les différents acteurs.

Objectif stratégique 2.2 : Définir les priorités statistiques pour la mise en œuvre des programmes d'intégration et de développement. Le recensement des priorités statistiques ainsi que la sélection et la définition d'indicateurs statistiques conduiront à l'élaboration d'un programme de travail harmonisé pour le Système statistique africain.

iii) Thème stratégique 3 : Renforcer durablement les capacités institutionnelles du Système statistique africain

Le renforcement des capacités institutionnelles du Système statistique africain est au cœur de cette stratégie du fait que, sans elles, les membres du Système statistique africain ne pourront pas produire et diffuser les statistiques harmonisées de qualité qu'exigent le processus de développement et l'intégration.

Objectif stratégique 3.1 : Réformer et renforcer les systèmes statistiques nationaux. Les activités au niveau national incluent : l'adoption de lois et d'un cadre réglementaire régissant les activités statistiques en conformité avec la Charte africaine de la statistique ; la création d'un Code de déontologie pour les statisticiens africains ; l'intégration de la statistique dans les processus nationaux de développement ; la formulation et la mise en œuvre de stratégies nationales de développement de la statistique. Ces mesures contribueront à une meilleure planification, à un développement durable et à une meilleure coordination des activités statistiques.

Objectif stratégique 3.2 : Réformer et renforcer les systèmes statistiques régionaux et continentaux, notamment par : la création d'unités statistiques au sein des secrétariats des CER qui n'en sont pas encore dotés (CEN-SAD, IGAD) ; le renforcement des fonctions statistiques des CER ; et la mise en œuvre opérationnelle de l'Institut de la statistique de l'Union Africaine (STATAFRIC). Les principaux résultats attendus sont des programmes harmonisés et une meilleure coordination du développement de la statistique à l'échelle du continent.

Objectif stratégique 3.3 : Renforcer durablement les capacités statistiques par : la formulation d'un programme de formation harmonisé ; la création et le renforcement de centres de formation en cours d'emploi au sein des offices statistiques nationaux ; le renforcement des établissements d'enseignement et de formation dans le domaine de la statistique et de la démographie ; le lancement du Centre de formation panafricain à la statistique, etc.

Objectif stratégique 3.4 : Mettre en place un environnement technologique efficace : par exemple, adopter des systèmes d'information de gestion pour faciliter i) le suivi du programme d'intégration ; ii) la création d'une base de données statistiques ; et iii) la normalisation des outils et plateformes de diffusion.

iv) Thème stratégique 4 : Promouvoir une culture de la qualité en matière de politiques publiques et de prise de décision

Une méconnaissance de l'importance de la statistique peut amener les gouvernements à financer insuffisamment des activités statistiques essentielles, ce qui entraîne une pénurie de données statistiques actualisées et fiables à l'échelle du continent.

Objectif stratégique 4.1 : Prendre des décisions fondées sur des données factuelles grâce au recours accru à la statistique. Il s'agit là d'encourager les décideurs et responsables politiques à utiliser les statistiques dans leurs discours et l'élaboration des politiques publiques.

Objectif stratégique 4.2 : Améliorer la communication des données statistiques. Il convient de formuler une stratégie de diffusion des données ainsi qu'un plan de communication, en vue d'une utilisation accrue de la statistique et d'une amélioration de la qualité des politiques et décisions publiques.

SHaSA, *Statistiques des recettes publiques en Afrique* et mobilisation des ressources nationales

Dans le même esprit que la stratégie SHaSA, les *Statistiques des recettes publiques en Afrique* répondent à la nécessité de disposer de statistiques de bonne qualité pour informer les politiques publiques et les réformes. En effet, cette publication relie deux grands objectifs des pays africains – améliorer les statistiques fiscales et mobiliser des ressources intérieures –, qui figurent au programme de l'Agenda 2063 de l'Union Africaine ainsi que dans les Objectifs de développement durable. L'amélioration des statistiques relatives aux recettes publiques permettra aux pays et aux organisations internationales de suivre les progrès accomplis et de formuler des stratégies d'accroissement des recettes publiques d'une manière durable, équitable et efficiente. L'harmonisation des données sur les recettes aidera en outre les pays à comparer leurs structures fiscales et leurs flux de recettes entre eux et au fil du temps, créant ainsi une appétence et des opportunités d'apprentissage entre pairs.

De plus, la disponibilité de données gratuites et faciles d'accès améliore la transparence et offre l'occasion de mieux rendre compte au public, tant au niveau national qu'international, ce qui peut ensuite créer des incitations à améliorer la gouvernance et les politiques dans les pays participants. Enfin, la participation à une initiative internationale peut améliorer la crédibilité des pays africains et leur capacité à mobiliser des ressources supplémentaires en faveur du développement auprès des investisseurs internationaux et des partenaires extérieurs.

Les *Statistiques des recettes publiques en Afrique* contribuent à promouvoir la vision du Système statistique africain ainsi que les quatre thèmes stratégiques de la SHaSA. En particulier, la publication concourt à :

- produire des statistiques de qualité pour l'Afrique grâce à la transformation des statistiques nationales en un corpus de statistiques comparables sur les recettes fiscales et non fiscales des pays africains. Ces statistiques sont produites selon les principes de classification du Guide d'interprétation de l'OCDE, qui est harmonisé avec toutes les grandes normes comptables nationales. Une fois harmonisées, les statistiques permettent de comparer directement les pays africains entre eux et avec les pays des autres régions participant aux *Statistiques des recettes publiques*. Ces données alimentent en outre une base de données unique, qui est mise gratuitement à la disposition du public ;

- coordonner la production de statistiques de qualité pour l'Afrique, grâce à une démarche de collaboration entre pays africains et organisations régionales partenaires, consistant à définir et valider ensemble les données pour chaque pays, sur la base d'une définition claire, pour chaque partie, des processus, résultats attendus, rôles et responsabilités. La clé de la réussite de cette démarche réside dans un dialogue continu et itératif, qui se conclut par la validation définitive des données statistiques par les pays concernés ;
- renforcer durablement les capacités institutionnelles du Système statistique africain grâce à une formation annuelle assurée dans le cadre des ateliers techniques destinés aux fonctionnaires africains des services statistiques et fiscaux qui participent aux *Statistiques des recettes publiques en Afrique*. Des échanges techniques réguliers avec chaque pays au sujet de la classification de leurs catégories de recettes contribuent à développer les capacités des administrations fiscales des pays africains en matière d'harmonisation des données ;
- promouvoir une culture de la qualité en matière de politiques publiques et de prise de décision grâce à la présentation aisément accessible de statistiques de recettes comparables entre pays et au suivi des effets des grandes réformes sur la mobilisation de recettes. S'ils peuvent étudier l'incidence quantitative de ces réformes depuis un niveau détaillé jusqu'au niveau global des catégories de recettes ainsi qu'au fil du temps, les responsables de la politique fiscale sont mieux à même de planifier leur action et les réformes de l'administration. Ils sont aussi mieux placés pour comparer leur pays à d'autres pays de la région et au-delà.

En résumé, le *Guide d'interprétation des statistiques des recettes publiques* propose un cadre pour l'harmonisation des statistiques de recettes publiques à l'échelle du continent africain. Il offre ainsi un cadre concret qui peut informer et appuyer la stratégie SHaSA, ce qui constitue un grand pas en avant vers la mise en place d'un cadre commun, complet et détaillé, pour l'harmonisation des statistiques dans tous les domaines de l'action publique dans l'ensemble de l'Afrique.

SHaSA : gouvernance et mise en œuvre

Gouvernance

Un ensemble de structures de gouvernance a été mis sur pied pour appliquer, suivre et évaluer la SHaSA, mais aussi pour rendre compte régulièrement des progrès de sa mise en œuvre. Ce mécanisme définit le rôle des instances de gouvernance, en tenant compte de leurs capacités existantes et de leurs domaines d'expertise et atouts particuliers, suivant le principe de la subsidiarité.

Mécanisme de mise en œuvre

Les *Groupes techniques spécialisés* (GTS) seront relancés afin qu'ils poursuivent leurs activités dans chacun des domaines statistiques recensés, sous la coordination des pays et la responsabilité de l'Institut de la statistique de l'UA. Les GTS prépareront et appliqueront des plans d'action sectoriels pour l'harmonisation statistique dans le domaine en question ; ils définiront ou adopteront des normes internationales et des principes méthodologiques pour l'harmonisation statistique dans leurs domaines respectifs. L'Institut de la statistique de l'UA aidera les pays africains à appliquer ces normes et méthodes. Le GTS Finances publiques, Secteur privé et Investissements, dont le champ d'action couvre les statistiques des recettes publiques, devrait commencer ses travaux afin d'établir une feuille de route détaillant précisément les activités à mener pour définir et adopter des normes, méthodes et classifications en vue de produire des statistiques de recettes publiques de bonne qualité et harmonisées dans tous les pays d'Afrique.

Des *pays champions ou chefs de file* seront désignés pour diriger les GTS. Des institutions panafricaines assureront le secrétariat des différents groupes. STATAFRIC établira le programme des activités des GTS (voir le document complet SHaSA-2 pour la liste des pays).

L'*Institut de la statistique de l'Union Africaine* (STATAFRIC) assurera le secrétariat des activités de mise en œuvre de la SHaSA. Il coordonnera les travaux des GTS et mènera des audits techniques dans les CER. L'harmonisation, la production et la validation des données statistiques officielles en Afrique relèveront de la responsabilité exclusive de STATAFRIC.

Le *Centre panafricain de formation en statistique* (PANSTAT) constitue une structure qui viendra compléter les établissements existants d'enseignement et de formation, et comblera les lacunes des programmes de formation.

Des partenariats renforcés pour la mise en œuvre de la SHaSA

Ce nouveau paysage statistique appelle d'autres types de partenariats, notamment avec le secteur privé, qui peuvent contribuer au financement des statistiques – fondations, société civile, partenaires de développement, chercheurs, universitaires, médias, journalistes et utilisateurs, entre autres, tant sur le continent africain qu'en dehors. La publication *Statistiques des recettes publiques en Afrique* est l'exemple d'un nouveau type de partenariat, dans lequel une nouvelle communauté de pratique et de nouvelles relations peuvent se construire en vue d'atteindre un but concret et des résultats tangibles. L'objectif est non seulement de satisfaire les besoins actuels de données mais aussi de mettre sur pied des processus plus efficients dans la perspective de futurs projets.

Volonté politique, capacité d'initiative et modification des comportements

Pour que le Système statistique africain fonctionne de la façon la plus efficace et efficiente possible au cours des années à venir et soit en mesure de répondre à la demande croissante de données, les responsables politiques seront tenus d'accorder une priorité élevée à la production de statistiques de qualité, tenues à jour, fiables et harmonisées à l'échelle du continent.

Favoriser la volonté et l'engagement politique

Pour encourager les pouvoirs publics à faire preuve de volonté et à s'engager, la Commission de l'Union Africaine continuera à plaider auprès de tous les pays qui n'ont pas encore ratifié la Charte africaine de la statistique pour qu'ils le fassent dès que possible, et à inviter les États membres à adapter leur législation nationale en matière de statistique pour la mettre en conformité avec les exigences de la Charte.

Il est largement reconnu que des activités statistiques de grande ampleur, telles que les recensements et les enquêtes, requièrent des ressources considérables. Au cours des 30 dernières années, 7 pays n'ont mené aucun recensement de la population et des logements, et 19 pays ne procèdent pas à un recensement décennal régulier (BAfD/OCDE/PNUD, 2015[1]). Il existe cependant de multiples activités moins coûteuses qui sont nécessaires pour assurer le fonctionnement efficace des systèmes statistiques, comme la promotion de l'utilisation des sources de données administratives. La décision prise par les chefs d'État et de gouvernement visant à allouer chaque année 0.15 % du budget national aux activités statistiques est par conséquent bienvenue. Toutefois, des engagements de ce type ne suffiront pas à créer des systèmes statistiques viables dans la durée s'ils ne se traduisent pas concrètement dans la réalité, sous forme de mesures budgétaires, comme il a été rappelé lors de la quatrième Conférence des ministres africains chargés de l'enregistrement et des statistiques d'état civil, réunis à Nouakchott en décembre 2017. L'Afrique du Sud a atteint cet objectif : elle a affecté en 2018 0.19 % de son budget aux statistiques.

L'engagement des pouvoirs publics en faveur d'un accroissement des ressources contribuerait à révolutionner la production des statistiques. Néanmoins, les responsables politiques doivent aussi s'engager à renforcer le plaidoyer pour la production de statistiques et leur utilisation efficace. Les acteurs de la sphère politique ont un rôle important à jouer pour souligner l'importance de la statistique en encourageant l'utilisation de ces données dans les processus clés d'élaboration des politiques publiques et de prise de décision.

Capacité d'initiative

Au niveau national, il revient avant tout aux directeurs généraux des instituts nationaux de statistique de jouer le rôle de coordinateurs et de veiller à l'harmonisation des statistiques dans l'ensemble du système statistique national. Cette activité est l'une des grandes priorités, voire la principale, de la SHaSA. À l'heure actuelle, le faible niveau d'engagement public en faveur de la statistique se traduit par un déficit chronique de financement à l'échelle du continent : ainsi, seuls 20 % environ des besoins sont financés par des ressources nationales. La forte dépendance à l'égard des ressources extérieures n'autorise pas une planification stratégique efficiente des activités statistiques et rend très difficile la mise en œuvre des stratégies nationales de développement de la statistique. De plus, sous-traiter la production des statistiques nationales peut amoindrir la capacité des pays à construire leur propre infrastructure statistique au fil du temps.

Concernant l'harmonisation et la coordination statistique à l'échelle du continent, les CER ont un rôle important à jouer au travers de la mise en œuvre de leurs politiques d'intégration, qui s'accompagnent souvent de mécanismes de convergence régionale. Il faut toutefois reconnaître que, à l'heure actuelle, certaines CER n'ont guère de capacités statistiques propres.

Au niveau continental, tout en gardant à l'esprit que la SHaSA constitue la feuille de route pour STATAFRIC et pour le Centre de formation panafricain à la statistique, les institutions panafricaines doivent continuer à travailler de façon complémentaire. À cet égard, la Commission de l'Union Africaine, qui a été mandatée pour assumer la direction politique du Système statistique africain et qui a mis en lumière le rôle de la statistique jusqu'aux plus hautes sphères politiques du continent, au niveau des chefs d'État et de gouvernement, continuera à jouer ce rôle dans la mise en œuvre de la SHaSA.

Modification des comportements

La mise en œuvre de la SHaSA nécessite un profond changement de comportement dans l'ensemble du Système statistique africain, tout spécialement parmi les statisticiens eux-mêmes, et en particulier au niveau national. Adoptant une attitude scientifique impartiale à l'égard de leur travail, déterminés à expliquer clairement leurs méthodes de travail et appliquant des méthodologies en toute transparence, les statisticiens doivent commencer à envisager leur rôle comme faisant partie intégrante du fonctionnement de l'économie et de la société de leur pays. De plus, ils doivent faire en sorte que des données statistiques soient fournies aux utilisateurs dans des délais raisonnables et conformément à un calendrier prédéterminé et communiqué, afin de renforcer la pertinence et la crédibilité de leurs produits.

Si les statisticiens doivent faire face à de nouvelles exigences considérables, ils doivent aussi prendre en considération la grande importance qui est accordée à la statistique et en tirer parti pour améliorer la production statistique. Ils doivent par conséquent se tenir prêts à adopter les innovations. Avec l'ouverture sur la société des systèmes statistiques nationaux, les statisticiens et les responsables des systèmes statistiques vont devoir construire et entretenir des partenariats avec des acteurs divers, issus du monde universitaire, des médias, des partenaires de développement, de la société civile et du secteur privé. Les dirigeants des systèmes statistiques nationaux doivent tirer parti de la volonté politique pour que la statistique figure au premier rang des priorités au plus haut niveau de l'État et demeure une question de souveraineté nationale.

Au niveau régional, le personnel des divisions statistiques des CER doit s'attaquer en priorité à la formulation et à l'application d'une stratégie régionale de développement de la statistique, conforme à leur programme d'intégration régionale, et interagir davantage avec les États membres de l'Union Africaine dans l'ensemble de ces processus.

Au niveau continental, tous les acteurs des institutions d'appui doivent continuer à placer le développement et l'harmonisation des statistiques au premier rang des priorités, notamment en dotant les institutions continentales de moyens suffisants.

Conclusion

Tout en répondant à la demande des responsables politiques et des utilisateurs, qui réclament des statistiques harmonisées de bonne qualité, nécessaires pour mettre en œuvre les programmes d'intégration et de développement du continent africain, la SHaSA répond au besoin du Système statistique africain de disposer d'un outil d'harmonisation des activités statistiques en Afrique. Le succès de la mise en œuvre de la SHaSA est subordonné à : i) l'émergence d'une volonté politique au plus haut niveau des autorités continentales ; ii) l'engagement des membres du Système statistique africain, y compris les responsables des systèmes statistiques nationaux, régionaux et continentaux ; iii) la mise en œuvre opérationnelle de l'Institut statistique de l'UA et du Centre panafricain de formation en statistique ; iv) une modification du comportement des acteurs de la statistique sur le continent ; v) l'application de la feuille de route pour une révolution des données ; et vi) la mobilisation de ressources suffisantes pour financer la mise en œuvre du plan d'action. Un plaidoyer continu et actif à tous les niveaux, ainsi que la diffusion, le suivi et l'évaluation de la SHaSA, assortis de rapports réguliers des organes de gouvernance, sont d'autres conditions critiques de sa bonne mise en œuvre.

Dans le domaine des recettes publiques, la publication *Statistiques des recettes publiques en Afrique* contribue déjà à faire progresser la réalisation de la SHaSA, et peut offrir des enseignements utiles pour l'harmonisation des statistiques dans d'autres domaines de l'action publique. En effet, elle propose des statistiques détaillées de bonne qualité sur les recettes publiques des pays africains ; elle se fonde sur un cadre d'harmonisation des statistiques de recettes qui pourrait être élargi à l'ensemble du continent ; elle développe les capacités statistiques au travers de sa séance annuelle de formation à la classification des recettes publiques ; et enfin elle apporte des éléments permettant aux pays participants de formuler des politiques et de prendre des décisions en s'appuyant sur des données factuelles.

Note

1. Aux termes de l'Article 1 de la Charte africaine de la statistique (entrée en vigueur : février 2015), le Système statistique africain est « le Partenariat regroupant les systèmes statistiques nationaux (fournisseurs, producteurs et utilisateurs de données, instituts de recherche et de formation statistiques et organismes de coordination statistique), les unités de statistiques des Communautés économiques régionales (CER), les organisations régionales de statistique, les centres régionaux de formation, les unités statistiques des organisations continentales et les instances de coordination au niveau continental. » (*https://au.int/sites/default/files/treaties/7794-treaty-0037_-_african_charter_on_statistics_f.pdf*)

Référence

BAfD/OCDE/PNUD (2015), *Perspectives économiques en Afrique 2015 : Développement territorial et inclusion spatiale*, Éditions OCDE, Paris, *https://doi.org/10.1787/aeo-2015-fr*. [1]

Chapter 4

Tax levels and tax structures, 1990-2016

Chapitre 4

Niveaux et structures des impôts, 1990-2016

Chapter 4 / Chapitre 4

Comparative tables, 1990-2016

In all of the following tables a ("..") indicates not available. The main series in this volume cover the years 1990 to 2016.

Figures referring to 1991-97 in Table 4.1 and figures relating to 1998-99, 2001-04 and 2006-09 in Tables 4.5 to 4.20 have been omitted because of lack of space. Complete series are, however, available on line at OECD/ATAF/AUC (2018), "Revenue Statistics in Africa: Comparative tables", *OECD Tax Statistics* (database), *http://dx.doi.org/10.1787/be755711-en*.

Tableaux comparatifs, 1990-2016

Dans tous les tableaux suivants le symbole (« .. ») signifie que l'information n'est pas disponible. Les principales séries dans ce volume couvrent les années 1990 à 2016.

Les années 1991 à 1997 dans le tableau 4.1 et les années 1998-99, 2001-04 et 2006-09 dans les tableaux 4.5 à 4.20 ont été omis en raison du manque d'espace. Les séries complètes sont cependant disponibles en ligne sur OCDE/ATAF/CUA (2018), « Statistiques des recettes publiques en Afrique : Tableaux comparatifs », *Statistiques fiscales de l'OCDE* (base de données), *http://dx.doi.org/10.1787/7f54581d-fr*.

Table 4.1. Total tax revenue as percentage of GDP, 1990-2016
Tableau 4.1. Total des recettes fiscales en pourcentage du PIB, 1990-2016

	1990	1998	1999	2000	2001	2002	2003	2004	2005	2006
Botswana	..	..	..	..	..	..	..	15.5	15.2	15.2
Burkina Faso	..	..	..	10.2	10.5	11.0	11.6	13.0	13.7	12.8
Cabo Verde	10.5	14.9	15.3	15.6	16.9	19.3	17.7	18.7	19.5	20.9
Cameroon / Cameroun	..	10.9	10.8	11.3	12.6	11.8	12.3	11.3	12.0	12.4
Congo	..	7.0	6.9	4.3	6.0	7.2	8.7	8.0	6.2	5.6
Congo, Dem. Rep. / Congo, Rép. dém.[1]	..	..	..	0.6	2.3	3.0	3.4	4.7	5.2	5.9
Côte d'Ivoire	21.6	15.9	15.9	15.3	15.6	15.9	14.6	15.9	15.6	16.2
Egypt / Égypte	..	..	..	..	..	16.2	16.3	16.8	16.4	18.4
Eswatini	..	10.5	11.1	10.4	10.1	10.5	11.4	11.1	11.4	11.5
Ghana	..	..	..	11.0	11.8	12.0	13.6	15.0	15.6	14.7
Kenya	..	..	..	..	16.6	16.1	16.7	17.1	18.4	17.5
Mali	..	..	..	11.4	11.4	12.3	13.9	14.9	14.5	14.1
Mauritius / Maurice[2]	23.3	18.9	19.0	19.3	17.2	16.7	18.0	18.1	18.7	18.7
Morocco / Maroc[3]	..	..	..	23.5	23.4	23.1	22.8	23.1	24.7	25.4
Niger	..	..	..	9.8	10.4	10.9	10.4	11.3	10.7	11.2
Rwanda[4]	..	10.8	10.8	10.2	11.3	12.4	12.2	12.1	12.1	11.9
Senegal / Sénégal[5]	..	15.4	16.1	16.8	16.8	17.7	17.7	18.2	19.3	19.7
South Africa / Afrique du Sud[6]	23.9	23.5	23.5	22.4	23.7	23.9	22.7	23.7	25.5	25.6
Togo	..	..	..	9.4	10.9	9.6	11.9	13.2	13.3	14.5
Tunisia / Tunisie[4]	..	..	..	24.4	24.8	24.8	24.2	24.1	24.2	24.4
Uganda / Ouganda	..	10.8	11.4	10.7	10.7	11.0	11.4	11.7	12.1	12.3
Africa (21) average / Moyenne Afrique (21)[7]	**..**	**..**	**..**	**13.1**	**13.8**	**14.3**	**14.6**	**15.1**	**15.4**	**15.6**
LAC average / Moyenne ALC[8]	**16.0**	**17.5**	**17.7**	**18.0**	**18.2**	**18.2**	**18.6**	**19.0**	**19.8**	**20.9**
OECD average / Moyenne OCDE[9]	**31.9**	**33.7**	**33.9**	**33.9**	**33.4**	**33.2**	**33.1**	**33.0**	**33.5**	**33.6**

	2007	2008	2009	2010	2011	2012	2013	2014	2015	2016
Botswana	13.7	17.1	15.8	15.7	15.7	13.8	14.7	15.2	12.7	14.0
Burkina Faso	14.2	13.4	14.1	15.3	15.8	17.2	18.1	16.4	17.4	18.1
Cabo Verde	20.8	21.2	18.4	18.4	19.6	17.7	17.8	16.9	18.8	19.0
Cameroon / Cameroun	12.8	12.5	13.1	12.1	13.0	13.5	14.1	14.4	14.7	14.4
Congo	6.7	6.6	7.8	7.1	7.4	8.4	14.0	11.5	16.6	16.0
Congo, Dem. Rep. / Congo, Rép. dém.[1]	7.1	8.8	8.0	8.9	9.3	11.4	10.1	9.5	9.7	7.6
Côte d'Ivoire	17.1	16.9	16.8	16.5	15.3	17.7	17.6	16.9	17.5	17.4
Egypt / Égypte	18.0	17.9	17.7	16.3	15.9	15.2	16.2	15.2	15.7	15.2
Eswatini	11.6	12.7	12.7	13.7	13.9	13.2	14.2	14.9	14.9	15.5
Ghana	14.8	14.3	14.1	14.5	16.1	16.2	15.0	16.7	17.2	17.6
Kenya	18.1	18.9	18.2	17.9	18.6	17.9	17.9	19.1	18.5	18.1
Mali	14.3	13.4	14.4	14.1	13.7	14.0	14.2	13.8	15.0	16.1
Mauritius / Maurice[2]	17.9	19.5	20.2	19.8	19.6	20.1	19.8	19.8	19.9	20.0
Morocco / Maroc[3]	27.7	30.2	26.9	27.7	28.5	29.5	28.1	27.0	25.9	26.4
Niger	12.0	12.1	14.0	13.2	13.9	14.4	16.9	16.3	16.9	14.4
Rwanda[4]	12.2	13.3	12.8	13.1	13.8	14.4	15.4	15.8	16.6	16.6
Senegal / Sénégal[5]	20.1	19.0	18.9	19.8	19.9	20.0	19.6	20.9	21.1	22.0
South Africa / Afrique du Sud[6]	26.9	26.8	25.1	24.8	25.4	26.4	27.1	27.6	28.9	28.6
Togo	15.2	14.4	14.6	15.0	18.0	19.0	19.5	20.9	21.6	22.2
Tunisia / Tunisie[4]	25.2	26.8	26.7	27.2	29.1	29.1	29.8	30.9	30.3	29.4
Uganda / Ouganda	12.3	12.1	11.1	10.4	10.6	10.9	11.3	11.6	12.6	13.1
Africa (21) average / Moyenne Afrique (21)[7]	**16.1**	**16.6**	**16.3**	**16.3**	**16.8**	**17.1**	**17.7**	**17.7**	**18.2**	**18.2**
LAC average / Moyenne ALC[8]	**21.2**	**21.3**	**20.8**	**20.9**	**21.4**	**21.9**	**21.9**	**22.4**	**23.1**	**22.7**
OECD average / Moyenne OCDE[9]	**33.7**	**33.0**	**32.3**	**32.5**	**32.8**	**33.3**	**33.6**	**33.9**	**34.0**	**34.3**

Table 4.1. **Total tax revenue as percentage of GDP, 1990-2016** *(cont.)*
Tableau 4.1. **Total des recettes fiscales en pourcentage du PIB, 1990-2016** *(suite)*

Note: The figures include sub-national government tax revenues for Eswatini (Swaziland in previous editions), Mauritius, Morocco and South Africa (for 2002-16). Sub-national government tax revenues are not available in other countries.

Heading 2000: Data on social security contributions are not available for the Republic of the Congo, the Democratic Republic of the Congo (prior to 2012), Togo and Uganda; and are only partially available in Cameroon and Senegal. Social security contributions for Botswana are deemed to be null as they do not meet the criteria to be classified as social security contributions set out in the OECD classification of taxes in the Interpretative Guide.

Heading 4000: In the Democratic Republic of the Congo, Ghana and Uganda, revenues from property taxes are mainly levied by local governments for which data on revenue are not available. In the Democratic Republic of the Congo only data for property taxes levied by the *Direction Générale des Recettes Administratives, Judiciaires, Domaniales et de Participation* (DGRAD) are available for 2010-16.

See the country tables in Chapter 5 for further information on data issues for individual countries.

1. The figures should be interpreted with caution as they are affected by macroeconomic instability in the early 2000s. For the years prior to 2010, the figures exclude some revenues collected by the *Direction Générale des Recettes Administratives, Judiciaires, Domaniales et de Participation* (DGRAD), which are estimated to be less than 1% of total tax revenue. See Table 5.6 in Chapter 5 for further information.
2. The fiscal year for Mauritius changed in 2010 and in 2015. Figures for 2015 needed to be estimated as a result.
3. Social security contributions in Morocco are estimated for years prior to 2002.
4. Rwanda and Tunisia do not include social security contributions in the tax-to-GDP ratio in their official publications as neither country considers them as taxes. They are included as tax revenue in this publication, following the classification set out in the OECD Interpretative Guide.
5. These figures include contributions to the Senegalese Pension Institute (IPRES) (estimated prior to 2006) and contributions to the social security fund (CSS) from 2012 as data for previous years are not available.
6. Includes payments made by South Africa to the Southern African Customs Union (SACU) pool.
7. Represents an unweighted average for the 21 African countries included in this publication. This average should be interpreted with caution due to missing and incomplete data for heading 2000 (social security contributions) and heading 4000 (property taxes). Due to lack of data availability, the Africa (21) average does not include Botswana prior to 2004, Egypt prior to 2002 and Kenya prior to 2001. These countries are included in the calculations of the Africa (21) average for subsequent years. Excluding these countries from the average does not substantially change the results.
8. Represents an unweighted average for the 25 Latin American and Caribbean (LAC) countries included in the publication *Revenue Statistics in Latin America and the Caribbean 2018*.
9. Represents an unweighted average for 35 OECD countries.

Note : Les chiffres incluent les recettes fiscales collectées par les administrations infranationales pour l'Afrique du Sud (pour les années 2002 à 2016), Eswatini (Swaziland dans les éditions précédentes), le Maroc et Maurice. Les données des recettes fiscales collectées par les administrations infranationales ne sont pas disponibles pour les autres pays.

Rubrique 2000: Les données des cotisations de sécurité sociale ne sont pas disponibles pour la République du Congo, la République démocratique du Congo (avant 2012), l'Ouganda et le Togo et ne sont que partiellement disponibles au Cameroun et au Sénégal. Les cotisations de sécurité sociale pour le Botswana sont nulles car elles ne répondent pas aux critères de classification des cotisations de sécurité sociale de la classification des impôts de l'OCDE du Guide d'interprétation.

Rubrique 4000: Au Ghana, en République démocratique du Congo et en Ouganda, les recettes provenant des impôts sur le patrimoine sont principalement perçues par les administrations locales pour lesquelles les données ne sont pas disponibles. En République démocratique du Congo, seules les données des impôts sur le patrimoine qui sont prélevées par la *Direction Générale des Recettes Administratives, Judiciaires, Domaniales et de Participation* (DGRAD) sont disponibles pour 2010-16.

Voir les tableaux des pays au chapitre 5 pour plus d'informations sur les problèmes de données pour les pays individuels.

1. Les chiffres doivent être interprétés avec prudence car ils sont affectés par une instabilité macroéconomique au début des années 2000. Pour les années antérieures à 2010, les chiffres excluent certaines recettes perçues par la *Direction Générale des Recettes Administratives, Judiciaires, Domaniales et de Participation* (DGRAD) estimées inférieures à 1 % du total des recettes fiscales. Voir le tableau 5.6 du chapitre 5 pour plus d'informations.
2. L'année fiscale pour Maurice a changé en 2010 et en 2015. Les chiffres pour 2015 ont dû être estimés en conséquence.
3. Les cotisations de sécurité sociale au Maroc antérieures à 2002 sont estimées.
4. Le Rwanda et la Tunisie n'incluent pas les cotisations de sécurité sociale dans le ratio impôts/PIB dans leurs publications officielles car ces deux pays ne les considèrent pas comme des impôts. Elles sont incluses dans les recettes fiscales de cette publication en accordance avec la classification des impôts établie dans le Guide d'interprétation de l'OCDE.
5. Les chiffres comprennent les cotisations de sécurité sociale de l'Institution de prévoyance retraite du Sénégal (IPRES) (estimées pour les années antérieures à 2006) et les cotisations de sécurité sociale de la Caisse de Sécurité Sociale (CSS) (à partir de 2012 car les données pour les années précédentes ne sont pas disponibles).
6. Comprend les paiements effectués par l'Afrique du Sud au fond collectif de l'Union douanière d'Afrique australe (SACU).
7. Représente la moyenne non pondérée des 21 pays d'Afrique inclus dans cette publication. Il convient d'interpréter cette moyenne avec prudence à cause de valeurs manquantes ou incomplètes pour la rubrique 2000 (cotisations de sécurité sociale) et la rubrique 4000 (taxes sur le patrimoine). En raison du manque de disponibilité des données, la moyenne Afrique (21) n'inclut pas le Botswana avant 2004, l'Égypte avant 2002 et le Kenya avant 2001. Ces pays sont inclus dans les calculs de la moyenne Afrique (21) pour les années suivantes. L'exclusion de ces pays de la moyenne ne modifie pas substantiellement les résultats.
8. Représente la moyenne non pondérée pour les 25 pays d'Amérique latine et des Caraïbes (ALC) inclus dans la publication *Revenue Statistics in Latin America and the Caribbean 2018*.
9. Représente la moyenne non pondérée pour 35 pays de l'OCDE.

StatLink https://doi.org/10.1787/888933820069

Table 4.2. **Total tax revenue (excluding social security) as percentage of GDP**
Tableau 4.2. **Total des recettes fiscales (sécurité sociale non comprise) en pourcentage du PIB**

	1990	1998	1999	2000	2001	2002	2003	2004	2005	2006
Botswana	..	..	..	..	..	..	..	15.5	15.2	15.2
Burkina Faso	..	..	..	9.5	9.8	10.3	10.9	12.1	12.9	11.9
Cabo Verde	10.5	14.9	15.3	14.8	16.5	18.9	17.2	18.2	18.9	20.4
Cameroon / Cameroun	..	10.1	9.9	10.4	11.6	10.8	11.3	10.3	11.1	11.6
Congo	..	7.0	6.9	4.3	6.0	7.2	8.7	8.0	6.2	5.6
Congo, Dem. Rep. / Congo, Rép. dém.[1]	..	..	..	0.6	2.3	3.0	3.4	4.7	5.2	5.9
Côte d'Ivoire	20.2	14.9	14.8	14.0	14.2	14.6	13.4	14.6	14.3	14.9
Egypt / Égypte	..	..	..	..	..	12.6	12.7	13.5	13.4	15.4
Eswatini	..	9.2	9.9	9.2	9.0	9.4	10.3	9.8	10.0	10.0
Ghana	..	..	..	10.0	10.6	10.7	12.4	13.7	14.4	13.2
Kenya	..	..	..	..	16.4	15.9	16.5	16.9	18.1	17.2
Mali	..	..	..	10.5	10.5	11.3	12.8	13.6	13.1	12.7
Mauritius / Maurice[2]	22.3	17.7	18.0	18.3	16.2	15.9	17.3	17.4	18.0	17.9
Morocco / Maroc	..	..	..	19.6	19.5	19.5	19.0	19.2	20.7	21.5
Niger	..	..	..	9.2	9.9	10.4	10.0	10.9	10.3	10.8
Rwanda	..	10.4	10.3	9.7	10.7	11.9	11.6	11.2	11.3	11.2
Senegal / Sénégal	..	14.8	15.5	16.1	16.1	16.9	17.0	17.4	18.5	18.8
South Africa / Afrique du Sud[3]	23.9	23.5	23.5	22.4	23.7	23.7	22.3	23.3	25.2	25.2
Togo	..	..	..	9.4	10.9	9.6	11.9	13.2	13.3	14.5
Tunisia / Tunisie	..	..	..	19.2	19.5	19.3	18.6	18.6	18.7	18.4
Uganda / Ouganda	..	10.8	11.4	10.7	10.7	11.0	11.4	11.7	12.1	12.3
Africa (21) average / Moyenne Afrique (21)[4]	**..**	**..**	**..**	**12.1**	**12.8**	**13.1**	**13.4**	**14.0**	**14.3**	**14.5**
LAC average / Moyenne ALC[5]	**13.9**	**15.1**	**15.2**	**15.4**	**15.6**	**15.5**	**15.9**	**16.3**	**17.1**	**18.1**
OECD average / Moyenne OCDE[6]	**24.6**	**25.1**	**25.3**	**25.3**	**24.8**	**24.5**	**24.4**	**24.5**	**25.0**	**25.2**

	2007	2008	2009	2010	2011	2012	2013	2014	2015	2016
Botswana	13.7	17.1	15.8	15.7	15.7	13.8	14.7	15.2	12.7	14.0
Burkina Faso	13.3	12.5	13.2	14.3	14.8	16.2	17.0	15.3	16.2	17.0
Cabo Verde	20.7	21.2	18.4	18.4	19.5	17.7	17.8	16.9	18.8	19.0
Cameroon / Cameroun	12.0	11.7	12.2	11.1	12.0	12.5	13.1	13.5	13.8	13.3
Congo	6.7	6.6	7.8	7.1	7.4	8.4	14.0	11.5	16.6	16.0
Congo, Dem. Rep. / Congo, Rép. dém.[1]	7.1	8.8	8.0	8.9	9.3	10.9	9.6	8.9	9.1	7.1
Côte d'Ivoire	15.8	15.6	15.5	15.2	14.3	16.0	15.6	14.9	15.6	15.4
Egypt / Égypte	15.2	15.3	15.5	13.9	13.7	12.9	13.8	12.7	13.0	13.3
Eswatini	10.0	11.2	11.0	11.8	12.2	11.6	12.7	13.4	13.3	13.9
Ghana	13.3	12.9	12.3	13.3	14.7	15.0	13.8	15.1	15.7	16.1
Kenya	17.9	18.7	18.0	17.7	18.4	17.7	17.8	19.0	18.3	17.9
Mali	12.8	11.9	12.9	12.8	12.3	12.5	12.8	12.3	13.5	14.3
Mauritius / Maurice[2]	17.1	18.8	19.2	18.8	18.7	19.2	18.8	18.8	18.8	19.0
Morocco / Maroc	23.8	26.5	23.0	22.8	23.2	24.1	22.8	22.4	21.5	21.9
Niger	11.5	11.5	13.4	12.5	13.1	13.7	16.1	15.5	16.1	13.7
Rwanda	11.4	12.4	11.9	12.3	12.9	13.4	14.3	14.8	15.6	15.5
Senegal / Sénégal	19.3	18.2	18.0	18.7	19.0	18.7	18.3	19.6	19.9	20.5
South Africa / Afrique du Sud[3]	26.5	26.4	24.7	24.4	25.0	26.0	26.7	27.2	28.5	28.2
Togo	15.2	14.4	14.6	15.0	18.0	19.0	19.5	20.9	21.6	22.2
Tunisia / Tunisie	19.0	20.4	19.7	19.8	21.1	20.8	21.2	22.4	21.3	20.1
Uganda / Ouganda	12.3	12.1	11.1	10.4	10.6	10.9	11.3	11.6	12.6	13.1
Africa (21) average / Moyenne Afrique (21)[4]	**15.0**	**15.4**	**15.1**	**15.0**	**15.5**	**15.8**	**16.3**	**16.3**	**16.8**	**16.7**
LAC average / Moyenne ALC[5]	**18.3**	**18.4**	**17.7**	**17.8**	**18.2**	**18.5**	**18.4**	**18.8**	**19.4**	**19.1**
OECD average / Moyenne OCDE[6]	**25.3**	**24.5**	**23.5**	**23.7**	**24.0**	**24.4**	**24.6**	**24.9**	**25.0**	**25.1**

Table 4.2. **Total tax revenue (excluding social security) as percentage of GDP** *(cont.)*
Tableau 4.2. **Total des recettes fiscales (sécurité sociale non comprise) en pourcentage du PIB** *(suite)*

Note: The figures include sub-national government tax revenues for Eswatini (Swaziland in previous editions), Mauritius, Morocco and South Africa (for 2002-16). Sub-national government tax revenues are not available in other countries.

Heading 4000: In the Democratic Republic of the Congo, Ghana and Uganda, revenues from property taxes are mainly levied by local governments for which data on revenue are not available. In the Democratic Republic of the Congo only data for property taxes levied by the *Direction Générale des Recettes Administratives, Judiciaires, Domaniales et de Participation* (DGRAD) are available for 2010-16.

See the country tables in Chapter 5 for further information on data issues for individual countries.

1. The figures should be interpreted with caution as they are affected by macroeconomic instability in the early 2000s. For the years prior to 2010, the figures exclude some revenues collected by the *Direction Générale des Recettes Administratives, Judiciaires, Domaniales et de Participation* (DGRAD) which are estimated to be less than 1 % of total tax revenue. See Table 5.6 in Chapter 5 for further information.
2. The fiscal year for Mauritius changed in 2010 and in 2015. Figures for 2015 needed to be estimated as a result.
3. Includes payments made by South Africa to the Southern African Customs Union (SACU) pool.
4. Represents an unweighted average for the 21 African countries included in this publication. This average should be interpreted with caution due to missing and incomplete data for heading 2000 (social security contributions) and heading 4000 (property taxes). Due to lack of data availability, the Africa (21) average does not include Botswana prior to 2004, Egypt prior to 2002 and Kenya prior to 2001. These countries are included in the calculations of the Africa (21) average for subsequent years. Excluding these countries from the average does not substantially change the results.
5. Represents an unweighted average for the 25 Latin American and Caribbean (LAC) countries included in the publication *Revenue Statistics in Latin America and the Caribbean 2018*.
6. Represents an unweighted average for 35 OECD countries.

Note : Les chiffres incluent les recettes fiscales collectées par les administrations infranationales pour l'Afrique du Sud (pour les années 2002 à 2016), Eswatini (Swaziland dans les éditions précédentes), le Maroc et Maurice. Les données des recettes fiscales collectées par les administrations infranationales ne sont pas disponibles pour les autres pays.

Rubrique 4000: Au Ghana, en République démocratique du Congo et en Ouganda, les recettes provenant des impôts sur le patrimoine sont principalement perçues par les administrations locales pour lesquelles les données ne sont pas disponibles. En République démocratique du Congo, seules les données des impôts sur le patrimoine qui sont prélevées par la *Direction Générale des Recettes Administratives, Judiciaires, Domaniales et de Participation* (DGRAD) sont disponibles pour 2010-16.

Voir les tableaux des pays au chapitre 5 pour plus d'informations sur les problèmes de données pour les pays individuels.

1. Les chiffres doivent être interprétés avec prudence car ils sont affectés par une instabilité macroéconomique au début des années 2000. Pour les années antérieures à 2010, les chiffres excluent certaines recettes perçues par la *Direction Générale des Recettes Administratives, Judiciaires, Domaniales et de Participation* (DGRAD) et sont estimées être inférieures à 1 % du total des recettes fiscales. Voir le tableau 5.6 du chapitre 5 pour plus d'informations.
2. L'année fiscale pour Maurice a changé en 2010 et en 2015. Les chiffres pour 2015 ont dû être estimés en conséquence.
3. Comprend les paiements effectués par l'Afrique du Sud au fond collectif de l'Union douanière d'Afrique australe (SACU).
4. Représente la moyenne non pondérée des 21 pays d'Afrique inclus dans cette publication. Il convient d'interpréter cette moyenne avec prudence à cause de valeurs manquantes ou incomplètes pour la rubrique 2000 (cotisations de sécurité sociale) et la rubrique 4000 (taxes sur le patrimoine). En raison du manque de disponibilité des données, la moyenne Afrique (21) n'inclut pas le Botswana avant 2004, l'Égypte avant 2002 et le Kenya avant 2001. Ces pays sont inclus dans les calculs de la moyenne Afrique (21) pour les années suivantes. L'exclusion de ces pays de la moyenne ne modifie pas substantiellement les résultats.
5. Représente la moyenne non pondérée pour les 25 pays d'Amérique latine et des Caraïbes (ALC) inclus dans la publication *Revenue Statistics in Latin America and the Caribbean 2018*.
6. Représente la moyenne non pondérée pour 35 pays de l'OCDE.

StatLink https://doi.org/10.1787/888933820088

Table 4.3. **Tax revenue of main headings as percentage of GDP, 2016**
Tableau 4.3. **Recettes fiscales sous les principales rubriques en pourcentage du PIB, 2016**

	1000 Income & profits / Impôts & profits	2000 Social security / Sécurité sociale	3000 Payroll / Salaires	4000 Property / Patrimoine	5000 Goods and services / Biens et services	6000 Other taxes / Autres impôts
Botswana	9.7	0.0	0.0	0.0	4.2	0.0
Burkina Faso	4.8	1.1	0.1	0.2	11.8	0.1
Cabo Verde	6.2	0.0	0.0	0.3	12.5	0.0
Cameroon / Cameroun	4.0	1.1	0.3	0.2	8.6	0.2
Congo	6.7	..	0.5	0.1	8.7	0.0
Congo, Dem. Rep. / Congo, Rép. dém.	2.3	0.5	0.1	0.0	4.6	0.1
Côte d'Ivoire	1.9	2.1	2.0	0.5	10.9	0.1
Egypt / Égypte	7.0	1.9	0.0	0.2	6.1	0.0
Eswatini	7.9	1.5	0.0	0.3	5.7	0.0
Ghana	4.8	1.5	0.0	..	11.2	0.0
Kenya	8.4	0.3	0.0	0.2	9.3	0.0
Mali	3.9	1.8	0.2	0.3	9.4	0.5
Mauritius / Maurice	4.9	1.0	0.1	1.1	12.8	0.0
Morocco / Maroc	8.3	4.5	0.0	2.0	11.3	0.3
Niger	3.8	0.8	0.1	0.0	8.8	0.9
Rwanda[1]	6.5	1.1	0.0	0.0	9.0	0.0
Senegal / Sénégal	5.9	1.5	0.2	0.6	13.6	0.2
South Africa / Afrique du Sud[2]	14.8	0.4	0.3	1.6	11.4	0.0
Togo	5.2	..	0.1	0.1	16.6	0.2
Tunisia / Tunisie[1]	8.2	9.3	0.4	0.3	10.5	0.7
Uganda / Ouganda	4.6	..	0.0	..	8.5	0.0
Africa (21) average / Moyenne Afrique (21)[3]	**6.2**	**1.7**	**0.2**	**0.4**	**9.8**	**0.2**
LAC average / Moyenne ALC[4]	**6.0**	**3.7**	**0.2**	**0.8**	**11.4**	**0.5**
OECD average / Moyenne OCDE[5]	**11.5**	**9.0**	**0.4**	**1.9**	**10.9**	**0.2**

Table 4.3. **Tax revenue of main headings as percentage of GDP, 2016** *(cont.)*
Tableau 4.3. **Recettes fiscales sous les principales rubriques en pourcentage du PIB, 2016** *(suite)*

Note: The figures include sub-national government tax revenues for Eswatini (Swaziland in previous editions), Mauritius, Morocco and South Africa (for 2002-16). Sub-national government tax revenues are not available in other countries.

Heading 2000: Data for social security contributions are not available for the Republic of the Congo, Togo and Uganda; and are only partially available in Cameroon and Senegal. Social security contributions for Botswana are deemed to be null as they do not meet the criteria to be classified as social security contributions set out in the OECD classification of taxes in the Interpretative Guide.

Heading 4000: In the Democratic Republic of the Congo, Ghana and Uganda, revenues from property taxes are mainly levied by local governments for which data on revenue are not available. In the Democratic Republic of the Congo only data for property tax revenues levied by the *Direction Générale des Recettes Administratives, Judiciaires, Domaniales et de Participation* (DGRAD) are available for 2010-16.

See the country tables in Chapter 5 for further information data issues for individual countries.

1. Rwanda and Tunisia do not include social security contributions in the tax-to-GDP ratios in their official publications as neither country considers them as taxes. They are included as tax revenue in this publication, following the classification set out in the OECD Interpretative Guide.
2. The figures for heading 5000 goods and services should be interpreted with caution as they include payments made by South Africa to the Southern African Customs Union (SACU) pool.
3. Represents an unweighted average for the 21 African countries included in this publication. The Africa (21) average should be interpreted with caution due to missing and incomplete data. The averages for heading 2000 (social security contributions) and heading 4000 (property taxes) exclude countries where these data were not available. This means that the Africa (21) average for the total tax revenues differs from the sum of average values for the subcategories. For example, in 2016, the average total tax revenue for Africa (21) as a percentage of GDP was 18.2%, but the sum of the average tax-to-GDP ratios for headings 1000, 2000, 3000, 4000, 5000, and 6000 was 18.5%.
4. Represents an unweighted average for the 25 Latin American and Caribbean (LAC) countries included in the publication *Revenue Statistics in Latin America and the Caribbean 2018.*
5. Represents an unweighted average for 35 OECD countries. Data are for 2015 as data for 2016 were not available at the date of publication.

Note : Les chiffres incluent les recettes fiscales collectées par les administrations infranationales pour l'Afrique du Sud (pour les années 2002 à 2016), Eswatini (Swaziland dans les éditions précédentes), le Maroc et Maurice. Les données des recettes fiscales collectées par les administrations infranationales ne sont pas disponibles pour les autres pays.

Rubrique 2000: Les données des cotisations de sécurité sociale ne sont pas disponibles pour la République du Congo, l'Ouganda et le Togo et ne sont que partiellement disponibles au Cameroun et au Sénégal. Les cotisations de sécurité sociale pour le Botswana sont nulles car elles ne répondent pas aux critères de classification des cotisations de sécurité sociale de la classification des impôts de l'OCDE du Guide d'interprétation.

Rubrique 4000: Au Ghana, en République démocratique du Congo et en Ouganda, les recettes provenant des impôts sur le patrimoine sont principalement perçues par les administrations locales pour lesquelles les données ne sont pas disponibles. En République démocratique du Congo, seules les données des impôts sur le patrimoine qui sont prélevées par la *Direction Générale des Recettes Administratives, Judiciaires, Domaniales et de Participation* (DGRAD) sont disponibles pour 2010-16.

Voir les tableaux des pays au chapitre 5 pour plus d'informations sur les problèmes de données pour les pays individuels.

1. Le Rwanda et la Tunisie n'incluent pas les cotisations de sécurité sociale dans le ratio impôts/PIB dans leurs publications officielles car aucun des deux pays ne les considère comme des impôts. Elles sont incluses comme recettes fiscales dans cette publication en accordance avec la classification des impôts établie dans le Guide d'interprétation de l'OCDE.
2. Les chiffres relatifs à la rubrique 5000 produits et services doivent être interprétés avec prudence car ils incluent les paiements effectués par l'Afrique du Sud à l'Union douanière d'Afrique australe (SACU).
3. Représente la moyenne non pondérée pour les 21 pays africains inclus dans cette publication. Il convient d'interpréter la moyenne Afrique (21) avec prudence à cause de valeurs manquantes ou incomplètes. Les moyennes pour la rubrique 2000 (cotisations de sécurité sociale) et la rubrique 4000 (taxes sur le patrimoine) excluent les pays pour lesquels ces données ne sont pas disponibles. Cela signifie que la moyenne Afrique (21) pour le total des recettes fiscales diffère de la somme des moyennes des sous-rubriques. Par exemple en 2016, la moyenne des recettes fiscales pour l'Afrique (21) en pourcentage du PIB s'élevait à 18.2 % alors que la somme des moyennes des recettes fiscales relatives aux catégories 1000, 2000, 3000, 4000, 5000 et 6000 était de 18.5%.
4. Représente la moyenne non pondérée pour les 25 pays d'Amérique latine et des Caraïbes (ALC) inclus dans la publication *Revenue Statistics in Latin America and the Caribbean 2018.*
5. Représente la moyenne non pondérée pour 35 pays de l'OCDE. Les données sont pour 2015 car les données pour 2016 n'étaient pas disponibles à la date de la publication.

StatLink https://doi.org/10.1787/888933820107

Table 4.4. **Tax revenue of main headings as percentage of total taxation, 2016**
Tableau 4.4. **Recettes fiscales sous les principales rubriques en pourcentage du total des recettes fiscales, 2016**

	1000 Income & profits / Impôts & profits	2000 Social security / Sécurité sociale	3000 Payroll / Salaires	4000 Property / Patrimoine	5000 Goods and services / Biens et services	6000 Other taxes / Autres impôts
Botswana	69.5	0.0	0.0	0.3	30.2	0.0
Burkina Faso	26.3	6.3	0.7	1.1	64.9	0.6
Cabo Verde	32.3	0.2	0.0	1.5	66.0	0.0
Cameroon / Cameroun	28.1	7.3	1.9	1.1	59.9	1.7
Congo	41.8	..	3.1	0.6	54.5	0.0
Congo, Dem. Rep. / Congo, Rép. dém.	30.3	7.0	1.3	0.5	59.8	1.2
Côte d'Ivoire	11.2	11.8	11.3	2.8	62.3	0.6
Egypt / Égypte	45.7	12.6	0.0	1.4	40.3	0.0
Eswatini	51.3	10.0	0.0	1.9	36.8	0.0
Ghana	27.4	8.8	0.0	..	63.8	0.0
Kenya	46.2	1.4	0.0	1.0	51.5	0.0
Mali	24.2	11.4	1.0	2.1	58.4	2.8
Mauritius / Maurice	24.4	5.2	0.7	5.6	64.0	0.1
Morocco / Maroc	31.3	17.1	0.0	7.5	42.8	1.3
Niger	26.4	5.5	0.5	0.3	60.9	6.3
Rwanda[1]	38.9	6.8	0.0	0.1	54.3	0.0
Senegal / Sénégal	26.9	6.7	0.9	2.7	61.8	1.0
South Africa / Afrique du Sud[2]	51.8	1.4	1.2	5.4	40.1	0.0
Togo	23.3	..	0.7	0.7	74.6	0.8
Tunisia / Tunisie[1]	27.8	31.6	1.3	1.1	35.8	2.4
Uganda / Ouganda	34.9	..	0.0	..	65.0	0.1
Africa (21) average / Moyenne Afrique (21)[3]	**34.3**	**8.4**	**1.2**	**2.0**	**54.6**	**0.9**
LAC average / Moyenne ALC[4]	**27.3**	**15.9**	**0.8**	**3.4**	**50.5**	**2.1**
OECD average / Moyenne OCDE[5]	**34.1**	**25.8**	**1.1**	**5.8**	**32.4**	**0.5**

Table 4.4. **Tax revenue of main headings as percentage of total taxation, 2016** *(cont.)*
Tableau 4.4. **Recettes fiscales sous les principales rubriques en pourcentage du total des recettes fiscales, 2016** *(suite)*

Note: The figures include sub-national government tax revenues for Eswatini (Swaziland in previous editions), Mauritius, Morocco and South Africa (for 2002-16). Sub-national government tax revenues are not available in other countries.

Heading 2000: Data for social security contributions are not available for the Republic of the Congo, Togo and Uganda; and are only partially available in Cameroon and Senegal. Social security contributions for Botswana are deemed to be null as they do not meet the criteria to be classified as social security contributions set out in the OECD classification of taxes in the Interpretative Guide.

Heading 4000: In the Democratic Republic of the Congo, Ghana and Uganda, revenues from property taxes are mainly levied by local governments for which data on revenue are not available. In the Democratic Republic of the Congo only data for property tax revenues levied by the *Direction Générale des Recettes Administratives, Judiciaires, Domaniales et de Participation* (DGRAD) are available for 2010-16.

See the country tables in Chapter 5 for further information data issues for individual countries.

1. Rwanda and Tunisia do not include social security contributions in the tax-to-GDP ratios in their official publications as neither country considers them as taxes. They are included as tax revenue in this publication, following the classification set out in the OECD Interpretative Guide.
2. The figures for heading 5000 goods and services should be interpreted with caution as they include payments made by South Africa to the Southern African Customs Union (SACU) pool.
3. Represents an unweighted average for the 21 African countries included in this publication. The Africa (21) average should be interpreted with caution due to missing and incomplete data. The average tax revenues as percentage of total tax revenue for headings 1000, 2000, 3000, 4000, 5000, and 6000 do not add up to 100% as the averages for heading 2000 (social security contributions) and heading 4000 (property taxes) exclude countries where these data were not available.
4. Represents an unweighted average for the 25 Latin American and Caribbean (LAC) countries included in the publication *Revenue Statistics in Latin America and the Caribbean 2018.*
5. Represents an unweighted average for 35 OECD countries. Data are for 2015 as data for 2016 were not available at the date of publication.

Note : Les chiffres incluent les recettes fiscales collectées par les administrations infranationales pour l'Afrique du Sud (pour les années 2002 à 2016), Eswatini (Swaziland dans les éditions précédentes), le Maroc et Maurice. Les données des recettes fiscales collectées par les administrations infranationales ne sont pas disponibles pour les autres pays.

Rubrique 2000: Les données des cotisations de sécurité sociale ne sont pas disponibles pour la République du Congo, l'Ouganda et le Togo et ne sont que partiellement disponibles au Cameroun et au Sénégal. Les cotisations de sécurité sociale pour le Botswana sont nulles car elles ne répondent pas aux critères de classification des cotisations de sécurité sociale de la classification des impôts de l'OCDE du Guide d'interprétation.

Rubrique 4000: Au Ghana, en République démocratique du Congo et en Ouganda, les recettes provenant des impôts sur le patrimoine sont principalement perçues par les administrations locales pour lesquelles les données ne sont pas disponibles. En République démocratique du Congo, seules les données des impôts sur le patrimoine qui sont prélevées par la *Direction Générale des Recettes Administratives, Judiciaires, Domaniales et de Participation* (DGRAD) sont disponibles pour 2010-16.

Voir les tableaux des pays au chapitre 5 pour plus d'informations sur les problèmes de données pour les pays individuels.

1. Le Rwanda et la Tunisie n'incluent pas les cotisations de sécurité sociale dans le ratio impôts/PIB dans leurs publications officielles car aucun des deux pays ne les considère comme des impôts. Elles sont incluses comme recettes fiscales dans cette publication en accordance avec la classification des impôts établie dans le Guide d'interprétation de l'OCDE.
2. Les chiffres relatifs à la rubrique 5000 produits et services doivent être interprétés avec prudence car ils incluent les paiements effectués par l'Afrique du Sud à l'Union douanière d'Afrique australe (SACU).
3. Représente la moyenne non pondérée pour les 21 pays africains inclus dans cette publication. Il convient d'interpréter la moyenne Afrique (21) avec prudence à cause de valeurs manquantes ou incomplètes. La somme des moyennes des recettes fiscales pour les rubriques 1000, 2000, 3000, 4000, 5000 et 6000 en pourcentage du total des recettes fiscales ne s'élève pas à 100 % car les moyennes pour la rubrique 2000 (cotisations de sécurité sociale) et la rubrique 4000 (taxes sur le patrimoine) excluent les pays pour lesquels ces données ne sont pas disponibles.
4. Représente la moyenne non pondérée pour les 25 pays d'Amérique latine et des Caraïbes (ALC) inclus dans la publication *Revenue Statistics in Latin America and the Caribbean 2018.*
5. Représente la moyenne non pondérée pour 35 pays de l'OCDE. Les données sont pour 2015 car les données pour 2016 n'étaient pas disponibles à la date de la publication.

StatLink https://doi.org/10.1787/888933820126

Table 4.5. **Taxes on income and profits (1000) as percentage of GDP**
Tableau 4.5. **Impôts sur le revenu et les bénéfices (1000) en pourcentage du PIB**

	1997	2000	2005	2010	2011	2012	2013	2014	2015	2016
Botswana	..	..	11.1	10.2	10.6	8.8	10.5	10.9	8.6	9.7
Burkina Faso	..	2.7	3.2	3.1	4.3	4.9	5.2	4.4	4.3	4.8
Cabo Verde	5.1	5.5	6.0	5.7	5.9	5.7	5.6	5.0	6.1	6.2
Cameroon / Cameroun	2.5	3.2	3.4	3.3	3.7	4.3	4.3	4.5	4.7	4.0
Congo	..	2.1	1.9	2.5	2.7	3.1	7.3	4.2	6.7	6.7
Congo, Dem. Rep. / Congo, Rép. dém.	..	0.2	1.0	2.4	2.3	2.5	2.6	3.0	3.4	2.3
Côte d'Ivoire	3.2	2.5	2.2	2.1	2.7	3.2	2.8	2.3	2.1	1.9
Egypt / Égypte	..	..	6.5	7.3	7.3	6.7	7.8	7.4	6.9	7.0
Eswatini	5.6	5.3	6.1	7.1	7.3	5.7	7.0	7.7	7.4	7.9
Ghana	..	3.2	4.1	5.3	5.9	6.5	5.9	6.5	5.5	4.8
Kenya	..	..	6.6	7.3	7.9	8.2	8.7	8.9	8.6	8.4
Mali	..	1.6	2.4	3.5	3.2	3.5	3.5	4.2	3.8	3.9
Mauritius / Maurice[1]	2.8	2.5	3.1	5.0	4.5	4.5	4.6	4.8	4.9	4.9
Morocco / Maroc	..	5.7	7.7	8.0	8.4	9.1	8.4	8.2	8.0	8.3
Niger	..	1.8	2.0	3.3	3.7	4.7	6.6	5.1	4.2	3.8
Rwanda	2.6	2.7	3.5	4.7	5.0	5.5	6.3	5.9	6.4	6.5
Senegal / Sénégal	3.2	3.7	4.5	5.1	4.9	5.3	5.1	5.3	5.4	5.9
South Africa / Afrique du Sud	12.8	12.7	13.4	13.4	13.6	13.8	13.9	14.3	15.0	14.8
Togo	..	2.0	3.3	2.6	2.9	2.8	3.7	4.3	3.9	5.2
Tunisia / Tunisie	..	5.5	7.0	8.1	9.2	8.4	9.2	9.8	9.1	8.2
Uganda / Ouganda	1.5	2.0	3.5	3.3	3.5	3.7	4.0	3.9	4.4	4.6
Africa (21) average / Moyenne Afrique (21)[2]	**..**	**3.6**	**4.9**	**5.4**	**5.7**	**5.8**	**6.3**	**6.2**	**6.2**	**6.2**
LAC average / Moyenne ALC[3]	**4.1**	**4.3**	**5.2**	**5.7**	**6.0**	**6.1**	**6.1**	**6.3**	**6.3**	**6.0**
OECD average / Moyenne OCDE[4]	**11.6**	**12.0**	**11.7**	**10.8**	**11.0**	**11.2**	**11.3**	**11.5**	**11.5**	**..**

Note: The figures include sub-national government tax revenues for Eswatini (Swaziland in previous editions), Mauritius, Morocco and South Africa (for 2002-16). Sub-national government tax revenues are not available in other countries.

1. The fiscal year for Mauritius changed in 2010 and in 2015. Figures for 2015 needed to be estimated as a result.
2. Represents an unweighted average for the 21 African countries included in this publication. Due to lack of data availability, the Africa (21) average does not include Botswana prior to 2004, Egypt prior to 2002 and Kenya prior to 2001. These countries are included in the calculations of the Africa (21) average for subsequent years.
3. Represents an unweighted average for the 25 Latin American and Caribbean (LAC) countries included in the publication *Revenue Statistics in Latin America and the Caribbean 2018*.
4. Represents an unweighted average for 35 OECD countries.

Note : Les chiffres incluent les recettes fiscales collectées par les administrations infranationales pour l'Afrique du Sud (pour les années 2002 à 2016), Eswatini (Swaziland dans les éditions précédentes), le Maroc et Maurice. Les données des recettes fiscales collectées par les administrations infranationales ne sont pas disponibles pour les autres pays.

1. L'année fiscale pour Maurice a changé en 2010 et en 2015. Les chiffres pour 2015 ont dû être estimés en conséquence.
2. Représente la moyenne non pondérée pour les 21 pays d'Afrique inclus dans cette publication. En raison du manque de disponibilité des données, la moyenne Afrique (21) n'inclut pas le Botswana avant 2004, l'Égypte avant 2002 et le Kenya avant 2001. Ces pays sont inclus dans les calculs de la moyenne Afrique (21) pour les années suivantes.
3. Représente la moyenne non pondérée pour les 25 pays d'Amérique latine et des Caraïbes (ALC) inclus dans la publication *Revenue Statistics in Latin America and the Caribbean 2018*.
4. Représente la moyenne non pondérée pour 35 pays de l'OCDE.

StatLink https://doi.org/10.1787/888933820145

Table 4.6. **Taxes on income and profits (1000) as percentage of total taxation**
Tableau 4.6. **Impôts sur le revenu et les bénéfices (1000) en pourcentage du total des recettes fiscales**

	1997	2000	2005	2010	2011	2012	2013	2014	2015	2016
Botswana	..	..	73.2	65.3	67.6	63.7	71.4	71.7	67.9	69.5
Burkina Faso	..	26.7	23.4	20.5	27.5	28.7	29.0	27.1	24.6	26.3
Cabo Verde	35.1	35.7	30.9	30.9	30.0	32.3	31.4	29.6	32.4	32.3
Cameroon / Cameroun	24.0	28.1	28.7	27.1	28.1	31.9	30.7	31.5	32.3	28.1
Congo	..	48.2	31.4	35.0	36.4	37.1	52.4	36.2	40.7	41.8
Congo, Dem. Rep. / Congo, Rép. dém.	..	34.0	18.6	26.8	25.2	21.8	25.6	32.0	35.6	30.3
Côte d'Ivoire	18.7	16.4	13.8	12.9	17.6	18.1	16.0	13.6	11.9	11.2
Egypt / Égypte	..	..	39.8	44.5	46.3	44.4	48.2	48.4	43.9	45.7
Eswatini	54.3	51.0	53.6	51.7	52.3	43.4	49.4	51.8	49.8	51.3
Ghana	..	28.9	25.9	36.1	36.9	40.0	39.0	38.9	32.1	27.4
Kenya	..	..	35.9	40.6	42.3	45.9	48.7	46.6	46.8	46.2
Mali	..	14.3	16.3	24.5	23.0	25.4	24.7	30.0	25.4	24.2
Mauritius / Maurice[1]	14.9	12.9	16.7	25.4	22.9	22.6	23.4	24.0	24.7	24.4
Morocco / Maroc	..	24.3	31.2	28.9	29.6	30.9	30.0	30.6	30.8	31.3
Niger	..	18.0	18.3	25.4	26.9	32.4	38.9	31.4	24.7	26.4
Rwanda	25.3	26.0	28.6	36.2	36.4	38.2	40.5	37.3	38.2	38.9
Senegal / Sénégal	21.0	22.1	23.1	25.9	24.7	26.5	26.0	25.2	25.5	26.9
South Africa / Afrique du Sud	56.6	56.7	52.6	54.0	53.7	52.1	51.2	51.7	52.0	51.8
Togo	..	21.6	24.6	17.3	15.9	14.5	19.1	20.3	18.2	23.3
Tunisia / Tunisie	..	22.6	28.9	29.7	31.7	28.9	30.7	31.8	30.0	27.8
Uganda / Ouganda	13.9	18.2	29.0	31.5	32.7	33.5	35.7	34.0	34.7	34.9
Africa (21) average / Moyenne Afrique (21)[2]	**..**	**28.1**	**30.7**	**32.9**	**33.7**	**33.9**	**36.3**	**35.4**	**34.4**	**34.3**
LAC average / Moyenne ALC[3]	**23.0**	**23.2**	**25.9**	**27.1**	**28.1**	**28.0**	**28.0**	**28.3**	**27.4**	**27.3**
OECD average / Moyenne OCDE[4]	**34.2**	**35.0**	**34.5**	**33.2**	**33.6**	**33.7**	**33.8**	**33.8**	**34.1**	**..**

Note: The figures include sub-national government tax revenues for Eswatini (Swaziland in previous editions), Mauritius, Morocco and South Africa (for 2002-16). Sub-national government tax revenues are not available in other countries.

1. The fiscal year for Mauritius changed in 2010 and in 2015. Figures for 2015 needed to be estimated as a result.
2. Represents an unweighted average for the 21 African countries included in this publication. Due to lack of data availability, the Africa (21) average does not include Botswana prior to 2004, Egypt prior to 2002 and Kenya prior to 2001. These countries are included in the calculations of the Africa (21) average for subsequent years.
3. Represents an unweighted average for the 25 Latin American and Caribbean (LAC) countries included in the publication *Revenue Statistics in Latin America and the Caribbean 2018*.
4. Represents an unweighted average for 35 OECD countries.

Note : Les chiffres incluent les recettes fiscales collectées par les administrations infranationales pour l'Afrique du Sud (pour les années 2002 à 2016), Eswatini (Swaziland dans les éditions précédentes), le Maroc et Maurice. Les données des recettes fiscales collectées par les administrations infranationales ne sont pas disponibles pour les autres pays.

1. L'année fiscale pour Maurice a changé en 2010 et en 2015. Les chiffres pour 2015 ont dû être estimés en conséquence.
2. Représente la moyenne non pondérée pour les 21 pays d'Afrique inclus dans cette publication. En raison du manque de disponibilité des données, la moyenne Afrique (21) n'inclut pas le Botswana avant 2004, l'Égypte avant 2002 et le Kenya avant 2001. Ces pays sont inclus dans les calculs de la moyenne Afrique (21) pour les années suivantes.
3. Représente la moyenne non pondérée pour les 25 pays d'Amérique latine et des Caraïbes (ALC) inclus dans la publication *Revenue Statistics in Latin America and the Caribbean 2018*.
4. Représente la moyenne non pondérée pour 35 pays de l'OCDE.

StatLink https://doi.org/10.1787/888933820164

Table 4.7. **Social security contributions (2000) as percentage of GDP**
Tableau 4.7. **Cotisations de sécurité sociale (2000) en pourcentage du PIB**

	1997	2000	2005	2010	2011	2012	2013	2014	2015	2016
Botswana	..	..	0.0	0.0	0.0	0.0	0.0	0.0	0.0	0.0
Burkina Faso	..	0.7	0.8	1.0	1.0	1.0	1.1	1.1	1.2	1.1
Cabo Verde	0.0	0.8	0.6	0.0	0.0	0.0	0.0	0.0	0.0	0.0
Cameroon / Cameroun	0.8	0.9	0.9	1.0	1.0	1.0	1.0	0.9	0.9	1.1
Congo	..	..	..	..	..	..	..	..	..	..
Congo, Dem. Rep. / Congo, Rép. dém.	..	..	..	..	..	0.5	0.6	0.6	0.6	0.5
Côte d'Ivoire	1.2	1.3	1.3	1.3	1.1	1.7	2.0	2.0	2.0	2.1
Egypt / Égypte	..	..	3.0	2.4	2.1	2.2	2.4	2.6	2.7	1.9
Eswatini	1.2	1.2	1.4	1.9	1.7	1.6	1.5	1.5	1.6	1.5
Ghana	..	1.0	1.2	1.3	1.4	1.2	1.2	1.6	1.5	1.5
Kenya	..	..	0.2	0.2	0.2	0.2	0.1	0.1	0.1	0.3
Mali	..	0.9	1.4	1.4	1.4	1.4	1.4	1.6	1.5	1.8
Mauritius / Maurice[1]	1.2	1.1	0.7	1.0	1.0	1.0	1.0	1.0	1.0	1.0
Morocco / Maroc[2]	..	3.9	4.0	4.9	5.3	5.4	5.3	4.6	4.4	4.5
Niger	..	0.5	0.4	0.7	0.7	0.7	0.8	0.8	0.8	0.8
Rwanda[3]	0.4	0.5	0.8	0.8	0.9	1.0	1.1	1.0	1.0	1.1
Senegal / Sénégal[4]	0.6	0.7	0.8	1.1	0.9	1.2	1.3	1.3	1.3	1.5
South Africa / Afrique du Sud	0.0	0.0	0.4	0.4	0.4	0.4	0.4	0.4	0.4	0.4
Togo	..	..	..	..	..	..	..	..	..	..
Tunisia / Tunisie[3]	..	5.3	5.5	7.3	8.1	8.3	8.7	8.5	8.9	9.3
Uganda / Ouganda	..	..	..	..	..	..	..	..	..	..
Africa (21) average / Moyenne Afrique (21)[5]	**..**	**1.3**	**1.4**	**1.6**	**1.6**	**1.6**	**1.7**	**1.6**	**1.7**	**1.7**
LAC average / Moyenne ALC[6]	**2.4**	**2.6**	**2.7**	**3.2**	**3.2**	**3.4**	**3.5**	**3.6**	**3.7**	**3.7**
OECD average / Moyenne OCDE[7]	**8.7**	**8.6**	**8.5**	**8.8**	**8.8**	**8.9**	**9.0**	**9.0**	**9.0**	**..**

Table 4.7. **Social security contributions (2000) as percentage of GDP** *(cont.)*
Tableau 4.7. **Cotisations de sécurité sociale (2000) en pourcentage du PIB** *(suite)*

Note: The figures include sub-national government tax revenues for Eswatini (Swaziland in previous editions), Mauritius, Morocco and South Africa (for 2002-16). Sub-national government tax revenues are not available in other countries.

Heading 2000: Data on social security contributions are not available for the Republic of the Congo, the Democratic Republic of Congo (prior to 2012), Togo and Uganda; and are only partially available in Cameroon and Senegal. Social security contributions for Botswana are deemed to be null as they do not meet the criteria to be classified as social security contributions set out in the OECD classification of taxes in the Interpretative Guide.

See the country tables in Chapter 5 for further information on data issues for individual countries.

1. The fiscal year for Mauritius changed in 2010 and in 2015. Figures for 2015 needed to be estimated as a result.
2. Estimated figures for years prior to 2002.
3. Rwanda and Tunisia do not include social security contributions in the tax-to-GDP ratios in their official publications as neither country considers them as taxes. They are included as tax revenue in this publication, following the classification set out in the OECD Interpretative Guide.
4. These figures include contributions to the Senegalese Pension Institute (IPRES) (estimated prior to 2006) and contributions to the social security fund (CSS) from 2012 as data for previous years are not available.
5. Represents an unweighted average for the 21 African countries included in this publication. The Africa (21) average should be interpreted with caution as data for social security contributions are not available or partially available in a few countries. Due to lack of data availability, the Africa (21) average does not include Botswana prior to 2004, Egypt prior to 2002 and Kenya prior to 2001. These countries are included in the calculations of the Africa (21) average for subsequent years.
6. Represents an unweighted average for the 25 Latin American and Caribbean (LAC) countries included in the publication *Revenue Statistics in Latin America and the Caribbean 2018*.
7. Represents an unweighted average for 35 OECD countries.

Note : Les chiffres incluent les recettes fiscales collectées par les administrations infranationales pour l'Afrique du Sud (pour les années 2002 à 2016), Eswatini (Swaziland dans les éditions précédentes), le Maroc et Maurice. Les données des recettes fiscales collectées par les administrations infranationales ne sont pas disponibles pour les autres pays.

Rubrique 2000 : Les données des cotisations de sécurité sociale ne sont pas disponibles pour la République du Congo, la République démocratique du Congo (avant 2012), l'Ouganda et le Togo et ne sont que partiellement disponibles au Cameroun et au Sénégal. Les cotisations de sécurité sociale pour le Botswana sont nulles car elles ne répondent pas aux critères de classification des cotisations de sécurité sociale de la classification des impôts de l'OCDE du Guide d'interprétation.

Voir les tableaux des pays au chapitre 5 pour plus d'informations sur les problèmes de données pour les pays individuels.

1. L'année fiscale pour Maurice a changé en 2010 et en 2015. Les chiffres pour 2015 ont dû être estimés en conséquence.
2. Les chiffres sont estimés pour les années antérieures à 2002.
3. Le Rwanda et la Tunisie n'incluent pas les cotisations de sécurité sociale dans le ratio impôts/PIB dans leurs publications officielles car aucun des deux pays ne les considère comme des impôts. Elles sont incluses comme recettes fiscales dans cette publication en accordance avec la classification des impôts établie dans le Guide d'interprétation de l'OCDE.
4. Les chiffres comprennent les cotisations de sécurité sociale de l'Institution de prévoyance retraite du Sénégal (IPRES) (estimées pour les années antérieures à 2006) et les cotisations de sécurité sociale de la Caisse de Sécurité Sociale (CSS) (à partir de 2012 car les données pour les années précédentes ne sont pas disponibles).
5. Représente la moyenne non pondérée pour les 21 pays d'Afrique inclus dans cette publication. Il convient d'interpréter la moyenne Afrique (21) avec prudence car les données pour les cotisations de sécurité sociale ne sont pas disponibles ou partiellement disponibles dans quelques pays. En raison du manque de disponibilité des données, la moyenne Afrique (21) n'inclut pas le Botswana avant 2004, l'Égypte avant 2002 et le Kenya avant 2001. Ces pays sont inclus dans les calculs de la moyenne Afrique (21) pour les années suivantes.
6. Représente la moyenne non pondérée pour les 25 pays d'Amérique latine et des Caraïbes (ALC) inclus dans la publication *Revenue Statistics in Latin America and the Caribbean 2018*.
7. Représente la moyenne non pondérée pour 35 pays de l'OCDE.

StatLink https://doi.org/10.1787/888933820183

Table 4.8. **Social security contributions (2000) as percentage of total taxation**
Tableau 4.8. **Cotisations de sécurité sociale (2000) en pourcentage du total des recettes fiscales**

	1997	2000	2005	2010	2011	2012	2013	2014	2015	2016
Botswana	..	..	0.0	0.0	0.0	0.0	0.0	0.0	0.0	0.0
Burkina Faso	..	7.0	5.9	6.2	6.6	5.6	6.1	6.6	7.0	6.3
Cabo Verde	0.0	5.2	2.8	0.2	0.1	0.2	0.2	0.2	0.2	0.2
Cameroon / Cameroun	7.8	8.1	7.4	8.6	8.0	7.4	7.1	6.2	6.0	7.3
Congo	..	..	..	..	..	..	..	..	..	..
Congo, Dem. Rep. / Congo, Rép. dém.	..	..	..	..	..	4.5	5.6	6.3	5.9	7.0
Côte d'Ivoire	7.1	8.8	8.3	8.0	7.0	9.7	11.3	11.6	11.2	11.8
Egypt / Égypte	..	..	18.3	14.6	13.4	14.8	15.0	16.8	17.0	12.6
Eswatini	11.7	11.6	11.9	13.6	12.3	12.1	10.6	10.0	10.7	10.0
Ghana	..	9.4	7.7	8.6	8.6	7.6	8.3	9.4	9.0	8.8
Kenya	..	..	1.3	1.1	1.1	1.0	0.7	0.6	0.7	1.4
Mali	..	7.7	9.5	9.8	10.3	10.3	9.9	11.3	10.1	11.4
Mauritius / Maurice[1]	6.2	5.5	4.0	4.9	4.9	4.8	5.0	5.2	5.3	5.2
Morocco / Maroc[2]	..	16.8	16.2	17.6	18.5	18.2	19.0	17.0	17.0	17.1
Niger	..	5.4	3.8	5.3	5.3	4.8	4.7	5.1	4.7	5.5
Rwanda[3]	3.4	5.0	6.9	6.4	6.6	6.6	7.0	6.4	6.0	6.8
Senegal / Sénégal[4]	3.9	4.0	4.1	5.8	4.4	6.2	6.7	6.3	6.0	6.7
South Africa / Afrique du Sud	0.0	0.0	1.5	1.6	1.6	1.6	1.5	1.5	1.5	1.4
Togo	..	..	..	..	..	..	..	..	..	..
Tunisia / Tunisie[3]	..	21.6	22.7	27.0	27.7	28.5	29.0	27.5	29.5	31.6
Uganda / Ouganda	..	..	..	..	..	..	..	..	..	..
Africa (21) average / Moyenne Afrique (21)[5]	..	**8.3**	**7.8**	**8.2**	**8.0**	**8.0**	**8.2**	**8.2**	**8.2**	**8.4**
LAC average / Moyenne ALC[6]	**13.6**	**14.5**	**14.0**	**14.9**	**14.8**	**15.4**	**15.8**	**15.9**	**16.0**	**15.9**
OECD average / Moyenne OCDE[7]	**25.1**	**24.7**	**25.1**	**26.4**	**26.3**	**26.2**	**26.1**	**26.0**	**25.8**	..

Table 4.8. **Social security contributions (2000) as percentage of total taxation** *(cont.)*
Tableau 4.8. **Cotisations de sécurité sociale (2000) en pourcentage du total des recettes fiscales** *(suite)*

Note: The figures include sub-national government tax revenues for Eswatini (Swaziland in previous editions), Mauritius, Morocco and South Africa (for 2002-16). Sub-national government tax revenues are not available in other countries.

Heading 2000: Data on social security contributions are not available for the Republic of the Congo, the Democratic Republic of Congo (prior to 2012), Togo and Uganda; and are only partially available in Cameroon and Senegal. Social security contributions for Botswana are deemed to be null as they do not meet the criteria to be classified as social security contributions set out in the OECD classification of taxes in the Interpretative Guide.

See the country tables in Chapter 5 for further information on data issues for individual countries.

1. The fiscal year for Mauritius changed in 2010 and in 2015. Figures for 2015 needed to be estimated as a result.
2. Estimated figures for years prior to 2002.
3. Rwanda and Tunisia do not include social security contributions in the tax-to-GDP ratios in their official publications as neither country considers them as taxes. They are included as tax revenue in this publication, following the classification set out in the OECD Interpretative Guide.
4. These figures include contributions to the Senegalese Pension Institute (IPRES) (estimated prior to 2006) and contributions to the social security fund (CSS) from 2012 as data for previous years are not available.
5. Represents an unweighted average for the 21 African countries included in this publication. The Africa (21) average should be interpreted with caution as data for social security contributions are not available or partially available in a few countries. Due to lack of data availability, the Africa (21) average does not include Botswana prior to 2004, Egypt prior to 2002 and Kenya prior to 2001. These countries are included in the calculations of the Africa (21) average for subsequent years.
6. Represents an unweighted average for the 25 Latin American and Caribbean (LAC) countries included in the publication *Revenue Statistics in Latin America and the Caribbean 2018*.
7. Represents an unweighted average for 35 OECD countries.

Note : Les chiffres incluent les recettes fiscales collectées par les administrations infranationales pour l'Afrique du Sud (pour les années 2002 à 2016), Eswatini (Swaziland dans les éditions précédentes), le Maroc et Maurice. Les données des recettes fiscales collectées par les administrations infranationales ne sont pas disponibles pour les autres pays.

Rubrique 2000 : Les données des cotisations de sécurité sociale ne sont pas disponibles pour la République du Congo, la République démocratique du Congo (avant 2012), l'Ouganda et le Togo et ne sont que partiellement disponibles au Cameroun et au Sénégal. Les cotisations de sécurité sociale pour le Botswana sont nulles car elles ne répondent pas aux critères de classification des cotisations de sécurité sociale de la classification des impôts de l'OCDE du Guide d'interprétation.

Voir les tableaux des pays au chapitre 5 pour plus d'informations sur les problèmes de données pour les pays individuels.

1. L'année fiscale pour Maurice a changé en 2010 et en 2015. Les chiffres pour 2015 ont dû être estimés en conséquence.
2. Les chiffres sont estimés pour les années antérieures à 2002.
3. Le Rwanda et la Tunisie n'incluent pas les cotisations de sécurité sociale dans le ratio impôts/PIB dans leurs publications officielles car aucun des deux pays ne les considère comme des impôts. Elles sont incluses comme recettes fiscales dans cette publication en accordance avec la classification des impôts établie dans le Guide d'interprétation de l'OCDE.
4. Les chiffres comprennent les cotisations de sécurité sociale de l'Institution de prévoyance retraite du Sénégal (IPRES) (estimées pour les années antérieures à 2006) et les cotisations de sécurité sociale de la Caisse de Sécurité Sociale (CSS) (à partir de 2012 car les données pour les années précédentes ne sont pas disponibles).
5. Représente la moyenne non pondérée pour les 21 pays d'Afrique inclus dans cette publication. Il convient d'interpréter la moyenne Afrique (21) avec prudence car les données pour les cotisations de sécurité sociale ne sont pas disponibles ou partiellement disponibles dans quelques pays. En raison du manque de disponibilité des données, la moyenne Afrique (21) n'inclut pas le Botswana avant 2004, l'Égypte avant 2002 et le Kenya avant 2001. Ces pays sont inclus dans les calculs de la moyenne Afrique (21) pour les années suivantes.
6. Représente la moyenne non pondérée pour les 25 pays d'Amérique latine et des Caraïbes (ALC) inclus dans la publication *Revenue Statistics in Latin America and the Caribbean 2018*.
7. Représente la moyenne non pondérée pour 35 pays de l'OCDE.

StatLink https://doi.org/10.1787/888933820202

Table 4.9. **Taxes on property (4000) as percentage of GDP**
Tableau 4.9. **Impôts sur le patrimoine (4000) en pourcentage du PIB**

	1997	2000	2005	2010	2011	2012	2013	2014	2015	2016
Botswana	..	..	0.0	0.1	0.1	0.0	0.0	0.0	0.0	0.0
Burkina Faso	..	0.1	0.1	0.1	0.1	0.1	0.1	0.2	0.2	0.2
Cabo Verde	0.8	0.8	0.8	0.5	0.6	0.4	0.4	0.4	0.4	0.3
Cameroon / Cameroun	0.1	0.2	0.1	0.1	0.1	0.1	0.1	0.1	0.1	0.2
Congo	..	0.1	0.0	0.0	0.1	0.1	0.1	0.1	0.2	0.1
Congo, Dem. Rep. / Congo, Rép. dém.[1]	..	..	..	0.1	0.0	0.0	0.0	0.0	0.0	0.0
Côte d'Ivoire	0.4	0.4	0.5	0.4	0.3	0.4	0.5	0.5	0.5	0.5
Egypt / Égypte	..	..	0.2	0.2	0.2	0.2	0.2	0.2	0.2	0.2
Eswatini	0.2	0.3	0.3	0.3	0.3	0.3	0.3	0.3	0.3	0.3
Ghana[1]	..	..	..	..	..	..	..	..	..	..
Kenya	..	..	0.1	0.2	0.2	0.2	0.2	0.2	0.2	0.2
Mali	..	0.1	0.2	0.2	0.2	0.2	0.2	0.2	0.2	0.3
Mauritius / Maurice[2]	1.4	1.2	1.0	1.1	1.0	1.1	1.0	1.1	1.0	1.1
Morocco / Maroc	..	1.3	1.5	1.6	1.6	1.8	1.9	1.9	2.0	2.0
Niger	..	0.1	0.1	0.1	0.1	0.1	0.0	0.0	0.1	0.0
Rwanda	0.0	0.0	0.0	0.0	0.0	0.0	0.0	0.0	0.0	0.0
Senegal / Sénégal	0.4	0.3	0.5	0.6	0.6	0.5	0.5	0.5	0.5	0.6
South Africa / Afrique du Sud	0.4	0.4	1.4	1.5	1.4	1.4	1.5	1.5	1.5	1.6
Togo	..	0.0	0.0	0.1	0.1	0.1	0.1	0.2	0.2	0.1
Tunisia / Tunisie	..	0.3	0.2	0.3	0.3	0.3	0.3	0.3	0.3	0.3
Uganda / Ouganda[1]	..	..	..	..	..	..	..	..	..	..
Africa (21) average / Moyenne Afrique (21)[3]	**..**	**0.4**	**0.4**	**0.4**	**0.4**	**0.4**	**0.4**	**0.4**	**0.4**	**0.4**
LAC average / Moyenne ALC[4]	**0.5**	**0.6**	**0.8**	**0.7**	**0.7**	**0.7**	**0.8**	**0.7**	**0.8**	**0.8**
OECD average / Moyenne OCDE[5]	**1.7**	**1.8**	**1.8**	**1.7**	**1.8**	**1.8**	**1.9**	**1.9**	**1.9**	**..**

Note: The figures include sub-national government tax revenues for Eswatini (Swaziland in previous editions), Mauritius, Morocco and South Africa (for 2002-16). Sub-national government tax revenues are not available in other countries.

1. In the Democratic Republic of the Congo, Ghana and Uganda, revenues from property taxes are mainly levied by local governments whose data are not available. In the Democratic Republic of the Congo, only data for property tax revenues levied by the *Direction Générale des Recettes Administratives, Judiciaires, Domaniales et de Participation* (DGRAD) are available for 2010-16. See the country tables in Chapter 5 for further information.
2. The fiscal year for Mauritius changed in 2010 and in 2015. Figures for 2015 needed to be estimated as a result.
3. Represents an unweighted average for the 21 African countries included in this publication. The Africa (21) average should be interpreted with caution as several countries collect property taxes at the local level, for which data is missing. Due to lack of data availability, the Africa (21) average does not include Botswana prior to 2004, Egypt prior to 2002 and Kenya prior to 2001. These countries are included in the calculations of the Africa (21) average for subsequent years.
4. Represents an unweighted average for the 25 Latin American and Caribbean (LAC) countries included in the publication *Revenue Statistics in Latin America and the Caribbean 2018.*
5. Represents an unweighted average for 35 OECD countries.

Note : Les chiffres incluent les recettes fiscales collectées par les administrations infranationales pour l'Afrique du Sud (pour les années 2002 à 2016), Eswatini (Swaziland dans les éditions précédentes), le Maroc et Maurice. Les données des recettes fiscales collectées par les administrations infranationales ne sont pas disponibles pour les autres pays.

1. En République démocratique du Congo, au Ghana et en Ouganda, les recettes provenant des impôts sur le patrimoine sont principalement perçues par les administrations locales pour lesquelles les données ne sont pas disponibles. En République démocratique du Congo, seules les données des recettes relatives aux impôts sur le patrimoine qui sont prélevées par la *Direction Générale des Recettes Administratives, Judiciaires, Domaniales et de Participation* (DGRAD) sont disponibles pour la période 2010-16. Voir les tableaux des pays au chapitre 5 pour plus d'informations.
2. L'année fiscale pour Maurice a changé en 2010 et en 2015. Les chiffres pour 2015 ont dû être estimés en conséquence.
3. Représente la moyenne non pondérée pour les 21 pays africains inclus dans cette publication. Il convient d'interpréter la moyenne Afrique (21) avec prudence car les données provenant des taxes foncières ne sont pas disponibles ou partiellement disponibles dans quelques pays. En raison du manque de disponibilité des données, la moyenne Afrique (21) n'inclut pas le Botswana avant 2004, l'Égypte avant 2002 et le Kenya avant 2001. Ces pays sont inclus dans les calculs de la moyenne Afrique (21) pour les années suivantes.
4. Représente la moyenne non pondérée pour les 25 pays d'Amérique latine et des Caraïbes (ALC) inclus dans la publication *Revenue Statistics in Latin America and the Caribbean 2018.*
5. Représente la moyenne non pondérée pour 35 pays de l'OCDE.

StatLink https://doi.org/10.1787/888933820221

Table 4.10. **Taxes on property (4000) as percentage of total taxation**
Tableau 4.10. **Impôts sur le patrimoine (4000) en pourcentage du total des recettes fiscales**

	1997	2000	2005	2010	2011	2012	2013	2014	2015	2016
Botswana	..	..	0.2	0.4	0.4	0.3	0.3	0.2	0.3	0.3
Burkina Faso	..	0.6	0.6	0.4	0.9	0.7	0.7	1.0	0.9	1.1
Cabo Verde	5.4	5.3	4.3	2.7	2.9	2.5	2.4	2.6	2.0	1.5
Cameroon / Cameroun	0.8	1.6	1.2	1.1	0.7	0.8	0.9	0.8	0.9	1.1
Congo	..	1.3	0.8	0.7	0.7	0.7	0.6	0.6	1.4	0.6
Congo, Dem. Rep. / Congo, Rép. dém.[1]	..	..	..	0.6	0.3	0.3	0.2	0.4	0.4	0.5
Côte d'Ivoire	2.6	2.8	3.1	2.4	2.1	2.5	3.0	2.7	2.6	2.8
Egypt / Égypte	..	..	1.5	1.3	1.2	1.2	1.0	1.2	1.1	1.4
Eswatini	2.0	2.6	2.3	2.0	2.0	2.0	2.1	1.9	1.9	1.9
Ghana[1]	..	..	..	..	..	..	..	..	..	..
Kenya	..	..	0.4	1.2	1.2	1.3	1.2	1.2	1.2	1.0
Mali	..	1.3	1.7	1.6	1.7	1.1	1.3	1.7	1.5	2.1
Mauritius / Maurice[2]	7.5	6.3	5.5	5.6	5.0	5.4	4.9	5.6	5.1	5.6
Morocco / Maroc	..	5.6	6.2	5.9	5.6	6.2	6.7	7.2	7.6	7.5
Niger	..	1.1	0.8	0.8	0.7	0.6	0.3	0.2	0.4	0.3
Rwanda	0.1	0.2	0.0	0.0	0.0	0.0	0.0	0.0	0.1	0.1
Senegal / Sénégal	2.4	2.0	2.6	3.1	2.8	2.6	2.5	2.5	2.4	2.7
South Africa / Afrique du Sud	1.6	1.8	5.6	5.9	5.5	5.4	5.4	5.5	5.0	5.4
Togo	..	0.3	0.3	0.7	0.6	0.6	0.6	0.7	0.7	0.7
Tunisia / Tunisie	..	1.1	1.0	1.0	1.2	1.1	1.1	1.0	1.1	1.1
Uganda / Ouganda[1]	..	..	..	..	..	..	..	..	..	..
Africa (21) average / Moyenne Afrique (21)[3]	**..**	**2.3**	**2.1**	**2.0**	**1.9**	**1.9**	**1.9**	**2.0**	**1.9**	**2.0**
LAC average / Moyenne ALC[4]	**2.6**	**2.8**	**3.9**	**3.2**	**3.1**	**3.2**	**3.4**	**3.2**	**3.4**	**3.4**
OECD average / Moyenne OCDE[5]	**5.3**	**5.5**	**5.6**	**5.5**	**5.5**	**5.5**	**5.6**	**5.7**	**5.8**	**..**

Note: The figures include sub-national government tax revenues for Eswatini (Swaziland in previous editions), Mauritius, Morocco and South Africa (for 2002-16). Sub-national government tax revenues are not available in other countries.

1. In the Democratic Republic of the Congo, Ghana and Uganda, revenues from property taxes are mainly levied by local governments whose data are not available. In the Democratic Republic of the Congo, only data for property tax revenues levied by the *Direction Générale des Recettes Administratives, Judiciaires, Domaniales et de Participation* (DGRAD) are available for 2010-16. See the country tables in Chapter 5 for further information.
2. The fiscal year for Mauritius changed in 2010 and in 2015. Figures for 2015 needed to be estimated as a result.
3. Represents an unweighted average for the 21 African countries included in this publication. The Africa (21) average should be interpreted with caution as several countries collect property taxes at the local level, for which data is missing. Due to lack of data availability, the Africa (21) average does not include Botswana prior to 2004, Egypt prior to 2002 and Kenya prior to 2001. These countries are included in the calculations of the Africa (21) average for subsequent years.
4. Represents an unweighted average for the 25 Latin American and Caribbean (LAC) countries included in the publication *Revenue Statistics in Latin America and the Caribbean 2018.*
5. Represents an unweighted average for 35 OECD countries.

Note : Les chiffres incluent les recettes fiscales collectées par les administrations infranationales pour l'Afrique du Sud (pour les années 2002 à 2016), Eswatini (Swaziland dans les éditions précédentes), le Maroc et Maurice. Les données des recettes fiscales collectées par les administrations infranationales ne sont pas disponibles pour les autres pays.

1. En République démocratique du Congo, au Ghana et en Ouganda, les recettes provenant des impôts sur le patrimoine sont principalement perçues par les administrations locales pour lesquelles les données ne sont pas disponibles. En République démocratique du Congo, seules les données des recettes relatives aux impôts sur le patrimoine qui sont prélevées par la *Direction Générale des Recettes Administratives, Judiciaires, Domaniales et de Participation* (DGRAD) sont disponibles pour la période 2010-16. Voir les tableaux des pays au chapitre 5 pour plus d'informations.
2. L'année fiscale pour Maurice a changé en 2010 et en 2015. Les chiffres pour 2015 ont dû être estimés en conséquence.
3. Représente la moyenne non pondérée pour les 21 pays africains inclus dans cette publication. Il convient d'interpréter la moyenne Afrique (21) avec prudence car les données provenant des taxes foncières ne sont pas disponibles ou partiellement disponibles dans quelques pays. En raison du manque de disponibilité des données, la moyenne Afrique (21) n'inclut pas le Botswana avant 2004, l'Égypte avant 2002 et le Kenya avant 2001. Ces pays sont inclus dans les calculs de la moyenne Afrique (21) pour les années suivantes.
4. Représente la moyenne non pondérée pour les 25 pays d'Amérique latine et des Caraïbes (ALC) inclus dans la publication *Revenue Statistics in Latin America and the Caribbean 2018.*
5. Représente la moyenne non pondérée pour 35 pays de l'OCDE.

StatLink https://doi.org/10.1787/888933820240

Table 4.11. **Taxes on goods and services (5000) as percentage of GDP**
Tableau 4.11. **Impôts sur les biens et services (5000) en pourcentage du PIB**

	1997	2000	2005	2010	2011	2012	2013	2014	2015	2016
Botswana	..	..	4.0	5.4	5.0	5.0	4.1	4.3	4.0	4.2
Burkina Faso	..	6.5	9.4	10.9	10.1	11.0	11.4	10.5	11.5	11.8
Cabo Verde	8.7	8.4	12.1	12.2	13.1	11.5	11.7	11.4	12.3	12.5
Cameroon / Cameroun	6.9	7.0	7.3	7.3	7.8	7.6	8.1	8.4	8.4	8.6
Congo	..	2.0	4.1	4.3	4.4	4.9	6.3	6.9	9.1	8.7
Congo, Dem. Rep. / Congo, Rép. dém.	..	0.4	3.5	5.9	6.2	7.6	6.3	5.2	5.3	4.6
Côte d'Ivoire	10.6	9.2	10.0	10.9	9.5	10.3	10.2	10.2	11.0	10.9
Egypt / Égypte	..	..	6.6	6.5	6.2	6.0	5.8	5.1	6.0	6.1
Eswatini	3.3	3.6	3.7	4.5	4.6	5.6	5.4	5.4	5.6	5.7
Ghana	..	6.8	10.4	8.0	8.7	8.5	7.9	8.6	10.1	11.2
Kenya	..	..	11.5	10.2	10.3	9.3	8.8	9.9	9.5	9.3
Mali	..	8.2	10.0	8.6	8.3	8.1	8.5	7.3	8.7	9.4
Mauritius / Maurice[1]	13.1	14.2	13.6	12.6	13.1	13.4	13.1	12.8	12.7	12.8
Morocco / Maroc	..	12.3	11.2	12.9	12.9	12.9	12.2	11.9	11.3	11.3
Niger	..	7.0	7.8	8.3	8.5	8.0	8.4	9.1	10.1	8.8
Rwanda	7.3	7.0	7.8	7.5	7.9	7.9	8.1	8.9	9.3	9.0
Senegal / Sénégal	10.7	11.6	13.1	12.6	13.1	12.5	12.3	13.4	13.4	13.6
South Africa / Afrique du Sud	9.2	8.9	9.9	9.2	9.6	10.4	11.0	11.0	11.6	11.4
Togo	..	7.0	9.6	11.7	14.4	15.5	15.0	15.8	17.0	16.6
Tunisia / Tunisie	..	12.7	10.9	10.7	10.6	11.2	10.8	11.3	10.8	10.5
Uganda / Ouganda	9.6	8.8	8.6	7.0	7.1	7.1	7.2	7.6	8.2	8.5
Africa (21) average / Moyenne Afrique (21)[2]	**..**	**7.9**	**8.8**	**8.9**	**9.1**	**9.3**	**9.2**	**9.3**	**9.8**	**9.8**
LAC average / Moyenne ALC[3]	**9.9**	**9.9**	**10.2**	**10.4**	**10.6**	**10.9**	**10.8**	**10.9**	**11.5**	**11.4**
OECD average / Moyenne OCDE[4]	**10.9**	**10.9**	**10.8**	**10.6**	**10.6**	**10.7**	**10.8**	**10.8**	**10.9**	**..**

Note: The figures include sub-national government tax revenues for Eswatini (Swaziland in previous editions), Mauritius, Morocco and South Africa (for 2002-16). Sub-national government tax revenues are not available in other countries.

1. The fiscal year for Mauritius changed in 2010 and in 2015. Figures for 2015 needed to be estimated as a result.
2. Represents an unweighted average for the 21 African countries included in this publication. Due to lack of data availability, the Africa (21) average does not include Botswana prior to 2004, Egypt prior to 2002 and Kenya prior to 2001. These countries are included in the calculations of the Africa (21) average for subsequent years.
3. Represents an unweighted average for the 25 Latin American and Caribbean (LAC) countries included in the publication *Revenue Statistics in Latin America and the Caribbean 2018.*
4. Represents an unweighted average for 35 OECD countries.

Note : Les chiffres incluent les recettes fiscales collectées par les administrations infranationales pour l'Afrique du Sud (pour les années 2002 à 2016), Eswatini (Swaziland dans les éditions précédentes), le Maroc et Maurice. Les données des recettes fiscales collectées par les administrations infranationales ne sont pas disponibles pour les autres pays.

1. L'année fiscale pour Maurice a changé en 2010 et en 2015. Les chiffres pour 2015 ont dû être estimés en conséquence.
2. Représente la moyenne non pondérée pour les 21 pays d'Afrique inclus dans cette publication. En raison du manque de disponibilité des données, la moyenne Afrique (21) n'inclut pas le Botswana avant 2004, l'Égypte avant 2002 et le Kenya avant 2001. Ces pays sont inclus dans les calculs de la moyenne Afrique (21) pour les années suivantes.
3. Représente la moyenne non pondérée pour les 25 pays d'Amérique latine et des Caraïbes (ALC) inclus dans la publication *Revenue Statistics in Latin America and the Caribbean 2018.*
4. Représente la moyenne non pondérée pour 35 pays de l'OCDE.

StatLink https://doi.org/10.1787/888933820259

Table 4.12. **Taxes on goods and services (5000) as percentage of total taxation**
Tableau 4.12. **Impôts sur les biens et services (5000) en pourcentage du total des recettes fiscales**

	1997	2000	2005	2010	2011	2012	2013	2014	2015	2016
Botswana	..	..	26.6	34.3	32.0	35.9	28.3	28.1	31.7	30.2
Burkina Faso	..	63.6	68.5	71.4	63.7	63.8	62.9	64.0	66.3	64.9
Cabo Verde	59.5	53.8	62.0	66.2	67.0	65.0	66.0	67.6	65.5	66.0
Cameroon / Cameroun	67.4	62.2	60.5	60.1	59.9	56.4	57.4	58.3	57.0	59.9
Congo	..	45.4	66.0	60.6	59.6	59.0	45.0	60.4	55.0	54.5
Congo, Dem. Rep. / Congo, Rép. dém.	..	65.3	67.7	65.7	66.5	66.4	61.8	55.1	54.4	59.8
Côte d'Ivoire	62.3	59.8	63.9	66.0	62.2	58.0	57.6	60.6	62.9	62.3
Egypt / Égypte	..	..	40.3	39.6	39.1	39.6	35.9	33.6	38.0	40.3
Eswatini	31.9	34.8	32.2	32.6	33.4	42.5	37.9	36.2	37.6	36.8
Ghana	..	61.7	66.4	55.3	54.5	52.4	52.8	51.7	58.9	63.8
Kenya	..	..	62.3	57.1	55.3	51.8	49.4	51.6	51.3	51.5
Mali	..	72.2	69.2	60.6	60.8	58.3	59.8	52.7	58.3	58.4
Mauritius / Maurice[1]	69.8	73.8	72.5	63.6	66.6	66.7	66.1	64.3	64.1	64.0
Morocco / Maroc	..	52.1	45.5	46.7	45.4	43.8	43.3	44.1	43.6	42.8
Niger	..	72.0	72.7	62.9	61.2	55.7	49.4	55.9	59.8	60.9
Rwanda	71.3	68.8	64.5	57.4	57.0	55.2	52.5	56.3	55.7	54.3
Senegal / Sénégal	69.9	69.2	67.8	63.4	66.1	62.8	62.6	63.9	63.6	61.8
South Africa / Afrique du Sud	40.7	39.9	38.9	37.2	37.8	39.5	40.7	40.0	40.2	40.1
Togo	..	74.2	72.2	78.0	80.0	81.6	77.1	75.3	78.9	74.6
Tunisia / Tunisie	..	51.8	45.0	39.5	36.5	38.5	36.2	36.4	35.8	35.8
Uganda / Ouganda	85.6	81.6	70.9	67.3	66.6	65.2	64.0	65.7	65.1	65.0
Africa (21) average / Moyenne Afrique (21)[2]	**..**	**61.2**	**58.8**	**56.4**	**55.8**	**55.2**	**52.7**	**53.4**	**54.5**	**54.6**
LAC average / Moyenne ALC[3]	**57.2**	**56.2**	**52.6**	**51.0**	**50.3**	**50.2**	**49.6**	**49.5**	**50.3**	**50.5**
OECD average / Moyenne OCDE[4]	**33.4**	**33.0**	**33.0**	**33.0**	**32.8**	**32.6**	**32.5**	**32.5**	**32.4**	**..**

Note: The figures include sub-national government tax revenues for Eswatini (Swaziland in previous editions), Mauritius, Morocco and South Africa (for 2002-16). Sub-national government tax revenues are not available in other countries.

1. The fiscal year for Mauritius changed in 2010 and in 2015. Figures for 2015 needed to be estimated as a result.
2. Represents an unweighted average for the 21 African countries included in this publication. Due to lack of data availability, the Africa (21) average does not include Botswana prior to 2004, Egypt prior to 2002 and Kenya prior to 2001. These countries are included in the calculations of the Africa (21) average for subsequent years.
3. Represents an unweighted average for the 25 Latin American and Caribbean (LAC) countries included in the publication *Revenue Statistics in Latin America and the Caribbean 2018.*
4. Represents an unweighted average for 35 OECD countries.

Note : Les chiffres incluent les recettes fiscales collectées par les administrations infranationales pour l'Afrique du Sud (pour les années 2002 à 2016), Eswatini (Swaziland dans les éditions précédentes), le Maroc et Maurice. Les données des recettes fiscales collectées par les administrations infranationales ne sont pas disponibles pour les autres pays.

1. L'année fiscale pour Maurice a changé en 2010 et en 2015. Les chiffres pour 2015 ont dû être estimés en conséquence.
2. Représente la moyenne non pondérée pour les 21 pays d'Afrique inclus dans cette publication. En raison du manque de disponibilité des données, la moyenne Afrique (21) n'inclut pas le Botswana avant 2004, l'Égypte avant 2002 et le Kenya avant 2001. Ces pays sont inclus dans les calculs de la moyenne Afrique (21) pour les années suivantes.
3. Représente la moyenne non pondérée pour les 25 pays d'Amérique latine et des Caraïbes (ALC) inclus dans la publication *Revenue Statistics in Latin America and the Caribbean 2018.*
4. Représente la moyenne non pondérée pour 35 pays de l'OCDE.

StatLink https://doi.org/10.1787/888933820278

Table 4.13. **Taxes on general consumption (5110) as percentage of GDP**
Tableau 4.13. **Impôts généraux sur la consommation (5110) en pourcentage du PIB**

	1997	2000	2005	2010	2011	2012	2013	2014	2015	2016
Botswana	..	..	3.5	4.9	4.4	4.5	3.6	3.8	3.6	3.8
Burkina Faso	..	3.3	5.7	5.5	5.9	6.5	6.8	5.8	6.3	6.5
Cabo Verde	0.0	0.0	6.6	7.2	7.6	6.5	6.5	6.1	6.8	6.7
Cameroon / Cameroun	3.1	3.6	3.8	3.8	4.3	4.1	4.6	4.8	4.8	4.9
Congo	..	1.7	2.4	2.6	2.6	2.9	3.7	4.3	5.5	5.4
Congo, Dem. Rep. / Congo, Rép. dém.	..	0.1	1.9	3.2	3.5	4.7	3.3	2.4	2.5	2.5
Côte d'Ivoire	3.7	3.3	3.2	4.0	3.1	3.8	3.7	3.5	3.5	3.3
Egypt / Égypte	..	..	3.4	3.3	3.0	2.9	2.8	2.6	2.8	2.8
Eswatini	2.7	2.9	3.1	3.7	3.7	4.4	3.9	4.0	4.1	4.2
Ghana	..	2.9	4.6	4.4	4.9	4.6	4.4	5.0	5.5	5.1
Kenya	..	..	4.8	4.7	5.0	4.4	4.1	4.6	4.6	4.3
Mali	..	3.9	5.9	5.0	5.1	4.5	5.1	3.9	4.3	4.8
Mauritius / Maurice[1]	3.0	4.8	6.7	7.0	7.1	7.3	7.1	6.8	6.9	7.0
Morocco / Maroc	..	5.2	5.9	8.3	8.7	8.8	8.4	8.1	7.6	7.5
Niger	..	2.7	4.5	4.8	4.4	4.6	4.8	5.6	6.0	5.1
Rwanda	1.4	2.0	4.0	3.9	4.0	4.1	4.5	5.1	5.1	4.9
Senegal / Sénégal	5.4	6.6	7.7	7.5	7.7	7.3	7.0	7.4	7.6	7.5
South Africa / Afrique du Sud	5.6	5.5	6.7	6.2	6.4	6.4	6.5	6.7	6.9	6.8
Togo	..	3.4	5.2	6.7	9.1	10.0	8.6	9.4	9.9	9.7
Tunisia / Tunisie	..	6.2	5.6	6.1	6.1	6.3	6.1	6.5	6.2	5.9
Uganda / Ouganda	3.3	3.5	4.0	3.4	3.4	3.5	3.8	3.7	4.1	4.3
Africa (21) average / Moyenne Afrique (21)[2]	**..**	**3.4**	**4.7**	**5.1**	**5.2**	**5.3**	**5.2**	**5.2**	**5.5**	**5.4**
LAC average / Moyenne ALC[3]	**5.4**	**5.8**	**6.5**	**6.7**	**6.8**	**7.1**	**7.1**	**7.2**	**7.5**	**7.5**
OECD average / Moyenne OCDE[4]	**6.6**	**6.6**	**6.8**	**6.6**	**6.7**	**6.8**	**6.8**	**6.9**	**6.9**	**..**

Note: The figures include sub-national government tax revenues for Eswatini (Swaziland in previous editions), Mauritius, Morocco and South Africa (for 2002-16). Sub-national government tax revenues are not available in other countries.

1. The fiscal year for Mauritius changed in 2010 and in 2015. Figures for 2015 needed to be estimated as a result.
2. Represents an unweighted average for the 21 African countries included in this publication. Due to lack of data availability, the Africa (21) average does not include Botswana prior to 2004, Egypt prior to 2002 and Kenya prior to 2001. These countries are included in the calculations of the Africa (21) average for subsequent years.
3. Represents an unweighted average for the 25 Latin American and Caribbean (LAC) countries included in the publication *Revenue Statistics in Latin America and the Caribbean 2018.*
4. Represents an unweighted average for 35 OECD countries.

Note : Les chiffres incluent les recettes fiscales collectées par les administrations infranationales pour l'Afrique du Sud (pour les années 2002 à 2016), Eswatini (Swaziland dans les éditions précédentes), le Maroc et Maurice. Les données des recettes fiscales collectées par les administrations infranationales ne sont pas disponibles pour les autres pays.

1. L'année fiscale pour Maurice a changé en 2010 et en 2015. Les chiffres pour 2015 ont dû être estimés en conséquence.
2. Représente la moyenne non pondérée pour les 21 pays d'Afrique inclus dans cette publication. En raison du manque de disponibilité des données, la moyenne Afrique (21) n'inclut pas le Botswana avant 2004, l'Égypte avant 2002 et le Kenya avant 2001. Ces pays sont inclus dans les calculs de la moyenne Afrique (21) pour les années suivantes.
3. Représente la moyenne non pondérée pour les 25 pays d'Amérique latine et des Caraïbes (ALC) inclus dans la publication *Revenue Statistics in Latin America and the Caribbean 2018.*
4. Représente la moyenne non pondérée pour 35 pays de l'OCDE.

StatLink https://doi.org/10.1787/888933820297

Table 4.14. **Taxes on general consumption (5110) as percentage of total taxation**
Tableau 4.14. **Impôts généraux sur la consommation (5110) en pourcentage du total des recettes fiscales**

	1997	2000	2005	2010	2011	2012	2013	2014	2015	2016
Botswana	..	..	23.2	31.3	28.3	32.6	24.6	25.3	28.2	27.1
Burkina Faso	..	32.0	41.8	36.1	37.1	37.6	37.5	35.4	36.1	35.8
Cabo Verde	0.0	0.0	34.0	39.3	38.8	36.5	36.5	36.2	36.3	35.5
Cameroon / Cameroun	30.8	32.2	31.7	31.2	33.2	30.6	32.9	33.2	32.9	33.8
Congo	..	40.2	39.4	36.4	34.8	34.1	26.7	37.1	33.4	33.6
Congo, Dem. Rep. / Congo, Rép. dém.	..	18.4	37.3	35.5	37.7	41.0	32.8	25.4	25.9	32.7
Côte d'Ivoire	21.5	21.8	20.5	24.1	20.4	21.6	21.3	21.0	20.1	19.1
Egypt / Égypte	..	..	20.9	20.5	19.0	19.4	17.0	17.1	18.2	18.1
Eswatini	26.2	28.0	27.5	27.4	26.6	33.3	27.2	26.7	27.4	27.1
Ghana	..	26.1	29.4	30.0	30.5	28.6	29.4	29.9	32.1	28.9
Kenya	..	..	26.2	26.1	26.8	24.5	22.8	24.1	24.7	23.9
Mali	..	33.9	40.5	35.0	37.1	32.3	35.7	28.5	28.4	29.5
Mauritius / Maurice[1]	15.9	25.0	35.9	35.6	36.1	36.3	36.1	34.1	34.9	34.9
Morocco / Maroc	..	22.1	23.9	30.1	30.5	29.9	29.8	30.1	29.4	28.2
Niger	..	27.4	42.0	36.7	31.7	31.7	28.4	34.1	35.6	35.2
Rwanda	13.3	20.0	33.1	29.9	29.0	28.8	28.9	32.3	30.8	29.8
Senegal / Sénégal	35.0	39.6	40.0	37.7	38.6	36.5	35.6	35.5	36.1	33.9
South Africa / Afrique du Sud	24.9	24.6	26.1	25.0	25.3	24.1	24.2	24.4	23.7	23.7
Togo	..	36.5	39.4	44.6	50.6	52.8	44.1	44.8	45.9	43.5
Tunisia / Tunisie	..	25.2	23.1	22.3	20.8	21.8	20.4	21.1	20.3	19.9
Uganda / Ouganda	29.6	33.0	33.0	32.3	31.9	31.6	33.4	32.4	32.3	32.4
Africa (21) average / Moyenne Afrique (21)[2]	**..**	**27.0**	**31.9**	**31.8**	**31.7**	**31.7**	**29.8**	**29.9**	**30.1**	**29.8**
LAC average / Moyenne ALC[3]	**30.4**	**31.2**	**31.8**	**31.9**	**31.8**	**31.9**	**31.9**	**31.9**	**32.3**	**32.9**
OECD average / Moyenne OCDE[4]	**20.1**	**19.9**	**20.6**	**20.7**	**20.7**	**20.5**	**20.5**	**20.7**	**20.6**	**..**

Note: The figures include sub-national government tax revenues for Eswatini (Swaziland in previous editions), Mauritius, Morocco and South Africa (for 2002-16). Sub-national government tax revenues are not available in other countries.

1. The fiscal year for Mauritius changed in 2010 and in 2015. Figures for 2015 needed to be estimated as a result.
2. Represents an unweighted average for the 21 African countries included in this publication. Due to lack of data availability, the Africa (21) average does not include Botswana prior to 2004, Egypt prior to 2002 and Kenya prior to 2001. These countries are included in the calculations of the Africa (21) average for subsequent years.
3. Represents an unweighted average for the 25 Latin American and Caribbean (LAC) countries included in the publication *Revenue Statistics in Latin America and the Caribbean 2018*.
4. Represents an unweighted average for 35 OECD countries.

Note : Les chiffres incluent les recettes fiscales collectées par les administrations infranationales pour l'Afrique du Sud (pour les années 2002 à 2016), Eswatini (Swaziland dans les éditions précédentes), le Maroc et Maurice. Les données des recettes fiscales collectées par les administrations infranationales ne sont pas disponibles pour les autres pays.

1. L'année fiscale pour Maurice a changé en 2010 et en 2015. Les chiffres pour 2015 ont dû être estimés en conséquence.
2. Représente la moyenne non pondérée pour les 21 pays d'Afrique inclus dans cette publication. En raison du manque de disponibilité des données, la moyenne Afrique (21) n'inclut pas le Botswana avant 2004, l'Égypte avant 2002 et le Kenya avant 2001. Ces pays sont inclus dans les calculs de la moyenne Afrique (21) pour les années suivantes.
3. Représente la moyenne non pondérée pour les 25 pays d'Amérique latine et des Caraïbes (ALC) inclus dans la publication *Revenue Statistics in Latin America and the Caribbean 2018*.
4. Représente la moyenne non pondérée pour 35 pays de l'OCDE.

StatLink https://doi.org/10.1787/888933820316

Table 4.15. **Taxes on specific goods and services (5120) as percentage of GDP**
Tableau 4.15. **Impôts sur les biens et services déterminés (5120) en pourcentage du PIB**

	1997	2000	2005	2010	2011	2012	2013	2014	2015	2016
Botswana	..	..	0.3	0.2	0.3	0.2	0.3	0.2	0.3	0.3
Burkina Faso	..	2.5	3.1	3.2	3.3	3.8	3.8	3.9	4.3	4.3
Cabo Verde	8.7	8.4	5.4	5.0	5.5	5.1	5.2	5.3	5.5	5.8
Cameroon / Cameroun	3.7	3.3	3.4	3.4	3.4	3.4	3.4	3.5	3.5	3.7
Congo	..	0.2	1.6	1.7	1.8	2.1	2.6	2.7	3.6	3.3
Congo, Dem. Rep. / Congo, Rép. dém.	..	0.3	1.6	2.6	2.6	2.8	2.9	2.8	2.7	2.0
Côte d'Ivoire	6.7	5.5	6.5	6.5	6.3	6.1	6.0	6.2	7.1	7.1
Egypt / Égypte	..	..	3.1	3.0	3.1	2.9	3.0	2.4	3.0	3.3
Eswatini	0.5	0.6	0.5	0.6	0.8	1.1	1.4	1.3	1.4	1.4
Ghana	..	3.9	5.8	3.7	3.9	3.9	3.5	3.6	4.6	6.1
Kenya	..	..	6.4	5.4	5.2	4.8	4.6	5.1	4.8	4.9
Mali	..	4.3	4.1	3.6	3.2	3.6	3.4	3.3	4.4	4.6
Mauritius / Maurice[1]	9.9	9.2	5.9	4.6	5.0	5.2	5.0	4.9	4.8	4.8
Morocco / Maroc	..	6.8	5.1	4.3	4.0	3.8	3.5	3.5	3.4	3.5
Niger	..	4.2	3.2	3.4	4.1	3.4	3.5	3.5	4.0	3.7
Rwanda	5.9	4.9	3.8	3.5	3.8	3.7	3.6	3.8	4.0	3.9
Senegal / Sénégal	5.3	4.9	5.3	5.0	5.4	5.2	5.2	5.8	5.7	6.0
South Africa / Afrique du Sud	3.6	3.4	3.1	2.8	3.0	3.9	4.3	4.1	4.6	4.5
Togo	..	3.6	4.3	5.0	5.3	5.4	6.4	6.3	7.1	6.8
Tunisia / Tunisie	..	6.3	5.0	4.4	4.4	4.6	4.5	4.5	4.4	4.4
Uganda / Ouganda	6.0	5.0	4.2	3.4	3.4	3.5	3.3	3.7	4.0	4.1
Africa (21) average / Moyenne Afrique (21)[2]	**..**	**4.3**	**3.9**	**3.6**	**3.7**	**3.7**	**3.8**	**3.8**	**4.2**	**4.2**
LAC average / Moyenne ALC[3]	**4.2**	**3.8**	**3.4**	**3.4**	**3.4**	**3.4**	**3.3**	**3.4**	**3.6**	**3.6**
OECD average / Moyenne OCDE[4]	**3.7**	**3.6**	**3.4**	**3.3**	**3.3**	**3.3**	**3.3**	**3.2**	**3.2**	**..**

Note: The figures include sub-national government tax revenues for Eswatini (Swaziland in previous editions), Mauritius, Morocco and South Africa (for 2002-16). Sub-national government tax revenues are not available in other countries.

1. The fiscal year for Mauritius changed in 2010 and in 2015. Figures for 2015 needed to be estimated as a result.
2. Represents an unweighted average for the 21 African countries included in this publication. Due to lack of data availability, the Africa (21) average does not include Botswana prior to 2004, Egypt prior to 2002 and Kenya prior to 2001. These countries are included in the calculations of the Africa (21) average for subsequent years.
3. Represents an unweighted average for the 25 Latin American and Caribbean (LAC) countries included in the publication *Revenue Statistics in Latin America and the Caribbean 2018*.
4. Represents an unweighted average for 35 OECD countries.

Note : Les chiffres incluent les recettes fiscales collectées par les administrations infranationales pour l'Afrique du Sud (pour les années 2002 à 2016), Eswatini (Swaziland dans les éditions précédentes), le Maroc et Maurice. Les données des recettes fiscales collectées par les administrations infranationales ne sont pas disponibles pour les autres pays.

1. L'année fiscale pour Maurice a changé en 2010 et en 2015. Les chiffres pour 2015 ont dû être estimés en conséquence.
2. Représente la moyenne non pondérée pour les 21 pays d'Afrique inclus dans cette publication. En raison du manque de disponibilité des données, la moyenne Afrique (21) n'inclut pas le Botswana avant 2004, l'Égypte avant 2002 et le Kenya avant 2001. Ces pays sont inclus dans les calculs de la moyenne Afrique (21) pour les années suivantes.
3. Représente la moyenne non pondérée pour les 25 pays d'Amérique latine et des Caraïbes (ALC) inclus dans la publication *Revenue Statistics in Latin America and the Caribbean 2018*.
4. Représente la moyenne non pondérée pour 35 pays de l'OCDE.

StatLink https://doi.org/10.1787/888933820335

Table 4.16. **Taxes on specific goods and services (5120) as percentage of total taxation**
Tableau 4.16. **Impôts sur les biens et services déterminés (5120) en pourcentage du total des recettes fiscales**

	1997	2000	2005	2010	2011	2012	2013	2014	2015	2016
Botswana	..	..	1.8	1.3	2.2	1.7	2.3	1.6	2.2	1.8
Burkina Faso	..	24.2	22.5	20.7	20.7	22.0	20.9	23.6	24.8	23.9
Cabo Verde	59.5	53.8	27.9	26.9	28.2	28.6	29.4	31.4	29.2	30.5
Cameroon / Cameroun	36.3	29.6	28.1	28.4	26.2	25.4	24.1	24.6	23.8	25.7
Congo	..	5.1	26.6	24.1	24.7	24.9	18.3	23.3	21.6	20.8
Congo, Dem. Rep. / Congo, Rép. dém.	..	45.6	30.2	28.7	28.3	24.8	28.7	29.2	28.1	26.5
Côte d'Ivoire	39.5	35.8	41.3	39.5	40.8	34.2	33.9	37.0	40.4	40.9
Egypt / Égypte	..	..	19.0	18.1	19.2	19.3	18.2	15.8	19.1	21.5
Eswatini	4.6	5.9	4.0	4.1	5.6	8.1	9.7	8.5	9.3	8.9
Ghana	..	35.6	36.9	25.3	24.0	23.9	23.4	21.8	26.9	34.9
Kenya	..	..	34.8	30.2	28.0	26.7	26.0	26.9	26.1	27.0
Mali	..	37.9	28.4	25.3	23.4	25.7	23.9	23.9	29.6	28.7
Mauritius / Maurice[1]	53.0	47.8	31.3	23.1	25.2	25.6	25.2	24.9	24.0	24.1
Morocco / Maroc	..	28.9	20.6	15.6	13.9	12.9	12.3	12.9	13.1	13.3
Niger	..	42.9	30.4	25.8	29.2	23.7	20.7	21.5	23.9	25.3
Rwanda	57.2	47.9	31.0	26.9	27.5	25.8	23.4	23.9	24.1	23.8
Senegal / Sénégal	34.4	29.2	27.4	25.4	27.1	25.8	26.6	27.9	27.0	27.3
South Africa / Afrique du Sud	15.8	15.3	12.0	11.4	11.7	14.6	15.8	14.9	15.9	15.7
Togo	..	37.6	32.6	33.3	29.2	28.7	32.7	30.3	32.7	30.7
Tunisia / Tunisie	..	25.7	20.8	16.3	14.9	15.9	15.0	14.5	14.7	15.1
Uganda / Ouganda	53.3	46.4	34.6	32.9	32.5	31.9	29.0	31.6	31.2	31.4
Africa (21) average / Moyenne Afrique (21)[2]	**..**	**33.1**	**25.8**	**23.0**	**23.0**	**22.4**	**21.9**	**22.4**	**23.2**	**23.7**
LAC average / Moyenne ALC[3]	**25.3**	**23.3**	**19.2**	**17.4**	**16.9**	**16.6**	**16.1**	**15.9**	**16.3**	**16.0**
OECD average / Moyenne OCDE[4]	**11.5**	**11.1**	**10.4**	**10.2**	**10.0**	**10.0**	**9.8**	**9.6**	**9.7**	**..**

Note: The figures include sub-national government tax revenues for Eswatini (Swaziland in previous editions), Mauritius, Morocco and South Africa (for 2002-16). Sub-national government tax revenues are not available in other countries.

1. The fiscal year for Mauritius changed in 2010 and in 2015. Figures for 2015 needed to be estimated as a result.
2. Represents an unweighted average for the 21 African countries included in this publication. Due to lack of data availability, the Africa (21) average does not include Botswana prior to 2004, Egypt prior to 2002 and Kenya prior to 2001. These countries are included in the calculations of the Africa (21) average for subsequent years.
3. Represents an unweighted average for the 25 Latin American and Caribbean (LAC) countries included in the publication *Revenue Statistics in Latin America and the Caribbean 2018.*
4. Represents an unweighted average for 35 OECD countries.

Note : Les chiffres incluent les recettes fiscales collectées par les administrations infranationales pour l'Afrique du Sud (pour les années 2002 à 2016), Eswatini (Swaziland dans les éditions précédentes), le Maroc et Maurice. Les données des recettes fiscales collectées par les administrations infranationales ne sont pas disponibles pour les autres pays.

1. L'année fiscale pour Maurice a changé en 2010 et en 2015. Les chiffres pour 2015 ont dû être estimés en conséquence.
2. Représente la moyenne non pondérée pour les 21 pays d'Afrique inclus dans cette publication. En raison du manque de disponibilité des données, la moyenne Afrique (21) n'inclut pas le Botswana avant 2004, l'Égypte avant 2002 et le Kenya avant 2001. Ces pays sont inclus dans les calculs de la moyenne Afrique (21) pour les années suivantes.
3. Représente la moyenne non pondérée pour les 25 pays d'Amérique latine et des Caraïbes (ALC) inclus dans la publication *Revenue Statistics in Latin America and the Caribbean 2018.*
4. Représente la moyenne non pondérée pour 35 pays de l'OCDE.

StatLink https://doi.org/10.1787/888933820354

Table 4.17. **Gross domestic product for tax reporting years at market prices, in national currency units**

Tableau 4.17. **Produit intérieur brut pour les années de déclaration fiscale au prix du marché, en monnaie nationale**

	1997	2000	2005	2010	2011	2012	2013	2014	2015	2016
Botswana[1]	18 807	30 165	52 841	91 227	106 202	113 692	130 336	145 918	152 197	172 282
Burkina Faso	1 428 629	1 874 781	2 882 208	4 447 570	5 060 322	5 700 578	5 904 400	6 119 941	6 162 670	6 704 200
Cabo Verde	50 292	70 536	96 690	138 569	147 924	150 351	153 723	154 436	158 699	163 381
Cameroon / Cameroun	5 686 260	7 179 525	9 464 932	12 948 432	13 843 139	14 858 604	15 981 280	17 276 469	18 285 382	19 104 989
Congo	1 355 700	2 292 500	3 210 700	6 082 520	6 982 455	6 971 923	6 927 242	6 959 940	5 056 482	4 615 600
Congo, Dem. Rep. / Congo, Rép. dém.	34 582	1 317 075	5 670 065	18 698 925	22 598 145	25 343 516	30 051 179	33 224 018	35 591 636	42 160 852
Côte d'Ivoire	6 841 856	7 630 266	9 011 755	12 324 723	12 112 687	13 677 317	15 445 759	17 461 003	19 595 381	21 561 686
Egypt / Égypte[2]	255 824	340 520	538 250	1 182 279	1 355 194	1 558 189	1 767 550	1 995 200	2 286 950	2 576 650
Eswatini[1]	9 399	12 794	21 152	33 546	36 293	39 941	43 656	47 512	51 737	57 415
Ghana	2 298	4 420	15 833	46 042	59 816	75 315	93 416	113 343	136 957	167 353
Kenya[2]	820 633	1 043 127	1 508 466	3 016 495	3 447 609	3 993 644	4 503 256	5 073 775	5 831 526	6 709 668
Mali	1 857 875	2 103 270	3 294 055	5 288 939	6 123 929	6 352 360	6 543 944	7 113 833	7 748 144	8 321 656
Mauritius / Maurice[2]	81 804	115 905	186 151	299 171	323 310	343 942	366 325	386 229	403 536	417 680
Morocco / Maroc	372 962	412 897	552 671	784 624	820 077	847 881	897 923	925 376	988 021	1 016 119
Niger	1 010 315	1 186 278	1 776 953	2 832 286	3 024 270	3 544 186	3 788 275	4 069 164	4 268 887	4 464 334
Rwanda	546 535	676 000	1 440 000	3 367 000	3 897 000	4 494 000	4 929 000	5 466 000	5 968 000	6 672 000
Senegal / Sénégal	2 727 198	3 331 768	4 592 673	6 400 738	6 783 016	7 263 157	7 346 007	7 568 099	8 081 807	8 722 341
South Africa / Afrique du Sud	703 117	946 324	1 639 254	2 748 009	3 023 659	3 253 852	3 539 977	3 805 349	4 051 421	4 350 314
Togo	1 078 972	1 059 553	1 202 931	1 696 830	1 824 891	1 977 542	2 134 464	2 259 047	2 471 777	2 643 472
Tunisia / Tunisie	22 944	29 433	41 871	63 055	64 492	70 354	75 152	80 816	84 656	90 376
Uganda / Ouganda[2]	6 617 801	9 300 795	16 049 113	40 868 624	48 630 513	57 311 079	64 068 475	69 712 050	77 174 036	84 121 496

1. The GDP for Botswana and Eswatini (Swaziland in previous editions) is adjusted using the following formula: GDP(n)*3/4+GDP(n+1))/4 in order to make it correspond more closely to an April(n)-to-March(n+1) fiscal year.
2. The GDP for Egypt, Kenya and Uganda in all years and for Mauritius in the years preceding 2010 and for Mauritius in 2016 are adjusted using the formula GDP(n)/2+GDP(n-1)/2. This is done in order to make the value of the GDP correspond more closely to a July(n-1)-to-June(n) fiscal year. The GDP for Mauritius is not adjusted from 2010 to 2015 because public finance data are reported on a calendar year for those years.

Source: IMF, *World Economic Outlook*, April 2018.

1. Le PIB pour Botswana et Eswatini (Swaziland dans les éditions précédentes) est ajusté selon la formule PIB(n)*3/4+PIB(n+1))/4 afin de le faire correspondre le mieux possible à une année fiscale de avril (n) à mars (n+1).
2. Le PIB pour l'Egypte, le Kenya et l'Ouganda, pour toutes les années et pour Maurice dans les années antérieures à 2010, est ajusté selon la formule suivante : PIB(n)/2+PIB(n-1)/2 afin de le faire correspondre le mieux possible à une année fiscale de juillet (n-1) à juin (n).

Source : FMI, *Perspectives de l'économie mondiale*, avril 2018.

StatLink https://doi.org/10.1787/888933820373

Table 4.18. **Gross domestic product for tax reporting years at market prices, in millions of US dollars at market exchange rates**

Tableau 4.18. **Produit intérieur brut pour les années de déclaration fiscale au prix du marché, en millions de dollars US aux taux de change du marché**

	1997	2000	2005	2010	2011	2012	2013	2014	2015	2016
Botswana[1]	4 973	5 731	10 053	13 419	15 572	15 811	15 251	15 806	15 126	11 745
Burkina Faso	2 448	2 633	5 474	8 963	10 734	11 172	11 955	12 398	10 425	11 310
Cabo Verde	540	589	1 090	1 664	1 865	1 752	1 851	1 861	1 597	1 640
Cameroon / Cameroun	10 509	9 802	17 974	26 193	29 364	29 121	32 358	34 999	30 932	32 230
Congo	2 323	3 220	6 097	12 304	14 811	13 664	14 026	14 099	8 554	7 787
Congo, Dem. Rep. / Congo, Rép. dém.	28 819	19 077	11 951	20 641	24 575	27 566	32 676	35 918	38 402	39 324
Côte d'Ivoire	11 735	10 748	17 115	24 931	25 693	26 805	31 274	35 373	33 148	36 375
Egypt / Égypte[2]	75 442	99 896	88 491	214 170	238 875	263 247	283 388	296 787	318 821	332 279
Eswatini[1]	1 948	1 748	3 271	4 593	4 847	4 671	4 391	4 208	4 070	2 886
Ghana	11 219	8 112	17 470	32 174	39 565	41 939	47 806	38 774	36 885	42 787
Kenya[2]	13 654	14 245	19 533	38 511	40 836	46 047	52 774	58 335	62 770	67 261
Mali	3 208	2 962	6 255	10 699	12 990	12 450	13 250	14 411	13 107	14 039
Mauritius / Maurice[2]	4 205	4 504	6 534	9 718	11 263	11 446	11 932	12 613	11 511	11 830
Morocco / Maroc	39 147	38 859	62 343	93 217	101 371	98 266	106 826	110 081	101 187	103 607
Niger	1 733	1 671	3 374	5 729	6 415	6 946	7 670	8 243	7 221	7 531
Rwanda	1 808	1 718	2 584	5 774	6 492	7 316	7 623	8 010	8 294	8 475
Senegal / Sénégal	4 672	4 692	8 721	12 948	14 388	14 235	14 874	15 332	13 671	14 715
South Africa / Afrique du Sud	152 611	136 453	257 667	375 304	416 879	396 332	366 821	350 901	317 698	295 678
Togo	1 849	1 493	2 283	3 432	3 871	3 876	4 322	4 576	4 181	4 460
Tunisia / Tunisie	20 747	21 473	32 272	44 054	45 810	45 044	46 253	47 605	43 156	42 074
Uganda / Ouganda[2]	6 212	6 003	8 944	19 396	20 660	22 806	25 157	26 879	26 578	25 258

1. The GDP for Botswana and Eswatini (Swaziland in previous editions) is adjusted using the following formula: GDP(n)*3/4+GDP(n+1))/4 in order to make it correspond more closely to an April(n)-to-March(n+1) fiscal year.
2. The GDP for Egypt, Kenya and Uganda in all years and for Mauritius in the years preceding 2010 and for Mauritius in 2016 are adjusted using the formula GDP(n)/2+GDP(n-1)/2. This is done in order to make the value of the GDP correspond more closely to a July(n-1)-to-June(n) fiscal year. The GDP for Mauritius is not adjusted from 2010 to 2015 because public finance data are reported on a calendar year for those years.

Source: IMF, *World Economic Outlook*, April 2018.

1. Le PIB pour Botswana et Eswatini (Swaziland dans les éditions précédentes) est ajusté selon la formule PIB(n)*3/4+PIB(n+1))/4 afin de le faire correspondre le mieux possible à une année fiscale de avril (n) à mars (n+1).
2. Le PIB pour l'Egypte, le Kenya et l'Ouganda, pour toutes les années et pour Maurice dans les années antérieures à 2010, est ajusté selon la formule suivante : PIB(n)/2+PIB(n-1)/2 afin de le faire correspondre le mieux possible à une année fiscale de juillet (n-1) à juin (n).

Source : FMI, *Perspectives de l'économie mondiale*, avril 2018.

StatLink https://doi.org/10.1787/888933820392

Table 4.19. **Exchange rates used, national currency per US dollar**
Tableau 4.19. **Taux de change utilisés, unités de monnaie nationale par dollar US**

	1997	2000	2005	2010	2011	2012	2013	2014	2015	2016
Botswana	3.78	5.26	5.26	6.80	6.82	7.19	8.55	9.23	10.06	14.67
Burkina Faso	583.67	711.98	526.55	496.24	471.43	510.24	493.89	493.63	591.15	592.76
Cabo Verde	93.18	119.69	88.67	83.26	79.32	85.82	83.05	82.98	99.37	99.64
Cameroon / Cameroun	541.11	732.49	526.60	494.36	471.43	510.24	493.89	493.63	591.15	592.76
Congo	583.70	711.98	526.60	494.36	471.43	510.24	493.89	493.63	591.15	592.76
Congo, Dem. Rep. / Congo, Rép. dém.	1.20	69.04	474.44	905.91	919.57	919.37	919.66	925.00	926.82	1 072.15
Côte d'Ivoire	583.05	709.89	526.55	494.36	471.43	510.24	493.89	493.63	591.15	592.76
Egypt / Égypte	3.39	3.41	6.08	5.52	5.67	5.92	6.24	6.72	7.17	7.75
Eswatini	4.82	7.32	6.47	7.30	7.49	8.55	9.94	11.29	12.71	19.89
Ghana	0.20	0.54	0.91	1.43	1.51	1.80	1.95	2.92	3.71	3.91
Kenya	60.10	73.23	77.23	78.33	84.43	86.73	85.33	86.98	92.90	99.76
Mali	579.17	710.04	526.60	494.36	471.43	510.24	493.89	493.63	591.15	592.76
Mauritius / Maurice	19.45	25.74	28.49	30.78	28.71	30.05	30.70	30.62	35.06	35.31
Morocco / Maroc	9.53	10.63	8.87	8.42	8.09	8.63	8.41	8.41	9.76	9.81
Niger	583.00	710.04	526.60	494.36	471.44	510.25	493.89	493.63	591.15	592.77
Rwanda	302.36	393.44	557.27	583.12	600.31	614.30	646.62	682.43	719.60	787.25
Senegal / Sénégal	583.70	710.04	526.60	494.36	471.43	510.24	493.89	493.63	591.15	592.76
South Africa / Afrique du Sud	4.61	6.94	6.36	7.32	7.25	8.21	9.65	10.84	12.75	14.71
Togo	583.67	709.60	526.90	494.36	471.43	510.24	493.89	493.63	591.15	592.76
Tunisia / Tunisie	1.11	1.37	1.30	1.43	1.41	1.56	1.62	1.70	1.96	2.15
Uganda / Ouganda	1 065.34	1 549.25	1 794.39	2 107.12	2 353.89	2 512.98	2 546.79	2 593.60	2 903.63	3 330.54

Note: The exchange rate is calculated by taking the ratio of the estimated fiscal year GDP in national currency for Table 4.17 to the estimated fiscal year GDP in US dollars in Table 4.18.

Note : Le taux de change est calculé en faisant le ratio du PIB de l'année budgétaire estimée en monnaie nationale du tableau 4.17 par rapport à l'année budgétaire estimée en dollars US du tableau 4.18.

StatLink https://doi.org/10.1787/888933820411

Table 4.20. **Total tax revenue in millions of US dollars at market exchange rates**
Tableau 4.20. **Total des recettes fiscales en millions de dollars US aux taux de change du marché**

	1997	2000	2005	2010	2011	2012	2013	2014	2015	2016
Botswana	..	..	1 529	2 103	2 440	2 179	2 238	2 400	1 921	1 646
Burkina Faso	..	270	748	1 370	1 696	1 922	2 158	2 032	1 815	2 052
Cabo Verde	79	92	212	307	365	311	329	315	300	312
Cameroon / Cameroun	1 076	1 106	2 156	3 179	3 821	3 918	4 573	5 036	4 547	4 629
Congo	..	138	377	871	1 102	1 143	1 957	1 621	1 419	1 243
Congo, Dem. Rep. / Congo, Rép. dém.	..	109	620	1 839	2 286	3 153	3 311	3 419	3 710	3 008
Côte d'Ivoire	2 001	1 647	2 674	4 123	3 942	4 749	5 511	5 968	5 815	6 346
Egypt / Égypte	..	..	14 474	34 895	37 932	39 922	46 042	45 183	49 918	50 657
Eswatini	202	181	372	628	674	617	623	628	605	447
Ghana	..	894	2 732	4 678	6 350	6 809	7 184	6 481	6 354	7 541
Kenya	..	..	3 589	6 896	7 598	8 235	9 439	11 146	11 592	12 195
Mali	..	337	905	1 514	1 782	1 740	1 885	1 993	1 961	2 267
Mauritius / Maurice	790	870	1 225	1 922	2 211	2 305	2 360	2 503	2 287	2 370
Morocco / Maroc	..	9 150	15 407	25 779	28 883	28 976	30 039	29 671	26 235	27 367
Niger	..	163	361	755	890	1 001	1 299	1 343	1 219	1 088
Rwanda	186	175	313	756	895	1 051	1 176	1 268	1 380	1 405
Senegal / Sénégal	715	788	1 685	2 565	2 857	2 841	2 913	3 206	2 890	3 240
South Africa / Afrique du Sud	34 415	30 506	65 833	93 052	105 744	104 701	99 272	96 898	91 786	84 468
Togo	..	141	303	514	696	736	844	957	904	991
Tunisia / Tunisie	..	5 250	7 820	11 977	13 349	13 111	13 791	14 725	13 057	12 381
Uganda / Ouganda	694	645	1 079	2 018	2 191	2 496	2 835	3 110	3 362	3 315

Note: The figures are derived by dividing the total tax revenue data in the tables from Chapter 5 by the exchange rate data in Table 4.19.

Note : Les chiffres sont calculés en divisant les données des recettes fiscales totales des tableaux du chapitre 5 par les données des taux de change du tableau 4.19.

StatLink https://doi.org/10.1787/888933820430

Chapter 5

Country tables – Tax revenues, 1997-2016

Chapitre 5

Tableaux pays – Recettes fiscales, 1997-2016

Chapter 5 / Chapitre 5

Country tables, 1997-2016

In all of the following tables a ("..") indicates not available or not applicable. The main series in this volume cover the years 1990 to 2016.

Figures referring to 1998-99, 2001-04 and 2006-09 in Tables 5.1 to 5.21 have been omitted because of lack of space. Complete series are, however, available on line at *http://dx.doi.org/10.1787/93add7a4-en*.

Tableaux pays, 1997-2016

Dans tous les tableaux suivants le symbole (« .. ») signifie que l'information n'est pas disponible ou qu'elle n'est pas applicable. Les principales séries dans ce volume couvrent les années 1990 à 2016.

Les années 1998-99, 2001-04 et 2006-09 dans les tableaux 5.1 à 5.21 ont été omis en raison du manque d'espace. Les séries complètes sont cependant disponibles en ligne sur *http://dx.doi.org/10.1787/ef1bbbc4-fr*.

Table 5.1. Botswana

Details of tax revenue / Recettes fiscales détaillées

Million BWP

	1997	2000	2005	2010	2011	2012	2013	2014	2015	2016
Total tax revenue	**..**	**..**	**8 039**	**14 300**	**16 640**	**15 668**	**19 122**	**22 160**	**19 332**	**24 139**
1000 Taxes on income, profits and capital gains	**..**	**..**	**5 887**	**9 345**	**11 242**	**9 985**	**13 659**	**15 882**	**13 134**	**16 777**
1100 Of individuals	..	..	..	..	..	..	..	..	..	..
1110 On income and profits	..	..	..	..	..	..	..	..	..	..
1120 On capital gains	..	..	..	..	..	..	..	..	..	..
1200 Corporate	..	..	..	..	..	..	..	..	..	..
1210 On profits	..	..	..	..	..	..	..	..	..	..
1220 On capital gains	..	..	..	..	..	..	..	..	..	..
1300 Unallocable between 1100 and 1200	..	..	5 887	9 345	11 242	9 985	13 659	15 882	13 134	16 777
Assessed income tax	..	..	3 877	5 168	6 861	5 279	8 157	9 365	6 825	9 454
Income tax arrears and deductions	..	..	1 171	3 114	3 620	3 950	4 508	5 185	5 259	5 172
Withholding tax	..	..	840	1 062	761	755	993	1 332	1 050	2 152
PAYE taxes	..	..	0	0	0	0	0	0	0	0
2000 Social security contributions[1]	**..**	**..**	**0**	**0**	**0**	**0**	**0**	**0**	**0**	**0**
2100 Employees	..	..	..	..	..	..	..	..	..	..
2110 On a payroll basis	..	..	..	..	..	..	..	..	..	..
2120 On an income tax basis	..	..	..	..	..	..	..	..	..	..
2200 Employers	..	..	..	..	..	..	..	..	..	..
2210 On a payroll basis	..	..	..	..	..	..	..	..	..	..
2220 On an income tax basis	..	..	..	..	..	..	..	..	..	..
2300 Self-employed or non-employed	..	..	..	..	..	..	..	..	..	..
2310 On a payroll basis	..	..	..	..	..	..	..	..	..	..
2320 On an income tax basis	..	..	..	..	..	..	..	..	..	..
2400 Unallocable between 2100, 2200 and 2300	..	..	..	..	..	..	..	..	..	..
2410 On a payroll basis	..	..	..	..	..	..	..	..	..	..
2420 On an income tax basis	..	..	..	..	..	..	..	..	..	..
3000 Taxes on payroll and workforce	**..**	**..**	**0**	**0**	**0**	**0**	**0**	**0**	**0**	**0**
4000 Taxes on property	**..**	**..**	**13**	**52**	**71**	**53**	**57**	**54**	**66**	**62**
4100 Recurrent taxes on immovable property	..	..	0	0	0	0	0	0	0	0
4110 Households	..	..	..	..	..	..	..	..	..	..
4120 Others	..	..	..	..	..	..	..	..	..	..
4200 Recurrent taxes on net wealth	..	..	0	0	0	0	0	0	0	0
4210 Individual	..	..	..	..	..	..	..	..	..	..
4220 Corporate	..	..	..	..	..	..	..	..	..	..
4300 Estate, inheritance and gift taxes	..	..	0	0	0	0	0	0	0	0
4310 Estate and inheritance taxes	..	..	..	..	..	..	..	..	..	..
4320 Gift taxes	..	..	..	..	..	..	..	..	..	..
4400 Taxes on financial and capital transactions	..	..	13	52	71	53	57	54	66	62
4500 Non-recurrent taxes	..	..	0	0	0	0	0	0	0	0
4510 On net wealth	..	..	..	..	..	..	..	..	..	..
4520 Other non-recurrent taxes	..	..	..	..	..	..	..	..	..	..
4600 Other recurrent taxes on property	..	..	0	0	0	0	0	0	0	0
5000 Taxes on goods and services	**..**	**..**	**2 138**	**4 903**	**5 326**	**5 631**	**5 407**	**6 223**	**6 132**	**7 300**
5100 Taxes on production, sale, transfer, etc	..	..	2 008	4 669	5 081	5 379	5 136	5 955	5 870	6 981
5110 General taxes	..	..	1 864	4 481	4 711	5 107	4 704	5 606	5 448	6 535
5111 Value added taxes	..	..	1 864	4 481	4 711	5 107	4 704	5 606	5 448	6 535
VAT - Revenue	..	..	1 832	4 481	4 711	5 107	4 704	5 606	5 448	6 535
VAT accrued interest	..	..	31	0	0	0	0	0	0	0
Refund of VAT - Revenue	..	..	1	0	0	0	0	0	0	0
5112 Sales tax	..	..	0	0	0	0	0	0	0	0
5113 Other	..	..	0	0	0	0	0	0	0	0
5120 Taxes on specific goods and services	..	..	144	188	370	271	433	349	422	446
5121 Excises	..	..	115	157	337	251	400	318	393	435
Alcohol Levy	..	..	0	0	197	76	218	214	284	327
Fuel Levy	..	..	115	157	140	175	182	104	109	107
5122 Profits of fiscal monopolies	..	..	0	0	0	0	0	0	0	0
5123 Customs and import duties	..	..	2	9	11	2	6	2	4	6
5124 Taxes on exports	..	..	0	2	1	2	2	2	2	3
5125 Taxes on investment goods	..	..	0	0	0	0	0	0	0	0
5126 Taxes on specific services	..	..	27	20	21	16	24	28	23	2
5127 Other taxes on internat. trade and transactions	..	..	0	0	0	0	0	0	0	0
5128 Other taxes	..	..	0	0	0	0	0	0	0	0
5130 Unallocable between 5110 and 5120	..	..	0	0	0	0	0	0	0	0
5200 Taxes on use of goods and perform activities	..	..	131	234	246	252	271	268	262	319
5210 Recurrent taxes	..	..	131	234	246	252	271	268	262	319
5211 Paid by households: motor vehicles	..	..	41	62	67	70	73	73	77	85
5212 Paid by others: motor vehicles	..	..	74	144	136	144	159	161	180	193
5213 Paid in respect of other goods	..	..	15	29	43	38	38	34	5	40

Table 5.1. **Botswana** *(cont.)*

Details of tax revenue / Recettes fiscales détaillées

Million BWP

	1997	2000	2005	2010	2011	2012	2013	2014	2015	2016
5220 Non-recurrent taxes	..	..	0	0	0	0	0	0	0	0
5300 Unallocable between 5100 and 5200	..	..	0	0	0	0	0	0	0	0
6000 Other taxes	**..**	**..**	**0**	**0**	**0**	**0**	**0**	**0**	**0**	**0**
6100 Paid solely by business	..	..	..	..	..	..	..	..	..	..
6200 Other	..	..	..	..	..	..	..	..	..	..

Note: Data are on a fiscal year basis beginning 1st April. For example, the data for 2015 represent April 2015 to March 2016.
Figures exclude tax revenues collected by sub-national governments as the data are not available.

1. Heading 2000: Social security contributions for Botswana are deemed to be null as they do not meet the criteria to be classified as social security contributions set out in the OECD classification of taxes in the Interpretative Guide.

Source: Botswana Ministry of Finance and Economic Development, and Statistics Botswana.

StatLink https://doi.org/10.1787/888933820449

Table 5.2. **Burkina Faso**

Details of tax revenue / Recettes fiscales détaillées

Million XOF

	1997	2000	2005	2010	2011	2012	2013	2014	2015	2016
Recettes fiscales totales	..	**191 898**	**393 892**	**679 620**	**799 719**	**980 576**	**1 065 945**	**1 003 247**	**1 072 731**	**1 216 194**
1000 Impôts sur revenu, bénéfices et gains en capital	..	**51 187**	**92 001**	**139 635**	**219 831**	**281 463**	**309 499**	**271 404**	**263 702**	**320 385**
1100 Des personnes physiques	..	17 673	49 354	53 094	73 750	84 845	85 480	67 134	78 696	93 206
1110 Sur le revenu et les bénéfices	..	17 673	49 354	53 094	73 750	84 845	85 480	67 134	78 696	93 206
Impôt sur les revenus	..	0	15 053	14	111	144	94	27	31	14
Impôt sur les bénéfices industriels, commerciaux et agricoles (pers. phys.)	..	3 242	8 342	3 566	11 979	10 364	8 122	2 847	4 551	7 885
Impôt sur les bénéfices non commerciaux (pers. phys.)	..	964	2 874	3 259	3 133	4 627	3 926	3 789	6 035	5 694
Impôt unique sur les traitements et salaires	..	13 468	23 084	46 255	58 527	69 710	73 338	60 471	68 079	78 997
Taxe sur les jeux de hasard	..	0	0	0	0	0	0	0	0	617
1120 Sur les gains en capital	..	..	..	..	..	..	..	..	..	..
1200 Des sociétés	..	31 935	40 415	83 097	142 607	193 660	220 561	199 958	180 821	222 402
1210 Sur les bénéfices	..	31 935	40 415	83 097	142 607	193 660	220 561	199 958	180 821	222 402
Impôt sur les sociétés	..	0	0	70 550	125 187	167 504	192 840	171 757	151 305	183 696
Contribution du secteur informel et des micro-entreprises	..	0	0	1 931	2 451	1 960	1 616	1 664	1 731	2 200
Impôt sur les bénéfices industriels, commerciaux et agricoles (pers. mor.)	..	28 308	34 986	0	0	0	0	0	0	0
Impôts sur le revenu des créances	..	519	1 178	5 085	2 523	3 447	4 683	4 659	4 743	6 525
Impôts sur le revenu des valeurs mobilières	..	3 108	4 251	5 530	12 445	20 750	21 422	21 879	23 042	29 980
1220 Sur les gains en capital	..	..	..	..	..	..	..	..	..	..
1300 Non ventilables entre 1100 et 1200	..	1 578	2 231	3 444	3 475	2 957	3 458	4 311	4 185	4 777
Impôts sur les revenus fonciers	..	1 454	1 572	3 409	3 113	2 425	3 033	4 122	3 787	3 964
Reversement des honoraires	..	69	416	4	11	92	18	0	0	0
Taxes sur les plus-values	..	56	244	31	350	440	407	189	398	814
2000 Cotisations de sécurité sociale	..	**13 416**	**23 185**	**42 286**	**53 080**	**54 922**	**64 819**	**66 383**	**74 759**	**76 711**
2100 A la charge des salariés	..	2 626	5 749	10 664	12 155	13 847	16 465	16 881	18 213	18 629
2110 Sur la base du salaire	..	2 626	5 749	10 664	12 155	13 847	16 465	16 881	18 213	18 629
2120 Sur la base de l'impôt sur les revenus	..	0	0	0	0	0	0	0	0	0
2200 A la charge des employeurs	..	10 806	17 447	31 628	40 930	41 079	48 357	49 504	55 050	56 458
2210 Sur la base du salaire	..	10 806	17 447	31 628	40 930	41 079	48 357	49 504	55 050	56 458
2220 Sur la base de l'impôt sur le revenu	..	0	0	0	0	0	0	0	0	0
2300 A charge des travailleurs indép. ou sans emploi	..	0	0	0	0	0	0	0	1 497	1 624
2310 Sur la base du salaire	..	0	0	0	0	0	0	0	1 497	1 624
2320 Sur la base de l'impôt sur le revenu	..	0	0	0	0	0	0	0	0	0
2400 Non ventilables entre 2100, 2200 et 2300	..	0	0	0	0	0	0	0	0	0
2410 Sur la base du salaire	..	..	..	..	..	..	..	..	..	..
2420 Sur la base de l'impôt sur le revenu	..	..	..	..	..	..	..	..	..	..
3000 Sur salaires ou main d'oeuvre	..	**2 719**	**4 390**	**5 465**	**4 968**	**6 156**	**7 559**	**7 407**	**8 246**	**9 026**
4000 Impôts sur le patrimoine	..	**1 117**	**2 319**	**2 499**	**7 009**	**6 612**	**7 959**	**10 172**	**9 291**	**12 976**
4100 Impôts périodiques sur la propriété immobilière	..	328	0	835	1 302	840	707	1 092	1 676	2 218
Contribution foncière	..	0	0	0	0	0	0	0	0	0
Taxe de résidence	..	238	0	521	964	524	526	558	486	865
Taxe sur les biens de mainmorte	..	89	0	314	338	316	181	534	1 190	1 353
4110 Ménages	..	..	..	..	..	..	..	..	..	..
4120 Autres agents	..	..	..	..	..	..	..	..	..	..
4200 Impôts périodiques sur l'actif net	..	0	0	0	0	0	0	0	0	0
4210 Personnes physiques	..	..	..	..	..	..	..	..	..	..
4220 Sociétés	..	..	..	..	..	..	..	..	..	..
4300 Impôts sur mut. par décès, succ. et donations	..	67	495	26	167	250	178	110	163	150
4310 Impôts sur mut. par décès et successions	..	60	34	24	143	217	117	95	151	131
4320 Impôts sur les donations	..	7	461	3	24	33	61	15	12	19
4400 Impôts sur transact. mobilières et immob.	..	568	1 136	518	3 550	4 285	5 558	7 571	6 000	8 834
4500 Impôts non-périodiques	..	155	688	1 120	1 990	1 237	1 515	1 399	1 452	1 774
4510 Sur l'actif net	..	0	0	0	0	0	0	0	0	0
4520 Autres non-périodiques	..	155	688	1 120	1 990	1 237	1 515	1 399	1 452	1 774
4600 Autres impôts périodiques sur patrimoine	..	0	0	0	0	0	0	0	0	0
5000 Impôts sur les biens et services	..	**122 119**	**269 745**	**485 055**	**509 373**	**626 032**	**670 749**	**642 028**	**711 082**	**789 358**
5100 Impôts sur production, vente, transfert, etc.	..	107 909	253 400	386 114	461 622	584 825	622 294	591 212	653 547	726 295
5110 Impôts généraux	..	61 490	164 795	245 498	296 371	368 863	399 599	354 724	387 215	435 112
5111 Taxes sur la valeur ajoutée	..	61 490	140 916	244 692	295 638	367 920	398 849	354 082	386 495	434 394
Taxes sur la valeur ajoutée (brute)	..	62 559	141 920	252 392	318 678	403 667	439 849	427 432	436 995	494 894
Remboursements TVA	..	-1 068	-1 004	-7 700	-23 040	-35 747	-41 000	-73 350	-50 500	-60 500
5112 Impôts sur les ventes	..	0	0	0	0	0	0	0	0	0
5113 Autres impôts	..	0	23 879	806	733	942	750	643	720	718
Taxe sur chiffre d'affaires	..	0	0	0	0	0	0	0	0	0
Taxe de développement touristique	..	0	23 879	806	733	942	750	643	720	718
5120 Impôts sur biens et services déterminés	..	46 419	88 605	140 616	165 251	215 963	222 695	236 488	266 333	291 183

Table 5.2. **Burkina Faso** *(cont.)*

Details of tax revenue / Recettes fiscales détaillées

Million XOF

	1997	2000	2005	2010	2011	2012	2013	2014	2015	2016
5121 Accises	..	16 130	31 146	46 536	54 816	67 460	57 364	78 489	94 108	105 387
Boissons	..	4 956	7 311	13 511	17 508	19 439	22 129	25 454	26 205	30 550
Taxes sur le café, le thé et les noix de cola	..	549	525	938	890	901	1 187	1 098	1 603	1 417
Taxe sur les produits pétroliers	..	10 515	23 169	31 710	35 490	46 335	33 021	50 988	65 266	71 818
Taxe sur les tabacs et allumettes	..	111	141	139	731	520	783	691	789	1 187
Autres accises	..	0	0	239	198	265	245	257	246	415
5122 Bénéfices de monopoles fiscaux	..	3 012	3 943	6 475	7 837	9 554	10 056	11 694	15 213	17 668
Monopole des tabacs	..	3 012	3 943	6 475	7 837	9 554	10 056	11 694	15 213	17 668
5123 Droits de douane et droits à l'importation	..	25 242	52 066	85 075	98 997	134 189	150 486	130 085	128 465	140 632
Redevance informatique et statistique	..	3 574	5 502	10 030	11 434	16 144	18 457	15 435	16 218	17 484
Droits de douanes	..	21 589	46 092	75 045	87 563	118 045	132 029	114 649	112 247	123 148
Taxe dégressive de protection	..	79	472	0	0	0	0	0	0	0
5124 Taxes à l'exportation	..	572	322	434	461	636	632	685	601	416
Contribution du secteur élevage	..	572	322	434	461	636	632	685	601	416
5125 Impôts sur biens d'équipement	..	0	0	0	0	0	0	0	0	0
5126 Impôts sur services déterminés	..	1 463	1 129	2 096	3 141	4 124	4 157	15 536	27 946	27 081
Taxe sur billets avions	..	3	176	349	531	1 060	709	608	543	597
Taxe spécifique sur les entreprises de télécommunication	..	0	0	0	0	0	245	13 078	23 562	22 104
Taxe sur les contrats d'assurance	..	1 460	952	1 748	2 609	3 064	3 203	1 850	3 842	4 379
5127 Autres impôts sur commerce et transact. internat.	..	0	0	0	0	0	0	0	0	0
5128 Autres impôts	..	0	0	0	0	0	0	0	0	0
5130 Non ventilables entre 5110 et 5120	..	0	0	0	0	0	0	0	0	0
5200 Impôts sur utilisation des biens et exerc. activites	..	10 492	13 135	97 500	46 068	39 699	44 566	50 123	54 923	59 286
5210 Impôts périodiques	..	3 862	5 898	72 197	19 829	14 731	16 186	11 143	22 435	26 713
5211 A la charge des ménages: véhicules à moteur	..	0	0	0	0	0	0	0	0	0
5212 A la charge autres agents: véhicules à moteur	..	0	0	0	0	0	0	0	0	0
5213 Autres impôts périodiques	..	3 862	5 898	72 197	19 829	14 731	16 186	11 143	22 435	26 713
Taxe sur les armes	..	15	0	27	34	42	29	31	26	36
Contribution des patentes	..	3 347	0	8 901	10 027	9 919	14 405	9 802	21 070	25 269
Taxe de visionnnement et de vérification	..	9	26	82	84	90	99	93	0	0
Matière forestière, faune sauvage et pêche	..	461	605	1 215	1 274	1 330	1 067	1 190	1 239	1 183
Recettes en matière d'hydraulique	..	0	0	0	0	0	10	0	0	0
Autorisation d'exploiter les hôtels et les restaurants	..	0	0	0	0	0	0	0	0	0
Licence de téléphonie mobile	..	0	0	61 793	8 165	3 000	0	0	0	0
Licence - vente à la consommation	..	30	5 267	180	245	350	575	26	99	224
5220 Impôts non-périodiques	..	6 630	7 237	25 303	26 238	24 968	28 380	38 981	32 489	32 573
Autres droits d'enregistrement	..	4 418	6 344	20 503	18 169	18 607	20 629	31 471	27 980	27 575
Taxe de jouissance	..	2 205	888	4 782	8 068	6 357	7 748	7 505	4 506	4 990
Licences d'agences et de guides touristiques	..	0	0	3	0	0	0	0	0	3
Agrément armes à feu	..	0	0	0	0	0	0	1	0	2
Agréments au code des investissements	..	7	5	14	1	3	2	4	2	3
5300 Non ventilables entre 5100 et 5200	..	3 717	3 210	1 441	1 683	1 508	3 889	693	2 611	3 778
Autres impôts non ventilables	..	65	318	110	209	188	612	236	423	932
Taxe préférentielle communautaire	..	3 154	1 890	0	0	246	0	0	0	0
Taxe pour le développement de la télévision	..	498	1 002	1 332	1 475	1 073	3 277	456	2 188	2 846
6000 Autres impôts	**..**	**1 339**	**2 251**	**4 680**	**5 458**	**5 391**	**5 361**	**5 853**	**5 650**	**7 737**
Droits de timbre	..	1 231	2 240	4 547	5 255	5 191	5 312	5 751	5 604	7 521
Autres recettes fiscales	..	107	11	133	203	199	49	102	46	217
6100 A la charge exclusive des entreprises	..	..	..	..	..	..	..	..	..	..
6200 A la charge d'autres agents	..	..	..	..	..	..	..	..	..	..

Note: Année civile se terminant le 31 décembre.

Les données sont sur la base des droits constatés.

Les chiffres n'incluent pas les recettes fiscales collectées par les collectivités locales car elles ne sont pas disponibles. Cependant, ils incluen des recettes collectées par l'administration centrale au profit des collectivités locales.

Les recettes provenant de la taxe de location de biens, des droits sur les titres miniers, des redevances minières et des frais administratif sont incluses dans les recettes non fiscales comme le préconise la classification OCDE (voir le guide d'interprétation en Annexe A). L classification nationale du Burkina Faso les comptabilise comme des recettes fiscales.

Source: Ministère de l'Économie, des Finances et du Développement du Burkina Faso.

StatLink https://doi.org/10.1787/888933820468

Table 5.3. **Cabo Verde**

Details of tax revenue / Recettes fiscales détaillées

Million CVE

	1997	2000	2005	2010	2011	2012	2013	2014	2015	2016
Recettes fiscales totales	**7 326**	**10 974**	**18 828**	**25 552**	**28 940**	**26 678**	**27 351**	**26 147**	**29 839**	**31 072**
1000 Impôts sur revenu, bénéfices et gains en capital	**2 571**	**3 913**	**5 815**	**7 892**	**8 678**	**8 616**	**8 596**	**7 747**	**9 669**	**10 050**
1100 Des personnes physiques	1 928	2 958	3 516	4 645	4 877	4 994	4 793	4 998	5 327	6 317
1110 Sur le revenu et les bénéfices	..	..	..	..	..	..	..	..	..	..
1120 Sur les gains en capital	..	..	..	..	..	..	..	..	..	..
1200 Des sociétés	643	955	2 299	3 247	3 801	3 622	3 802	2 749	4 342	3 733
1210 Sur les bénéfices	..	..	..	..	..	..	..	..	..	..
1220 Sur les gains en capital	..	..	..	..	..	..	..	..	..	..
1300 Non ventilables entre 1100 et 1200	0	0	0	0	0	0	0	0	0	0
2000 Cotisations de sécurité sociale	**0**	**569**	**533**	**42**	**37**	**41**	**43**	**56**	**46**	**56**
2100 A la charge des salariés	..	..	..	..	..	..	..	..	..	..
2110 Sur la base du salaire	..	..	..	..	..	..	..	..	..	..
2120 Sur la base de l'impôt sur les revenus	..	..	..	..	..	..	..	..	..	..
2200 A la charge des employeurs	..	..	..	..	..	..	..	..	..	..
2210 Sur la base du salaire	..	..	..	..	..	..	..	..	..	..
2220 Sur la base de l'impôt sur le revenu	..	..	..	..	..	..	..	..	..	..
2300 A charge des travailleurs indép. ou sans emploi	..	..	..	..	..	..	..	..	..	..
2310 Sur la base du salaire	..	..	..	..	..	..	..	..	..	..
2320 Sur la base de l'impôt sur le revenu	..	..	..	..	..	..	..	..	..	..
2400 Non ventilables entre 2100, 2200 et 2300	..	569	533	42	37	41	43	56	46	56
2410 Sur la base du salaire	..	569	533	42	37	41	43	56	46	56
Contributions pour la sécurité sociale	..	11	1	28	26	34	38	49	40	56
Taxe sociale unique	..	558	532	14	10	8	5	7	5	0
2420 Sur la base de l'impôt sur le revenu	..	0	0	0	0	0	0	0	0	0
3000 Sur salaires ou main d'oeuvre	**0**	**0**	**0**	**0**	**0**	**0**	**0**	**0**	**0**	**0**
4000 Impôts sur le patrimoine	**394**	**584**	**810**	**701**	**835**	**668**	**668**	**668**	**582**	**472**
4100 Impôts périodiques sur la propriété immobilière	0	0	0	0	0	0	0	0	0	0
4110 Ménages	..	..	..	..	..	..	..	..	..	..
4120 Autres agents	..	..	..	..	..	..	..	..	..	..
4200 Impôts périodiques sur l'actif net	0	0	0	0	0	0	0	0	0	0
4210 Personnes physiques	..	..	..	..	..	..	..	..	..	..
4220 Sociétés	..	..	..	..	..	..	..	..	..	..
4300 Impôts sur mut. par décès, succ. et donations	0	0	0	0	0	0	0	0	0	0
4310 Impôts sur mut. par décès et successions	..	..	..	..	..	..	..	..	..	..
4320 Impôts sur les donations	..	..	..	..	..	..	..	..	..	..
4400 Impôts sur transact. mobilières et immob.	394	584	810	701	835	668	668	668	582	472
4500 Impôts non-périodiques	0	0	0	0	0	0	0	0	0	0
4510 Sur l'actif net	..	..	..	..	..	..	..	..	..	..
4520 Autres non-périodiques	..	..	..	..	..	..	..	..	..	..
4600 Autres impôts périodiques sur patrimoine	0	0	0	0	0	0	0	0	0	0
5000 Impôts sur les biens et services	**4 361**	**5 908**	**11 670**	**16 917**	**19 390**	**17 353**	**18 044**	**17 676**	**19 542**	**20 494**
5100 Impôts sur production, vente, transfert, etc.	4 361	5 908	11 670	16 917	19 390	17 353	18 044	17 676	19 542	20 494
5110 Impôts généraux	0	0	6 409	10 035	11 216	9 730	9 996	9 458	10 824	11 017
5111 Taxes sur la valeur ajoutée	..	..	6 409	10 035	11 216	9 730	9 996	9 458	10 824	11 017
TVA brute sur les importations (DGA)	..	..	4 192	6 180	7 544	6 515	6 602	6 253	6 358	6 601
TVA brute sur le marché intérieur (DGCI)	..	..	2 359	4 341	4 060	3 890	3 921	3 917	4 935	5 385
Remboursements TVA	..	..	-143	-486	-387	-674	-526	-712	-469	-969
5112 Impôts sur les ventes	..	..	0	0	0	0	0	0	0	0
5113 Autres impôts	..	..	0	0	0	0	0	0	0	0
5120 Impôts sur biens et services déterminés	4 361	5 908	5 261	6 882	8 174	7 623	8 047	8 219	8 718	9 477
5121 Accises	1 518	1 938	1 030	1 494	2 236	2 041	2 235	2 065	2 073	2 228
Taxe spéciale sur la consommation	1 518	1 812	838	1 227	1 706	1 498	1 664	1 507	1 478	1 550
Taxe écologique	0	126	192	267	531	543	571	558	595	678
5122 Bénéfices des monopoles fiscaux	0	0	0	0	0	0	0	0	0	0
5123 Droits de douane et droits à l'importation	2 843	3 971	4 231	5 388	5 938	5 516	5 434	5 497	5 827	6 523
5124 Taxes à l'exportation	0	0	0	0	0	0	0	0	0	0
5125 Impôts sur biens d'équipement	0	0	0	0	0	0	0	0	0	0
5126 Impôts sur services déterminés	0	0	0	0	0	66	378	657	817	726
Contribution touristique	..	..	..	..	..	0	329	598	645	711
Autres (taxe incendie, taxe touristique)	..	..	..	..	..	66	49	59	172	16
5127 Autres impôts sur commerce et transact. internat.	0	0	0	0	0	0	0	0	0	0
5128 Autres impôts	0	0	0	0	0	0	0	0	0	0
5130 Non ventilables entre 5110 et 5120	0	0	0	0	0	0	0	0	0	0
5200 Impôts sur utilisation des biens et exerc. activites	0	0	0	0	0	0	0	0	0	0
5210 Impôts périodiques	..	..	..	..	..	..	..	..	..	..
5211 A la charge des ménages: véhicules à moteur	..	..	..	..	..	..	..	..	..	..
5212 A la charge autres agents: véhicules à moteur	..	..	..	..	..	..	..	..	..	..
5213 Autres impôts périodiques	..	..	..	..	..	..	..	..	..	..

Table 5.3. **Cabo Verde** *(cont.)*

Details of tax revenue / Recettes fiscales détaillées

Million CVE

	1997	2000	2005	2010	2011	2012	2013	2014	2015	2016
5220 Impôts non-périodiques	..	..	..	..	..	..	..	..	..	..
5300 Non ventilables entre 5100 et 5200	0	0	0	0	0	0	0	0	0	0
6000 Autres impôts	**0**	**0**	**0**	**0**	**0**	**0**	**0**	**0**	**0**	**0**
6100 A la charge exclusive des entreprises	..	..	..	..	..	..	..	..	..	..
6200 A la charge d'autres agents	..	..	..	..	..	..	..	..	..	..

Note: Année civile se terminant le 31 décembre.

Les données sont sur la base des encaissements.

Les chiffres n'incluent pas les recettes fiscales collectées par les collectivités locales car elles ne sont pas disponibles.

Le prélèvement communautaire de la CEDEAO (Communauté économique des États de l'Afrique de l'Ouest) n'est pas compris parmi les impôts selon le guide d'interprétation de l'OCDE (voir § 4). La classification nationale du Cabo Verde le comptabilise comme une recette fiscale. Cette recette qui n'est pas comprise dans le total des recettes fiscales ou des recettes non fiscales est présentée à titre de rubrique « Pour mémoire ».dans le tableau 6.8 du chapitre 6.

Source: Ministère des Finances.

StatLink https://doi.org/10.1787/888933820487

Table 5.4. **Cameroon / Cameroun**

Details of tax revenue / Recettes fiscales détaillées

Million XAF

	1997	2000	2005	2010	2011	2012	2013	2014	2015	2016
Recettes fiscales totales	**582 398**	**810 500**	**1 135 257**	**1 571 695**	**1 801 174**	**1 999 143**	**2 258 738**	**2 486 045**	**2 687 926**	**2 743 908**
1000 Impôts sur revenu, bénéfices et gains en capital	**140 000**	**228 100**	**325 764**	**425 741**	**505 594**	**637 416**	**693 317**	**784 122**	**867 834**	**771 155**
1100 Des personnes physiques	66 400	87 100	66 598	102 793	116 950	130 516	158 622	175 021	185 512	179 475
1110 Sur le revenu et les bénéfices	66 400	87 100	66 548	102 728	116 928	130 483	158 338	174 190	184 213	177 669
Traitements, salaires, pensions et rentes viagères	40 100	60 800	17 722	86 440	96 097	101 245	120 908	127 331	135 738	131 524
Revenus fonciers	0	0	2 225	2 402	4 487	5 346	6 135	13 247	12 405	12 716
Bénéfices artisanaux, industriels et commerciaux	0	0	3 904	5 342	6 609	11 648	16 267	13 648	21 010	15 689
Bénéfices agricoles	0	0	77	47	7	14	22	27	56	31
Bénéfices des professions non commerciales	0	0	249	295	397	577	612	592	2 875	5 687
Autres impôts sur le revenu	26 300	26 300	42 372	8 202	9 331	11 653	14 394	19 345	12 130	12 022
1120 Sur les gains en capital	0	0	50	65	22	33	284	831	1 299	1 806
Impôts sur plus-values sur cession immobilière	..	..	46	46	8	17	263	830	1 297	1 803
Impôts sur les autres gains en capital	..	..	3	19	14	16	21	1	2	3
1200 Des sociétés	57 100	119 400	217 495	256 404	311 102	421 796	428 360	460 571	538 969	460 785
1210 Sur les bénéfices	57 100	119 400	217 495	256 404	311 102	421 796	428 360	460 571	538 969	460 785
Bénéfices des sociétés pétrolières	19 000	39 000	76 523	83 764	96 729	160 588	169 689	161 724	171 891	108 966
Bénéfices des sociétés non pétrolières	38 100	80 400	140 972	172 639	214 373	261 207	258 671	298 847	367 078	351 818
1220 Sur les gains en capital	..	..	..	0	0	0	0	0	0	0
1300 Non ventilables entre 1100 et 1200	16 500	21 600	41 671	66 544	77 542	85 105	106 335	148 530	143 352	130 896
Taxe spéciale sur les revenus payés à l'étranger	11 000	12 400	19 198	38 877	42 626	43 572	61 708	97 511	84 412	68 691
Impôts sur les revenus des capitaux mobiliers	5 500	9 200	21 619	27 629	32 441	38 313	40 177	44 489	48 774	39 350
Centimes communaux sur l'impôt sur le revenu	0	0	854	39	2 475	3 219	4 450	6 530	10 166	22 855
2000 Cotisations de sécurité sociale	**45 598**	**65 500**	**83 903**	**135 747**	**143 734**	**147 543**	**160 134**	**153 707**	**160 992**	**200 960**
2100 A la charge des salariés	11 998	19 747	24 123	33 297	34 741	34 414	42 212	40 917	44 669	44 655
2110 Sur la base du salaire	11 998	19 747	24 123	33 297	34 741	34 414	42 212	40 917	44 669	44 655
2120 Sur la base de l'impôt sur le revenu	0	0	0	0	0	0	0	0	0	0
2200 A la charge des employeurs	..	..	..	..	..	..	..	..	..	..
2210 Sur la base du salaire	..	..	..	..	..	..	..	..	..	..
2220 Sur la base de l'impôt sur le revenu	..	..	..	..	..	..	..	..	..	..
2300 A charge des travailleurs indép. ou sans emploi	..	..	..	..	..	..	..	..	..	..
2310 Sur la base du salaire	..	..	..	..	..	..	..	..	..	..
2320 Sur la base de l'impôt sur le revenu	..	..	..	..	..	..	..	..	..	..
2400 Non ventilables entre 2100, 2200 et 2300	33 600	45 753	59 780	102 450	108 993	113 129	117 922	112 790	116 323	156 305
2410 Sur la base du salaire	33 600	45 753	59 780	102 450	108 993	113 129	117 922	112 790	116 323	156 305
2420 Sur la base de l'impôt sur le revenu	0	0	0	0	0	0	0	0	0	0
3000 Sur salaires ou main d'oeuvre	**0**	**0**	**8 644**	**17 860**	**30 792**	**40 427**	**39 817**	**46 902**	**53 572**	**52 826**
4000 Impôts sur le patrimoine	**4 500**	**13 100**	**13 361**	**18 003**	**12 973**	**15 087**	**20 816**	**21 024**	**25 437**	**30 471**
4100 Impôts périodiques sur la propriété immobilière	100	500	1 318	1 552	386	59	1 714	1 692	1 743	3 905
4110 Ménages	..	..	..	..	..	..	..	..	..	..
4120 Autres agents	..	..	..	..	..	..	..	..	..	..
4200 Impôts périodiques sur l'actif net	0	0	0	0	0	0	0	0	0	0
4210 Personnes physiques	..	..	..	..	..	..	..	..	..	..
4220 Sociétés	..	..	..	..	..	..	..	..	..	..
4300 Impôts sur mut. par décès, succ. et donations	0	0	33	39	176	176	157	214	62	160
4310 Impôts sur mut. par décès et successions	..	..	33	39	176	176	157	214	62	160
4320 Impôts sur les donations	..	..	0	0	0	0	0	0	0	0
4400 Impôts sur transact. mobilières et immob.	4 400	12 600	12 010	16 412	12 411	14 853	18 945	19 117	23 632	26 406
Droits d'enregistrement sur les mutations entre vifs	..	..	82	32	96	96	287	586	391	376
Droits d'enregistrement sur les mutations immobilières	..	..	1 909	2 747	411	3 650	3 343	3 250	3 080	2 921
Droits de bail	..	..	3 976	4 602	3 373	2 575	2 337	2 725	2 364	2 425
Droits autres mutations et transactions	..	..	6 043	9 031	8 532	8 532	12 978	12 556	17 797	20 685
4500 Impôts non-périodiques	0	0	0	0	0	0	0	0	0	0
4510 Sur l'actif net	..	..	..	..	..	..	..	..	..	..
4520 Autres non-périodiques	..	..	..	..	..	..	..	..	..	..
4600 Autres impôts périodiques sur patrimoine	0	0	0	0	0	0	0	0	0	0
5000 Impôts sur les biens et services	**392 300**	**503 800**	**686 416**	**944 412**	**1 078 788**	**1 126 840**	**1 296 237**	**1 448 405**	**1 532 668**	**1 642 804**
5100 Impôts sur production, vente, transfert, etc.	390 600	501 100	679 379	936 564	1 071 238	1 119 094	1 287 824	1 438 522	1 522 834	1 632 420
5110 Impôts généraux	179 100	260 900	360 218	490 521	598 625	611 802	743 099	826 250	883 618	928 368
5111 Taxes sur la valeur ajoutée	0	260 900	360 218	490 513	598 603	611 792	743 078	826 225	883 580	928 368
Valeur ajoutée intérieure (brute)	..	186 500	251 019	299 504	373 531	373 916	472 885	532 980	604 046	629 355
Valeur ajoutée à la porte (brute)	..	107 300	157 799	259 343	278 633	311 007	315 945	358 184	354 701	355 033
Remboursements credits de TVA	..	-32 900	-48 600	-68 333	-53 561	-73 132	-45 752	-64 938	-75 167	-56 020
5112 Impôts sur les ventes	0	0	0	0	0	0	0	0	0	0
5113 Autres impôts	179 100	0	0	8	23	10	20	25	39	0
5120 Impôts sur biens et services déterminés	211 500	240 200	319 161	446 043	472 613	507 292	544 726	612 272	639 216	704 052

Table 5.4. **Cameroon / Cameroun** *(cont.)*

Details of tax revenue / Recettes fiscales détaillées

Million XAF

	1997	2000	2005	2010	2011	2012	2013	2014	2015	2016
5121 Accises	77 400	84 000	114 306	164 943	182 730	198 030	220 643	240 269	289 280	323 562
Droits d'accises intérieure	19 300	26 500	42 754	68 414	81 616	84 068	95 553	98 327	170 164	204 785
Droits d'accises à la porte	1 100	1 900	2 198	12 936	15 861	15 867	14 817	14 762	14 608	12 662
Taxe spéciale sur les produits pétroliers	57 000	55 600	69 345	82 962	84 580	97 423	109 598	118 515	103 773	105 579
Vignette sur tabac et produits manufacturés	0	0	8	632	672	672	675	8 665	736	537
5122 Bénéfices des monopoles fiscaux	0	0	0	0	0	0	0	0	0	0
5123 Droits de douane et droits à l'importation	85 700	119 900	189 364	261 731	268 897	289 838	299 976	345 511	320 314	350 705
5124 Taxes à l'exportation	45 900	24 300	1 725	8 793	8 082	7 481	13 054	15 089	17 133	16 330
5125 Impôts sur biens d'équipement	0	0	0	0	0	0	0	0	0	0
5126 Impôts sur services déterminés	1 200	1 100	3 108	3 600	4 392	4 603	4 930	5 238	5 035	6 387
5127 Autres impôts sur commerce et transact. internat.	0	0	0	0	0	0	0	0	0	0
5128 Autres impôts	1 300	10 900	10 658	6 977	8 512	7 340	6 123	6 165	7 454	7 068
5130 Non ventilables entre 5110 et 5120	0	0	0	0	0	0	0	0	0	0
5200 Impôts sur utilisation des biens et exerc. activités	1 700	2 700	7 037	7 848	7 550	7 746	8 413	9 883	9 835	10 385
5210 Impôts périodiques	1 700	2 700	7 037	7 848	7 550	7 746	8 413	9 883	9 835	10 385
5211 A la charge des ménages: véhicules à moteur	1 300	1 600	4 987	6 111	5 803	6 138	6 640	7 819	7 539	8 050
5212 A la charge autres agents: véhicules à moteur	400	1 100	1 902	1 663	1 676	1 530	1 707	1 985	2 213	2 205
5213 Autres impôts périodiques	0	0	149	74	71	78	67	79	83	130
5220 Impôts non-périodiques	0	0	0	0	0	0	0	0	0	0
5300 Non ventilables entre 5100 et 5200	0	0	0	0	0	0	0	0	0	0
6000 Autres impôts	**0**	**0**	**17 169**	**29 932**	**29 292**	**31 829**	**48 416**	**31 885**	**47 424**	**45 692**
6100 A la charge exclusive des entreprises	..	..	..	..	..	..	..	..	..	..
6200 A la charge d'autres agents	..	..	..	..	..	..	..	..	..	..

Note: Année civile se terminant le 31 décembre.

Les données sont sur la base des encaissements.

Les chiffres n'incluent pas les recettes fiscales collectées par les collectivités locales car elles ne sont pas disponibles.

Rubrique 2000 : Les cotisations de sécurité sociale du secteur public (APU) incluent uniquement les cotisations pour les retraites et ne couvrent pas les prestations familiales et d'invalidité.

Rubrique 5111 : Les données antérieures à 1999 correspondent aux recettes de la taxe sur le chiffre d'affaire (TCA) et ont été reclassées dans la rubrique « 5113 Autres impôts généraux sur les biens et services » La TVA a été introduite au Cameroun en 1999. Dans cette édition, les données de recettes TVA sont présentées nettes de remboursements TVA comme le préconise la classification OCDE (voir le guide d'interprétation en Annexe A).

Source: Ministère des Finances du Cameroun.

StatLink https://doi.org/10.1787/888933820506

Table 5.5. **Congo**

Details of tax revenue / Recettes fiscales détaillées

Million XAF

	1997	2000	2005	2010	2011	2012	2013	2014	2015	2016
Recettes fiscales totales	**..**	**98 591**	**198 670**	**430 810**	**519 330**	**583 057**	**966 510**	**800 381**	**838 742**	**736 706**
1000 Impôts sur revenu, bénéfices et gains en capital	**..**	**47 544**	**62 458**	**150 800**	**189 193**	**216 378**	**506 588**	**289 623**	**341 292**	**308 200**
1100 Des personnes physiques	..	22 850	28 265	64 372	86 655	108 208	365 190	149 837	144 150	148 447
1110 Sur le revenu et les bénéfices	..	22 385	24 190	57 196	73 759	85 606	92 131	112 717	109 709	106 822
Traitements et salaires	..	21 836	22 581	54 793	69 382	82 062	87 556	107 849	103 976	100 477
Revenus fonciers	..	549	1 079	2 259	2 883	3 250	4 043	4 752	5 531	6 020
Bénéfices non commerciaux (BNC)	..	0	62	23	1 377	268	469	50	50	19
Bénéfices industriels et commerciaux (BIC)	..	0	468	122	117	27	63	67	152	307
1120 Sur les gains en capital	..	466	4 075	7 176	12 896	22 602	273 059	37 120	34 441	41 625
1200 Des sociétés	..	24 694	34 193	86 428	102 538	108 170	141 398	139 786	197 141	159 753
1210 Sur les bénéfices	..	24 694	34 193	86 428	102 538	108 170	141 398	139 786	197 141	159 753
1220 Sur les gains en capital	..	..	..	..	..	..	..	..	..	..
1300 Non ventilables entre 1100 et 1200	..	0	0	0	0	0	0	0	0	0
2000 Cotisations de sécurité sociale	**..**	**..**	**..**	**..**	**..**	**..**	**..**	**..**	**..**	**..**
2100 A la charge des salariés	..	..	..	..	..	..	..	..	..	..
2110 Sur la base du salaire	..	..	..	..	..	..	..	..	..	..
2120 Sur la base de l'impôt sur les revenus	..	..	..	..	..	..	..	..	..	..
2200 A la charge des employeurs	..	..	..	..	..	..	..	..	..	..
2210 Sur la base du salaire	..	..	..	..	..	..	..	..	..	..
2220 Sur la base de l'impôt sur le revenu	..	..	..	..	..	..	..	..	..	..
2300 A charge des travailleurs indép. ou sans emploi	..	..	..	..	..	..	..	..	..	..
2310 Sur la base du salaire	..	..	..	..	..	..	..	..	..	..
2320 Sur la base de l'impôt sur le revenu	..	..	..	..	..	..	..	..	..	..
2400 Non ventilables entre 2100, 2200 et 2300	..	..	..	..	..	..	..	..	..	..
2410 Sur la base du salaire	..	..	..	..	..	..	..	..	..	..
2420 Sur la base de l'impôt sur le revenu	..	..	..	..	..	..	..	..	..	..
3000 Sur salaires ou main d'oeuvre	**..**	**4 965**	**3 455**	**16 007**	**17 010**	**18 177**	**19 059**	**22 646**	**24 528**	**22 754**
4000 Impôts sur le patrimoine	**..**	**1 299**	**1 571**	**2 934**	**3 839**	**4 259**	**5 591**	**4 790**	**11 585**	**4 471**
4100 Impôts périodiques sur la propriété immobilière	..	0	0	0	0	0	0	0	0	0
4110 Ménages	..	..	..	..	..	..	..	..	..	..
4120 Autres agents	..	..	..	..	..	..	..	..	..	..
4200 Impôts périodiques sur l'actif net	..	0	0	0	0	0	0	0	0	0
4210 Personnes physiques	..	..	..	..	..	..	..	..	..	..
4220 Sociétés	..	..	..	..	..	..	..	..	..	..
4300 Impôts sur mut. par décès, succ. et donations	..	0	0	0	0	0	0	0	0	0
4310 Impôts sur mut. par décès et successions	..	..	..	..	..	..	..	..	..	..
4320 Impôts sur les donations	..	..	..	..	..	..	..	..	..	..
4400 Impôts sur transact. mobilières et immob.	..	1 299	1 571	2 934	3 839	4 259	5 591	4 790	11 585	4 471
4500 Impôts non-périodiques	..	0	0	0	0	0	0	0	0	0
4510 Sur l'actif net	..	..	..	..	..	..	..	..	..	..
4520 Autres non-périodiques	..	..	..	..	..	..	..	..	..	..
4600 Autres impôts périodiques sur patrimoine	..	0	0	0	0	0	0	0	0	0
5000 Impôts sur les biens et services	**..**	**44 783**	**131 186**	**261 069**	**309 288**	**344 243**	**435 272**	**483 322**	**461 337**	**401 281**
5100 Impôts sur production, vente, transfert, etc.	..	44 783	131 186	261 069	309 288	344 243	435 272	483 322	461 337	401 281
5110 Impôts généraux	..	39 641	78 187	156 770	180 474	198 880	257 900	296 773	280 123	247 767
5111 Taxes sur la valeur ajoutée	..	36 889	75 247	147 032	169 125	184 430	239 267	273 943	253 875	221 768
TVA Intérieure	..	38 962	54 294	92 054	99 769	106 271	146 920	177 038	163 875	140 255
TVA Douane	..	0	23 744	57 110	69 357	78 924	92 347	96 905	90 000	81 512
Remboursements TVA	..	-2 073	-2 791	-2 132	0	-764	0	0	0	0
5112 Impôts sur les ventes	..	0	0	0	0	0	0	0	0	0
5113 Autres impôts	..	2 753	2 940	9 738	11 349	14 449	18 633	22 830	26 248	25 999
5120 Impôts sur biens et services déterminés	..	5 033	52 858	103 721	128 081	145 082	176 955	186 545	181 214	153 514
5121 Accises	..	4 966	8 313	17 603	11 800	11 256	11 862	13 035	13 197	12 792
5122 Bénéfices des monopoles fiscaux	..	0	0	0	0	0	0	0	0	0
5123 Droits de douane et droits à l'importation	..	0	44 446	85 775	115 816	132 399	164 469	172 774	166 613	139 716
Recettes import/export	..	..	41 022	77 852	104 544	117 550	147 620	155 030	148 444	125 944
Recettes douanes hors budget	..	..	3 424	7 923	11 272	14 849	16 849	17 745	18 169	13 771
5124 Taxes à l'exportation	..	0	0	0	0	0	0	0	0	0
5125 Impôts sur biens d'équipement	..	0	0	0	0	0	0	0	0	0
5126 Impôts sur services déterminés	..	67	98	343	464	1 428	625	736	1 405	1 006
5127 Autres impôts sur commerce et transact. internat.	..	0	0	0	0	0	0	0	0	0
5128 Autres impôts	..	0	0	0	0	0	0	0	0	0
5130 Non ventilables entre 5110 et 5120	..	109	141	578	733	281	417	4	0	0
5200 Impôts sur utilisation des biens et exerc. activites	..	0	0	0	0	0	0	0	0	0
5210 Impôts périodiques	..	..	..	..	..	..	..	..	..	..
5211 A la charge des ménages: véhicules à moteur	..	..	..	..	..	..	..	..	..	..
5212 A la charge autres agents: véhicules à moteur	..	..	..	..	..	..	..	..	..	..
5213 Autres impôts périodiques	..	..	..	..	..	..	..	..	..	..

Table 5.5. **Congo** *(cont.)*

Details of tax revenue / Recettes fiscales détaillées

Million XAF

	1997	2000	2005	2010	2011	2012	2013	2014	2015	2016
5220 Impôts non-périodiques	..	..	..	..	..	..	..	..	..	..
5300 Non ventilables entre 5100 et 5200	..	0	0	0	0	0	0	0	0	0
6000 Autres impôts	**..**	**0**	**0**	**0**	**0**	**0**	**0**	**0**	**0**	**0**
6100 A la charge exclusive des entreprises	..	..	..	..	..	..	..	..	..	..
6200 A la charge d'autres agents	..	..	..	..	..	..	..	..	..	..

Note: Année civile se terminant le 31 décembre.

Les données sont sur la base des encaissements.

Les chiffres n'incluent pas les recettes fiscales collectées par les collectivités locales car elles ne sont pas disponibles.

Source: Ministère des Finances de la République du Congo.

StatLink https://doi.org/10.1787/888933820525

Table 5.6. **Congo, Dem. Rep./Congo, Rép. dém**

Details of tax revenue / Recettes fiscales détaillées

Million CDF

	1997	2000	2005	2010	2011	2012	2013	2014	2015	2016
Recettes fiscales totales	..	**7 551**	**293 945**	**1 665 702**	**2 101 842**	**2 898 542**	**3 045 373**	**3 162 493**	**3 438 900**	**3 224 662**
1000 Impôts sur revenu, bénéfices et gains en capital	..	**2 565**	**54 761**	**447 039**	**529 008**	**633 044**	**778 242**	**1 012 377**	**1 225 021**	**976 671**
1100 Des personnes physiques	..	996	24 243	208 715	275 090	398 726	480 564	516 536	515 851	509 354
1110 Sur le revenu et les bénéfices	..	996	24 243	208 715	275 090	398 726	480 564	516 536	515 851	509 354
Impôt sur les revenus (IR) des nationaux	..	899	15 444	162 931	228 883	332 907	394 400	421 427	417 442	409 977
IR/ Institutions Politiques	..	0	0	1 842	13 375	17 583	16 089	20 027	16 698	18 828
IR/ Fonctionnaire et Agents publics	..	0	0	0	0	0	4 900	9 298	12 825	12 789
IR/ Régies financières	..	0	0	0	0	0	7 237	9 727	8 186	5 094
IR/ Expatriés	..	81	7 513	43 779	31 371	45 402	55 787	55 507	59 921	62 241
IR/ Proféssions libérales	..	15	1 286	44	1 319	2 612	1 653	0	0	0
Taxe ad valorem sur les gains des parieurs (DGRAD)	..	0	0	119	142	222	498	548	779	424
1120 Sur les gains en capital	..	..	..	..	..	..	..	..	..	..
1200 Des sociétés	..	1 569	30 518	237 937	253 837	234 285	297 669	495 784	709 095	467 230
Impôts sur les revenus des capitaux mobiliers	..	30	2 065	23 356	27 053	37 918	45 672	49 931	53 212	53 445
1210 Sur les bénéfices	..	1 539	28 453	214 582	226 785	196 367	251 997	445 853	655 884	413 785
Impôt sur les bénéfices / sociétés non pétrolières	..	1 061	22 942	194 758	203 431	171 735	220 318	390 544	607 004	365 466
Impôt sur les bénéfices / non résidents	..	0	0	0	0	0	23 360	42 882	46 124	45 450
Impôt sur les bénéfices / entreprises individuelles	..	410	3 523	19 823	23 354	24 633	8 320	12 426	2 756	2 869
Impôts sur les revenus locatifs	..	69	1 988	0	0	0	0	0	0	0
1220 Sur les gains en capital	..	..	..	..	..	..	..	..	..	..
1300 Non ventilables entre 1100 et 1200	..	..	..	386	80	33	9	57	75	87
2000 Cotisations de sécurité sociale	..	..	..	..	..	**129 002**	**169 836**	**199 653**	**201 805**	**225 592**
2100 A la charge des salariés	..	..	..	..	..	36 106	47 534	55 885	56 493	75 746
2110 Sur la base du salaire	..	..	..	..	..	36 106	47 534	55 885	56 493	75 746
2120 Sur la base de l'impôt sur les revenus	..	..	..	..	..	0	0	0	0	0
2200 A la charge des employeurs	..	..	..	..	..	92 844	122 231	143 705	145 268	149 803
2210 Sur la base du salaire	..	..	..	..	..	92 844	122 231	143 705	145 268	149 803
2220 Sur la base de l'impôt sur le revenu	..	..	..	..	..	0	0	0	0	0
2300 A charge des travailleurs indép. ou sans emploi	..	..	..	..	..	0	0	0	0	0
2310 Sur la base du salaire	..	..	..	..	..	..	..	..	..	..
2320 Sur la base de l'impôt sur le revenu	..	..	..	..	..	..	..	..	..	..
2400 Non ventilables entre 2100, 2200 et 2300	..	..	..	..	..	52	71	63	44	43
2410 Sur la base du salaire	..	..	..	..	..	..	..	..	..	..
2420 Sur la base de l'impôt sur le revenu	..	..	..	..	..	..	..	..	..	..
3000 Sur salaires ou main d'oeuvre	..	**56**	**2 630**	**15 370**	**18 107**	**37 328**	**49 092**	**49 047**	**48 503**	**43 343**
Impôt sur les rémunérations des expatriés (IERE)	..	56	2 630	15 370	18 107	37 328	49 092	49 047	48 503	43 343
4000 Impôts sur le patrimoine	..	..	..	**9 644**	**5 363**	**9 431**	**4 918**	**13 731**	**12 983**	**14 854**
4100 Impôts périodiques sur la propriété immobilière	..	..	..	3 695	2 828	6 288	3 113	9 743	8 817	9 254
4110 Ménages	..	..	..	..	..	..	..	..	..	..
4120 Autres agents	..	..	..	..	..	..	..	..	..	..
4200 Impôts périodiques sur l'actif net	..	..	..	0	0	0	0	0	0	0
4210 Personnes physiques	..	..	..	..	..	..	..	..	..	..
4220 Sociétés	..	..	..	..	..	..	..	..	..	..
4300 Impôts sur mut. par décès, succ. et donations	..	..	..	0	0	0	0	0	0	0
4310 Impôts sur mut. par décès et successions	..	..	..	..	..	..	..	..	..	..
4320 Impôts sur les donations	..	..	..	..	..	..	..	..	..	..
4400 Impôts sur transact. mobilières et immob.	..	..	..	5 949	2 534	3 143	1 804	3 988	4 166	5 600
4500 Impôts non-périodiques	..	..	..	0	0	0	0	0	0	0
4510 Sur l'actif net	..	..	..	..	..	..	..	..	..	..
4520 Autres non-périodiques	..	..	..	..	..	..	..	..	..	..
4600 Autres impôts périodiques sur patrimoine	..	..	..	0	0	0	0	0	0	0
5000 Impôts sur les biens et services	..	**4 931**	**199 076**	**1 094 565**	**1 398 438**	**1 925 721**	**1 881 940**	**1 741 343**	**1 871 774**	**1 926 860**
5100 Impôts sur production, vente, transfert, etc.	..	4 833	198 497	1 068 789	1 387 159	1 905 589	1 873 921	1 726 836	1 857 276	1 909 324
5110 Impôts généraux	..	1 390	109 602	590 594	792 547	1 188 022	999 363	804 138	891 546	1 056 005
5111 Taxes sur la valeur ajoutée	..	0	0	0	0	1 126 091	971 594	802 236	891 404	1 055 955
TVA intérieure (brute)	..	..	..	..	..	475 159	583 798	585 321	639 995	619 212
TVA à l'importation (brute)	..	..	..	..	..	893 457	864 543	873 055	879 549	561 978
Remboursements TVA	..	..	..	..	..	-242 525	-476 747	-656 140	-628 140	-125 234
5112 Impôts sur les ventes	..	..	..	110	0	0	0	0	0	0
5113 Autres impôts	..	1 390	109 602	590 484	792 547	61 930	27 770	1 903	143	50
Impôt sur le chiffre d'affaires (ICA)/ ventes locales	..	194	20 440	110 004	119 016	15 250	7 912	405	143	47
ICA/ Prestations de services	..	409	28 534	181 338	261 441	45 428	16 411	1 310	0	0
ICA/ Travaux immobiliers	..	14	3 971	5 969	7 297	1 173	3 426	186	0	0
ICA/ Exportation produits miniers	..	0	2	0	0	0	0	0	0	0
ICA/ Exportation hors produits miniers	..	6	0	0	0	0	0	0	0	0
ICA/ Importation	..	768	56 654	291 557	403 323	0	0	0	0	0
Autres impôts généraux sur les biens et services (DGRAD)	..	0	0	1 616	1 470	79	20	2	0	2

Table 5.6. **Congo, Dem. Rep./Congo, Rép. dém** *(cont.)*

Details of tax revenue / Recettes fiscales détaillées

Million CDF

	1997	2000	2005	2010	2011	2012	2013	2014	2015	2016
5120 Impôts sur biens et services déterminés	..	3 442	88 896	478 194	594 613	717 567	874 558	922 697	965 729	853 319
5121 Accises	..	1 417	26 357	195 837	210 455	242 066	331 946	331 403	396 426	424 083
Redevances sur produits spécifiques (DGRAD)	..	0	0	12 259	788	1 499	425	807	3 256	1 303
Droits d'accises perçus en régime intérieur	..	1 380	19 891	153 005	180 379	200 454	259 580	243 462	239 329	233 433
Accises (intérieur) - Boissons	..	..	..	62 785	74 701	81 214	139 922	145 392	148 179	133 236
Accises (intérieur) - Tabacs et allumettes	..	..	..	40 034	46 276	53 190	39 465	14 316	2 643	9 149
Accises (intérieur) - Télécommunication	..	..	..	49 338	58 750	63 070	74 521	78 063	86 315	88 198
Accises (intérieur) - Autres produits	..	..	..	848	652	2 981	5 672	5 691	2 193	2 850
Droits d'accises perçus à l'importation	..	37	6 465	30 573	29 288	40 113	71 940	87 134	153 841	189 347
Accises (importation) - Boissons	..	..	..	2 431	2 914	3 767	12 475	10 474	13 556	13 847
Accises (importation) - Tabacs et allumettes	..	..	..	4 739	4 517	13 046	18 368	35 609	59 422	46 449
Accises (importation) - Produits pétroliers	..	..	..	9 257	4 926	6 221	9 504	12 671	53 350	102 829
Accises (importation) - Véhicules	..	..	..	9 901	12 104	12 124	12 757	11 961	15 878	12 022
Accises (importation) - Autres produits	..	..	..	4 246	4 827	4 955	18 836	16 420	11 635	14 200
5122 Bénéfices des monopoles fiscaux	..	0	0	0	0	0	0	0	0	0
5123 Droits de douane et droits à l'importation	..	1 942	56 349	270 089	370 539	463 492	533 071	580 820	560 340	420 432
5124 Taxes à l'exportation	..	83	6 190	7 725	10 799	8 182	7 311	7 171	5 446	4 529
Droits de sortie sur les minerais	..	82	5 623	3 850	4 940	3 245	2 551	2 791	3 238	2 774
Droits de sortie sur les produits agricoles	..	1	567	3 046	5 845	4 937	4 760	4 379	2 208	1 755
Droits de sortie sur les autres produits	..	0	0	829	15	0	0	0	0	0
5125 Impôts sur biens d'équipement	..	0	0	0	0	0	0	0	0	0
5126 Impôts sur services déterminés	..	0	0	4 543	2 820	3 827	2 231	3 304	3 518	4 275
5127 Autres impôts sur commerce et transact. internat.	..	0	0	0	0	0	0	0	0	0
5128 Autres impôts	..	0	0	0	0	0	0	0	0	0
5130 Non ventilables entre 5110 et 5120	..	0	0	0	0	0	0	0	0	0
5200 Impôts sur utilisation des biens et exerc. activites	..	98	579	25 776	11 279	20 132	8 019	14 508	14 499	17 536
5210 Impôts périodiques	..	0	0	1 564	1 979	1 637	450	947	881	2 461
5211 A la charge des ménages: véhicules à moteur	..	..	..	0	0	0	0	0	0	0
5212 A la charge autres agents: véhicules à moteur	..	..	..	3	9	63	2	37	7	17
5213 Autres impôts périodiques	..	..	..	1 561	1 970	1 574	448	910	874	2 443
5220 Impôts non-périodiques	..	98	579	24 212	9 300	18 496	7 570	13 561	13 617	15 076
Immatriculation des véhicules routiers (plaques)	..	98	579	2 681	3 623	2 513	2 353	2 507	1 366	1 373
Autorisations d'exportation et d'importation	..	0	0	2 909	901	5 172	688	1 791	3 567	2 642
Taxe d'implementation (DGRAD)	..	0	0	1 203	437	2 428	525	3 079	2 849	3 184
Autres autorisations (DGRAD)	..	0	0	17 419	4 340	8 382	4 004	6 184	5 835	7 877
5300 Non ventilables entre 5100 et 5200	..	0	0	0	0	0	0	0	0	0
6000 Autres impôts	**..**	**0**	**37 477**	**99 085**	**150 926**	**164 016**	**161 344**	**146 341**	**78 815**	**37 342**
Recettes des produits pétroliers	..	..	37 477	98 431	150 622	163 425	161 220	144 910	78 417	35 540
Droits proportionnels sur les S.A.R.L. (DGRAD)	..	..	0	654	304	591	123	1 431	398	1 803
6100 A la charge exclusive des entreprises	..	..	..	..	..	..	..	..	..	..
6200 A la charge d'autres agents	..	..	..	..	..	..	..	..	..	..

Note: Année civile se terminant le 31 décembre.

Les données sont sur la base des encaissements.

Les chiffres n'incluent pas les recettes fiscales collectées par les collectivités locales car elles ne sont pas disponibles.

Les données entre 2000 à 2003 doivent être interprétées avec prudence car elles augmentent de façon significative. L'aboutissement du processus de réunification sur la période 2001-03 conjugué aux réformes mises en œuvre à la suite de la reprise des relations avec les institutions de Bretton Woods en 2001 ont permis la maîtrise de l'hyperinflation et expliquent l'accroissement significatif des recettes fiscales à partir de 2001

Rubrique 2000 : Les données de cotisations de sécurité sociale (à partir de 2012) sont disponibles pour la première fois pour cette édition.

Les recettes provenant de la vente des imprimés sont incluses dans les recettes non fiscales (Ventes de biens et services) comme le préconise la classification OCDE (voir le guide d'interprétation en Annexe A). Elles sont considérées comme des recettes fiscales dans la catégorie « Autres recettes » en République démocratique du Congo.

Rubriques 1110, 5113, 5121, 5220, 6000 : Pour la période 2010-16, ces rubriques contiennent des recettes provenant de la *Direction Générale des Recettes Administratives, Judiciaires, Domaniales et de Participation* (DGRAD) et sont annotées comme telles. Elles sont incluses dans les recettes fiscales comme le préconise la classification OCDE (voir le guide d'interprétation en Annexe A) mais considérées comme des recettes non fiscales en République démocratique du Congo.

Rubriques 1300, 4100, 4400, 5112, 5126, 5128, 5212, 5213: Pour la période 2010-16, ces rubriques contiennent des recettes provenant de la DGRAD. Elles sont incluses dans les recettes fiscales comme le préconise la classification OCDE (voir le guide d'interprétation en Annexe A) mais considérées comme des recettes non fiscales en République démocratique du Congo. Le total des recettes provenant de la DGRAD considérées comme recettes fiscales représentent en moyenne 1 % du total des recettes fiscales.

Source: Ministère des Finances de la République démocratique du Congo.

StatLink https://doi.org/10.1787/888933820544

Table 5.7. **Côte d'Ivoire**

Details of tax revenue / Recettes fiscales détaillées

Million XOF

	1997	2000	2005	2010	2011	2012	2013	2014	2015	2016
Recettes fiscales totales	**1 166 891**	**1 169 373**	**1 408 231**	**2 038 010**	**1 858 500**	**2 423 117**	**2 721 780**	**2 946 103**	**3 437 730**	**3 761 418**
1000 Impôts sur revenu, bénéfices et gains en capital	**218 661**	**192 048**	**193 850**	**263 342**	**327 466**	**439 778**	**436 606**	**401 740**	**408 880**	**419 405**
1100 Des personnes physiques	5 455	5 108	6 184	6 970	5 735	7 339	9 202	9 430	10 054	18 110
1110 Sur le revenu et les bénéfices	5 433	5 093	6 164	6 937	5 709	7 300	9 166	9 388	10 011	18 059
Impôt général sur le revenu	0	0	323	1 420	115	761	995	635	817	8 011
Impôt BIC hors pétrole-gaz (personnes physiques)	5 392	5 045	5 770	5 431	5 504	6 424	8 017	8 610	9 008	9 859
IR des valeurs mobilières (pers. physiques)	41	48	71	86	90	115	154	143	186	189
1120 Sur les gains en capital	22	16	20	33	27	39	36	42	42	51
IR des capitaux (pers. physiques)	22	16	20	33	27	39	36	42	42	51
1200 Des sociétés	157 299	148 900	176 272	240 768	306 584	415 300	407 968	371 821	375 893	384 251
1210 Sur les bénéfices	149 971	143 602	169 683	229 732	297 735	402 448	395 918	357 867	361 782	367 300
Impôt BIC pétrole-gaz	..	..	..	63 649	128 537	201 519	141 732	92 389	71 985	54 962
Impôt BIC hors pétrole-gaz (personnes morales)	136 507	127 710	146 074	137 500	139 347	162 629	202 948	217 980	228 043	249 588
IR des valeurs mobilieres (pers. morales)	13 464	15 892	23 609	28 583	29 851	38 300	51 237	47 499	61 753	62 750
1220 Sur les gains en capital	7 328	5 297	6 589	11 036	8 849	12 852	12 050	13 954	14 111	16 951
Impôt sur le revenu des capitaux (personnes morales)	7 328	5 297	6 589	11 036	8 849	12 852	12 050	13 954	14 111	16 951
1300 Non ventilables entre 1100 et 1200	55 907	38 040	11 394	15 604	15 146	17 139	19 436	20 489	22 934	17 044
L'acompte d'impôt sur le revenu du secteur informel (ex ASDI)	52 369	33 983	5 882	7 624	6 850	9 128	12 286	12 509	14 637	663
Impôt synthétique	3 538	4 057	5 512	7 980	8 296	8 011	7 150	7 980	8 296	16 380
2000 Cotisations de sécurité sociale	**83 054**	**102 700**	**116 818**	**162 754**	**131 021**	**235 903**	**307 259**	**340 667**	**383 540**	**443 310**
2100 A la charge des salariés	..	..	..	64 364	51 191	93 605	121 401	135 406	151 728	177 045
CNPS	..	..	..	39 044	29 030	57 798	73 287	84 360	92 206	113 016
CGRAE	..	..	..	25 320	22 161	35 806	48 114	51 046	59 522	64 029
2110 Sur la base du salaire	..	..	..	..	..	..	..	..	..	..
2120 Sur la base de l'impôt sur les revenus	..	..	..	..	..	..	..	..	..	..
2200 A la charge des employeurs	..	..	..	98 390	79 830	142 298	185 858	205 261	231 812	266 265
CNPS	..	..	..	47 721	35 482	70 643	89 572	103 107	112 697	138 130
CGRAE	..	..	..	50 669	44 348	71 656	96 286	102 154	119 115	128 135
2210 Sur la base du salaire	..	..	..	..	..	..	..	..	..	..
2220 Sur la base de l'impôt sur le revenu	..	..	..	..	..	..	..	..	..	..
2300 A charge des travailleurs indép. ou sans emploi	..	..	..	0	0	0	0	0	0	0
2310 Sur la base du salaire	..	..	..	..	..	..	..	..	..	..
2320 Sur la base de l'impôt sur le revenu	..	..	..	..	..	..	..	..	..	..
2400 Non ventilables entre 2100, 2200 et 2300	83 054	102 700	116 818	0	0	0	0	0	0	0
2410 Sur la base du salaire	..	..	..	..	..	..	..	..	..	..
2420 Sur la base de l'impôt sur le revenu	..	..	..	..	..	..	..	..	..	..
3000 Sur salaires ou main d'oeuvre	**104 982**	**138 023**	**148 912**	**207 243**	**198 848**	**269 501**	**313 695**	**322 884**	**372 524**	**424 516**
Fonds de formation professionnelle	6 089	6 990	7 473	9 776	8 012	10 754	12 783	12 483	11 805	13 336
Impôt sur traitements et salaires (ITS), solde	98 893	131 033	141 439	197 467	190 836	258 748	300 912	310 400	360 719	411 180
4000 Impôts sur le patrimoine	**30 581**	**32 732**	**43 879**	**49 706**	**38 442**	**61 144**	**82 326**	**79 839**	**89 040**	**106 691**
4100 Impôts périodiques sur la propriété immobilière	21 824	24 664	34 032	38 009	30 278	49 013	61 322	64 645	72 299	79 627
4110 Ménages	..	..	..	..	..	..	..	..	..	..
4120 Autres agents	..	..	..	..	..	..	..	..	..	..
4200 Impôts périodiques sur l'actif net	0	0	0	0	0	0	0	0	0	0
4210 Personnes physiques	..	..	..	..	..	..	..	..	..	..
4220 Sociétés	..	..	..	..	..	..	..	..	..	..
4300 Impôts sur mut. par décès, succ. et donations	0	0	0	0	0	0	0	0	0	0
4310 Impôts sur mut. par décès et successions	..	..	..	..	..	..	..	..	..	..
4320 Impôts sur les donations	..	..	..	..	..	..	..	..	..	..
4400 Impôts sur transact. mobilières et immob.	8 757	8 068	9 847	11 697	8 164	12 131	21 004	15 194	16 741	27 064
4500 Impôts non-périodiques	0	0	0	0	0	0	0	0	0	0
4510 Sur l'actif net	..	..	..	..	..	..	..	..	..	..
4520 Autres non-périodiques	..	..	..	..	..	..	..	..	..	..
4600 Autres impôts périodiques sur patrimoine	0	0	0	0	0	0	0	0	0	0
5000 Impôts sur les biens et services	**727 054**	**699 518**	**899 719**	**1 344 200**	**1 156 614**	**1 405 960**	**1 568 130**	**1 783 891**	**2 162 691**	**2 344 944**
5100 Impôts sur production, vente, transfert, etc.	712 481	674 206	870 744	1 294 834	1 136 339	1 353 779	1 502 963	1 710 241	2 081 303	2 254 458
5110 Impôts généraux	251 446	255 297	288 885	490 520	378 695	524 503	579 050	619 100	692 416	717 606
5111 Taxes sur la valeur ajoutée	251 446	255 297	267 106	473 711	369 742	514 898	570 444	610 020	680 080	703 825
Taxes sur la valeur ajoutée (DGI)	82 346	106 797	104 204	178 761	145 883	195 936	228 450	255 464	286 170	316 361
Taxes sur la valeur ajoutée brute (DGI)	..	..	112 304	194 241	160 418	214 791	247 890	280 819	327 995	354 521
Remboursements credits de TVA (DGI)	..	..	-8 100	-15 480	-14 535	-18 855	-19 440	-25 355	-41 825	-38 159
Taxes sur la valeur ajoutée (DGD)	169 100	148 500	162 902	294 950	223 859	318 962	341 994	354 556	393 909	387 463
Taxes sur la valeur ajoutée brute (DGD)	..	..	172 802	313 870	241 624	342 007	365 754	385 546	445 028	446 235
Remboursements credits de TVA (DGD)	..	..	-9 900	-18 920	-17 765	-23 045	-23 760	-30 989	-51 119	-58 772
5112 Impôts sur les ventes	0	0	0	0	0	0	0	0	0	0

Table 5.7. **Côte d'Ivoire** *(cont.)*

Details of tax revenue / Recettes fiscales détaillées

Million XOF

	1997	2000	2005	2010	2011	2012	2013	2014	2015	2016
5113 Autres impôts	0	0	21 779	16 809	8 953	9 605	8 606	9 080	12 336	13 782
Taxe ad-valorem (taxe domaniale)	..	..	0	0	0	8 917	7 972	8 760	12 185	13 679
Contribution à la reconstitution nationale	..	..	21 779	1 567	296	436	123	63	71	68
Taxe de solidarité pour la sortie de crise	..	..	0	15 243	8 656	251	511	257	80	35
5120 Impôts sur biens et services déterminés	461 035	418 909	581 859	804 314	757 644	829 277	923 913	1 091 140	1 388 888	1 536 852
5121 Accises	75 919	74 908	59 977	128 698	73 865	97 017	122 689	130 450	243 162	304 695
Taxe SIDA	0	0	0	740	767	845	832	908	821	621
Taxe sur le caoutchouc	0	0	0	0	0	16 828	17 780	3 124	78	168
Taxe sur le tabac pour le dévelopment du sport	0	0	0	1 708	1 568	1 954	1 946	2 158	2 029	1 529
Taxe sur les sacs et sachets en matière plastique	-11	-8	-3	0	0	4	179	172	113	37
Taxe sur les boissons	1 779	3 642	2 986	5 050	4 885	6 100	7 609	14 563	18 213	19 084
Taxes sur le carburant	242	290	122	81	61	80	81	95	105	123
Taxes sur le tabac	12 898	15 518	10 933	12 040	12 096	13 307	13 191	19 817	14 771	10 731
Diverses taxes spécifiques à la DGD	61 000	50 300	38 391	96 560	43 842	44 380	64 166	72 567	183 719	242 824
Diverses accises spécifiques à la DGD	0	5 158	7 545	12 520	10 646	13 519	16 904	17 046	23 314	29 577
5122 Bénéfices des monopoles fiscaux	0	0	0	0	0	0	0	0	0	0
5123 Droits de douane et droits à l'importation	178 700	126 512	167 701	288 039	256 698	344 173	383 583	459 675	510 175	528 936
5124 Taxes à l'exportation	173 200	185 114	320 201	331 261	374 771	304 216	326 539	363 222	473 333	520 798
Droits d'enregistrement du café et cacao	..	21 114	58 039	103 669	95 775	74 308	27 389	38 033	86 244	128 522
Taxe sur le cacao et café (DGD)	165 900	156 700	253 148	221 180	273 686	222 760	291 819	316 371	377 418	383 637
Taxe sur le bois et autres produits (DGD)	7 300	7 300	9 014	6 412	5 310	7 149	7 331	8 819	9 671	8 639
5125 Impôts sur biens d'équipement	0	0	0	0	0	0	0	0	0	0
5126 Impôts sur services déterminés	33 217	32 375	33 980	56 315	52 310	83 871	91 102	137 792	162 218	182 423
Contribution de solidarité sur les billets d'avion	0	0	0	216	249	279	709	1 273	3 088	488
Taxe sur le transport aérien	0	0	0	799	608	1 332	1 680	2 054	2 569	2 434
Taxe pour la promotion de la culture	0	0	0	1 598	1 172	1 610	1 874	2 279	1 884	1 855
Taxe développement des NTICs en zone rurale	0	0	0	11 486	10 088	14 150	14 938	16 528	16 977	17 318
Taxe sur les télécommunications	0	0	0	0	0	17 925	22 176	43 080	50 618	62 459
Taxes sur les transports urbains	0	0	0	1 019	412	613	394	174	3	7
Prélèvement aux jeux de casino	449	168	339	378	13	230	245	273	163	7
Taxe d'abattage	2 522	2 434	1 810	1 125	716	1 349	1 335	1 280	1 299	1 354
Taxe sur la publicité	19	137	93	300	328	408	508	411	437	258
Taxe pour le développement touristique	0	0	0	0	0	1 085	972	1 001	1 298	1 420
Communications téléphoniques	0	0	0	0	0	0	0	16 667	20 425	23 395
Taxe sur les assurances	8 238	6 942	8 666	7 739	7 500	11 512	11 466	12 214	14 435	15 076
Taxe sur les encours bancaires	1 966	2 002	2 030	3 627	3 739	1 106	2	3	0	581
Taxe sur les opérations bancaires	20 023	20 692	21 042	28 028	27 487	32 273	34 805	40 554	49 023	55 770
5127 Autres impôts sur commerce et transact. internat.	0	0	0	0	0	0	0	0	0	0
5128 Autres impôts	0	0	0	0	0	0	0	0	0	0
5130 Non ventilables entre 5110 et 5120	0	0	0	0	0	0	0	0	0	0
5200 Impôts sur utilisation des biens et exerc. activites	14 573	25 312	28 975	49 366	20 274	52 180	65 167	73 651	81 388	90 486
5210 Impôts périodiques	14 573	25 312	28 975	49 366	20 274	52 180	65 167	73 651	81 388	90 486
5211 A la charge des ménages: véhicules à moteur	2 354	4 176	5 942	9 171	283	10 197	12 183	13 403	14 926	16 103
5212 A la charge autres agents: véhicules à moteur	0	0	0	0	0	0	0	0	0	0
5213 Autres impôts périodiques	12 218	21 136	23 033	40 195	19 991	41 983	52 984	60 248	66 462	74 383
5220 Impôts non-périodiques	0	0	0	0	0	0	0	0	0	0
5300 Non ventilables entre 5100 et 5200	0	0	0	0	0	0	0	0	0	0
6000 Autres impôts	**2 560**	**4 352**	**5 053**	**10 765**	**6 109**	**10 831**	**13 764**	**17 082**	**21 055**	**22 551**
6100 A la charge exclusive des entreprises	0	0	0	3 732	4 005	5 822	5 428	5 622	6 979	7 719
Fonds de soutien à l'habitat	..	..	..	45	0	0	0	0	0	0
Fonds interprofessionnel	..	..	..	3 687	4 005	5 822	5 428	5 622	6 979	7 719
6200 A la charge d'autres agents	2 560	4 352	5 053	7 033	2 104	5 008	8 336	11 460	14 076	14 833

Table 5.7. **Côte d'Ivoire** *(cont.)*

Details of tax revenue / Recettes fiscales détaillées

Note: Année civile se terminant le 31 décembre.

Les données sont sur la base des encaissements.

les chiffres n'incluent pas les recettes fiscales collectées par les collectivités locales.

Rubrique 2000 : Des données plus détaillées sont disponibles pour la première fois pour cette édition.

La rubrique 5113 comprend la taxe ad-valorem, une taxe domaniale. Les recettes autres que celles de la taxe ad-valorem sont considérées comme des recettes non fiscales selon la classification OCDE (voir le guide d'interprétation en Annexe A). La classification nationale de la Côte d'Ivoire les comptabilise comme des recettes fiscales.

La rubrique 5113 comprend la Contribution à la reconstruction nationale (CRN) instituée en 2004 pour cinq ans et arrivée à expiration en 2009. Elle a été remplacée par la Contribution pour la sortie de crise. Celle-ci était basée sur les charges d'exploitation des entreprises réalisant un chiffre d'affaire annuel supérieur ou égal à 1 milliard de francs, au titre de l'exercice clos au 31 décembre 2009.

La rubrique 6100 comprend le Fonds de soutien à l'habitat (FSH) alimenté par des recettes fiscales affectées (contribution patronale sur la masse salariale, taxes sur services déterminés et taxe sur le carburant). Il n'est pas possible de distinguer ces différents éléments d'où sa classification dans la rubrique 6100. Cette taxe a été supprimée en 2010.

Les recettes de la taxe audiovisuelle et la redevance radiodiffusion télévision ivoirienne (RTI) sont considérées comme des recettes non fiscales selon la classification OCDE (voir le guide d'interprétation en Annexe A) et ont été classifiées dans la rubrique « vente de biens et services ». La classification nationale de la Côte d'Ivoire les comptabilise comme des recettes fiscales.

Source: Ministère de l'Économie et des Finances.

StatLink https://doi.org/10.1787/888933820563

Table 5.8. **Egypt / Égypte**

Details of tax revenue / Recettes fiscales détaillées

Million EGP

	1997	2000	2005	2010	2011	2012	2013	2014	2015	2016
Total tax revenue	..	..	**88 038**	**192 630**	**215 197**	**236 303**	**287 172**	**303 752**	**358 069**	**392 820**
1000 Taxes on income, profits and capital gains	..	..	**35 054**	**85 767**	**99 595**	**105 000**	**138 327**	**146 954**	**157 032**	**179 538**
1100 Of individuals	..	..	8 839	16 368	19 047	21 694	26 228	31 411	38 213	42 352
1110 On income and profits	..	..	8 834	16 285	18 869	21 590	26 141	31 193	37 934	42 009
Tax on domestic salaries	..	..	3 991	9 623	11 247	13 756	16 912	19 336	23 803	28 098
Taxes on industrial and commercial profits	..	..	3 523	4 570	5 163	5 263	6 100	8 431	10 589	9 247
Stamp duty on salaries	..	..	1 180	1 778	2 146	2 254	2 796	2 916	2 998	3 933
Tax on professionals income	..	..	139	314	314	317	333	509	544	731
1120 On capital gains	..	..	5	84	177	104	87	218	279	343
1200 Corporate	..	..	22 257	66 022	77 248	79 453	104 700	104 768	108 285	125 457
1210 On profits	..	..	22 257	66 022	77 248	79 453	104 700	104 768	108 285	125 457
EGPC and foreign partner	..	..	4 030	32 181	34 308	34 075	45 816	46 060	36 000	37 313
Suez Canal Authority	..	..	7 343	9 443	10 900	11 800	12 150	14 312	13 400	14 903
Central Bank of Egypt	..	..	212	0	0	0	8 290	4 042	3 691	13 245
Other companies	..	..	10 672	18 591	25 330	23 674	25 275	25 099	38 512	36 926
Interest income from T-Bills and Bonds	..	..	0	5 808	6 711	9 903	13 168	15 256	16 682	23 069
1220 On capital gains	..	..	0	0	0	0	0	0	0	0
1300 Unallocable between 1100 and 1200	..	..	3 959	3 377	3 300	3 854	7 400	10 775	10 534	11 729
Tax on movable capital revenues from C.B.E	..	..	3 959	3 243	3 093	3 676	7 204	10 604	10 228	10 965
Delayed tax income	..	..	0	134	207	177	196	171	306	765
2000 Social security contributions	..	..	**16 141**	**28 032**	**28 942**	**34 898**	**42 990**	**51 139**	**60 693**	**49 331**
2100 Employees	..	..	..	..	..	..	..	..	..	..
2110 On a payroll basis	..	..	..	..	..	..	..	..	..	..
2120 On an income tax basis	..	..	..	..	..	..	..	..	..	..
2200 Employers	..	..	..	..	..	..	..	..	..	..
2210 On a payroll basis	..	..	..	..	..	..	..	..	..	..
2220 On an income tax basis	..	..	..	..	..	..	..	..	..	..
2300 Self-employed or non-employed	..	..	..	..	..	..	..	..	..	..
2310 On a payroll basis	..	..	..	..	..	..	..	..	..	..
2320 On an income tax basis	..	..	..	..	..	..	..	..	..	..
2400 Unallocable between 2100, 2200 and 2300	..	..	16 141	28 032	28 942	34 898	42 990	51 139	60 693	49 331
2410 On a payroll basis	..	..	..	..	..	..	..	..	..	..
2420 On an income tax basis	..	..	..	..	..	..	..	..	..	..
3000 Taxes on payroll and workforce	..	..	**0**	**0**	**0**	**0**	**0**	**0**	**0**	**0**
4000 Taxes on property	..	..	**1 323**	**2 533**	**2 596**	**2 928**	**2 791**	**3 504**	**4 113**	**5 578**
4100 Recurrent taxes on immovable property	..	..	327	518	317	520	531	428	637	1 172
4110 Households	..	..	..	..	..	..	..	..	..	..
4120 Others	..	..	..	..	..	..	..	..	..	..
4200 Recurrent taxes on net wealth	..	..	0	0	0	0	0	0	0	0
4210 Individual	..	..	..	..	..	..	..	..	..	..
4220 Corporate	..	..	..	..	..	..	..	..	..	..
4300 Estate, inheritance and gift taxes	..	..	0	0	0	0	0	0	0	0
4310 Estate and inheritance taxes	..	..	..	..	..	..	..	..	..	..
4320 Gift taxes	..	..	..	..	..	..	..	..	..	..
4400 Taxes on financial and capital transactions	..	..	996	2 014	2 279	2 407	2 260	3 076	3 476	4 407
Property transferring fees	..	..	312	607	612	672	737	799	948	1 002
Stamps taxes	..	..	684	1 407	1 667	1 735	1 523	2 278	2 528	3 405
4500 Non-recurrent taxes	..	..	0	0	0	0	0	0	0	0
4510 On net wealth	..	..	..	..	..	..	..	..	..	..
4520 Other non-recurrent taxes	..	..	..	..	..	..	..	..	..	..
4600 Other recurrent taxes on property	..	..	0	0	0	0	0	0	0	0
5000 Taxes on goods and services	..	..	**35 520**	**76 298**	**84 065**	**93 477**	**103 064**	**102 155**	**136 232**	**158 373**
5100 Taxes on production, sale, transfer, etc	..	..	35 096	74 414	82 236	91 465	101 027	99 858	133 365	155 605
5110 General taxes	..	..	18 397	39 519	40 856	45 952	48 854	51 997	64 996	71 015
5111 Value added taxes	..	..	18 397	39 519	40 856	45 952	48 854	51 997	64 996	71 015
Local commodities	..	..	5 257	11 735	12 923	15 566	14 038	14 577	18 415	21 102
Imported goods	..	..	8 548	18 977	18 950	21 607	25 458	28 398	35 010	36 352
Hotel and restaurant services for tourists	..	..	1 126	2 172	2 082	1 740	1 997	1 704	2 334	2 157
Operating services for others	..	..	1 555	2 936	3 020	3 110	3 409	3 442	4 844	6 845
International and local communication services	..	..	1 911	3 700	3 882	3 928	3 952	3 877	4 393	4 559
Gross value added taxes	..	..	19 215	40 142	41 567	46 368	49 368	52 537	65 708	71 785
VAT refunds	..	..	-819	-623	-711	-416	-515	-540	-712	-770
5112 Sales tax	..	..	0	0	0	0	0	0	0	0
5113 Other	..	..	0	0	0	0	0	0	0	0
5120 Taxes on specific goods and services	..	..	16 700	34 896	41 380	45 513	52 173	47 861	68 369	84 590

Table 5.8. **Egypt / Égypte** *(cont.)*

Details of tax revenue / Recettes fiscales détaillées

Million EGP

	1997	2000	2005	2010	2011	2012	2013	2014	2015	2016
5121 Excises	..	..	6 539	17 170	24 588	27 664	31 864	25 822	41 207	49 468
Tobacco and cigarettes	..	..	3 987	6 997	14 105	15 959	17 251	19 588	26 463	33 584
Petroleum products	..	..	818	7 563	8 093	9 120	12 328	3 934	12 004	13 181
Stamp taxes on specific goods	..	..	536	1 603	1 411	1 608	1 334	1 258	1 198	948
Other excises	..	..	1 197	1 006	979	977	951	1 042	1 543	1 755
5122 Profits of fiscal monopolies	..	..	80	0	0	0	0	0	0	0
5123 Customs and import duties	..	..	7 664	13 733	13 455	14 395	16 054	17 352	21 460	27 534
5124 Taxes on exports	..	..	1	819	289	302	597	183	180	216
5125 Taxes on investment goods	..	..	0	0	0	0	0	0	0	0
5126 Taxes on specific services	..	..	1 520	1 804	1 874	2 012	2 208	2 865	2 462	2 456
Stamp taxes on specific services	..	..	515	681	813	981	940	1 520	936	439
Other taxes on specific services	..	..	1 005	1 123	1 061	1 031	1 267	1 345	1 526	2 017
5127 Other taxes on internat. trade and transactions	..	..	0	0	0	0	0	0	0	0
5128 Other taxes	..	..	897	1 371	1 174	1 140	1 450	1 639	3 059	4 916
5130 Unallocable between 5110 and 5120	..	..	0	0	0	0	0	0	0	0
5200 Taxes on use of goods and perform activities	..	..	424	1 884	1 829	2 012	2 038	2 297	2 867	2 768
5210 Recurrent taxes	..	..	424	1 884	1 829	2 012	2 038	2 297	2 867	2 768
5211 Paid by households: motor vehicles	..	..	394	1 837	1 813	1 993	2 017	2 279	2 841	2 747
5212 Paid by others: motor vehicles	..	..	0	0	0	0	0	0	0	0
5213 Paid in respect of other goods	..	..	30	47	16	19	21	18	26	21
5220 Non-recurrent taxes	..	..	0	0	0	0	0	0	0	0
5300 Unallocable between 5100 and 5200	..	..	0	0	0	0	0	0	0	0
6000 Other taxes	**..**	**..**	**0**	**0**	**0**	**0**	**0**	**0**	**0**	**0**
6100 Paid solely by business	..	..	..	..	..	..	..	..	..	..
6200 Other	..	..	..	..	..	..	..	..	..	..

Note: Fiscal year ends on 30 June. For example, the data for 2016 represent July 2015 to June 2016.

The data are on a cash basis.

Heading 2000: Egypt does not include social security contributions in its tax revenue data as the Egyptian authorities do not consider them as taxes.

Royalties on the Suez Canal as well as other royalties, development fees and administrative fees are reported as taxes in Egypt. These revenues are considered as non-tax revenues according to the OECD classification, described in the Interpretative Guide in Annex A.

Source: Ministry of Finance.

StatLink https://doi.org/10.1787/888933820582

Table 5.9. **Eswatini**

Details of tax revenue / Recettes fiscales détaillées

Million SZL

	1997	2000	2005	2010	2011	2012	2013	2014	2015	2016
Total tax revenue	**973**	**1 327**	**2 406**	**4 588**	**5 049**	**5 276**	**6 196**	**7 091**	**7 690**	**8 890**
1000 Taxes on income, profits and capital gains	**529**	**677**	**1 289**	**2 373**	**2 641**	**2 289**	**3 062**	**3 676**	**3 830**	**4 560**
1100 Of individuals	256	428	804	1 449	1 605	1 364	1 772	2 062	2 254	2 735
1110 On income and profits	256	428	804	1 449	1 605	1 364	1 772	2 062	2 254	2 735
Pay-as-you-earn tax (PAYE)	249	421	733	1 321	1 510	1 327	1 752	2 049	2 176	2 662
Provisional income tax	2	2	16	75	69	16	0	0	0	0
Taxes on interest, dividends and trust income	0	0	8	35	8	13	1	0	1	1
Personal income tax on non-residents	0	0	0	3	3	5	1	1	1	2
Tax on benefits	0	0	5	11	12	0	17	10	15	15
Withholding tax on resident suppliers	0	0	40	0	0	0	0	0	0	0
Personal income tax on the self employed	5	4	0	1	0	2	0	0	59	52
Lottery levy	0	1	1	2	2	2	2	2	2	3
1120 On capital gains	..	..	..	..	..	..	..	..	..	..
1200 Corporate	251	236	461	905	968	873	1 216	1 570	1 507	1 730
1210 On profits	251	236	461	905	968	873	1 216	1 570	1 507	1 730
Corporate income tax on resident companies	250	233	394	739	815	737	1 060	1 468	1 358	1 527
Taxes on royalties	0	0	54	144	132	124	45	27	42	58
Corporate income tax on non-resident companies	1	3	13	22	22	12	111	75	107	145
1220 On capital gains	..	..	..	..	..	..	..	..	..	..
1300 Unallocable between 1100 and 1200	22	14	23	20	68	52	74	44	68	95
Income taxes on non-residents	20	11	20	15	63	50	72	43	67	93
Other taxes on income	2	3	3	4	5	2	2	1	2	2
2000 Social security contributions	**114**	**154**	**287**	**626**	**620**	**637**	**654**	**710**	**823**	**888**
2100 Employees	29	38	72	157	159	160	164	178	206	222
2110 On a payroll basis	..	..	..	..	..	..	..	..	..	..
2120 On an income tax basis	..	..	..	..	..	..	..	..	..	..
2200 Employers	86	115	215	469	461	478	490	533	617	666
2210 On a payroll basis	..	..	..	..	..	..	..	..	..	..
2220 On an income tax basis	..	..	..	..	..	..	..	..	..	..
2300 Self-employed or non-employed	0	0	0	0	0	0	0	0	0	0
2310 On a payroll basis	..	..	..	..	..	..	..	..	..	..
2320 On an income tax basis	..	..	..	..	..	..	..	..	..	..
2400 Unallocable between 2100, 2200 and 2300	0	0	0	0	0	0	0	0	0	0
2410 On a payroll basis	..	..	..	..	..	..	..	..	..	..
2420 On an income tax basis	..	..	..	..	..	..	..	..	..	..
3000 Taxes on payroll and workforce	**0**	**0**	**0**	**0**	**0**	**0**	**0**	**0**	**0**	**0**
4000 Taxes on property	**20**	**34**	**55**	**92**	**103**	**108**	**131**	**137**	**148**	**168**
4100 Recurrent taxes on immovable property	12	24	30	54	57	63	64	71	78	77
Local property taxes	12	24	30	54	57	63	64	71	78	77
4110 Households	..	..	..	..	..	..	..	..	..	..
4120 Others	..	..	..	..	..	..	..	..	..	..
4200 Recurrent taxes on net wealth	..	..	0	0	0	0	0	0	0	0
4210 Individual	..	..	..	..	..	..	..	..	..	..
4220 Corporate	..	..	..	..	..	..	..	..	..	..
4300 Estate, inheritance and gift taxes	..	..	0	0	0	0	16	9	15	21
4310 Estate and inheritance taxes	..	..	0	..	..	..	16	9	15	21
Tax on trust beneficiaries	..	..	0	..	..	..	16	9	15	21
4320 Gift taxes	..	..	0	..	..	..	0	0	0	0
4400 Taxes on financial and capital transactions	8	10	25	39	46	45	51	57	56	70
Transfer duties	3	5	13	26	24	27	34	33	30	46
Stamp duties	5	5	12	12	22	18	17	23	25	24
4500 Non-recurrent taxes	0	0	0	0	0	0	0	0	0	0
4510 On net wealth	..	..	..	..	..	..	..	..	..	..
4520 Other non-recurrent taxes	..	..	..	..	..	..	..	..	..	..
4600 Other recurrent taxes on property	0	0	0	0	0	0	0	0	0	0
5000 Taxes on goods and services	**311**	**462**	**776**	**1 496**	**1 685**	**2 242**	**2 348**	**2 567**	**2 889**	**3 274**
5100 Taxes on production, sale, transfer, etc	300	449	758	1 442	1 624	2 182	2 283	2 499	2 821	3 200
5110 General taxes	255	372	661	1 255	1 342	1 756	1 684	1 895	2 107	2 407
5111 Value added taxes	0	0	0	0	0	1 623	1 648	1 883	2 107	2 407
Gross VAT revenues	..	..	..	..	..	2 187	2 390	2 787	3 048	3 337
VAT refunds	..	..	..	..	..	-564	-742	-904	-941	-929
5112 Sales tax	255	372	661	1 255	1 342	133	36	12	0	0
5113 Other	0	0	0	0	0	0	0	0	0	0
5120 Taxes on specific goods and services	45	78	97	186	281	426	599	604	714	793
5121 Excises	42	75	73	148	206	381	549	573	667	732
Fuel taxes	42	75	73	148	206	381	549	573	667	732
5122 Profits of fiscal monopolies	0	0	0	0	0	0	0	0	0	0
5123 Customs and import duties	0	0	0	0	0	0	0	0	0	0

Table 5.9. **Eswatini** *(cont.)*

Details of tax revenue / Recettes fiscales détaillées

Million SZL

	1997	2000	2005	2010	2011	2012	2013	2014	2015	2016
5124 Taxes on exports	0	0	0	0	0	0	0	0	0	0
Cattle export tax	0	0	0	0	0	0	0	0	0	0
5125 Taxes on investment goods	0	0	0	0	0	0	0	0	0	0
5126 Taxes on specific services	3	2	23	39	75	44	50	31	47	61
Tax on management fees	0	0	17	37	73	43	45	27	42	58
Taxes on lotteries, gaming and betting	3	2	7	2	2	2	5	4	5	3
Other taxes on services and hospitality	0	0	0	0	0	0	0	0	0	0
5127 Other taxes on internat. trade and transactions	0	0	0	0	0	0	0	0	0	0
5128 Other taxes	0	0	0	0	0	0	0	0	0	0
5130 Unallocable between 5110 and 5120	0	0	0	0	0	0	0	0	0	0
5200 Taxes on use of goods and perform activities	11	12	18	54	61	60	65	68	68	74
5210 Recurrent taxes	7	8	13	30	32	32	35	38	38	43
5211 Paid by households: motor vehicles	4	4	1	11	12	12	14	15	16	18
5212 Paid by others: motor vehicles	0	0	0	0	0	0	0	0	0	0
5213 Paid in respect of other goods	3	3	11	19	20	20	22	23	22	25
Trading licences	1	1	8	11	13	12	13	14	14	16
Company licences	1	1	2	7	7	7	7	8	7	8
Special licences	0	1	1	1	1	1	1	1	1	1
5220 Non-recurrent taxes	4	5	5	25	29	28	29	31	31	31
Road tolls	3	4	4	24	28	27	29	30	30	30
Firearm registration fees	0	0	1	1	1	1	1	1	1	1
5300 Unallocable between 5100 and 5200	0	0	0	0	0	0	0	0	0	0
6000 Other taxes	**0**	**0**	**0**	**0**	**0**	**0**	**0**	**0**	**0**	**0**
6100 Paid solely by business	..	..	..	..	..	..	..	..	..	..
6200 Other	..	..	..	..	..	..	..	..	..	..

Note: Eswatini was referred to as Swaziland in the previous editions of *Revenue Statistics in Africa*.

Data are reported on a fiscal year basis beginning 1st April. For example, the data for 2015 represent April 2015 to March 2016.

The data are on a cash basis.

Heading 4000: Data gaps in previous years' editions have been filled with newly available local data for numerous subcategories.

Heading 5211: This heading includes revenue from motor vehicle licences, the change of ownership fees and the registration of new motor vehicles. These revenues are considered as tax revenue according to the OECD classification, described in the Interpretative Guide in Annex A. The national classification of Eswatini classifies these revenues as non-tax revenues.

Heading 5213: This heading includes revenue from business and sundry licences. These revenues are considered as tax revenues according to the OECD classification, described in the Interpretative Guide in Annex A. The national classification of Eswatini classifies them as non-tax revenues.

Heading 5220: This heading includes revenue from the registrations of specific goods (e.g firearms). These revenues are considered as tax revenues under the OECD classification, as set out in the Interpretative Guide in Annex A. The national classification of Eswatini classifies these revenues as non-tax revenues.

Revenue from PAYE penalties, tax interest and penalties on taxes are considered as non-tax revenue under the OECD classification, as set out in the Interpretative Guide in Annex A. The national classification of Eswatini classifies these revenues as tax revenues.

Source: Eswatini Revenue Authority

StatLink https://doi.org/10.1787/888933820601

Table 5.10. **Ghana**

Details of tax revenue / Recettes fiscales détaillées

Million GHS

	1997	2000	2005	2010	2011	2012	2013	2014	2015	2016
Total tax revenue	..	**487**	**2 476**	**6 695**	**9 601**	**12 228**	**14 038**	**18 944**	**23 592**	**29 495**
1000 Taxes on income, profits and capital gains	..	**141**	**642**	**2 417**	**3 542**	**4 885**	**5 470**	**7 360**	**7 570**	**8 084**
1100 Of individuals	..	56	269	1 115	1 493	2 368	2 549	3 219	3 570	3 702
1110 On income and profits	..	56	269	1 115	1 493	2 368	2 549	3 219	3 570	3 702
Employees income tax	..	48	232	1 015	1 361	2 204	2 367	3 000	3 310	3 466
Self employers income/profit tax	..	8	37	100	132	164	182	219	260	237
1120 On capital gains	..	..	..	..	..	..	..	..	..	..
1200 Corporate	..	70	303	1 080	1 699	2 385	2 785	3 992	3 837	4 233
1210 On profits	..	70	303	1 080	1 699	2 385	2 785	3 992	3 837	4 233
Income/profit tax on companies (excl. oil)	..	70	303	988	1 568	2 362	2 316	3 034	3 620	4 052
Income/profit tax on oil companies	..	0	0	0	0	0	419	797	45	42
National Fiscal Stabilisation Levy (NFSL)	..	0	0	85	129	23	50	162	172	139
National Reconstruction Levy (NRL)	..	0	0	7	3	0	0	0	0	0
1220 On capital gains	..	..	..	..	..	..	..	..	..	..
1300 Unallocable between 1100 and 1200	..	15	70	222	349	132	136	149	163	148
Other direct taxes aside from oil and mineral royalties	..	15	70	222	349	132	136	149	163	148
2000 Social security contributions	..	**46**	**191**	**577**	**826**	**934**	**1 160**	**1 784**	**2 122**	**2 593**
2100 Employees	..	..	..	..	..	..	..	..	..	..
2110 On a payroll basis	..	..	..	..	..	..	..	..	..	..
2120 On an income tax basis	..	..	..	..	..	..	..	..	..	..
2200 Employers	..	..	..	..	..	..	..	..	..	..
2210 On a payroll basis	..	..	..	..	..	..	..	..	..	..
2220 On an income tax basis	..	..	..	..	..	..	..	..	..	..
2300 Self-employed or non-employed	..	..	..	..	..	..	..	..	..	..
2310 On a payroll basis	..	..	..	..	..	..	..	..	..	..
2320 On an income tax basis	..	..	..	..	..	..	..	..	..	..
2400 Unallocable between 2100, 2200 and 2300	..	46	191	577	826	934	1 160	1 784	2 122	2 593
2410 On a payroll basis	..	..	..	..	..	..	..	..	..	..
2420 On an income tax basis	..	..	..	..	..	..	..	..	..	..
3000 Taxes on payroll and workforce	..	**0**	**0**	**0**	**0**	**0**	**0**	**0**	**0**	**0**
4000 Taxes on property	..	..	..	..	..	..	..	..	..	..
4100 Recurrent taxes on immovable property	..	..	..	..	..	..	..	..	..	..
4110 Households	..	..	..	..	..	..	..	..	..	..
4120 Others	..	..	..	..	..	..	..	..	..	..
4200 Recurrent taxes on net wealth	..	..	..	..	..	..	..	..	..	..
4210 Individual	..	..	..	..	..	..	..	..	..	..
4220 Corporate	..	..	..	..	..	..	..	..	..	..
4300 Estate, inheritance and gift taxes	..	..	..	..	..	..	..	..	..	..
4310 Estate and inheritance taxes	..	..	..	..	..	..	..	..	..	..
4320 Gift taxes	..	..	..	..	..	..	..	..	..	..
4400 Taxes on financial and capital transactions	..	..	..	..	..	..	..	..	..	..
4500 Non-recurrent taxes	..	..	..	..	..	..	..	..	..	..
4510 On net wealth	..	..	..	..	..	..	..	..	..	..
4520 Other non-recurrent taxes	..	..	..	..	..	..	..	..	..	..
4600 Other recurrent taxes on property	..	..	..	..	..	..	..	..	..	..
5000 Taxes on goods and services	..	**301**	**1 643**	**3 701**	**5 233**	**6 409**	**7 409**	**9 799**	**13 900**	**18 817**
5100 Taxes on production, sale, transfer, etc	..	301	1 643	3 701	5 233	6 409	7 409	9 799	13 900	18 817
5110 General taxes	..	127	729	2 006	2 926	3 491	4 124	5 672	7 562	8 530
5111 Value added taxes	..	127	729	2 006	2 926	3 491	4 124	5 672	7 562	8 530
Value added taxes	..	127	595	1 618	2 376	2 777	3 317	4 672	6 254	7 130
VAT (external collection)	..	89	399	970	1 389	1 716	1 983	2 757	3 489	4 108
VAT (domestic collection)	..	39	196	649	987	1 061	1 334	1 915	2 766	3 022
National Health Insurance Levy (NHIL)	..	0	134	316	472	576	648	782	1 019	1 119
National Health Insurance Levy (customs collection)	..	..	..	183	285	364	405	463	558	613
National Health Insurance Levy (domestic collection)	..	..	..	133	186	212	243	319	461	506
Social Security and National Insurance Trust (SSNIT) contributions to the National Health Insurance Scheme (NHIS)	..	..	..	72	79	138	159	218	289	280
5112 Sales tax	..	0	0	0	0	0	0	0	0	0
5113 Other	..	0	0	0	0	0	0	0	0	0
5120 Taxes on specific goods and services	..	173	915	1 695	2 306	2 918	3 285	4 127	6 337	10 287

Table 5.10. **Ghana** *(cont.)*

Details of tax revenue / Recettes fiscales détaillées

Million GHS

	1997	2000	2005	2010	2011	2012	2013	2014	2015	2016
5121 Excises	..	75	477	374	606	730	694	764	2 402	5 289
Petroleum taxes aside from EFL and RFL	..	53	403	221	407	544	525	617	2 163	2 319
Energy Fund Levy (EFL)	..	0	0	36	32	0	0	0	0	25
Road Fund Levy (RFL)	..	0	0	0	0	0	0	0	0	1 002
Energy Debt Recovery Levy	..	0	0	0	0	0	0	0	0	1 320
Price Stabilisation and Recovery Levy	..	0	0	0	0	0	0	0	0	326
Other excise duties	..	21	74	118	168	186	169	147	239	297
5122 Profits of fiscal monopolies	..	0	0	0	0	0	0	0	0	0
5123 Customs and import duties	..	81	377	1 051	1 511	1 887	2 231	2 773	3 078	4 122
5124 Taxes on exports	..	18	61	95	5	103	100	319	371	269
Levies on cocoa exports	..	18	61	95	5	103	100	319	371	269
5125 Taxes on investment goods	..	0	0	0	0	0	0	0	0	0
5126 Taxes on specific services	..	0	0	174	184	197	260	272	486	608
Communication service tax	..	..	..	137	135	128	174	217	252	339
Airport tax	..	..	..	37	49	69	86	55	235	269
5127 Other taxes on internat. trade and transactions	..	0	0	0	0	0	0	0	0	0
5128 Other taxes	..	0	0	0	0	0	0	0	0	0
5130 Unallocable between 5110 and 5120	..	0	0	0	0	0	0	0	0	0
5200 Taxes on use of goods and perform activities	..	0	0	0	0	0	0	0	0	0
5210 Recurrent taxes	..	..	..	..	..	..	..	..	..	..
5211 Paid by households: motor vehicles	..	..	..	..	..	..	..	..	..	..
5212 Paid by others: motor vehicles	..	..	..	..	..	..	..	..	..	..
5213 Paid in respect of other goods	..	..	..	..	..	..	..	..	..	..
5220 Non-recurrent taxes	..	..	..	..	..	..	..	..	..	..
5300 Unallocable between 5100 and 5200	..	0	0	0	0	0	0	0	0	0
6000 Other taxes	..	**0**	**0**	**0**	**0**	**0**	**0**	**0**	**0**	**0**
6100 Paid solely by business	..	..	..	..	..	..	..	..	..	..
6200 Other	..	..	..	..	..	..	..	..	..	..

Note: Year ending 31st December.

The data are on a cash basis.

Figures exclude tax revenues collected by sub-national governments as the data are not available.

The data covering the years 2000-09 are more detailed than what was used previously. This affects Headings 1110, 1210, 1300, and 5126.

Heading 2000: The data are not available from 2000 to 2007.

Heading 4000: Property tax is levied annually by local authorities and is not available for this report.

Heading 5111: The national health insurance levy is a tax on goods and services whose funds are allocated to the National Health Insurance Scheme (NHIS).

Heading 6000: In previous years, VAT refunds were included under "Other taxes" (heading 6000), however VAT revenues (heading 5111) are now presented net of refunds.

Royalties from oil and mineral royalties are reported as taxes on income and property in Ghana's budget documents. These revenues are classified as non-tax revenue (Heading "Rents and royalties") in accordance with the OECD classification, as set out in the Interpretative Guide in Annex A.

Source: Ghana Statistical Service.

StatLink https://doi.org/10.1787/888933820620

Table 5.11. **Kenya**

Details of tax revenue / Recettes fiscales détaillées

Million KES

	1997	2000	2005	2010	2011	2012	2013	2014	2015	2016
Total tax revenue	..	..	**277 202**	**540 164**	**641 469**	**714 186**	**805 423**	**969 469**	**1 076 958**	**1 216 558**
1000 Taxes on income, profits and capital gains	..	..	**99 557**	**219 227**	**271 603**	**327 903**	**392 395**	**451 793**	**504 077**	**561 792**
1100 Of individuals	..	..	55 818	124 392	148 483	180 716	216 416	259 007	284 222	322 885
1110 On income and profits	..	..	55 818	124 392	148 483	180 716	216 416	259 007	284 222	322 885
Paye As You Earn (PAYE)	..	..	52 767	120 593	143 785	175 141	211 061	252 974	277 068	312 032
Individual income tax	..	..	3 051	3 799	4 698	5 575	5 355	6 033	7 154	8 821
Tax on rental income	..	..	0	0	0	0	0	0	0	2 033
1120 On capital gains	..	..	..	..	..	..	..	..	..	..
1200 Corporate	..	..	31 947	67 661	86 352	94 643	110 626	135 971	126 541	152 407
1210 On profits	..	..	31 947	67 661	86 352	94 643	110 626	135 971	126 541	152 407
Corporation tax	..	..	31 947	67 661	86 352	94 643	110 626	135 971	126 541	152 407
1220 On capital gains	..	..	..	..	..	..	..	..	..	..
1300 Unallocable between 1100 and 1200	..	..	11 792	27 174	36 768	52 544	65 354	56 816	93 313	86 500
Withholding tax	..	..	11 792	27 174	36 768	52 544	65 354	56 816	92 678	82 690
Capital gains tax	..	..	0	0	0	0	0	0	636	3 811
2000 Social security contributions	..	..	**3 675**	**6 026**	**6 766**	**7 015**	**5 582**	**6 185**	**7 565**	**16 782**
2100 Employees	..	..	558	0	0	0	0	0	0	0
Women and children's pension	..	..	558	0	0	0	0	0	0	0
2110 On a payroll basis	..	..	..	..	..	..	..	..	..	..
2120 On an income tax basis	..	..	..	..	..	..	..	..	..	..
2200 Employers	..	..	..	..	..	..	..	..	..	..
2210 On a payroll basis	..	..	..	..	..	..	..	..	..	..
2220 On an income tax basis	..	..	..	..	..	..	..	..	..	..
2300 Self-employed or non-employed	..	..	..	..	..	..	..	..	..	..
2310 On a payroll basis	..	..	..	..	..	..	..	..	..	..
2320 On an income tax basis	..	..	..	..	..	..	..	..	..	..
2400 Unallocable between 2100, 2200 and 2300	..	..	3 117	6 026	6 766	7 015	5 582	6 185	7 565	16 782
2410 On a payroll basis	..	..	..	..	..	..	..	..	..	..
2420 On an income tax basis	..	..	..	..	..	..	..	..	..	..
3000 Taxes on payroll and workforce	..	..	**0**	**0**	**0**	**0**	**0**	**0**	**0**	**0**
4000 Taxes on property	..	..	**1 244**	**6 465**	**7 851**	**9 097**	**9 670**	**11 203**	**12 630**	**11 654**
4100 Recurrent taxes on immovable property	..	..	185	1 133	1 045	1 206	1 076	1 133	1 051	1 237
Immovable property (Stand premia on town plots)	..	..	7	86	133	83	0	63	6	36
Land rates	..	..	178	0	0	0	0	0	0	0
Land rent	..	..	0	1 047	913	1 123	1 076	1 071	1 045	1 201
4110 Households	..	..	..	..	..	..	..	..	..	..
4120 Others	..	..	..	..	..	..	..	..	..	..
4200 Recurrent taxes on net wealth	..	..	0	0	0	0	0	0	0	0
4210 Individual	..	..	..	..	..	..	..	..	..	..
4220 Corporate	..	..	..	..	..	..	..	..	..	..
4300 Estate, inheritance and gift taxes	..	..	0	0	0	0	0	0	0	0
4310 Estate and inheritance taxes	..	..	..	..	..	..	..	..	..	..
4320 Gift taxes	..	..	..	..	..	..	..	..	..	..
4400 Taxes on financial and capital transactions	..	..	1 059	5 332	6 805	7 891	8 594	10 069	11 579	10 417
Stamp duty-domestic taxes	..	..	940	5 332	6 805	7 891	8 594	10 069	11 579	10 417
Stamp duty-other taxes	..	..	0	0	0	0	0	0	0	0
Stamp duty-customs services	..	..	119	0	0	0	0	0	0	0
4500 Non-recurrent taxes	..	..	0	0	0	0	0	0	0	0
4510 On net wealth	..	..	..	..	..	..	..	..	..	..
4520 Other non-recurrent taxes	..	..	..	..	..	..	..	..	..	..
4600 Other recurrent taxes on property	..	..	0	0	0	0	0	0	0	0
5000 Taxes on goods and services	..	..	**172 726**	**308 283**	**355 050**	**369 975**	**397 570**	**500 039**	**552 536**	**626 168**
5100 Taxes on production, sale, transfer, etc	..	..	169 176	304 497	351 121	365 723	392 618	494 128	546 051	619 129
5110 General taxes	..	..	72 656	141 152	171 809	174 933	183 404	233 724	265 501	291 229
5111 Value added taxes	..	..	72 656	141 041	171 679	174 788	183 219	233 558	264 872	290 843
VAT-Ordinary imports	..	..	28 287	57 594	74 535	85 744	88 023	114 556	127 744	125 105
VAT-Oil imports	..	..	4 186	5 352	6 860	8 608	6 661	10 621	7 894	6 368
VAT - Domestic (Refunds)	..	..	40 183	78 095	90 284	80 436	88 534	108 380	129 234	159 370
VAT - Domestic (Net)	..	..	48 583	92 255	103 300	93 371	101 446	123 068	143 922	174 051
VAT - Domestic (Gross)	..	..	8 400	14 160	13 016	12 935	12 912	14 688	14 688	14 681
5112 Sales tax	..	..	0	0	0	0	0	0	0	0
5113 Other	..	..	0	111	130	145	185	166	630	385
Turnover tax	..	..	0	111	130	145	185	166	630	385
5120 Taxes on specific goods and services	..	..	96 520	163 345	179 312	190 791	209 215	260 404	280 550	327 900

Table 5.11. **Kenya** *(cont.)*

Details of tax revenue / Recettes fiscales détaillées

Million KES

	1997	2000	2005	2010	2011	2012	2013	2014	2015	2016
5121 Excises	..	..	57 314	93 803	99 712	98 291	105 288	119 122	130 910	168 286
Excise duty-Oil	..	..	24 876	35 780	35 459	30 759	33 148	38 416	42 687	51 611
Excise duty-Domestic	..	..	15 744	23 755	28 573	30 878	33 260	35 855	38 246	48 986
Road maintenance levy	..	..	9 645	23 780	24 101	24 184	25 002	28 163	30 890	45 407
Excise duty-Imports	..	..	4 235	6 994	8 016	8 584	10 307	13 151	15 175	18 096
Sugar levy	..	..	1 587	1 590	1 638	1 748	1 726	1 585	1 329	1 357
Petroleum development levy	..	..	1 041	1 585	1 570	1 595	1 702	1 794	1 817	1 974
Petroleum regulatory levy	..	..	0	134	135	136	143	158	301	485
Second hand motor vehicles purchase tax	..	..	186	183	219	407	0	0	466	369
5122 Profits of fiscal monopolies	..	..	0	0	0	0	0	0	0	0
5123 Customs and import duties	..	..	32 873	57 047	66 349	76 878	82 743	113 701	120 612	125 025
Import duty-Ordinary	..	..	22 722	40 382	44 860	50 944	56 734	65 580	72 346	79 372
Import declaration fees	..	..	9 724	15 836	20 467	24 846	24 270	26 627	27 119	25 851
Railway development levy	..	..	0	0	0	0	0	19 721	18 940	17 273
Import duty-Oil	..	..	427	797	923	969	1 163	1 016	1 387	1 595
Merchant superintendent shipping levy	..	..	0	32	99	118	576	757	820	934
5124 Taxes on exports	..	..	0	0	0	0	0	0	0	0
5125 Taxes on investment goods	..	..	0	0	0	0	0	0	0	0
5126 Taxes on specific services	..	..	6 333	12 495	13 250	15 622	21 184	27 580	29 028	34 589
Excise on air time	..	..	2 982	7 893	7 796	8 984	11 315	12 302	13 122	14 884
Airport revenue	..	..	1 846	2 464	3 026	3 460	6 281	6 837	6 619	6 570
Aviation revenue	..	..	1 505	2 138	2 428	3 178	3 589	3 468	3 565	4 122
Excise on financial services	..	..	0	0	0	0	0	4 973	5 722	9 013
5127 Other taxes on internat. trade and transactions	..	..	0	0	0	0	0	0	0	0
5128 Other taxes	..	..	0	0	0	0	0	0	0	0
5130 Unallocable between 5110 and 5120	..	..	0	0	0	0	0	0	0	0
5200 Taxes on use of goods and perform activities	..	..	3 550	3 786	3 929	4 252	4 952	5 911	6 485	7 039
5210 Recurrent taxes	..	..	3 550	3 786	3 929	4 252	4 952	5 911	6 485	7 039
5211 Paid by households: motor vehicles	..	..	3 266	3 367	3 499	3 840	4 488	5 415	6 010	6 564
Road transport fees	..	..	2 793	2 499	2 648	2 767	3 027	3 691	3 947	3 911
Foreign motor vehicles tax	..	..	0	0	0	0	0	0	0	0
Advance and other taxes	..	..	473	868	851	1 073	1 461	1 725	2 064	2 653
5212 Paid by others: motor vehicles	..	..	0	0	0	0	0	0	0	0
5213 Paid in respect of other goods	..	..	284	419	430	412	464	496	475	475
Kenya Bureau of Standards (KEBS) tax	..	..	284	419	430	412	464	496	475	475
5220 Non-recurrent taxes	..	..	0	0	0	0	0	0	0	0
5300 Unallocable between 5100 and 5200	..	..	0	0	0	0	0	0	0	0
6000 Other taxes	**..**	**..**	**0**	**164**	**199**	**196**	**206**	**250**	**150**	**161**
Other taxes[1]	..	..	..	164	199	196	206	250	150	161
6100 Paid solely by business	..	..	..	..	..	..	..	..	..	..
6200 Other taxes not solely paid by business	..	..	..	..	..	..	..	..	..	..

Note: Data are reported on a fiscal year basis beginning 1st July. For example, the data for 2016 represent July 2015 to June 2016.

The data are on a cash basis.

Figures exclude tax revenues collected by sub-national governments as the data are not available.

The majority of taxes are collected by the Kenya Revenue Authority (KRA). Some revenues are collected by the KRA on behalf of other agencies (please see 1). Other revenues are collected by respective government ministries

Heading 2000: Data on social security have been included in this edition for the first time. The mandatory contributions by employees are proxied by the membership in the National Health Insurance Fund. The social security contributions are deducted by employers and remitted to National Health Insurance Fund.

1. These revenues are collected by the Kenya Revenue Authority (KRA) on behalf of other agencies. The national classification of Kenya classifies all agency revenues as non-tax revenues.

Source: Kenya Revenue Authority (KRA).

StatLink https://doi.org/10.1787/888933820639

Table 5.12. **Mali**

Details of tax revenue / Recettes fiscales détaillées

Million XOF

	1997	2000	2005	2010	2011	2012	2013	2014	2015	2016
Recettes fiscales totales	..	**239 362**	**476 775**	**748 245**	**840 002**	**887 628**	**930 886**	**983 596**	**1 159 330**	**1 343 499**
1000 Impôts sur revenu, bénéfices et gains en capital	..	**34 218**	**77 530**	**183 548**	**193 092**	**225 075**	**229 742**	**295 236**	**294 843**	**325 600**
1100 Des personnes physiques	..	32 095	39 902	61 018	63 150	72 066	69 954	88 538	92 395	101 312
1110 Sur le revenu et les bénéfices	..	32 095	39 902	61 018	63 150	72 066	69 954	88 538	92 395	101 312
ITS retenue, secteur privé	..	12 374	25 119	39 859	48 533	59 539	56 021	63 658	71 153	76 734
ITS retenue, secteur public	..	3 311	7 125	8 624	9 071	8 360	9 425	8 797	13 904	13 882
BIC secteur privé	..	15 996	6 589	10 643	3 272	2 539	2 695	14 171	5 024	7 643
BIC secteur état	..	38	30	0	0	0	0	0	0	0
Impôts sur les revenus fonciers	..	376	1 039	1 892	2 274	1 628	1 813	1 912	2 314	3 053
1120 Sur les gains en capital	..	..	..	..	..	..	..	..	..	..
1200 Des sociétés	..	0	31 767	107 703	110 060	132 707	141 576	182 280	174 434	199 055
1210 Sur les bénéfices	..	0	31 767	107 703	110 060	132 707	141 576	182 280	174 434	199 055
Impôt sur les societés (IS privé)	..	0	31 767	107 582	109 996	130 299	141 574	182 231	174 433	199 055
Impôt sur les societés (IS état)	..	0	0	121	64	2 408	2	49	1	0
1220 Sur les gains en capital	..	..	..	..	..	..	..	..	..	..
1300 Non ventilables entre 1100 et 1200	..	2 123	5 861	14 827	19 882	20 302	18 212	24 418	28 014	25 233
2000 Cotisations de sécurité sociale	..	**18 442**	**45 497**	**73 600**	**86 719**	**91 665**	**91 693**	**110 925**	**116 702**	**153 398**
2100 A la charge des salariés	..	..	..	..	..	..	..	..	..	..
2110 Sur la base du salaire	..	..	..	..	..	..	..	..	..	..
2120 Sur la base de l'impôt sur les revenus	..	..	..	..	..	..	..	..	..	..
2200 A la charge des employeurs	..	..	..	..	..	..	..	..	..	..
2210 Sur la base du salaire	..	..	..	..	..	..	..	..	..	..
2220 Sur la base de l'impôt sur le revenu	..	..	..	..	..	..	..	..	..	..
2300 A charge des travailleurs indép. ou sans emploi	..	..	..	..	..	..	..	..	..	..
2310 Sur la base du salaire	..	..	..	..	..	..	..	..	..	..
2320 Sur la base de l'impôt sur le revenu	..	..	..	..	..	..	..	..	..	..
2400 Non ventilables entre 2100, 2200 et 2300	..	18 442	45 497	73 600	86 719	91 665	91 693	110 925	116 702	153 398
Social security contributions (CMSS)	..	..	9 259	12 834	15 245	16 859	22 570	24 444	26 550	45 311
Social security contributions (INPS)	..	18 442	36 238	60 766	71 474	74 807	69 123	86 481	90 152	108 086
2410 Sur la base du salaire	..	..	..	..	..	..	..	..	..	..
2420 Sur la base de l'impôt sur le revenu	..	..	..	..	..	..	..	..	..	..
3000 Sur salaires ou main d'oeuvre	..	**4 671**	**8 381**	**6 278**	**7 848**	**9 878**	**8 451**	**9 881**	**11 567**	**13 192**
4000 Impôts sur le patrimoine	..	**3 149**	**7 909**	**12 062**	**14 019**	**9 760**	**12 450**	**16 512**	**17 933**	**28 489**
4100 Impôts périodiques sur la propriété immobilière	..	119	930	979	752	666	923	1 380	1 561	1 590
Droits de conservation de la propriété	..	119	930	979	752	659	913	1 341	1 549	1 572
Taxe sur les locations des particuliers	..	0	0	0	0	7	10	39	12	18
4110 Ménages	..	..	..	..	..	..	..	..	..	..
4120 Autres agents	..	..	..	..	..	..	..	..	..	..
4200 Impôts périodiques sur l'actif net	..	0	0	0	0	0	0	0	0	0
4210 Personnes physiques	..	..	..	..	..	..	..	..	..	..
4220 Sociétés	..	..	..	..	..	..	..	..	..	..
4300 Impôts sur mut. par décès, succ. et donations	..	0	0	0	0	0	0	0	0	0
4310 Impôts sur mut. par décès et successions	..	..	..	..	..	..	..	..	..	..
4320 Impôts sur les donations	..	..	..	..	..	..	..	..	..	..
4400 Impôts sur transact. mobilières et immob.	..	3 030	6 979	11 083	13 267	9 094	11 527	15 132	16 372	26 899
Droits d'enregistrements (DGI)	..	2 934	3 414	6 928	6 621	4 068	6 677	8 726	11 023	18 390
Droits d'enregistrements (DND)	..	0	3 055	4 107	6 399	4 741	4 584	6 150	5 321	8 436
Transfert lettre et permis OCC en TF	..	96	510	0	0	0	0	0	0	0
Taxe sur les frais d'édilité	..	0	0	48	247	285	266	256	28	73
4500 Impôts non-périodiques	..	0	0	0	0	0	0	0	0	0
4510 Sur l'actif net	..	..	..	..	..	..	..	..	..	..
4520 Autres non-périodiques	..	..	..	..	..	..	..	..	..	..
4600 Autres impôts périodiques sur patrimoine	..	0	0	0	0	0	0	0	0	0
5000 Impôts sur les biens et services	..	**172 751**	**329 994**	**453 154**	**510 662**	**517 144**	**556 400**	**518 514**	**675 842**	**784 971**
5100 Impôts sur production, vente, transfert, etc.	..	171 923	328 837	451 425	508 634	515 068	554 301	516 161	673 184	781 685
5110 Impôts généraux	..	81 113	193 276	261 811	311 817	286 922	331 998	280 616	329 598	396 055
5111 Taxes sur la valeur ajoutée	..	80 633	191 827	260 599	310 489	285 289	330 695	279 167	328 157	394 552
TVA Importations	..	46 622	119 548	161 656	185 505	170 709	203 494	176 270	210 431	232 434
TVA Privé	..	31 218	67 629	95 383	121 369	104 380	120 244	99 994	113 512	150 102
TVA État	..	2 793	4 650	3 560	3 615	10 200	6 957	2 903	4 214	12 016
5112 Impôts sur les ventes	..	0	0	0	0	0	0	0	0	0
5113 Autres impôts	..	480	1 449	1 212	1 328	1 633	1 303	1 449	1 441	1 503
5120 Impôts sur biens et services déterminés	..	90 810	135 561	189 614	196 817	228 146	222 303	235 545	343 586	385 630

Table 5.12. **Mali** *(cont.)*

Details of tax revenue / Recettes fiscales détaillées

Million XOF

	1997	2000	2005	2010	2011	2012	2013	2014	2015	2016
5121 Accises	..	45 791	42 725	56 909	42 530	70 801	62 716	68 459	136 898	159 013
Taxes intérieures sur produits petroliers (TIPP)	..	33 694	26 389	25 660	4 684	25 232	22 286	27 793	93 264	100 648
Taxe Ad Valorem (entreprises minières) (DNDC)	..	4 233	9 811	20 479	24 682	31 754	28 889	25 474	25 253	30 605
Taxes locales sur les tabacs	..	816	3 285	5 385	6 518	6 608	3 650	6 445	8 264	12 787
Taxes sur les boissons alcoolisés	..	1 169	1 317	1 777	2 173	2 383	1 912	2 880	3 611	3 672
Impôt spécial sur les boissons	..	1 680	1 609	2 275	2 673	3 463	3 390	3 616	4 354	5 763
Taxe sur autres produits	..	4 199	314	1 333	1 800	1 361	2 589	2 251	2 152	5 538
5122 Bénéfices des monopoles fiscaux	..	0	0	0	0	0	0	0	0	0
5123 Droits de douane et droits à l'importation	..	30 734	67 175	86 853	103 072	91 234	104 534	105 683	124 049	139 263
Droits de douanes	..	29 328	60 305	76 287	91 594	80 753	93 269	93 480	111 062	124 320
Redevance Statistique	..	315	6 485	9 702	10 418	9 390	10 634	11 125	12 940	14 803
Taxe dégréssive de protection (TDP)	..	6	373	831	1 017	1 036	542	969	0	0
Taxe conjoncturelle à l'importation	..	1 085	12	33	43	55	89	109	47	140
5124 Taxes à l'exportation	..	4 046	9 922	20 503	23 694	33 857	26 383	26 407	30 243	29 288
5125 Impôts sur biens d'équipement	..	0	0	0	0	0	0	0	0	0
5126 Impôts sur services déterminés	..	10 239	15 739	25 349	27 521	32 254	28 670	34 996	52 396	58 066
Taxes sur les Activités Financières	..	5 785	9 995	17 828	18 799	22 852	18 378	23 112	39 608	41 562
Ristournes sur PMU et CASINO	..	1 515	1 955	3 061	3 611	3 449	4 173	5 173	5 966	6 821
Taxes sur les transporteurs routiers	..	1 676	2 287	2 659	2 897	2 736	2 962	3 243	3 499	4 890
Taxes sur les contrats d'assurances	..	1 261	1 475	1 787	2 209	3 216	3 155	3 465	3 321	4 783
Autres taxes sur les services déterminés	..	2	27	14	5	1	2	3	2	10
5127 Autres impôts sur commerce et transact. internat.	..	0	0	0	0	0	0	0	0	0
5128 Autres impôts	..	0	0	0	0	0	0	0	0	0
5130 Non ventilables entre 5110 et 5120	..	0	0	0	0	0	0	0	0	0
5200 Impôts sur utilisation des biens et exerc. activites	..	828	1 157	1 729	2 028	2 076	2 099	2 353	2 658	3 286
5210 Impôts périodiques	..	828	1 157	1 729	2 028	2 076	2 099	2 353	2 658	3 286
5211 A la charge des ménages: véhicules à moteur	..	716	1 140	1 715	2 007	2 068	2 083	2 336	2 658	3 286
5212 A la charge autres agents: véhicules à moteur	..	0	0	0	0	0	0	0	0	0
5213 Autres impôts périodiques	..	112	17	14	21	8	16	17	0	0
5220 Impôts non-périodiques	..	0	0	0	0	0	0	0	0	0
5300 Non ventilables entre 5100 et 5200	..	0	0	0	0	0	0	0	0	0
6000 Autres impôts	**..**	**6 131**	**7 464**	**19 603**	**27 662**	**34 106**	**32 150**	**32 528**	**42 443**	**37 849**
Droits de Timbres (DGI)	..	4 188	6 172	10 797	11 414	11 769	14 719	15 000	16 840	18 821
Droits de timbres (DND)	..	0	911	143	186	136	390	500	235	277
Recettes sur exercices antérieurs	..	1 943	381	8 663	16 062	22 201	17 041	17 028	25 368	18 751
6100 A la charge exclusive des entreprises	..	..	..	..	..	..	..	..	..	..
6200 A la charge d'autres agents	..	..	..	..	..	..	..	..	..	..

Note: Année civile se terminant le 31 décembre.

Les données sont sur la base des encaissements.

Les chiffres n'incluent pas les recettes fiscales collectées par les collectivités locales car elles ne sont pas disponibles.

Les données sur les cotisations de la Caisse Malienne de Sécurité Sociale (CMSS) et les données de l'Institut National de Prévoyance Sociale (INPS) ne sont disponibles qu'à partir de 2004 et 2006 respectivement. Ces recettes ne sont pas incluses dans les recettes de l'État du Mali.

Rubrique 5123 : Les recettes de la CEDEAO (Communauté économique des États de l'Afrique de l'Ouest), y compris les redevances statistiques, le prélèvement communautaire, et la taxe dégressive de protection, ne sont pas considérées comme des recettes fiscales ou des recettes non fiscales selon le guide d'interprétation de l'OCDE (voir § 4).

Source: Ministère de l'Économie et des Finances du Mali.

StatLink https://doi.org/10.1787/888933820658

Table 5.13. **Mauritius / Maurice**

Details of tax revenue / Recettes fiscales détaillées

Million MUR

	1997	2000	2005	2010	2011	2012	2013	2014	2015	2016
Total tax revenue	**15 367**	**22 390**	**34 901**	**59 165**	**63 455**	**69 268**	**72 463**	**76 647**	**80 186**	**83 672**
1000 Taxes on income, profits and capital gains	**2 287**	**2 881**	**5 829**	**15 005**	**14 560**	**15 642**	**16 956**	**18 385**	**19 793**	**20 403**
1100 Of individuals	1 220	1 540	2 553	4 583	4 913	5 331	6 214	7 049	7 614	7 621
1110 On income and profits	..	..	..	..	..	..	..	..	..	..
1120 On capital gains	..	..	..	..	..	..	..	..	..	..
1200 Corporate	1 067	1 341	3 276	9 457	8 788	9 380	9 763	10 268	10 993	11 686
1210 On profits	1 067	1 341	3 276	9 457	8 788	9 380	9 763	10 268	10 993	11 686
Income Tax - companies & bodies corporate	..	..	..	8 428	7 847	8 372	8 727	8 972	9 788	10 459
Special levy on banks	..	..	..	455	448	482	473	772	748	771
Solidarity levy on telecommunication companies	..	..	..	424	376	397	438	358	331	308
Corporate social responsibility	..	..	..	150	116	130	125	166	126	147
Special contribution from hotels	..	..	..	0	0	0	0	0	0	0
1220 On capital gains	..	..	..	..	..	..	..	..	..	..
1300 Unallocable between 1100 and 1200	..	..	..	965	859	931	978	1 068	1 186	1 096
Tax deduction at source	..	..	..	965	859	931	978	1 068	1 186	1 096
2000 Social security contributions	**948**	**1 230**	**1 387**	**2 880**	**3 100**	**3 302**	**3 658**	**3 959**	**4 210**	**4 315**
2100 Employees	..	..	462	713	782	840	904	1 004	1 065	1 097
2110 On a payroll basis	..	..	..	..	..	..	..	..	..	..
2120 On an income tax basis	..	..	..	..	..	..	..	..	..	..
2200 Employers	..	..	925	1 426	1 564	1 680	1 807	2 009	2 130	2 193
2210 On a payroll basis	..	..	..	..	..	..	..	..	..	..
2220 On an income tax basis	..	..	..	..	..	..	..	..	..	..
2300 Self-employed or non-employed	..	..	0	0	0	1	1	1	1	1
2310 On a payroll basis	..	..	..	..	..	..	..	..	..	..
2320 On an income tax basis	..	..	..	..	..	..	..	..	..	..
2400 Unallocable between 2100, 2200 and 2300	948	1 230	0	741	753	782	947	945	1 014	1 025
2410 On a payroll basis	..	..	..	..	..	..	..	..	..	..
2420 On an income tax basis	..	..	..	..	..	..	..	..	..	..
3000 Taxes on payroll and workforce	**101**	**140**	**204**	**176**	**187**	**201**	**235**	**507**	**474**	**592**
Extra-budgetary taxes on payroll and workforce	101	140	204	176	187	201	235	507	474	592
4000 Taxes on property	**1 147**	**1 411**	**1 920**	**3 328**	**3 184**	**3 718**	**3 568**	**4 299**	**4 109**	**4 680**
4100 Recurrent taxes on immovable property	171	205	240	417	417	238	267	279	146	296
4110 Households	0	0	0	0	0	0	0	0	0	0
4120 Others	171	205	240	417	417	238	267	279	146	296
Local government recurrent taxes on immovable property	171	205	240	410	410	235	261	275	143	292
Campement taxes	0	0	0	6	6	4	6	4	3	4
4200 Recurrent taxes on net wealth	0	0	0	0	0	0	0	0	0	0
4210 Individual	..	..	..	..	..	..	..	..	..	..
4220 Corporate	..	..	..	..	..	..	..	..	..	..
4300 Estate, inheritance and gift taxes	0	0	0	0	0	0	0	0	0	0
4310 Estate and inheritance taxes	..	..	..	..	..	..	..	..	..	..
4320 Gift taxes	..	..	..	..	..	..	..	..	..	..
4400 Taxes on financial and capital transactions	976	1 206	1 680	2 902	2 747	3 471	3 277	4 000	3 907	4 337
Land transfer tax	..	..	409	1 190	1 243	1 618	1 496	1 652	1 650	1 831
Registration duty on transfer of immovable property	..	..	562	1 180	959	1 382	1 239	1 522	1 708	1 943
Tax on transfer of leasehold rights in state lands	..	..	0	175	119	187	272	374	157	119
Registration duty on transfer of shares	..	..	0	84	121	32	24	182	122	174
Registration duty on fixed and floating charges	..	..	116	180	213	168	169	162	157	164
Stamp duties	..	..	14	75	81	85	78	109	112	105
Registration duty on loans	..	..	0	9	4	0	0	0	0	0
Mortgages, inscriptions and transcriptions	..	..	10	11	8	0	0	0	0	0
Other taxes on financial and capital transactions	..	..	568	0	0	0	0	0	0	0
4500 Non-recurrent taxes	0	0	0	10	20	9	24	20	55	47
4510 On net wealth	..	..	..	0	0	0	0	0	0	0
4520 Other non-recurrent taxes	..	..	..	10	20	9	24	20	55	47
4600 Other recurrent taxes on property	0	0	0	0	0	0	0	0	0	0
5000 Taxes on goods and services	**10 727**	**16 514**	**25 300**	**37 611**	**42 240**	**46 215**	**47 880**	**49 309**	**51 412**	**53 571**
5100 Taxes on production, sale, transfer, etc	10 581	16 312	23 445	34 748	38 932	42 888	44 466	45 229	47 243	49 345
5110 General taxes	2 442	5 604	12 529	21 088	22 918	25 171	26 174	26 154	28 025	29 203
5111 Value added taxes	0	5 604	12 529	21 088	22 710	24 926	26 016	25 989	28 025	29 203
Gross VAT revenues	..	..	..	26 583	29 002	31 325	31 816	32 783	33 291	34 540
VAT refunds	..	..	..	-5 495	-6 292	-6 399	-5 800	-6 794	-5 267	-5 337
5112 Sales tax	2 442	0	0	0	0	0	0	0	0	0
5113 Other	0	0	0	0	207	245	158	165	0	0
Extra-budgetary taxes on goods and services	..	..	..	..	136	148	158	165	0	0
Local taxes on goods and services	..	..	..	..	72	97	0	0	0	0

Table 5.13. **Mauritius / Maurice** *(cont.)*

Details of tax revenue / Recettes fiscales détaillées

Million MUR

	1997	2000	2005	2010	2011	2012	2013	2014	2015	2016
5120 Taxes on specific goods and services	8 139	10 707	10 916	13 660	16 014	17 716	18 293	19 075	19 218	20 142
Unallocated taxes on goods and services	..	..	3 279	0	0	0	0	0	0	0
5121 Excises	..	..	2 840	9 331	11 502	13 052	13 569	14 423	14 834	15 633
Spirits, liquors and alcoholic beverages	..	..	1 220	2 351	3 097	3 705	4 122	4 170	4 448	4 603
Tobacco products	..	..	1 617	2 371	3 039	3 420	3 697	3 823	3 851	4 196
Motor vehicles and motor cycles	..	..	0	1 928	1 942	2 340	2 054	2 400	2 471	2 582
Petro. products (incl. MIDL)	..	..	0	2 421	3 018	3 099	3 069	3 219	3 292	3 438
PET bottles and other plastic products	..	..	0	159	205	255	223	242	250	235
Sugar content of soft drinks	..	..	0	0	0	0	177	330	344	345
Energy inefficient products	..	..	0	0	0	0	1	5	3	2
Sugar brokerage	..	..	1	0	0	0	0	0	0	0
Extra-budgetary excise taxes	..	..	0	0	15	13	13	0	0	0
Other excises	..	..	1	101	186	220	214	233	175	231
5122 Profits of fiscal monopolies	..	..	0	0	0	0	0	0	0	0
5123 Customs and import duties	..	..	3 899	1 525	1 560	1 506	1 389	1 239	1 302	1 347
5124 Taxes on exports	..	..	0	0	0	0	0	0	0	0
5125 Taxes on investment goods	..	..	0	0	0	0	0	0	0	0
5126 Taxes on specific services	..	..	898	2 731	2 945	3 152	3 334	3 413	3 083	3 163
Taxes on the national lottery and other lotteries	..	..	14	693	623	588	682	652	436	387
Betting taxes on horse racing, football, etc.	..	..	269	658	786	773	793	934	837	887
Gaming taxes on casinos and gaming houses	..	..	614	818	744	495	541	529	591	652
Passenger fee on air tickets	..	..	0	561	793	1 204	1 219	1 213	1 173	1 230
Levy on messaging services	..	..	0	0	0	92	99	85	46	7
Hotel and restaurant tax	..	..	0	0	0	0	0	0	0	0
5127 Other taxes on internat. trade and transactions	..	..	0	0	0	0	0	0	0	0
5128 Other taxes	..	..	0	73	7	7	0	0	0	0
Temporary solidarity tax on hotels	..	..	0	0	0	0	0	0	0	0
Local government taxes on goods and services	..	..	0	73	7	7	0	0	0	0
5130 Unallocable between 5110 and 5120	0	0	0	0	0	0	0	0	0	0
5200 Taxes on use of goods and perform activities	146	203	1 750	2 765	3 295	3 313	3 414	4 080	4 169	4 226
5210 Recurrent taxes	146	203	1 287	1 934	2 292	2 368	2 343	2 363	2 702	2 792
5211 Paid by households: motor vehicles	0	0	652	1 117	1 155	1 211	1 291	1 345	1 362	1 430
5212 Paid by others: motor vehicles	0	0	0	0	0	0	0	0	0	0
5213 Paid in respect of other goods	146	203	635	816	1 137	1 157	1 052	1 018	1 341	1 362
Company licences	..	..	103	148	156	160	235	235	306	196
Incorporation & lodging fees, search duty, etc.	..	..	5	9	10	9	17	18	18	16
Tourist enterprise licences	..	..	33	74	81	81	85	85	91	110
Gambling licences	..	..	48	100	224	349	352	317	368	438
Liquor licences	..	..	10	10	25	21	24	23	25	23
Freeport licences	..	..	0	0	0	2	8	7	6	7
Pharmacy licences	..	..	0	1	1	1	1	1	2	2
Fishing vessel licences	..	..	38	52	39	43	64	54	43	52
Registration of factories	..	..	2	2	3	3	3	3	3	3
Registration of associations	..	..	1	2	2	2	1	0	1	1
Recruitment licences	..	..	0	2	0	0	0	0	0	1
Environment protection fee	..	..	132	141	302	145	130	159	391	399
Advertising structure fee	..	..	0	0	0	62	68	67	63	64
Regional taxes on permission to use goods	0	0	2	2	3	2	2	3	2	2
Local taxes on permission to use goods	146	203	244	255	271	251	0	0	0	0
Other recurrent taxes on goods and activities	..	..	16	20	21	27	62	45	23	48
5220 Non-recurrent taxes	0	0	463	832	1 003	944	1 071	1 716	1 467	1 434
Processing fee on acquisitions schemes	..	..	0	0	0	0	2	3	5	5
Registration duty on transfer of motor vehicles	..	..	463	794	818	895	972	1 195	1 277	1 266
Land conversion tax	..	..	0	38	185	49	96	518	185	163
5300 Unallocable between 5100 and 5200	0	0	105	98	14	15	0	0	0	0
Extra-budgetary taxes on goods and services	0	0	105	98	14	15	0	0	0	0
6000 Other taxes	**157**	**215**	**260**	**164**	**183**	**189**	**165**	**189**	**188**	**111**
Mauritius Revenue Authority penalties	0	0	0	0	0	34	34	59	74	22
Unidentified local government taxes	0	0	0	0	0	18	0	0	0	0
Unidentified taxes	157	215	260	164	183	137	131	130	114	89
6100 Paid solely by business	..	..	..	..	..	..	..	..	..	..
6200 Other	..	..	..	..	..	..	..	..	..	..

Table 5.13. **Mauritius / Maurice** *(cont.)*

Details of tax revenue / Recettes fiscales détaillées

Note: Data for 2016 and for years prior to 2010 are on a fiscal year basis beginning 1st July. For example, the data for 2009 represent July 2008 to June 2009 and 2016 represents July 2015 to June 2016. The data for years 2010-15 are on a calendar year (January-December) basis.

Mauritius budget statements cover January-June 2015 and July 2015 to June 2016, but neither the fiscal nor the calendar year for 2015. Figures for 2015 are therefore estimated using quarterly revenue figures at the aggregate level and fiscal year revenue data. Linear projections were used in 2015 and 2016 for social security contributions (2000) and for extra-budgetary taxes on payroll and the workforce (3000).

Data for the central government budgetary tax prior to 2007 and all extra-budgetary, regional and local data were classified according to the IMF Government Finance Statistics Manual. The 1986 manual was used for data up to 2009 and the 2001 manual for data up to 2009 onwards. Data from 2007 onwards are classified under the OECD classification, as set out in the Interpretative Guide in Annex A.

Heading 1210: the solidarity levy on telecommunications companies, the corporate social responsibility tax and the special contribution from hotels are classified as "other taxes" by the Mauritius Revenue Authority.

Heading 5213: the Environment Protection Fee and Advertising Structure Fee are classified as other taxes by the Mauritius Revenue Authority.

Heading 5220: includes the registration duty on transfer of motor vehicles and the land conversion tax that are classified as taxes on property by the Mauritius Revenue Authority.

Headings 5113, 5213 and 6000: due to an administrative change, some categories of local revenues were reclassified. Local taxes that were previously classified as local taxes on goods, as well as taxes on the use of goods and permission to use goods, and some revenues classified as miscellaneous revenues were recorded as sales of goods and services from 2013 onwards.

Source: Mauritius Revenue Authority for central government budgetary tax revenue data from 2007 to 2015; Statistics Mauritius for extra budgetary, local and regional government non-tax revenues from 1990 to 2015; Statistics Mauritius for budgetary central government non-tax revenues up to 2006; Ministry of Finance budget estimates for detailed revenue figures for the period July 2005-June 2008, for 2015-16 and for the figures used to estimate calendar year 2015 revenues.

StatLink https://doi.org/10.1787/888933820677

Table 5.14. **Morocco / Maroc**

Details of tax revenue / Recettes fiscales détaillées

Million MAD

	1997	2000	2005	2010	2011	2012	2013	2014	2015	2016
Recettes fiscales totales	**..**	**97 226**	**136 587**	**216 987**	**233 661**	**250 022**	**252 490**	**249 422**	**256 163**	**268 399**
1000 Impôts sur revenu, bénéfices et gains en capital	**..**	**23 656**	**42 613**	**62 646**	**69 071**	**77 317**	**75 636**	**76 342**	**78 952**	**84 111**
1100 Des personnes physiques	..	14 540	23 661	26 598	29 405	33 717	34 846	34 573	37 214	39 792
1110 Sur le revenu et les bénéfices	..	12 473	21 009	22 391	24 727	28 492	30 046	30 651	32 797	35 082
Salaires	..	10 829	18 830	19 409	21 769	25 052	25 815	26 452	28 277	30 833
Revenus professionnels	..	1 645	2 179	2 982	2 958	3 440	4 232	4 199	4 519	4 249
1120 Sur les gains en capital	..	2 067	2 653	4 207	4 678	5 225	4 799	3 922	4 417	4 710
1200 Des sociétés	..	9 116	18 952	36 049	39 667	43 600	40 790	41 769	41 738	44 319
1210 Sur les bénéfices	..	9 116	18 952	36 049	39 667	43 600	40 790	41 769	41 738	44 319
Bénéfices	..	8 870	18 484	34 266	37 799	40 561	38 792	38 459	39 598	42 303
Produits bruts versés aux sociétés étrangères	..	246	468	1 783	1 868	3 039	1 999	3 310	2 140	2 016
1220 Sur les gains en capital	..	..	..	..	..	..	..	..	..	..
1300 Non ventilables entre 1100 et 1200	..	0	0	0	0	0	0	0	0	0
2000 Cotisations de sécurité sociale	**..**	**16 309**	**22 130**	**38 142**	**43 330**	**45 568**	**47 979**	**42 476**	**43 511**	**45 974**
2100 A la charge des salariés	..	..	..	..	..	..	..	..	..	..
2110 Sur la base du salaire	..	..	..	..	..	..	..	..	..	..
2120 Sur la base de l'impôt sur les revenus	..	..	..	..	..	..	..	..	..	..
2200 A la charge des employeurs	..	..	..	..	..	..	..	..	..	..
2210 Sur la base du salaire	..	..	..	..	..	..	..	..	..	..
2220 Sur la base de l'impôt sur le revenu	..	..	..	..	..	..	..	..	..	..
2300 A charge des travailleurs indép. ou sans emploi	..	..	..	..	..	..	..	..	..	..
2310 Sur la base du salaire	..	..	..	..	..	..	..	..	..	..
2320 Sur la base de l'impôt sur le revenu	..	..	..	..	..	..	..	..	..	..
2400 Non ventilables entre 2100, 2200 et 2300	..	16 309	22 130	38 142	43 330	45 568	47 979	42 476	43 511	45 974
2410 Sur la base du salaire	..	..	..	..	..	..	..	..	..	..
2420 Sur la base de l'impôt sur le revenu	..	..	..	..	..	..	..	..	..	..
3000 Sur salaires ou main d'oeuvre	**..**	**0**	**0**	**0**	**0**	**0**	**0**	**0**	**0**	**0**
4000 Impôts sur le patrimoine	**..**	**5 405**	**8 403**	**12 702**	**13 137**	**15 456**	**17 002**	**17 926**	**19 536**	**20 182**
4100 Impôts périodiques sur la propriété immobilière	..	3 340	4 415	5 740	5 485	5 770	7 397	6 101	6 859	7 477
4110 Ménages	..	1 989	2 866	3 898	3 564	3 770	4 878	3 888	4 414	4 781
Taxe d'habitation	..	517	696	382	297	290	430	301	364	320
Taxe sur les terrains non bâtis	..	135	236	839	627	831	1 121	901	1 113	1 163
Taxe sur les services communaux	..	1 337	1 934	2 677	2 640	2 649	3 327	2 685	2 937	3 298
4120 Autres agents	..	1 351	1 549	1 842	1 920	2 000	2 519	2 213	2 445	2 696
4200 Impôts périodiques sur l'actif net	..	0	0	0	0	0	0	0	0	0
4210 Personnes physiques	..	..	..	..	..	..	..	..	..	..
4220 Sociétés	..	..	..	..	..	..	..	..	..	..
4300 Impôts sur mut. par décès, succ. et donations	..	0	0	0	0	0	0	0	0	0
4310 Impôts sur mut. par décès et successions	..	..	..	..	..	..	..	..	..	..
4320 Impôts sur les donations	..	..	..	..	..	..	..	..	..	..
4400 Impôts sur transact. mobilières et immob.	..	2 065	3 988	6 962	7 652	9 686	9 605	11 825	12 677	12 705
4500 Impôts non-périodiques	..	0	0	0	0	0	0	0	0	0
4510 Sur l'actif net	..	..	..	..	..	..	..	..	..	..
4520 Autres non-périodiques	..	..	..	..	..	..	..	..	..	..
4600 Autres impôts périodiques sur patrimoine	..	0	0	0	0	0	0	0	0	0
5000 Impôts sur les biens et services	**..**	**50 655**	**62 100**	**101 384**	**106 168**	**109 460**	**109 215**	**110 024**	**111 766**	**114 743**
5100 Impôts sur production, vente, transfert, etc.	..	49 539	60 701	99 056	103 842	106 929	106 303	107 068	108 848	111 457
5110 Impôts généraux	..	21 476	32 607	65 247	71 321	74 772	75 260	74 995	75 271	75 735
5111 Taxes sur la valeur ajoutée	..	21 476	32 607	65 247	71 321	74 772	75 260	74 995	75 271	75 735
5112 Impôts sur les ventes	..	0	0	0	0	0	0	0	0	0
5113 Autres impôts	..	0	0	0	0	0	0	0	0	0
5120 Impôts sur biens et services déterminés	..	28 063	28 094	33 809	32 521	32 157	31 043	32 073	33 577	35 722
5121 Accises	..	15 223	15 631	21 382	22 086	22 983	23 150	24 119	25 661	26 451
Taxes intérieures de consommation	..	15 183	15 544	21 132	21 861	22 731	22 873	23 849	25 366	26 134
Taxe sur la vente de produits forestiers	..	4	18	26	24	24	31	20	29	29
Taxe sur les débits de boissons	..	23	37	143	131	138	161	156	162	167
Taxe sur les eaux minerales et de table	..	13	31	81	70	90	85	94	104	121
5122 Bénéfices des monopoles fiscaux	..	0	0	0	0	0	0	0	0	0
5123 Droits de douane et droits à l'importation	..	12 810	12 386	12 242	10 262	9 003	7 681	7 738	7 715	9 074
5124 Taxes à l'exportation	..	0	0	0	0	0	0	0	0	0
5125 Impôts sur biens d'équipement	..	0	0	0	0	0	0	0	0	0
5126 Impôts sur services déterminés	..	30	77	184	174	170	212	216	201	197
Taxe de séjour	..	26	67	160	155	149	178	191	173	168
Taxe sur le transport public de voyageurs	..	4	10	24	19	21	34	25	28	29
5127 Autres impôts sur commerce et transact. internat.	..	0	0	0	0	0	0	0	0	0
5128 Autres impôts	..	0	0	0	0	0	0	0	0	0
5130 Non ventilables entre 5110 et 5120	..	0	0	0	0	0	0	0	0	0
5200 Impôts sur utilisation des biens et exerc. activites	..	1 116	1 398	2 328	2 326	2 531	2 913	2 956	2 918	3 286

Table 5.14. **Morocco / Maroc** *(cont.)*

Details of tax revenue / Recettes fiscales détaillées

Million MAD

	1997	2000	2005	2010	2011	2012	2013	2014	2015	2016
5210 Impôts périodiques	..	964	1 134	1 385	1 448	1 560	1 933	1 973	1 955	2 348
5211 A la charge des ménages: véhicules à moteur	..	959	1 119	1 351	1 418	1 525	1 898	1 937	1 920	2 310
5212 A la charge autres agents: véhicules à moteur	..	0	0	0	0	0	0	0	0	0
5213 Autres impôts périodiques	..	5	15	33	30	35	35	36	35	38
5220 Impôts non-périodiques	..	152	265	943	878	971	980	983	963	938
Taxe sur les opérations de construction	..	113	230	703	664	722	720	718	709	709
Taxe sur les opérations de lotissement	..	39	35	240	214	249	260	265	254	229
5300 Non ventilables entre 5100 et 5200	..	0	0	0	0	0	0	0	0	0
6000 Autres impôts	**..**	**1 201**	**1 341**	**2 112**	**1 955**	**2 221**	**2 657**	**2 654**	**2 398**	**3 390**
Droits de timbres	..	1 132	1 260	1 683	1 601	1 853	2 061	2 010	2 092	3 090
Taxes locales	..	69	81	429	354	368	596	644	306	300
6100 A la charge exclusive des entreprises	..	..	..	..	..	..	..	..	..	..
6200 A la charge d'autres agents	..	..	..	..	..	..	..	..	..	..

Note: Année civile se terminant le 31 décembre.
Les données sont sur la base des encaissements.
Les parts d'impôts affectées aux Comptes spéciaux du Trésor sont comprises dans les données.
Rubrique 2000 : Les données de cotisations de sécurité sociale sont estimées pour les années 2000 et 2001.
Les recettes des majorations et pénalités relatives aux impôts sont désormais considérées comme des recettes non fiscales. La classification nationale du Maroc les comptabilise comme des recettes fiscales.

Source: Ministère de l'Économie et des Finances.

StatLink https://doi.org/10.1787/888933820696

Table 5.15. **Niger**

Details of tax revenue / Recettes fiscales détaillées

Million XOF

	1997	2000	2005	2010	2011	2012	2013	2014	2015	2016
Recettes fiscales totales	..	**115 819**	**190 218**	**373 461**	**419 409**	**510 995**	**641 408**	**663 171**	**720 540**	**644 899**
1000 Impôts sur revenu, bénéfices et gains en capital	..	**20 891**	**34 848**	**94 839**	**112 673**	**165 625**	**249 555**	**208 402**	**177 695**	**170 506**
1100 Des personnes physiques	..	9 634	12 268	19 756	23 876	33 695	43 022	45 697	45 501	50 942
1110 Sur le revenu et les bénéfices	..	9 634	12 217	19 623	23 658	33 494	42 693	45 468	45 294	50 508
Impôt sur les traitements et salaires	..	8 000	11 207	18 575	22 551	32 633	41 663	44 638	44 198	49 415
Impôt synthétique	..	1 530	803	974	1 023	785	881	762	1 030	1 047
Impôt général sur le revenu (IGR)	..	103	207	74	84	77	150	68	66	47
1120 Sur les gains en capital	..	0	51	133	218	201	328	229	208	434
Plus-values de cessions immob. (IPVCI)	..	0	51	133	218	201	328	229	208	434
1200 Des sociétés	..	11 257	22 580	75 083	88 797	131 930	206 534	162 705	132 194	119 564
1210 Sur les bénéfices	..	11 257	22 580	75 083	88 797	131 930	206 534	162 705	132 194	119 564
Impôt sur les bénéfices (ISB)	..	10 933	21 605	67 863	76 340	117 387	192 631	146 385	121 448	109 509
Bénéfices non commerciaux (BNC) (arriérés)	..	126	239	0	0	0	0	0	0	0
Impôt sur le revenu des valeurs mobilières (IRVM)	..	198	736	5 695	7 665	12 767	10 428	11 484	7 900	7 966
Recettes portuaires	..	0	0	1 525	4 792	1 775	3 475	4 836	2 846	2 089
1220 Sur les gains en capital	..	0	0	0	0	0	0	0	0	0
1300 Non ventilables entre 1100 et 1200	..	0	0	0	0	0	0	0	0	0
2000 Cotisations de sécurité sociale	..	**6 216**	**7 305**	**19 950**	**22 243**	**24 740**	**29 972**	**33 610**	**34 117**	**35 453**
2100 A la charge des salariés	..	..	..	..	..	..	..	..	..	..
2110 Sur la base du salaire	..	..	..	..	..	..	..	..	..	..
2120 Sur la base de l'impôt sur les revenus	..	..	..	..	..	..	..	..	..	..
2200 A la charge des employeurs	..	..	..	..	..	..	..	..	..	..
2210 Sur la base du salaire	..	..	..	..	..	..	..	..	..	..
2220 Sur la base de l'impôt sur le revenu	..	..	..	..	..	..	..	..	..	..
2300 A charge des travailleurs indép. ou sans emploi	..	..	..	..	..	..	..	..	..	..
2310 Sur la base du salaire	..	..	..	..	..	..	..	..	..	..
2320 Sur la base de l'impôt sur le revenu	..	..	..	..	..	..	..	..	..	..
2400 Non ventilables entre 2100, 2200 et 2300	..	6 216	7 305	19 950	22 243	24 740	29 972	33 610	34 117	35 453
2410 Sur la base du salaire	..	..	..	..	..	..	..	..	..	..
2420 Sur la base de l'impôt sur le revenu	..	..	..	..	..	..	..	..	..	..
3000 Sur salaires ou main d'oeuvre	..	**401**	**533**	**1 121**	**1 513**	**1 732**	**2 816**	**3 478**	**3 978**	**3 472**
Taxe d'apprentissage (TAP)	..	401	533	1 121	1 513	1 732	2 816	3 478	3 978	3 472
4000 Impôts sur le patrimoine	..	**1 252**	**1 590**	**2 906**	**2 899**	**3 297**	**1 729**	**1 612**	**2 742**	**2 117**
4100 Impôts périodiques sur la propriété immobilière	..	1 252	1 590	2 906	2 899	3 297	1 729	1 612	2 742	2 117
Taxe immobilière	..	1 015	1 150	2 904	2 898	3 297	1 728	1 612	2 742	2 117
Taxe foncière	..	238	440	0	0	0	0	0	0	0
Impôt forfaitaire de droit de propriétés	..	0	0	2	1	0	0	0	0	0
4110 Ménages	..	..	..	..	..	..	..	..	..	..
4120 Autres agents	..	..	..	..	..	..	..	..	..	..
4200 Impôts périodiques sur l'actif net	..	0	0	0	0	0	0	0	0	0
4210 Personnes physiques	..	..	..	..	..	..	..	..	..	..
4220 Sociétés	..	..	..	..	..	..	..	..	..	..
4300 Impôts sur mut. par décès, succ. et donations	..	0	0	0	0	0	0	0	0	0
4310 Impôts sur mut. par décès et successions	..	..	..	..	..	..	..	..	..	..
4320 Impôts sur les donations	..	..	..	..	..	..	..	..	..	..
4400 Impôts sur transact. mobilières et immob.	..	0	0	0	0	0	0	0	0	0
4500 Impôts non-périodiques	..	0	0	0	0	0	0	0	0	0
4510 Sur l'actif net	..	..	..	..	..	..	..	..	..	..
4520 Autres non-périodiques	..	..	..	..	..	..	..	..	..	..
4600 Autres impôts périodiques sur patrimoine	..	0	0	0	0	0	0	0	0	0
5000 Impôts sur les biens et services	..	**83 383**	**138 312**	**234 839**	**256 826**	**284 525**	**316 593**	**370 745**	**431 233**	**392 894**
5100 Impôts sur production, vente, transfert, etc.	..	81 489	137 675	233 477	255 507	282 855	314 669	368 641	428 892	390 385
5110 Impôts généraux	..	31 766	79 938	136 966	132 886	161 766	181 930	225 855	256 546	227 121
5111 Taxes sur la valeur ajoutée	..	31 766	79 938	136 966	132 886	139 400	154 469	197 683	237 621	204 248
TVA intérieure	..	12 375	31 686	76 999	64 184	86 318	91 790	130 060	145 529	123 186
TVA à la douane (DGD)	..	19 391	48 252	59 967	68 702	53 082	62 679	67 623	92 092	81 062
5112 Impôts sur les ventes	..	0	0	0	0	0	0	0	0	0
5113 Autres impôts	..	0	0	0	0	22 366	27 461	28 171	18 925	22 873
Redevance ad valorem	..	0	0	0	0	22 366	27 461	28 171	18 925	22 873
5120 Impôts sur biens et services déterminés	..	49 722	57 737	96 511	122 621	121 089	132 739	142 787	172 345	163 263
5121 Accises	..	13 754	17 716	28 505	34 374	45 255	43 727	39 124	51 081	46 307
Taxe intérieure sur les produits pétroliers (TIPP) (y compris DGD)	..	4 313	6 654	11 694	12 860	19 146	14 195	11 913	19 375	12 703
Taxe sur les tabacs et les cigarettes	..	4 600	4 862	11 279	14 736	13 520	17 084	14 001	17 926	20 295
Taxe sur les boissons alcoolisés (TBA)	..	882	1 033	1 263	1 437	3 579	2 619	1 817	2 684	2 345
Taxe d'exploitation artisanale (TEA)	..	0	0	0	0	0	0	2	22	44
Autres droits d'accises	..	3 959	5 166	4 269	5 341	9 011	9 829	11 391	11 074	10 919
5122 Bénéfices des monopoles fiscaux	..	0	0	0	0	0	0	0	0	0

Table 5.15. **Niger** *(cont.)*

Details of tax revenue / Recettes fiscales détaillées

Million XOF

	1997	2000	2005	2010	2011	2012	2013	2014	2015	2016
5123 Droits de douane et droits à l'importation	..	22 930	26 854	36 286	42 370	36 126	45 430	46 536	59 517	53 482
Droits de douane	..	14 722	24 354	28 141	35 982	32 329	40 170	40 976	53 226	48 392
Redevance statistique à l'importation	..	1 652	2 493	8 144	6 389	3 790	5 260	5 558	6 283	5 087
Droits divers (y compris T.C.I.)	..	6 556	7	0	0	7	0	1	8	3
5124 Taxes à l'exportation	..	11 671	12 012	27 567	38 613	32 817	36 352	37 377	31 025	27 590
Taxes sur les réexportations	..	9 997	11 069	25 405	35 396	26 880	28 647	30 923	25 657	23 056
Redevance statistique à l'exportation	..	1 673	943	1 465	2 408	5 904	7 682	6 340	5 342	4 524
Taxe forfaitaire sur la réexportation et/ou transit de tabacs et cigarettes	..	0	0	696	809	33	23	113	25	10
5125 Impôts sur biens d'équipement	..	0	0	0	0	0	0	0	0	0
5126 Impôts sur services déterminés	..	1 238	901	3 080	6 157	5 772	6 614	19 074	30 399	35 691
Taxe sur la terminaison du trafic international entrant (TATTIE)	..	0	0	0	0	0	0	12 184	18 666	25 706
Taxe sur l'utilisation du réseau de télécommunication (TURTEL)	..	0	0	0	2 672	1 929	2 133	2 332	5 349	4 973
Taxe sur les recettes des loteries	..	877	104	1 303	1 517	1 835	2 040	2 238	3 377	2 474
Taxe unique sur les assurances (TUA)	..	361	792	1 490	1 607	1 725	2 114	2 007	2 310	2 291
Impôt sur les gains des loteries	..	0	5	0	26	30	29	25	550	7
Taxe sur les jeux de hasard (TJH)	..	0	0	246	301	219	294	284	140	240
Taxe sur la publicité commerciale extérieure (TPCE)	..	0	0	41	33	34	4	3	8	0
5127 Autres impôts sur commerce et transact. internat.	..	0	0	0	0	0	0	0	0	0
5128 Autres impôts	..	130	254	1 074	1 107	1 120	616	677	324	193
Droits miniers	..	130	254	1 074	1 107	1 120	616	667	295	120
Droit fixe mine	..	0	0	0	0	0	0	9	28	67
Droit fixe pétrole	..	0	0	0	0	0	0	0	1	6
5130 Non ventilables entre 5110 et 5120	..	0	0	0	0	0	0	0	0	0
5200 Impôts sur utilisation des biens et exerc. activites	..	894	637	1 362	1 319	1 670	1 925	2 104	2 341	2 509
5210 Impôts périodiques	..	529	637	1 362	1 319	1 670	1 914	2 073	2 316	2 474
Vignette	..	520	625	1 354	1 311	1 664	1 903	2 054	2 310	2 471
5211 A la charge des ménages: véhicules à moteur	..	0	0	0	0	0	0	0	0	0
5212 A la charge autres agents: véhicules à moteur	..	0	0	0	0	0	0	0	0	0
5213 Autres impôts périodiques	..	9	12	8	8	7	11	18	6	3
Permis de chasse et visite	..	0	1	0	3	1	2	9	2	0
Taxe sur les armes à feu (TAF)	..	9	11	8	5	5	8	9	4	3
5220 Impôts non-périodiques	..	365	0	0	0	0	11	31	25	35
Péage routier	..	365	..	..	..	..	0	0	0	0
Redevance plaque d'immatriculation	..	0	..	..	..	..	11	31	25	35
5300 Non ventilables entre 5100 et 5200	..	1 000	0	0	0	0	0	0	0	0
6000 Autres impôts	**..**	**3 676**	**7 630**	**19 807**	**23 255**	**31 076**	**40 743**	**45 324**	**70 775**	**40 457**
Droits d'enregistrement	..	2 166	4 834	8 048	10 981	18 026	27 711	29 642	51 113	24 353
Prélèvement pour compte des collectivités locales	..	0	0	6 512	6 731	7 671	6 463	8 161	11 727	8 577
Taxe sur certains frais généraux des entreprises (TCFGE)	..	310	776	1 963	2 266	2 323	3 211	4 060	4 132	4 045
Droits de timbre	..	1 201	2 019	3 283	3 277	3 056	3 358	3 460	3 803	3 481
6100 A la charge exclusive des entreprises	..	..	..	..	..	..	..	..	..	..
6200 A la charge d'autres agents	..	..	..	..	..	..	..	..	..	..

Note: Année civile se terminant le 31 décembre.

Les données sont sur la base des encaissements.

Les chiffres n'incluent pas les recettes fiscales collectées par les collectivités locales car elles ne sont pas disponibles.

Les recettes provenant du domaine public, des redevances minières, des redevances superficiaires des mines et du pétrole et des amendes e pénalités relatives aux impôts sont incluses dans les recettes non fiscales dans cette publication comme le préconise la classification OCDI (voir le guide d'interprétation en Annexe A). La classification du Niger comptabilise ces recettes comme des recettes fiscales.

Rubriques 5111 et 5121 : Ces rubriques contiennent des recettes provenant de la Direction Générale des Douanes (DGD) et sont annotée comme telles.

Rubrique 5220 : Cette rubrique comprend les recettes de la redevance plaques d'immatriculation collectées par la Direction Générale dı Trésor et de la Comptabilité Publique (DGTCP) entre 2005 et 2016 comme le préconise la classification OCDE (voir le guide d'interprétation eı Annexe A). La classification du Niger comptabilise ces recettes comme des recettes non fiscales.

Source: Institut National de la Statistique.

StatLink https://doi.org/10.1787/888933820715

Table 5.16. **Rwanda**

Details of tax revenue / Recettes fiscales détaillées

Million RWF

	1997	2000	2005	2010	2011	2012	2013	2014	2015	2016
Total tax revenue	**56 249**	**68 909**	**174 606**	**440 724**	**537 439**	**645 448**	**760 158**	**865 554**	**993 047**	**1 106 163**
1000 Taxes on income, profits and capital gains	**14 205**	**17 943**	**49 911**	**159 567**	**195 395**	**246 467**	**308 107**	**322 827**	**379 676**	**430 431**
1100 Of individuals	4 312	6 621	24 587	102 037	124 133	157 814	182 996	193 212	224 553	253 893
1110 On income and profits	4 312	6 621	24 587	102 037	124 133	157 814	182 996	193 212	224 553	253 893
Pay As You Earn	..	..	..	..	..	..	..	..	216 750	245 138
Rental income tax	..	..	..	..	..	..	..	..	7 803	8 754
1120 On capital gains	..	..	..	..	..	..	..	..	..	..
1200 Corporate	9 893	11 322	25 324	57 530	71 262	88 653	125 111	129 615	155 123	176 538
1210 On profits	9 893	11 322	25 324	57 530	71 262	88 653	125 111	129 615	155 123	176 538
Corporate income tax	7 245	3 603	11 606	26 459	30 756	32 815	48 962	39 157	49 571	58 645
Withholding tax	545	59	605	10 764	16 227	32 382	42 363	49 948	58 422	71 929
Personal income tax	1 045	868	2 210	7 316	7 264	7 530	7 828	6 950	7 358	8 752
Other taxes on profits	1 058	6 792	10 903	12 991	17 015	15 926	25 958	33 561	39 772	37 212
1220 On capital gains	..	..	..	..	..	..	..	..	..	..
1300 Unallocable between 1100 and 1200	0	0	0	0	0	0	0	0	0	0
2000 Social security contributions	**1 915**	**3 423**	**11 988**	**28 235**	**35 636**	**42 890**	**53 123**	**55 530**	**59 687**	**74 728**
2100 Employees	717	1 283	4 493	10 586	13 361	16 081	19 918	20 820	22 379	28 014
2110 On a payroll basis	717	1 283	4 493	10 586	13 361	16 081	19 918	20 820	22 379	28 014
2120 On an income tax basis	0	0	0	0	0	0	0	0	0	0
2200 Employers	1 196	2 138	7 488	17 644	22 269	26 802	33 197	34 701	37 299	46 702
2210 On a payroll basis	1 196	2 138	7 488	17 644	22 269	26 802	33 197	34 701	37 299	46 702
2220 On an income tax basis	0	0	0	0	0	0	0	0	0	0
2300 Self-employed or non-employed	2	3	6	4	5	7	8	9	9	11
2310 On a payroll basis	2	3	6	4	5	7	8	9	9	11
2320 On an income tax basis	0	0	0	0	0	0	0	0	0	0
2400 Unallocable between 2100, 2200 and 2300	0	0	0	0	0	0	0	0	0	0
2410 On a payroll basis	..	..	..	..	..	..	..	..	..	..
2420 On an income tax basis	..	..	..	..	..	..	..	..	..	..
3000 Taxes on payroll and workforce	**0**	**0**	**0**	**0**	**0**	**0**	**0**	**0**	**0**	**0**
4000 Taxes on property	**48**	**130**	**43**	**97**	**69**	**28**	**18**	**19**	**632**	**779**
4100 Recurrent taxes on immovable property	48	130	42	96	69	28	18	19	632	779
4110 Households	48	130	42	96	69	28	18	19	632	779
4120 Others	0	0	0	0	0	0	0	0	0	0
4200 Recurrent taxes on net wealth	0	0	0	0	0	0	0	0	0	0
4210 Individual	..	..	..	..	..	..	..	..	..	..
4220 Corporate	..	..	..	..	..	..	..	..	..	..
4300 Estate, inheritance and gift taxes	0	0	0	0	0	0	0	0	0	0
4310 Estate and inheritance taxes	..	..	..	..	..	..	..	..	..	..
4320 Gift taxes	..	..	..	..	..	..	..	..	..	..
4400 Taxes on financial and capital transactions	0	0	0	0	0	0	0	0	0	0
4500 Non-recurrent taxes	0	0	0	0	0	0	0	0	0	0
4510 On net wealth	..	..	..	..	..	..	..	..	..	..
4520 Other non-recurrent taxes	..	..	..	..	..	..	..	..	..	..
4600 Other recurrent taxes on property	0	0	1	0	0	0	0	0	0	0
5000 Taxes on goods and services	**40 081**	**47 413**	**112 664**	**252 826**	**306 339**	**356 062**	**398 910**	**487 178**	**553 053**	**600 225**
5100 Taxes on production, sale, transfer, etc	39 683	46 777	111 848	250 214	304 131	352 857	397 084	485 735	545 092	592 167
5110 General taxes	7 485	13 777	57 747	131 665	156 082	186 015	219 501	279 275	305 544	329 331
5111 Value added taxes	0	0	57 747	131 665	156 082	186 015	219 501	279 275	305 544	329 331
Gross Value Added	..	..	64 163	146 295	173 424	206 684	243 890	310 305	339 493	365 923
VAT Refunds	..	..	-6 416	-14 629	-17 342	-20 668	-24 389	-31 031	-33 949	-36 592
5112 Sales tax	7 485	13 777	0	0	0	0	0	0	0	0
5113 Other	0	0	0	0	0	0	0	0	0	0
5120 Taxes on specific goods and services	32 198	32 999	54 101	118 548	148 049	166 841	177 583	206 461	239 548	262 836
5121 Excises	11 637	18 849	22 614	75 236	98 005	99 071	105 304	121 220	134 076	134 216
Beers	8 109	7 146	9 371	22 548	28 760	33 372	34 318	36 872	45 950	42 510
Petroleum	539	7 857	6 515	30 941	40 346	33 489	35 982	37 283	47 043	49 761
Strategic Reserve Levy	0	0	0	0	0	0	0	0	4 185	9 485
Other Excises	2 988	3 846	6 728	21 746	28 900	32 210	35 003	47 065	36 899	32 461
5122 Profits of fiscal monopolies	0	0	0	0	0	0	0	0	0	0
5123 Customs and import duties	16 299	14 151	31 488	43 313	50 044	67 770	72 280	85 241	105 472	128 620
Import duties	12 447	9 260	22 071	26 215	31 413	45 891	46 448	55 106	69 731	72 062
Road Maintenance Fund	2 077	2 531	3 644	14 843	17 219	20 588	23 865	25 167	29 620	43 062
Infrastructure development levy	0	0	0	0	0	0	0	0	3 837	10 069
Other customs and import duties	1 776	2 360	5 773	2 254	1 412	1 292	1 967	4 968	2 284	3 426
5124 Taxes on exports	4 262	0	0	0	0	0	0	0	0	0
5125 Taxes on investment goods	0	0	0	0	0	0	0	0	0	0
5126 Taxes on specific services	0	0	0	0	0	0	0	0	0	0
5127 Other taxes on internat. trade and transactions	0	0	0	0	0	0	0	0	0	0

Table 5.16. **Rwanda** *(cont.)*

Details of tax revenue / Recettes fiscales détaillées

Million RWF

	1997	2000	2005	2010	2011	2012	2013	2014	2015	2016
5128 Other taxes	0	0	0	0	0	0	0	0	0	0
5130 Unallocable between 5110 and 5120	0	0	0	0	0	0	0	0	0	0
5200 Taxes on use of goods and perform activities	398	636	816	2 612	2 208	3 205	1 825	1 442	7 961	8 058
5210 Recurrent taxes	398	636	816	2 612	2 208	3 205	1 825	1 442	7 961	8 058
5211 Paid by households: motor vehicles	398	636	816	2 612	2 208	3 205	1 825	1 442	3 252	2 947
5212 Paid by others: motor vehicles	0	0	0	0	0	0	0	0	0	0
5213 Paid in respect of other goods	0	0	0	0	0	0	0	0	4 709	5 111
5220 Non-recurrent taxes	0	0	0	0	0	0	0	0	0	0
5300 Unallocable between 5100 and 5200	0	0	0	0	0	0	0	0	0	0
6000 Other taxes	**0**	**0**	**0**	**0**	**0**	**0**	**0**	**0**	**0**	**0**
6100 Paid solely by business	..	..	..	..	..	..	..	..	..	..
6200 Other	..	..	..	..	..	..	..	..	..	..

Note: Year ending 31st December. From 2008, the figures for social security contributions are on a fiscal year basis beginning 1st July. For example, data for 2016 represent July 2015 to June 2016.

The data are on a cash basis.

Figures exclude tax revenues collected by sub-national governments as the data are not available.

Figures include fines related to tax revenues as it is not possible to split these out from tax revenues. These revenues are now classified as non-tax revenues following a change in the OECD classification. Rwanda considers these revenues as tax revenues.

Heading 2000: Rwanda does not include social security contributions in their tax revenue data as the Rwandan authorities do not consider them as taxes.

Heading 5111: In this edition, data prior to 2001 have been reclassified as 5112 Sales Tax. A value-added tax replaced the sales tax in 2001.

Source: Rwanda Revenue Authority.

StatLink https://doi.org/10.1787/888933820734

Table 5.17. **Senegal / Sénégal**

Details of tax revenue / Recettes fiscales détaillées

Million XOF

	1997	2000	2005	2010	2011	2012	2013	2014	2015	2016
Recettes fiscales totales	**417 544**	**559 295**	**887 248**	**1 267 799**	**1 346 757**	**1 449 805**	**1 438 502**	**1 582 376**	**1 708 631**	**1 920 628**
1000 Impôts sur revenu, bénéfices et gains en capital	**87 500**	**123 771**	**204 800**	**328 200**	**333 200**	**384 040**	**373 800**	**398 500**	**435 600**	**516 600**
1100 Des personnes physiques	53 600	64 021	102 600	192 900	213 700	240 640	217 300	238 200	261 000	314 500
1110 Sur le revenu et les bénéfices	53 000	63 370	101 100	191 000	211 400	238 140	214 400	234 700	257 900	310 800
1120 Sur les gains en capital	600	651	1 500	1 900	2 300	2 500	2 900	3 500	3 100	3 700
1200 Des sociétés	29 000	49 418	83 900	106 100	98 000	113 900	135 700	133 800	147 300	165 500
1210 Sur les bénéfices	29 000	49 418	83 900	106 100	98 000	113 900	135 700	133 800	147 300	165 500
1220 Sur les gains en capital	..	..	..	..	..	..	..	..	..	..
1300 Non ventilables entre 1100 et 1200	4 900	10 332	18 300	29 200	21 500	29 500	20 800	26 500	27 300	36 600
2000 Cotisations de sécurité sociale	**16 474**	**22 215**	**36 568**	**72 999**	**59 627**	**90 525**	**95 782**	**99 897**	**101 760**	**129 334**
2100 A la charge des salariés	..	..	..	..	..	..	..	..	..	..
2110 Sur la base du salaire	..	..	..	..	..	..	..	..	..	..
2120 Sur la base de l'impôt sur les revenus	..	..	..	..	..	..	..	..	..	..
2200 A la charge des employeurs	..	..	..	..	..	..	..	..	..	..
2210 Sur la base du salaire	..	..	..	..	..	..	..	..	..	..
2220 Sur la base de l'impôt sur le revenu	..	..	..	..	..	..	..	..	..	..
2300 A charge des travailleurs indép. ou sans emploi	..	..	..	..	..	..	..	..	..	..
2310 Sur la base du salaire	..	..	..	..	..	..	..	..	..	..
2320 Sur la base de l'impôt sur le revenu	..	..	..	..	..	..	..	..	..	..
2400 Non ventilables entre 2100, 2200 et 2300	16 474	22 215	36 568	72 999	59 627	90 525	95 782	99 897	101 760	129 334
Institution de Prévoyance Retraite du Sénégal (IPRES)	16 474	22 215	36 568	72 999	59 627	67 611	72 493	73 446	74 958	101 359
Caisse de Sécurité Sociale (CSS)	..	..	..	..	..	22 914	23 289	26 451	26 802	27 975
2410 Sur la base du salaire	..	..	..	..	..	..	..	..	..	..
2420 Sur la base de l'impôt sur le revenu	..	..	..	..	..	..	..	..	..	..
3000 Sur salaires ou main d'oeuvre	**5 650**	**6 668**	**9 440**	**10 800**	**12 400**	**15 100**	**16 100**	**16 900**	**20 200**	**17 310**
4000 Impôts sur le patrimoine	**9 900**	**11 200**	**23 200**	**39 100**	**38 200**	**37 200**	**36 600**	**39 600**	**41 500**	**51 984**
4100 Impôts périodiques sur la propriété immobilière	0	0	0	0	0	0	0	0	0	0
4110 Ménages	..	..	..	..	..	..	..	..	..	..
4120 Autres agents	..	..	..	..	..	..	..	..	..	..
4200 Impôts périodiques sur l'actif net	0	0	0	0	0	0	0	0	0	0
4210 Personnes physiques	..	..	..	..	..	..	..	..	..	..
4220 Sociétés	..	..	..	..	..	..	..	..	..	..
4300 Impôts sur mut. par décès, succ. et donations	2 178	2 464	5 104	12 445	9 669	7 651	7 809	8 086	13 060	14 872
4310 Impôts sur mut. par décès et successions	..	..	..	..	..	..	..	..	..	..
4320 Impôts sur les donations	..	..	..	..	..	..	..	..	..	..
4400 Impôts sur transact. mobilières et immob.	7 722	8 736	18 096	26 655	28 531	29 549	28 791	31 514	28 440	37 111
Droits de mutation (immeubles)	..	..	..	15 418	15 710	19 398	15 713	18 352	11 267	11 685
Droits d'enregistrement autre que patrimoine	..	..	..	11 237	12 821	10 151	13 078	13 162	17 173	25 426
4500 Impôts non-périodiques	0	0	0	0	0	0	0	0	0	0
4510 Sur l'actif net	..	..	..	..	..	..	..	..	..	..
4520 Autres non-périodiques	..	..	..	..	..	..	..	..	..	..
4600 Autres impôts périodiques sur patrimoine	0	0	0	0	0	0	0	0	0	0
5000 Impôts sur les biens et services	**291 820**	**386 940**	**601 700**	**804 400**	**890 330**	**910 440**	**900 820**	**1 010 679**	**1 086 871**	**1 187 100**
5100 Impôts sur production, vente, transfert, etc.	289 920	384 590	597 700	799 400	884 330	904 440	894 420	1 002 679	1 078 171	1 175 000
5110 Impôts généraux	146 240	221 410	354 800	478 000	519 200	529 700	512 200	561 400	617 000	651 300
5111 Taxes sur la valeur ajoutée	146 240	221 410	354 800	478 000	519 200	529 700	512 200	561 400	617 000	651 300
5112 Impôts sur les ventes	0	0	0	0	0	0	0	0	0	0
5113 Autres impôts	0	0	0	0	0	0	0	0	0	0
5120 Impôts sur biens et services déterminés	143 680	163 180	242 900	321 400	365 130	374 740	382 220	441 279	461 171	523 700
5121 Accises	6 140	61 100	82 700	82 600	77 800	79 800	76 095	84 079	88 821	106 600
Taxe spécifique sur les produits pétroliers	..	..	62 600	63 900	55 600	53 800	53 740	59 579	61 520	73 759
Taxes sur les tabacs	..	..	8 483	9 647	9 931	13 116	13 205	13 289	14 565	15 252
Taxes sur les corps gras	..	..	4 148	978	993	1 375	2 648	1 447	1 964	4 712
Taxes sur les alcools	..	..	3 535	5 297	5 278	4 975	5 498	5 382	5 516	6 824
Taxe sur la cola	..	..	278	273	203	183	48	26	19	8
Taxe sur les thés	..	..	121	154	95	102	125	124	153	228
Taxe sur le café	..	..	140	175	216	153	285	367	428	441
Taxe sur les produits comestiques	..	..	0	0	0	0	500	1 400	1 465	1 604
Autres accises non classées ailleurs	..	..	3 395	2 176	5 484	6 096	45	2 466	3 189	3 771
5122 Bénéfices des monopoles fiscaux	0	0	0	0	0	0	0	0	0	0
5123 Droits de douane et droits à l'importation	129 500	90 340	138 900	181 600	203 800	195 200	218 000	221 100	227 600	234 600
5124 Taxes à l'exportation	0	0	0	0	0	0	0	0	0	0
5125 Impôts sur biens d'équipement	0	0	0	0	0	0	0	0	0	0
5126 Impôts sur services déterminés	8 040	11 740	21 300	45 000	55 900	62 500	63 825	69 500	71 200	76 100
Taxe sur les activités financières (TAF)	6 400	9 340	17 600	30 600	34 300	39 100	40 340	45 800	47 700	51 600
Redevance d'utilisation des télécommunications	0	0	0	10 000	16 700	18 600	18 645	18 700	19 500	18 600
Taxe sur les contrats d'assurances	1 640	2 400	3 700	4 400	4 900	4 800	4 840	5 000	4 000	5 900

Table 5.17. **Senegal / Sénégal** *(cont.)*

Details of tax revenue / Recettes fiscales détaillées

Million XOF

	1997	2000	2005	2010	2011	2012	2013	2014	2015	2016
5127 Autres impôts sur commerce et transact. internat.	0	0	0	0	0	0	0	0	0	0
5128 Autres impôts	0	0	0	12 200	27 630	37 240	24 300	66 600	73 551	106 400
Fonds de sécurisation des importations de produits pétroliers	..	..	..	12 200	27 630	32 240	19 400	62 600	69 451	104 600
Contributions spéciales (mines et carrières)	..	..	..	0	0	5 000	4 900	4 000	4 100	1 800
5130 Non ventilables entre 5110 et 5120	0	0	0	0	0	0	0	0	0	0
5200 Impôts sur utilisation des biens et exerc. activites	1 900	2 350	4 000	5 000	6 000	6 000	6 400	8 000	8 700	12 100
5210 Impôts périodiques	1 900	2 350	4 000	5 000	6 000	6 000	6 400	8 000	8 700	12 100
5211 A la charge des ménages: véhicules à moteur	..	..	..	..	..	..	..	..	..	..
5212 A la charge autres agents: véhicules à moteur	..	..	..	..	..	..	..	..	..	..
5213 Autres impôts périodiques	..	..	..	..	..	..	..	..	..	..
5220 Impôts non-périodiques	0	0	0	0	0	0	0	0	0	0
5300 Non ventilables entre 5100 et 5200	0	0	0	0	0	0	0	0	0	0
6000 Autres impôts	**6 200**	**8 500**	**11 540**	**12 300**	**13 000**	**12 500**	**15 400**	**16 800**	**22 700**	**18 300**
6100 A la charge exclusive des entreprises	..	..	..	..	..	..	..	..	..	..
6200 A la charge d'autres agents	..	..	..	..	..	..	..	..	..	..

Note: Année civile se terminant le 31 décembre.

Les données sont sur la base des encaissements.

Les chiffres n'incluent pas les recettes fiscales collectées par les collectivités locales car elles ne sont pas disponibles.

Les chiffres ne comprennent pas les taxes parafiscales car elles ne sont pas disponibles. Les taxes parafiscales pourraient s'élever à un montant d'environ 70 milliards, objectif programmé du gouvernement dans la loi de finances 2015.

La rubrique 2000 comprend les cotisations de sécurité sociale de l'Institution de prévoyance retraite du Sénégal (IPRES) à partir de 2006 et pour la première fois pour cette édition les cotisations de sécurité sociale de la Caisse de Sécurité Sociale (CSS) à partir de 2012. Les cotisations de sécurité sociale au Sénégal antérieures à 2006 sont estimées. Les chiffres de 2016 restent à titre indicatif.

La rubrique 5126 comprend la redevance sur l'accès ou l'utilisation du réseau des télécommunications publiques (RUTEL) classifiée comme accise au Sénégal.

Les recettes fiscales incluent les amendes et pénalités sur impôts et taxes considérées comme des recettes non fiscales. Il n'a pas été possible pour cette édition de séparer le versement des amendes et pénalités des recettes correspondant aux impôts auxquels ces amendes et pénalités se rattachent. La classification nationale du Sénégal les comptabilise comme des recettes fiscales.

Source: Ministère de l'Économie, des Finances et du Plan.

StatLink https://doi.org/10.1787/888933820753

Table 5.18. **South Africa / Afrique du Sud**

Details of tax revenue / Recettes fiscales détaillées

Million ZAR

	1997	2000	2005	2010	2011	2012	2013	2014	2015	2016
Total tax revenue	**158 556**	**211 561**	**418 823**	**681 333**	**766 967**	**859 587**	**958 015**	**1 050 810**	**1 170 499**	**1 242 771**
1000 Taxes on income, profits and capital gains	**89 772**	**119 979**	**220 197**	**368 118**	**412 135**	**447 923**	**490 305**	**543 216**	**608 227**	**644 259**
1100 Of individuals	65 681	87 105	122 279	219 886	243 056	267 952	300 559	340 708	393 232	418 548
1110 On income and profits	65 681	87 105	122 279	219 886	243 056	267 952	300 559	340 708	393 232	418 548
Employees tax	..	..	..	213 113	238 108	264 366	295 824	332 863	379 535	402 200
PIT Provisional tax	..	..	..	15 719	14 826	15 888	17 188	19 944	24 200	27 313
PIT Assessment payments	..	..	..	7 425	6 820	7 183	8 849	8 682	9 970	11 594
PIT Refunds	..	..	..	-16 372	-16 698	-19 485	-21 301	-20 781	-20 474	-22 559
1120 On capital gains	..	..	..	..	..	..	..	..	..	..
1200 Corporate	19 409	23 987	82 628	132 275	149 777	155 751	173 738	182 022	191 348	200 765
1210 On profits	19 409	23 987	82 628	132 275	149 777	155 751	173 738	182 022	191 348	200 765
CIT Provisional tax	..	..	..	136 615	155 438	162 076	177 034	181 491	190 437	202 636
CIT Assessment payments	..	..	..	9 051	9 078	9 279	9 170	12 040	11 119	10 291
Royalties	..	..	..	161	201	248	325	276	369	544
CIT Refunds	..	..	..	-13 552	-14 940	-15 852	-12 791	-11 784	-10 577	-12 706
1220 On capital gains	..	..	..	..	..	..	..	..	..	..
1300 Unallocable between 1100 and 1200	4 682	8 887	15 290	15 957	19 303	24 220	16 008	20 486	23 647	24 946
2000 Social security contributions	**0**	**0**	**6 477**	**11 117**	**12 557**	**14 078**	**14 181**	**15 600**	**17 136**	**17 785**
2100 Employees	..	..	3 254	5 740	6 583	7 184	7 226	7 931	8 722	9 048
2110 On a payroll basis	..	..	31	363	610	290	271	263	308	312
2120 On an income tax basis	..	..	3 223	5 377	5 973	6 894	6 955	7 668	8 414	8 737
2200 Employers	..	..	3 223	5 377	5 973	6 894	6 955	7 668	8 414	8 737
2210 On a payroll basis	..	..	0	0	0	0	0	0	0	0
2220 On an income tax basis	..	..	3 223	5 377	5 973	6 894	6 955	7 668	8 414	8 737
2300 Self-employed or non-employed	..	..	0	0	0	0	0	0	0	0
2310 On a payroll basis	..	..	..	..	..	..	..	..	..	..
2320 On an income tax basis	..	..	..	..	..	..	..	..	..	..
2400 Unallocable between 2100, 2200 and 2300	..	..	0	0	0	0	0	0	0	0
2410 On a payroll basis	..	..	..	..	..	..	..	..	..	..
2420 On an income tax basis	..	..	..	..	..	..	..	..	..	..
3000 Taxes on payroll and workforce	**0**	**870**	**4 839**	**8 240**	**9 885**	**11 334**	**11 900**	**13 264**	**15 111**	**15 092**
4000 Taxes on property	**2 592**	**3 829**	**23 530**	**40 108**	**42 238**	**46 295**	**51 453**	**58 303**	**59 110**	**67 554**
4100 Recurrent taxes on immovable property	0	0	12 906	31 041	33 984	38 150	41 421	46 291	44 618	51 668
4110 Households	..	..	12 258	30 533	33 502	37 659	40 896	45 807	44 169	51 133
4120 Others	..	..	648	508	482	491	525	484	449	535
4200 Recurrent taxes on net wealth	0	0	0	0	0	0	0	0	0	0
4210 Individual	..	..	..	..	..	..	..	..	..	..
4220 Corporate	..	..	..	..	..	..	..	..	..	..
4300 Estate, inheritance and gift taxes	304	436	626	855	1 065	887	1 266	1 519	2 065	1 832
4310 Estate and inheritance taxes	287	417	598	794	1 013	820	1 163	1 349	1 918	1 612
4320 Gift taxes	17	19	28	61	53	67	103	170	147	220
4400 Taxes on financial and capital transactions	439	1 094	1 718	2 912	2 919	3 147	3 617	4 098	5 069	6 081
4500 Non-recurrent taxes	1 850	2 299	8 280	5 300	4 270	4 112	5 149	6 394	7 358	7 974
4510 On net wealth	0	0	0	0	0	0	0	0	0	0
4520 Other non-recurrent taxes	1 850	2 299	8 280	5 300	4 270	4 112	5 149	6 394	7 358	7 974
4600 Other recurrent taxes on property	0	0	0	0	0	0	0	0	0	0
5000 Taxes on goods and services	**64 471**	**84 462**	**162 918**	**253 728**	**290 172**	**339 927**	**390 171**	**420 457**	**470 916**	**498 073**
5100 Taxes on production, sale, transfer, etc	64 471	84 462	159 589	248 406	284 098	333 186	382 810	412 874	463 058	489 342
5110 General taxes	39 461	52 054	109 274	170 548	194 296	207 480	231 545	256 482	277 532	294 694
5111 Value added taxes	39 461	52 054	109 274	170 552	194 295	207 472	231 528	256 464	277 530	294 674
Domestic VAT	21 211	52 547	126 492	202 535	214 673	237 373	258 213	281 236	303 285	314 734
VAT on Imports	18 250	25 148	42 615	78 645	94 286	109 839	124 906	134 535	148 392	150 986
VAT Refunds	0	-25 641	-59 833	-110 627	-114 664	-139 740	-151 592	-159 307	-174 147	-171 046
5112 Sales tax	0	0	0	-5	1	9	16	17	2	20
5113 Other	0	0	0	0	0	0	0	0	0	0
5120 Taxes on specific goods and services	25 010	32 408	50 315	77 858	89 802	125 706	151 265	156 392	185 526	194 647
5121 Excises	19 091	24 341	35 490	76 239	87 407	96 044	103 156	112 440	137 512	143 337
Specific excise tax - Domestic	..	..	..	22 448	25 216	27 671	28 290	31 400	34 588	35 714
Ad valorem excise - Domestic	..	..	..	1 569	1 756	2 093	2 198	2 848	3 295	3 238
Fuel levy	..	..	..	32 758	36 568	39 248	42 656	46 802	56 694	61 064
Plastic bags	..	..	..	177	-26	286	200	139	213	221
Electricity levy	..	..	..	5 065	6 157	7 324	8 968	8 541	8 481	8 507
Incandescent light bulb levy	..	..	..	180	125	148	116	68	35	66
CO_2 tax - motor vehicle emissions	..	..	..	205	1 545	1 571	1 669	1 591	1 429	1 177
RAF	..	..	..	13 837	16 067	17 702	19 058	21 051	32 778	33 350
5122 Profits of fiscal monopolies	0	0	0	0	0	0	0	0	0	0

Table 5.18. **South Africa / Afrique du Sud** *(cont.)*

Details of tax revenue / Recettes fiscales détaillées

Million ZAR

	1997	2000	2005	2010	2011	2012	2013	2014	2015	2016
5123 Customs and import duties	6 273	7 714	13 294	0	0	26 544	42 794	41 857	43 965	47 438
Import duties	..	..	..	0	0	20 430	30 708	31 616	32 130	33 855
Ad valorem Imported	..	..	..	0	0	4 251	8 011	7 573	8 495	8 701
Excise Imported	..	..	..	0	0	1 862	4 076	2 668	3 340	4 882
5124 Taxes on exports	0	0	0	61	65	60	72	118	121	116
5125 Taxes on investment goods	0	0	0	0	0	0	0	0	0	0
5126 Taxes on specific services	0	0	1 320	2 252	2 404	2 792	2 967	2 992	3 224	3 401
5127 Other taxes on internat. trade and transactions	-354	353	211	-695	-74	266	2 276	-1 015	703	355
5128 Other taxes	0	0	0	0	0	0	0	0	0	0
5130 Unallocable between 5110 and 5120	0	0	0	0	0	0	0	0	0	0
5200 Taxes on use of goods and perform activities	0	0	3 328	5 322	6 073	6 741	7 361	7 583	7 858	8 732
5210 Recurrent taxes	..	..	3 328	5 322	6 073	6 741	7 361	7 583	7 858	8 732
5211 Paid by households: motor vehicles	..	..	2 644	4 046	4 762	5 224	5 742	5 879	6 234	6 565
5212 Paid by others: motor vehicles	..	..	661	1 012	1 191	1 306	1 435	1 470	1 558	1 641
5213 Paid in respect of other goods	..	..	23	264	120	210	184	234	66	525
5220 Non-recurrent taxes	0	0	0	0	0	0	0	0	0	0
5300 Unallocable between 5100 and 5200	0	0	0	0	0	0	0	0	0	0
6000 Other taxes	**1 721**	**2 420**	**863**	**23**	**-20**	**29**	**5**	**-29**	**-1**	**9**
6100 Paid solely by business	0	0	0	0	0	0	0	0	0	0
6200 Other	1 721	2 420	863	23	-20	29	5	-29	-1	9
Stamp duties and fees	..	..	..	9	-1	-1	31	0	0	0
Unallocated Tax Revenue	..	..	..	14	-19	30	-26	-29	-1	9

Table 5.18. **South Africa / Afrique du Sud** *(cont.)*

Details of tax revenue / Recettes fiscales détaillées

Note: Year ending 31st December. Some fiscal year data have been adjusted to align to calendar years. Social security contributions and taxes at provincial and local level are reported on a fiscal year basis beginning 1st April. For example, the data for 2016 represent April 2016 to March 2017.

Data prior to 1995/96 were restated retrospectively to aggregate the revenues from TBVC States and Self-Governing Territories.

With the adoption of the interim Constitution in 1994, these were abolished.

-TBVC States: Transkei, Bophuthatswana, Venda and Ciskei.

-Self-Governing Territories: Gazankulu, Kangwane, Kwandebele, Kwazulu, Lebowa and Qwaqwa.

Tax revenues on national and provincial government level in South Africa are on a cash basis, while local authorities and public entities are on an accrual basis.

Tax revenues at the local and provincial levels are only available from 2003 (representing fiscal year 2003/04).

Headings 1110 and 1120: The figures include Capital Gains Tax (CGT). CGT cannot been listed separately under 1120 and 1220 because the data that South African Revenue Service (SARS) collated for CGT are for liability raised and not actual CGT collections received. The figures exclude interest and fines from 1994 onwards.

Heading 1300: includes revenue from the small business tax amnesty, the tax on retirement funds, the SDC/dividends tax and other small revenues.

Heading 2000: the social security contributions in South Africa consist of contributions to the Unemployment Insurance Fund (UIF). Standard practice in South Africa is to classify UIF under non-tax revenue. The methodology applied in the compilation of the data was to allocate 50% of the total social security contributions (UIF) to each of employees and employers.

Heading 4120: the figures refer to penalties and collection charges on property rates.

Heading 5111: includes interests and fines.

Heading 5121: following the OECD classification, the Road Accident Fund (RAF) is classified as an excise. The national classification of South Africa classifies this revenue as a social security contribution.

Headings 5121 and 5123: The data for customs duties and excise include revenue on import duties plus specific and ad valorem excise duties that will be paid to Botswana, Eswatini, Lesotho and Namibia (BELN) through the revenue sharing agreement.

Heading 5123: SARS only started separately reporting ordinary custom duties on imported goods, specific excise duties on imported goods and ad valorem duties on imported goods from April 2012. From April 2014 onwards, the Customs Duty amounts for the specific tariff headings under chapter 27 (Mineral Fuels) were treated as fuel levies (5121 Excises).

Headings 5127 and 6200: include negative figures due to refund accounting adjustments.

Heading 5211: an 80:20 ratio was used to split provincial recurrent motor vehicle taxes based on research about South Africa's commercial and private household motor vehicle fleet.

Heading 6200: includes stamp duties and fees plus unallocated tax revenue.

Taxes that were discontinued and introduced (causing breaks in the data) include the following:

a. Ordinary levy discontinued in March 2003 (heading 5127).

b. Demutualisation charge has been included in heading 4400. There were two collections in March 1999 and August 1999.

c. Secondary Tax on Companies (STC) in heading 1300 effective from July 1993 and changed to Dividends Tax (DT) in April 2012.

d. Small business tax amnesty (heading 1300) effective from March 2007.

e. VAT (heading 5111) effective from September 1991 at a rate of 10% and increased to 14% in 1993. Prior to that, sales tax data was restated to VAT.

f. Levy on financial services (heading 4400) effective from January 1992.

g. Skills development levy (heading 3000) effective from May 2000.

h. Excises (5121)

- Plastic bags effective from June 2005.
- Electricity levy effective from August 2009.
- Incandescent light bulbs effective from March 2010.
- CO_2 tax effective from September 2010.

i. Air departure tax (heading 5126) effective from December 2000.

j. Universal services fund (heading 5213) effective from March 2006.

Source: Data on national government taxation from the South African Revenue Service (SARS); data on social security contributions, and taxes levied at the provincial and local level from the National Treasury of South Africa.

StatLink https://doi.org/10.1787/888933820772

Table 5.19. **Togo**

Details of tax revenue / Recettes fiscales détaillées

Million XOF

	1997	2000	2005	2010	2011	2012	2013	2014	2015	2016
Recettes fiscales totales	..	**100 017**	**159 896**	**254 242**	**328 123**	**375 436**	**416 628**	**472 307**	**534 357**	**587 505**
1000 Impôts sur revenu, bénéfices et gains en capital	..	**21 640**	**39 315**	**43 948**	**52 088**	**54 449**	**79 422**	**96 011**	**97 374**	**137 065**
1100 Des personnes physiques	..	8 962	16 158	15 677	17 294	19 057	24 686	17 935	23 848	28 542
1110 Sur le revenu et les bénéfices	..	8 962	16 158	15 677	17 294	19 057	24 686	17 935	23 848	28 542
Impôt sur le revenu (IR) des transporteurs routiers	..	451	514	393	186	265	204	266	374	487
Retenue sur les revenus des capitaux mobiliers	..	912	1 582	5 071	4 040	3 131	4 457	3 454	3 456	5 276
IR des personnes physiques	..	7 598	14 062	10 212	13 069	15 658	20 023	14 215	20 018	22 773
IR des personnes physiques (transferts aux collectivités locales)	..	..	..	1	0	3	2	0	0	5
1120 Sur les gains en capital	..	0	0	0	0	0	0	0	0	0
1200 Des sociétés	..	12 678	23 157	28 271	34 794	35 392	54 736	78 076	73 526	108 523
1210 Sur les bénéfices	..	12 678	23 157	28 271	34 794	35 392	54 736	78 076	73 526	108 523
Impôt sur les sociétés	..	7 672	13 440	13 435	19 363	19 139	28 622	31 195	35 840	42 354
Recouvrement des exercices antérieurs	..	2 525	5 878	9 919	12 644	13 776	23 247	41 104	30 996	58 113
Prélèvement bénéf. industriels et commerciaux (BIC)	..	2 481	3 839	4 917	2 787	2 477	2 867	5 776	6 691	8 056
1220 Sur les gains en capital	..	0	0	0	0	0	0	0	0	0
1300 Non ventilables entre 1100 et 1200	..	0	0	0	0	0	0	0	0	0
2000 Cotisations de sécurité sociale	..	..	..	..	..	..	..	..	..	..
2100 A la charge des salariés	..	..	..	..	..	..	..	..	..	..
2110 Sur la base du salaire	..	..	..	..	..	..	..	..	..	..
2120 Sur la base de l'impôt sur les revenus	..	..	..	..	..	..	..	..	..	..
2200 A la charge des employeurs	..	..	..	..	..	..	..	..	..	..
2210 Sur la base du salaire	..	..	..	..	..	..	..	..	..	..
2220 Sur la base de l'impôt sur le revenu	..	..	..	..	..	..	..	..	..	..
2300 A charge des travailleurs indép. ou sans emploi	..	..	..	..	..	..	..	..	..	..
2310 Sur la base du salaire	..	..	..	..	..	..	..	..	..	..
2320 Sur la base de l'impôt sur le revenu	..	..	..	..	..	..	..	..	..	..
2400 Non ventilables entre 2100, 2200 et 2300	..	..	..	..	..	..	..	..	..	..
2410 Sur la base du salaire	..	..	..	..	..	..	..	..	..	..
2420 Sur la base de l'impôt sur le revenu	..	..	..	..	..	..	..	..	..	..
3000 Sur salaires ou main d'oeuvre	..	**1 865**	**2 213**	**4 879**	**4 529**	**5 579**	**4 865**	**7 911**	**3 639**	**3 889**
Taxe complémentaire à l'impôt sur le revenu	..	36	70	1 044	538	1 015	1 220	5 159	630	572
Taxes/salaires	..	1 829	2 144	3 702	3 851	4 380	3 415	2 440	2 698	2 928
Taxe complémentaire à l'Impôt sur le revenu (transferts aux collectivités locales)	..	..	..	134	140	183	230	312	311	389
4000 Impôts sur le patrimoine	..	**339**	**519**	**1 668**	**1 832**	**2 144**	**2 519**	**3 447**	**3 756**	**3 923**
4100 Impôts périodiques sur la propriété immobilière	..	339	519	1 668	1 832	2 144	2 519	3 447	3 756	3 923
Taxe foncière sur les propriétés bâties	..	243	355	425	480	504	469	699	861	664
Droits d'immatriculation des propriétés foncières	..	96	164	335	355	487	502	521	613	783
Taxe d'enlèvement des ordures (transferts aux collectivités locales)	..	..	..	129	129	156	212	288	315	360
Taxe foncière sur les propriétés bâties (transferts aux collectivités locales)	..	..	..	553	695	726	977	1 551	1 404	1 494
4110 Ménages	..	0	0	226	174	270	359	388	563	623
Taxe d'habitation (transferts aux collectivités locales)	..	..	..	226	174	270	359	388	563	623
4120 Autres agents	..	0	0	0	0	0	0	0	0	0
4200 Impôts périodiques sur l'actif net	..	0	0	0	0	0	0	0	0	0
4210 Personnes physiques	..	..	..	..	..	..	..	..	..	..
4220 Sociétés	..	..	..	..	..	..	..	..	..	..
4300 Impôts sur mut. par décès, succ. et donations	..	0	0	0	0	0	0	0	0	0
4310 Impôts sur mut. par décès et successions	..	..	..	..	..	..	..	..	..	..
4320 Impôts sur les donations	..	..	..	..	..	..	..	..	..	..
4400 Impôts sur transact. mobilières et immob.	..	0	0	0	0	0	0	0	0	0
4500 Impôts non-périodiques	..	0	0	0	0	0	0	0	0	0
4510 Sur l'actif net	..	..	..	..	..	..	..	..	..	..
4520 Autres non-périodiques	..	..	..	..	..	..	..	..	..	..
4600 Autres impôts périodiques sur patrimoine	..	0	0	0	0	0	0	0	0	0
5000 Impôts sur les biens et services	..	**74 249**	**115 428**	**198 311**	**262 529**	**306 524**	**321 018**	**355 839**	**421 368**	**438 001**
5100 Impôts sur production, vente, transfert, etc.	..	74 148	115 286	197 915	261 998	305 864	320 200	354 407	419 655	436 016
5110 Impôts généraux	..	36 489	63 068	113 329	166 051	198 276	183 938	211 447	245 065	255 661
5111 Taxes sur la valeur ajoutée	..	35 655	62 014	108 743	160 911	192 124	175 635	200 493	231 388	240 029
Taxe sur la valeur ajoutée (Douanes)	..	25 101	44 182	69 840	89 433	98 240	97 847	128 864	161 480	168 358
Taxe sur la valeur ajoutée (Intérieure)	..	10 553	17 832	35 203	38 978	51 344	39 114	57 653	64 160	67 594
Soutien à la politique pétrolière	..	0	0	3 700	32 500	42 540	38 675	13 976	5 748	4 077
5112 Impôts sur les ventes	..	0	0	0	0	0	0	0	0	0

Table 5.19. **Togo** *(cont.)*

Details of tax revenue / Recettes fiscales détaillées

Million XOF

	1997	2000	2005	2010	2011	2012	2013	2014	2015	2016
5113 Autres impôts	..	834	1 054	4 586	5 140	6 152	8 302	10 954	13 677	15 632
Taxe professionnelle unique	..	143	148	317	365	357	312	346	471	475
Taxe professionnelle	..	691	906	1 451	1 650	1 950	3 042	3 629	6 006	7 590
Taxe professionnelle unique (transferts aux collectivités locales)	..	..	..	206	190	241	332	423	507	572
Taxe professionnelle (transferts aux collectivités locales)	..	..	..	2 613	2 936	3 604	4 616	6 556	6 693	6 995
5120 Impôts sur biens et services déterminés	..	37 634	52 191	84 553	95 913	107 578	136 262	142 959	174 590	180 355
5121 Accises	..	12 750	14 721	16 090	15 862	20 206	30 270	29 358	35 126	43 517
Droits d'accises/produits pétroliers	..	11 738	11 771	11 468	12 748	13 947	19 722	16 850	17 954	20 941
Autres droits d'accises	..	1 012	2 950	4 622	3 114	6 259	3 847	7 033	8 240	10 741
Prélèvement dette secteur pétrolier	..	0	0	0	0	0	6 701	5 474	8 932	11 836
5122 Bénéfices des monopoles fiscaux	..	0	0	0	0	0	0	0	0	0
5123 Droits de douane et droits à l'importation	..	22 559	35 143	61 676	71 528	76 984	93 471	99 201	122 750	119 825
Droits de douane	..	18 519	30 023	52 941	60 999	65 744	80 115	83 234	101 730	98 020
Redevance statistique	..	2 717	3 720	6 763	7 968	8 379	10 103	12 740	13 578	14 021
Timbre douanier	..	94	138	297	321	336	424	359	424	298
Cartes et vignettes	..	186	209	237	372	441	406	385	369	600
Taxe de protection et d'entretien des infrastructures	..	1 039	1 050	1 434	1 863	2 078	2 418	2 476	2 958	3 252
Produits des crédits en douane	..	2	2	2	1	1	4	6	5	9
Prélèvement national de solidarité	..	0	0	0	0	0	0	0	3 686	3 625
Remises	..	1	0	0	0	0	0	0	0	0
Entrepôts fictifs	..	1	2	2	3	4	0	1	0	0
5124 Taxes à l'exportation	..	302	314	1 430	1 756	1 506	1 881	2 544	2 728	2 476
Taxe spéciale de réexportation	..	302	314	1 430	1 756	1 506	1 235	1 947	2 260	2 015
Redevance minière (66,67%)	..	0	0	0	0	0	646	597	468	461
5125 Impôts sur biens d'équipement	..	0	0	0	0	0	0	0	0	0
5126 Impôts sur services déterminés	..	2 022	2 012	5 357	6 767	8 882	10 641	11 857	13 987	14 537
Taxe sur les produits des jeux de hasard	..	149	201	343	280	736	882	643	899	1 047
Taxe/convention d'assurance	..	207	332	747	811	1 158	1 227	1 275	1 812	2 086
Taxe sur les activités financières	..	1 666	1 480	4 171	5 594	6 871	8 377	9 756	11 035	11 142
Taxe sur les produits des jeux de hasard (transferts aux collectivités locales)	..	..	..	94	76	116	151	171	228	262
Taxe sur les spectacles (transferts aux collectivités locales)	..	..	..	2	6	1	5	13	13	0
5127 Autres impôts sur commerce et transact. internat.	..	0	0	0	0	0	0	0	0	0
5128 Autres impôts	..	0	0	0	0	0	0	0	0	0
5130 Non ventilables entre 5110 et 5120	..	25	28	33	34	10	0	0	0	0
5200 Impôts sur utilisation des biens et exerc. activites	..	101	141	396	530	660	818	1 432	1 713	1 985
5210 Impôts périodiques	..	101	141	396	530	660	818	1 432	1 713	1 985
5211 A la charge des ménages: véhicules à moteur	..	0	0	0	0	0	0	0	0	0
5212 A la charge autres agents: véhicules à moteur	..	0	0	0	0	0	3	26	61	98
5213 Autres impôts périodiques	..	101	141	396	530	660	814	1 406	1 652	1 887
Taxe spéc. sur la fabric. et le commerce des boissons	..	101	141	132	258	330	375	797	1 027	1 130
Taxe spéc. sur la fabric. et le commerce des boissons (transferts aux collectivités locales)	..	..	..	264	273	331	439	609	625	757
5220 Impôts non-périodiques	..	0	0	0	0	0	0	0	0	0
5300 Non ventilables entre 5100 et 5200	..	0	0	0	0	0	0	0	0	0
6000 Autres impôts	**..**	**1 922**	**2 422**	**5 437**	**7 146**	**6 740**	**8 805**	**9 099**	**8 220**	**4 628**
Droits de timbres	..	1 457	1 637	3 078	2 655	3 250	2 849	2 760	3 418	3 623
Droits d'enregistrement	..	465	784	2 317	4 488	3 405	5 891	6 333	4 800	791
Taxe d'enregistrement (transferts aux collectivités locales)	..	..	..	41	3	86	64	6	2	214
6100 A la charge exclusive des entreprises	..	..	..	..	..	..	..	..	..	..
6200 A la charge d'autres agents	..	..	..	..	..	..	..	..	..	..

Table 5.19. **Togo** *(cont.)*

Details of tax revenue / Recettes fiscales détaillées

Note: Année civile se terminant le 31 décembre.

Les données sont sur la base des encaissements.

Les chiffres sous les rubriques 1110, 3000, 4100, 5113, 5126, 5213, et 6000 incluent pour la première fois les recettes recouvrées par l'administration fiscale togolaise pour le compte des collectivités locales. Ce traitement s'applique sur la période 2008-16 et les lignes concernées sont mises en exergue avec la mention « transferts aux collectivités locales ». Ces recettes sont classifiées comme des recettes du gouvernement central conformément au guide d'interprétation de l'OCDE. Le Togo ne les comptabilise pas dans les recettes du budget de l'État.

Rubrique 2000 : Les données de cotisations de sécurité sociale ne sont pas disponibles.

Rubrique 5111 : Les recettes au soutien à la politique pétrolière sont prélevées à partir de la TVA recouvrée par la Douane.

Rubrique 5121 : Le prélèvement pour l'apurement de la dette du secteur pétrolier (PADSP) est considéré comme une recette fiscale dans cette publication comme le préconise la classification OCDE (voir le guide d'interprétation en Annexe A). La classification nationale du Togo considère ces recettes comme des recettes non fiscales.

Les données sur les remboursements de TVA ne sont pas disponibles car au Togo, les crédits de TVA ne font pas l'objet de remboursement avec les moyens classiques de paiement (virement, chèque, espèces...). Lorsqu'un contribuable dispose d'un crédit de TVA, il adresse une demande de remboursement à l'administration fiscale qui lui délivre un certificat de détaxe. Ce certificat lui permet de payer non seulement ses déclarations ultérieures de TVA mais aussi les autres impôts.

La classification nationale du Togo considère les amendes et pénalités relatives aux impôts, les confiscations et ventes en douane et les remboursements du prélèvement communautaire de solidarité comme des recettes fiscales. Ces recettes sont classifiées comme des recettes non fiscales dans cette publication comme le préconise la classification OCDE (voir le guide d'interprétation en Annexe A).

Source: Office Togolais des Recettes.

StatLink https://doi.org/10.1787/888933820791

Table 5.20. **Tunisia / Tunisie**

Details of tax revenue / Recettes fiscales détaillées

Million TND

	1997	2000	2005	2010	2011	2012	2013	2014	2015	2016
Recettes fiscales totales	..	**7 196**	**10 146**	**17 143**	**18 794**	**20 478**	**22 407**	**24 998**	**25 613**	**26 596**
1000 Impôts sur revenu, bénéfices et gains en capital	..	**1 624**	**2 927**	**5 091**	**5 959**	**5 921**	**6 878**	**7 955**	**7 678**	**7 384**
1100 Des personnes physiques	..	1 049	1 565	2 658	2 918	3 188	3 711	4 096	5 003	5 931
1110 Sur le revenu et les bénéfices	..	1 037	1 560	2 644	2 905	3 173	3 686	4 058	4 965	5 887
Traitements et salaires	..	742	1 160	2 006	2 326	2 640	3 068	3 260	3 549	4 107
Honoraires, commissions, courtage et loyers	..	20	93	184	177	180	205	236	364	483
Intérêts des dépôts des comptes spéciaux d'épargne	..	65	43	68	90	82	102	125	159	176
Revenus des capitaux mobiliers	..	32	63	75	62	57	69	87	212	269
Avances sur les marchés	..	27	24	50	45	41	46	56	313	508
Bénéfices industriels et commerciaux	..	43	56	94	78	76	95	98	119	142
Bénéfices non commerciaux	..	17	24	49	44	41	46	71	76	79
Impôt forfaitaire	..	14	16	25	13	23	22	31	36	37
Revenus agricoles	..	5	4	8	5	9	11	15	19	22
Revenus fonciers et autres	..	5	4	8	7	9	10	12	14	22
Autres impôts sur le revenu et bénéfices	..	66	73	78	59	15	13	67	105	42
1120 Sur les gains en capital	..	12	5	13	12	15	24	38	39	45
1200 Des sociétés	..	575	1 360	2 432	3 041	2 730	3 165	3 855	2 673	1 450
1210 Sur les bénéfices	..	575	1 359	2 424	3 035	2 722	3 159	3 848	2 658	1 442
Sociétés pétrolières	..	96	459	813	999	1 117	1 438	1 575	950	346
Sociétés non-pétrolières	..	359	644	864	1 258	822	779	1 137	1 088	806
Avances sur les marchés	..	33	97	356	346	331	389	478	222	46
Avance au titre des importations	..	7	28	111	124	156	166	184	198	198
Revenus des capitaux mobiliers	..	58	68	113	144	141	174	215	72	27
Honoraires, commissions, courtage et loyers	..	16	52	125	125	127	169	183	86	2
Redevances servies aux non résidents	..	3	8	39	35	26	36	53	18	9
Autres impôts sur les bénéfices	..	3	3	3	3	2	8	22	25	9
1220 Sur les gains en capital	..	0	1	7	6	7	6	7	14	7
1300 Non ventilables entre 1100 et 1200	..	0	2	2	1	3	3	4	2	4
2000 Cotisations de sécurité sociale	..	**1 551**	**2 307**	**4 629**	**5 210**	**5 839**	**6 504**	**6 882**	**7 549**	**8 415**
2100 A la charge des salariés	..	..	..	..	..	..	..	..	..	..
2110 Sur la base du salaire	..	..	..	..	..	..	..	..	..	..
2120 Sur la base de l'impôt sur les revenus	..	..	..	..	..	..	..	..	..	..
2200 A la charge des employeurs	..	..	..	..	..	..	..	..	..	..
2210 Sur la base du salaire	..	..	..	..	..	..	..	..	..	..
2220 Sur la base de l'impôt sur le revenu	..	..	..	..	..	..	..	..	..	..
2300 A charge des travailleurs indép. ou sans emploi	..	..	..	..	..	..	..	..	..	..
2310 Sur la base du salaire	..	..	..	..	..	..	..	..	..	..
2320 Sur la base de l'impôt sur le revenu	..	..	..	..	..	..	..	..	..	..
2400 Non ventilables entre 2100, 2200 et 2300	..	1 551	2 307	4 629	5 210	5 839	6 504	6 882	7 549	8 415
2410 Sur la base du salaire	..	..	..	..	..	..	..	..	..	..
2420 Sur la base de l'impôt sur le revenu	..	..	..	..	..	..	..	..	..	..
3000 Sur salaires ou main d'oeuvre	..	**107**	**114**	**199**	**212**	**224**	**242**	**285**	**315**	**345**
Fonds de promotion des logements	..	71	74	124	136	143	147	177	191	215
Taxe de formation professionnelle	..	35	40	75	76	81	95	107	124	130
4000 Impôts sur le patrimoine	..	**81**	**104**	**177**	**218**	**228**	**244**	**257**	**282**	**299**
4100 Impôts périodiques sur la propriété immobilière	..	7	7	10	4	8	8	8	11	11
4110 Ménages	..	7	7	10	4	8	8	8	11	11
4120 Autres agents	..	0	0	0	0	0	0	0	0	0
4200 Impôts périodiques sur l'actif net	..	0	0	0	0	0	0	0	0	0
4210 Personnes physiques	..	..	..	..	..	..	..	..	..	..
4220 Sociétés	..	..	..	..	..	..	..	..	..	..
4300 Impôts sur mut. par décès, succ. et donations	..	0	0	0	0	0	0	0	0	0
4310 Impôts sur mut. par décès et successions	..	..	..	..	..	..	..	..	..	..
4320 Impôts sur les donations	..	..	..	..	..	..	..	..	..	..
4400 Impôts sur transact. mobilières et immob.	..	74	97	168	213	220	236	248	271	288
4500 Impôts non-périodiques	..	0	0	0	0	0	0	0	0	0
4510 Sur l'actif net	..	..	..	..	..	..	..	..	..	..
4520 Autres non-périodiques	..	..	..	..	..	..	..	..	..	..
4600 Autres impôts périodiques sur patrimoine	..	0	0	0	0	0	0	0	0	0
5000 Impôts sur les biens et services	..	**3 729**	**4 567**	**6 768**	**6 866**	**7 892**	**8 116**	**9 099**	**9 168**	**9 523**
5100 Impôts sur production, vente, transfert, etc.	..	3 665	4 458	6 612	6 724	7 726	7 948	8 903	8 977	9 300
5110 Impôts généraux	..	1 814	2 347	3 819	3 918	4 465	4 581	5 267	5 211	5 288
5111 Taxes sur la valeur ajoutée	..	1 792	2 301	3 750	3 850	4 383	4 460	5 117	5 068	5 118
Recettes brutes de la TVA	..	..	2 419	4 163	4 231	4 794	5 130	5 544	5 684	5 771
Remboursements TVA	..	..	-118	-413	-381	-411	-670	-427	-617	-653
5112 Impôts sur les ventes	..	0	0	0	0	0	0	0	0	0
5113 Autres impôts	..	21	46	69	69	82	121	150	144	170

Table 5.20. **Tunisia / Tunisie** *(cont.)*

Details of tax revenue / Recettes fiscales détaillées

Million TND

	1997	2000	2005	2010	2011	2012	2013	2014	2015	2016
5120 Impôts sur biens et services déterminés	..	1 851	2 111	2 793	2 806	3 261	3 367	3 637	3 765	4 012
5121 Accises	..	1 023	1 340	1 814	1 801	2 109	2 143	2 315	2 397	2 876
Tabac	..	371	601	799	893	1 033	1 014	1 085	1 087	1 248
Boissons alcoolisées	..	147	146	174	164	218	267	303	290	336
Essences et huiles	..	260	269	268	266	263	258	279	305	649
Voitures	..	86	91	242	167	241	251	251	289	285
Produits alimentaires	..	19	28	31	31	32	35	45	41	44
Ciment	..	11	13	17	17	16	18	20	17	15
Autres accises	..	131	192	282	262	306	299	332	369	299
5122 Bénéfices des monopoles fiscaux	..	0	0	0	0	0	0	0	0	0
5123 Droits de douane et droits à l'importation	..	654	524	620	617	763	796	882	918	742
Hors tabac	..	565	424	428	432	562	570	603	639	429
Redevances sur prestations douanières à l'importation	..	68	81	142	138	157	166	182	155	188
Taxe conjoncturelle sur ventes du ciment importé	..	0	0	0	0	0	18	41	61	28
Tabac	..	9	12	23	22	28	27	31	27	37
Autres droits de douane	..	0	4	4	2	2	2	2	1	0
Prèlevements à l'importation	..	12	3	20	19	11	11	18	29	45
Autres taxes et prélèvements à l'importation	..	1	1	3	4	3	3	5	7	15
5124 Taxes à l'exportation	..	11	9	27	36	43	38	38	41	30
5125 Impôts sur biens d'équipement	..	0	0	0	0	0	0	0	0	0
5126 Impôts sur services déterminés	..	162	236	330	352	346	389	401	409	363
Taxe sur les télécommunications	..	72	91	136	150	139	160	151	147	153
Taxe de compensation sur les transports	..	55	84	105	102	113	119	123	126	67
Taxe sur les assurances	..	33	59	86	97	92	109	120	129	138
Autres impôts sur services déterminés	..	2	2	3	3	2	2	8	7	5
5127 Autres impôts sur commerce et transact. internat.	..	0	0	0	0	0	0	0	0	0
5128 Autres impôts	..	0	1	1	1	1	1	1	1	0
5130 Non ventilables entre 5110 et 5120	..	0	0	0	0	0	0	0	0	0
5200 Impôts sur utilisation des biens et exerc. activites	..	64	109	156	142	166	168	196	191	223
5210 Impôts périodiques	..	55	77	103	97	111	116	124	134	160
5211 A la charge des ménages: véhicules à moteur	..	35	44	60	56	64	69	74	81	91
5212 A la charge autres agents: véhicules à moteur	..	18	28	43	41	47	46	49	53	69
5213 Autres impôts périodiques	..	1	6	0	0	0	0	0	0	0
5220 Impôts non-périodiques	..	9	32	53	44	56	52	72	57	63
5300 Non ventilables entre 5100 et 5200	..	0	0	0	0	0	0	0	0	0
6000 Autres impôts	**..**	**104**	**126**	**279**	**329**	**374**	**423**	**520**	**622**	**630**
Droits de timbres	..	25	32	133	215	208	256	288	334	350
Droits d'enregistrements	..	40	67	107	85	103	124	145	181	201
Droits sur les voyages à l'étranger	..	12	12	21	19	24	26	30	33	35
Divers	..	28	15	17	9	39	17	57	75	43
6100 A la charge exclusive des entreprises	..	..	..	..	..	..	..	..	..	..
6200 A la charge d'autres agents	..	..	..	..	..	..	..	..	..	..

Note: Année civile se terminant le 31 décembre.

Les données sont sur la base des encaissements.

Les chiffres n'incluent pas les recettes fiscales collectées par les collectivités locales car elles ne sont pas disponibles.

Les impôts affectés aux Fonds spéciaux du Trésor et aux Fonds de concours sont compris dans les données pour la période 2000-16.

La rubrique 1210 exclut les redevances des compagnies pétrolières. En Tunisie, elles sont considérées comme un complément de l'impôt sur les sociétés depuis avril 2012.

Les cotisations de sécurité sociale sous la rubrique 2000 ne sont pas considérées comme des recettes fiscales en Tunisie.

Source: Ministère des Finances pour toutes les données des recettes fiscales. Ministère des Affaires sociales pour les données de cotisations de sécurité sociale.

StatLink https://doi.org/10.1787/888933820810

Table 5.21. **Uganda / Ouganda**

Details of tax revenue / Recettes fiscales détaillées

Million UGX

	1997	2000	2005	2010	2011	2012	2013	2014	2015	2016
Total tax revenue	**738 886**	**999 659**	**1 935 472**	**4 252 022**	**5 158 308**	**6 272 330**	**7 220 835**	**8 065 069**	**9 761 430**	**11 042 302**
1000 Taxes on income, profits and capital gains	**102 453**	**181 905**	**560 351**	**1 340 327**	**1 686 313**	**2 104 213**	**2 578 064**	**2 744 735**	**3 387 902**	**3 854 687**
1100 Of individuals	79 577	142 306	400 329	968 399	1 208 508	1 448 015	1 757 795	1 989 167	2 382 729	2 767 373
1110 On income and profits	79 577	142 306	400 329	968 399	1 208 508	1 448 015	1 757 795	1 989 167	2 382 729	2 767 373
PAYE	38 332	83 471	245 325	657 920	825 644	996 933	1 196 504	1 397 556	1 613 243	1 803 532
Rental income tax	2 800	5 500	8 292	10 105	15 350	0	0	0	27 649	55 034
Other income tax (not counting WHT)	9 319	11 220	13 899	19 001	8 014	1 685	17 898	53 616	42 189	44 322
Withholding taxes	29 125	42 115	132 813	281 373	359 500	449 398	543 392	537 995	699 648	864 485
WHT on imports	15 499	23 349	47 399	68 581	84 766	120 477	154 012	131 294	152 787	165 145
WHT on general supplies	0	0	85 414	120 061	218 314	234 302	223 256	232 028	282 825	330 729
WHT on government payments	0	0	0	44 446	55 672	94 159	154 236	60 016	89 367	150 824
WHT management and professional fees	0	0	0	24 886	84	0	1 982	35 883	45 447	61 860
WHT on dividends	0	0	0	11 237	70	28	5 455	33 926	61 823	69 110
WHT non residents	0	0	0	1 356	14	296	4 451	44 832	57 106	79 583
Other WHT or unclassified	13 627	18 766	0	10 806	581	135	1	16	10 293	7 234
1120 On capital gains	..	..	..	..	..	..	..	..	..	..
1200 Corporate	22 849	35 391	151 738	305 274	404 237	553 927	597 635	486 636	714 772	732 159
1210 On profits	22 849	35 391	151 738	305 274	404 237	553 927	597 635	486 636	714 772	732 159
1220 On capital gains	..	..	..	..	..	..	..	..	..	..
1300 Unallocable between 1100 and 1200	27	4 207	8 284	66 654	73 568	102 271	222 634	268 932	290 401	355 154
2000 Social security contributions	**..**	**..**	**..**	**..**	**..**	**..**	**..**	**..**	**..**	**..**
2100 Employees	..	..	..	..	..	..	..	..	..	..
2110 On a payroll basis	..	..	..	..	..	..	..	..	..	..
2120 On an income tax basis	..	..	..	..	..	..	..	..	..	..
2200 Employers	..	..	..	..	..	..	..	..	..	..
2210 On a payroll basis	..	..	..	..	..	..	..	..	..	..
2220 On an income tax basis	..	..	..	..	..	..	..	..	..	..
2300 Self-employed or non-employed	..	..	..	..	..	..	..	..	..	..
2310 On a payroll basis	..	..	..	..	..	..	..	..	..	..
2320 On an income tax basis	..	..	..	..	..	..	..	..	..	..
2400 Unallocable between 2100, 2200 and 2300	..	..	..	..	..	..	..	..	..	..
2410 On a payroll basis	..	..	..	..	..	..	..	..	..	..
2420 On an income tax basis	..	..	..	..	..	..	..	..	..	..
3000 Taxes on payroll and workforce	**0**	**0**	**0**	**0**	**0**	**0**	**0**	**0**	**0**	**0**
4000 Taxes on property	**..**	**..**	**..**	**..**	**..**	**..**	**..**	**..**	**..**	**..**
4100 Recurrent taxes on immovable property	..	..	..	..	..	..	..	..	..	..
4110 Households	..	..	..	..	..	..	..	..	..	..
4120 Others	..	..	..	..	..	..	..	..	..	..
4200 Recurrent taxes on net wealth	..	..	..	..	..	..	..	..	..	..
4210 Individual	..	..	..	..	..	..	..	..	..	..
4220 Corporate	..	..	..	..	..	..	..	..	..	..
4300 Estate, inheritance and gift taxes	..	..	..	..	..	..	..	..	..	..
4310 Estate and inheritance taxes	..	..	..	..	..	..	..	..	..	..
4320 Gift taxes	..	..	..	..	..	..	..	..	..	..
4400 Taxes on financial and capital transactions	..	..	..	..	..	..	..	..	..	..
4500 Non-recurrent taxes	..	..	..	..	..	..	..	..	..	..
4510 On net wealth	..	..	..	..	..	..	..	..	..	..
4520 Other non-recurrent taxes	..	..	..	..	..	..	..	..	..	..
4600 Other recurrent taxes on property	..	..	..	..	..	..	..	..	..	..
5000 Taxes on goods and services	**632 132**	**815 835**	**1 372 355**	**2 861 862**	**3 434 069**	**4 091 556**	**4 623 565**	**5 301 667**	**6 350 601**	**7 182 036**
5100 Taxes on production, sale, transfer, etc	612 846	793 285	1 308 282	2 772 331	3 321 504	3 985 244	4 504 786	5 158 322	6 201 129	7 050 396
5110 General taxes	219 057	329 755	638 773	1 371 561	1 645 234	1 984 392	2 411 866	2 611 779	3 150 723	3 580 638
5111 Value added taxes	219 057	329 755	638 773	1 371 561	1 645 234	1 984 392	2 411 866	2 611 779	3 150 723	3 580 638
VAT on imports (government taxes)	4 190	16 628	10 444	35 775	24 486	30 936	33 787	20 344	0	0
VAT on imports (non-government taxes)	129 264	178 868	365 418	763 398	986 521	1 164 581	1 254 531	1 404 415	1 783 518	1 952 821
VAT on phone talk time	0	0	0	93 277	68 244	98 331	142 033	141 352	151 747	181 944
VAT on beer	11 542	11 586	16 771	37 034	52 441	75 167	97 365	96 412	108 831	120 513
VAT on electricity	0	0	0	74 584	45 062	60 668	135 306	162 673	112 811	114 679
VAT on sugar	0	0	0	64 276	72 225	62 439	109 802	71 294	110 801	120 363
VAT on soft drinks	5 018	5 139	12 028	15 846	25 845	28 283	34 901	30 268	32 385	35 449
VAT on cement	0	0	0	25 161	21 017	24 228	30 237	37 356	53 086	72 014
VAT on cigarettes	8 074	6 904	6 641	1 411	1 406	1 223	2 538	6 767	16 759	9 366
Other VAT	63 196	140 630	263 679	359 821	438 002	572 908	726 989	807 772	923 754	1 117 807
VAT refunds	-2 228	-30 000	-36 208	-99 023	-90 015	-134 371	-155 623	-166 874	-142 970	-144 320
5112 Sales tax	0	0	0	0	0	0	0	0	0	0
5113 Other	0	0	0	0	0	0	0	0	0	0
5120 Taxes on specific goods and services	393 789	463 530	669 509	1 400 770	1 676 269	2 000 852	2 092 921	2 546 543	3 050 407	3 469 758

Table 5.21. **Uganda / Ouganda** *(cont.)*

Details of tax revenue / Recettes fiscales détaillées

Million UGX

	1997	2000	2005	2010	2011	2012	2013	2014	2015	2016
5121 Excises	104 264	132 953	187 615	275 929	316 626	472 853	610 214	700 426	834 589	878 166
Excise tax on beer	40 704	59 938	60 704	98 864	118 781	159 485	170 717	144 222	146 853	177 678
Excise tax on phone talk time	0	0	24 901	99 490	100 751	113 826	147 560	170 432	184 175	166 780
Excise tax on soft drinks	14 439	13 348	15 304	27 907	37 834	47 616	53 520	59 338	71 799	83 125
Excise tax on cigarettes	29 761	33 572	28 632	7 698	6 553	7 386	9 911	14 246	14 979	12 617
Excise tax on spirits / waragi	1 353	915	6 463	10 376	17 999	19 664	34 240	45 555	53 331	58 203
Excise on international calls	0	0	0	0	0	0	0	68 162	65 142	34 230
Excise tax on sugar	0	0	0	17 187	13 744	5 539	7 351	7 479	17 854	18 220
Excise tax on cement	1	1	1	8 228	11 719	10 898	13 179	15 729	17 773	20 784
Other excise taxes	18 007	25 180	51 610	84 179	101 543	140 312	173 737	175 262	262 684	306 530
Tax refunds due to diesel tax exemption	0	0	0	-77 999	-92 297	-31 872	0	0	0	0
5122 Profits of fiscal monopolies	0	0	0	0	0	0	0	0	0	0
5123 Customs and import duties	288 233	330 339	480 361	1 122 850	1 346 919	1 522 021	1 475 304	1 831 978	2 188 774	2 519 584
Petroleum duty	197 456	197 202	309 024	716 234	821 181	920 898	794 836	984 245	1 197 749	1 382 952
Surcharge on used imports	0	0	0	38 621	47 760	50 268	61 213	72 889	95 895	136 280
Non-oil imports	2 233	5 301	3 653	21 651	30 798	45 091	20 780	27 702	0	0
Commission on imports	16 271	22 746	19 567	2	0	0	0	0	0	0
Infrastructure Levy	0	0	0	0	0	0	0	0	57 268	62 936
Other import duties	72 274	105 090	153 667	346 621	447 420	506 063	598 735	747 533	841 381	940 066
Fixed duty drawbacks	0	0	-5 550	-280	-240	-300	-260	-390	-3 520	-2 650
5124 Taxes on exports	0	0	1 165	122	7 929	586	1	3 126	13 186	15 878
5125 Taxes on investment goods	0	0	0	0	0	0	0	0	0	0
5126 Taxes on specific services	1 293	238	368	1 869	4 795	5 392	7 401	11 012	13 858	56 130
Casino and lottery tax	1 293	238	368	1 869	4 795	5 392	7 401	11 012	13 858	17 416
Bank charges	0	0	0	0	0	0	0	0	0	38 714
5127 Other taxes on internat. trade and transactions	0	0	0	0	0	0	0	0	0	0
5128 Other taxes	0	0	0	0	0	0	0	0	0	0
5130 Unallocable between 5110 and 5120	0	0	0	0	0	0	0	0	0	0
5200 Taxes on use of goods and perform activities	19 285	22 551	64 073	89 531	112 565	106 312	118 779	143 345	149 472	131 640
5210 Recurrent taxes	16 823	17 890	52 440	64 096	67 421	63 786	69 983	92 857	91 886	73 350
5211 Paid by households: motor vehicles	16 823	17 890	52 440	64 096	67 421	63 786	69 983	92 857	91 886	73 350
Fees and licences	16 823	17 890	52 440	64 096	67 421	63 786	69 983	92 857	91 886	73 350
Road user charges	0	0	0	0	0	0	0	0	0	0
5212 Paid by others: motor vehicles	0	0	0	0	0	0	0	0	0	0
5213 Paid in respect of other goods	0	0	0	0	0	0	0	0	0	0
5220 Non-recurrent taxes	2 462	4 660	11 633	25 434	45 144	42 525	48 796	50 488	57 586	58 290
5300 Unallocable between 5100 and 5200	0	0	0	0	0	0	0	0	0	0
6000 Other taxes	**4 302**	**1 919**	**2 766**	**49 833**	**37 926**	**76 561**	**19 205**	**18 668**	**22 927**	**5 580**
6100 Paid solely by business	0	0	0	0	0	0	0	0	0	0
6200 Other	4 302	1 919	2 766	49 833	37 926	76 561	19 205	18 668	22 927	5 580
Stamp duties and embossing fees	1 818	1 919	6 946	26 256	32 018	106 749	26 620	39 558	48 557	60 130
Coffee stabilisation tax	2 484	0	0	0	0	0	0	0	0	0
Government payments on behalf of private companies	0	0	0	0	0	0	15 059	0	0	0
Un-allocated revenue	0	0	0	29 457	58 767	2 772	2 046	0	0	0
Tax refunds	0	0	-4 180	-5 880	-52 860	-32 960	-24 520	-20 890	-25 630	-54 550

Note: Data are reported on a fiscal year basis beginning 1st July. For example, the data for 2016 represent July 2015 to June 2016.

The data are on a cash basis.

Figures exclude tax revenues collected by sub-national governments as the data are not available.

Heading 4000: Property tax is levied annually by local authorities. Revenue from property tax is not available.

Heading 5111: VAT refunds are included for the first time, allowing for total VAT revenues to be reported on a net, rather than a gross basis "Other VAT revenues" combines revenues from spirits/waragi, bottled water, water, and other goods and services.

Heading 5121: The "other excises taxes" category combines excise revenues from bottled water, cosmetics and mobile money transfers (a three in the "Indirect Domestic Taxes: excises" section of the Uganda Revenue Authority's budget document) with revenue from the excis duty (in the "taxes on international trade" section) and the excise duty (in the "government taxes" section).

Heading 6200: For this edition, the main tax refunds could be allocated to the appropriate tax category.

Revenue from driver permits are considered non-tax revenue under the OECD classification, as set out in the Interpretative Guide in Annex A The national classification of Uganda classifies this revenue as tax revenue.

Source: Uganda Revenue Authority.

StatLink https://doi.org/10.1787/888933820829

Chapter 6

Country tables – Non-tax revenues, 1997-2016

Chapitre 6

Tableaux pays – Recettes non fiscales, 1997-2016

Chapter 6 / Chapitre 6

Non-tax revenue tables, 1997-2016

In all of the following tables a ("..") indicates not available or not applicable. The main series in this volume cover the years 1990 to 2016.

Figures referring to 1998-99, 2001-04 and 2006-09 in Table 6.1 and Tables 6.4 to 6.21 have been omitted because of lack of space. Complete series are, however, available on line at *http://dx.doi.org/10.1787/93add7a4-en.*

Tableaux des recettes non fiscales, 1997-2016

Dans tous les tableaux suivants le symbole (« .. ») signifie que l'information n'est pas disponible ou qu'elle n'est pas applicable. Les principales séries dans ce volume couvrent les années 1990 à 2016.

Les années 1998-99, 2001-04 et 2006-09 dans le tableau 6.1 et les tableaux 6.4 à 6.20 ont été omis en raison du manque d'espace. Les séries complètes sont cependant disponibles en ligne sur *http://dx.doi.org/10.1787/ef1bbbc4-fr.*

Table 6.1. **Total non-tax revenue as percentage of GDP, 1997-2016**
Tableau 6.1. **Total des recettes non fiscales en pourcentage du PIB, 1997-2016**

	1997	2000	2005	2010	2011	2012	2013	2014	2015	2016
Botswana	..	..	26.6	19.1	20.0	22.4	22.3	22.8	18.4	18.2
Burkina Faso	..	8.6	5.6	5.7	6.9	7.0	8.0	6.3	6.2	5.6
Cabo Verde	16.1	7.6	9.2	9.7	5.6	6.0	6.2	5.3	7.6	7.2
Cameroon / Cameroun	5.0	7.3	6.3	4.3	5.7	4.6	4.5	3.9	3.9	2.7
Congo[1]	..	20.7	31.9	29.0	33.2	33.0	33.5	27.3	7.9	9.4
Congo, Dem. Rep. / Congo, Rép. dém.	..	..	..	6.5	4.4	5.7	3.6	6.4	4.7	3.7
Côte d'Ivoire	1.4	1.1	2.3	1.7	1.5	1.9	2.5	2.6	3.3	1.9
Egypt / Égypte	..	..	7.1	8.7	5.8	6.5	6.0	10.2	7.3	5.7
Eswatini	12.3	12.1	15.5	8.0	6.6	19.1	17.0	16.8	14.6	11.2
Ghana[2]	..	2.2	4.2	5.0	5.3	6.1	6.2	5.6	6.2	4.0
Kenya[3]	..	..	3.2	1.1	..	..	1.4	1.5	2.0	1.7
Mali	..	6.8	5.4	4.9	5.6	1.4	4.2	3.3	2.8	2.5
Mauritius / Maurice[4]	4.0	2.8	2.5	3.8	3.5	3.1	3.2	3.0	2.9	2.8
Morocco / Maroc	..	2.2	3.0	3.6	3.9	3.7	4.1	3.8	3.9	3.5
Niger	..	5.5	8.2	6.3	4.9	8.0	9.5	8.0	7.6	7.0
Rwanda	7.5	11.8	12.7	12.3	12.3	8.8	11.2	9.4	8.9	7.8
Senegal / Sénégal	2.4	2.7	2.3	3.2	2.9	3.8	4.2	5.2	4.5	5.8
South Africa / Afrique du Sud	0.5	0.4	0.5	0.6	0.6	0.6	0.6	0.5	0.4	0.5
Togo	..	1.8	2.7	11.2	9.3	6.3	5.3	4.3	4.1	4.3
Tunisia / Tunisie	..	2.5	2.6	2.9	4.0	3.5	3.6	2.4	2.1	1.7
Uganda / Ouganda	..	..	5.7	2.3	2.5	1.7	1.3	1.5	1.7	1.4

Note: The figures include sub-national government non-tax revenues for Eswatini (Swaziland in previous editions), Kenya (for the years 2014-16), Mauritius and Morocco. Sub-national government non-tax revenues are not available in other countries.

1. Data on non-tax revenues were only available for oil revenues and grants.
2. The figures should be treated with caution prior to 2010. The data prior to 2010 exclude oil and mineral royalties that could not be distinguished from tax revenues.
3. The data are incomplete for 2011 and 2012 and a figure for total non-tax revenue is not included for these years.
4. Some of the figures used for 2015 represented collections over the Jan-June period.

Note : Les chiffres incluent les recettes non fiscales des collectivités infranationales pour l'Eswatini (Swaziland dans les précédentes éditions), le Kenya (pour les années 2014-16), le Maroc et Maurice. Les recettes non fiscales des collectivités infranationales des autres pays ne sont pas disponibles.

1. Seules les données des recettes non fiscales relatives aux recettes pétrolières et aux dons sont disponibles.
2. Les chiffres doivent être interprétés avec prudence. Les données antérieures à 2010 excluent les redevances pétrolières et minérales qui ne peuvent être distinguées des recettes fiscales.
3. Les données sont incomplètes pour 2011 et 2012 et un chiffre des recettes non fiscales totales n'a pas été calculé pour ces années.
4. Certains chiffres utilisés de 2015 représentent les recettes sur la période janvier-juin.

StatLink https://doi.org/10.1787/888933820848

Table 6.2. **Non-tax revenue of main headings as percentage of GDP, 2016**
Tableau 6.2. **Recettes non fiscales sous les principales rubriques en pourcentage du PIB, 2016**

	Grants / Dons	Property income / Revenus de la propriété	Sales of goods and services / Ventes de biens et de services	Fines, penalties and forfeits / Amendes, pénalités et confiscations	Miscellaneous and unidentified revenue / Recettes diverses et non identifiées
Botswana	0.0	10.7	0.7	0.0	6.8
Burkina Faso	2.7	1.1	0.7	0.9	0.3
Cabo Verde	2.8	0.7	3.1	0.4	0.3
Cameroon / Cameroun	0.3	2.1	0.2	0.1	0.1
Congo	0.9	8.6	..	..	..
Congo, Dem. Rep. / Congo, Rép. dém.	2.5	0.6	0.4	0.2	0.0
Côte d'Ivoire	1.2	0.3	0.2	0.0	0.2
Egypt / Égypte	0.1	2.8	1.1	0.1	1.5
Eswatini	0.2	1.3	0.4	0.1	9.2
Ghana	0.7	1.1	2.3	0.0	0.0
Kenya	0.5	0.3	0.7	0.0	0.2
Mali	1.2	0.4	0.7	0.2	0.1
Mauritius / Maurice[1]	0.1	1.2	0.9	0.1	0.5
Morocco / Maroc	0.0	0.9	1.5	0.3	0.8
Niger	6.1	0.7	0.1	0.1	0.1
Rwanda[2]	5.1	..	..	..	2.7
Senegal / Sénégal	2.8	1.0	0.0	0.0	2.0
South Africa / Afrique du Sud	0.0	0.3	0.1	0.1	0.0
Togo	2.9	0.8	0.3	0.0	0.3
Tunisia / Tunisie	0.1	1.0	0.0	0.3	0.2
Uganda / Ouganda	1.1	0.0	0.3	0.0	0.0

Note: The figures include sub-national government non-tax revenues for Eswatini (Swaziland in previous editions), Kenya (for the years 2014-16), Mauritius and Morocco. Sub-national government non-tax revenues are not available in other countries.

1. Some of the figures used for 2015 represented collections over the Jan-June period.
2. Data for property income, sales of goods and services and fines, penalties and forfeits are included in miscellaneous and unidentified revenue.

Note : Les chiffres incluent les recettes non fiscales des collectivités infranationales pour l'Eswatini (Swaziland dans les précédentes éditions), le Kenya (pour les années 2014-16), le Maroc et Maurice. Les recettes non fiscales des collectivités infranationales des autres pays ne sont pas disponibles.

1. Certains chiffres utilisés de 2015 représentent les recettes sur la période janvier-juin.
2. Les données relatives aux revenus de propriété, les ventes de biens et de services, les amendes, les pénalités et les confiscations sont incluses dans la rubrique « recettes diverses et non identifiées ».

StatLink https://doi.org/10.1787/888933820867

Table 6.3. **Non-tax revenue of main headings as percentage of total non-tax revenues, 2016**

Tableau 6.3. **Recettes non fiscales sous les principales rubriques en pourcentage du total des recettes non fiscales, 2016**

	Grants / Dons	Property income / Revenus de la propriété	Sales of goods and services / Ventes de biens et de services	Fines, penalties and forfeits / Amendes, pénalités et confiscations	Miscellaneous and unidentified revenue / Recettes diverses et non identifiées
Botswana	0.0	58.7	3.6	0.2	37.5
Burkina Faso	47.8	19.8	11.8	15.4	5.1
Cabo Verde	38.3	9.2	42.8	5.8	4.0
Cameroon / Cameroun	10.6	77.7	5.7	3.0	3.0
Congo	9.3	90.7	..	..	..
Congo, Dem. Rep. / Congo, Rép. dém.	68.1	16.8	10.5	4.2	0.3
Côte d'Ivoire	63.2	17.0	10.9	0.0	8.9
Egypt / Égypte	2.4	48.9	19.4	2.4	26.8
Eswatini	1.9	11.8	3.4	0.6	82.3
Ghana	16.8	26.6	56.6	0.0	0.0
Kenya	26.8	19.2	40.5	1.3	12.1
Mali	46.6	16.0	28.0	7.2	2.2
Mauritius / Maurice[1]	2.9	42.8	32.5	2.1	19.6
Morocco / Maroc	0.0	26.8	41.9	9.0	22.4
Niger	86.3	10.2	0.9	1.3	1.3
Rwanda[2]	65.2	..	..	..	34.8
Senegal / Sénégal	48.6	16.6	0.0	0.0	34.8
South Africa / Afrique du Sud	8.9	55.3	12.8	20.8	2.2
Togo	66.4	18.6	7.9	0.2	6.8
Tunisia / Tunisie	8.4	59.5	2.0	17.7	12.3
Uganda / Ouganda	79.1	0.9	20.0	0.0	0.0

Note: The figures include sub-national government non-tax revenues for Eswatini (Swaziland in previous editions), Kenya (for the years 2014-16), Mauritius and Morocco. Sub-national government non-tax revenues are not available in other countries.

1. Some of the figures used for 2015 represented collections over the Jan-June period.
2. Data for property income, sales of goods and services and fines, penalties and forfeits are included in miscellaneous and unidentified revenue.

Note : Les chiffres incluent les recettes non fiscales des collectivités infranationales pour l'Eswatini (Swaziland dans les précédentes éditions), le Kenya (pour les années 2014-16), le Maroc et Maurice. Les recettes non fiscales des collectivités infranationales des autres pays ne sont pas disponibles.

1. Certains chiffres utilisés de 2015 représentent les recettes sur la période janvier-juin.
2. Les données relatives aux revenus de propriété, les ventes de biens et de services, les amendes, les pénalités et les confiscations sont incluses dans la rubrique « recettes diverses et non identifiées ».

StatLink https://doi.org/10.1787/888933820886

Table 6.4. **Total non-tax revenue in millions of US dollars at market exchange rates**

Tableau 6.4. **Totale des recettes non fiscales en millions de dollars américains au taux de change du marché**

	1997	2000	2005	2010	2011	2012	2013	2014	2015	2016
Botswana	..	..	2 670	2 561	3 111	3 548	3 403	3 596	2 778	2 142
Burkina Faso	..	225	304	512	744	788	960	776	649	635
Cabo Verde	87	45	100	161	105	106	115	99	122	118
Cameroon / Cameroun	524	720	1 140	1 134	1 661	1 336	1 462	1 351	1 220	860
Congo	..	667	1 948	3 565	4 917	4 509	4 702	3 854	678	734
Congo, Dem. Rep. / Congo, Rép. dém.	..	..	..	1 340	1 093	1 564	1 169	2 300	1 787	1 439
Côte d'Ivoire	163	121	387	415	394	499	771	906	1 108	677
Egypt / Égypte	..	..	6 275	18 722	13 898	17 154	16 929	30 274	23 308	19 037
Eswatini	239	211	507	365	321	894	745	709	593	322
Ghana	..	178	730	1 612	2 112	2 559	2 943	2 179	2 292	1 733
Kenya	..	..	617	430	..	..	764	879	1 224	1 164
Mali	..	202	335	525	730	177	560	479	367	356
Mauritius / Maurice	169	128	161	372	393	353	381	376	339	332
Morocco / Maroc	..	873	1 889	3 323	3 949	3 607	4 407	4 153	3 940	3 592
Niger	..	92	275	363	317	557	728	662	548	528
Rwanda	135	203	327	712	799	647	853	754	736	661
Senegal / Sénégal	112	125	200	412	423	544	617	800	621	848
South Africa / Afrique du Sud	780	596	1 399	2 211	2 575	2 284	2 112	1 837	1 406	1 375
Togo	..	27	61	384	360	245	231	195	173	192
Tunisia / Tunisie	..	529	831	1 257	1 835	1 570	1 664	1 121	891	716
Uganda / Ouganda	..	..	510	450	508	399	316	407	456	361

Note: This table is derived by dividing the total non-tax revenue figures for each country (in millions of national currency) by the exchange rate figures shown in Table 4.19.

Note : Ce tableau est obtenu en divisant les chiffres des recettes non fiscales en millions de monnaie nationale pour chaque pays par les taux de change du tableau 4.19.

StatLink https://doi.org/10.1787/888933820905

Table 6.5. **Botswana**

Details of non-tax revenue / Recettes non fiscales détaillées

Million BWP

	1997	2000	2005	2010	2011	2012	2013	2014	2015	2016
Total non-tax revenue	**..**	**..**	**14 034**	**17 412**	**21 219**	**25 515**	**29 081**	**33 197**	**27 953**	**31 412**
Grants	..	..	0	210	118	1	125	316	74	1
Grants	..	..	..	210	118	1	125	316	74	1
IMF Gold Sales	..	..	..	0	0	0	0	0	0	0
Property income	..	..	9 159	9 914	11 722	10 390	14 967	16 402	11 152	18 424
Rents and royalties	..	..	1 589	2 071	3 765	2 374	3 228	3 775	3 223	3 320
Mineral Royalties	..	..	1 577	2 057	3 754	2 364	3 221	3 766	3 215	3 307
Royalties and Dividends	..	..	0	0	0	0	0	0	0	0
Rent of Land	..	..	12	14	11	10	7	9	8	13
Interest and dividends	..	..	7 569	7 842	7 957	8 016	11 739	12 627	7 929	15 104
Mineral Dividends	..	..	6 573	7 054	6 933	6 450	9 032	10 267	6 766	11 976
Bank of Botswana Revenue	..	..	741	700	864	1 490	1 900	2 079	1 133	2 842
Profits From Public Enterprises	..	..	171	61	123	56	13	48	18	67
Interest: Parastatals (DDF)	..	..	38	20	32	15	790	229	8	215
Interest: Local Authorities	..	..	1	0	0	0	0	0	0	0
Interest: Deposits	..	..	46	8	6	5	4	4	4	4
Other property income	..	..	0	0	0	0	0	0	0	0
Sales of goods and services	..	..	908	1 047	893	825	768	715	811	1 137
Motor vehicle revenues	..	..	342	363	78	53	52	49	50	40
Petrol, Oil and Lubricants - Revenue	..	..	54	182	195	231	235	158	231	259
Water revenues	..	..	167	42	7	9	1	1	2	2
Fees and charges	..	..	84	107	122	133	127	133	129	123
Rent of Buildings & Equipment	..	..	73	86	86	88	93	93	97	95
Sale of Livestock	..	..	2	5	56	4	2	2	2	1
Registrations, licenses and certificates	..	..	19	22	30	39	37	37	33	34
Other sales of goods and services	..	..	167	242	319	269	221	242	269	583
Fines, penalties and forfeits	..	..	36	31	57	77	46	67	93	65
Traffic fines	..	..	0	0	0	0	0	0	44	25
Court fines	..	..	19	20	44	42	32	52	38	23
Bond revenues	..	..	1	1	2	19	2	1	1	3
Income tax penalty	..	..	11	0	0	0	0	0	0	0
Other fines, penalties and forfeits	..	..	5	10	11	16	12	14	11	14
Miscellaneous and unidentified revenue	..	..	3 931	6 210	8 430	14 223	13 175	15 697	15 823	11 784
SACU Revenue	..	..	3 930	6 207	8 424	14 216	13 170	15 691	15 818	11 773
Recovery of Arrears of Revenue	..	..	0	3	5	5	4	6	5	10
Revenue from Local Authorities	..	..	0	0	0	0	0	0	0	0
Reimbursement of Medical Claims (Revenue)	..	..	1	1	1	2	1	0	1	1
Total tax and non-tax revenue	..	..	22 072	31 712	37 859	41 184	48 204	55 357	47 285	55 551

Note: Data are on a fiscal year basis beginning 1st April. For example, the data for 2015 represent April 2015 to March 2016.
Data are on cash basis.
Figures exclude non-tax revenues collected by sub-national governments as the data are not available.

Source: Botswana Ministry of Finance and Economic Development, and Statistics Botswana.

StatLink https://doi.org/10.1787/888933820924

Table 6.6. **Burkina Faso**

Details of non-tax revenue / Recettes non fiscales détaillées

Million XOF

	1997	2000	2005	2010	2011	2012	2013	2014	2015	2016
Total des recettes non fiscales	..	**160 524**	**160 036**	**254 029**	**350 611**	**401 885**	**474 011**	**382 954**	**383 766**	**376 586**
Dons	..	143 716	131 541	198 940	253 670	277 501	324 364	256 447	230 041	180 190
Revenus de la propriété	..	6 326	9 148	15 447	48 284	57 447	58 336	66 261	57 875	74 704
Loyers et redevances	..	411	508	12 453	34 048	42 365	36 759	36 225	37 938	45 182
Droits sur les titres miniers et redevances minières	..	324	508	12 453	34 048	42 365	36 759	36 225	37 938	45 182
Redevance sureté	..	87	0	0	0	0	0	0	0	0
Intérêts et dividendes	..	5 915	8 640	2 993	14 236	15 082	21 577	30 036	19 937	29 522
Intérêts en douane	..	42	36	40	77	90	87	223	493	295
Portefeuille de l'Etat et plus value	..	5 873	8 604	2 954	14 159	14 993	21 490	29 813	19 443	29 227
Autres revenus de la propriété	..	0	0	0	0	0	0	0	0	0
Ventes de biens et de services	..	6 420	12 000	24 521	25 763	35 636	38 593	41 957	39 978	44 377
Diverses prestations de services	..	2 376	4 876	10 841	10 505	16 590	16 806	22 054	19 015	20 869
Location de biens	..	8	39	398	39	227	221	159	75	72
Frais douanes	..	2 493	5 031	6 667	7 637	10 987	12 206	9 166	9 795	12 533
Frais visas, papiers d'identite et permis de conduire	..	431	1 007	2 986	2 865	2 758	3 320	4 605	4 582	5 201
Autres frais administratifs	..	1 113	1 048	3 629	4 717	5 075	6 041	5 971	6 511	5 702
Amendes, pénalités et confiscations	..	1 272	2 689	4 505	9 828	21 413	28 180	6 153	41 421	58 166
Recettes diverses et non identifiées	..	2 790	4 658	10 618	13 066	9 888	24 538	12 137	14 451	19 148
Reversement des intérêts	..	2 382	2 071	3 618	3 713	3 468	3 209	3 570	2 534	785
Autres produits	..	408	2 588	7 000	9 354	6 419	21 328	8 568	11 917	18 363
Total des recettes fiscales et non fiscales	..	195 273	399 191	692 417	843 575	1 050 034	1 150 770	1 063 369	1 151 695	1 335 879
Pour mémoire : Prélèvement communautaire de solidarité (UEMOA)	..	1	6	6	7 145	10 020	10 681	9 003	9 855	11 433
Pour mémoire : Prélèvement communautaire (CEDEAO)	..	1 144	2 249	4 243	4 910	7 009	7 622	6 734	7 018	7 504

Note: Année civile se terminant le 31 décembre.

Les données sont sur la base des droits constatés.

Les chiffres n'incluent pas les recettes non fiscales collectées par les collectivités locales car elles ne sont pas disponibles.

Les recettes provenant de la taxe de location de biens, des droits sur les titres miniers, redevances minières et des frais administratifs sont incluses dans les recettes non fiscales comme le préconise la classification OCDE (voir le guide d'interprétation en Annexe A). La classification nationale du Burkina Faso les comptabilise comme des recettes fiscales.

Source: Ministère de l'Économie, des Finances et du Développement du Burkina Faso.

StatLink https://doi.org/10.1787/888933820943

Table 6.7. **Cabo Verde**

Details of non-tax revenue / Recettes non fiscales détaillées

Million CVE

	1997	2000	2005	2010	2011	2012	2013	2014	2015	2016
Total des recettes non fiscales	**8 119**	**5 372**	**8 902**	**13 396**	**8 298**	**9 074**	**9 574**	**8 211**	**12 116**	**11 777**
Dons	6 360	3 931	6 610	9 440	4 342	4 203	4 024	2 787	3 958	4 507
Transferts courants de gouvernements étrangers	6 360	0	0	0	0	0	254	228	370	461
Aide budgétaire	0	..	..	..	..	..	0	0	0	0
Aide alimentaire	949	..	..	..	..	..	0	0	0	0
Dons directs	4 606	..	..	..	..	..	253	228	353	449
Autre transfert courants	805	..	..	..	..	..	1	0	17	13
Transferts en capital de gouvernements étrangers	0	3 931	6 610	9 440	4 342	4 203	3 769	2 559	3 588	4 046
Aide budgétaire	..	0	551	3 085	1 711	573	1 199	1 041	1 282	1 312
Aide alimentaire	..	672	750	338	389	230	329	17	0	60
Dons directs	..	3 259	5 138	6 018	2 242	3 399	2 235	1 501	2 048	2 542
Autre dons en capital	..	0	171	0	0	0	6	0	259	132
Revenus de la propriété	367	364	95	316	339	384	476	209	1 022	1 083
Loyers et redevances	..	..	..	..	..	..	..	..	..	..
Intérêts et dividendes	..	..	..	..	..	..	..	..	..	..
Autres revenus de la propriété	..	..	..	..	..	..	..	..	..	..
Ventes de biens et de services	489	592	1 496	3 077	3 143	3 874	3 897	4 010	4 652	5 042
Prestations de service	201	448	1 445	3 003	3 043	3 796	3 734	3 823	4 492	4 738
Ventes de biens courants	288	144	51	74	100	77	163	187	160	303
Amendes, pénalités et confiscations	67	54	169	376	280	332	511	706	404	679
Recettes diverses et non identifiées	836	431	532	187	194	281	666	499	2 079	467
Autres transferts	257	413	150	41	85	195	32	128	36	35
Autres recettes diverses et non spécifiées	579	18	382	146	109	86	635	371	2 043	432
Total des recettes fiscales et non fiscales	15 445	16 346	27 731	38 948	37 238	35 752	36 924	34 358	41 955	42 849
Pour mémoire : Prélèvement communautaire de la CEDEAO[1]	0	67	156	245	290	262	266	258	254	290

Note: Année civile se terminant le 31 décembre.

Les données sont sur la base des encaissements.

Les chiffres n'incluent pas les recettes non fiscales collectées par les collectivités locales car elles ne sont pas disponibles.

La présente publication n'inclut pas le produit de la vente d'actifs non financiers rapporté dans les documents budgétaires du Cabo Verde. La classification nationale du Cabo Verde comptabilise le produit de la vente d'actifs non financiers comme des recettes non fiscales. Selon la classification de l'OCDE (voir le guide d'interprétation en Annexe B), le produit de la vente d'actifs n'est pas considéré comme une recette (fiscale ou non fiscale).

1. Le prélèvement communautaire de la CEDEAO (Communauté économique des États de l'Afrique de l'Ouest) n'est pas compris dans le total des recettes non fiscales ou fiscales et est présenté à titre de rubrique « Pour mémoire ». Le prélèvement communautaire de la CEDEAO est considéré comme une recette fiscale au Cabo Verde. Selon la classification de l'OCDE (voir le guide d'interprétation en Annexe A § 4), ce paiement n'est pas compris parmi les impôts.

Source: Ministère des Finances.

StatLink https://doi.org/10.1787/888933820962

Table 6.8. **Cameroon / Cameroun**

Details of non-tax revenue / Recettes non fiscales détaillées

Million XAF

	1997	2000	2005	2010	2011	2012	2013	2014	2015	2016
Total des recettes non fiscales	**283 502**	**527 053**	**600 552**	**560 690**	**782 963**	**681 934**	**722 010**	**666 820**	**721 082**	**509 962**
Dons	0	6 900	91 404	78 805	62 084	56 049	75 879	23 813	18 089	54 100
Revenus de la propriété[1]	221 100	404 500	446 825	442 296	668 984	566 680	577 877	580 497	465 541	396 033
Loyers et redevances	221 100	404 500	410 657	437 650	662 428	556 891	568 962	570 574	445 587	376 734
Redevance pétrolière	219 000	399 300	367 955	418 971	541 153	532 375	538 732	517 040	384 630	316 005
Droits de passage du pipeline	0	0	14 065	9 080	8 248	7 747	8 802	24 675	36 201	31 953
Autres loyers et redevances	2 100	5 200	28 637	9 599	113 027	16 769	21 428	28 860	24 756	28 776
Intérêts et dividendes	0	0	36 169	4 646	6 556	9 789	8 915	9 922	19 954	19 299
Autres revenus de la propriété	0	0	0	0	0	0	0	0	0	0
Ventes de biens et de services	30 400	33 500	40 262	37 732	41 027	47 664	62 682	52 990	188 402	29 094
Amendes, pénalités et confiscations	0	0	444	1 857	1 664	2 498	5 362	3 975	26 849	15 487
Recettes diverses et non identifiées[2]	32 002	82 153	21 616	0	9 204	9 043	211	5 546	22 201	15 248
Total des recettes fiscales et non fiscales	865 900	1 337 553	1 735 808	2 132 385	2 584 137	2 681 077	2 980 748	3 152 865	3 409 008	3 253 870

Note: Année civile se terminant le 31 décembre.

Les données sont sur la base des encaissements.

Les chiffres n'incluent pas les recettes non fiscales collectées par les collectivités locales car elles ne sont pas disponibles.

1. Cette rubrique inclut les taxes domaniales, la taxe à l'extraction des carrières et la redevance à la production des eaux comme le préconise la classification OCDE (voir le guide d'interprétation en Annexe B). La classification nationale du Cameroun les comptabilise comme des recettes fiscales.
2. Y compris transferts de capitaux non compris ailleurs et transferts volontaires autres que les dons.

Source: Ministère des Finances du Cameroun.

StatLink https://doi.org/10.1787/888933820981

Table 6.9. **Congo**

Details of non-tax revenue / Recettes non fiscales détaillées

Million XAF

	1997	2000	2005	2010	2011	2012	2013	2014	2015	2016
Total des recettes non fiscales	..	**474 909**	**1 025 700**	**1 762 400**	**2 318 200**	**2 300 700**	**2 322 100**	**1 902 300**	**400 800**	**435 100**
Dons	..	6 800	5 900	4 100	35 400	10 000	26 900	31 100	41 400	40 400
Revenus de la propriété	..	468 109	1 019 800	1 758 300	2 282 800	2 290 700	2 295 200	1 871 200	359 400	394 700
Loyers et redevances	..	468 109	1 019 800	1 758 300	2 282 800	2 290 700	2 295 200	1 871 200	359 400	394 700
Intérêts et dividendes	..	..	..	..	..	..	..	..	..	..
Autres revenus de la propriété	..	..	..	..	..	..	..	..	..	..
Ventes de biens et de services	..	..	..	..	..	..	..	..	..	..
Amendes, pénalités et confiscations	..	..	..	..	..	..	..	..	..	..
Recettes diverses et non identifiées	..	..	..	..	..	..	..	..	..	..
Total des recettes fiscales et non fiscales	..	573 499	1 224 370	2 193 210	2 837 530	2 883 757	3 288 610	2 702 681	1 239 542	1 171 806

Note: Année civile se terminant le 31 décembre.

Les données sont sur la base des encaissements.

Les chiffres n'incluent pas de recettes non fiscales à part les dons et les recettes pétrolières. Les données des dons et des recettes pétrolières sont issues de la base de données de la publication PEM 2018 (*Perspectives de l'économie mondiale 2018*) publiée par le FMI.

Source: Ministère des Finances et du Budget de la République du Congo, FMI.

StatLink https://doi.org/10.1787/888933821000

Table 6.10. **Congo, Dem. Rep./Congo, Rép. dém**

Details of non-tax revenue / Recettes non fiscales détaillées

Million CDF

	1997	2000	2005	2010	2011	2012	2013	2014	2015	2016
Total des recettes non fiscales	**..**	**..**	**..**	**1 213 982**	**1 004 824**	**1 437 667**	**1 075 255**	**2 127 683**	**1 656 103**	**1 542 559**
Dons	..	..	110 362	656 421	421 965	536 194	522 072	1 444 380	1 108 062	1 050 733
Revenus de la propriété	..	..	0	397 774	417 901	762 112	415 292	464 141	330 992	259 619
Loyers et redevances	..	..	..	358 125	317 811	638 268	345 027	400 379	292 678	237 299
Royalties des sociétés pétrolières	..	..	..	39 705	37 475	43 745	40 763	38 717	19 050	15 218
Redevance et royalty minières	..	..	..	65 476	64 416	90 355	110 013	148 882	138 244	114 681
Droits superficie annuels	..	..	..	25 340	25 294	21 638	20 788	20 172	20 102	14 522
Bonus de signature/renouvellement	..	..	..	4 566	631	3 294	521	820	624	1 015
Redevance annuelle sur l'exploitation et autres	..	..	..	50 599	26 005	44 297	33 755	37 086	38 632	50 465
Autorisation de concessions, extractions et autres autorisations	..	..	..	9 126	7 876	56 607	137	18 639	5 789	113
Permis ressources forestières et faune	..	..	..	3 541	5 156	1 549	1 487	1 730	387	638
Marge distribuable (recettes pétrolières)	..	..	..	84 491	125 412	124 474	132 450	123 433	52 694	34 918
Redevances superficiaires sur permis d'exploration et sur concession	..	..	..	10	3	2 435	13	4 197	8 791	4 280
Autres loyers	..	..	..	75 272	25 541	249 873	5 099	6 703	8 365	1 450
Intérêts et dividendes	..	..	..	39 301	99 704	123 073	69 526	62 272	37 159	22 228
Dividendes on shore (recettes pétrolières)	..	..	..	8 068	14 100	20 020	21 846	17 375	14 665	3 916
Participations off shore (recettes pétrolières)	..	..	..	25 347	50 190	37 339	39 726	36 372	15 806	10 463
Autres dividendes et participations	..	..	..	5 886	35 415	65 713	7 953	8 524	6 688	7 848
Autres revenus de la propriété	..	..	..	348	386	771	740	1 490	1 155	92
Ventes de biens et de services	..	158	7	123 659	71 485	90 036	96 777	146 328	164 250	162 253
Vente des imprimés[1]	..	158	7	1 106	3 118	1 292	1 312	1 881	690	218
Taxe de numérotation[2]	..	0	0	16 464	9 734	8 659	17 414	21 121	26 110	26 898
Taxe de régulation et taxe de modification des titres obtenus / télécommunications	..	0	0	13 180	25 885	16 446	22 433	28 709	36 198	38 820
Passeport, visa et carte de travail	..	0	0	20 344	15 877	17 673	18 917	26 288	30 957	26 053
Taxes sur le gardiennage par la Police Nationale Congolaise[2]	..	0	0	4 247	1 149	3 058	3 346	10 346	11 337	10 597
Contrôle des produits d'origine toxique, soporifique et stupéfiante	..	0	0	647	711	5 034	1 582	7 699	7 328	6 862
Redevance sur la désinfection et le contrôle sanitaire des friperies	..	0	0	3 828	176	1 565	64	2 292	3 111	2 586
Agréments	..	0	0	1 359	182	334	278	1 340	1 045	404
Autres	..	0	0	62 483	14 653	34 142	29 562	44 827	44 950	45 686
Loyers, Institut National de Sécurité Sociale (INSS)	..	0	0	0	0	1 834	1 868	1 825	2 524	4 128
Amendes, pénalités et confiscations	..	420	42	35 378	28 779	48 152	36 630	71 428	50 772	64 953
Amendes et pénalités (Direction générale des impôts)	..	418	2	15 455	14 737	25 696	30 848	42 138	15 160	40 058
Amendes et pénalités (DGDA)	..	2	40	1 561	6 941	3 429	1 424	1 615	4 093	2 525
Amendes et pénalités (DGRAD)	..	0	0	18 363	7 100	19 027	4 358	27 676	31 518	22 369
Recettes diverses et non identifiées	..	0	0	750	64 694	1 172	4 483	1 407	2 027	5 002
Total des recettes fiscales et non fiscales	..	..	..	2 879 684	3 106 666	4 336 209	4 120 628	5 290 176	5 095 003	4 767 222

Note: Année civile se terminant le 31 décembre.

Les données sont sur la base des encaissements.

Les chiffres n'incluent pas les recettes non fiscales collectées par les collectivités locales car elles ne sont pas disponibles.

Les données des dons sont issues de la base de données de la publication PEM 2018 (*Perspectives de l'économie mondiale 2018*) publiée par le FMI.

Les données autres que les dons sont disponibles à partir de 2010.

Pour la période 2010-16, 5 % en moyenne des recettes considérées comme non fiscales par la République démocratique du Congo ont été classifiées comme recettes fiscales dans cette publication comme le préconise la classification OCDE (voir le guide d'interprétation en Annexe A). Ces recettes collectées par la DGRAD (Direction Générale des Recettes Administratives, Judiciaires, Domaniales et de Participations) sont entre autres les redevances sur produits spécifiques, les droits proportionnels sur les S.A.R.L, la taxe ad valorem sur les gains des parieurs, les autorisations d'exportation et d'importation, la taxe d'implantation des établissements dangereux/insalubres/incommodes et diverses autorisations.

1. Les recettes provenant de la vente des imprimés sont incluses dans les recettes non fiscales comme le préconise la classification OCDE (voir le guide d'interprétation en Annexe B). La classification nationale en République démocratique du Congo classifie les recettes de la vente des imprimés comme des recettes fiscales.
2. Ces recettes sont considérées comme des droits administratifs car elles sont proportionnelles au coût d'une prestation de service rendue par une administration publique et sont donc classifiées comme des recettes non fiscales comme le préconise la classification OCDE (voir le guide d'interprétation en Annexe B).

Source: Ministère des Finances de la République démocratique du Congo.

StatLink https://doi.org/10.1787/888933821019

Table 6.11. **Côte d'Ivoire**

Details of non-tax revenue / Recettes non fiscales détaillées

Million XOF

	1997	2000	2005	2010	2011	2012	2013	2014	2015	2016
Total des recettes non fiscales	**95 048**	**86 004**	**203 671**	**205 073**	**185 612**	**254 640**	**380 736**	**447 046**	**654 836**	**401 313**
Dons	44 069	33 500	94 628	106 540	81 208	81 208	201 460	303 989	282 200	253 518
Revenus de la propriété	2 895	4 204	5 555	76 308	88 874	148 815	149 233	91 828	285 955	68 211
Loyers et redevances[1]	2 895	4 204	5 555	44 902	74 620	137 504	119 015	82 046	255 515	57 736
Revenus du domaine	0	0	0	283	172	396	941	1 363	2 111	2 972
Taxe d'exploitation pétrolière	0	0	0	27 275	60 966	87 079	60 764	39 595	30 851	23 555
Taxes domaniales[2]	2 895	4 204	5 555	7 696	7 852	22 309	37 395	31 737	37 224	25 697
Autres loyers et redevances	0	0	0	9 647	5 630	27 720	19 915	9 351	185 329	5 512
Intérêts et dividendes	0	0	0	27 981	13 678	11 230	29 973	9 693	30 440	10 475
Autres revenus de la propriété	0	0	0	3 426	576	80	245	89	0	0
Ventes de biens et de services	0	0	13 200	21 700	15 177	24 306	28 097	31 556	35 414	43 920
Redevance RTI (Radiodiffusion Télévision Ivoirienne)[3]	..	..	0	4 107	2 340	5 564	5 568	6 021	6 244	7 275
Taxe audiovisuelle	..	..	0	0	0	0	0	0	0	0
Autres ventes de biens et de services	..	..	13 200	17 592	12 837	18 742	22 529	25 535	29 170	36 645
Amendes, pénalités et confiscations	0	0	0	173	99	99	219	291	0	0
Recettes diverses et non identifiées[4]	48 084	48 300	90 288	353	253	213	1 727	19 382	51 267	35 664
Total des recettes fiscales et non fiscales	1 261 939	1 255 377	1 611 902	2 243 084	2 044 112	2 677 757	3 102 515	3 393 148	4 092 566	4 162 731

Note: Année civile se terminant le 31 décembre.

Les données sont sur la base des encaissements.

Les chiffres n'incluent pas les recettes non fiscales collectées par les collectivités locales car elles ne sont pas disponibles.

1. Les recettes des taxes domaniales, la taxe ad valorem et la taxe d'exploitation sont considérées comme des recettes non fiscales selon la classification OCDE (voir le guide d'interprétation en Annexe B). La classification nationale de la Côte d'Ivoire les comptabilise comme des recettes fiscales.
2. Les recettes des taxes domaniales sont hors taxe ad-valorem pour la période 2012 à 2016, période pour laquelle il a été possible de distinguer ces recettes.
3. La taxe audiovisuelle et la redevance radiodiffusion télévision ivoirienne (RTI) sont considérées comme des recettes non fiscales selon la classification OCDE (voir le guide d'interprétation en Annexe B). La classification nationale de la Côte d'Ivoire les comptabilise comme des recettes fiscales.
4. Les recettes diverses et non identifiées comprennent les transferts de capitaux non compris ailleurs et transferts volontaires autres que les dons.

Source: Ministère de l'Économie et des Finances.

StatLink https://doi.org/10.1787/888933821038

Table 6.12. **Egypt / Égypte**

Details of non-tax revenue / Recettes non fiscales détaillées

Million EGP

	1997	2000	2005	2010	2011	2012	2013	2014	2015	2016
Total non-tax revenue	**..**	**..**	**38 171**	**103 350**	**78 846**	**101 539**	**105 589**	**203 525**	**167 195**	**147 623**
Grants	..	..	2 853	4 333	2 287	10 104	5 208	95 856	25 437	3 543
Property income	..	..	18 672	56 512	43 124	58 023	58 634	59 384	84 164	72 246
Rents and royalties	..	..	1 114	7 839	3 564	5 101	5 499	4 425	9 005	7 633
Royalties on petroleum	..	..	0	2 750	1 465	2 800	2 933	1 737	5 964	4 139
Royalties on Suez Canal	..	..	1 068	1 354	1 402	1 568	1 617	1 867	1 945	2 059
Other royalties	..	..	47	3 734	696	733	949	821	1 096	1 436
Interest and dividends	..	..	17 233	47 115	42 469	53 453	52 770	54 709	74 894	64 264
SCA	..	..	9 651	12 729	15 252	16 118	16 375	18 084	19 214	14 755
C.B.E.	..	..	4 999	205	498	15 012	11 317	9 283	13 417	29 462
Economic authorities	..	..	402	1 431	1 287	2 207	1 915	1 630	10 093	7 820
Public and private companies and enterprises	..	..	245	3 272	3 266	3 991	3 539	3 157	3 295	3 433
EGPC	..	..	154	25 546	21 010	15 027	18 785	21 809	25 414	7 820
Other dividends and interests	..	..	1 782	3 930	1 157	1 099	839	747	3 460	974
Other property income	..	..	324	1 559	-2 909	-531	366	250	265	350
Sales of goods and services	..	..	8 463	24 113	13 854	13 235	13 503	20 693	25 837	28 698
Administrative fees	..	..	1 505	2 681	2 761	2 993	3 705	3 745	4 482	4 453
Development fees	..	..	455	917	940	777	821	811	1 046	1 137
Service fees	..	..	2 494	3 505	2 358	2 486	2 564	10 001	6 620	7 168
Capital revenues	..	..	3 986	16 962	7 747	6 935	6 264	6 029	13 610	15 824
Other sales of goods and services	..	..	24	49	48	44	150	108	80	116
Fines, penalties and forfeits	..	..	969	1 854	1 735	1 441	1 602	1 917	2 823	3 540
Miscellaneous and unidentified revenue	..	..	7 212	16 538	17 847	18 736	26 642	25 674	28 934	39 597
Current revenues from special accounts and funds	..	..	4 842	12 268	13 741	14 290	18 946	17 052	17 797	19 627
Voluntary transfers other than grants	..	..	1 084	684	916	673	612	1 061	901	1 455
Current revenues	..	..	1 114	3 312	2 815	3 482	6 721	7 215	9 827	17 968
Other revenues	..	..	173	275	375	292	363	346	408	547
Total tax and non-tax revenue	..	..	110 068	267 948	265 101	302 944	349 772	456 137	464 572	491 112

Note: Data are reported on a fiscal year basis beginning 1st July. For example, the data for 2016 represent July 2015 to June 2016.

The data are on a cash basis.

Figures exclude non-tax revenues collected by sub-national governments as the data are not available.

Royalties on the Suez Canal as well as other royalties, development fees and administrative fees are reported as tax revenues in Egypt. In accordance with the OECD classification, as set out in the Interpetative Guide in Annex A, these revenues are considered non-tax revenues.

Source: Ministry of Finance.

StatLink https://doi.org/10.1787/888933821057

Table 6.13. **Eswatini**

Details of non-tax revenue / Recettes non fiscales détaillées

Million SZL

	1997	2000	2005	2010	2011	2012	2013	2014	2015	2016
Total non-tax revenue	**1 152**	**1 546**	**3 279**	**2 668**	**2 405**	**7 643**	**7 409**	**8 003**	**7 542**	**6 412**
Grants	0	0	0	1	0	136	101	134	99	122
Property income	103	95	67	553	115	173	173	264	394	757
Rents and royalties	0	0	0	3	4	4	4	14	25	28
Land concession rents, postal revenue	0	0	0	0	0	0	0	0	0	0
Rents attributed to social security funds	0	0	0	3	4	4	4	14	25	28
Interest and dividends	90	91	65	548	107	166	161	238	339	484
Local interest collected by central government	28	21	25	538	19	16	24	0	60	7
Central bank profit	4	0	0	0	74	120	110	214	245	287
External interest and interest on capital	54	69	13	0	2	5	5	11	0	2
Dividends	4	1	27	8	11	22	13	0	11	115
Interest and dividends collected by social security funds	0	0	0	1	1	2	10	12	23	73
Other property income	13	4	1	1	4	4	8	13	31	244
Quitrents	..	0	0	0	0	0	0	0	0	..
Local government property income	..	4	1	1	4	4	8	13	31	..
Sales of goods and services	39	40	63	115	97	82	76	71	73	216
Sundry fees	13	13	40	38	40	25	22	6	6	144
Passports, citizenship and resident permits	7	5	5	25	23	23	23	25	25	29
Rental of government real estate	2	3	6	7	8	8	10	10	11	12
Driver's licences, motor vehicle certification	1	1	3	8	8	6	7	8	11	15
Hospital and medical services	1	5	4	6	6	6	7	7	6	7
Hire of government plants and vehicles	0	0	0	21	0	3	0	0	0	0
Aviation fees	12	12	1	0	0	0	0	0	0	0
Sale of government furniture and vehicles	0	0	0	6	6	5	0	6	7	1
Sale of agricultural products and services	2	2	1	1	1	2	2	3	2	3
Public service transport fees	1	0	1	1	1	1	1	2	1	1
Sale of government publications	0	0	0	1	1	1	1	1	1	2
Prison industry sales	0	0	0	0	0	0	0	0	0	0
Local government sales of goods and services	0	0	1	1	2	2	2	2	2	3
Fines, penalties and forfeits	3	4	11	28	28	55	30	32	33	38
Traffic fines	2	2	5	15	15	14	15	15	13	14
Judicial fines and other penalties	0	1	4	10	10	11	12	15	18	22
Interest and penalties on late tax payments	0	0	1	1	1	8	2	2	2	1
PAYE penalties[1]	0	1	1	1	2	22	0	0	0	0
Fines, penalties and forfeits (local non-tax revenue)	0	0	0	0	0	0	0	0	0	0
Miscellaneous and unidentified revenue	1 007	1 407	3 138	1 972	2 166	7 197	7 029	7 502	6 942	5 280
SACU revenue	1 007	1 406	3 136	1 969	2 161	7 192	7 025	7 487	6 931	5 252
SACU penalties	0	0	1	2	3	3	0	14	9	12
Miscellaneous and unidentified revenue (local non-tax revenue)	0	0	0	2	2	2	4	1	3	16
Total tax and non-tax revenue	2 125	2 872	5 685	7 256	7 454	12 919	13 604	15 094	15 231	15 302

Note: Eswatini was referred to as Swaziland in the first two editions of *Revenue Statistics in Africa*.

Data are reported on a fiscal year basis beginning 1st April. For example, the data for 2016 represent April 2016 to March 2017.

The data are on a cash basis.

Revenues from motor vehicle licences, the change of ownership fees and the registration of new motor vehicles are considered as tax revenue under the OECD classification as set out in the Interpretative Guide in Annex A and are classified under heading 5211 (Recurrent taxes paid by households: motor vehicles). The national classification of Eswatini classifies these revenues as non-tax revenues.

The revenues from business and sundry licences are considered as tax revenue under the OECD classification, as set out in the Interpretative Guide in Annex A and are classified under heading 5211 (Recurrent taxes paid on use of goods and perform activities other than on motor vehicles). The national classification of Eswatini classifies these revenues as non-tax revenues.

The revenues from the registrations of specific goods (e.g. firearms) are considered as tax revenue under the OECD classification, as set out in the Interpretative Guide in Annex A and are classified under heading 5220 (Non-recurrent taxes on use of goods and perform activities). The national classification of Eswatini classifies these revenues as non-tax revenues.

The revenues from the education loans' repayments do not represent an increase of net worth resulting from a transaction and therefore are not considered as revenues under the OECD classification, as set out in the Interpretative Guide in Annex B.

1. Revenue from PAYE Penalties, tax interests and penalties on taxes are considered as non-tax revenue under the OECD classification, as set out in the Interpretative Guide in Annex A. The national classification of Eswatini classifies it as tax revenues.

Source: Eswatini Revenue Authority.

StatLink https://doi.org/10.1787/888933821076

Table 6.14. **Ghana**

Details of non-tax revenue / Recettes non fiscales détaillées

Million GHS

	1997	2000	2005	2010	2011	2012	2013	2014	2015	2016
Total non-tax revenue	**..**	**97**	**661**	**2 306**	**3 193**	**4 595**	**5 751**	**6 369**	**8 512**	**6 777**
Grants	..	57	535	1 080	1 231	1 160	739	814	2 689	1 141
Project grants	..	24	284	591	708	512	374	787	1 744	1 034
Programme grants	..	34	135	288	281	503	158	27	945	106
International debt relief	..	0	116	201	242	146	207	0	0	0
Property income	..	7	18	347	927	1 283	2 123	2 727	2 628	1 803
Rents and royalties	..	..	..	..	445	583	748	1 075	908	757
Mineral royalties (aside from oil)	..	..	..	..	261	312	408	517	518	578
Oil revenues	..	..	..	..	184	270	339	554	384	176
Lodgements to MDAs and MMDAs: surface rentals from oil/PHF interest	..	..	..	..	0	1	2	4	6	3
Lodgements to MDAs and MMDAs: fees from granting of new stability agreements	..	..	..	..	0	0	0	0	0	0
Revenue from oil companies (includes corporate tax)	..	..	..	..	0	0	0	0	0	0
Interest and dividends	..	7	18	347	482	700	1 375	1 653	1 720	1 046
Lodgements to MDAs and MMDAs: dividend, interest and profits from oil companies	..	0	0	0	482	700	875	1 435	995	491
Lodgements to MDAs and MMDAs: dividend, interest and profits aside from oil companies	..	7	18	347	0	0	500	218	726	556
Other property income	..	..	..	..	..	..	..	..	..	..
Sales of goods and services	..	32	108	879	1 034	2 152	2 888	2 827	3 195	3 833
Retentions by MDAs and MMDAs	..	23	78	685	722	1 791	2 516	2 497	2 531	3 368
Lodgements to MDAs and MMDAs: fees and charges	..	10	30	194	312	362	372	330	663	466
Lodgements to MDAs and MMDAs: gas receipts	..	0	0	0	0	0	0	0	2	0
Fines, penalties and forfeits	..	0	0	0	0	0	0	0	0	0
Miscellaneous and unidentified revenue	..	0	0	0	0	0	0	0	0	0
Total tax and non-tax revenue	..	584	3 138	9 001	12 793	16 824	19 789	25 312	32 104	36 272

Note: Year ending 31st December.
The data are on a cash basis.
Figures exclude non-tax revenues collected by sub-national governments as the data are not available.
Revenues for MDAs (Municipalities, Departments and Agencies) and MMDAs (Metropolitan, Municipal and District Assemblies) contain a mixture of revenues collected at the local level, and revenues collected at a federal level. These are reported as revenues to the central government.

Source: Ghana Statistical Service.

StatLink https://doi.org/10.1787/888933821095

Table 6.15. **Kenya**

Details of non-tax revenue / Recettes non fiscales détaillées

Million KES

	1997	2000	2005	2010	2011	2012	2013	2014	2015	2016
Total non-tax revenue	..	..	**47 672**	**33 643**	..	..	**65 178**	**76 489**	**113 718**	**116 082**
Grants	..	..	29 810	14 060	..	..	26 155	27 397	29 501	31 160
Foreign governments-capital	..	..	14 905	0	..	..	5 459	7 355	2 644	2 641
Foreign governments-current	..	..	0	0	..	..	0	0	0	0
Foreign governments-cash through exchequer	..	..	5 564	3 108	..	..	2 566	514	1 383	1 573
Foreign governments-direct payments treated as Appropriations in Aid (AIA)	..	..	9 341	6 107	..	..	2 893	6 841	16 098	16 275
International organisations-capital	..	..	0	0	..	..	0	0	5 533	5 914
International organisations-current	..	..	0	0	..	..	4	0	3 843	4 757
International organisations-cash through exchequer	..	..	0	4 845	..	..	2 622	5 205	0	0
International organisations-direct payments-treated as Appropriations in Aid (AIA)	..	..	0	0	..	..	12 611	7 482	0	0
Property income	..	..	5 255	9 921	13 002	17 001	18 508	11 876	16 216	22 309
Rents and royalties	..	..	727	1 184	1 157	1 633	1 887	1 694	695	743
Rent of land	..	..	674	1 108	1 073	1 544	1 789	1 588	8	25
Kenya Airports Authority (KAA) concession fees	..	..	53	77	84	89	99	106	113	114
Base titanium royalty	..	..	0	0	0	0	0	0	338	356
Mining royalties	..	..	0	0	0	0	0	0	136	143
Royalties from soda ash	..	..	0	0	0	0	0	0	100	105
Interest and dividends	..	..	2 027	8 736	11 845	15 367	16 621	5 865	10 781	18 225
Profits and dividends	..	..	1 185	8 354	11 086	14 132	15 264	5 865	9 002	15 919
Interests	..	..	843	382	759	1 236	1 356	0	1 779	2 306
Other property income	..	..	2 500	0	0	0	0	4 317	4 740	3 341
Surplus funds from regulatory authority	..	..	2 500	0	0	0	0	4 317	4 740	3 341
Sales of goods and services	..	..	1 548	2 302	0	0	12 479	28 990	45 303	47 042
Work permits	..	..	0	0	..	..	4 277	900	4 098	5 226
Road transit toll	..	..	293	457	468	591	546	495	562	674
Immigration visas and other consular fees	..	..	0	0	..	..	2 751	606	2 822	3 063
Fees under traffic act	..	..	304	1 188	..	..	548	108	0	0
Land administration fees	..	..	55	0	..	..	64	148	1 826	586
Motor driver's licences	..	..	376	656	..	..	762	0	0	0
Passport fees	..	..	0	0	..	..	502	125	570	845
Rent of government buildings and housing	..	..	520	0	..	365	274	54	135	213
Other fees for administrative services	..	..	0	0	..	..	2 606	128	556	542
Hire of security service fees	..	..	0	0	..	..	9	18	372	321
Registration of organisations, professionals and agreements	..	..	0	0	..	..	70	46	296	360
Registration of births, deaths and marriages	..	..	0	0	..	..	71	62	214	193
Other non-tax revenue collected by local government	..	..	..	..	..	..	..	26 300	33 850	35 020
Fines, penalties and forfeits	..	..	200	229	290	1 079	1 465	1 443	1 459	1 470
Miscellaneous and unidentified revenue	..	..	10 859	7 131	15 649	9 081	6 571	6 784	21 239	14 101
Contribution from government employees to social and welfare schemes within government	..	..	558	341	660	111	0	204	871	462
National Social Security Fund	..	..	4 097	6 790	7 166	6 781	6 571	6 580	9 168	12 312
Other Miscellaneous	..	..	6 204	0	7 823	2 189	0	0	11 200	1 327
Total tax and non-tax revenue	..	..	324 873	573 806	6 766	7 015	870 602	1 045 958	1 190 676	1 332 640

Note: Data are reported on a fiscal year basis beginning 1st July. For example, the data for 2016 represent July 2016 to June 2017.

The data are on a cash basis.

Detailed non-tax revenue data are not readily available for 2001, 2002, 2003, 2004, 2006, 2011 and 2012.

Figures exclude non-tax revenues collected by sub-national governments prior to 2014 as the data are not available.

The national classification of Kenya classifies revenues from the airport revenue, aviation revenue, petroleum development levy, FMV, road maintenance levy, sugar levy, petroleum regulatory levy, merchant superintendent shipping levy, railway development levy, revenue stamps, KEBS, land rates and contributions to the national social security fund as non-tax revenues. They are considered in this publication as tax revenues under the OECD classification, as set out in the Interpretative Guide in Annex A.

Heading miscellaneous and unidentified revenues: Other non-tax revenue included non-tax revenue collected by local government. These data are available for the first time in this edition.

Source: Kenya Revenue Authority and the National Treasury.

StatLink https://doi.org/10.1787/888933821114

Table 6.16. **Mali**

Details of non-tax revenue / Recettes non fiscales détaillées

Million XOF

	1997	2000	2005	2010	2011	2012	2013	2014	2015	2016
Total des recettes non fiscales	..	**143 652**	**176 548**	**259 490**	**344 252**	**90 229**	**276 786**	**236 384**	**217 220**	**211 001**
Dons	..	102 481	138 317	190 540	276 866	7 568	206 507	162 500	112 124	98 310
Dons - programmes des gouvernements étrangers	..	..	0	22 263	35 100	0	10 006	18 188	20 665	8 639
Dons - projets des institutions internationales	..	..	0	0	5 608	0	0	0	0	0
Ressources PPTE	..	..	22 633	7 909	13 619	6 555	11 313	12 909	12 393	17 729
Ressources exceptionnelles: reconversion dette monétaire fonds de concours	..	..	0	0	0	0	14 169	3 874	0	0
Autres dons et subventions	..	102 481	115 684	160 368	222 539	1 013	171 019	127 529	79 066	71 942
Revenus de la propriété	..	9 669	12 421	34 564	31 669	47 402	38 062	35 055	46 966	33 747
Loyers et redevances	..	358	507	650	856	513	564	756	1 735	750
Concessions ordinaires	..	336	257	262	350	292	378	401	1 315	276
Redevances superficiaires	..	22	241	388	506	209	153	263	262	240
Taxe d'extraction	..	0	9	0	0	12	33	92	158	234
Intérêts et dividendes	..	9 311	11 914	32 873	30 293	46 319	37 159	34 118	44 810	32 544
Revenus des valeurs mobilières, des titres et des dividendes	..	9 296	11 908	30 500	28 698	43 848	34 169	30 745	41 261	29 761
Autres intérêts et dividendes (budget d'état)	..	15	6	0	0	0	0	0	0	0
Interêts des comptes bancaires (INPS)	..	0	0	2 373	1 595	2 471	2 990	3 373	3 549	2 783
Autres revenus de la propriété	..	0	0	1 041	520	569	338	181	420	453
Autres revenus de la propriété (CMSS)	..	0	0	0	6	6	88	48	140	142
Autres revenus de la propriété (INPS)	..	0	0	1 041	513	564	250	133	281	311
Ventes de biens et de services	..	24 754	10 541	16 046	20 004	12 733	18 018	21 059	42 574	59 044
Aliénation d'immeubles (DNDC)	..	20 857	3 102	2 858	3 443	3 402	4 125	3 641	4 219	7 443
Taxe sur Accès au Reseau de Télécom Ouvert au Public (TARTOP)	..	0	0	0	0	0	0	5 365	15 530	27 650
Droits de chancellerie	..	886	1 949	2 152	2 658	2 678	2 455	2 225	4 310	3 033
Passeports et cartes d'identités,	..	473	1 466	2 609	2 580	2 786	3 239	3 487	2 680	1 494
Recettes sur rôles (Trésor - BN)	..	981	154	91	26	0	0	0	0	0
Frais d'administration, voitures	..	497	591	813	1 018	859	960	1 021	1 200	1 342
Ventes en douanes	..	15	24	117	73	54	15	12	26	66
Location des immeubles de l'état	..	393	36	0	0	0	0	0	0	29
Autres ventes de biens et de services (budget d'état)	..	652	148	6 440	7 134	562	5 139	3 663	12 574	14 531
Recettes de la Caisse Malienne de Sécurité Sociale (CMSS) - hors cotisations	..	0	403	699	912	1 165	1 150	999	995	1 672
Recettes de l'Institut National de Prévoyance Sociale (INPS) - hors cotisations	..	0	2 668	267	2 160	1 227	935	646	1 040	1 784
Amendes, pénalités et confiscations	..	2 786	4 656	8 010	11 551	15 753	9 661	9 782	12 764	15 196
Pénalités sur impots directs	..	352	1 154	3 939	5 364	10 102	5 592	4 742	4 753	7 580
Pénalités sur impôts indirects	..	1 528	2 602	1 418	3 982	4 190	1 792	2 729	3 101	3 794
Amendes et confiscations	..	710	592	1 268	1 243	599	937	1 292	2 738	2 357
Transactions forestières, pêche et chasse	..	98	45	153	134	100	121	137	0	0
Frais et amendes judiciaires	..	98	243	249	5	195	229	258	397	386
Autres pénalités (budget d'état)	..	0	20	77	326	50	85	87	624	69
Pénalités et frais contentieux (INPS)	..	0	0	906	497	517	905	537	1 151	1 010
Recettes diverses et non identifiées	..	3 962	10 613	10 329	4 163	6 774	4 537	7 988	2 793	4 705
Compensations des moins values de recettes	..	0	5 260	0	0	0	0	0	0	0
Amendes arbitrées	..	268	41	66	269	79	127	112	41	80
Autres recettes diverses	..	3 694	5 312	10 263	3 894	6 695	4 410	7 876	2 752	4 625
Total des recettes fiscales et non fiscales	..	383 014	653 323	1 007 735	1 184 255	977 858	1 207 672	1 219 980	1 376 550	1 554 500
Pour mémoire : Redevances Statistiques (taxe UEMOA)	..	1 394	0	0	0	0	0	0	0	0

Note: Année civile se terminant le 31 décembre.

Les données sont sur la base des encaissements.

Les chiffres n'incluent pas les recettes non fiscales collectées par les collectivités locales car elles ne sont pas disponibles.

Source: Ministère de l'Économie et des Finances du Mali.

StatLink https://doi.org/10.1787/888933821133

Table 6.17. **Mauritius**

Details of non-tax revenue / Recettes non fiscales détaillées

Million MUR

	1997	2000	2005	2010	2011	2012	2013	2014	2015	2016
Total non-tax revenue	**3 286**	**3 293**	**4 590**	**11 458**	**11 275**	**10 620**	**11 688**	**11 517**	**11 887**	**11 704**
Grants	63	161	444	1 991	2 345	2 398	1 416	940	1 202	345
Grants from foreign governments	..	..	..	2	222	122	121	569	183	122
Grants from international organizations	..	..	..	1 989	2 122	2 276	1 295	371	1 019	223
Property income	2 577	2 370	2 395	5 020	4 328	4 846	5 315	5 233	4 668	5 012
Rents and royalties	0	0	0	1 284	1 167	1 068	1 219	1 087	1 019	961
Interest and dividends	0	0	0	979	1 018	1 074	1 827	1 404	1 031	644
Interest	..	..	..	392	376	589	408	461	451	325
Dividends	..	..	..	587	643	484	1 418	943	580	319
Other property income	2 577	2 370	2 395	2 756	2 142	2 705	2 269	2 741	2 618	3 408
Budgetary	1 954	1 692	1 235	1 549	1 127	1 167	1 066	1 437	2 028	2 289
Extra-budgetary	43	58	136	349	341	325	272	211	36	22
Social security funds	527	544	973	777	598	1 131	756	1 038	529	1 058
Regional government	0	0	6	11	11	10	14	11	5	5
Local government	54	76	45	71	64	73	161	46	20	34
Sales of goods and services	520	626	1 385	2 028	2 427	2 576	3 002	3 698	4 111	3 807
Work/occupational permits	0	0	47	95	112	125	163	205	194	203
Extra-budgetary fees, charges, and non-industrial sales	185	177	397	543	621	689	689	1 078	1 216	1 054
Fees, charges, and non-industrial sales by social security funds	22	20	40	51	145	216	234	140	78	156
Regional government sales of goods and services	0	0	6	5	7	8	7	7	4	4
Local government sales of goods and services	32	60	96	113	127	101	419	691	353	713
Other sales of goods and services	282	370	799	1 222	1 415	1 436	1 489	1 577	2 266	1 675
Fines, penalties and forfeits	44	65	152	272	306	282	313	332	360	247
Budgetary fines, penalties and forfeits	44	65	151	269	302	276	308	326	358	244
Extra-budgetary fines, penalties and forfeits	0	0	0	0	0	1	1	2	0	0
Regional government fines, penalties and forfeits	0	0	1	3	4	6	4	4	2	2
Local government fines, penalties and forfeits	0	0	0	0	0	0	0	0	0	0
Miscellaneous and unidentified revenue	83	70	214	2 147	1 870	518	1 642	1 314	1 546	2 294
Budgetary miscellaneous and unidentified revenue	4	10	13	1 803	1 468	187	1 360	140	454	522
Extra-budgetary miscellaneous and unidentified revenue	75	44	185	293	223	267	280	1 173	1 092	1 771
Miscellaneous and unidentified revenue for social security funds	0	4	0	3	117	0	0	0	0	0
Regional government miscellaneous and unidentified revenue	0	0	0	1	1	1	2	1	0	1
Local government miscellaneous and unidentified revenue	4	13	16	47	61	64	0	0	0	0
Total tax and non-tax revenue	18 654	25 684	39 491	70 623	74 730	79 888	84 151	88 164	92 073	95 377

Note: Data are on a fiscal year basis beginning 1st July for years prior to 2010 (for example, the data for 2009 represent July 2008 to June 2009) and are on a calendar year basis from 2010-2015.

Mauritius went back to a July-June fiscal year in 2015. Figures for 2016 correspond to the July-June 2015/16 fiscal year, while figures for 2015 correspond to the January-December calendar year. The calendar year 2015 is not used in national budget reporting by Mauritius, which means that official figures are not available for all revenue categories for this period. Where data were missing for 2015, quarterly revenue figures at the aggregate level were used along with fiscal year revenue data to produce estimates.

The data are on a cash basis, except for revenue from grants, which is reported on an accrual basis.

Due to an administrative change, some categories of local revenues were reclassified. Local taxes that were previously classified as local taxes on goods, as well as taxes on the use of goods and permission to use goods, and some revenues classified as miscellaneous revenues were recorded as sales of goods and services from 2013 onwards.

Source: Mauritius Revenue Authority for central government budgetary non-tax revenue data from 2007 to 2015; Statistics Mauritius for extra budgetary, local and regional government non-tax revenues from 1990 to 2016; Statistics Mauritius for budgetary central government non-tax revenues up to 2006; Ministry of Finance budget estimates for detailed revenue figures for the period July 2005-June 2008, for 2015-16 and for the figures used to estimate calendar year 2015 revenues.

StatLink https://doi.org/10.1787/888933821152

Table 6.18. **Morocco / Maroc**

Details of non-tax revenue / Recettes non fiscales détaillées

Million MAR

	1997	2000	2005	2010	2011	2012	2013	2014	2015	2016
Total des recettes non fiscales	**..**	**9 278**	**16 745**	**27 970**	**31 945**	**31 121**	**37 039**	**34 913**	**38 472**	**35 225**
Dons	..	2	1 163	199	9	8	7	0	0	0
Revenus de la propriété	..	3 125	4 878	9 786	12 181	12 257	13 063	10 938	8 933	9 425
Loyers et redevances	..	1 507	2 892	3 868	5 279	4 577	5 360	5 387	5 191	4 237
Redevance gazoduc	..	298	1 369	1 442	2 151	2 146	2 327	2 438	1 765	999
Redevances et contributions pour licence de pêche en haute mer	..	94	38	329	635	3	177	538	520	593
Redevances pour l'occupation du domaine public	..	132	214	331	325	289	566	279	281	195
Autres redevances reçues par l'administration centrale	..	7	8	63	3	3	9	3	6	10
Loyers et redevances reçues par les collectivités locales	..	977	1 262	1 703	2 165	2 136	2 281	2 128	2 619	2 440
Intérêts et dividendes	..	1 618	1 986	5 918	6 902	7 680	7 702	5 551	3 742	5 188
Dividendes des monopoles	..	1 008	1 540	5 584	6 510	7 376	7 378	4 970	3 236	4 675
Intérêts sur placements et avances	..	419	198	96	158	74	73	322	195	199
Interêts et dividendes reçus par les collectivités locales	..	191	248	239	234	230	251	259	311	315
Autres revenus de la propriété	..	0	0	0	0	0	0	0	0	0
Ventes de biens et de services	..	4 573	7 315	10 286	11 745	11 796	14 244	14 417	15 791	14 746
Cartes d'identité, passeports et divers documents	..	453	511	567	555	515	489	220	498	718
Produits de certains établissements publics	..	1 544	3 038	2 990	3 684	3 855	5 410	4 551	5 462	3 149
Revenus des immeubles domaniaux (loyers, charges locatives …)	..	137	172	250	184	287	239	217	265	312
Autres produits de l'administration centrale	..	175	824	646	1 494	649	801	864	773	791
Ventes de biens et de services par les collectivités locales	..	2 265	2 770	5 832	5 828	6 490	7 304	8 566	8 794	9 777
Amendes, pénalités et confiscations	..	398	851	2 802	2 262	2 364	2 526	2 690	2 994	3 179
Amendes et condamnations pécuniaires	..	17	42	21	23	32	46	56	61	68
Amendes transactionnelles	..	36	90	130	183	345	485	893	706	593
Autres (produits des confiscations, pénalités et amendes autres que fiscales)	..	6	9	1	1	1	1	1	0	0
Majorations et pénalités (DGI)[1]	..	339	709	2 650	2 055	1 986	1 994	1 740	2 226	2 518
Recettes diverses et non identifiées	..	1 180	2 539	4 897	5 748	4 696	7 200	6 868	10 755	7 875
Fonds de concours	..	147	968	3 597	3 624	2 246	4 441	2 564	3 453	2 187
Recettes en atténuation des dépenses de la dette	..	801	879	480	1 044	725	1 024	2 230	4 386	1 894
Reversements sur traitements et salaires	..	55	157	99	106	155	96	63	62	60
Créances sur le trésor prescrites	..	30	224	39	56	186	112	78	97	163
Autres (divers remboursements à l'État) reçues par l'administration centrale	..	7	29	6	133	198	281	396	254	254
Recettes diverses et non identifiées des collectivités locales	..	139	281	677	785	1 186	1 246	1 536	2 503	3 316
Total des recettes fiscales et non fiscales	..	106 504	153 332	244 956	265 606	281 143	289 529	284 335	294 635	303 625

Note: Année civile se terminant le 31 décembre.

Les données sont sur la base des encaissements.

1. Les recettes des majorations et pénalités relatives aux impôts sont considérées comme des recettes non fiscales. La classification nationale du Maroc les comptabilise comme des recettes fiscales.

Source: Ministère de l'Économie et des Finances.

StatLink https://doi.org/10.1787/888933821171

Table 6.19. **Niger**

Details of non-tax revenue / Recettes non fiscales détaillées

Million XOF

	1997	2000	2005	2010	2011	2012	2013	2014	2015	2016
Total des recettes non fiscales	..	**65 671**	**145 019**	**179 681**	**149 542**	**284 036**	**359 601**	**326 622**	**323 732**	**313 103**
Dons	..	59 240	134 000	130 144	113 497	216 542	304 855	222 124	232 611	270 255
Revenus de la propriété	..	4 751	5 998	28 436	28 501	53 475	35 440	42 838	40 249	31 921
Loyers et redevances	..	4 673	5 156	14 977	18 299	22 452	20 173	34 589	32 963	19 974
Bonus de signature	..	0	0	0	0	0	0	16 082	17 044	0
Redevance minière (RM)	..	4 519	4 732	14 381	16 832	21 334	18 526	13 195	11 323	13 105
Redevance superficaire pétrole	..	0	0	0	0	0	0	3 064	2 776	3 093
Publicité foncière	..	50	281	429	801	711	979	1 024	950	1 476
Redevance superficaire mine	..	0	0	0	0	0	0	396	449	1 001
Retenue pour logements	..	6	3	25	23	43	193	276	173	165
Concessions provisoires	..	0	73	86	550	289	299	212	164	740
Permis de coupe de bois	..	65	18	42	62	54	125	277	52	358
Bornage de terrains	..	4	13	9	20	19	14	32	20	23
Concessions définitives	..	29	35	5	11	2	37	31	12	12
Intérêts et dividendes	..	0	653	13 166	9 973	30 828	15 018	7 990	6 996	11 613
Dividendes	..	..	653	12 081	9 630	28 814	9 663	2 994	2 990	3 990
Bénéfices pétroliers	..	..	0	0	0	1 671	5 190	4 857	3 577	3 674
Intérêts créditeurs	..	..	0	1 084	343	343	165	140	430	3 949
Autres revenus de la propriété	..	78	189	293	228	195	249	259	290	334
Droits d'occupation du domaine public	..	78	189	293	228	195	249	259	290	334
Ventes de biens et de services	..	85	281	289	870	647	3 568	39 120	36 492	2 730
Vente de licence de téléphonie cellulaire	..	0	0	0	0	0	0	34 000	34 000	0
Commission sur transferts banque centrale (BCEAO)	..	0	0	42	0	1	2 002	3 691	1 090	799
Vente passeports/visa interpol	..	0	0	0	0	0	669	288	469	961
Vaccination internationale	..	0	0	0	0	0	215	201	239	275
Emission cartes grises/transport	..	0	0	0	0	0	125	141	143	121
Recettes des régies forestières	..	30	110	159	175	202	280	263	127	46
Ventes imprimés DGI/DGD	..	0	0	0	0	0	70	90	104	51
Droit de chancellerie	..	0	4	3	4	6	12	4	76	8
Location d'immeubles	..	9	135	63	279	89	41	22	9	27
Autres ventes de biens et services	..	46	32	21	412	349	155	419	235	442
Amendes, pénalités et confiscations	..	1 348	1 700	3 816	3 221	3 303	6 040	6 653	6 744	4 215
Amendes et pénalités de la DGI	..	1 188	1 062	2 296	1 812	1 588	4 108	4 289	4 035	2 281
Amendes et frais de police	..	0	76	482	384	543	655	916	1 230	820
Amendes et confiscations	..	159	122	214	220	328	414	478	842	628
Amendes, frais et pénalités (gendarmerie et police)	..	0	402	769	749	785	807	861	595	428
Amendes et saisies forêts et chasse	..	1	27	45	43	42	47	84	26	9
Amendes et frais de justice	..	0	4	8	10	7	3	18	9	42
Amendes et saisies sur contrôle des prix-poids-mesure	..	0	6	1	1	9	5	7	8	7
Recettes diverses et non identifiées	..	248	3 040	16 995	3 454	10 068	9 698	15 887	7 635	3 983
Autres recettes diverses - Trésor National	..	0	0	16 461	2 899	9 737	9 241	15 155	4 921	3 021
Autres recettes diverses	..	248	250	420	555	323	457	732	779	962
Reversement UEMOA et produits divers de l'African Risk Capacity (ARC)	..	0	2 790	114	0	8	0	0	1 935	0
Total des recettes fiscales et non fiscales	..	181 490	335 237	553 142	568 952	795 030	1 001 009	989 793	1 044 271	958 003
Pour mémoire : Prélèvement communautaire de la CEDEAO[1]	..	448	1 479	5 302	5 109	5 044	3 893	4 433	4 893	3 961
Pour mémoire : Prélèvement communautaire UEMOA	..	866	0	0	0	0	0	0	0	4 518

Note: Année civile se terminant le 31 décembre.

Les données sont sur la base des encaissements.

Les chiffres n'incluent pas les recettes non fiscales collectées par les collectivités locales car elles ne sont pas disponibles.

Les données pour la période 2000-04 doivent être interprétées avec prudence car les données non fiscales collectées par la Direction Générale du Trésor et de la Comptabilité Publique (DGTCP) ne sont pas disponibles pour cette période. Selon la classification OCDE (voir le guide d'interprétation en Annexe B), le produit de la vente d'immeuble bâtis n'est pas considéré comme une recette (fiscale ou non fiscale) car il ne représente pas une augmentation de la valeur nette résultant d'une transaction. La classification du Niger comptabilise ces recettes comme des recettes non fiscales.

1. Le prélèvement communautaire de la CEDEAO (Communauté économique des États de l'Afrique de l'Ouest) et le prélèvement communautaire de solidarité de l'UEMOA (Union Economique et Monétaire Ouest Africaine) ne sont pas compris dans le total des recettes fiscales ou des recettes non fiscales comme le préconise la classification OCDE (voir le guide d'interprétation en Annexe A) et est présenté ici à titre de rubrique « Pour mémoire ». La classification du Niger les comptabilise comme des recettes.

Source: Institut National de la Statistique.

StatLink https://doi.org/10.1787/888933821190

Table 6.20. **Rwanda**

Details of non-tax revenue / Recettes non fiscales détaillées

Million RWF

	1997	2000	2005	2010	2011	2012	2013	2014	2015	2016
Total non-tax revenue	**40 858**	**79 888**	**182 339**	**415 465**	**479 815**	**397 600**	**551 411**	**514 565**	**529 400**	**520 541**
Grants	37 731	76 710	164 477	397 352	443 150	345 510	459 200	421 821	374 600	339 336
Property income	..	..	..	..	..	..	..	..	..	..
Rents and royalties	..	..	..	..	..	..	..	..	..	..
Interest and dividends	..	..	..	..	..	..	..	..	..	..
Other property income	..	..	..	..	..	..	..	..	..	..
Sales of goods and services	..	..	..	..	..	..	..	..	..	..
Fines, penalties and forfeits	..	..	..	..	..	..	..	..	..	..
Miscellaneous and unidentified revenue[1]	3 127	3 178	17 862	18 113	36 665	52 090	92 211	92 745	154 800	181 205
Total tax and non-tax revenue	97 107	148 797	356 945	856 189	1 017 253	1 043 048	1 311 569	1 380 119	1 522 447	1 626 704

Note: Year ending 31st December.

The data are on a cash basis.

Figures exclude non-tax revenues collected by sub-national governments as the data are not available.

Figures exclude fines related to tax revenues as it is not possible to split these out from tax revenues. Revenues from fines related to taxes are now classified as non-tax revenues following a change in the OECD classification. Rwanda considers these revenues as tax revenues.

1. This category includes non-tax fines, administrative fees and revenue from public property and public assets for Rwanda. These data could not be disaggregated to allocate revenue to the relevant non-tax revenue categories.

Source: Rwanda Revenue Authority.

StatLink https://doi.org/10.1787/888933821209

Table 6.21. **Senegal / Sénégal**

Details of non-tax revenue / Recettes non fiscales détaillées

Million XOF

	1997	2000	2005	2010	2011	2012	2013	2014	2015	2016
Total des recettes non fiscales	**65 600**	**89 100**	**105 200**	**203 550**	**199 300**	**277 800**	**304 935**	**394 700**	**366 943**	**502 731**
Dons	65 600	64 000	75 600	161 850	150 000	206 300	187 540	253 500	232 034	244 348
Revenus de la propriété	0	21 100	26 500	39 600	40 100	66 700	88 795	81 300	84 990	83 413
Loyers et redevances	..	..	14 600	20 300	15 800	38 000	45 420	25 200	35 790	31 943
Intérêts et dividendes	..	..	11 900	19 300	24 300	28 700	43 375	56 100	49 200	51 470
Autres revenus de la propriété	..	..	0	0	0	0	0	0	0	0
Ventes de biens et de services	0	0	0	0	0	0	0	0	0	0
Amendes, pénalités et confiscations[1]	0	0	0	0	0	0	27 100	49 000	28 220	0
Recettes diverses et non identifiées	0	4 000	3 100	2 100	9 200	4 800	1 500	10 900	21 700	174 970
Recettes exceptionnelles (Swapp et Sonatel)	..	0	0	0	0	0	0	0	0	139 770
Divers reversements[2]	..	4 000	3 100	2 100	9 200	4 800	1 500	10 900	21 700	35 200
Total des recettes fiscales et non fiscales	483 144	648 395	992 448	1 471 349	1 546 057	1 727 605	1 743 437	1 977 076	2 075 574	2 423 358

Note: Année civile se terminant le 31 décembre.

Les données sont sur la base des encaissements.

Les chiffres n'incluent pas les recettes non fiscales collectées par les collectivités locales car elles ne sont pas disponibles.

La nomenclature actuelle des recettes budgétaires du Sénégal ne considère pas les dons comme une recette non fiscale.

1. Les recettes des amendes et les pénalités sur impôts et taxes sont considérées comme des recettes non fiscales. Cependant, ne disposant pas des moyens de dissocier les recettes fiscales des recettes non fiscales tirées de ces amendes et pénalités, ces recettes sont toutes comptabilisés avec les recettes fiscales dans ce rapport et excluent des recettes non fiscales. La classification nationale du Sénégal les comptabilise comme des recettes fiscales.
2. Y compris transferts de capitaux non compris ailleurs.

Source: Ministère de l'Économie, des Finances et du Plan.

StatLink https://doi.org/10.1787/888933821228

Table 6.22. **South Africa / Afrique du Sud**

Details of non-tax revenue / Recettes non fiscales détaillées

Million ZAR

	1997	2000	2005	2010	2011	2012	2013	2014	2015	2016
Total non-tax revenue	**3 595**	**4 135**	**8 899**	**16 192**	**18 676**	**18 750**	**20 382**	**19 922**	**17 934**	**20 233**
Grants[1]	265	637	1 118	1 012	1 480	1 966	2 335	1 960	1 467	1 800
Property income	1 379	1 378	5 208	8 170	10 340	10 220	11 172	12 102	10 112	11 188
Rents and royalties	158	0	271	4 448	5 787	5 123	6 648	5 489	3 772	5 948
Interest and dividends	1 222	1 378	4 937	3 721	4 554	5 097	4 524	6 613	6 340	5 240
Interest	1 153	714	2 570	2 524	2 959	3 224	2 585	4 467	4 487	3 981
Dividends	68	664	2 366	1 197	1 595	1 874	1 939	2 146	1 853	1 259
Other property income	0	0	0	0	0	0	0	0	0	0
Sales of goods and services	1 648	2 006	2 243	2 335	2 894	2 620	1 671	1 663	2 158	2 591
Fines, penalties and forfeits	134	114	280	4 425	3 602	3 373	4 782	3 647	3 665	4 206
Interest on overdue tax: individuals	..	..	..	1 225	983	908	1 009	918	993	1 301
Interest on overdue tax: companies	..	..	..	1 744	1 685	1 473	2 306	1 554	1 707	2 239
Other fines, penalties and forfeits	134	114	280	1 457	934	993	1 466	1 174	965	667
Miscellaneous and unidentified revenue	169	0	50	251	360	571	422	550	531	448
Total tax and non-tax revenue	162 151	215 696	427 722	697 526	785 643	878 337	978 397	1 070 732	1 188 433	1 263 004
***Memo items:** SACU expenditure*[2]	..	..	14 107	17 862	21 719	42 108	41 979	51 661	50 289	39 388

Note: Data are reported on a fiscal year basis beginning 1st April. For example, the data for 2016 represent April 2016 to March 2017.
The data are on a cash basis.
Figures exclude non-tax revenues collected by sub-national governments as the data are not available.

1. The grants data represent total grants and donations received mainly from foreign governments and multilateral institutions. Moreover, this flow does not go through the Government Revenue fund, it is earmarked for specific projects implemented across government (by line departments).
2. Memo items: the Southern African Customs Union (SACU) expenditure records the difference between South Africa contributions to the SACU pool and the South Africa revenue share from the SACU pool that includes the balance of the "surplus/deficit" for that fiscal year and allocations to the SACU secretariat.

Source: National Treasury of South Africa. Data for grants are from the financial statements of the Reconstruction and Development Fund Programme (RDP) Fund administered by the office of Accountant General.

StatLink https://doi.org/10.1787/888933821247

Table 6.23. **Togo**

Details of non-tax revenue / Recettes non fiscales détaillées

Million XOF

	1997	2000	2005	2010	2011	2012	2013	2014	2015	2016
Total des recettes non fiscales	..	**18 964**	**31 886**	**189 643**	**169 511**	**125 000**	**114 019**	**96 255**	**102 156**	**113 821**
Dons	..	4 292	13 110	80 357	113 503	56 980	73 511	45 762	57 238	75 601
Dons projets	..	4 292	13 110	62 257	84 603	40 692	62 786	45 762	47 539	64 333
Dons programmes	..	0	0	18 100	28 900	16 288	10 725	0	9 699	11 267
Revenus de la propriété	..	10 040	11 942	92 473	42 318	57 417	30 852	29 585	25 555	21 201
Loyers et redevances	..	5 548	3 221	42 400	18 200	15 590	6 368	8 468	3 837	3 640
Redevances minières	..	0	0	0	0	0	3 181	7 367	1 270	1 372
Redevances de réhabilitation de l'Aéroport International Gnassingbé Eyadéma (AIGE)	..	5 548	3 221	0	0	0	35	1 101	2 240	1 819
Redevance contour global	..	0	0	0	0	0	0	0	0	408
Autres recettes domaniales	..	0	0	42 400	18 200	15 590	3 152	0	327	42
Intérêts et dividendes	..	4 492	8 721	50 073	24 118	41 827	24 484	21 117	21 718	17 560
Dividendes	..	2 416	2 696	6 745	4 451	18 088	16 453	13 172	16 179	11 335
Intérêts de placement	..	771	1 838	985	1 464	8 148	301	7 507	4 307	307
Produits divers (commissions, transferts BCEAO et intérêts)	..	0	0	0	0	0	0	190	201	4 642
Autres produits financiers	..	1 304	4 187	42 344	18 202	15 591	7 729	248	1 032	1 276
Autres revenus de la propriété	..	0	0	0	0	0	0	0	0	0
Ventes de biens et de services	..	1 365	850	140	1 011	2 045	6 450	17 690	7 692	9 017
Loyers d'immeuble	..	0	0	0	0	0	0	428	201	1 626
Redevances téléphoniques	..	0	0	0	0	0	2 000	11 949	2 000	1 500
Recettes de services	..	1 365	850	140	1 011	2 045	3 710	4 261	4 752	5 286
Recettes consulaires	..	0	0	0	0	0	740	1 052	739	605
Amendes, pénalités et confiscations	..	1 199	580	393	409	517	1 033	1 323	558	261
Amendes et pénalités (recettes fiscales)[1]	..	932	442	161	219	339	409	103	188	62
Amendes et penalités (recettes douanières)	..	267	138	232	190	178	624	1 219	369	199
Recettes diverses et non identifiées	..	2 069	5 403	16 280	12 270	8 040	2 173	1 895	11 114	7 741
Confiscations et ventes en douane[2]	..	0	0	0	0	0	0	385	954	4 226
Ordre de recettes (gestion antérieure)	..	0	0	0	0	0	166	0	6	262
Ordre de recettes (gestion courante)	..	0	0	0	0	0	0	85	95	53
Divers reversements	..	785	1 216	0	0	0	1 923	1 271	9 754	2 985
Autres recettes non fiscales	..	1 284	4 187	16 280	12 270	8 040	85	154	305	216
Total des recettes fiscales et non fiscales	..	118 981	191 782	443 885	497 634	500 436	530 648	568 562	636 513	701 326

Note: Année civile se terminant le 31 décembre.

Les données sont sur la base des encaissements.

Les chiffres n'incluent pas des autres recettes collectées par les collectivités locales pour leur propre compte, car elles ne sont pas disponibles.

La classification nationale du Togo considère le *Prélèvement pour apurement de la dette du secteur pétrolier* (PADSP) comme une recette non fiscale. Cette recette est considérée comme une recette fiscale dans cette publication comme le préconise la classification OCDE (voir le guide d'interprétation en Annexe A).

1. Ces recettes sont classifiées comme des recettes non fiscales dans cette publication comme le préconise la classification OCDE (voir le guide d'interprétation en Annexe B). La classification nationale du Togo comptabilise ces recettes comme des recettes fiscales.
2. Cette rubrique comprend les recettes provenant des confiscations et ventes en douane et les reversements du prélèvement communautaire de solidarité qui sont classifiés comme des recettes non fiscales dans cette publication comme le préconise la classification OCDE (voir le guide d'interprétation en Annexe B. La classification nationale du Togo considère ces recettes comme des recettes fiscales douanières. Avant 2014, ces recettes étaient comptabilisés dans la rubrique « Amendes et pénalités (recettes douanières) ».

Source: Office Togolais des Recettes et Direction de l'Économie.

StatLink https://doi.org/10.1787/888933821266

Table 6.24. **Tunisia / Tunisie**

Details of non-tax revenue / Recettes non fiscales détaillées

Million TND

	1997	2000	2005	2010	2011	2012	2013	2014	2015	2016
Total des recettes non fiscales	**..**	**725**	**1 078**	**1 799**	**2 584**	**2 452**	**2 704**	**1 903**	**1 749**	**1 539**
Dons[1]	..	7	70	54	207	633	225	368	292	130
Revenus de la propriété	..	525	703	1 299	2 044	1 267	1 514	976	863	915
Loyers et redevances	..	185	295	435	419	394	372	357	350	388
Redevances pétrolières et du gaz	..	177	284	415	410	379	353	337	328	366
Loyers	..	8	11	19	10	15	18	20	22	23
Intérêts et dividendes	..	341	408	864	1 625	872	1 143	618	513	527
Intérêts	..	56	87	56	49	66	31	42	41	8
Transferts des entreprises publiques et bénéfices de la Banque Centrale	..	274	311	796	1 567	757	1 070	503	430	447
Remises sur crédit	..	3	3	2	2	2	2	3	3	4
Autres intérêts et dividendes non compris ailleurs	..	9	8	10	8	46	39	70	39	68
Autres revenus de la propriété	..	0	0	0	0	0	0	0	0	0
Ventes de biens et de services	..	22	38	40	20	54	26	24	28	32
Ventes de produits divers	..	21	37	38	19	53	25	22	26	30
Frais administratifs	..	1	1	2	1	1	2	2	2	2
Amendes, pénalités et confiscations	..	87	127	186	98	355	730	346	378	273
Recettes diverses et non identifiées[2]	..	85	139	220	214	143	208	188	189	190
Total des recettes fiscales et non fiscales	..	7 922	11 223	18 942	21 378	22 929	25 112	26 901	27 362	28 135

Note: Année civile se terminant le 31 décembre.

Les données sont sur la base des encaissements.

Les chiffres n'incluent pas les recettes non fiscales collectées par les collectivités locales car elles ne sont pas disponibles.

1. Les dons affectés pour les Fonds spéciaux du Trésor et les Fonds de concours sont compris dans les données des dons des gouvernements et institutions étrangers.
2. Les recettes diverses et non identifiées incluent entre autres des recettes accidentelles à divers titres et des recettes non fiscales des Fonds spéciaux du Trésor et des Fonds de concours.

Source: Ministère des Finances.

StatLink https://doi.org/10.1787/888933821285

Table 6.25. **Uganda / Ouganda**

Details of non-tax revenue / Recettes non fiscales détaillées

Million UGX

	1997	2000	2005	2010	2011	2012	2013	2014	2015	2016
Total non-tax revenue	**..**	**..**	**914 434**	**948 353**	**1 196 307**	**1 001 459**	**805 360**	**1 055 407**	**1 325 469**	**1 201 242**
Grants	397 552	784 473	897 515	890 502	1 129 253	936 181	702 488	930 809	1 147 209	949 743
Budget support	193 411	365 249	484 362	515 470	575 979	198 668	191 442	258 151	339 676	259 263
Project grants	204 141	419 223	413 153	375 032	553 274	737 513	511 046	672 658	807 533	690 480
Property income	..	..	2 355	4 061	9 138	7 660	7 442	8 237	8 684	10 914
Rents and royalties	..	..	2 355	4 061	9 138	7 660	7 442	8 237	8 684	10 914
Interest and dividends	..	..	0	0	0	0	0	0	0	0
Other property income	..	..	0	0	0	0	0	0	0	0
Sales of goods and services	..	..	14 564	53 790	57 915	57 618	95 431	116 361	169 575	240 585
Driver's permits[1]	1 503	1 919	3 877	12 373	11 823	13 520	13 655	14 147	15 921	18 240
Migration fees	..	..	3 822	23 317	21 658	34 082	41 740	49 993	90 913	123 251
Passport fees	..	..	2 523	4 614	6 593	6 076	7 980	10 413	12 800	21 660
Uganda Registration Services Bureau	..	..	0	0	0	0	0	20 490	23 470	24 417
Other administrative fees	..	..	4 342	13 486	17 841	3 940	32 056	21 317	26 472	53 017
Fines, penalties and forfeits	..	..	0	0	0	0	0	0	0	0
Miscellaneous and unidentified revenue[2]	..	..	0	0	0	0	0	0	0	0
Total tax and non-tax revenue	..	..	2 849 905	5 200 374	6 354 615	7 273 790	8 026 195	9 120 476	11 086 899	12 243 544

Note: Data are reported on a fiscal year basis beginning 1st July. For example, the data for 2016 represent July 2015 to June 2016.

The data are on a cash basis.

Figures exclude non-tax revenues collected by sub-national governments as the data are not available.

1. Revenue from drivers permits are considered as non-tax revenue according the OECD classification described in the Interpretative Guide. The national classification of Uganda classifies it as tax revenues.
2. This category includes non-tax fines, administrative fees and revenue from public property and public assets. These data could not be disaggregated to allocate revenue to the relevant non-tax revenue categories.

Source: Uganda Revenue Authority.

StatLink https://doi.org/10.1787/888933821304

Revenue Statistics in Africa 1990-2016/Statistiques des recettes publiques en Afrique 1990-2016

Annex A

The OECD classification of taxes and interpretative guide[1]

Table of contents

A.1. The OECD classification of taxes

1. 1000 Taxes on income, profits and capital gains
   - 1100 Taxes on income, profits and capital gains of individuals
     - 1110 On income and profits
     - 1120 On capital gains
   - 1200 Corporate taxes on income, profits and capital gains
     - 1210 On income and profits
     - 1220 On capital gains
   - 1300 Unallocable as between 1100 and 1200
2. 2000 Social security contributions
   - 2100 Employees
     - 2110 On a payroll basis
     - 2120 On an income tax basis
   - 2200 Employers
     - 2210 On a payroll basis
     - 2220 On an income tax basis
   - 2300 Self-employed or non-employed
     - 2310 On a payroll basis
     - 2320 On an income tax basis
   - 2400 Unallocable as between 2100, 2200 and 2300
     - 2410 On a payroll basis
     - 2420 On an income tax basis
3. 3000 Taxes on payroll and workforce
4. 4000 Taxes on property
   - 4100 Recurrent taxes on immovable property
     - 4110 Households
     - 4120 Other
   - 4200 Recurrent taxes on net wealth
     - 4210 Individual
     - 4220 Corporate
   - 4300 Estate, inheritance and gift taxes
     - 4310 Estate and inheritance taxes
     - 4320 Gift taxes
   - 4400 Taxes on financial and capital transactions
   - 4500 Other non-recurrent taxes on property
     - 4510 On net wealth
     - 4520 Other non-recurrent taxes
   - 4600 Other recurrent taxes on property

5. 5000 Taxes on goods and services

5100 Taxes on production, sale, transfer, leasing and delivery of goods and rendering of services

5110 General taxes

5111 Value added taxes

5112 Sales taxes

5113 Other general taxes on goods and services

5120 Taxes on specific goods and services

5121 Excises

5122 Paid by other than business or unidentifiable

5123 Paid by other than business or unidentifiable

5124 Paid by other than business or unidentifiable

5125 Taxes on investment goods

5126 Taxes on specific services

5127 Other taxes on international trade and transactions

5128 Other taxes on specific goods and services

5130 Unallocable as between 5110 and 5120

5200 Taxes on use of goods, or on permission to use goods or perform activities

5210 Recurrent taxes

5211 Paid by households in respect of motor vehicles

5212 Paid by others in respect of motor vehicles

5213 Other recurrent taxes

5220 Non-recurrent taxes

5300 Unallocable as between 5100 and 5200

6. 6000 Other taxes

6100 Paid solely by business

6200 Paid by other than business or unidentifiable

A.2. Coverage

General criteria

1. In the OECD classification the term "taxes" is confined to compulsory unrequited payments to general government. Taxes are unrequited in the sense that benefits provided by government to taxpayers are not normally in proportion to their payments.

2. The term "tax" does not include fines, penalties and compulsory loans paid to government. Borderline cases between tax and non-tax revenues in relation to certain fees and charges are discussed in §11–14.

3. General government consists of the central administration, agencies whose operations are under its effective control, state and local governments and their administrations, certain social security schemes and autonomous governmental entities, excluding public enterprises. This definition of government follows that of the 2008 *System of National Accounts* (SNA).[2] In that publication, the general government sector and its sub-sectors are defined in Chapter 4, paragraphs 4.117 to 4.165.

4. Extra-budgetary units are part of the general government system. These are general government entities with individual budgets that are not fully covered by the main or general budget. These entities operate under the authority or control of a central, state, or local government. Extra-budgetary entities may have their own revenue sources, which may be supplemented by grants (transfers) from the general budget or from other sources. Even though their budgets may be subject to approval by the legislature, similar to that of budgetary accounts, they have discretion over the volume and composition of their spending. Such entities may be established to carry out specific government functions, such as road construction, or the nonmarket production of health or education services. Budgetary arrangements vary widely across countries, and various terms are used to describe these entities, but they are often referred to as "extra-budgetary funds" or "decentralised agencies."

5. Compulsory payments to supra-national bodies and their agencies are no longer included as taxes as from 1998, with some exceptions. However, custom duties collected by EU member states on behalf of the European Union are still identified as memorandum items and included in overall tax revenue amounts in the country tables of the country in which they are collected (See §99). In countries where the church forms part of general government church taxes are included, provided they meet the criteria set out in §1 above. As the data refer to receipts of general government, levies paid to non-government bodies, welfare agencies or social insurance schemes outside general government, trade unions or trade associations, even where such levies are compulsory, are excluded. Compulsory payments to general government earmarked for such bodies are, however, included, provided that the government is not simply acting in an agency capacity.[3] Profits from fiscal monopolies are distinguished from those of other public enterprises and are treated as taxes because they reflect the exercise of the taxing power of the state by the use of monopoly powers (see §65–67), as are profits received by the government from the purchase and sale of foreign exchange at different rates (see §74).

6. Taxes paid by governments (e.g., social security contributions and payroll taxes paid by governments in their capacity as an employer, consumption taxes on their purchases or taxes on their property) are not excluded from the data provided. However, where it is possible to identify the amounts of revenue involved,[4] they are shown in Chapter 4.2 of this Report.

7. The relationship between this classification and that of the System of National Accounts (SNA) is set out in Sections A.9 and A.11 below. Because of the differences between the two classifications, the data shown in national accounts are sometimes calculated or classified differently from the practice set out in this guide. These and other differences are mentioned where appropriate (e.g., in §30 below) but it is not possible to refer to all of them. There may also be some differences between this classification and that employed domestically by certain national administrations (e.g., see §12 below), so that OECD and national statistics data may not always be consistent: any such differences, however, are likely to be very slight in terms of amounts of revenues involved.

Social security contributions

8. Compulsory social security contributions, as defined in §39, and paid to general government, are treated here as tax revenues. Being compulsory payments to general government they clearly resemble taxes. They may, however, differ from other taxes in that the receipt of social security benefits depends, in most countries, upon appropriate contributions having been made, although the size of the benefits is not necessarily related to the amount of the contributions. Better comparability between countries is obtained by treating social security contributions as taxes, but they are listed under a separate heading so that they can be distinguished in any analysis.

9. The strict dividing line between tax revenues (compulsory unrequited payments to general government) and non-tax compulsory payments (NTCPs) (payments that are either requited or made to other institutions) is clearly defined. However, within the range of different compulsory payments to governments existing across countries, it is not always straightforward in practice to decide whether specific payments are either taxes or NTCPs. For example, compulsory pension savings that are controlled by general government and that accumulate on an individual account earning a market return or a rate that compensates for inflation would at first sight be categorised as NTCPs as opposed to taxes. However, even these payments might still be 'unrequited' and therefore classify as taxes instead of NTCPs (for example if these pension savings are not paid out when the taxpayer dies before reaching the pension age and the funds are then used to provide a minimum pension to all taxpayers that are insured). These issues result in the social security revenue figures reported for most countries being based on the premise that all types of compulsory payments to general government are judged to some extent to have a re-distributional element. It should be noted that this conclusion is based on a typically broad interpretation of the term 'unrequited' in the tax definition.

10. Social security contributions which are either voluntary or not payable to general government (see §1) are not treated as taxes, though in some countries, as indicated in the country footnotes, there are difficulties in completely eliminating voluntary contributions and certain compulsory payments to the private sector from the revenue figures. Imputed social security contributions are also not treated as taxes.

Fees, user charges and licence fees

11. Apart from vehicle licence fees, which are universally regarded as taxes, it is not easy to distinguish between those fees and user charges which are to be treated as taxes and those which are not, since, whilst a fee or charge is levied in connection with a specific service or activity, the strength of the link between the fee and the service provided may vary considerably, as may the relation between the amount of the fee and the cost of providing

the service. Where the recipient of a service pays a fee clearly related to the cost of providing the service, the levy may be regarded as requited and under the definition of §1 would not be considered as a tax. In the following cases, however, a levy could be considered as 'unrequited':

a. where the charge greatly exceeds the cost of providing the service;

b. where the payer of the levy is not the receiver of the benefit (e.g., a fee collected from slaughterhouses to finance a service which is provided to farmers);

c. where government is not providing a specific service in return for the levy which it receives even though a licence may be issued to the payer (e.g., where the government grants a hunting, fishing or shooting licence which is not accompanied by the right to use a specific area of government land);

d. where benefits are received only by those paying the levy but the benefits received by each individual are not necessarily in proportion to his payments (e.g., a milk marketing levy paid by dairy farmers and used to promote the consumption of milk).

12. In marginal cases, however, the application of the criteria set out in §1 can be particularly difficult. The solution adopted — given the desirability of international uniformity and the relatively small amounts of revenue usually involved — is to follow the predominant practice among tax administrations rather than to allow each country to adopt its own view as to whether such levies are regarded as taxes or as non-tax revenue.[5]

13. A list of the main fees and charges in question and their normal[6] treatment in this publication is as follows:

- *Non-tax revenues:* court fees; driving licence fees; harbour fees; passport fees; radio and television licence fees where public authorities provide the service.
- *Taxes within heading* 5200: permission to perform such activities as distributing films; hunting, fishing and shooting; providing entertainment or gambling facilities; selling alcohol or tobacco; permission to own dogs or to use or own motor vehicles or guns; severance taxes.

14. In practice it may not always be possible to isolate tax receipts from non-tax revenue receipts when they are recorded together. If it is estimated that the bulk of the receipts derive from non-tax revenues, the whole amount involved is treated as a non-tax revenue; otherwise, such government receipts are included and classified according to the rules provided in §32 below.

Royalties

15. The ownership of subsoil assets in the form of deposits of minerals or fossil fuels (coal, oil, or natural gas) depends upon the way in which property rights are defined by law and also on international agreements in the case of deposits below international waters. In some cases, either the ground below which the mineral deposits are located, the deposits themselves or both may belong to a local or central government unit.

16. In such cases, these general government units may grant leases to other institutional units that permit them to extract these deposits over a specified period of time in return for a payment or series of payments. These payments are often described as 'royalties' but they are essentially rent that accrues to owners of natural resources in return for putting these assets at the disposal of other units for specified periods of time. The rent may take the form of periodic payments of fixed amounts, irrespective of the rate of extraction, or, more commonly, they may be a function of the quantity, volume, or value of the asset extracted. Enterprises engaged in exploration on government land may make payments to general government units

in exchange for the right to undertake test drilling or otherwise investigate the existence and location of subsoil assets. Such payments are also recorded as rents even though no extraction may take place. These payments are therefore classified as non-tax revenues.

17. The same principles apply when other institutional units are granted leases that permit them to fell timber in natural forests on land owned by general government units. These payments are also classified as non-tax revenues.

18. These rents or royalties paid to general government should not be confused with taxes on income and profits, severance taxes, business licenses, or other taxes. If the payments are levied on the profits from the extraction activity, then they should be classified as taxes on incomes, profits and gains (1000). In addition, any severance payments that are imposed on the extraction of minerals and fossil fuels from reserves owned privately or by another government should be classified as taxes. Payments related to the gross value of production should be classified as other taxes on goods and services (5128). Payments for a license or permit to conduct extraction operations should be classified as taxes on use of goods and on permission to use goods or perform activities (5213).

Fines and penalties

19. In principle, fines and penalties charged on overdue taxes or penalties imposed for the attempted evasion of taxes should not be recorded as tax revenues. However it may not be possible to separate payments of fines or other penalties from the revenues from the taxes to which they relate. In this case the fines and penalties relating to a particular tax are recorded together with the revenues from that tax and fines and penalties paid with revenue from unidentifiable taxes are classified as other taxes in Category 6000. Fines not relating to tax offences (e.g., for parking offences), or not identifiable as relating to tax offences, are also not treated as tax revenues.

A.3. Basis of reporting

Accrual reporting

20. The data reported in this publication for recent years are predominantly recorded on an accrual basis, i.e. recorded at the time that the tax liability was created. Further information is provided in the footnotes to the country table in Chapter 4 of the Report.

21. However, data for earlier years are still predominantly recorded on a cash basis, i.e. at the time at which the payment was received by government. Thus, for example, taxes withheld by employers in one year but paid to the government in the following year and taxes due in one year but actually paid in the following year are both included in the receipts of the second year. Corrective transactions, such as refunds, repayments and drawbacks, are deducted from gross revenues of the period in which they are made.

22. Data on tax revenues are recorded without offsets for the administrative expenses connected with tax collection. Similarly, where the proceeds of tax are used to subsidise particular members of the community, the subsidy is not deducted from the yield of the tax, though the tax may be shown net of subsidies in the national records of some countries.

23. As regards fiscal monopolies (heading 5122), only the amount actually transferred to the government is included in government revenues. However, if any expenditures of fiscal monopolies are considered to be government expenditures (e.g., social expenditures undertaken by fiscal monopolies at the direction of the government) they are added back for the purpose of arriving at tax revenue figures (see §65 below).

The distinction between tax and expenditure provisions[7]

24. Because this publication is concerned only with the revenue side of government operations, no account being taken of the expenditure side, a distinction has to be made between tax and expenditure provisions. Normally there is no difficulty in making this distinction as expenditures are made outside the tax system and the tax accounts and under legislation separate from the tax legislation. In borderline cases, cash flow is used to distinguish between tax provisions and expenditure provisions. Insofar as a provision affects the flow of tax payments from the taxpayer to the government, it is regarded as a tax provision and is taken into account in the data shown in this publication. A provision which does not affect this flow is seen as an expenditure provision and is disregarded in the data recorded in this publication.

25. Tax allowances, exemptions and deductions against the tax base clearly affect the amount of tax paid to the government and are therefore considered as tax provisions. At the other extreme, those subsidies which cannot be offset against tax liability and which are clearly not connected with the assessment process, do not reduce tax revenues as recorded in this publication. Tax credits are amounts deductible from tax payable (as distinct from deductions from the tax base). Two types of tax credits are distinguished, those (referred to here as wastable tax credits) which are limited to the amount of the tax liability and therefore cannot give rise to a payment by the authorities to the taxpayer, and those (referred to as non-wastable tax credits) which are not so limited, so that the excess of the credit over the tax liability can be paid to the taxpayer.[8] A wastable tax credit, like a tax allowance, clearly affects the amount of tax paid to the government, and is therefore considered as a tax provision. The practice followed for non-wastable tax credits[9] is to distinguish between the 'tax expenditure component',[10] which is that portion of the credit that is used to reduce or eliminate a taxpayer's liability, and the 'transfer component', which is the portion that exceeds the taxpayer's liability and is paid to that taxpayer. Reported tax revenues should be reduced by the amount of the tax expenditure component but not by the amount of the transfer component. In addition, the amounts of the tax expenditure and transfer components should be reported as memorandum items in the country tables. Countries that are unable to distinguish between the tax expenditure and transfer components should indicate whether or not the tax revenues have been reduced by the total of these components, and provide any available estimates of the amounts of the two components. Further information is given in Chapter 1 of the Report, which illustrates the effect of alternative treatments of non-wastable tax credits on tax to GDP.

Calendar and fiscal years

26. National authorities whose fiscal years do not correspond to the calendar year show data, where possible, on a calendar year basis to permit maximum comparability with the data of other countries. There remain a few countries where data refer to fiscal years. For these the GDP data used in the comparative tables also correspond to the fiscal years.

A.4. General classification criteria

The main classification criteria

27. The classification of receipts among the main headings (1000, 2000, 3000, 4000, 5000 and 6000) is generally governed by the base on which the tax is levied: 1000 income, profits and capital gains; 2000 and 3000 earnings, payroll or number of employees; 4000 property; 5000 goods and services; 6000 multiple bases, other bases or unidentifiable bases. Where a

tax is calculated on more than one base, the receipts are, where possible, split among the various headings (see §32 and §81). The headings 4000 and 5000 cover not only taxes where the tax base is the property, goods or services themselves but also certain related taxes. Thus, taxes on the transfer of property are included in 4400[11] and taxes on the use of goods or on permission to perform activities in 5200. In headings 4000 and 5000 a distinction is made in certain sub-headings between recurrent and non-recurrent taxes: recurrent taxes are defined as those levied at regular intervals (usually annually) and non-recurrent taxes are levied once and for all (see also §47 to §50, §53, §54 and §79 for particular applications of this distinction).

28. Earmarking of a tax for specific purposes does not affect the classification of tax receipts. However, as explained in §39 on the classification of social security contributions, the conferment of an entitlement to social benefits is crucial to the definition of the 2000 main heading.

29. The way that a tax is levied or collected (e.g., by use of stamps) does not affect classification.

Classification of taxpayers

30. In certain sub-headings distinctions are made between different categories of taxpayers. These distinctions vary from tax to tax:

a. *Between individuals and corporations in relation to income and net wealth taxes*

The basic distinction is that corporation income taxes, as distinct from individual income taxes, are levied on the corporation as an entity, not on the individuals who own it, and without regard to the personal circumstances of these individuals. The same distinction applies to net wealth taxes on corporations and those on individuals. Taxes paid on the profits of partnerships and the income of institutions, such as life insurance or pension funds, are classified according to the same rule. They are classified as corporate taxes (1200) if they are charged on the partnership or institution as an entity without regard to the personal circumstances of the owners. Otherwise, they are treated as individual taxes (1100). Usually, there is different legislation for the corporation taxes and for the individual taxes.[12] The distinction made here between individuals and corporations does not follow the sector classification between households, enterprises, and so on of the System of National Accounts for income and outlay accounts. The SNA classification requires certain unincorporated businesses[13] to be excluded from the household sector and included with non-financial enterprises and financial institutions. The tax on the profits of these businesses, however, cannot always be separated from the tax on the other income of their owners, or can be separated only on an arbitrary basis. No attempt at this separation is made here and the whole of the individual income tax is shown together without regard to the nature of the income chargeable.

b. *Between households and others in relation to taxes on immovable property*

Here the distinction is that adopted by the SNA for the production and consumption expenditure accounts. The distinction is between households as consumers (i.e. excluding non-incorporated business) on the one hand and producers on the other hand. However, taxes on dwellings occupied by households, whether paid by owner-occupiers, tenants or landlords, are classified under households. This follows the common distinction made between taxes on domestic property versus taxes on business property. Some countries are not, however, in a position to make this distinction.

c. *Between households and others in relation to motor vehicle licences*

Here the distinction is between households as consumers on the one hand and producers on the other, as in the production and consumption expenditure accounts of the SNA.

d. *Between business and others in relation to the residual taxes (6000)*

The distinction is the same as in c) above between producers on the one hand and households as consumers on the other hand. Taxes which are included under the heading 6000 because they involve more than one tax base or because the tax base does not fall within any of the previous categories but which are identifiable as levyable only on producers and not on households are included under 'business'. The rest of the taxes which are included under the heading 6000 are shown as 'other' or non-identified.

Surcharges

31. Receipts from surcharges in respect of particular taxes are usually classified with the receipts from the relevant tax whether or not the surcharge is temporary. If, however, the surcharge has a characteristic which would render it classifiable in a different heading of the OECD list, receipts from the surcharge are classified under that heading separately from the relevant tax.

Unidentifiable tax receipts and residual sub-headings

32. A number of cases arise where taxes cannot be identified as belonging entirely to a heading or sub-heading of the OECD classification and the following practices are applied in such cases:

a. The heading is known, but it is not known how receipts should be allocated between sub-headings: receipts are classified in the appropriate residual sub-heading (1300, 2400, 4520, 4600, 5130, 5300 or 6200).

b. It is known that the bulk of receipts from a group of taxes (usually local taxes) is derived from taxes within a particular heading or sub-heading, but some of the taxes in the group whose amount cannot be precisely ascertained may be classifiable in other headings or sub-headings: receipts are shown in the heading or sub-heading under which most of the receipts fall.

c. Either the heading nor sub-heading of a tax (usually local) can be identified: the tax is classified in 6200 unless it is known that it is a tax on business in which case it is classified in 6100.

A.5. Commentaries on items of the list

1000 — Taxes on income, profits and capital gains

33. This heading covers taxes levied on the net income or profits (i.e. gross income minus allowable tax reliefs) of individuals and enterprises. Also covered are taxes levied on the capital gains of individuals and enterprises, and gains from gambling.

34. Included in the heading are:

a. taxes levied predominantly on income or profits, though partially on other bases. Taxes on various bases which are not predominantly income or profits are classified according to the principles laid down in §32 and §81;

b. taxes on property, which are levied on a presumed or estimated income as part of an income tax (see also §47(a), (c) and (d));

c. compulsory payments to social security fund contributions that are levied on income but do not confer an entitlement to social benefits. When such contributions do confer an entitlement to social benefits, they are included in heading 2000 (see §39);

d. receipts from integrated scheduler income tax systems are classified as a whole in this heading, even though certain of the scheduler taxes may be based upon gross income and may not take into account the personal circumstances of the taxpayer.

35. The main subdivision of this heading is between levies on individuals (1100) and those on corporate enterprises (1200). Under each subdivision a distinction is made between taxes on income and profits (1110 and 1210), and taxes on capital gains (1120 and 1220). If certain receipts cannot be identified as appropriate to either 1100 or 1200, or if in practice this distinction cannot be made (e.g., because there are no reliable data on the recipients of payments from which withholding taxes are deducted) they are classified in 1300 as not-allocable.

Treatment of credits under imputation systems

36. Under imputation systems of corporate income tax, a company's shareholders are wholly or partly relieved of their liability to income tax on dividends paid by the company out of income or profits liable to corporate income tax. In countries with such systems,[14] part of the tax on the company's profits is available to provide relief against the shareholders' own tax liability. The relief to the shareholder takes the form of a tax credit, the amount of which may be less than, equal to, or more than the shareholder's overall tax liability. If the tax credit exceeds this tax liability the excess may be payable to the shareholder. As this type of tax credit is an integral part of the imputation system of corporate income tax, any payment to the shareholders is treated as a repayment of tax and not as expenditure (compare the treatment of other tax credits described in §25).

37. As the tax credit under imputation systems (even when exceeding tax liability) is to be regarded as a tax provision, the question arises whether it should be deducted from individual income tax receipts (1110) or corporate income tax receipts (1210). In this Report, the full amount of corporate income tax paid is shown under 1210 and no imputed tax is included under 1110. Thus, the full amount of the credit reduces the amount of 1110 whether the credit results in a reduction of personal income tax liability or whether an actual refund is made because the credit exceeds the income tax liability. (Where, however, such tax credits are deducted from corporation tax in respect of dividends paid to corporations the amounts are deducted from the receipts of 1210).

1120 and 1220 — Taxes on capital gains

38. These sub-headings comprise taxes imposed on capital gains, 1120 covering those levied on the gains of individuals and 1220 those levied on the gains of corporate enterprises, where receipts from such taxes can be separately identified. In many countries this is not the case and the receipts from such taxes are then classified with those from the income tax. Heading 1120 also includes taxes on gains from gambling.

2000 — Social security contributions

39. Classified here are all compulsory payments that confer an entitlement to receive a (contingent) future social benefit. Such payments are usually earmarked to finance social benefits and are often paid to institutions of general government that provide such benefits. However, such earmarking is not part of the definition of social security contributions

and is not required for a tax to be classified here. However, conferment of an entitlement is required for a tax to be classified under this heading. So, levies on income or payroll that are earmarked for social security funds but do not confer an entitlement to benefit are excluded from this heading and shown under personal income taxes (1100) or taxes on payroll and workforce (3000). Taxes on other bases, such as goods and services, which are earmarked for social security benefits are not shown here but are classified according to their respective bases because they generally confer no entitlement to social security benefits.

40. Contributions for the following types of social security benefits would, *inter alia*, be included: unemployment insurance benefits and supplements, accident, injury and sickness benefits, old-age, disability and survivors' pensions, family allowances, reimbursements for medical and hospital expenses or provision of hospital or medical services. Contributions may be levied on both employees and employers.

41. Contributions may be based on earnings or payroll ('on a payroll basis') or on net income after deductions and exemptions for personal circumstances ('on an income tax basis'), and the revenues from the two bases should be separately identified if possible. However, where contributions to a general social security scheme are on a payroll basis, but the contributions of particular groups (such as the self-employed) cannot be assessed on this basis and net income is used as a proxy for gross earnings, the receipts may still be classified as being on a payroll basis. In principle, this heading excludes voluntary contributions paid to social security schemes. When separately identifiable these are shown in the memorandum item on the financing of social security benefits. In practice, however, they cannot always be separately identified from compulsory contributions, in which case they are included in this heading.

42. Contributions to social insurance schemes which are not institutions of general government and to other types of insurance schemes, provident funds, pension funds, friendly societies or other saving schemes are not considered as social security contributions. Provident funds are arrangements under which the contributions of each employee and of the corresponding employer on his/her behalf are kept in a separate account earning interest and withdrawable under specific circumstances. Pension funds are separately organised schemes negotiated between employees and employers and carry provisions for different contributions and benefits, sometimes more directly tied to salary levels and length of service than under social security schemes. When contributions to these schemes are compulsory or quasi-compulsory (e.g., by virtue of agreement with professional and union organisations) they are shown in the memorandum item (refer to Chapter 4.2 of the Report).

43. Contributions by government employees and by governments in respect of their employees, to social security schemes classified within general government are included in this heading. Contributions to separate schemes for government employees, which can be regarded as replacing general social security schemes, are also regarded as taxes.[15] Where, however, a separate scheme is not seen as replacing a general scheme and has been negotiated between the government, in its role as an employer, and its employees, it is not regarded as social security and contributions to it are not regarded as taxes, even though the scheme may have been established by legislation.

44. This heading excludes 'imputed' contributions, which correspond to social benefits paid directly by employers to their employees or former employees or to their representatives (e.g., when employers are legally obliged to pay sickness benefits for a certain period).

45. Contributions are divided into those of employees (2100), employers (2200), and self-employed or non-employed (2300), and then further sub-divided according to the basis on which they are levied. Employees are defined for this purpose as all persons engaged in activities of business units, government bodies, private non-profit institutions, or other paid employment, except the proprietors and their unpaid family members in the case of unincorporated businesses. Members of the armed forces are included, irrespective of the duration and type of their service, if they contribute to social security schemes. The contributions of employers are defined as their payments on account of their employees to social security schemes. Where employees or employers are required to continue the payment of social security contributions when the employee becomes unemployed these contributions, data permitting, are shown in 2100 and 2200 respectively. Accordingly, the sub-heading 2300 is confined to contributions paid by the self-employed and by those outside of the labour force (e.g., disabled or retired individuals).

3000 — Taxes on payroll and workforce

46. These consist of taxes payable by enterprises assessed either as a proportion of the wages or salaries paid or as a fixed amount per person employed. They do not include compulsory social security contributions paid by employers or any taxes paid by employees themselves out of their wages or salaries

4000 — Taxes on property

47. This heading covers recurrent and non-recurrent taxes on the use, ownership or transfer of property. These include taxes on immovable property or net wealth, taxes on the change of ownership of property through inheritance or gift and taxes on financial and capital transactions. The following kinds of tax are excluded from this heading:

a. taxes on capital gains resulting from the sale of a property (1120 or 1220);

b. taxes on the use of goods or on permission to use goods or perform activities (5200); see §76;

c. taxes on immovable property levied on the basis of a presumed net income which take into account the personal circumstances of the taxpayer. They are classified as income taxes along with taxes on income and capital gains derived from property (1100);

d. taxes on the use of property for residence, where the tax is payable by either proprietor or tenant and the amount payable is a function of the user's personal circumstances (pay, dependants, and so on). They are classified as taxes on income (1100);

e. taxes on building in excess of permitted maximum density, taxes on the enlargement, construction or alteration of certain buildings beyond a permitted value and taxes on building construction. They are classified as taxes on permission to perform activities (5200);

f. taxes on the use of one's own property for special trading purposes like selling alcohol, tobacco, meat or for exploitation of land resources (e.g., United States severance taxes). They are classified as taxes on permission to perform activities (5200).

4100 — *Recurrent taxes on immovable property*

48. This sub-heading covers taxes levied regularly in respect of the use or ownership of immovable property.

- these taxes are levied on land and buildings;
- they can be in the form of a percentage of an assessed property value based on a national rental income, sales price, or capitalised yield; or in terms of other characteristics of real property, (for example size or location) from which a presumed rent or capital value can be derived.
- such taxes can be levied on proprietors, tenants, or both. They can also be paid by one level of government to another level of government in respect of property under the jurisdiction of the latter.
- debts are not taken into account in the assessment of these taxes, and they differ from taxes on net wealth in this respect.

49. Taxes on immovable property are further sub-divided into those paid by households (4110) and those paid by other entities (4120), according to the criteria set out in §30(*b*) above.

4200 — *Recurrent taxes on net wealth*

50. This sub-heading covers taxes levied regularly (in most cases annually) on net wealth, i.e. taxes on a wide range of movable and immovable property, net of debt. It is sub-divided into taxes paid by individuals (4210) and taxes paid by corporate enterprises (4220) according to the criteria set out in §30(*a*) above. If separate figures exist for receipts paid by institutions, the tax payments involved are added to those paid by corporations.

4300 — *Estate, inheritance and gift taxes*

51. This sub-heading is divided into taxes on estates and inheritances (4310) and taxes on gifts (4320).[16] Estate taxes are charged on the amount of the total estate whereas inheritance taxes are charged on the shares of the individual recipients; in addition the latter may take into account the relationship of the individual recipients to the deceased.

4400 — *Taxes on financial and capital transactions*

52. This sub-heading comprises, *inter alia*, taxes on the issue, transfer, purchase and sale of securities, taxes on cheques, and taxes levied on specific legal transactions such as validation of contracts and the sale of immovable property. The heading does not include:

a. taxes on the use of goods or property or permission to perform certain activities (5200);

b. fees paid to cover court charges, charges for birth, marriage or death certificates, which are normally regarded as non-tax revenues (see §11);

c. taxes on capital gains (1000);

d. recurrent taxes on immovable property (4100);

e. recurrent taxes on net wealth (4200);

f. once-and-for-all levies on property or wealth (4500).

4500 — *Other non-recurrent taxes on property*[16]

53. This sub-heading covers once-and-for-all, as distinct from recurrent, levies on property. It is divided into taxes on net wealth (4510) and other non-recurrent taxes on property (4520). Heading 4510 would include taxes levied to meet emergency expenditures, or for

redistribution purposes. Heading 4520 would cover taxes levied to take account of increases in land value due to permission given to develop or provision of additional local facilities by general government, any taxes on the revaluation of capital and once-and-for-all taxes on particular items of property.

4600 — Other recurrent taxes on property

54. These rarely exist in OECD member countries, but the heading would include taxes on goods such as cattle, jewellery, windows, and other external signs of wealth.

5000 — Taxes on goods and services

55. All taxes and duties levied on the production, extraction, sale, transfer, leasing or delivery of goods, and the rendering of services (5100), or in respect of the use of goods or permission to use goods or to perform activities (5200) are included here. The heading thus covers:

a. multi-stage cumulative taxes;

b. general sales taxes — whether levied at manufacture/production, wholesale or retail level;

c. value-added taxes;

d. excises;

e. taxes levied on the import and export of goods;

f. taxes levied in respect of the use of goods and taxes on permission to use goods, or perform certain activities;

g. taxes on the extraction, processing or production of minerals and other products.

56. Borderline cases between this heading and heading 4000 (taxes on property) and 6100 (other taxes on business) are referred to in §47, §52 and §78. Residual sub-headings (5300) and (5130) cover tax receipts which cannot be allocated between 5100 and 5200 and between 5110 and 5120, respectively; see §32.

5100 — Taxes on the production, sale, transfer, leasing and delivery of goods and rendering of services

57. This sub-heading consists of all taxes, levied on transactions in goods and services on the basis of their intrinsic characteristics (e.g., value, weight of tobacco, strength of alcohol, and so on) as distinct from taxes imposed on the use of goods, or permission to use goods or perform activities, which fall under 5200.

5110 — General taxes on goods and services

58. This sub-heading includes all taxes, other than import and export duties (5123 and 5124), levied on the production, leasing, transfer, delivery or sales of a wide range of goods and/or the rendering of a wide range of services, irrespective of whether they are domestically produced or imported and irrespective of the stage of production or distribution at which they are levied. It thus covers value-added taxes, sales taxes and multi-stage cumulative taxes. Receipts from border adjustments in respect of such taxes when goods are imported are added to gross receipts for this category, and repayments of such taxes when goods are exported are deducted. These taxes are subdivided into 5111 value-added taxes, 5112 sales taxes, 5113 turnover and other general taxes on goods and services.

59. Borderline cases arise between this heading and taxes on specific goods (5120) when taxes are levied on a large number of goods, for example, the United Kingdom purchase tax

(repealed in 1973) and the Japanese commodity tax (repealed in 1988). In conformity with national views, the former United Kingdom purchase tax is classified as a general tax (5112) and the former Japanese commodity tax as excises (5121).

5111 — *Value-added taxes*

60. All general consumption taxes charged on value-added are classified in this sub-heading, irrespective of the method of deduction and the stages at which the taxes are levied. In practice, all OECD countries with value-added taxes normally allow immediate deduction of taxes on purchases by all but the final consumer and impose tax at all stages. In some countries the heading may include certain taxes, such as those on financial and insurance activities, either because receipts from them cannot be identified separately from those from the value-added tax, or because they are regarded as an integral part of the value-added tax, even though similar taxes in other countries might be classified elsewhere (e.g., 5126 as taxes on services or 4400 as taxes on financial and capital transactions).

5112 — *Sales taxes*

61. All general taxes levied at one stage only, whether at manufacturing or production, wholesale or retail stage are classified here.

5113 — *Turnover and other general taxes on goods and services*

62. These are multi-stage cumulative taxes and taxes where elements of consumption taxes are combined with multistage taxes. These taxes are levied each time a transaction takes place without deduction for taxes paid on inputs. Multi-stage taxes can be combined with elements of value-added or sales taxes.

5120 — *Taxes on specific goods and services*

63. Excises, profits generated and transferred from fiscal monopolies, and customs and imports duties as well as taxes on exports, foreign exchange transactions, investment goods and betting stakes and special taxes on services, which do not form part of a general tax of 5110, are included in this category.

5121 — Excises

64. Excises are taxes levied as a product specific unit tax on a predefined limited range of goods. Excises are usually levied at differentiated rates on nonessential or luxury goods, alcoholic beverages, tobacco, and energy. Excises may be imposed at any stage of production or distribution and are usually assessed as a specific charge per unit based on characteristics by reference to the value, weight, strength, or quantity of the product. Included are special taxes on individual products such as sugar, sugar beets, matches, and chocolates; taxes levied at varying rates on a certain range of goods; and taxes levied on tobacco goods, alcoholic drinks, motor fuels, and hydrocarbon oils. If a tax collected principally on imported goods also applies, or would apply, under the same law to comparable domestically produced goods, then the revenue from this tax is classified as arising from excises rather than from import duties. This principle applies even if there is no comparable domestic production or no possibility of such production. Taxes on the use of utilities such as water, electricity, gas, and energy are regarded as excises rather than taxes on specific services (5126). Excises exclude those taxes that are levied as general taxes on goods and services (5110); profits of fiscal monopolies (5122); customs and other import duties (5123); or taxes on exports (5124).

5122 — *Profits of fiscal monopolies*

65. This sub-heading covers that part of the profits of fiscal monopolies which is transferred to general government or which is used to finance any expenditures considered to be government expenditures (see §23). Amounts are shown when they are transferred to general government or used to make expenditures considered to be government expenditures.

66. Fiscal monopolies reflect the exercise of the taxing power of government by the use of monopoly powers. Fiscal monopolies are non-financial public enterprises exercising a monopoly in most cases over the production or distribution of tobacco, alcoholic beverages, salt, matches, playing cards and petroleum or agricultural products (i.e. on the kind of products which are likely to be, alternatively or additionally, subject to the excises of 5121), to raise the government revenues which in other countries are gathered through taxes on dealings in such commodities by private business units. The government monopoly may be at the production stage or, as in the case of government-owned and controlled liquor stores, at the distribution stage.

67. Fiscal monopolies are distinguished from public utilities such as rail transport, electricity, post offices, and other communications, which may enjoy a monopoly or quasi-monopoly position but where the primary purpose is normally to provide basic services rather than to raise revenue for government. Transfers from such other public enterprises to the government are considered as non-tax revenues. The traditional concept of fiscal monopoly is not generally extended to include state lotteries, the profits of which are usually accordingly regarded as non-tax revenues. However, they can be included as tax revenues if the prime reason for their operation is to raise revenues to finance government expenditure. Fiscal monopoly profits are distinguished from export and import monopoly profits (5127) transferred from marketing boards or other enterprises dealing with international trade.

5123 — *Customs and other import duties*

68. Taxes, stamp duties and surcharges restricted by law to imported products are included here. Also included are levies on imported agricultural products which are imposed in member countries of the European Union and amounts paid by certain of these countries under the Monetary Compensation Accounts (MCA) system.[17] Starting from 1998, customs duties collected by European Union member states on behalf of the European Union are no longer reported under this heading in the country tables (in Chapter 4 of the Report). Excluded here are taxes collected on imports as part of a general tax on goods and services, or an excise applicable to both imported and domestically produced goods.

5124 — *Taxes on exports*

69. In the 1970s, export duties were levied in Australia, Canada and Portugal as a regular measure and they have been used in Finland for counter-cyclical purposes. Some member countries of the European Union pay, as part of the MCA system, a levy on exports (see note 16 to §68). Where these amounts are identifiable, they are shown in this heading. This heading does not include repayments of general consumption taxes or excises or customs duties on exported goods, which should be deducted from the gross receipts under 5110, 5121 or 5123, as appropriate.

5125 — *Taxes on investment goods*

70. This sub-heading covers taxes on investment goods, such as machinery. These taxes may be imposed for a number of years or temporarily for counter-cyclical purposes. Taxes

on industrial inputs which are also levied on consumers [e.g., the Swedish energy tax which is classified under (5121)] are not included here.

5126 — *Taxes on specific services*

71. All taxes assessed on the payment for specific services, such as taxes on insurance premiums, banking services, gambling and betting stakes (e.g., from horse races, football pools, lottery tickets), transport, entertainment, restaurant and advertising charges, fall into this category. Taxes levied on the gross income of companies providing the service (e.g., gross insurance premiums or gambling stakes received by the company) are also classified under this heading. Tax revenues from bank levies and payments to deposit insurance and financial stability schemes are provisionally included here for the 2012 edition. The detailed classification is set out in §108.

72. Excluded from this sub-heading are:

a. taxes on services forming part of a general tax on goods and services (5110);

b. taxes on electricity, gas and energy (5121 as excises);

c. taxes on individual gains from gambling (1120 as taxes on capital gains of individuals and non-corporate enterprises) and lump-sum taxes on the transfer of private lotteries or on the permission to set up lotteries (5200);[18]

d. taxes on cheques and on the issue, transfer or redemption of securities (4400 as taxes on financial and capital transactions).

5127 — *Other taxes on international trade and transactions*

73. This sub-heading covers revenue received by the government from the purchase and sale of foreign exchange at different rates. When the government exercises monopoly powers to extract a margin between the purchase and sales price of foreign exchange, other than to cover administrative costs, the revenue derived constitutes a compulsory levy exacted in indeterminate proportions from both purchaser and seller of foreign exchange. It is the common equivalent of an import duty and export duty levied in a single exchange rate system or of a tax on the sale or purchase of foreign exchange. Like the profits of fiscal monopolies and import or export monopolies transferred to government, it represents the exercise of monopoly powers for tax purposes and is included in tax revenues.

74. The sub-heading covers also the profits of export or import monopolies, which do not however exist in OECD countries, taxes on purchase or sale of foreign exchange, and any other taxes levied specifically on international trade or transactions.

5128 — *Other taxes on specific goods and services*

75. This item includes taxes on the extraction of minerals, fossil fuels and other exhaustible resources from deposits owned privately or by another government together with any other unidentifiable receipts from taxes on specific goods and services. Taxes on the extraction of exhaustible resources are usually a fixed amount per unit of quality or weight, but can be a percentage of value. The taxes are recorded when the resources are extracted. Payments from the extraction of exhaustible resources from deposits owned by the government unit receiving the payment are classified as rent.

5200 — *Taxes on use of goods or on permission to use goods or perform activities*

76. This sub-heading covers taxes which are levied in respect of the use of goods as distinct from taxes on the goods themselves. Unlike the latter taxes – reported under 5100 –, they are

not assessed on the value of the goods but usually as fixed amounts. Taxes on permission to use goods or to perform activities are also included here, as are pollution taxes not based upon the value of particular goods. It is sometimes difficult to distinguish between compulsory user charges and licence fees which are regarded as taxes and those which are excluded as non-tax revenues. The criteria which are employed are noted in §11–12.

77. Although the sub-heading refers to the 'use' of goods, registration of ownership rather than use may be what generates liability to tax, so that the taxes of this heading may apply to the ownership of animals or goods rather than their use (e.g., race horses, dogs and motor vehicles) and may apply even to unusable goods (e.g., unusable motor vehicles or guns).

78. Borderline cases arise with:

a. taxes on the permission to perform business activities which are levied on a combined income, payroll or turnover base and, accordingly, are classified following the rules in §81;

b. taxes on the ownership or use of property of headings 4100, 4200 and 4600. The heading 4100 is confined to taxes on the ownership or tenancy of immovable property and – unlike the taxes of 5200 – they are related to the value of the property. The net wealth taxes and taxes on chattels of 4200 and 4600 respectively are confined to the ownership rather than the use of assets, apply to groups of assets rather than particular goods and again are related to the value of the assets,

5210 — *Recurrent taxes on use of goods and on permission to use goods or perform activities*

79. The principal characteristic of taxes classified here is that they are levied at regular intervals and that they are usually fixed amounts. The most important item in terms of revenue receipts is vehicle licence taxes. This sub-heading also covers taxes on permission to hunt, shoot, fish or to sell certain products and taxes on the ownership of dogs and on the performance of certain services, provided that they meet the criteria set out in §11–12. The sub-divisions of 5210 are user taxes on motor vehicles paid by households (5211) and those paid by others (5212). Sub-heading 5213 covers dog licences and user charges for permission to perform activities such as selling meat or liquor when the levies are on a recurring basis. It also covers recurrent general licences for hunting, shooting and fishing where the right to carry out these activities is not granted as part of a normal commercial transaction (e.g., the granting of the licence is not accompanied by the right to use a specific area which is owned by government).

5220 — *Non-recurrent taxes on use of goods and on permission to use goods or perform activities*

80. This section covers non-recurrent taxes levied on the use of goods or on permission to use goods or perform activities and taxes levied each time goods are used. It includes taxes levied on the emission or discharge into the environment of noxious gases, liquids or other harmful substances.

- Payments for tradable emission permits issued by governments under cap and trade schemes should be recorded here at the time the emissions occur. No revenue should be recorded for permits that governments issue free of charge. The accrual basis of recording means that there can be a timing difference between the cash being received by government for the permits and the time the emission occurs. In the national accounts, this timing gives rise to a financial liability for government during the period.

- Payments made for the collection and disposal of waste or noxious substances by public authorities should be excluded as they constitute a sale of services to enterprises.

81. Other taxes falling under heading 5200 that are not levied recurrently are also included here. Thus, once-and-for-all payments for permission to sell liquor or tobacco or to set up betting shops are included provided they meet the criteria set out in §11–12.

6000 — Other taxes

82. Taxes levied on a base, or bases, other than those described under headings 1000, 3000, 4000 and 5000, or on bases of which cannot be considered to be related to any one of these headings, are included here. Where taxes are levied on a multiple base and it is possible to estimate the receipts related to each base the separate amounts are included under the appropriate headings. If separate amounts cannot be estimated and it is known that most of the receipts are derived from one base, the whole of the receipts are classified according to that base. Otherwise, they are classified here. Other revenues included here are presumptive taxes not included elsewhere in the classification system, taxes on individuals in the form of a poll tax or capitation tax, stamp taxes not related to financial and capital transactions nor falling exclusively on a single category of transaction, expenditure taxes where personal deductions or exemptions are applied and unidentifiable tax receipts. A subdivision is made between taxes levied wholly or predominantly on business (6100) and those levied on others (6200).

A.6. Conciliation with National Accounts

83. This section of the tables provides a re-conciliation between the OECD calculation of total tax revenues and the total of all taxes and social contributions paid to general government as recorded in the country's National Accounts. Where the country is a member of the European Union (EU), the comparison is between the OECD calculation of total tax revenues and the sum of tax revenues and social contributions recorded in the combination of the general government and the institutions of the EU sectors of the National Accounts.

A.7. Memorandum item on the financing of social security benefits

84. In view of the varying relationship between taxation and social security contributions and the cases referred to in §39 to §45, a memorandum item collects together all payments earmarked for social security-type benefits, other than voluntary payments to the private sector. Data are presented as follows (refer to Chapter 4.2 of the Report):

a. Taxes of 2000 series.

b. Taxes earmarked for social security benefits.

c. Voluntary contributions to the government.

d. Compulsory contributions to the private sector.

Guidance on the breakdown of (a) to (d) above is provided in §39 to §45.

A.8. Memorandum item on identifiable taxes paid by government

85. Identifiable taxes actually paid by government are presented in a memorandum item classified by the main headings of the OECD classification of taxes. In the vast majority of countries, only social security contributions and payroll taxes paid by government can

be identified. These are, however, usually the most important taxes paid by governments (refer to Chapter 4.2 of the Report).

A.9. Relation of OECD classification of taxes to national accounting systems

86. A system of national accounts (SNA) seeks to provide a coherent framework for recording and presenting the main flows relating respectively to production, consumption, accumulation and external transactions of a given economic area, usually a country or a major region within a country. Government revenues are an important part of the transactions recorded in SNA. The final version of the 2008 SNA was jointly published by five international organisations: the United Nations, the International Monetary Fund, the European Union, the Organisation for Economic Co-operation and Development, and the World Bank in August 2009. The *System* is a comprehensive, consistent and flexible set of macroeconomic accounts. It is designed for use in countries with market economies, whatever their stage of economic development, and also in countries in transition to market economies. The important parts of the SNA's conceptual framework and its definitions of the various sectors of the economy have been reflected in the OECD's classification of taxes.

87. There are, however, some differences between the OECD classification of taxes and SNA concepts that are listed below. They arise because the aim of the former is to provide the maximum disaggregation of statistical data on what are generally regarded as taxes by tax administrations.

a. OECD includes compulsory social security contributions paid to general government in total tax revenues. Imputed and voluntary contributions plus those paid to private funds are not treated as taxes (§8 and §10 above);

b. there are different points of view on whether or not some levies and fees are classified as taxes (§11 and §12 above);

c. OECD excludes imputed taxes or subsidies resulting from the operation of official multiple exchange rates or from the central bank paying a rate of interest on required reserves that is different from other market rates;

d. there are differences in the treatment of non-wastable tax credits

88. As noted in §1 and §2, headings 1000 to 6000 of the OECD list of taxes cover all unrequited payments to general government, other than compulsory loans and fines. Such unrequited payments including fines, but excluding compulsory loans can be obtained from adding together the following figures in the 2008 SNA

- value-added type taxes (D.211);
- taxes and duties on imports, excluding VAT (D.212);
- export taxes (D.213);
- taxes on products, excluding VAT, import and export taxes (D.214);
- other taxes on production (D.29);
- taxes on income (D.51);
- other current taxes (D.59);
- social contributions (D.61), excluding voluntary contributions;
- capital taxes (D.91).

A.10. The OECD classification of taxes and the International Monetary Fund (GFS) system

89. The coverage and valuation of tax revenues in the GFS system and the 2008 SNA are very similar. Therefore, the differences between the OECD classification and that of the 2008 SNA (see §87 above) also apply to the GFS. In addition the International Monetary Fund subdivides the OECD 5000 heading into section IV (Domestic Taxes on Goods and Services) and section V (Taxes on International Trade and Transactions). This reflects the fact that while the latter usually yield insignificant amounts of revenue in OECD countries, this is not the case in many non-OECD countries.

A.11. Comparison of the OECD classification of taxes with other international classifications

90. The table below describes an item by item comparison of the OECD classification of taxes and the classifications used in the following:

a. System of National Accounts (2008 SNA);

b. European System of Accounts (2010 ESA);

c. IMF *Government Finance Statistics Manual* (GFSM2014).

91. These comparisons represent those that would be expected to apply in the majority of cases. However in practice some flexibility should be used in their application. This is because in particular cases, countries can adopt varying approaches to the classification of revenues in National Accounts.

OECD Classification	2008 SNA	2010 ESA	GFSM2014
1000 Taxes on income, profits and capital gains			
1100 Individuals			
1110 Income and profits	D51-8.61a	D51A	1111
1120 Capital gains	D51-8.61c, d	D51C, D	1111
1200 Corporations			
1210 Income and profits	D51-8.61b	D51B	1112
1220 Capital gains	D51-8.61c	D51C	1112
1300 Unallocable as between 1100 and 1200			1113
2000 Social security contributions			
2100 Employees	D613-8.85	D613	1211
2200 Employers	D611-8.83	D611	1212
2300 Self-employed, non-employed	D613-8.85	D613	1213
2400 Unallocable as between 2100, 2200 and 2300			1214
3000 Taxes on payroll and workforce	D29-7.97a	D29C	112
4000 Taxes on property			
4100 Recurrent taxes on immovable property			
4110 Households	D59-8.63a	D59A	1131
4120 Other	D29-7.97b	D29A	1131
4200 Recurrent net wealth taxes			
4210 Individual	D59-8.63b	D59A	1132
4220 Corporations	D59-8.63b	D59A	1132
4300 Estate, inheritance and gift taxes			
4310 Estate and inheritance taxes	D91-10.207b	D91A	1133
4320 Gift taxes	D91-10.207b	D91A	1133
4400 Taxes on financial and capital transactions	D59-7.96d; D29-7.97e	D214B, C	114114; 1161
4500 Other non-recurrent taxes on property	D91-10.207a	D91B	1135
4600 Other recurrent taxes on property	D59-8.63c	D59A	1136

OECD Classification	2008 SNA	2010 ESA	GFSM2014
5000 Taxes on goods and services			
5100 Taxes on production, sale and transfer of goods and services			
5110 General taxes on goods and services			
5111 Value-added taxes	D211-7.89	D211; D29G	11411
5112 Sales taxes	D2122-7.94a; D214-7.96a	D21224; D214I	11412
5113 Other general taxes on goods and services	D214-7.96a	D214I	11413
5120 Taxes on specific goods and services			
5121 Excises	D2122-7.94b; D214-7.96b	D21223; D214A, B, D	1142
5122 Profits of fiscal monopolies	D214-7.96e	D214J	1143
5123 Customs and other import duties	D2121-7.93	D2121; D21221, 2	1151
5124 On exports	D213-7.95a	D214K	1152-4
5125 On investment goods			
5126 On specific services	D2122-7.94c; D214-7.96c	D21225; D214E, F, G, H; D29F	1144; 1156
5127 Other taxes on international trade and transactions	D2122-7.94d D29-7.95b D29-7.97g D59-8.64d	D21226; D29D; D59E	1153; 1155-6
5128 Other taxes on specific goods and services			1146
5130 Unallocable between 5110 and 5120			
5200 Taxes on use of goods and on permission to use goods or perform activities			
5210 Recurrent taxes on use of goods and on permission to use goods or perform activities			
5211 Motor vehicle taxes households	D59-8.64c	D59D	11451
5212 Motor vehicles taxes others	D29-7.97d	D214D; D29B	11451
5213 Other recurrent taxes on use of goods and on permission to use goods or perform activities	D29-7.97c, d, f D59-8.64c	D29B, E, F; D59D	11452
5220 Non-recurrent taxes on permission to use goods or perform activities			11452
5300 Unallocable as between 5100 and 5200			
6000 Other taxes			
6100 Payable solely by business			1161
6200 Payable by other than business, or unidentifiable	D59-8.64a, b	D59B, C	1162

A.12. Attribution of tax revenues by sub-sectors of general government

92. The OECD classification requires a breakdown of tax revenues by sub-sectors of government. The definition of each sub-sector and the criteria to be used to attribute tax revenues between these sub-sectors are set out below. They follow the guidance of the 2008 SNA and GFSM 2014.

Sub-sectors of general government to be identified

a) Central government

93. The central government sub-sector includes all governmental departments, offices, establishments and other bodies which are agencies or instruments of the central authority whose competence extends over the whole territory, with the exception of the administration of social security funds. Central government therefore has the authority to impose taxes on all resident and non-resident units engaged in economic activities within the country.

b) State, provincial or regional government

94. This sub-sector consists of intermediate units of government exercising a competence at a level below that of central government. It includes all such units operating independently of central government in a part of a country's territory encompassing a number of smaller

localities, with the exception of the administration of social security funds. In unitary countries, regional governments may be considered to have a separate existence where they have substantial autonomy to raise a significant proportion of their revenues from sources within their control and their officers are independent of external administrative control in the actual operation of the unit's activities.

95. At present, federal countries comprise the majority of cases where revenues attributed to intermediate units of government are identified separately. Spain is the only unitary country in this position. In the remaining unitary countries, regional revenues are included with those of local governments.

c) *Local government*

96. This sub-sector includes all other units of government exercising an independent competence in part of the territory of a country, with the exception of the administration of social security funds. It encompasses various urban and/or rural jurisdictions (e.g., local authorities, municipalities, cities, boroughs, districts).

d) Social security funds

97. Social security funds form a separate sub-sector of general government. The social security sub-sector is defined in the 2008 SNA by the following extracts from paragraphs 4.124 to 4.126 and 4.147:

> *"Social security schemes are social insurance schemes covering the community as a whole or large section of the community that are imposed and controlled by government units. The schemes cover a wide variety of programmes, providing benefits in cash or in kind for old age, invalidity or death, survivors, sickness and maternity, work injury, unemployment, family allowance, health care, etc. There is not necessarily a direct link between the amount of the contribution paid by an individual and the benefits he or she may receive." (Paragraph 4.124).*

> *"When social security schemes are separately organised from the other activities of government units and hold their assets and liabilities separately from the latter and engage in financial transactions on their own account they qualify as institutional units that are described as social security funds." (Paragraph 4.125).*

> *"The amounts raised, and paid out, in social security contributions and benefits may be deliberately varied in order to achieve objectives of government policy that have no direct connection with the concept of social security as a scheme to provide social benefits to members of the community. They may be raised or lowered in order to influence the level of aggregate demand in the economy, for example. Nevertheless, so long as they remain separately constituted funds, they must be treated as separate institutional units in the SNA. (Paragraph 4.126).*

> *"The social security funds sub-sector (of general government) consists of the social security funds operating at all levels of government. Such funds are social insurance schemes covering the community as a whole or large section of the community that are imposed by government units." (Paragraph 4.147).*

98. This definition of social security funds is followed in the OECD classification with the two following exceptions which are excluded

- Schemes imposed by government and operated by bodies outside the general government sector, as defined in §3 of this manual; and
- Schemes to which all contributions are voluntary.

Supra-national Authorities

99. This sub-sector covers the revenue-raising operations of supra-national authorities within a country. In practice, the only relevant supra-national authority in the OECD area is that of the institutions of the European Union (EU). As from 1998, supra-national authorities are no longer included in the *Revenue Statistics*, to achieve consistency with the SNA definition of general government which excludes them. For example, income taxes and social security contributions collected by European Institutions and paid by European civil servants who are resident of EU member countries should not be included. However the specific levies paid by the member states of the EU continue to be included in total tax revenues and they are shown under this heading.

Criteria to be used for the attribution of tax revenues

100. When a government collects taxes and pays them over in whole or in part to other governments, it is necessary to determine whether the revenues should be considered to be those of the collecting government which it distributes to others as grants, or those of the beneficiary governments which the collecting government receives and passes on only as their agent. The criteria to be used in the attribution of revenues are set out in §101 to §104 which replicate paragraphs 3.70 to 3.73 from the 2008 SNA.

101. In general, a tax is attributed to the government unit that

a. exercises the authority to impose the tax (either as a principal or through the delegated authority of the principal),

b. has final discretion to set and vary the rate of the tax

102. Where an amount is collected by one government for and on behalf of another government, and the latter government has the authority to impose the tax, and set and vary its rate, then the former is acting as an agent for the latter and the tax is reassigned. Any amount retained by the collecting government as a collection charge should be treated as a payment for a service. Any other amount retained by the collecting government, such as under a tax-sharing arrangement, should be treated as a current grant. If the collecting government was delegated the authority to set and vary the rate, then the amount collected should be treated as tax revenue of this government.

103. Where different governments jointly and equally set the rate of a tax and jointly and equally decide on the distribution of the proceeds, with no individual government having ultimate overriding authority, then the tax revenues are attributed to each government according to its respective share of the proceeds. If an arrangement allows one government unit to exercise ultimate overriding authority, then all of the tax revenue is attributed to that unit.

104. There may also be the circumstance where a tax is imposed under the constitutional or other authority of one government, but other governments individually set the tax rate in their jurisdictions. The proceeds of the tax generated in each respective government's jurisdiction are attributed as tax revenues of that government.

Levies paid by member states of the European Union

105. The levies paid by the member states of the EU take the form specific levies which include

a. custom duties and levies on agricultural goods (5123),

b. gross monetary compensation accounts (5123 if relating to imports and 5124 if relating to exports); and

c. Steel, coal, sugar and milk levies (5128).

106. The custom duties collected by member states on behalf of the EU are recorded

- on a gross of collection fee basis;
- using figures adjusted so that duties are shown on a 'final destination' as opposed to a 'country of first entry' basis where such adjustments can be made. These adjustments concern in particular duties collected at important (sea) ports. Although the EU duties are collected by the authorities of the country of first entry, when possible these duties should be excluded from the revenue of the collecting country and be included in the revenue of the country of final destination

107. This is the specific EU levy that most clearly conforms to the attribution criterion described in §99 above. Consequently as from 1998, these amounts are footnoted as a memorandum item to EU member state country tables and no longer shown under heading 5123. However the figures are included in the total tax revenue figures on the top line for all the relevant years shown in the tables.

A.13. Provisional classification of revenues from bank levies and payments to deposit insurance and financial stability schemes

108. The OECD have adopted the following interim approach to reporting revenue from bank levies plus deposit insurance and stability fees for the 2012 and subsequent editions of *OECD Revenue Statistics*. It is recommended that the amounts should be recorded under category 5126.

- Compulsory payments of stability fees, bank levies and deposit insurance should generally be treated as tax revenues where the payments are made to General Government and allocated to the governments' consolidated or general funds so that the Government is free to make immediate use of the money for the purposes that it chooses. This principle would apply regardless of whether the Government is promising to make payments to guarantee the banks' customer deposits in some future contingency.
- If the compulsory payments are made to general government and placed in funds that are earmarked to be entirely channelled back to the sector of the economy that comprises the companies that are subject to the payment, they would still generally be treated as tax revenues on the grounds that the funds would be available for the government and would reduce its budget deficit, the fee is unrequited for an individual entity and the amounts raised could be unrelated to any eventual pay out to depositors or expenditure on wider support for the financial sector.
- Payments to made to the smaller long-standing schemes for insuring 'retail' deposits, where the payment levels are consistent with the costs of insurance should be classified as fee for service.
- Any payments which involve governments realising the assets of a failed institution or receiving a priority claim on its assets in liquidation in order to fund payments of compensation to customers for their lost deposits would be treated as a fee for a service as opposed to tax revenues.
- Compulsory payments that are made to funds operated outside the government sector and non-state institutions backed by the deposit takers and all payments to voluntary schemes should not be treated as tax revenues.

Notes

1. References in this OECD Interpretative Guide to Sections or Parts of "this Report" refer to OECD (2017), Revenue Statistics 2017 , OECD Publishing, Paris
2. All references to SNA are to the 2008 edition.
3. See section A.12 of this guide for a discussion of the concept of agency capacity.
4. It is usually possible to identify amounts of social security contributions and payroll taxes, but not other taxes paid by government.
5. If, however, a levy which is considered as non-tax revenue by most countries is regarded as a tax — or raises substantial revenue — in one or more countries, the amounts collected are footnoted at the end of the relevant country tables, even though the amounts are not included in total tax revenues.
6. Names, however, can frequently be misleading. For example, though a passport fee would normally be considered a non-tax revenue, if a supplementary levy on passports (as is the case in Portugal) were imposed in order to raise substantial amounts of revenue relative to the cost of providing the passport, the levy would be regarded as a tax under 5200.
7. A more detailed explanation of this distinction can be found in the special feature, 'Current issues in reporting tax revenues', in the 2001 edition of the *Revenue Statistics*.
8. Sometimes the terms 'non-refundable' and 'refundable' are used, but it may be considered illogical to talk of 'refundable' when nothing has been paid.
9. A different treatment, however, is accorded to non-wastable tax credits under imputation systems of corporate income tax (§36–38).
10. This is not strictly a true tax expenditure in the formal sense. Such tax expenditures require identification of a benchmark tax system for each country or, preferably, a common international benchmark. In practice it has not been possible to reach agreement on a common international benchmark.
11. Unless based on the profit made on a sale, in which case they would be classified as capital gains taxes under 1120 or 1220.
12. In some countries the same legislation applies to both individual and corporate enterprises for particular taxes on income. However, the receipts from such taxes are usually allocable between individuals and enterprises and can therefore be shown in the appropriate sub-heading.
13. For example, "...sufficiently self-contained and independent that they behave in the same way as corporations.......(including) keeping a complete set of accounts" (2008 SNA, section 4.44).
14. In Canada — a country also referred to as having an imputation system — the (wastable) tax credit for the shareholder is in respect of domestic corporation tax deemed to have been paid whether or not a corporation tax liability has arisen. As there is no integral connection between the corporation tax liability and the credit given against income tax under such systems, these credits for dividends are treated, along with other tax credits, on the lines described in §25.
15. This may also apply where a scheme for government employees existed prior to the introduction of a general social security scheme.
16. In the 2008 SNA these are regarded as capital transfers and not as taxes (see section A.8).
17. This is the system by which the European Union adjusts for differences between the exchange rates used to determine prices under the Common Market Agricultural Policy and actual exchange rates. Payments under the system may relate to imports or exports and where these amounts are separately identifiable they are shown under the appropriate heading (5123 or 5124). In this Report, these amounts are shown gross (i.e. without deducting any subsidies paid out under the MCA system).
18. Transfers of profits of State lotteries are regarded as non-tax revenues (see also §67).

Revenue Statistics in Africa 1990-2016/Statistiques des recettes publiques en Afrique 1990-2016

Annexe A

Classification des impôts de l'OCDE et Guide d'interprétation[1]

Table des matières

A.1. Classification des impôts de l'OCDE

1. 1000 Impôts sur le revenu, les bénéfices et les gains en capital
   - 1100 Impôts sur le revenu, les bénéfices et les gains en capital des personnes physiques
     - 1110 Sur le revenu et les bénéfices
     - 1120 Sur les gains en capital
   - 1200 Impôts sur le revenu, les bénéfices et les gains en capital des sociétés
     - 1210 Sur le revenu et les bénéfices
     - 1220 Sur les gains en capital
   - 1300 Non ventilables entres les rubriques 110 et 1200
2. 2000 Cotisations de sécurité sociale
   - 2100 A la charge des salariés
     - 2110 Sur la base du salaire
     - 2120 Sur la base de l'impôt sur le revenu
   - 2200 A la charge des employeurs
     - 2210 Sur la base du salaire
     - 2220 Sur la base de l'impôt sur le revenu
   - 2300 A la charge des travailleurs indépendants ou des personnes n'occupant pas d'emploi
     - 2310 Sur la base du salaire
     - 2320 Sur la base de l'impôt sur le revenu
   - 2400 Non ventilables entre les rubriques 2100, 2200 et 2300
     - 2410 Sur la base du salaire
     - 2420 Sur la base de l'impôt sur le revenu
3. 3000 Impôts sur les salaires et la main-d'œuvre
4. 4000 Impôts sur le patrimoine
   - 4100 Impôts périodiques sur la propriété immobilière
     - 4110 Ménages
     - 4120 Autres agents
   - 4200 Impôts périodiques sur l'actif net
     - 4210 Personnes physiques
     - 4220 Sociétés
   - 4300 Impôts sur les mutations par décès, les successions et les donations
     - 4310 Impôts sur les mutations par décès et les successions
     - 4320 Impôts sur les donations
   - 4400 Impôts sur les transactions mobilières et immobilières
   - 4500 Autres impôts non périodiques sur le patrimoine
     - 4510 Impôts sur l'actif net
     - 4520 Autres impôts non périodiques
   - 4600 Autres impôts périodiques sur le patrimoine

5. 5000 Impôts sur les biens et services

5100 Impôts sur la production, la vente, le transfert, la location et la livraison des biens et la prestation de services

5110 Impôts généraux

5111 Taxes sur la valeur ajoutée

5112 Impôts sur les ventes

5113 Impôts sur le chiffre d'affaires et autres impôts généraux sur les biens et services

5120 Impôts sur des biens et des services déterminés

5121 Accises

5122 Bénéfices des monopoles fiscaux

5123 Droits de douane et autres droits à l'importation

5124 Taxes à l'exportation

5125 Impôts sur les biens d'équipement

5126 Impôts sur des services déterminés

5127 Autres impôts sur les transactions et les échanges internationaux

5128 Autres impôts sur des biens et services déterminés

5130 Non ventilables entre les rubriques 5110 et 5120

5200 Impôts sur l'utilisation des biens ou l'autorisation d'utiliser des biens ou d'exercer des activités

5210 Impôts périodiques

5211 A la charge des ménages au titre de véhicules à moteur

5212 A la charge d'autres agents au titre de véhicules à moteur

5213 Autres impôts périodiques

5220 Impôts non périodiques

5300 Non ventilables entre les rubriques 5100 et 5200

6. 6000 Autres impôts

6100 A la charge exclusive des entreprises

6200 A la charge d'autre agents que les entreprises ou non identifiables

A.2. Champ couvert

Principes généraux

1. Dans la classification de l'OCDE, le terme « impôts » désigne uniquement les versements obligatoires effectués sans contrepartie au profit des administrations publiques. Les impôts n'ont pas de contrepartie en ce sens que, normalement, les prestations fournies par les administrations au contribuable ne sont pas proportionnelles à ses versements.

2. Le terme « impôts » ne couvre pas les amendes, les pénalités, ni les prêts obligatoires aux administrations. Les cas dans lesquels la délimitation entre recettes fiscales et non fiscales est délicate à tracer, pour certains droits et taxes d'utilisation, sont examinés dans les § 11 à 14.

3. Les administrations publiques comprennent l'administration centrale et les organismes dont les opérations sont sous son contrôle effectif, les administrations régionales et locales et leurs services, les organismes de sécurité sociale et les entités publiques autonomes, à l'exception des entreprises publiques. Cette définition des administrations est calquée sur celle du Système de comptabilité nationale 2008 (SCN)[2]. Dans cette publication, les administrations publiques et leurs sous-secteurs sont décrits dans le chapitre 4, paragraphes 4.117 à 4.165.

4. Les unités extrabudgétaires sont des composantes du système des administrations publiques. Il s'agit d'entités d'administration publique dotées de budgets distincts, qui ne sont pas intégralement financés par le budget central ou général. Ces organismes fonctionnent sous l'autorité ou le contrôle d'une administration centrale, d'un État fédéré ou d'une collectivité locale. Les entités extrabudgétaires peuvent disposer de leurs propres sources de recettes, qui peuvent être complétées par des dotations (transferts) provenant du budget général ou d'autres sources. Même si leurs budgets peuvent être soumis à l'approbation du corps législatif, comme les comptes budgétaires, elles disposent d'une certaine latitude quant au volume et à la composition de leurs dépenses. Ces entités peuvent être mises en place pour exercer des fonctions spécifiques des administrations publiques, telles que la construction de routes ou la production non marchande de services de santé ou d'éducation. Les dispositions budgétaires peuvent varier grandement suivant les pays, et différents termes sont utilisés pour décrire ces entités, mais elles sont souvent qualifiées de « fonds extrabudgétaires » ou d'« organismes autonomes ».

5. Les paiements obligatoires à des organismes supranationaux et aux organismes qui en dépendent ne sont plus compris depuis 1998 parmi les impôts sauf quelques exceptions. En effet, les droits de douane collectés par les États membres de l'Union européenne pour le compte de celle-ci sont toujours présentés à titre de rubrique « Pour mémoire » et compris dans le total des recettes fiscales (voir § 99). Dans les pays où les églises font partie des administrations publiques, les impôts sur les cultes sont inclus dans ces paiements, à condition qu'ils répondent aux critères énoncés au § 1 ci-dessus. Comme les données se réfèrent aux montants encaissés par les administrations publiques, les contributions versées à des organismes privés, aux organismes sociaux ou régimes de sécurité sociale extérieurs aux administrations publiques, aux syndicats ou aux associations professionnelles sont exclues, même si elles sont obligatoires. Sont toutefois inclus les versements obligatoires aux administrations publiques dont le montant est affecté à ces organismes, à condition que l'administration ne fasse pas simplement office d'agent collecteur[3]. On a distingué les bénéfices des monopoles fiscaux de ceux d'autres entreprises publiques et on les a considérés comme des impôts parce qu'ils reflètent l'exercice du pouvoir d'imposition de l'État par l'intermédiaire du monopole (voir § 65 à 67), comme le sont les bénéfices de l'État provenant de l'achat et de la vente de monnaies étrangères à des taux différents (voir § 74).

6. Les impôts payés par les administrations elles-mêmes (tels que les cotisations de sécurité sociale et les impôts sur les salaires payés par les administrations en tant qu'employeurs (2200 et 3000), les impôts sur la consommation qu'elles acquittent à l'occasion de leurs achats ou les impôts sur leur patrimoine) sont inclus dans les données présentées. Toutefois, lorsqu'il est possible de les isoler, les montants provenant de ces impôts[4] sont indiqués dans le chapitre 4.2 de cette publication.

7. Les rapports entre cette classification et celle du Système de comptabilité nationale (SCN) sont indiqués dans les sections A.9 et A.11. À cause des différences qui existent entre les deux classifications, les statistiques de la comptabilité nationale ne sont pas toujours établies ou classées suivant la pratique adoptée dans le présent guide. Ces différences et d'autres encore sont mentionnées dans les cas appropriés (voir par exemple § 30), mais il est impossible de toutes les signaler. Il peut y avoir aussi certaines différences entre cette classification et celle utilisée par certaines administrations nationales (voir par exemple § 12), aussi les statistiques nationales et celles de l'OCDE ne peuvent pas toujours être compatibles ; ces différences, cependant, sont vraisemblablement très insignifiantes dans les montants des recettes en cause.

Cotisations de sécurité sociale

8. Les cotisations obligatoires de sécurité sociale, définies au § 39, qui sont versées aux administrations publiques, font partie des recettes fiscales. Elles sont évidemment assimilables à des impôts puisqu'il s'agit de versements obligatoires à des administrations publiques. Mais elles peuvent différer toutefois des autres impôts du fait que le paiement des prestations de sécurité sociale dépend dans la plupart des pays du versement des cotisations appropriées, encore qu'il n'y ait pas forcément un lien entre l'importance des prestations et le montant des cotisations. La comparabilité entre les pays sera meilleure si on considère les cotisations de sécurité sociale comme des impôts ; elles figurent cependant sous une rubrique distincte de façon à permettre un traitement séparé pour n'importe quelle analyse.

9. La distinction stricte entre les recettes fiscales (qui sont des paiements obligatoires sans contrepartie aux administrations publiques) et les prélèvements obligatoires non fiscaux (PONF) (qui sont soit des paiements avec contrepartie aux administrations publiques, soit des paiements destinés à d'autres organismes) est clairement définie. Néanmoins, dans la palette des divers prélèvements obligatoires destinés aux administrations publiques qui existent dans les différents pays, il n'est pas toujours évident de déterminer en pratique si tel ou tel prélèvement est un impôt ou un PONF. Ainsi, l'épargne-retraite obligatoire qui est placée sous le contrôle des administrations publiques et qui s'accumule sur un compte individuel rémunéré à un taux correspondant au rendement du marché ou destiné à compenser l'inflation semble, à première vue, constituer une forme de PONF, et non d'impôt. Toutefois, ces paiements peuvent encore être considérés comme « sans contrepartie » et, par conséquent, être classés dans les impôts et non dans les PONF (par exemple si cette épargne-retraite n'est pas remboursée au cas où le contribuable décède avant d'atteindre l'âge de la retraite, et si les fonds en question sont utilisés ensuite pour verser une pension minimale à tous les contribuables qui sont assurés). En conséquence, les chiffres relatifs aux recettes de sécurité sociale indiqués pour la plupart des pays reposent sur l'hypothèse que l'on considère que tous les types de prélèvements obligatoires destinés aux administrations publiques comportent, dans une certaine mesure, un élément redistributif. Il convient de noter que cette conclusion découle d'une interprétation généralement large du terme « sans contrepartie » dans la définition de l'impôt.

10. Les cotisations de sécurité sociale qui sont facultatives ou qui ne sont pas versées à des administrations publiques (voir § 1) ne sont pas considérées comme des impôts, bien que dans certains pays (comme il est indiqué dans les notes correspondantes), il soit difficile d'éliminer complètement les cotisations facultatives et certains versements obligatoires au secteur privé des statistiques relatives aux recettes publiques. Les cotisations de sécurité sociale imputées ne sont pas considérées comme des impôts.

Droits, taxes d'utilisation et droits de licence

11. Si l'on excepte les droits perçus sur les permis de circulation des véhicules à moteur, qui sont universellement considérés comme des impôts, il n'est pas facile de distinguer les droits et taxes d'utilisation qui doivent être traitées comme des impôts de celles qui ne doivent pas l'être. Si, en effet, un droit ou une taxe est perçu au titre d'un service ou d'une activité déterminée, le lien entre ce prélèvement et la prestation fournie peut être plus ou moins important, de même que la relation entre le montant du prélèvement et le coût de la prestation. Lorsque le bénéficiaire d'une prestation acquitte un droit dont le montant est clairement lié au coût de la prestation fournie, on peut considérer que le prélèvement comporte une contrepartie, et d'après la définition donnée au § 1, il ne sera pas traité comme un impôt. Toutefois, dans les cas suivants, les prélèvements seraient 'sans contrepartie':

a. lorsque le prélèvement est très supérieur au coût de la prestation fournie ;

b. lorsque le redevable de la contribution n'est pas le bénéficiaire de la prestation correspondante (par exemple, un droit perçu sur l'abattage du bétail pour financer un service qui est fourni aux agriculteurs) ;

c. lorsque l'État ne fournit pas un service déterminé en contrepartie du droit qu'il perçoit, même si un permis est délivré à celui qui acquitte le droit (par exemple, lorsque l'État délivre des permis de chasse, de pêche ou de port d'armes qui ne sont pas assortis du droit d'utiliser une parcelle déterminée de terres appartenant à l'État) ;

d. lorsque les bénéficiaires de la prestation sont les personnes qui ont acquitté le droit, mais que la prestation dont chacun bénéficie n'est pas nécessairement en rapport avec le montant de ses propres versements (par exemple, le droit de commercialisation du lait acquitté par les fermiers qui sert à promouvoir la consommation de lait.

12. Dans des cas limites, cependant, l'application des critères énoncés au § 1 peut être particulièrement difficile. La solution adoptée, dans un souci d'uniformité entre les pays et eu égard aux montants relativement faibles des recettes en cause, consiste à s'en tenir à la pratique prépondérante des administrations fiscales plutôt que de laisser chaque pays décider si ces prélèvements sont des impôts ou des recettes non fiscales[5].

13. On trouvera ci-après la liste des principaux droits et taxes en question et leur traitement normal[6] dans la présente publication :

- *Recettes non fiscales* : frais de justice ; droits de délivrance de permis de conduire ; droits portuaires ; redevances de passeport ; redevances de radio et de télévision lorsque le service est assuré par les pouvoirs publics.
- *Impôts du sous-groupe 5200:* autorisation d'exercer certaines activités telles que : distribution de films ; chasse, pêche et utilisation d'armes à feu ; organisation de spectacles ou de jeux et paris ; vente de boissons alcoolisées ou de tabacs ; autorisation de posséder des chiens et d'utiliser ou posséder des véhicules à moteur ou des armes à feu ; taxes d'extraction.

14. Dans la pratique, il se peut qu'il ne soit pas toujours possible d'isoler les recettes fiscales des recettes non fiscales quand elles sont enregistrées ensemble. Si l'on estime qu'il s'agit surtout de recettes non fiscales, l'ensemble sera traité comme tel ; dans le cas contraire, les recettes seront comptabilisées et classées conformément aux règles énoncées au § 32.

Redevances

15. La propriété des gisements prenant la forme de minéraux ou de combustibles fossiles (charbon, pétrole ou gaz naturel) dépend de la façon dont les droits de propriété sont définis par la loi, et aussi par les conventions internationales quand les gisements sont situés sous les eaux internationales. Dans certains cas, soit le terrain sous lequel les gisements sont situés, soit les gisements eux-mêmes, soit les deux peuvent appartenir à une administration publique centrale ou locale.

16. Ces unités des administrations publiques peuvent alors consentir un bail à d'autres unités institutionnelles en les autorisant à exploiter ces gisements pendant une période déterminée, en contrepartie d'un paiement ou d'une série de paiements. Ces paiements sont souvent qualifiés de redevances (« royalties »), mais ils n'en constituent pas moins essentiellement des loyers, qui reviennent aux propriétaires des ressources naturelles considérées parce qu'ils mettent ces actifs à la disposition d'autres unités institutionnelles pour des durées déterminées. Ces loyers peuvent prendre la forme de versements périodiques d'un montant fixe, indépendant du rythme d'extraction ; plus vraisemblablement, ils peuvent être fonction de la quantité, du volume ou de la valeur des actifs extraits. Les entreprises engagées dans des activités de prospection sur des terrains publics peuvent effectuer des paiements aux unités de l'administration publique concernées, en contrepartie de l'autorisation de procéder à des forages d'essai ou de réaliser par d'autres moyens des recherches concernant l'existence et la localisation de gisements. Ces paiements sont également considérés comme des loyers, même en l'absence d'extraction. Ils sont donc classés dans les recettes non fiscales.

17. Les mêmes principes s'appliquent lorsque d'autres unités institutionnelles se voient consentir un bail leur permettant de couper du bois dans des forêts naturelles sur des terrains appartenant à des unités des administrations publiques. Ces paiements sont également classés dans les recettes non fiscales.

18. Ces loyers ou redevances versés aux administrations publiques ne doivent pas être confondus avec les impôts sur le revenu et les bénéfices, les taxes d'extraction, les taxes professionnelles ou d'autres impôts. Si ces paiements sont prélevés sur les bénéfices tirés des activités d'extraction, ils doivent être classés dans les impôts sur le revenu, les bénéfices et les gains en capital (1000). En outre, toute taxe d'extraction relative à des minéraux ou des combustibles fossiles extraits de réserves privées ou appartenant à d'autres administrations publiques doit être classée dans les impôts. Les paiements liés à la valeur brute de la production doivent être classés dans les autres impôts sur des biens et services déterminés (5128). Les paiements effectués en contrepartie d'une autorisation ou d'un permis d'extraction doivent être classés dans les impôts sur l'utilisation des biens ou l'autorisation d'utiliser des biens ou d'exercer des activités (5200).

Amendes et pénalités

19. En principe, les amendes et pénalités portant sur les impôts impayés ou les pénalités appliquées en cas de tentative d'évasion fiscale ne doivent pas être enregistrées comme des recettes fiscales. Cependant, il se peut qu'il ne soit pas possible de séparer le versement des amendes et pénalités des recettes correspondant aux impôts auxquels ces amendes et

pénalités se rattachent. Dans ce cas, les amendes et pénalités associés à un impôt particulier sont enregistrées avec les recettes correspondant à cet impôt alors que les amendes et pénalités liées à des recettes correspondant à des impôts non-identifiés sont classées comme autres impôts dans la catégorie 6000. Les amendes qui ne concernent pas des infractions fiscales (comme les infractions au stationnement), ou qui ne sont pas identifiables en tant que telles, ne sont pas non plus considérées comme des recettes fiscales.

A.3. Bases de comptabilisation

Droits constatés

20. Les données enregistrées dans cette publication pour les années récentes sont essentiellement indiquées en droits constatés, c'est-à-dire qu'elles sont enregistrées au moment du fait générateur de l'impôt. D'autres informations sont fournies dans les notes des tableaux par pays au chapitre 4 de ce rapport.

21. Toutefois, les données des années antérieures sont encore principalement comptabilisées sur la base des décaissements, c'est-à-dire au moment où l'administration reçoit le versement. Ainsi, les impôts retenus à la source par les employeurs au cours d'un exercice, mais versés à l'administration au cours de l'exercice suivant, et les impôts dus au titre d'une année mais effectivement versés l'année suivante, figurent les uns et les autres dans les recettes du second exercice. Les restitutions, remboursements et retraits résultant d'opérations rectificatives sont déduits des recettes brutes de la période au cours de laquelle ces opérations sont effectuées.

22. Les données relatives aux recettes fiscales sont comptabilisées, sans déduction compensatoire des dépenses administratives liées au recouvrement de l'impôt. De même, lorsque le produit d'un impôt sert à subventionner certains membres de la collectivité, la subvention n'est pas déduite du rendement de l'impôt, encore que certains pays fassent figurer dans leurs données l'impôt après déduction des subventions.

23. Pour les monopoles fiscaux (sous-groupe 5122), seul le montant effectivement transféré à l'État est inclus dans les recettes publiques. Toutefois, les dépenses des monopoles fiscaux qui sont considérées comme des dépenses publiques (par exemple, des dépenses de caractère social engagées par les monopoles fiscaux à l'instigation de l'État) sont ajoutées après coup pour calculer le montant des recettes fiscales (voir § 65).

La distinction entre dispositions fiscales et dépenses directes[7]

24. Étant donné que la présente publication ne vise que les recettes publiques en faisant abstraction des dépenses, il convient de distinguer entre les dispositions fiscales et les dépenses directes. Normalement, cette distinction ne soulève aucune difficulté, car les dépenses directes sont effectuées en dehors du système fiscal et des comptes fiscaux et en vertu de dispositions législatives distinctes. Dans les cas limites, on recourt, pour établir la distinction, au principe de la comptabilisation sur la base des paiements. Dans la mesure où une disposition affecte le montant des paiements du contribuable à l'État, elle est considérée comme une disposition fiscale dont il est tenu compte dans les données figurant dans cette publication. Une disposition qui n'affecte pas ce montant est considérée comme une dépense directe dont il n'est pas tenu compte dans les données reproduites dans cette publication.

25. Il est clair que les abattements fiscaux, exonérations et déductions de l'assiette de l'impôt modifient le montant de l'impôt acquitté à l'État ; il s'agit donc de dispositions fiscales. Inversement, les formes d'aides qui ne sont pas imputables sur l'impôt et n'ont

donc aucun lien avec le processus d'imposition, ne réduisent pas les recettes publiques qui sont consignées dans ce volume. Les crédits d'impôt sont des montants déductibles de l'impôt à acquitter (par opposition aux déductions, qui sont opérées sur l'assiette de l'impôt). On distingue deux catégories de crédits d'impôt : ceux (que l'on qualifiera ici de 'non récupérables') qui sont limités au montant de l'impôt à acquitter et ne peuvent donc donner lieu à un versement de l'administration au contribuable, et ceux (qualifiés ici de 'récupérables') qui n'ont pas cette limite, de sorte que l'excédent du crédit sur l'impôt peut être versé au contribuable[8]. Le crédit d'impôt non récupérable, comme un abattement fiscal, affecte évidemment le montant de l'impôt acquitté à l'État ; aussi est-il considéré comme une disposition fiscale. La solution adoptée pour les crédits d'impôts récupérables[9] consiste à distinguer l'élément de « dépense fiscale »[10], qui est la part du crédit utilisée pour réduire ou supprimer l'impôt dû par le contribuable, et l'« élément de transfert », qui correspond à la part excédant l'impôt dû par le contribuable et qui lui est reversée. Les recettes fiscales rapportées doivent être diminuées du montant de l'élément de dépense, mais non de l'élément de transfert. En outre, les montants de l'élément de dépense fiscale et de l'élément de transfert doivent être indiqués pour mémoire dans les tableaux par pays. Les pays qui ne sont pas en mesure de faire la distinction entre l'élément de dépense fiscale et l'élément de transfert doivent indiquer si leurs recettes fiscales ont été ou non diminuées du montant total de ces éléments, et fournir toutes les estimations dont ils disposent concernant les montants de ces deux éléments. Des informations complémentaires figurent dans le chapitre 1 de ce Rapport, qui fait apparaître les effets des différents traitements possibles des crédits d'impôts récupérables sur les ratios impôt rapportant les impôts au PIB.

Année civile et année fiscale (exercice budgétaire)

26. Les autorités nationales dont l'exercice budgétaire ne correspond pas à l'année civile fournissent, autant que possible, leurs données sur la base de l'année civile afin de faciliter au maximum la comparaison avec les données des autres pays. Les données d'un petit nombre de pays se réfèrent à l'exercice budgétaire. Pour ceux-ci, les statistiques de PIB utilisées dans les tableaux comparatifs portent aussi sur les exercices budgétaires.

A.4. Principes généraux de classification

Les fondements essentiels de la classification

27. Les recettes sont classées par groupes principaux (1000, 2000, 3000, 4000, 5000, 6000) suivant l'assiette de l'impôt : 1000 revenus, bénéfices et gains en capital ; 2000 et 3000 salaires et nombre d'employés ; 4000 patrimoine ; 5000 biens et services ; 6000 assiettes diverses, autres ou non identifiables. Lorsqu'un impôt est calculé en fonction de plusieurs assiettes, les recettes sont, chaque fois que c'est possible, réparties entre les divers groupes (voir § 32 et § 81). Les groupes 4000 et 5000 ne comprennent pas seulement les impôts ayant pour assiette le patrimoine, les biens ou les services eux-mêmes, mais aussi certains impôts connexes. Ainsi, les impôts sur les mutations du patrimoine sont classés dans le groupe 4400[11] et les impôts sur l'utilisation des biens, ou l'autorisation d'exercer une activité, dans le groupe 5200. Dans les groupes 4000 et 5000, une distinction est faite dans certains sous-groupes entre impôts périodiques et impôts non périodiques : on entend par impôts périodiques ceux qui sont perçus à intervalles réguliers (ordinairement tous les ans) et par impôts non périodiques ceux qui ne sont perçus qu'une seule fois (voir aussi les § 47 à 50, § 53, § 54, et § 79 pour une application particulière de cette distinction).

28. L'affectation spéciale de certaines recettes fiscales n'influe pas sur leur classification. Toutefois comme explicité au § 39 sur la classification des cotisations de sécurité sociale, l'octroi d'un droit aux prestations sociales est crucial dans la définition de la rubrique principale 2000.

29. La manière selon laquelle un impôt est perçu ou recouvré (par exemple, au moyen de timbres) n'affecte pas sa classification.

Classification des contribuables

30. Dans certains sous-groupes, des distinctions sont faites entre les différentes catégories de contribuables. Ces distinctions varient d'un impôt à l'autre :

a. Ventilation des impôts sur le revenu et sur l'actif net entre personnes physiques et sociétés

La distinction fondamentale entre les impôts sur le revenu des sociétés et les impôts sur le revenu des personnes physiques est que les premiers sont perçus sur la société en tant qu'entité et non sur les personnes physiques qui en sont propriétaires, donc sans tenir compte de la situation personnelle de celles-ci. La même distinction est applicable aux impôts sur l'actif net des sociétés et des personnes physiques. Les impôts perçus sur les bénéfices des sociétés de personnes et sur le revenu de certaines institutions comme les caisses d'assurance-vie ou de retraite, sont classés selon le même principe. Ils sont compris dans les impôts sur les sociétés (1200) lorsqu'ils sont perçus sur la société de personnes ou l'institution en tant qu'entité sans que la situation personnelle des propriétaires entre en ligne de compte ; dans les autres cas, ils sont considérés comme des impôts sur les personnes physiques (1100). Ordinairement, les impôts sur les sociétés et les impôts sur les personnes physiques sont régis par des dispositions législatives différentes[12]. La distinction qui est faite ici entre personnes physiques et sociétés ne reprend pas la classification par secteur (ménages, entreprises, etc.) adoptée dans les comptes de revenus et de dépenses du SCN. Cette dernière classification exclut du secteur des ménages certaines entreprises non constituées en sociétés[13] et les fait figurer parmi les entreprises non financières et les institutions financières. Toutefois, l'impôt sur les bénéfices de ces entreprises ne peut pas toujours être isolé de l'impôt sur les autres revenus des propriétaires de ces entreprises, ou ne peut l'être que d'une façon arbitraire. On n'a pas cherché ici à faire la distinction et l'impôt sur le revenu des personnes physiques figure globalement, quelle que soit la nature du revenu imposable.

b. Ventilation des impôts sur les biens immobiliers entre ménages et autres agents

En l'occurrence, la distinction est celle qui a été adoptée par le SCN dans les comptes de production et de consommation. On distingue, en effet, les ménages en tant que consommateurs d'une part (c'est-à-dire à l'exclusion des entreprises individuelles), et les producteurs d'autre part. Cependant, les impôts sur les logements occupés par les ménages, qu'ils soient à la charge des propriétaires qui les occupent, du locataire ou du propriétaire, sont classés comme étant à la charge des ménages. C'est la distinction faite habituellement entre les impôts sur les biens des personnes et les impôts sur les biens des entreprises. Toutefois, certains pays ne sont pas en mesure d'établir cette distinction.

c. Ventilation des permis de circuler des véhicules à moteur entre taxes à la charge des ménages et à la charge d'autres agents

On distingue ici les ménages en tant que consommateurs d'une part, et producteurs d'autre part, comme dans les comptes de production et de consommation du SCN.

d. Ventilation des autres impôts (6000) entre les entreprises et les autres agents

Il est fait la même distinction qu'au point (c) ci-dessus entre les producteurs, d'une part, et les ménages consommateurs d'autre part. Les impôts qui figurent dans le groupe 6000 parce qu'ils ne comportent pas une assiette unique ou parce que leur assiette ne relève d'aucune des catégories précédentes, mais qui ne sont manifestement perçus que sur les producteurs et non sur les ménages, sont classés comme étant 'à la charge des entreprises'. Les autres impôts du groupe 6000 figurent sous la rubrique 'à la charge d'autres agents' ou 'non identifiés'.

Surtaxes

31. Les recettes des surtaxes relatives à des impôts particuliers sont classées ordinairement avec les recettes de l'impôt correspondant, que la surtaxe ait ou non un caractère temporaire. Toutefois, si l'une des caractéristiques de la surtaxe permet de la classer sous une rubrique différente de la classification de l'OCDE, les recettes de cette surtaxe sont classées sous cette rubrique et non pas avec les recettes de l'impôt correspondant

Recettes fiscales non identifiables et sous-groupes résiduels

32. Il arrive parfois qu'on ne puisse déterminer si des impôts relèvent entièrement d'un groupe ou d'un sous-groupe de la classification de l'OCDE ; dans ces cas on applique les méthodes suivantes :

a. le groupe est connu, mais on ne sait pas comment répartir les recettes entre les sous-groupes ; les recettes sont alors classées dans le sous-groupe résiduel approprié (1300, 2400, 4520, 4600, 5130, 5300 ou 6200) ;

b. on sait que l'ensemble des recettes d'un groupe d'impôts (ordinairement des impôts locaux) provient d'impôts relevant d'un groupe ou sous-groupe particulier, mais certains impôts du groupe, dont le montant ne peut être déterminé avec précision, peuvent être classés dans d'autres groupes ou sous-groupes ; dans ce cas les recettes sont comptabilisées dans le groupe ou sous-groupe dont relève l'essentiel des recettes ;

c. il est impossible d'identifier le groupe ou le sous-groupe d'un impôt (ordinairement un impôt local) ; l'impôt est alors classé dans le groupe 6200, à moins qu'il ne s'agisse d'un impôt manifestement à la charge des entreprises, auquel cas il est classé dans le sous-groupe 6100.

A.5. Commentaires sur les postes de la liste

1000 — Impôts sur le revenu, les bénéfices et les gains en capital

33. Ce groupe couvre les impôts prélevés sur le revenu ou le bénéfice net (c'est-à-dire le revenu brut déduction faite des abattements autorisés) des personnes physiques et des entreprises. Sont aussi couverts les impôts prélevés sur les gains en capital des personnes physiques et des entreprises et sur les gains provenant de jeux.

34. Ce groupe comprend :

a. les impôts perçus principalement sur les revenus ou les bénéfices, bien qu'ils puissent l'être partiellement sur d'autres bases. Les impôts qui ont une autre assiette principale que le revenu ou les bénéfices sont classés selon les principes énoncés aux § 32 et § 81 ;

b. les impôts sur la propriété immobilière, qui sont perçus sur la base d'un revenu présumé ou estimé faisant partie de l'assiette de l'impôt sur le revenu (voir aussi § 47 (a), (c) et (d)) ;

c. les versements obligatoires aux caisses de sécurité sociale qui sont prélevés sur les revenus mais ne donnent pas droit à des prestations sociales. Lorsque ces contributions donnent droit à des prestations sociales, elles figurent à la rubrique 2000 (voir § 39) ;

d. les recettes provenant d'impôts cédulaires sur le revenu intégrés dans le régime général qui sont globalement classés dans ce groupe, bien que certains de ces impôts soient sur le revenu brut et ne tiennent pas toujours compte de la situation personnelle du contribuable.

35. Les impôts figurant dans ce groupe sont subdivisés en deux grands sous-groupes, les impôts sur le revenu des personnes physiques (1100) et les impôts sur le revenu des sociétés (1200), une ventilation étant faite dans chacun d'eux entre les impôts sur le revenu et les bénéfices (1110 et 1210) et les impôts sur les gains en capital (1120 et 1220). Si certaines recettes ne peuvent être identifiées comme relevant soit du sous-groupe 1100, soit du sous-groupe 1200, ou si cette distinction ne peut être faite dans la pratique (parce qu'il n'y a pas de données fiables sur les bénéficiaires des paiements sur lesquels la retenue à la source est faite), elles sont classées dans le sous-groupe 1300 (non ventilables).

Traitement des crédits d'impôt dans les systèmes d'imputation

36. Dans les régimes d'imputation de l'impôt sur les bénéfices des sociétés, les actionnaires bénéficient d'une compensation totale ou partielle d'imposition sur les dividendes que la société leur a versés et pour lesquels elle a acquitté l'impôt sur le revenu des sociétés. Dans les pays qui appliquent un tel régime, une fraction de l'impôt sur les bénéfices des sociétés sert à alléger l'impôt dû par l'actionnaire. Cet allégement prend la forme d'un crédit d'impôt, dont le montant peut être inférieur, égal ou supérieur au montant total de l'impôt dont il est redevable. Si le crédit d'impôt dépasse ce montant, l'excédent peut être versé à l'actionnaire. Comme ce type de crédit d'impôt fait partie intégrante des systèmes d'imputation de l'impôt sur le revenu des sociétés, tout paiement à l'actionnaire est considéré comme un remboursement d'impôt et non comme une dépense (se référer au traitement des autres crédits d'impôt exposé au § 25).

37. Puisque, dans les systèmes d'imputation, le crédit d'impôt (même lorsqu'il dépasse l'impôt dû) est censé être une disposition fiscale, on peut se demander s'il doit être déduit des recettes de l'impôt sur le revenu des personnes physiques (1110) ou de celles de l'impôt sur les bénéfices de sociétés (1210). Dans ce Rapport le montant intégral de l'impôt acquitté sur les bénéfices des sociétés figure sous le poste 1210 et aucun impôt imputé n'est inclus dans le poste 1110. Le montant total du crédit d'impôt réduit donc le montant des recettes du poste 1110, que ce crédit se traduise par une réduction de l'impôt dû sur le revenu des personnes physiques ou par un remboursement réel du fait que le crédit dépasse le montant de l'impôt. (Cependant, lorsque ces crédits sont déduits de l'impôt sur les sociétés au titre de dividendes versés à des sociétés, le montant est déduit des recettes du poste 1210).

1120 et 1220 — Impôts sur les gains en capital

38. Ces postes comprennent les impôts perçus sur les gains en capital, le sous-groupe 1120 comptabilisant les impôts prélevés sur les gains des personnes physiques et le sous-groupe 1220 ceux qui sont perçus sur les gains des entreprises constituées sous forme de sociétés,

lorsque ces recettes peuvent être ventilées. Ce n'est pas le cas dans de nombreux pays et les recettes de ces impôts sont alors classées avec celles de l'impôt sur le revenu. Les impôts sur les gains provenant de jeux sont aussi classés sous le poste 1120.

2000 — Cotisations de sécurité sociale

39. Figurent dans ce groupe tous les versements obligatoires qui donnent le droit de bénéficier d'une prestation sociale future (éventuelle). Ces versements sont généralement affectés au financement de prestations sociales et souvent effectués au profit d'institutions ou d'administrations publiques qui fournissent de telles prestations. Cependant, cette affectation n'entre pas dans la définition des cotisations de sécurité sociale et n'est pas nécessaire pour qu'un impôt soit classé dans cette rubrique. Cependant, il faut qu'un impôt confère un droit pour être classé dans cette rubrique. Par conséquent, les prélèvements sur les revenus ou la masse salariale qui sont affectés aux caisses de sécurité sociale mais ne donnent aucun droit à des prestations sont exclus de cette rubrique et figurent à celle des impôts sur le revenu des personnes physiques (1100) ou des impôts sur les salaires et la main-d'œuvre (3000). Les impôts assis sur d'autres bases, telles que les biens et services, qui sont affectés à des prestations de sécurité sociale, ne sont pas indiqués ici, mais sont classés en fonction de leurs bases respectives parce qu'en général ils ne donnent pas droit à des prestations de sécurité sociale.

40. Seraient entre autres incluses les cotisations au titre des catégories suivantes de prestations de sécurité sociale : les allocations d'assurance-chômage et les compléments, les allocations pour accidents, blessures et maladie, les pensions de retraite, d'invalidité et de survivant, les allocations familiales, les remboursements de dépenses médicales et d'hospitalisation ou la fourniture de services médicaux ou hospitaliers. Les cotisations peuvent être collectées à la fois auprès des employés et des employeurs.

41. Les cotisations peuvent être assises sur les gains ou la masse salariale (« sur la base du salaire ») ou sur le revenu net après déductions et exemptions en fonction de la situation personnelle (« sur la base de l'impôt sur le revenu ») et les recettes correspondant à ces deux bases doivent être identifiées séparément si possible. Cependant, lorsque les cotisations à un régime général de sécurité sociale sont assises sur la masse salariale, mais que les cotisations de groupes particuliers (tels que les travailleurs indépendants) ne peuvent être évaluées sur cette base et que le revenu net est utilisé comme valeur rapprochée des gains bruts, les recettes peuvent encore être considérées comme assises sur la masse salariale. En principe, cette rubrique exclut les cotisations facultatives à des régimes de sécurité sociale. Lorsqu'elles peuvent être identifiées séparément, elles figurent pour mémoire dans le tableau indiquant le financement des prestations de sécurité sociale. Toutefois, en pratique, elles ne peuvent pas toujours être distinguées des cotisations facultatives, et dans ce cas elles figurent à cette rubrique.

42. Les cotisations à des régimes d'assurance sociale qui ne relèvent pas des pouvoirs publics et à d'autres régimes d'assurance ou de prévoyance, aux caisses de retraite, sociétés de secours mutuel ou autres systèmes d'épargne, ne sont pas considérées comme des cotisations de sécurité sociale. Les caisses de prévoyance résultant d'arrangements aux termes desquels les cotisations de chaque salarié et celles que l'employeur verse en son nom sont comptabilisées séparément dans un compte productif d'intérêts d'où elles peuvent être retirées dans des conditions biens déterminées. Les caisses de retraite sont des régimes autonomes organisés par négociations entre salariés et employeurs, qui comportent diverses contributions et prestations, parfois liées plus directement au salaire et à la durée

d'activité que dans les régimes de sécurité sociale. Lorsque les cotisations à ces régimes sont obligatoires ou quasi obligatoires (par exemple en vertu d'un accord entre organisations professionnelles et syndicales), elles sont comptabilisées dans le poste pour mémoire (voir le chapitre 4.2 du rapport).

43. Les cotisations versées par les agents des administrations et par les administrations au titre de leurs agents à des régimes de sécurité sociale relevant des pouvoirs publics sont incluses dans ce groupe. Sont aussi assimilées à des impôts les cotisations à des régimes particuliers réservés aux agents des administrations qui sont censés remplacer un régime général de la sécurité sociale[14]. Par contre, lorsqu'un régime distinct n'est pas censé remplacer un régime général et résulte de négociations entre l'administration, agissant en qualité d'employeur, et ses agents, il n'est pas considéré comme un régime de sécurité sociale et les cotisations à ce titre ne sont pas assimilées à des impôts, même si le régime a été institué par des dispositions législatives.

44. Cette rubrique ne comprend pas les cotisations 'imputées', qui correspondent aux prestations sociales versées directement par les employeurs à leurs salariés, ou anciens salariés, ou à leurs représentants (par exemple, lorsque des employeurs sont légalement tenus de verser des prestations maladies pendant une certaine période).

45. Le groupe comprend les cotisations à la charge des salariés (2100), à la charge des employeurs (2200), et à la charge des travailleurs indépendants ou des personnes n'occupant pas d'emploi (2300). À cet effet, on entend par salariés toutes les personnes qui exercent une activité dans des entreprises, des administrations, des institutions privées sans but lucratif, ou qui occupent d'autres emplois rémunérés, à l'exception des propriétaires et des membres de leur famille non rémunérés dans le cas d'entreprises individuelles. Sont également compris les membres des forces armées, quelle que soit la durée et la nature de leurs services, s'ils cotisent à un régime de sécurité sociale. Par cotisations à la charge des employeurs, on entend les versements qu'ils effectuent au régime de sécurité sociale pour le compte de leurs salariés. Si, en cas de chômage, les salariés ou employeurs sont tenus de continuer à effectuer ces versements, ces derniers doivent figurer respectivement dans les sous-groupes 2100 et 2200. En conséquence, le sous-groupe 2300 est réservé aux cotisations versées par les travailleurs indépendants et par ceux qui n'appartiennent pas à la population active (comme les handicapés ou les retraités).

3000 — Impôts sur les salaires et la main-d'œuvre

46. Il s'agit d'impôts que doivent acquitter les entreprises, déterminés en proportion des salaires et des traitements payés, ou d'après un montant fixe par personne employée. Ils ne comprennent pas les cotisations obligatoires de sécurité sociale payées par les employeurs, ni les impôts payés par les salariés sur leurs traitements et leurs salaires.

4000 — Impôts sur le patrimoine

47. Ce groupe couvre les impôts périodiques et non périodiques sur l'utilisation, la propriété ou la mutation des biens. Sont comptabilisés ici les impôts sur la propriété immobilière et sur l'actif net, les impôts sur les mutations par décès, les successions et les donations, et les impôts sur les transactions mobilières et immobilières. Sont exclus de ce groupe :

a. les impôts sur les gains en capital provenant de la vente d'un bien (1120 ou 1220) ;

b. les impôts sur l'utilisation des biens ou l'autorisation d'utiliser des biens ou d'exercer des activités (5200) [voir § 76] ;

c. les impôts immobiliers perçus sur la base d'un revenu net présumé qui tiennent compte de la situation personnelle du contribuable. Ces impôts sont classés dans le groupe 1100 en tant qu'impôts sur le revenu, avec les impôts sur le revenu et les gains en capital provenant des biens immobiliers ;

d. les impôts sur l'utilisation de biens immobiliers aux fins d'habitation qui sont à la charge du propriétaire ou du locataire et dont le montant est fonction de la situation personnelle de l'utilisateur (salaire, personnes à charge, etc.). Ils sont classés dans le groupe 1100 en tant qu'impôts sur le revenu ;

e. les impôts sur les constructions dépassant la densité autorisée, les impôts sur l'extension, la construction ou la modification de certains immeubles au-delà d'une valeur autorisée et les impôts sur la construction d'immeubles. Ces impôts sont classés dans le poste 5200 en tant qu'impôts sur l'autorisation d'exercer certaines activités ;

f. les impôts sur l'utilisation de biens immobiliers par le propriétaire à des fins commerciales particulières, comme la vente de boissons alcoolisées, de tabac, de viande, ou pour l'exploitation de sols ou terrains (par exemple aux États-Unis, les taxes d'extraction). Ils sont classés dans le poste 5200 en tant qu'impôts sur l'autorisation d'exercer certaines activités.

4100 — Impôts périodiques sur la propriété immobilière

48. Ce sous-groupe comprend les impôts prélevés régulièrement au titre de l'utilisation ou de la propriété de biens immobiliers.

- ces impôts sont prélevés sur les terrains et les bâtiments ;
- ces impôts sont calculés en pourcentage de la valeur du bien évalué d'après un revenu locatif fictif, le prix de vente ou le rendement capitalisé, ou en fonction d'autres caractéristiques du bien, comme sa dimension ou son emplacement, d'où l'on peut déduire une valeur locative présumée ou la valeur du capital.
- ces impôts sont à la charge du propriétaire, du locataire ou des deux. Ils peuvent également être payés par une administration à une autre administration au titre d'un bien relevant de la compétence de cette dernière.
- il n'est pas tenu compte des dettes pour la détermination de l'assiette de ces impôts, contrairement aux impôts sur l'actif net.

49. Les impôts sur la propriété immobilière sont en outre subdivisés en impôts acquittés par les ménages (4110) et impôts acquittés par d'autres agents (4120), suivant les critères exposés au § 30(*b*) ci-dessus.

4200 — Impôts périodiques sur l'actif net

50. Ce sous-groupe comprend les impôts prélevés régulièrement (dans la plupart des cas annuellement) sur l'actif net, c'est-à-dire les impôts perçus sur un large éventail de biens mobiliers et immobiliers, endettement déduit. Il est subdivisé en impôts acquittés par des personnes physiques (4210), et en impôts acquittés par des sociétés (4220) selon les critères exposés plus haut au § 30(a). Si les recettes provenant des institutions sont comptabilisées à part, 66res doivent être ajoutées aux impôts des entreprises.

4300 — Impôts sur les mutations par décès, les successions et les donations

51. Ce sous-groupe comprend les impôts sur les mutations par décès et les successions (4310) et les impôts sur les donations (4320). Les impôts sur les mutations par décès sont calculés soit sur l'ensemble de la masse successorale, soit en fonction de la part de chacun des bénéficiaires (« part héréditaire ») ; en outre, ces derniers impôts peuvent tenir compte du degré de parenté entre chacun des bénéficiaires et le défunt.

4400 — Impôts sur les transactions mobilières et immobilières

52. Sont compris, entre autres, dans ce sous-groupe les impôts sur l'émission, le transfert, l'achat et la vente de valeurs mobilières, les impôts sur les chèques, ainsi que les droits perçus à l'occasion d'actes juridiques déterminés, comme la validation de contrats et la vente de biens immobiliers. Sont exclus :

a. les impôts sur l'utilisation de biens, mobiliers ou immobiliers, ou l'autorisation d'exercer certaines activités (5200) ;

b. les droits acquittés au titre de frais de justice, ou pour la délivrance de certificats de naissance, de mariage ou de décès, car ces droits sont considérés comme des recettes non fiscales (voir § 11) ;

c. les impôts sur les gains en capital (1000) ;

d. les impôts périodiques sur la propriété immobilière (4100) ;

e. les impôts périodiques sur l'actif net (4200) ;

f. les prélèvements sur le patrimoine ou sur l'actif net effectués une fois pour toutes (4500) ;

4500 — Autres impôts non périodiques sur le patrimoine[16]

53. Ce sous-groupe comprend les prélèvements sur le patrimoine effectués une fois pour toutes (par opposition aux prélèvements périodiques). Il est subdivisé en impôts sur l'actif net (4510) et en autres impôts non périodiques sur le patrimoine (4520). Le poste 4510 inclurait les impôts perçus pour couvrir des dépenses exceptionnelles ou à des fins de redistribution. Le poste 4520 comprendrait les impôts prélevés pour tenir compte d'une plus-value prise par les terrains du fait que les administrations publiques ont autorisé l'extension ou l'aménagement d'installations locales, ainsi que les impôts sur la réévaluation du capital ou les impôts perçus une seule fois sur certains biens déterminés.

4600 — Autres impôts périodiques sur le patrimoine

54. Ils sont rares dans des pays Membres de l'OCDE ; ce sous-groupe comprendrait les impôts sur des biens tels que le cheptel, les bijoux, les fenêtres et les signes extérieurs de richesse.

5000 — Impôts sur les biens et services

55. Ce poste couvre tous les impôts et droits perçus sur la production, l'extraction, la vente, le transfert, la location ou la livraison de biens et la prestation de services (5100), ou sur l'utilisation ou l'autorisation d'utiliser des biens ou d'exercer des activités (5200). Ce groupe comprend donc :

a. les taxes cumulatives en cascade ;

b. les taxes générales sur les ventes — perçues au stade de la production ou de la fabrication, du gros ou du détail ;

c. les taxes sur la valeur ajoutée ;

d. les accises ;

e. les taxes perçues à l'importation et à l'exportation de biens ;

f. les impôts perçus sur l'utilisation de biens et sur l'autorisation d'utiliser des biens ou d'exercer certaines activités ;

g. les impôts sur l'extraction, le traitement ou la production de minéraux et autres produits.

56. Les cas douteux de délimitation entre ce groupe et le groupe 4000 (impôts sur le patrimoine) et le sous-groupe 6100 (autres impôts à la charge des entreprises) sont examinés aux § 47, § 52 et § 78. Des postes résiduels (5300 et 5130) ont été prévus pour comptabiliser les recettes fiscales qui ne peuvent être ventilées respectivement entre les postes 5100 et 5200 et entre les postes 5110 et 5120 (voir § 32).

5100 — *Impôts sur la production, la vente, le transfert, la location et la livraison de biens et la prestation de services*

57. Ce sous-groupe comprend tous les impôts perçus sur les transactions afférentes à des biens ou services, en fonction de leurs caractéristiques propres (comme la valeur, le poids du tabac, le degré d'alcool, etc.), à la différence des impôts perçus au titre de l'utilisation ou de l'autorisation d'utiliser des biens ou d'exercer des activités, qui entrent dans le sous-groupe 5200.

5110 — *Impôts généraux sur les biens et services*

58. Ce sous-groupe comprend tous les impôts, autres que les droits à l'importation et à l'exportation (5123 et 5124), perçus sur la production, la location, le transfert, la livraison ou la vente d'une gamme de biens ou la prestation d'une gamme de services, qu'ils soient produits dans le pays ou importés, et quel que soit le stade de la production ou de la distribution aux quel ils sont perçus. Il couvre ainsi les taxes sur la valeur ajoutée, les taxes sur les ventes et les taxes de caractère cumulatif en cascade. On a ajouté aux recettes brutes de cette catégorie les recettes provenant de la compensation à la frontière de ces impôts lorsque les biens sont importés, et déduit les remboursements d'impôts effectués lorsque les marchandises sont exportées. Ces impôts sont ventilés en : taxes sur la valeur ajoutée (5111), impôts sur les ventes (5112), impôts sur le chiffre d'affaires et autres impôts généraux sur les biens et services (5113).

59. Certains cas se trouvent à la limite entre ce sous-groupe et celui des impôts sur des biens et services déterminés (5120) lorsque ces impôts sont perçus sur un grand nombre de biens, comme dans le cas de la « *purchase tax* » au Royaume-Uni (abrogée en 1973) et l'impôt japonais sur les biens marchands (abrogé en 1988). Conformément aux options nationales, la « *purchase tax* » britannique est classée impôt général (5112) et l'impôt japonais dans les accises (5121).

5111 — *Taxes sur la valeur ajoutée*

60. Sont classés dans ce sous-groupe tous les impôts généraux sur la consommation prélevée sur la valeur ajoutée, quels que soient le mode de déduction et les stades auxquels ils sont perçus. En pratique, tous les pays de l'OCDE où existe une taxe sur la valeur ajoutée autorisent normalement la déduction immédiate des taxes sur les achats par tous les redevables, à l'exception du consommateur final, et imposent la taxe à tous les stades. Dans certains pays, le poste peut inclure aussi certains impôts, comme les taxes sur les activités

financières et les assurances, soit parce que les recettes correspondantes ne peuvent être dissociées de celles de la taxe sur la valeur ajoutée, soit parce qu'elles sont considérées comme faisant partie intégrante de la taxe sur la valeur ajoutée, même si les taxes similaires qui existent dans d'autres pays peuvent être classées autrement (par exemple, sous le poste 5126 comme impôts sur les services ou sous le poste 4400 comme impôts sur les transactions mobilières et immobilières).

5112 — *Impôts sur les ventes*

61. Sont classés ici tous les impôts perçus à un stade unique, que ce soit celui de la fabrication, de la production, du gros ou du détail.

5113 — *Impôts sur le chiffre d'affaires et autres impôts généraux sur les biens et services*

62. Il s'agit des taxes cumulatives en cascade et des taxes qui combinent des éléments de taxe sur la consommation et des taxes en cascade. Ces impôts sont prélevés sur chaque transaction sans déduction des taxes acquittées en amont. Les taxes en cascade peuvent être combinées avec des éléments de taxe sur la valeur ajoutée ou d'impôts sur les ventes.

5120 — *Impôts sur des biens et des services déterminés*

63. Ce sous-groupe couvre les accises, les bénéfices engendrés et transférés par les monopoles fiscaux, et les droits de douane et à l'importation, ainsi que les taxes à l'exportation, les opérations de change, les biens d'équipement et les paris, et aussi les impôts spéciaux sur les services qui ne font pas partie d'un impôt général du sous-groupe 5110.

5121 — *Accises*

64. Les accises sont des impôts spécifiques perçus par unité produite sur une gamme limitée de biens prédéfinie. Les accises sont généralement prélevées à des taux différenciés sur des biens non essentiels ou de luxe, les boissons alcoolisées, les produits à base de tabac et l'énergie. Les accises peuvent être perçues à un stade quelconque de la production ou de la distribution et sont calculées généralement sur la base d'un prélèvement spécifique par unité correspondant aux caractéristiques du produit considéré, par référence à sa valeur, son poids, son degré ou son volume. Cette subdivision couvre ainsi les impôts spéciaux sur certains produits tels que le sucre, la betterave, les allumettes et le chocolat ; les impôts prélevés à des taux variables sur une gamme déterminée de produits ; ainsi que les impôts perçus sur les produits à base de tabac, les boissons alcoolisées, les combustibles et les hydrocarbures. Si un impôt frappant principalement des produits importés doit ou devrait également être perçu sur des produits nationaux comparables, suivant la même législation, les recettes de cet impôt doivent alors être classées dans la catégorie des accises et non dans celle des droits à l'importation. Ce principe vaut également même s'il n'existe pas, ou ne peut exister, de production nationale comparable. Les impôts prélevés sur la consommation de services d'utilité publique (eau, électricité, gaz et autres formes d'énergie) sont considérés comme des accises, et non comme des impôts sur des services déterminés (5126). Ne sont pas inclus dans les accises les prélèvements entrant dans les catégories des impôts généraux sur les biens et services (5110), des bénéfices des monopoles fiscaux (5122), des droits de douane et autres droits à l'importation (5123) ou des taxes à l'exportation (5124).

5122 — *Bénéfices des monopoles fiscaux*

65. Ce sous-groupe couvre la fraction des bénéfices des monopoles fiscaux qui est transférée aux administrations publiques ou qui sert à financer des dépenses considérées comme

dépenses publiques (voir § 23). Les montants sont comptabilisés lorsqu'ils sont transférés aux administrations publiques ou utilisés pour effectuer des dépenses considérées comme des dépenses publiques.

66. Les monopoles fiscaux reflètent l'exercice du pouvoir d'imposition de l'État par l'intermédiaire du monopole. Les monopoles fiscaux sont des entreprises publiques non financières, qui exercent dans la plupart des cas un monopole sur la production ou la distribution du tabac, des boissons alcoolisées, du sel, des allumettes, des cartes à jouer et des produits pétroliers ou agricoles (c'est-à-dire, sur le genre de produits qui peuvent être soumis, principalement ou accessoirement, aux accises du poste 5121), pour procurer des recettes publiques qui, dans d'autres pays, sont obtenues par le biais d'impôts frappant les transactions sur ces produits d'entreprises privées. Le monopole d'État peut être exercé au stade de la production, ou au stade de la distribution comme dans le cas des magasins de vente de boissons alcoolisées qui appartiennent à l'État et sont contrôlés par lui.

67. Les monopoles fiscaux sont différents des services publics, comme les chemins de fer, l'électricité, les postes et autres moyens de communication, qui peuvent avoir une position de monopole ou de quasi-monopole, mais dont l'objet principal est, normalement, de fournir des services essentiels et non pas de procurer des recettes à l'État. Les transferts à l'administration de ces autres entreprises publiques sont considérés comme des recettes non fiscales. La notion traditionnelle de monopole fiscal n'a généralement pas été élargie pour inclure les loteries nationales, dont les bénéfices sont habituellement considérés comme des recettes non fiscales. Cependant, ces bénéfices peuvent être considérés comme des recettes fiscales quand la raison principale de la mise en œuvre de ces loteries est l'augmentation des recettes pour financer les dépenses publiques. On distingue les bénéfices des monopoles fiscaux des bénéfices des monopoles d'exportation et d'importation (5127), qui sont transférés des offices de commercialisation ou d'autres entreprises s'occupant du commerce international.

5123 — *Droits de douane et autres droits à l'importation*

68. Figurent ici les taxes, droits de timbre et surtaxes qui, selon la loi sont perçus exclusivement sur des produits importés. Sont aussi inclus dans ce poste les droits perçus sur l'importation de denrées agricoles dans les pays Membres de l'Union Européenne et les montants acquittés par certains de ces pays en vertu du Système de Montants Compensatoires[15]. À partir de 1998 les droits de douane collectés par les États membres de l'Union européenne pour le compte de l'Union européenne ne sont plus reportés sous cette rubrique dans les tableaux par pays (chapitre 4 de ce rapport). Sont exclues ici les taxes perçues sur les importations au titre d'un impôt général sur les biens et les services ou d'une accise applicable aussi bien aux produits importés qu'aux produits fabriqués dans le pays.

5124 — *Taxes à l'exportation*

69. Pendant les années 70, les droits à l'exportation étaient perçus normalement en Australie, au Canada et au Portugal, et ils étaient utilisés en Finlande à des fins conjoncturelles. Certains pays Membres de l'Union Européenne acquittent, dans le cadre du système des montants compensatoires, une taxe sur les exportations (voir la note 16 du § 68). Lorsque ces montants sont identifiables, ils sont inclus dans ce poste. Ce dernier ne comprend pas les remboursements effectués au titre d'impôts généraux sur la consommation d'accises ou de droits de douane sur des biens exportés, qui doivent être déduits des recettes brutes comptabilisées, selon le cas, sous le poste 5110, 5121 ou 5123.

5125 — *Impôts sur les biens d'équipement*

70. Ce sous-groupe comprend les impôts perçus sur les biens d'équipement, comme les machines. Ils peuvent exister depuis un certain nombre d'années ou avoir un caractère temporaire et être prélevés à des fins conjoncturelles. Ne sont pas inclus les impôts sur les 'inputs' industriels qui frappent aussi les consommateurs (comme l'impôt suédois sur l'énergie qui est classé sous le poste 5121).

5126 — *Impôts sur des services déterminés*

71. Sous ce poste figurent tous les impôts calculés sur la rémunération de services spécifiques, comme les taxes sur les primes d'assurance, les taxes sur les services bancaires, sur les jeux et paris (par exemple : courses de chevaux, pronostics de football, billets de loterie nationale), les transports, les spectacles, les restaurants et la publicité. Les impôts prélevés sur le revenu brut des sociétés prestataires d'un service (exemple : primes d'assurance brutes, mises de jeux encaissées par les sociétés) sont classés sous ce poste. Les recettes fiscales provenant des prélèvements sur les banques et des contributions aux mécanismes de garantie des dépôts et de stabilité financière sont provisoirement classés ici pour l'édition 2012. La classification détaillée est présentée au § 108.

72. Ne figurent pas sous ce poste :

a. les impôts sur les services qui font partie d'un impôt général sur les biens et services et sont classés sous le poste 5110 ;

b. les taxes sur l'électricité, le gaz et l'énergie (classées sous le poste 5121 en tant qu'accises) ;

c. les taxes sur les gains personnels tirés de jeux et paris (qui sont classées sous le poste 1120, en tant qu'impôts sur les gains en capital des personnes physiques et entreprises individuelles) et les montants forfaitaires perçus sur le transfert de loteries privées ou sur l'autorisation de créer des loteries (5200)[16] ;

d. les impôts sur les chèques et sur l'émission, le transfert ou le remboursement de valeurs mobilières, (qui sont classés sous le poste 4400, en tant qu'impôts sur les transactions mobilières et immobilières).

5127 — *Autres impôts sur les transactions et les échanges internationaux*

73. Ce sous-groupe couvre les recettes perçues par l'État sur l'achat et la vente de monnaies étrangères à des taux différents. Lorsque l'État exerce le privilège exclusif dont il dispose pour s'assurer une marge entre le prix d'achat et le prix de vente de devises qui ne se réduit pas à la simple couverture des frais administratifs, ce bénéfice représente un prélèvement obligatoire imposé dans des proportions indéterminées à l'acheteur et au vendeur des monnaies étrangères. Il équivaut normalement au droit à l'importation et au droit à l'exportation perçus dans un système de taux de change unique, ou à une taxe sur la vente ou l'achat de monnaies étrangères. Comme les bénéfices des monopoles fiscaux et des monopoles d'importation ou d'exportation transférés à l'État, il représente l'exercice d'un monopole aux fins d'imposition et est inclus dans les recettes fiscales.

74. Ce sous-groupe comprend aussi les bénéfices des monopoles d'exportation ou d'importation, bien qu'il n'en existe pas dans les pays de l'OCDE, les impôts sur l'achat ou la vente de devises et tous les autres impôts perçus spécifiquement sur les opérations ou les échanges internationaux.

5128 — *Autres impôts sur des biens et services déterminés*

75. Cette rubrique comprend les impôts sur l'extraction de minéraux, combustibles fossiles et autres ressources non renouvelables provenant de gisements privés ou détenus par une autre administration, ainsi que toute autre recette non ventilable provenant des impôts sur des biens et services déterminés. Les impôts sur l'extraction de ressources non renouvelables correspondent généralement à un montant forfaitaire par unité de qualité ou de poids, mais peuvent être calculés ad valorem. Les impôts sont comptabilisés à la date d'extraction des ressources. Les versements tirés de l'extraction de ressources non renouvelables issues de gisements appartenant à l'administration publique qui perçoit ces versements sont classés en tant que loyers.

5200 — *Impôts sur l'utilisation des biens ou l'autorisation d'utiliser des biens ou d'exercer des activités*

76. Ce sous-groupe comprend les taxes prélevées en raison de l'utilisation de biens, indépendamment des impôts frappant les biens eux-mêmes. Contrairement à ceux-ci (5100), les impôts du sous-groupe 5200 ne sont pas calculés d'après la valeur des biens, mais ordinairement d'après un montant forfaitaire. Sont aussi couverts les impôts perçus au titre du droit d'utiliser des biens ou d'exercer des activités, comme les taxes sur la pollution qui ne reposent pas sur la valeur de biens déterminés. Il est parfois difficile de distinguer les taxes d'utilisation et droits de licence obligatoires, qui sont considérés comme des impôts, de ceux qui ne le sont pas parce qu'ils sont assimilés à des recettes non fiscales ; les critères appliqués sont ceux indiqués aux § 11 et 12.

77. Bien que le sous-groupe se réfère à l'utilisation des biens, le fait générateur de l'impôt peut être aussi bien l'enregistrement de la propriété, de sorte que les impôts relevant de ce sous-groupe peuvent viser la possession d'animaux ou de biens plutôt que leur utilisation (par exemple, les chevaux de course, les chiens, les véhicules à moteur) et même s'appliquer à des biens inutilisables (comme les véhicules à moteur ou les fusils inutilisables).

78. Les cas limites concernent :

a. les impôts sur l'autorisation d'exercer des activités commerciales, qui sont classés selon les règles exposées au § 81 lorsqu'ils ont une assiette mixte associant le revenu, les salaires versés ou le chiffre d'affaires ;

b. les impôts sur la propriété ou l'utilisation de la propriété de biens visés par les postes 4100, 4200 et 4600. Le poste 4100 ne vise que les impôts sur la propriété ou la location de biens immobiliers et, contrairement aux impôts du sous-groupe 5200, ils sont fonction de la valeur du bien. Les impôts sur l'actif net et les impôts sur les biens meubles des sous-groupes 4200 et 4600 visent la propriété et non pas l'utilisation des biens, couvrent un groupe d'actifs et non pas de biens particuliers et sont aussi fonction de la valeur du bien.

5210 — *Impôts périodiques sur l'utilisation de biens ou sur l'autorisation d'utiliser des biens ou d'exercer certaines activités*

79. Ces impôts ont pour principale caractéristique d'être perçus à intervalles réguliers et de représenter ordinairement des montants forfaitaires. Le poste le plus important, du point de vue du volume des recettes, est constitué par les permis de circulation des véhicules. Ce sous-groupe inclut aussi les taxes perçues lors de la délivrance de permis de chasse, de tir ou de pêche, ou l'autorisation de vendre certains produits, ainsi que les taxes sur la possession de chiens et sur la prestation de certains services à condition qu'elles

répondent aux critères définis aux § 11 et 12. Les subdivisions du poste 5210 comprennent les taxes d'utilisation de véhicules à moteur à la charge des ménages (5211) et à la charge d'autres agents (5212). Le poste 5213 couvre les plaques de chiens et les taxes perçues pour l'autorisation d'exercer certaines activités, comme la vente de viande et d'alcool, lorsque les prélèvements ont un caractère périodique. Il couvre aussi les permis généraux de chasse, de port d'armes et de pêche, lorsque le droit d'exercer ces activités n'est pas accordé au titre d'une opération commerciale normale (par exemple, la délivrance du permis ne comporte pas le droit d'utiliser une parcelle déterminée de terrain appartenant à l'État).

5220 — Impôts non périodiques sur l'utilisation de biens ou sur l'autorisation d'utiliser des biens ou d'exercer certaines activités

80. Cette rubrique recouvre les taxes non périodiques perçues sur l'utilisation de biens ou sur l'autorisation d'utiliser des biens ou d'exercer certaines activités et celles qui sont prélevées chaque fois que des biens sont utilisés.

- Les impôts prélevés sur l'émission ou le rejet dans l'environnement de gaz toxiques, liquides nocifs ou autres substances dangereuses figurent ici. Les paiements au titre des permis d'émission négociables délivrés par les administrations publiques dans le cadre des dispositifs de plafonnement et d'échange doivent également être comptabilisés sous cette rubrique au moment où les émissions sont produites. Les permis délivrés gratuitement par les administrations ne donnent lieu à aucun enregistrement comptable de recettes.
- La comptabilisation en droits constatés implique un éventuel délai entre la date à laquelle l'administration perçoit le règlement des permis et la date à laquelle les émissions sont produites. Dans les comptes nationaux, ce délai se traduit pour l'administration par un engagement financier sur la période.
- Il convient d'exclure les paiements effectués au titre de la collecte et de l'élimination de déchets ou de substances nocives par les autorités publiques, étant donné qu'il s'agit là de vente de services aux entreprises.

81. D'autres impôts non périodiques qui relèvent du poste 5200 sont aussi classés dans cette rubrique. Ainsi figurent les paiements uniques effectués au titre de l'autorisation de vendre des boissons alcoolisées ou des tabacs ou d'ouvrir des guichets de « paris mutuels », à condition qu'ils répondent aux critères définis aux § 11 et 12.

6000 — Autres impôts

82. Ce groupe couvre les impôts prélevés sur une ou plusieurs assiettes différentes de celles qui sont indiquées pour les groupes 1000, 3000, 4000 et 5000, ou sur des assiettes qui ne peuvent être considérées comme liées à l'une de celles afférentes à ces groupes. Lorsque des impôts sont perçus sur plusieurs assiettes différentes, et qu'il est possible d'évaluer les recettes liées à chaque assiette, les montants correspondants sont inclus dans le groupe approprié. S'il est impossible d'évaluer le montant correspondant à chaque assiette, et si l'on sait que l'essentiel des recettes provient des impôts perçus sur une assiette donnée, la totalité des recettes est classée en fonction de cette assiette. Sinon, les impôts sont classés dans le présent groupe. Sont également inclus dans ce groupe les impôts forfaitaires non inclus ailleurs dans le système de classification, les impôts prélevés sur les personnes physiques sous la forme de taxe civique ou d'impôt de capitation, les droits de timbre qui ne sont pas liés à des transactions mobilières ou immobilières et qui n'entrent pas exclusivement dans une catégorie de transactions, les impôts sur les dépenses dès lors qu'ils s'accompagnent

d'abattements et d'exonérations individuels, ainsi que les recettes fiscales non identifiables. Ce poste est divisé en impôts exclusivement ou principalement à la charge des entreprises (6100) et en impôts à la charge d'autres contribuables (6200).

A.6. Conciliation avec les comptes nationaux

83. Cette section des tableaux permet de concilier les calculs des recettes fiscales totales de l'OCDE et l'ensemble des impôts et cotisations sociales versés aux administrations publiques qui sont enregistrés dans les comptes nationaux par pays. Lorsque le pays en question est membre de l'Union européenne (UE) la comparaison est effectuée entre les calculs des recettes fiscales totales des pays de l'OCDE et la somme des recettes fiscales et cotisations de sécurité sociale perçues par les administrations publiques et les institutions des secteurs de l'Union européenne des comptes nationaux.

A.7. Poste pour mémoire relatif au financement des prestations de sécurité sociale

84. Le rapport entre les impôts et les cotisations de sécurité sociale étant variable, et en raison des problèmes évoqués aux § 39 à 45, on a réuni dans un poste pour mémoire l'ensemble des versements affectés à des prestations du type sécurité sociale, en dehors des versements facultatifs au secteur privé. Les données sont présentées de la façon suivante (voir le chapitre 4.2)

a. impôts du groupe 2000 ;

b. impôts affectés aux prestations de sécurité sociale ;

c. cotisations facultatives à l'administration ;

d. cotisations obligatoires au secteur privé.

Les § 39 à 45 ci-dessus contiennent des directives pour la ventilation entre ces quatre catégories

A.8. Poste pour mémoire relatif aux impôts identifiables payés par les administrations

85. Les impôts effectivement payés par les administrations elles-mêmes et que l'on peut identifier sont indiqués dans un poste pour mémoire et classés suivant les grandes rubriques de la classification des impôts de l'OCDE. Dans la très grande majorité des pays, seuls peuvent être identifiées en l'occurrence les cotisations de sécurité sociale et les impôts sur les salaires, mais il s'agit là en général des impôts les plus importants acquittés par les administrations (voir le chapitre 4.2 de cette publication).

A.9. Rapport de la classification des impôts de l'OCDE avec les systèmes nationaux de comptabilité nationale

86. Un système de comptabilité nationale (SCN) tend à fournir un cadre cohérent pour enregistrer et présenter les principaux flux relatifs à la production, à la consommation, à l'accumulation et aux transactions extérieures d'une zone économique donnée, d'ordinaire un pays ou une grande région d'un pays. Les recettes publiques sont une partie importante des transactions enregistrées dans le SCN. La version finale du SCN 2008 a été diffusée conjointement par cinq organisations internationales : les Nations Unies, le Fonds Monétaire International, l'Union européenne, l'Organisation de Coopération et de Développement Économiques et la Banque Mondiale, en août 2009. Le Système est un ensemble complet,

cohérent et souple de comptes macro-économiques. Il est élaboré pour être utilisé dans les pays à économie de marché quel que soit leur niveau de développement économique ainsi que dans les pays en transition vers l'économie de marché. De larges extraits du cadre théorique ainsi que les définitions des divers secteurs de l'économie du SCN figurent dans la classification des impôts de l'OCDE.

87. Il existe cependant un certain nombre de différences entre la classification des impôts de l'OCDE et les concepts du SCN qui sont indiqués ci-dessous. Ils proviennent du fait que l'objectif de cette classification est de permettre une ventilation aussi large que possible des données statistiques pour ce que les administrations fiscales conviennent de considérer de manière générale comme des impôts.

a. l'OCDE inclut les cotisations obligatoires de sécurité sociale payées aux administrations publiques dans les recettes fiscales totales. Les cotisations sociales facultatives et imputées ainsi que celles versées aux caisses privées ne sont pas considérées comme des impôts (§ 8 et 10 ci-dessus) ;

b. les avis diffèrent sur la question de savoir s'il y a lieu de classer certains prélèvements et redevances dans les impôts (§ 11 et 12 ci-dessus) ;

c. l'OCDE exclut les impôts imputés ou les subventions résultant d'opérations de taux de change officiels multiples et ceux résultant du fait que la banque centrale paye un taux d'intérêt sur les réserves obligatoires différent des autres taux du marché ;

d. il existe des différences dans le traitement des crédits d'impôt récupérables.

88. Comme on l'a noté aux § 1 et 2, les groupes 1000 à 6000 de la classification de l'OCDE comprennent tous les versements sans contrepartie aux administrations publiques, à l'exclusion des prêts obligatoires et des amendes. On peut obtenir le total de ces versements sans contrepartie, amendes incluses, mais prêts obligatoires exclus, en additionnant les postes suivants du SCN 2008 :

- impôts du type valeur ajoutée (D.211) ;
- droits et taxes sur les importations à l'exclusion de la TVA (D.212) ;
- droits sur les exportations (D.213) ;
- taxes sur les produits, à l'exclusion de la TVA, des droits sur les importations et les exportations (D.214) ;
- autres impôts sur la production (D.29) ;
- impôts sur le revenu (D.51) ;
- autres impôts périodiques (D.59) ;
- cotisations de sécurité sociale (D.61) à l'exclusion des cotisations facultatives ;
- impôts sur le capital (D.91).

A.10. La classification des impôts de l'OCDE et le système du Fonds monétaire international (SFP)

89. Le périmètre et l'évaluation des recettes fiscales dans le système de statistiques de finances publiques (SFP) et dans le système de comptabilité nationale de 2008 (SCN 2008) sont très proches. Par conséquent, les différences entre la classification de l'OCDE et celle du SCN 2008 (voir § 87 ci-dessus) sont également valables pour les SFP. En outre, le Fonds monétaire international subdivise le groupe 5000 de la classification de l'OCDE en une section iv (Taxes intérieures sur les biens et services) et une section v (Taxes sur

les transactions et les échanges internationaux). Cela tient à ce que le rendement de ces dernières taxes représente généralement des sommes infimes dans les pays de l'OCDE ce qui n'est pas le cas dans beaucoup de pays non membres.

A.11. Comparaison de la classification des impôts de l'OCDE et des autres classifications internationales des recettes publiques

90. Le tableau ci-dessous décrit point par point la comparaison entre la classification des impôts de l'OCDE et les classifications suivantes :

a. Système des comptes nationaux (SCN 2008) ;
b. Système européen des comptes (SEC 2010) ;
c. Manuel de statistiques des finances publiques du Fonds monétaire international (MSFP 2014).

91. Ces comparaisons correspondent à celles qui devraient s'appliquer dans la majorité des cas. Toutefois, en pratique il faut faire preuve d'une certaine souplesse dans leur application. En effet, dans certains cas, les pays peuvent adopter des méthodes diverses de classification des recettes dans les comptes nationaux.

OECD Classification	2008 SNA	2010 ESA	GFSM2014
1000 Taxes on income, profits and capital gains			
1100 Individuals			
1110 Income and profits	D51-8.61a	D51A	1111
1120 Capital gains	D51-8.61c, d	D51C, D	1111
1200 Corporations			
1210 Income and profits	D51-8.61b	D51B	1112
1220 Capital gains	D51-8.61c	D51C	1112
1300 Unallocable as between 1100 and 1200			1113
2000 Social security contributions			
2100 Employees	D613-8.85	D613	1211
2200 Employers	D611-8.83	D611	1212
2300 Self-employed, non-employed	D613-8.85	D613	1213
2400 Unallocable as between 2100, 2200 and 2300			1214
3000 Taxes on payroll and workforce	D29-7.97a	D29C	112
4000 Taxes on property			
4100 Recurrent taxes on immovable property			
4110 Households	D59-8.63a	D59A	1131
4120 Other	D29-7.97b	D29A	1131
4200 Recurrent net wealth taxes			
4210 Individual	D59-8.63b	D59A	1132
4220 Corporations	D59-8.63b	D59A	1132
4300 Estate, inheritance and gift taxes			
4310 Estate and inheritance taxes	D91-10.207b	D91A	1133
4320 Gift taxes	D91-10.207b	D91A	1133
4400 Taxes on financial and capital transactions	D59-7.96d; D29-7.97e	D214B, C	114114; 1161
4500 Other non-recurrent taxes on property	D91-10.207a	D91B	1135
4600 Other recurrent taxes on property	D59-8.63c	D59A	1136
5000 Taxes on goods and services			
5100 Taxes on production, sale and transfer of goods and services			
5110 General taxes on goods and services			
5111 Value-added taxes	D211-7.89	D211; D29G	11411
5112 Sales taxes	D2122-7.94a; D214-7.96a	D21224; D214I	11412
5113 Other general taxes on goods and services	D214-7.96a	D214I	11413

OECD Classification	2008 SNA	2010 ESA	GFSM2014
5120 Taxes on specific goods and services			
5121 Excises	D2122-7.94b; D214-7.96b	D21223; D214A, B, D	1142
5122 Profits of fiscal monopolies	D214-7.96e	D214J	1143
5123 Customs and other import duties	D2121-7.93	D2121; D21221, 2	1151
5124 On exports	D213-7.95a	D214K	1152-4
5125 On investment goods			
5126 On specific services	D2122-7.94c; D214-7.96c	D21225; D214E, F, G, H; D29F	1144; 1156
5127 Other taxes on international trade and transactions	D2122-7.94d; D29-7.95b D29-7.97g; D59-8.64d	D21226; D29D; D59E	1153; 1155-6
5128 Other taxes on specific goods and services			1146
5130 Unallocable between 5110 and 5120			
5200 Taxes on use of goods and on permission to use goods or perform activities			
5210 Recurrent taxes on use of goods and on permission to use goods or perform activities			
5211 Motor vehicle taxes households	D59-8.64c	D59D	11451
5212 Motor vehicles taxes others	D29-7.97d	D214D; D29B	11451
5213 Other recurrent taxes on use of goods and on permission to use goods or perform activities	D29-7.97c, d, f D59-8.64c	D29B, E, F; D59D	11452
5220 Non-recurrent taxes on permission to use goods or perform activities			11452
5300 Unallocable as between 5100 and 5200			
6000 Other taxes			
6100 Payable solely by business			1161
6200 Payable by other than business, or unidentifiable	D59-8.64a, b	D59B, C	1162

A.12. Répartition des recettes fiscales par sous-secteurs d'administration publique

92. La classification de l'OCDE appelle une ventilation des recettes fiscales par sous-secteurs d'administration. On trouvera ci-après la définition de chaque sous-secteur et les critères à utiliser pour répartir entre eux les recettes fiscales. Ces définitions et critères suivent les orientations qui figurent dans le SCN 2008 et le MSFP 2014.

Sous-secteurs des administrations publiques à identifier

a) Administration centrale

93. Le sous-secteur des administrations centrales groupe tous les ministères, bureaux, établissements et autres organismes qui sont des services ou des moyens d'action du pouvoir central et dont la compétence s'étend à la totalité du territoire, à l'exception de l'administration des caisses de sécurité sociale. L'administration centrale a donc le pouvoir de prélever des impôts sur toutes les unités résidentes et non résidentes exerçant des activités économiques à l'intérieur du pays.

b) Administration d'un État fédéré, d'une province ou d'une région

94. Ce sous-secteur comprend les unités administratives intermédiaires et inclut toutes les unités administratives dont la compétence s'exerce indépendamment de l'Administration centrale sur une partie du territoire englobant un certain nombre de petites localités, à l'exception des caisses de sécurité sociale. Dans les pays unitaires, les administrations régionales peuvent être considérées comme dotées d'une existence distincte lorsqu'elles

disposent d'une autonomie substantielle pour percevoir une part importante de leurs recettes de sources placées sous leur contrôle et lorsque leurs agents ne sont pas soumis à un contrôle administratif externe dans l'exercice des activités de l'unité.

95. Actuellement, les pays à structure fédérale représentent la majorité des cas dans lesquels les recettes attribuées aux unités administratives intermédiaires sont identifiées séparément. L'Espagne est le seul pays à structure unitaire qui se trouve dans cette situation. Dans les autres pays unitaires, les recettes des administrations régionales sont incluses dans celles des administrations locales.

c) Collectivités locales

96. Ce sous-secteur comprend toutes les autres unités administratives exerçant une compétence indépendante sur une partie du territoire d'un pays, à l'exception des administrations des caisses de sécurité sociale. Il englobe les diverses circonscriptions urbaines et/ou rurales (par exemple les collectivités locales, les municipalités, les villes, les bourgs ou les districts).

d) Caisses de sécurité sociale

97. Les caisses de sécurité sociale constituent un sous-secteur distinct des administrations publiques. Le sous-secteur de la sécurité sociale est défini dans le SCN de 2008 par les extraits suivants des paragraphes 4.124 à 4.126 et 4.147 :

> *« Les systèmes de sécurité sociale sont des systèmes d'assurance sociale qui couvrent l'ensemble de la collectivité ou d'importants sous-ensembles de la collectivité : ces systèmes sont imposés et contrôlés par les administrations publiques. Ces systèmes couvrent une grande variété de programmes qui consistent à fournir des prestations, en espèces ou en nature, au titre des circonstances suivantes : vieillesse, invalidité ou décès, survie, maladie et maternité, accident du travail, chômage, allocations familiales, soins de santé etc. Il n'existe pas nécessairement de lien direct entre le montant de la cotisation versée par un particulier et les prestations qu'il est susceptible de recevoir » (paragraphe 4.124).*

> *« Lorsque les systèmes de sécurité sociale ont une organisation distincte des autres activités des administrations publiques et détiennent des actifs et des engagements indépendamment de ces dernières et effectuent des opérations financières pour leur propre compte, ils peuvent être considérés comme des unités institutionnelles désignées sous le nom de caisses de sécurité sociale » (paragraphe 4.125).*

> *« Il est possible de faire varier de façon discrétionnaire les montants prélevés et versés sous forme de cotisations de sécurité sociale et de prestations afin d'atteindre des objectifs de politique publique qui n'ont pas de lien direct avec la notion de sécurité sociale en tant que système visant à fournir des prestations à des membres de la collectivité. Ainsi, ces cotisations ou prestations peuvent être augmentées ou diminuées afin d'influer sur le niveau de la demande globale au sein de l'économie. Néanmoins, tant que ces caisses restent indépendantes, elles doivent être traitées comme des unités institutionnelles distinctes dans le SCN ». (paragraphe 4.126).*

> *« Le sous-secteur des administrations de sécurité sociale comprend les administrations de sécurité sociale opérant à tous les niveaux des administrations publiques. Les administrations de sécurité sociale sont des systèmes couvrant l'ensemble de la collectivité ou d'importants sous-ensembles de la collectivité qui sont rendus obligatoires et contrôlés par des administrations publiques » (paragraphe 4.147).*

98. Cette définition des administrations de sécurité sociale est suivie dans la classification de l'OCDE à l'exception des régimes suivants :

- Les régimes imposés par l'administration et exploités par des organismes extérieurs au secteur des administrations publiques, tel qu'il est défini au § 3 de ce manuel et
- Les régimes qui perçoivent des cotisations facultatives.

Autorités supranationales

99. Ce sous-secteur s'applique aux activités de collecte de recettes publiques des autorités supranationales sur le territoire d'un pays. En pratique, le seul cas d'autorité supranationale de la zone de l'OCDE est celui des institutions de l'Union européenne (UE). Depuis 1998, les autorités supranationales ne figurent plus dans les Statistiques des recettes publiques dans un souci de cohérence avec la définition du SCN des administrations publiques qui les exclut. Par exemple, les impôts sur le revenu et des contributions de sécurité sociale rassemblées par des Institutions européennes et payé par les fonctionnaires européens qui sont résidents de pays membres de l'Union européenne ne devraient pas être inclus. Toutefois, les prélèvements spécifiques versés par les États membres à l'Union européenne continuent à être inclus dans les recettes fiscales totales et ils sont indiqués sous cette rubrique.

Critères à utiliser pour l'attribution des recettes fiscales

100. Lorsqu'une administration collecte l'impôt et le reverse, en totalité ou en partie, à d'autres administrations, il est nécessaire de déterminer si ces recettes doivent être considérées comme étant celles de l'administration qui les perçoit et les répartit entre d'autres administrations ou celles des administrations bénéficiaires auxquelles l'administration qui les a perçues les a transférées en simple qualité d'agent. Les critères à utiliser dans l'attribution des recettes sont indiqués aux § 101 à 104, qui reprennent les paragraphes 3.70 à 3.73 du SCN 2008.

101. En général, un impôt est attribué à l'Unité administrative qui :

a. exerce le pouvoir de percevoir l'impôt (soit en tant que détenteur de ce pouvoir soit par délégation de l'autorité qui le détient),

b. dispose du pouvoir discrétionnaire final de fixer et de faire varier le taux de l'impôt.

102. Lorsqu'une somme est collectée par une administration au profit d'une autre administration et en son nom, et que cette dernière a le pouvoir de percevoir l'impôt et de fixer et de faire varier son taux, la première intervient comme agent pour le compte de la dernière et l'impôt est réaffecté. Toute somme retenue par l'administration collectrice au titre des frais de recouvrement doit être considérée comme la rémunération d'un service rendu. Toute autre somme conservée par l'administration collectrice, notamment dans le cadre d'un accord de partage d'impôt, doit être considérée comme une subvention courante. Si l'administration collectrice s'est vu déléguer le pouvoir de fixer et de faire varier le taux, le montant recouvré doit être considéré comme une recette fiscale de cette administration.

103. Lorsque des administrations différentes fixent conjointement et sur un pied d'égalité la répartition du produit de cet impôt, aucune administration ne disposant d'un pouvoir prépondérant en dernier ressort, les recettes fiscales sont attribuées à chaque administration en fonction de sa part respective du produit de l'impôt. Si un accord permet à une unité administrative d'exercer un pouvoir prépondérant en dernier ressort, la totalité des recettes fiscales est attribuée à cette unité.

104. Dans certains cas aussi, un impôt est perçu dans le cadre des compétences d'une administration qui résulte de la constitution ou d'autres dispositions mais d'autres administrations fixent individuellement le taux d'imposition sur leurs territoires. Le produit de l'impôt généré sur les territoires respectifs de chaque administration est attribué à l'administration en question comme constituant ses recettes fiscales.

Versements effectués par les États membres de l'Union européenne

105. Les versements effectués par les États membres de l'Union européenne prennent la forme de prélèvements spécifiques qui comprennent :

a. les droits de douane et les prélèvements agricoles (5123),

b. les montants compensatoires monétaires bruts (5123 si relatifs aux importations et 5124 si relatifs aux exportations), et

c. les prélèvements de la CECA, les cotisations sucre et les taxes de coresponsabilité sur le lait (5128).

106. Les droits de douane collectés par les États membres pour le compte de l'Union européenne sont comptabilisés :

- sur une base qui ne tient pas compte des droits d'encaissement,
- en utilisant des chiffres corrigés de manière à exprimer les droits sur la base de la « destination finale » et non du « pays de première entrée » lorsque de telles corrections sont possibles. Ces corrections concernent en particulier les droits prélevés dans des ports (maritimes) importants. Bien que les droits de l'UE soient prélevés par les autorités du pays de première entrée, ces droits doivent être dans la mesure du possible déduits des recettes du pays qui les recouvre et inclus dans les recettes du pays de destination finale.

107. Ces droits de l'UE sont le plus clairement conformes au critère d'attribution décrit au § 99 ci-dessus. En conséquence, à partir de 1998, ces montants sont mentionnés dans une note de bas de page à titre de rubrique « Pour mémoire » dans les tableaux des États membres de l'UE (chapitre 4 du Rapport) et ne figurent plus sous la rubrique 5123. Toutefois, ces montants sont inclus dans les grands totaux des recettes fiscales à la ligne supérieure pour toutes les années indiquées dans les tableaux.

A.13. Classification provisoire des recettes provenant des prélèvements sur les banques et des contributions aux mécanismes de garantie des dépôts et de stabilité financière

108. L'OCDE a provisoirement adopté, depuis l'édition 2012 de ses *Statistiques des recettes publiques*, le principe suivant concernant l'enregistrement comptable des recettes issues des prélèvements sur les banques ainsi que des redevances acquittées au titre de la garantie des dépôts et de la stabilité financière. Il est recommandé que les montants concernés soient comptabilisés à la rubrique 5126.

- Les redevances de stabilité, les prélèvements sur les banques et les contributions à la garantie des dépôts, qu'il est obligatoire d'acquitter, doivent généralement être traitées comme des recettes fiscales lorsque les versements sont effectués au profit de l'administration publique et affectés au budget consolidé ou général des administrations de sorte que les pouvoirs publics soient libres d'utiliser les fonds sans délai aux fins qu'ils jugent opportunes. Ce principe s'appliquerait indépendamment du fait que l'administration promette ou non d'effectuer des versements pour garantir les dépôts des clients des établissements bancaires si la situation l'exigeait à l'avenir.

- Si les paiements obligatoires sont effectués au profit de l'administration publique et imputés à des budgets dont les ressources doivent être entièrement réaffectées au secteur de l'économie qui englobe les entreprises assujetties à ces paiements, ceux-ci seront toujours traités, en règle générale, comme des recettes fiscales étant donné que les fonds seraient disponibles pour l'administration et réduiraient son déficit budgétaire, que la redevance est sans contrepartie pour les entités individuelles et que les montants collectés pourraient être dissociés de tout versement en faveur des déposants ou de toute dépense visant à soutenir plus largement le secteur financier.
- Les contributions aux mécanismes traditionnels de moindre envergure destinés à garantir les dépôts de détail, contributions dont le montant est aligné sur le coût de la garantie, doivent être classées en tant que redevances pour services rendus.
- Tout versement au titre de la réalisation par une administration des actifs d'un établissement en faillite ou du recouvrement par cette administration d'une créance prioritaire sur les actifs de l'établissement en cours de liquidation, effectué en vue de financer l'indemnisation des clients ayant perdu leurs dépôts, serait traité comme une redevance par opposition aux recettes fiscales.

Les contributions obligatoires aux fonds administrés en-dehors du secteur public et aux organismes non étatiques bénéficiant du soutien des institutions collectrices de dépôts ainsi que toutes les contributions aux mécanismes facultatifs ne doivent pas être traitées comme des recettes fiscales.

Notes

1. « Les références dans cette annexe aux chapitres ou aux sections de « ce rapport » sont issues de OCDE (2017), Statistiques des recettes publiques 1965-2016, Éditions OCDE, Paris. »
2. Toutes les références au SCN concernent l'édition de 2008.
3. Se reporter à la section A.12 de ce manuel pour l'examen de cette notion.
4. Il est en général possible d'identifier les montants des cotisations de sécurité sociale et les impôts sur les salaires, mais pas les autres impôts payés par les administrations.
5. En revanche, si un ou plusieurs pays considèrent comme un impôt un droit que la plupart des pays font entrer dans les recettes non fiscales ou qui procure des recettes substantielles, les montants ainsi perçus figureront dans une note de renvoi à la fin des tableaux par pays correspondants, même s'ils ne sont pas inclus dans le total des recettes fiscales.
6. Les appellations peuvent cependant être souvent trompeuses. Ainsi, une redevance de passeport sera normalement considérée comme une recette non fiscale, alors qu'un prélèvement additionnel sur les passeports (comme c'est le cas au Portugal), qui a pour but de procurer un montant substantiel de recettes eu égard au coût de délivrance du passeport, sera considéré comme un impôt du sous-groupe 5200.
7. On trouvera des précisions sur cette distinction dans l'étude spéciale intitulée « L'information sur les recettes fiscales : problèmes actuels », de l'édition de 2001 des *Statistiques des recettes publiques*.
8. On utilise parfois les expressions « non remboursable » et « remboursable » mais il peut paraître illogique de parler de « remboursement » lorsque rien n'a été versé.
9. Toutefois, dans les systèmes d'imputation de l'impôt sur les sociétés, les crédits d'impôts récupérables sont traités différemment (§ 36 à 38).
10. Il ne s'agit pas d'une véritable dépense fiscale au sens strict. De telles dépenses fiscales supposent que l'on identifie un système fiscal de référence pour chaque pays ou, de préférence, une norme internationale commune. En pratique, il n'a pas été possible de parvenir à un accord sur une norme internationale commune.
11. Sauf s'ils sont calculés sur le bénéfice résultant de la vente, auquel cas ils seraient classés parmi les impôts sur les gains en capital dans le sous-groupe 1120 ou 1220.

12. Dans certains pays, la même législation est applicable aux personnes physiques et aux entreprises dans le cas d'impôts sur le revenu particulier. Cependant, les recettes procurées par ces impôts peuvent, en général, être ventilées et figurent donc dans les deux sous-groupes appropriés.

13. Ainsi, « celles qui sont suffisamment autonomes et indépendantes pour que leur fonctionnement soit comparable à celui d'une société... (y compris) la tenue de comptes complets » (2008 SCN section 4.44).

14. Il peut en être ainsi lorsqu'un régime en faveur des administrations existait avant l'instauration d'un régime général de sécurité sociale.

15. Système selon lequel l'Union Européenne ajuste les effets des différences entre les taux de change utilisés pour fixer les prix des produits agricoles dans le cadre de la politique agricole commune, et le taux de change réel. Les paiements effectués selon ce système portent sur les importations ou les exportations; lorsqu'ils sont identifiables, ces montants figurent dans la rubrique appropriée (5123 ou 5124). Dans ce guide, sont inclus les montants bruts, c'est-à-dire sans déduction d'aucune prime payée dans le cadre du système des montants compensatoires.

16. Les transferts de bénéfices de loteries d'État sont considérés comme des recettes non fiscales (voir aussi § 67).

Revenue Statistics in Africa 1990-2016/Statistiques des recettes publiques en Afrique 1990-2016

ANNEX B

Interpretative guide to non-tax revenue in Revenue Statistics in Africa

Table of contents

B.1. Coverage

The definition of non-tax revenues and the main subcategories identified in this publication generally correspond to the concepts laid out in the 2014 IMF Government Finance Statistics Manual (GSFM). Non-tax revenues refer to increases in government net worth resulting from transactions other than tax revenues. They exclude funds arising from the repayment of previous lending by governments or from borrowing, or proceeds derived from sales of fixed capital assets, stocks, land and intangible assets or private gifts.

Non-tax revenues are made up of the following elements.

B.2. Grants

The GSFM 2014 states "Grants are transfers receivable by government units from non-resident government units or international organisations without the receipt of any goods, services, or assets in return. Grants are normally receivable in cash, but may also take the form of the receipt of goods or services (in kind)". These transfers are un-refundable and unrequited. Grants encompass reparations and gifts given for particular projects or programmes. The term "grants" is not used to refer to transfers to or from non-governmental units and excludes inter-governmental transfers. The remission of funds collected by one government for another in an agency capacity should not be shown as receipt of a grant by the beneficiary government but as its direct receipt of revenue.

B.3. Property income

This category includes income to government arising from their ownership of property, enterprises, financial assets, or intangible assets when government units place them at the disposal of other units. Sales of non-financial assets such as the sales of lands are not recorded as revenue because disposal of such an asset does not increase the net worth. Similarly, repayments on loans and loan disbursements are not revenue. Property income may take the form of dividends, interest, land rents, royalties, or withdrawals from entrepreneurial income. The main components are:

- Interest and dividends: Interest is the revenue earned by the government unit from a financial asset by putting it at the disposal of another institutional unit. Dividends are the revenue earned by placing equity funds at the disposal of a corporation (resident or non-resident corporation). This category also consists of profits of state-owned enterprises except those classified as fiscal monopolies (see §62-§64 of the OECD Interpretative Guide to tax revenue in Annex A), export and import monopoly profits (see §70-§71 of the same document) or those providing public utilities such as rail transport, electricity, post offices and other communications. In this category are included revenue from public financial institutions such as the central banks' profits, profits transferred or distributed from the operation of monetary authority functions outside the central bank and the profits of state lotteries transferred to the government. Transfers from public utilities enterprises are recorded as non-tax revenue under "sales of goods and services" whereas profits for fiscal, export or import monopolies are classified as tax revenue.
- Rents or royalties: Rent is the revenue generated from natural resources, such as land, mining, or oil resources, when a government unit places these at the disposal of private or foreign entities. The rents received relate to a resource lease-giving agreement for the exploitation and extraction of a natural resource by the lessee in return for a payment.

Payments for exploration rights are also treated as rent. Rents should not be confused with other payments a government may receive related to the exploitation of subsoil and similar assets, such as severance taxes, business licenses, or other taxes (e.g. value added taxes, excises, taxes on exports, etc.). They should also not be taken to mean incomes from the rental of buildings and equipment, which are treated as sales of goods and services. Revenues from rents and royalties are in some cases difficult to establish and depend on the agreement between the government unit and the lessee. For example rents, royalties and taxes such as corporate income taxes and VAT are sometimes encompassed in a single payment to the general government. In such cases the revenue should be classified under the category to which the majority of revenue belongs (see §71 of Annex A for further explanation.)

- Other property income: This includes revenue earned by a government unit placing funds at a disposal of quasi-corporations.[1] Conceptually this source of revenue is equivalent to that of dividends from a corporation but by definition, quasi-corporations cannot distribute income in the form of dividends. This category of "other property income" also includes retained or reinvested earnings, i.e. the percentage of distributable revenue not paid out as dividends, but retained by the corporation or quasi-corporation on foreign investment; property income from investment income disbursements and unidentified property income.

B.4. Sales of goods and services

Revenue under the category "sales of goods and services" is generally reported on a gross basis, without deduction of costs. Since these costs can represent a significant proportion of revenues, they cannot be regarded in total as funds available for governments to finance their general activities. This contrasts with tax revenues, where the collection costs are usually a small proportion of revenue. This difference implies that it may not be meaningful to sum tax and non-tax revenues as part of a calculation of generally available funds.

The proceeds of sales of nonfinancial assets such as the sale of buildings or lands are not classified as revenues since their disposal does not increase the net worth.

Sales of goods and services consist of:

- Sales by market establishments.[2]
- Administrative fees for services (i.e. fees for drivers' licences, passports, visas, court fees, harbour fees, fees for birth, marriage or death certificates, patent registrations, radio and television licenses when public authorities provide general broadcasting services).
- Administrative fees that are sales of services associated with a regulatory function of government (such as fees for the inspection of premises before delivering a business licence) and considered to be proportional to the cost of producing the service are included in this category. If the fee in return for the service provided by the government unit is disproportionate, then the fee will be classified as a tax. Specific examples of fees that are considered taxes include fees for permission to perform activities such as hunting, fishing and shooting; and fees for business registration where this is a legal requirement for the business to operate.
- Sales by nonmarket establishments such as fees at government hospitals, tuition fees at government schools and admission fees to museums and parks.
- Leasing of buildings and equipment.

B.5. Fines, penalties and forfeits

The GSFM 2014 states "Fines and penalties are compulsory transfers imposed by courts of law or bodies for violations of laws or administrative rules. Out-of-court agreements are also included (...). Forfeits are amounts deposited with a general government unit pending a legal or administrative proceeding, and that will be transferred to the unit upon resolution". For example traffic fines are included here. Fines and penalties charged on overdue taxes or penalties imposed for the evasion of taxes should be recorded in this category and not as taxes. However if it is not possible to separate the amounts paid in taxes and fines, the whole amount should be classified under the tax to which the fine relates (see §14 of Annex A for further explanation).

B.6. Other social contributions

This category includes the actual and imputed contributions to social insurance schemes operated by governments as employers on behalf of their employees that do not create a future defined liability. This category also includes the sum of the total voluntary contributions.[3] Excluded from this category are any contributions to funds in which the contributions of each participant and of his employer on his behalf are kept in a separate account earning interest and withdrawable under specified circumstances or any contributions to a pension fund autonomous to the general government. This category is not included in this publication.

B.7. Miscellaneous and unidentified revenue

This category consists of unidentified non-tax revenues or those that do not fit into any of the other categories listed above. It includes revenue such as gifts and transfers from individuals, private non-profit institutions, nongovernmental foundations, corporations, or sources other than governments and international organisations. Major non-recurrent payments receivable in compensation for extensive damages or serious injuries not covered by insurance policies are also included, such as payments of compensation for damages caused by major explosions; oil spillages; or payments receivable for damage to property other than payments from an insurance settlement.

Notes

1. Quasi-corporations are unincorporated enterprises that exercise some functions of corporations, but have not been granted separate legal personality by statute.
2. A market establishment is an establishment that charges economically significant prices.
3. The IMF includes these contributions as part of their total of social security contributions.

Revenue Statistics in Africa 1990-2016/Statistiques des recettes publiques en Afrique 1990-2016

Annexe B

Guide d'interprétation des recettes non fiscales dans les Statistiques des recettes publiques en Afrique

Table des matières

B.1. Champ couvert

La définition des recettes non fiscales et des principales sous-catégories décrites dans la présente publication coïncident en grande partie avec les notions retenues dans le manuel des statistiques de finances publiques du FMI de 2014 (manuel SFP 2014). Les recettes non fiscales désignent des augmentations de la valeur nette résultant d'une transaction et qui ne sont pas des recettes fiscales. Elles excluent les fonds relatifs au remboursement de prêts consentis antérieurement par les administrations ou liés à des emprunts, ainsi que le produit de la cession d'actifs immobilisés, d'éléments de stocks, de terrains, d'actifs immatériels et les dons à titre privé.

Les recettes non fiscales se composent des éléments suivants.

B.2. Dons

Selon le manuel SFP 2014, les dons sont des transferts qu'une administration publique reçoit d'une autre administration publique étrangère ou d'une organisation internationale, sans recevoir de cette dernière un bien, un service ou un actif en contrepartie directe. Les dons sont habituellement reçus en espèces, mais peuvent aussi prendre la forme de biens ou de services (en nature). Ces transferts sont non remboursables et sans contrepartie. Les dons recouvrent les réparations et dons assignés à des projets ou programmes particuliers. Le terme de « dons » n'est pas employé pour désigner les transferts réalisés par des entités autres que des administrations publiques ou effectués en leur faveur et exclut les transferts entre administrations. Le versement de fonds collectés par une administration qui agit en qualité de mandataire ne devrait pas entrer dans la catégorie des dons perçus par l'administration bénéficiaire, mais bien s'ajouter aux recettes directement perçues par cette dernière.

B.3. Revenus de la propriété

Cette catégorie regroupe les recettes publiques découlant de la détention de biens fonciers, de parts de sociétés, d'actifs financiers ou d'actifs immatériels que certaines unités administratives ont mis à la disposition d'autres unités administratives. Les cessions d'actifs non financiers comme la vente de terrains ne sont pas enregistrées en tant que recettes parce que la cession de tels actifs n'a pas d'effet sur la valeur nette. De même, les remboursements de prêts et les prêts octroyés ne sont pas des recettes. Les revenus de la propriété peuvent prendre la forme de dividendes, d'intérêts, de revenus fonciers, de redevances, ou de prélèvements sur des revenus d'entreprises. Les principales composantes en sont les suivantes :

- Intérêts et dividendes : Les intérêts sont les revenus perçus par une unité administrative au titre d'un actif financier qu'elle met à la disposition d'une autre unité institutionnelle. Les dividendes sont les recettes perçues par une unité qui met des capitaux à la disposition d'une société (qu'elle soit ou non un résident du pays concerné). Cette catégorie recouvre également les bénéfices d'entreprises détenues par une administration, en excluant les monopoles fiscaux (voir paragraphes 62 à 64 du Guide d'interprétation de l'OCDE en Annexe A), les monopoles d'exportation et d'importation (voir paragraphes 70 et 71 du même document) ainsi que les entreprises qui fournissent des services publics comme les chemins de fer, l'électricité, les postes et autres moyens de communication. Sont regroupés dans cette catégorie les revenus provenant d'institutions financières publiques comme les bénéfices de la banque centrale, les bénéfices transférés ou distribués au titre de fonctions de l'autorité monétaire exercées en dehors de la banque centrale et les bénéfices liés aux loteries nationales qui sont transférés à l'administration. Les transferts émanant d'entreprises qui assurent des services publics sont comptabilisés dans la rubrique « ventes de biens et de services » alors que les bénéfices des monopoles fiscaux, d'exportation ou d'importation constituent des recettes fiscales.

- Loyers et redevances : Les loyers sont des revenus générés lorsqu'une unité administrative met à la disposition d'autres entités privées ou étrangères des ressources naturelles, comme des terrains ou des gisements de minéraux ou de pétrole. Les loyers perçus sont liés à des accords de concession relatifs à l'exploitation et à l'extraction d'une ressource naturelle par un concessionnaire en contrepartie d'un paiement. Les paiements en échange de droits de prospection doivent également être traités comme des loyers. Les loyers sont à distinguer des autres paiements qu'une administration publique peut recevoir pour l'exploitation d'actifs du sous-sol et d'autres actifs du même type, par exemple les paiements de taxes d'extraction, patentes ou autres impôts (taxes sur la valeur ajoutée, accises, taxes à l'exportation, etc.). Il ne faut pas non plus confondre loyers et revenus de la location de bâtiments et d'équipements, par exemple, qui sont classés dans les ventes de biens et de services. Les revenus liés aux loyers et redevances sont parfois difficiles à déterminer car ils dépendent de la nature de l'accord conclu entre l'unité administration et le concessionnaire. À titre d'exemple, un versement unique effectué en faveur des administrations publiques peut regrouper le paiement de loyers, de redevances et d'autres obligations fiscales comme l'impôt sur les bénéfices des sociétés ou la TVA. Dans un tel cas, le paiement est classé dans la catégorie qui correspond à la majeure partie du versement considéré (voir paragraphe 71 en Annexe A pour plus de précisions).
- Autres revenus de la propriété : Cette catégorie inclut les recettes perçues par une unité administrative qui met des capitaux à la disposition de quasi-sociétés[1]. Cette source de recettes est en substance équivalente à des dividendes versés par une société mais, par définition, les quasi-sociétés ne distribuent pas de bénéfices sous forme de dividendes. Cette catégorie englobe de plus les bénéfices non distribués ou réinvestis, à savoir la fraction du bénéfice distribuable qui n'a pas été versée sous forme de dividendes, mais conservée par la société ou quasi-société sur des investissements étrangers ; les revenus de la propriété provenant de versements de revenus d'investissements et revenus de la propriété non identifiés.

B.4. Ventes de biens et de services

Les recettes qui entrent dans cette catégorie sont enregistrées en valeur brute, sans déduction de coûts. Dans la mesure où les coûts peuvent représenter une part importante des recettes, le montant total des ventes biens et de services ne peut pas être considéré comme un montant dont l'administration dispose dans son intégralité pour financer ses activités générales. C'est une différence notable avec les recettes fiscales, auxquelles sont associés des coûts de recouvrement qui ne représentent le plus souvent qu'une faible part des recettes. De ce fait, le montant obtenu par addition des recettes fiscales et non fiscales ne fournit pas forcément une bonne évaluation des fonds généralement disponibles.

Le produit généré par la cession d'actifs non financiers tels que des bâtiments ou des terrains n'est pas enregistré en tant que recettes étant donné que la cession de tels actifs n'a pas d'effet sur la valeur nette.

Les ventes de biens et de services se composent des éléments suivants :

- les ventes des établissements marchands[2].

- les droits administratifs pour services fournis (droits sur les permis de conduire, sur les passeports, sur les visas ; droits de procédure ; droits portuaires ; droits pour l'établissement d'actes de naissance, de mariage, de décès ; frais de dépôt de brevet ; licences de radio et télévision lorsque les autorités publiques fournissent des services généraux de radiodiffusion).
- Les droits administratifs qui sont des ventes de biens et de services associés à une fonction régulatrice des administrations publiques (comme les droits perçus au titre d'une inspection d'installations menée en vue de la délivrance d'un permis d'exploitation) sont inclus lorsqu'ils sont considérés comme étant proportionnels au coût de production du service en question. Lorsque les droits perçus en contrepartie d'un service fourni par l'administration sont disproportionnés par rapport aux coûts, ils sont considérés comme des impôts. Parmi les droits ainsi classés dans la catégorie des recettes fiscales figurent notamment les droits perçus pour l'octroi de permis d'exercer des activités telles que la chasse, la pêche et l'utilisation d'armes à feu ; et les droits d'enregistrement d'une société dès lors que les entreprises sont tenues par la loi de procéder à un tel enregistrement pour pouvoir exercer leur activité.
- les ventes par les établissements non marchands, comme les droits prélevés par les hôpitaux publics, les droits de scolarité des écoles publiques et les droits d'entrée aux musées et parcs.
- la location de bâtiments et d'équipements.

B.5. Amendes, pénalités et confiscations

Le manuel des statistiques de finances publiques du FMI de 2014 définit les amendes et pénalités comme des transferts obligatoires imposés aux unités par des tribunaux ou des organismes pour infraction à la loi ou aux règlements administratifs. Les accords extra-judiciaires sont également inclus. Les confiscations sont les montants déposés auprès d'une unité d'administration publique pendant le déroulement d'une procédure judiciaire ou administrative puis transférés à cette unité au moment du règlement de celle-ci. À titre d'exemple, les amendes sanctionnant les contraventions au code de la route entrent dans cette catégorie. Les amendes et pénalités appliquées au titre d'arriérés d'impôts ou les pénalités pour fraude fiscale devraient également être comptabilisées ici et non comme des recettes fiscales. Toutefois, s'il est impossible de distinguer les montants qui correspondent respectivement à l'impôt et aux pénalités, la somme totale est rattachée aux recettes générées par l'impôt qui a motivé l'application des pénalités (voir paragraphe 14 en Annexe A pour plus de précisions).

B.6. Autres cotisations sociales

Cette catégorie englobe les cotisations sociales effectives et imputées aux régimes d'assurance sociale gérés par des administrations publiques en qualité d'employeurs pour le compte de leurs employés qui ne génèrent pas de passif défini dans des périodes futures. Cette catégorie inclut également la somme des contributions volontaires totales[3]. Toutefois, sont exclues les cotisations à des fonds dans lesquels les cotisations de chaque salarié et celles que l'employeur verse en son nom sont comptabilisées séparément dans un compte productif d'intérêts d'où elles peuvent être retirées dans des conditions biens déterminées, ainsi que les cotisations à des fonds de pension autonomes vis-à-vis des administrations publiques. Cette catégorie n'est pas incluse aux fins de la présente publication.

B.7. Recettes diverses et non identifiées

Cette catégorie regroupe toutes les recettes non fiscales qui ne peuvent être identifiées ou qui n'entrent dans aucune des catégories décrites précédemment. Elle englobe des dons et transferts provenant de personnes physiques, d'institutions privées sans but lucratif, de fondations non gouvernementales, de sociétés ou de sources autres que les administrations publiques et les organisations internationales. Les paiements non récurrents d'un montant élevé reçus par les administrations publiques en compensation de dommages importants non couverts par des polices d'assurance sont également inclus, ainsi que des paiements d'indemnités en compensation de dommages causés par des explosions de grande ampleur, le déversement d'hydrocarbures, ou des paiements exigibles en cas de dommages matériels autres que les paiements au titre d'une indemnisation par une assurance.

Notes

1. Les quasi-sociétés sont des entreprises non constituées en sociétés qui exercent certaines de leurs activités comme des sociétés, mais n'ont pas reçu de personnalité juridique distincte en vertu de la loi.
2. Un établissement marchand est une entité qui pratique des prix économiquement significatifs.
3. Le FMI comptabilise ces cotisations dans le total des cotisations de sécurité sociale.